Communicating About Health

Communicating About Health

Current Issues and Perspectives

FIFTH EDITION

Athena du Pré
University of West Florida

New York Oxford
Oxford University Press

Oxford University Press is a department of the University of Oxford. It furthers the University's objective of excellence in research, scholarship, and education by publishing worldwide. Oxford is a registered trade mark of Oxford University Press in the UK and certain other countries.

Published in the United States of America by Oxford University Press
198 Madison Avenue, New York, NY 10016, United States of America.

For titles covered by Section 112 of the US Higher Education Opportunity Act, please visit www.oup.com/us/he for the latest information about pricing and alternate formats.

Library of Congress Cataloging-in-Publication Data
Names: DuPré, Athena.
Title: Communicating about health : current issues and perspectives / Athena du Pré, University of West Florida.
Description: Fifth edition. | New York : Oxford University Press, [2017] | Includes bibliographical references and indexes.
Identifiers: LCCN 2015046594 | ISBN 9780190275686
Subjects: LCSH: Communication in medicine. | Medical personnel and patient. | Health education. | Health promotion.
Classification: LCC R118 .D87 2017 | DDC 362.1—dc23 LC record available at http://lccn.loc.gov/2015046594

9 8 7 6 5 4 3 2 1

Printed by RR Donnelley, USA

Brief Contents

Contents

Preface

My fascination with health communication began with people who were generous enough to share their stories with me. I have been lucky to occupy roles in which the marvels of health care have played out before my eyes.

- As a health news reporter, I stood, awed, in the hospital room of a woman who invited me to be there when the bandages were removed from her eyes and she saw her children for the first time in 20 years.
- As director of hospital public relations, I met other remarkable people, including a 34-year-old police officer, nestled to the left in a hospital bed in his parents' front room, the right side reserved for his faithful canine companion, Shep, who, along with hospice, provided warmth and comfort during the final joyful and sad months of his life.
- Years later, as a health communication researcher, I met a young woman who said, "If you have a minute, I have a remarkable story to tell you." Indeed, she did. It forever changed my feelings about dying and convinced me that, maybe, the connections between people both living and dead are never lost.
- One of my greatest privileges has been befriending Samantha Rodzwicz, who, despite being paralyzed from the neck down, was one of the most dynamic, energetic, and brilliant people I have ever met. She was the teacher and I the student. (Sam is pictured in Chapter 8.)

Stories such as these occur every day in health settings. They are the reasons we do what we do—be that designing health campaigns, caring for patients, serving in leadership roles, researching and teaching health communication, or studying the issues so that we and our loved ones will be better prepared when we are the patients.

In this edition of *Communicating About Health: Current Issues and Perspectives* my objective is twofold: (1) to update coverage of the latest issues and research (and there is a lot of exciting news to cover) and (2) to give voice to the stories of people who live and embody the issues we study. If I have been successful, you will find this to be an insightful, rich, and thorough overview of health communication. My wish is that readers come away with sophisticated knowledge about current issues and research, a real-life appreciation of the human side of health care and advocacy, and practical strategies for communicating more effectively and ethically about health.

My Approach

Because health care is so dynamic and complex, it is difficult to keep up with everything. We feel we are doing well to stay up to date in any one sector. That's understandable. But it is also the greatest weakness in the system, and it can be a fatal flaw. We miss opportunities for innovative teamwork. Our efforts are often duplicative and contradictory. And we often don't see the larger patterns at work. As the great systems theorist Peter Senge (2006) observes, "*Structures of which we are unaware hold us prisoner*" (p. 93).

In health care, this often equates to mistakes and duplications, expensive care that might have been avoided, well-intentioned campaigns that don't work, and administrative oversight that is cumbersome and distracting rather than smooth, supportive, and integrated. Effective communication isn't a nicety. It's good medicine, and it's good business.

Communicating About Health is readable enough to serve as an introduction to the field. But as feedback from experienced health professionals bears out, this is not a skim-the-surface book. It offers deep insights that are helpful even for experienced practitioners and researchers. By the book's end, readers should be able to speak knowledgeably, not just about one aspect of health care, but about how the many pieces fit together and influence each other.

Intended Audience

This book is designed primarily for people pursuing careers in the health industry and those with a research interest in health communication. This includes care providers, health care administrators, marketing and public relations professionals, media planners and producers, public health promoters, educators, human resources personnel, researchers, educators, and others.

It may seem that such a diverse audience could not be served by the same text, and that is true to some extent. By all means, read other works as well. Explore specialized texts. But my advice is to read this book first or alongside the others. It provides something that specific-interest books cannot—a revealing overview of how various professions, cultures, and current concerns converge in health care. I believe that, where health is concerned, understanding the big picture is as important as mastering a particular skill set. Your success will be enhanced if you are able to speak knowledgeably about current issues in the health care field overall. (And truth be told, I'm counting on you to address some of the challenges in health care.)

My Background

I have a professional and a theoretical interest in health communication. In recent years, I have devoted myself to teaching health communication, studying health transactions, consulting with health care organizations, and writing books and articles on the subject. Earlier in my career, I covered health news for newspaper and television audiences and supervised advertising and public relations for a large medical center. In these capacities, I wrote news stories, directed public health campaigns, designed advertising, produced a monthly television program about health issues, assisted in strategic planning and marketing efforts, and worked alongside health caregivers and administrators.

As a former journalist, I understand the difficulties in keeping the public informed, and I am uncomfortably aware that unethical practices sometimes degrade the value of what the media has to say. My experience in a health care organization reminds me of how challenging it is to maintain morale, encourage open communication, and adjust to market pressures. As a scholar and researcher, I appreciate more than ever how important and difficult it is to manage the multiple goals and diverse influences on health communication.

Together, these experiences make me especially sensitive to the weaknesses and strengths of health communication. It is impossible to observe (and be part of) health communication efforts and believe that they are all good or all bad. You will notice throughout the book that issues are described in terms of their potential advantages and drawbacks. For instance, public health promotion is an immensely valuable way to inform and motivate people. However, promoters must be careful to avoid stigmatizing ill persons and making people unnecessarily anxious. I believe communicators are most effective when they have given careful thought and ethical consideration to the communication strategies available to them.

Another result of studying and working in the health industry is my immense respect for the diverse people who comprise it. I am frustrated by scholars who criticize the actions of health professionals and patients without also acknowledging what they are up against—time limits, stress, overwhelming emotional demands, and so on. I believe health communication can be improved in many respects, but it is naive to call for reform or expect it to happen without understanding and modifying the factors that influence it. This book provides insight about many of those factors.

Strengths of the Book

Communicating About Health has several advantages. For one, it offers up-to-date coverage of issues and research. It describes how managed care, telehealth, health care reform, and other factors are changing the nature of health communication. More than most health communication texts, this one goes beyond research data to explain the larger social issues and policies that influence health care and health advocacy.

Second, this book provides extensive coverage of diversity in health care. It describes culturally diverse ways of thinking about health and healing and reveals how such factors as gender identity, age, and race influence health communication. Readers are able to look at health care through the eyes of care providers, patients, administrators, health promoters, and others who contribute to the process.

Third, *Communicating About Health* is a useful guide for people interested in improving their health-related communication skills. It includes suggestions for encouraging patient participation, providing social support, listening, developing cultural competence, working in teams, designing health promotion campaigns, and more.

Fourth, this text situates health communication within the contexts of history, culture, and philosophy. This gives a depth of understanding and allows readers better to grasp the significance of health communication phenomena. For instance, evidence that physicians tend to dominate medical transactions takes on added importance when readers understand the influence of science and technology on medicine.

Fifth, this book is designed to promote critical thinking and discussion. It poses ethical considerations and discussion questions, and is supported by an instructor's manual that presents a wide range of class activities and discussion starters. Additionally, case studies and interviews with health professionals bring health communication to life.

In summary, *Communicating About Health* is much more than a literature review. It explores the diverse perspectives of people involved in health communication and shows how they blend and negotiate their ideas to create communication episodes. The book integrates research, theories, current issues, and real-life examples. This blend of information enables students to understand the implications of various communication phenomena. At the same time, readers learn how they can contribute to health communication in a positive way as professionals, patients, and researchers.

Features in the New Edition

A great deal has happened in the last few years, including enactment of the Affordable Care Act and the proliferation of eHealth. At the same time, research and theory continue to evolve, embracing a broader range of perspectives than in the early days of the discipline. Following is an overview of key features in this edition. (A more detailed list of changes appears in the instructor's manual.)

DIVERSITY

Coverage of diversity, always a strength of this book, is enhanced in this edition. Chapter 1 now includes discussion of the sociocultural model of health. Chapter 6, Diversity and Health Care, explores how social structures and personal identity influence health and health communication. It includes diverse perspectives in terms of gender, race, age, ability, socioeconomic status, and more. Chapter 7, Cultural Conceptions of Health and Illness, has been substantially revised, with new features on cultural competence and diverse conceptualizations of health and healing around the world.

Perspectives boxes throughout the book describe actual episodes of health communication as described by patients, professionals, family members, health care leaders, and others. This edition also includes expanded coverage of a wide array of professional perspectives, including those of health care administrators, pharmacists, allied health personnel, dentists, therapists, physicians, nurses, public health professionals, marketing and public relations professionals, and others.

CURRENT ISSUES

A rich and thoughtful appreciation for health communication requires one to understand the issues that are reshaping health care as we know it. Chapter 2, The Landscape for Health Communication, features up-to-date coverage of global health concerns, population shifts, the move toward patient empowerment, and the impact of managed care and the Affordable Care Act. This chapter illustrates that health communication is influenced at every level by social structures, cultural ideals, and public policies. Current events and issues appear throughout the book as well, as when we explore the role of communication in the controversy over childhood vaccines in Chapter 12.

COMMUNICATION TECHNOLOGY

This edition features up-to-date information about the impact of technology on health communication. Chapter 9, eHealth, mHealth, and Telehealth, considers the impact of mobile technology, social media, and computer-mediated health care encounters. Readers are exposed to innovations unimagined just a few years ago and encouraged to consider the pros and cons in terms of health communication. In addition, new *Health and Communication Technology* boxes throughout the book describe emerging innovations.

CAREER OPPORTUNITIES

Those considering careers in the health care industry may appreciate links and resources that provide information about salaries, desired qualifications, market demand, and job duties for more than 125 careers.

CRITICAL THINKING PROMPTS

Boxed features such as *What Do You Think?*, *Can You Guess?*, and *In Your Experience* stimulate critical thinking and discussion, not just at the end of each chapter, but as readers explore the text. The new edition also includes more photos and graphics.

Ethical Considerations boxes present the pros and cons of issues such as paternalism, privacy, the politics of prevention, health care rationing, and more. To stimulate further exploration, *Resources* and *Check It Out!* boxes suggest relevant articles, books, organizations, websites, and online video footage.

PRACTICAL APPLICATIONS

Communication Skill Builder sections feature practical strategies for communicating with patients and caregivers, avoiding burnout, stimulating teamwork, designing public health campaigns, and more.

INSTRUCTIONAL RESOURCES

Ancillary Resource Center (**ARC**) at www.oup-arc.com/dupre is a convenient, instructor-focused website that provides access to all of the teaching resources for this text—at any time—while guaranteeing the security of grade-significant resources. In addition, it allows OUP to keep instructors informed when new content becomes available. The following items are available on the ARC:

- The **Instructor's Manual** features sample syllabi, class activities, audiovisual materials, and more. Lesson plans in the instructor's manual correspond to PowerPoint and Prezi presentations designed to stimulate student engagement either in person or online.
- The **Computerized Test Bank** offers 500 exam questions in multiple-choice, true-false, and short-answer and essay formats, with each item tagged to the corresponding page and section references in the text.
- **PowerPoint** and **Prezi slides** present key concepts, video clips, discussion prompts, and activities in coordination with the instructor's manual.

With this brief overview in mind, here is a more detailed look at components of the book.

Overview of the Book

PART I: ESTABLISHING A CONTEXT FOR HEALTH COMMUNICATION

The first two chapters provide an introduction to health communication. Chapter 1 establishes the nature and definition of health communication, current issues, and important reasons to study health communication. This edition features expanded coverage of communication as a collaborative endeavor. It also includes a new section on the sociocultural model of health. Chapter 1 provides tips for making the most of features such as *Ethical Considerations*, *Theoretical Foundations*, and *Career Opportunities* boxes that appear throughout the book.

Chapter 2 explores how health communication is evolving within the context of social and public issues. Understanding these issues allows for deeper appreciation of topics described in the rest of the book. The chapter culminates with a look at how provisions of the Affordable Care Act influence health communication (previously covered in Chapter 12).

PART II: THE ROLES OF PATIENTS AND CAREGIVERS

Part II focuses on interpersonal communication between patients and professional caregivers. Chapter 3 describes patient–caregiver communication in terms of who usually talks, who listens, and how medical decisions are made. It features a broader array of caregivers than in the past, thanks to emerging research about nurses, pharmacists, paramedics, physical therapists, technicians, and others. The chapter features a discussion of narrative medicine and real-life examples of patient–caregiver communication. It also presents a list of journals relevant to health communication and career opportunities for people with expertise in health communication research.

Chapter 4 examines health communication through patients' eyes, considering what motivates patients, what they typically like and do not like about health care, and how people express themselves in health encounters. This edition looks closely at how communication is influenced by the nature of illness, patient disposition, and threats to personal identity. It includes information about communication skills training for patients and updated information about patient narratives and self-advocacy. The chapter provides resources and career information for people who wish to serve as patient advocates.

In Chapter 5, readers view health from the perspective of professional care providers. This edition explores the philosophy behind caregiver training programs and how that has changed through the years. (This is a condensed version of content previously covered in Chapter 2.) As in Chapter 3, coverage includes a broader array of professionals than in the past. This edition features a new section on mindfulness and expanded coverage of other strategies to help care providers remain emotionally resilient. The chapter also features new coverage of interprofessional education and updated tips for communicating with difficult patients, communicating when time is limited, and disclosing medical mistakes. It concludes with a unit on multidisciplinary teamwork. Information is provided on more than 30 careers in medicine, dentistry, nursing, and allied health.

PART III: SOCIOCULTURAL ISSUES

Chapter 6 focuses on diversity among patients and health professionals. It begins with a new feature on intersectionality theory and includes expanded coverage of nuanced gender identities. The chapter presents information and strategies for communicating effectively with people who differ in terms of social status, gender, race, language, ability, and age. The section on health literacy is substantially updated. Case studies describe the experiences of a Spanish-speaking woman in an English-speaking hospital and a college student coping with a physical disability. The chapter features career information for diversity officers, interpreters, and Equal Employment Opportunity Commission personnel.

Chapter 7 describes social and cultural conceptions of health and healing. It presents a model of cultural competence and exposes readers to ideas about health around the world, including conceptualizations of health as a balance between the physical and spiritual, between elements of "hot" and "cold," between different types of life energy, and more. Coverage of holistic medicine appears in this chapter, as do diverse expectations about the roles of patients and caregivers. The chapter includes a feature about the theory of health as expanded consciousness and many examples illustrating diverse perspectives.

PART IV: COPING AND HEALTH RESOURCES

Part IV focuses on the array of resources we may use to maintain and regain health, and when that is not possible, to cope at the end of life.

Chapter 8 illustrates the importance of social support and provides tips for supportive communication. This edition features updated coverage about the role of communication in family caregiving and end-of-life experiences. It includes new coverage of online social support for family caregivers. The chapter also examines instances of social support "gone wrong"—episodes in which people's efforts to help actually hurt, and how we can avoid making the same mistakes. Another section within the chapter explores the notion of animals as supportive companions. The chapter includes sections on transformative health care experiences and organ donation decisions. A *Career Opportunities* box showcases careers in social services and mental health.

Chapter 9 presents updated information about eHealth, mHealth, and telehealth. It presents evidence that, around the world, more people now have mobile technology than have electricity in their homes. We explore how health communication specialists are trying to make the most of this new information resource to benefit big-city dwellers and people in the most remote regions of the world. The chapter addresses such questions as *Why and under what circumstances do people seek electronic health information? Is eHealth information mostly helpful or counterproductive?* and *How does eHealth communication compare with face-to-face transactions?* Theorists and researchers reflect on opportunities for people to actively create and share information with worldwide audiences. Readers will learn more about the emergence of virtual hospitals and debate the pros and cons of telehealth in terms of health communication. Information about medical information and technology careers is presented.

PART V: COMMUNICATION IN HEALTH ORGANIZATIONS

In Chapter 10, readers follow a health care administrator in charge of marketing, public relations, and crisis management through the fascinating challenges that come up when one's job is to handle the unexpected, sometimes while the cameras are running.

The chapter is loaded with theories and expert tips for being a servant leader, promoting a shared vision, working in teams, and rewriting the rules by which health care organizations operate. It culminates with tips for service excellence from some of the best medical centers in the world. Coverage includes theories and related stories from professionals in the field.

PART VI: MEDIA, PUBLIC POLICY, AND HEALTH PROMOTION

Chapter 11 provides the latest information about health images in advertising, news, and entertainment. It features new coverage about body image and highly advertised children's toys as well as media influences on obesity, alcohol and tobacco use, sex, and violence. The chapter also includes a section on the international impact of entertainment-education and information about careers in health journalism. It includes tips for reporting health news, using interactive media to present health information, and developing media literacy.

In Chapter 12, readers explore the real-life lessons of health communication professionals involved with Ebola, AIDS, MERS, anthrax, avian flu, and other health threats. The chapter presents advice for preventing and minimizing crises, responding in the heat of the moment, and managing public fears and information needs. The emphasis is on collaborative communication that is timely, data based, and culturally sensitive. A *Career Opportunities* box features information about careers in public health. (Health care reform coverage previously in this chapter now appears in Chapter 2.)

Chapters 13 and 14 guide readers through the creation and evaluation of public health campaigns. Both chapters include real-life campaign exemplars and sample PSAs, as well as expanded coverage of campaign design resources and message framing. An updated section discusses the lessons of the critical-cultural approach as we contemplate the ethics of persuading people in diverse cultures to reexamine health-related behaviors. These chapters showcase careers in health promotion and health campaign design.

Acknowledgments

A great number of people have contributed to the creation of this text. My first thanks go to Toni Magyar, Paul Longo, Mark Haynes, Keith Faivre, James Fraleigh, and their colleagues at Oxford University Press for their remarkable guidance, enthusiasm, and good humor. I am also grateful to the following reviewers who suggested ideas for this edition:

Rebecca de Souza, *University of Minnesota, Duluth*
Kate Joeckel, *Bellevue University*
Elizabeth Edgecomb, *Xavier University of Louisiana*
Brooke Hildebrand Clubbs, *Southeast Missouri State University*
Patrick J. Dillon, *University of Memphis*
Crystal Daugherty, *University of Memphis*
Tricia Burke, *Texas State University*
Jo Anna Grant, *California State University, San Bernardino*
Christina Sabee, *San Francisco State University*
Cheri Niedzwiecki, *University of Wisconsin–La Crosse*
Christine Parkhurst, *MCPHS University*
Christine Skubisz, *Emerson College*
Virginia McDermott, *High Point University*
Vernon F. Humphrey, *Columbus State University*
Laurie A. Grosik, *Saint Francis University*
Alan Zemel, *University at Albany*
Elizabeth Petrun, *University of Maryland*
Salome Brooks, *Springfield College*
Daniel Steinberg, *Otterbein University*
Jessica Elton, *Eastern Michigan University*
Joy Cypher, *Rowan University*

I continue to be grateful, as well, to those who have edited and reviewed previous editions, including Peter Labella, Josh Hawkins, Nanette Giles, Holly Allen, Mariaelena Bartesaghi, Maria Brann, Ellen R. Cohn, Randa Garden, Chris R. Morse, Loretta L. Pecchioni, Richard L. Street Jr., Julie E. Volkman, Ken Watkins, Elaine Wittenberg-Lyles, Debra L. Worthington, Jill Yamasaki, Michael Dennis, Stephen Haas, Amy Hedman, Haywood Joiner, JJ McIntyre, Jill O'Brien, Jim Query, Pam Secklin, Jiunn-Jye Sheu, Juliann C. Scholl, Sharlene Thompson, Kandi Walker, Catherine Woells, Kevin Wright, Mary L. Brown, Rebecca Cline, June Flora, Stephen Hines, Katherine Miller, Donna Pawlowski, Rajiv N. Rimal, Claire F. Sullivan, Teresa Thompson, Monique Mitchell Turner, and Gust A. Yep.

I would also like to thank colleagues and students who have contributed ideas, narratives, and feedback, most notably Annina Dahlstrom, Beth McPherson,

Josh Newby, Chris Elkins, Alejandra Escobar Ryan, Patricia Barlow, Jennifer Terry, Susanne Fillmore, Dawn Murray, Praewa Tanuthep, Beverly Davis Willi, Jennifer Seneca, Lori Juneau, Stefanie Howell, Melanie Barnes, Amy Jenkins, Bridget King, Micah Nickens, Samantha Olivier, Gwynné Williams, Brittany Jay, Dustin Saulmon, Vickie Payne, Chris Thomas, Nicole Yeakos, Drew Bryson, and Evelyn Briere.

I owe heartfelt thanks to Grant Brown, whose support, inspiration, and patience are astonishing and much appreciated.

As always, I am indebted to mentors Sandy Ragan, Jon Nussbaum, Sonia Crandall, and the late Larry Wieder and Jung-Sook Lee. Heartfelt thanks also to Betty Adams and Cris Berard, who will always be the kind editors in my head. Finally, to my family (Ginger, Ed, Jordan, Hannah, Matt, Benjamin, Sarah, Katherine, and Bethany), who accommodated the many hours devoted to this project and provided endless support. I am forever grateful.

PART I

Establishing a Context for Health Communication

A lot has happened in the last decade. Passage of the Patient Protection and Affordable Care Act opened the way for the United States to become the last industrialized nation to offer health coverage to all citizens. As with any decision of this magnitude, it incited a mixture of controversy, optimism, concern, joy, and renunciation. No matter which of these describes your reactions, one thing is certain: It is an exciting time to study health communication. To contribute in meaningful ways, we must be up to date, well informed, and aware of the big picture. This section lays the groundwork for that. You can read the rest of the book in any order you like, but begin with this section. In Chapters 1 and 2, you will learn about philosophical perspectives and recent events that have led us to the current moment. Understanding that journey makes it easier to envision the future—and ways that you can make a difference in it.

There are decades when nothing happens, and there are weeks when decades happen.

—VLADIMIR ILYICH LENIN

CHAPTER 1

Introduction

Phil Bretthauer's doctor was worried. Despite frequent and expensive care, Phil's health was steadily weakening. He was in and out of the hospital with heart attacks, respiratory problems, and prostate cancer.

"It's a demoralizing position to be in," said his doctor. Although he was concerned about his patient, he felt powerless to reverse his decline. It is no wonder that Phil himself was discouraged. "If it's going to happen, it's going to happen to me," said the discouraged 70-year-old. As it turned out, a turning point in Phil's case resulted from improved communication.

Phil Bretthauer reviews medications with home health nurse Tammy Bennett. In addition to helping Bretthauer with biomedical concerns, Bennett spends time listening to and talking with him. As a result of their communication, she found volunteer opportunities in the community for him to lessen his sense of boredom and isolation.

Phil's story is part of a feature by Jenny Gold (2013) for Kaiser Health News and National Public Radio. Gold describes a new health care delivery model in the United States that encourages more two-way communication between patients and health professionals and more teamwork between care providers. As you will see in a moment, Phil's life changed after his physician became part of this new model, in the form of an **accountable care organization** (**ACO**). An ACO is a network of service providers who, together, provide care for a specified group of Medicare subscribers. The goal is to keep these people well, not just to treat them when they become ill.

Based on provisions of the Affordable Care Act passed in 2010, accountable care organizations that improve the health of their members *and* save costs get a financial bonus. Regardless of what happens with ACOs, most people agree on the principle underlying them—that cost-effective, high-quality care will require a greater degree of open communication, creative thinking, and teamwork than ever before.

Phil's case is an example of multidisciplinary teamwork (which we explore more fully in Chapter 5) and the theory of collaborative medical communication (Chapter 3), which casts patients and health professionals as peers who talk openly about goals and options (Balint & Shelton, 1996; Laine & Davidoff, 1996). Phil's physician became part of a multidisciplinary care team when he joined an accountable care organization. Among other measures, the team decided to schedule Phil for regular visits by a home nurse.

Phil's home health nurse, Tammy Bennett, took a collaborative approach. She spent time talking with Phil about his daily routines and general outlook on life as well as his medical needs. When she realized Phil had been taking some of his medication incorrectly, Bennett helped him get back on track and avoid the side effects of overdosing. Through their interactions, she also learned that Phil was depressed and lonely, just sitting at home all day. Aware that he had once been a NASCAR announcer, she found opportunities for him to be a volunteer announcer at Little League games and a bingo caller at a local rehab center. As he became more socially involved, Phil's health and his outlook improved. He was in the hospital less, which was good for him and for the budget (Gold, 2013).

Phil's case reminds us that health involves medications and procedures, but it also involves being well informed, listening to one another, social interaction, teamwork, and a great deal more. We are all involved in health communication. Our ideas about health are shaped by personal experiences and our interactions with professionals, friends, family members, coworkers, and educators. We are also influenced by Internet content, movies, television shows, public service announcements, and more. At the same time, we influence the people around us with our own actions and thoughts about health.

In this chapter, we consider what health and health communication are all about. We examine philosophical perspectives of health and healing. Then we focus on how and why people communicate as they do about health. The chapter concludes with key reasons to study health communication, including particularly promising career growth. (See Box 1.1 for a list of health-related careers featured throughout the book.)

WHAT DO YOU THINK?

Think beyond the boundaries of conventional care to design a team ideally suited to help you stay healthy.

- Who would you want on your team? Perhaps a nurse, a dietician, a physician, a yoga instructor, a counselor, and/or a massage therapist? Who else?
- By what means would you prefer to communicate with these people? What would you most like to talk about?
- Do you think your health would be affected if your wishes became reality? If so, how?

The Philosophy Behind This Book

It is an exciting and challenging time to be involved with health communication. Perhaps more than ever before, health care leaders are open to innovative

BOX 1.1 CAREER OPPORTUNITIES

Profiles of More Than 125 Health-Related Jobs

Career boxes throughout the book showcase careers related to health and health care. Each box provides links where you can find more information and job listings. Here is a list of jobs profiled in each chapter.

CHAPTER 3 Research/Education

- Consultant
- Professor
- Researcher

CHAPTER 4 Patient Advocacy

- Case manager
- Patient advocate
- Patient care coordinator
- Patient navigator
- Social worker

CHAPTER 5 Caregivers

- Clinical laboratory assistant
- Dental assistant
- Dental hygienist
- Dentist
- Doctor of osteopathic medicine
- Emergency medical technician
- Hospitalist
- Licensed practical nurse
- Medical records technician
- Medical doctor
- Nurse practitioner
- Occupational health/safety technician
- Occupational therapist
- Pharmacist
- Pharmacy technician
- Physical therapist
- Physician assistant
- Psychiatric technician or aide
- Psychiatrist
- Psychologist
- Radiology technologist
- Recreational therapist
- Registered nurse
- Respiratory therapist
- Speech-language therapist
- Surgeon
- Surgical technologist

CHAPTER 6 Diversity

- Diversity officer
- Health care interpreter
- Equal Employment Opportunity (EEO) officer

CHAPTER 7 Holistic Medicine

- Acupuncturist
- Chiropractor
- Holistic nurse
- Massage therapist
- Midwife
- Naturopathic physician
- Nutritionist/dietician
- Reiki practitioner
- Yoga instructor

CHAPTER 8 Mental Health

- Mental health counselor
- Social worker
- Psychologist
- Social service manager
- Hospice/palliative care provider
- Home health aide
- Senior citizen services providers

CHAPTER 9 Medical Technology

- Computer and information systems manager
- Health information administrator or technician
- Software developer

CHAPTER 10 Health Care Administration

- Chief financial officer
- Chief operating officer
- Departmental director
- Director of human resources
- Health information manager
- Medical director
- Medical office manager
- Nursing director
- President or CEO
- Strategic planning director

Health Care Human Resources

- Compensation and benefits manager
- Customer service representative
- Human resource manager
- Recruiter
- Training and development specialist

Health Care Marketing and Public Relations

- Advertising designer
- Community services director
- In-house communication director
- Marketing professional
- Pharmaceutical sales representative
- Physician marketing coordinator
- Public relations professional
- Strategic planning manager

CHAPTER 11 Health Journalism

- Health news editor/reporter
- Health publication editor
- Journal or magazine editor
- Media relations specialist
- Nonprofit organization publicity manager

CHAPTER 12 Public Health

- Business or billing manager
- Communication specialist
- Emergency management director
- Environmentalist
- Epidemiologist
- Fundraiser
- Health campaign designer
- Health department administrator
- Health educator
- Health inspector
- Health researcher
- Media relations professional
- Nonprofit organization director
- Nutritionist/dietician
- Nurse
- Patient advocate or navigator
- Physician
- Public policy advisor
- Risk/crisis communication specialist
- Social worker

CHAPTER 13 Health Promotion and Education

- Community health educator
- Corporate wellness director
- Fitness instructor
- Health campaign designer/manager
- Health information publication designer
- Hospital-based health educator
- Patient advocate or patient navigator
- School-based health educator

CHAPTER 14 Health Campaigns

- Communication director
- Director of nonprofit organization
- Media relations specialist
- Public relations specialist
- Publication designer
- Professor/educator

ideas. They are also facing critical challenges—to control costs, attract clients, and earn employees' loyalty. The changes are both destabilizing and exciting. The good news is that disequilibrium, although it can be stressful, opens the field to new ways of thinking and behaving. People involved with health care today have the potential to reshape and improve the system. In Chapter 10, we discuss innovative ways that people in health care organizations are pursuing these goals.

TIPS ON READING THIS BOOK

- *Do not overlook boxes and sidebars.* Sometimes a feature works best standing on its own. That does not mean it's less important than the rest. Key terms and theories appear in boxes as well as in the main text.
- *Engage in critical thinking.* Questions throughout the book prompt you to reflect on your viewpoints and experiences. Critical thinking, the ability to link abstract ideas to actual practices, is one of the most useful ways to put what you learn to good use.

At the same time, we must keep in mind that health communication is more than business and economics. It involves life and joy and, sometimes, heartbreak. Phil's experiences remind us that physical regimens are not always enough to make us feel better, and that caring for others involves a mixture of knowledge and compassion.

A central theme of this book is that to be our best (and our best is required), we must understand health communication from a wide range of perspectives. Here are some examples of what can go wrong when people focus on one area of communication but neglect others:

- A patient is well treated, but his or her family feels distraught and uninformed.
- A campaign director unfamiliar with cultural ideas about health creates messages that are unappealing or offensive to the target audience.
- A marketing/public relations director who does not understand the dynamics of patient–caregiver communication is unable to help shape and promote services that meet stakeholders' needs.
- A team member uninformed about health care administration and current issues misses out on leadership opportunities.
- Health professionals who do not communicate effectively with each other confuse patients and their loved ones with contradictory information.
- Health communication researchers focus only on individual actions rather than recognizing the social and organizational constraints that may limit people's options.

The list goes on. Knowledge gaps are understandable, even among people who have been in health-related careers for some time. The field is changing rapidly. Whereas specialization was once encouraged, now effective health care scholars and practitioners are attuned to broader contexts and more diverse ideas. They must be aware of the historical, cultural, and market pressures that influence health. Success also relies on their ability to encourage feedback, to listen, to analyze, to experiment with new communication techniques, and to sell their ideas to others.

WHAT DO YOU THINK?

Off the top of your head, define what *health* means to you. Then keep reading to see how your definition compares to that of the World Health Organization. In Chapter 7, we examine different ways of viewing health in cultures around the world.

This book is designed to give readers an up-to-date look at health communication from many perspectives. After establishing the context for current issues in health communication in Part I, we focus on interpersonal connections between patients and professional caregivers in Part II, and then broaden the scope in Part III to consider the influence of diversity and culture. Part IV explores health care resources, including social support and technology. In Part V, we consider the ways that people in health care organizations use communication to lead, inspire, and support team members, and to partner with the community.

The book concludes, in Part VI, with coverage of health communication in the media, public health, and health care campaigns. In this way, we move largely from one-on-one communication to macro-level issues. In real life, of course, we encounter these factors simultaneously rather than one by one. Keep the interplay between them in mind.

Perhaps the most rewarding aspect of learning about health communication is putting what we learn to good use. Throughout the book, *Communication Skill Builder* sections present practical tips for communicating effectively about health. Experts suggest strategies for communicating with diverse people, presenting our concerns as patients, being effective leaders, using social media, designing health campaigns, and more. (See Box 1.2 for ideas about how you can put your skills to work in a service-learning project or internship.)

BOX 1.2

Learn While You Make a Difference

Whether it is a service-learning project, an internship, or a volunteer effort, there are many ways that you can gain experience and learn about health care while you make a difference in people's lives. It helps to establish learning objectives and goals at the beginning and to reflect on what you have learned and accomplished when the project is complete. Here are a few ideas.

Work with a Nonprofit

- Help with strategic planning
- Create a media packet and marketing plan
- Publicize an event or program
- Provide assistance with training
- Recruit volunteers
- Help with an event already scheduled
- Conduct surveys
- Host a health fair booth
- Help develop a crisis management plan
- Stage a mock crisis for practice

Plan, Publicize, and Host an Event

- Fundraiser
- Awards banquet
- Celebration
- Cleanup or spruce-up activity
- Image-building outreach activity
- Health-enhancing event

Advocate

- Focus on a particular need, risk, or group of people
- Research the issue
- Partner with people in need; honor their agenda
- Identify needed resources and/or policies
- Educate the public
- Meet with policy-makers and community leaders
- Host strategy sessions
- Create coalitions and long-term plans

Educate People

- Host a public lecture
- Organize a symposium
- Hold a mini-conference
- Present communication workshops
- Write articles and PSAs for the media

Raise Money

- Host a fundraising event
- Collect contributions
- Recruit sponsors and partners
- Sell items of value
- Host a chance drawing

Health Campaigns

- Conduct market research
- Create a campaign or assist with one
  - Promote healthy behaviors
  - Raise awareness of risks
- Assess campaign exposure
- Evaluate outcomes

What Is Health?

It sounds like an easy question. We know when we are healthy and when we are sick. At least that is how it feels most of the time. But sometimes we are not even sure ourselves. There is space in the middle. And depending on our personal and cultural perspectives, our very idea of being *healthy* can differ from other people's definitions.

The World Health Organization (WHO) defines **health** as "a state of complete physical, mental and social well-being and not merely the absence of disease or infirmity" (WHO, 1948, p. 1). This definition, unchanged for more than 60 years, reminds us that *healthy* is not the opposite of *sick*. Health often involves a sense of harmony and equilibrium between many aspects of life. It may call into play our feelings, physical abilities, and relationships with others. Throughout the book, we discuss diverse theories about the nature of health and its relation to communication.

What Is Health Communication?

Health communication is shaped by many influences, including personal goals, skills, cultural values, situational factors, and consideration of other people's feelings. The definitions presented in this section emphasize the interdependence of these factors. As communicators, we influence—and are simultaneously influenced by—the people and circumstances around us. We rely on others to help us meet goals and make sense of life events. Sometimes the most important thing we do is simply be present for others.

DEFINING COMMUNICATION

Communication is anything but simple. Imagine a scenario in which a person says to you, "I'm pregnant." If we believe that meaning lies only in the words we use, this is a simple two-word parcel of information. As we know, however, communication involves a lot more than that. Even in the case of relatively simple interactions, people negotiate a myriad of potential meanings and implications.

The **transactional model of communication** proposes that people collaborate to construct meaning in a process of ongoing, reciprocal influence (Barnlund, 1970). If you were asked to comment on the "I'm pregnant" statement, you would probably want answers to a number of questions first: *Who said it? Under what circumstances? Did the speaker look and sound happy, sad, fearful, or some other way? Is the person who made this statement my wife? My teenage daughter? My cashier in the grocery store?* The transactional communication model reminds us that communication is a sophisticated process. It does not happen within people, but between them, in the midst of many factors that influence how they behave and what sense they make of the situation and each other. To clarify, let's take a closer look at three key aspects of transactional communication: collaboration, multiple levels of meaning, and the importance of context and culture.

Collaborative Sense-Making

A central tenet of transactional communication is that meaning does not lie in discrete units of information or in any one person. Rather, it emerges within experiences that are cocreated by the participants.

BOX 1.3 PERSPECTIVES

True Stories About Health Communication Experiences

In *Perspectives* boxes throughout the book you will read about the real-life experiences of people involved with health communication. These accounts represent the viewpoints of patients, loved ones, caregivers, executives, social activists, health campaign managers, and others. They provide insight about how people of different races, cultures, ages, languages, abilities, sexual orientations, and educational levels experience health communication.

To return to the previous example, if a friend tells you she is pregnant, you are likely to notice her nonverbal cues, do a quick mental inventory of her situation and prior comments, and experience feelings of your own. Your reaction to the news may show on your face even before the words are completely out of her mouth. In a study of couples coping with infertility, one woman described feeling happy when a friend announced her pregnancy, but discouraged by the comparison to her own situation. Her internal dialogue went something like this: "Congratulations. I know that it's a joyful experience but at the same time, it's kind of a sick analogy, but if someone lost their leg, you don't go around saying, 'Oh, I've got two legs, I can run'" (Palmer-Wackerly & Krieger, 2015, p. 618). In such a situation, the speaker may pick up on her friend's dismayed reaction and reframe the announcement and even how she feels about it. Ultimately, whether the exchange takes on the key of celebrating, comforting, or any number of other options depends on how the people involved coconstruct it.

One implication of transactional communication is that participants do not take turns being senders or receivers. Instead, they simultaneously send and receive messages all the time. Even a blank expression is likely to be considered feedback, suggesting that the listener is bored, uninterested, or so on. Thus, the transactional model highlights the importance, not only of words, but of ever-present nonverbal cues.

As you will see in Chapter 3, many people criticize the traditional model of patient–caregiver communication in which patients are mostly silent and health professionals do most of the talking. This is likely to result in misunderstandings and in a power differential that limits patients' opportunities to help shape their own care. From a transactional perspective, the blame does not lie solely with health professionals, however (Kreps 1990; T. L. Thompson, 1984). Patients are often observed to be quiet and submissive. Whether they realize it or not, they may contribute to the very dynamic they dislike.

Multiple Levels of Meaning

Transactional communication is consistent with a **relational approach**, which proposes that meaning is interpreted at both a content and a relational level (L. E. Rogers & Escudero, 2004; Watzlawick, Beavin, & Jackson, 1967). At a content level, meaning is considered to be mostly denotative—that is, subject to literal interpretation. "I'm pregnant" is a simple statement of fact.

At a relational level, participants consider the implications of communication in terms of their relative status and feelings about each other. Relational messages are often conveyed implicitly, as by considering *how* something is said, *who* says it and *when*, and what they *do not* say. Although relational cues may be subtle, they often convey powerful implications regarding the expectations, emotions, power, and status of the participants. For example, in Chapter 8 we discuss the conundrum that individuals often over-assist people with physical limitations. Although their intentions are good, the relational-level implications may be that "you are needy and incapable" and

> **IN YOUR EXPERIENCE**
>
> - Have you ever felt like the underdog in a health care encounter?
> - If so, what contributed to this feeling? Is there anything you or other people might have done differently?

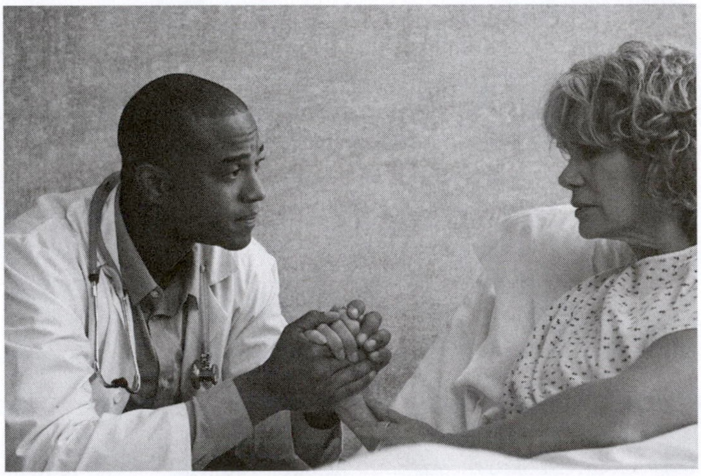

At a relational level, people may use touch, eye contact, space, silence, and other cues to suggest who they are to each other and what they are accomplishing in terms of communication. What do the nonverbal cues in this photo suggest to you about the nature of the relationship and the type of communication involved?

"you are different from me and from other people." In reality, people with physical challenges often say they prefer to be treated just like anyone else (e.g., Nemeth, 2000). In a similar way, a person may feel gratified by a health professional who treats him as an equal but put off by one who insinuates that he is ignorant or irresponsible about his health. (Bear in the mind that, as a collaborator in the process, the person's response will help to shape the ultimate meaning and tone of that encounter.)

Context and Culture

The anthropologist Clifford Geertz (1973) famously observed that people are suspended in "webs of significance" (p. 5). In other words, none of us exists in isolation. We are influenced by larger environments and contexts—such as our past experiences, the neighborhoods in which we live, the cultures with which we identify, and so on. Each of these is likely to influence what we consider acceptable and how we interpret what happens around us.

In Chapter 2, we consider how health care has evolved over time and the effects of recent reform efforts. On the surface, these happenings may seem irrelevant to the way we communicate about health as individuals. However, they probably influence us more than most people realize. For example, a health professional might wish to spend an hour with each patient but be prohibited from doing so by organizational rules and structures. Patients who criticize the professional for being "hurried and inattentive" may miss the reality that the system is more to blame than the individual.

From a transactional perspective, cultural mores are woven into the sense-making endeavors of everyday communication. Cultural expectations influence how we behave as patients (Chapter 4), how society regards health concerns such as mental illness and obesity (Chapters 6 and 7), and so on. You might know someone who does not seek care for depression because, in the culture in which she was raised, mental illness is considered shameful.

One way of honoring diverse contexts is to avoid imposing one's worldview on others as much as possible. For example, before designing a campaign to promote physical activity among African American men, researchers interviewed members of the target audience to learn more about their preferences and attitudes. The men interviewed suggested that the health promoters use a combination of media messages and word of mouth, that they target messages to African American men specifically, and that they focus on the idea that fitness helps men feel better, live longer, and be there for their families (D. B. Friedman, Hooker, Wilcox, Burroughs, & Rheaume, 2012).

As we will discuss throughout the book, people who do not understand and respect cultural differences often do harm even when they are trying to help (Dutta & de Souza, 2008). See Chapters 6, 7, 13, and 14 for more on this.

In summary, the transactional perspective reminds us that communication episodes are collaborative and unique accomplishments. The people involved interactively shape the meanings that emerge at both a content and relational level, and they do so within many layers of context. Awareness of this perspective may help you appreciate the sophisticated nature of health communication phenomena you read about in this book and avoid drawing simplistic conclusions about them. That being said, do not expect every communication study that is described to be transactional in nature. Researchers sometimes single out or isolate particular aspects of health communication for study, and rightfully so. With an understanding of transactional communication, perhaps you can appreciate these as components of a larger process as you continue to learn and put the pieces together.

PERSPECTIVES

"When I first began working at a continuing care retirement community I would speak loudly, lean close to people, and draw out my words. Finally, a resident gave me a little advice: 'Just relax, we can hear you fine. You're the one that may need to listen better.' I began to listen to their stories, exchange jokes, and ask them for advice. I quickly realized I was surrounded by people with wisdom and history that far exceed mine."

—*Chris*

DEFINING HEALTH COMMUNICATION

Gary Kreps and Barbara Thornton (1992) define **health communication** as "the way we seek, process, and share health information" (p. 2). We search out and pass along messages and mingle what we hear and see with our own ideas and experiences. In this way,

BOX 1.4 THEORETICAL FOUNDATIONS

The Basis for Health Communication

He who loves practice without theory is like the sailor who boards the ship without a rudder and compass and never knows where he may cast.

—LEONARDO DA VINCI

As we explore the field of health communication, theories connect the dots, just as constellations reveal patterns in the stars. Good theories make sense of diverse information and help us to get our bearings. They help us know, in advance, where we are headed and what paths are available to us. *Theoretical Foundations* segments (sometimes in the text, sometimes in boxes of their own) showcase theories relevant to health communication. These theories address such issues as:

- What is health?
- How do we make sense of health crises?
- What behaviors enhance and compromise coping efforts?
- How do interpersonal relationships influence health?
- How does multiculturalism influence health and health care?
- How can health care organizations stimulate teamwork and innovation?
- In what ways do media messages influence our health?
- How do people respond to public health campaigns?
- What factors influence people to become more knowledgeable and proactive about their own health?

we are actively involved in health communication, not just passive recipients of information. A great deal of health communication involves professional caregivers, such as doctors, nurses, pharmacists, aides, therapists, counselors, and technicians. But we serve as caregivers for friends and loved ones as well. Chapter 8 demonstrates the value of social support when we are ill, healthy, and even (perhaps especially) when we cope with death and dying.

THE HISTORY OF HEALTH COMMUNICATION

Health communication emerged as a defined area of study in the late 1960s. Interest was spurred most notably by researchers and practitioners in psychology, medicine, sociology, and persuasion who recognized that communication is central to the process of health and healing (Kreps, Query, & Bonaguro, 2008, p. 5). Health communication has also flourished as a component of communication, business, nursing, public health, and allied health programs, to name just a few.

One lesson that has emerged is that communication is not separate from health care, but is therapeutic in itself. It is also the vehicle through which people learn about health and reach agreement about what is wrong and what could be better. This involves individual health as well as organizational structures and public policy.

Health communication scholars have also brought attention to social factors. It is common to think about health in terms of personal choices—a good diet, an active lifestyle, regular checkups, and good information. But the evidence is clear (see Chapters 6 and 14) that these options are not available to everyone in the same measure. Improving the health of a community requires that we also consider social equity, community resources, access to care, and the environment.

Health communication is often persuasive in nature. Communication—be it through news stories, PSAs, entertainment programming, or conversations with health professionals or loved ones—has an impact on whether we smoke, exercise, drink and drive, get enough sleep, take part in health screenings, and so on. Persuasive communication is a powerful tool. How, and under what circumstances, should we use it to influence people's behavior? What persuasive appeals are most effective? Which are unethical? We examine answers to these questions and others in Part VI.

Today, health communication research is a thriving field. Notable publications include the journal *Health Communication,* first published in 1989 and still led by founding editor Teresa Thompson at the University of Dayton, as well as *Qualitative Health Research*, the *Journal of Health Communication*, *Communication & Medicine*, *The Routledge Handbook of Health Communication* (T. L. Thompson, Parrott, & Nussbaum, 2011), and many others. (See Box 1.5 for a list of relevant organizations, and see Chapter 3 for a more comprehensive list of journals.)

As you probably realize by now, health communication is quite diverse. It unites interdisciplinary practitioners and scholars and covers a gamut of issues ranging from interpersonal communication, to culture, media, public health, education, and more. It involves the work of scholars around the world—from Europe to Australia and New Zealand, Asia, Canada, the United Kingdom, and the Americas (Thompson et al., 2011).

The following section introduces three approaches to health care that are fundamental to how and why people communicate as they do.

BOX 1.5 RESOURCES

Health Communication Organizations and Resources

This book is designed to give you a rich and current overview of health communication. We will visit a number of locations (social settings, doctors' offices, board rooms, movie theatres, and more) and look at health through different people's eyes. My hope is that, as you explore each perspective, your appreciation of the nuances that influence health and health communication will increase. Along the way you will probably want to know more than can be fit into one book, so *Resources* boxes provide information about relevant websites, organizations, publications, and more.

To get you started, here is a list of organizations and websites you might wish to investigate for more information about health communication:

- American College of Health Care Administrators: http://www.achca.org
- American College of Health Care Executives: http://www.healthmanagementcareers.org
- American Communication Association: www.americancomm.org
- American Public Health Association: www.apha.org
- American Society for Healthcare Human Resource Administration: http://www.ashhra.org
- Association for Education in Journalism & Mass Communication: www.aejmc.org
- Centers for Disease Control and Prevention: http://www.cdc.gov
- Central States Communication Association: www.csca-net.org
- Coalition for Healthcare Communication: www.cohealthcom.org
- Eastern Communication Association: www.ecasite.org
- European Association for Communication in Healthcare: www.each.eu
- European Public Health Association: www.eupha.org
- Health Care Public Relations Association: https://www.hcpra.org
- International Communication Association (Health Communication Division): www.icahdq.org
- International Union for Health Promotion and Education: www.iuhpe.org
- National Cancer Institute: http://www.cancer.gov
- National Center for Health Marketing: www.cdc.gov/healthmarketing
- National Communication Association (Health Communication Division): www.natcom.org
- National Institute of Health: www.nih.gov
- National Prevention Information Network: https://npin.cdc.gov
- Public Relations Society of America, Health Academy: healthacademy.prsa.org/index.html
- South Asian Public Health Forum: www.saphf.org
- Southern States Communication Association: www.ssca.net
- U.S. Department of Human Services Health Communication Activities: www.health.gov/communication
- Western States Communication Association: www.westcomm.org
- World Federation of Public Health Associations: www.wfpha.org
- World Health Organization: www.who.int/en

Health Care Models

What causes ill health? If your answer is germs, you have probably been influenced by the biomedical model, which is not surprising, considering that it has been the primary basis of conventional Western medicine for the last 100 years. But if you believe that illness is caused by a variety of factors—such as people's frame of mind, their values, and the communities in which they live—your views more closely reflect a biopsychosocial or sociocultural model. Following is a description of each model and its impact on health communication.

BIOMEDICAL

The **biomedical** model is based on the premise that ill health is a physical phenomenon that can be explained, identified, and treated through physical means. Biomedicine is well suited to a culture familiar with engines and computers. "Repairing a body, in this view, is analogous to fixing a machine," writes Charles Longino (1997, p. 14). Physicians are like scientists or mechanics. They collect information about a problem, try to identify the source of it, and fix it.

The focus is often reductionist. That is, in accordance with the scientific method, health professionals try to isolate key variables by bracketing out extraneous information. A medical interview may sound a lot like this: *When did the symptoms start? . . . Does it hurt when I do this? . . . On a scale of 1 to 10, how bad is the pain? . . . Have you had a fever?* Health communication influenced by the biomedical model is typically focused and specific. Health professionals' questions require only brief answers, such as *two weeks ago* and *yes*.

Biomedical talk tends to have its own vocabulary, which can be puzzling and intimidating to patients. A mother summoned to the hospital after her son had been injured remembers:

> *When I walked into the trauma center, they told me Justin had suffered severe trauma to his brain, a subarachnoid hemorrhage in the sylvian fissure and right posterior fossa, frontal lobe contusions, diffuse axonal shearing injuries, and a non-displaced vertical fracture of the C6 vertebra. What I heard was "brain damage, broken neck."*

Although her son's condition was critical, he eventually recovered. His mother says she feels lucky about the outcome, but she will never forget the terror of being confronted with medical jargon that frightened and confused her, rather than helping her understand what was really wrong.

Experts agree that the future of health care must involve greater collaboration between diverse care providers, health care leaders, and others. The challenge is to develop the communication skills necessary to make the most of multidisciplinary teamwork and problem solving.

At its best, the biomedical approach is efficient and definitive. Medical tests and observations may yield evidence that can be logically analyzed and treated with well-established methods. One criticism of the model, however, is that it marginalizes patients' feelings and social experiences, sometimes to the extent of treating people as impersonal collections of parts or symptoms. People are often dissatisfied when caregivers do not listen to their concerns surrounding an illness, and they may mistrust diagnoses if they feel that caregivers do not fully understand their problems.

BIOPSYCHOSOCIAL

The **biopsychosocial** perspective takes into account people's physical conditions (biology), their thoughts and beliefs (psychology), and their social expectations. From this perspective, health experiences are not solely physical phenomena but are also influenced by people's feelings, their ideas about health, and the events of their lives.

The biopsychosocial perspective emphasizes that no one approach works well with everyone. For example, some family caregivers welcome loved ones' help, whereas others find it disruptive. A caregiver interviewed by Elaine Wittenberg-Lyles and colleagues put it this way: "After not having anybody for a while and then having somebody here all the time kind of makes me—adds to my stress" (p. 906). The researchers observe that more social support is not always better. A more important consideration is how well it meets the recipient's preferences and psychological needs (Wittenberg-Lyles, Washington, Demiris, Oliver, & Shaunfield, 2014).

There is evidence to support the biopsychosocial premise that people's thoughts and emotions have an influence on their overall health and coping ability. Researchers have long known that emotional stress tends to elevate people's heart rates and blood pressure. They are now finding that excessive stress reduces the body's resistance to disease (e.g., Lovell, Moss, & Wetherell, 2011). On the bright side, health is sometimes enhanced by good humor, a positive attitude, and social support (e.g., Gallagher, Phillips, Ferraro, Drayson, & Carroll, 2008).

BOX 1.6 PERSPECTIVES

A Memorable Hospital Experience

In my short 27 years I have visited hospitals in four states, and only one stands out in my memory: St. Jude Children's Research Hospital in Memphis, Tennessee. My family spent nearly two years of our lives walking in and out of the doors of St. Jude while my sister was being treated for leukemia.

Walking into the administrative office the first day we arrived was like being in Grandma's house seated by a warm, open fireplace. During those first hours of our shock and fear over my sister's diagnosis, the hospital staff worked quickly on her paperwork without making us feel the least bit rushed. The warmth and tone of their voices was like that of a family member. We were assured we could always reach them—if not at work, at home! They were our new family.

The doctors at St. Jude stopped and spoke with families and patients and answered any questions they were asked. The doctors were not the only gems in the hospital, though. I remember two very special nurses, Jackie and Mary. One night my parents and I went to eat and were late getting back (it was shrimp night!). We found Mary, who had gotten off work 1½ hours earlier, reading to my sister. Jackie assisted my sister with manicuring her nails, even though it was not part of her technical duties. The nurses at St. Jude stepped out of their textbook roles to accommodate the needs of their patients.

Members of the housekeeping and dietary staff were always helpful, too. When my sister thought she had an appetite for a hamburger or macaroni and cheese, they always did their best to get some up to her before she realized she did not want anything at all.

The last person I recall from the support staff was Mrs. Fran, our social worker. She was a dream, not just a friend you could talk to but one you could count on to take care of the little things you naturally forget in situations such as ours. When my sister died, Mrs. Fran was there for my family and made all the arrangements to get us back home to Louisiana.

There were many difficulties in dealing with the death of a loved one, and my sister was only 15. However, my parents and I feel an incredible debt to St. Jude. We have founded a fundraising chapter for St. Jude in Baton Rouge and I hope to pursue a career to help caregivers, families, and the public understand the importance of interpersonal communication skills in hospitals and other health care centers.

—GWYNNÉ WILLIAMS

SOCIOCULTURAL

From a **sociocultural** perspective, health reflects a complex array of factors involving personal choice, social dynamics, and culture. Social variables include wealth, poverty, prejudice, access to health services, and living conditions, to name a few. Culture is embodied in shared values, traditions, and rituals.

The sociocultural perspective rejects the notion, on the one hand, that health is purely personal, and on the other hand, that people are simply products of their environment. Instead, it recognizes that these factors are mutually reflexive. Therefore, focusing on only one factor is typically counterproductive.

As an example, the popular Drug Abuse Resistance Education (DARE) program has been largely ineffective at changing schoolchildren's long-term attitudes and behavior concerning illegal drugs (Birkeland, Murphy-Graham, & Weiss, 2005). After studying the data, Nicole Stephens and colleagues concluded that DARE's impact is limited because it has focused almost exclusively on drug use as a matter of personal choice. The larger reality, they found, is that some young people live in environments in which drug use is prevalent, highly encouraged by their peers, and considered normal. Those youth "may find it harder to resist drug use by simply 'saying no,'" the researchers assert. "Instead, a different set of intervention strategies—for example, decreasing students' exposure to situations where drug use is likely—may be more useful or effective" (Stephens, Markus, & Fryberg, 2012, p. 729).

Ultimately, no medical model is comprehensive enough to cover all facets of health. The best option may be awareness that health can be approached in different ways and the versatility to use dimensions of these models appropriately. The biopsychosocial and sociocultural models are appealing for their thoroughness and personal concern (see Boxes 1.6 and 1.8). However, implementing a holistic approach is no easy task, and sometimes a biomedical solution is enough. In Chapters 3 through 5, we explore patterns and techniques of patient–caregiver communication. In Chapters 6 and 7, we investigate the link between health and sociocultural factors such as social status, race, gender, age, and ability. Then we return to the idea in Chapter 14, where we consider how a critical-cultural perspective can help health promoters give voice to marginalized groups and allow them to challenge and perhaps transform inequitable social structures.

IN YOUR EXPERIENCE

- Have your health care experiences been characterized more by the biomedical, the biopsychosocial, or the sociocultural model? How?
- Which do you prefer and why?

The Importance of Health Communication

Health communication is important to individuals, organizations, and society overall. It is crucial to meeting medical goals, enhancing personal well-being, saving time and money, and making the most of health information. Following are six reasons to study health communication. Each of these is addressed more fully in the chapters that follow.

First, *communication is crucial to the success of health care encounters*. Without it, caregivers cannot hear patients' concerns, make diagnoses, share their recommendations, or follow up on treatment outcomes. "Health communication is the singularly most important tool health professionals have to provide health care to their clients," write Kreps and Thornton (1992, p. 2). Patients who take an active role in medical encounters are more likely than others to be satisfied with their care (Ashraf et al., 2013).

Interpersonal communication is crucial, considering that about 32 million people in the United States (roughly 1 in 7 adults) are unable to read more than a simple children's storybook (U.S. Department of Education, 2015). Added to that figure are people who, although they can read, have language differences and physical challenges that make it difficult to understand and use health information. All of these fall within the category of health literacy. People with health literacy challenges are usually less knowledgeable about health issues than others, and they may miss appointments, avoid medical care because they are embarrassed or frustrated, prepare incorrectly for surgery and other procedures, misinterpret the instructions for medications, and more. Experts estimate that health literacy challenges result in avoidable medical costs totaling more than $106 billion a year in the United States (Vernon,

BOX 1.7 ETHICAL CONSIDERATIONS

An Essential Component of Health Communication

Our customers routinely bare their bodies, as well as their souls, within our organizations. I can think of no other enterprise in our society where so much is placed in the hands of others.

—LARRY SANDERS, CHAIR OF THE AMERICAN COLLEGE OF HEALTH CARE EXECUTIVES

Sanders (2003) advises those who provide and study health care, "One of the most significant ways we can demonstrate how much we care about those we serve is to visibly display our personal commitment to operating with extraordinary integrity, ethics and morality each and every day" (p. 46).

It is imperative that people involved with health care understand the ethical implications of their actions and conduct themselves with honor and integrity. They must also be aware of the perceptions of others. If people perceive—rightly or wrongly—that health-related professionals are unethical, they may experience stress, avoid medical care, lie to health care providers, or withhold information to protect themselves.

Many of the ethical dilemmas that people in health care face are essentially matters of communication. They involve honesty, privacy, power, conflicts of interest, social stigmas, media images, advertising, and persuasive messages about health. In most cases, there is more than one option, but no simple solution. What seems right in one situation may be wrong in another. Personal preference and culture, among other factors, shape what people want and expect. Even so, there is value in thinking through the implications and exploring diverse reactions with others.

An *Ethical Considerations* box in each chapter presents an ethical dilemma and a list of discussion questions and additional resources. I encourage you to discuss and debate these issues, eliciting diverse views. Do not be afraid to change your mind or to argue both sides of an issue. It is usually easier to behave ethically if you have thought the issues through *before* you find yourself in a real-life dilemma. Following are some questions you might ask yourself as you consider your options concerning ethical challenges posed in this book and elsewhere.

- Is this option legal?
- Is it honest? Is deception or omission of the truth involved?
- Who will be hurt? Who will be helped?
- Will the decision benefit me personally but hurt others?
- Are the results worth the hardship involved?
- Is it culturally acceptable?
- Will my decision compromise people's privacy or trust?
- Will my decision be demeaning or degrading to anyone?
- Is it fair? Will my action unfairly discriminate against anyone?
- Is the action appropriate for the situation?
- Have I considered all the options?
- How would I wish to be treated in the same situation?
- How would I feel if my decision or action were published in tomorrow's newspaper?

Trujillo, Rosenbaum, & DeBuono, 2007), and the loss in productivity and quality of life is immeasurable. Effective communication can offset the tragic and costly consequences of low literacy (Chapter 6).

Second, *wise use of mass media and social media can help people learn about health and minimize the influence of unhealthy and unrealistic media portrayals.* Media consumers—especially those who rely on newspapers, magazines, and computers—are likely to be well informed about health issues and to take an active role in maintaining their own health (Koch-Weser, Bradshaw, Gualtieri, & Gallagher, 2010; Rains, 2008a). However, the media is also filled with glamorous images of people engaging in unhealthy behaviors, making media literacy especially important. In Chapter 9, we survey innovative ways that health promoters are making use of online and mobile communication. In Chapters 11, 13, and 14 we explore health

BOX 1.8 PERSPECTIVES

Down, But Not Out

As a high school baseball pitcher, it was devastating to hurt my shoulder just three weeks from the playoffs. My doctor helped to lighten the mood a bit by saying, "You're a great kid and I like you, but I hate seeing you here in my office. That means something's wrong." I always felt comfortable with him because he knew how to connect with me and assure me that whatever the problem was, he would get it fixed and get me back out on the field.

As it turned out, I didn't need surgery, but I did need physical therapy five days a week. The therapists were really great. They were very strict when it came to my rehab and throwing program. "Absolutely no throwing if you feel any pain whatsoever. You got it?" one therapist said to me. They treated me like royalty, even though I wasn't, and made sure I was doing the right things to get healthy again. With the urgency to get back in the game quickly, they placed me on a fast-paced, demanding rehabilitation regimen. They made sure I received the appropriate amount of work every day, and they repeatedly asked me how my shoulder was coming along.

I can't say enough about how helpful and flexible they were with me. It was tough for me to come in during office hours, so they sacrificed their own time to come in early and stay late for me. Not once did they complain. They always had smiles on their faces and always seemed positive and excited to be helping me.

After two weeks of the well-conditioned rehab they put me through, I felt completely pain free and ready to pitch again. "Now if you ever need to come in again for any therapy or some shoulder exercises, you just come on in. Don't hesitate. We'll be here," the head physical therapist told me. "Yes ma'am, I appreciate everything you all have done for me," I replied. I am thankful to have had those professionals who gave me their best effort and went to the absolute maximum to ensure that I was taken care of and treated properly. I can never repay them for what they did for me.

—DREW

Drew went on to earn titles as Pitcher of the Year in Alabama, All-County Pitcher of the Year, and Most Valuable Pitcher of the Year, in addition to pitching for his college team.

images in the media, media literacy, and how to create effective health campaigns.

Third, *communication is an important source of personal confidence and coping ability.* Health professionals are less likely to experience burnout and less likely to leave the profession if they are satisfied (Dyrbye et al., 2013). Likewise, patients cope best when they feel comfortable talking about delicate subjects such as pain and death. And people involved in support groups often cope better and even live longer than similar persons who are not members (Chapter 8). In short, good communication is conducive to good health.

Fourth, *effective communication saves time and money.* Caregivers who listen attentively and communicate a sense of caring and warmth are less likely than others to be sued for malpractice (Dym, 2008). Likewise, patients who communicate clearly with their caregivers have the best chance of having their concerns immediately addressed, which is likely to improve their health and save time and money.

Fifth, *communication helps health care organizations operate effectively.* Communication skills are useful in recruiting employees, establishing innovative teams, creating efficient systems, and sustaining service excellence (Chapter 10). Studies show that supervisors' communication skills are one of the most important determinants of employees' satisfaction and their intention to stay on the job. Organizational leaders can also use communication to assess market needs and respond to patient preferences.

Sixth, *health communication may be important to you because of career opportunities.* The health industry already employees about 15.6 million people in the United States, and that number is expected to skyrocket to more than 20 million within a few years.

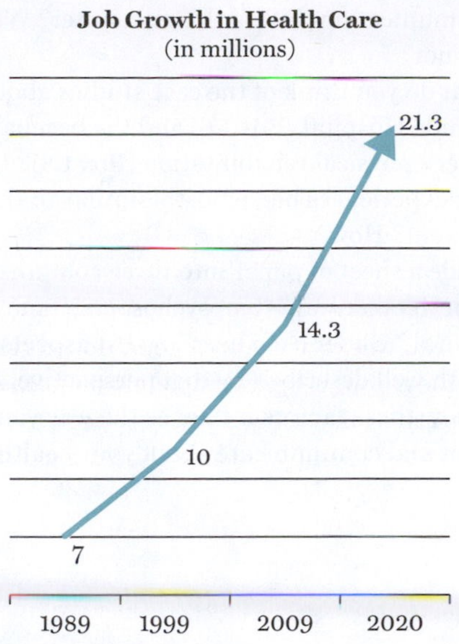

FIGURE 1.1 The job outlook in health care is better than in any other segment of the economy.

Sources: Hatch & Clinton, 2000; U.S. BLS, 2013

Experts predict that nearly one-third of the U.S. jobs created between 2012 and 2022 will be in health care (U.S. BLS, 2013). This includes jobs in clinical care, public relations, marketing, health care administration, human resources, education, community outreach, crisis management, patient advocacy, and more. (See Figure 1.1.)

Reasons for the notable job growth are threefold: (1) Baby boomers are retiring, which diminishes the current pool of professionals in health care; (2) health needs are simultaneously escalating as the average age of the population increases; and (3) health care reform has the potential to add 20 to 30 million Americans to health insurance rosters, qualifying them to receive medical care. Labor analysts predict a particularly high demand for nurses, allied health professionals, health educators, public health specialists, and health care administrators. Communication skills are a valuable asset in these and every other aspect of the health industry.

Summary

Health communication is accomplished within a complex array of influences. Teamwork skills, listening, and intercultural competence are central to the goals of empowering people and addressing their health needs, ideally *before* they become ill or injured.

From a transactional perspective, meanings and relationships are mutually and continually coconstructed by the people involved, who are themselves influenced by contexts, culture, and past experiences. Content-level meanings are explicit, but relational messages are typically implicit reflections on the power and status of people involved in communication transactions.

Three of the most popular ways of looking at health care are the biomedical, biopsychosocial, and sociocultural models. The biomedical model assumes that disease is best understood and treated in physical terms. The biopsychosocial model treats health as a broad concept that includes social, personal, and physical factors. The sociocultural model proposes that health-related behaviors reflect both personal choices and the larger dynamics in which people live.

Health communication is important for several reasons. It allows patients and caregivers to share concerns and establish trust. It helps people cope and build self-confidence. Communicating well saves time and money and helps organizations solicit, organize, and implement new ideas. Finally, media messages have the potential to improve or discourage healthy habits.

If health communication is good or bad, we have a host of people to thank or to blame. Almost always we are among those people. We influence the process throughout our lives. We all have something to gain by understanding the process and, hopefully, something to contribute as well.

Key Terms and Theories

accountable care organization (ACO)
health
transactional model of communication
relational approach
health communication
biomedical
biopsychosocial
sociocultural

Discussion Questions

1. Imagine that you have been given responsibility for your family members' health. You can hire any collection of professionals you like, but you should

not limit your thinking to traditional aspects of health care. What factors would you consider in terms of each person's health? Who would you involve in making sure that your healthy family members stay healthy?

2. Spend a few minutes writing about a health care encounter you have experienced as a patient, loved one, or health professional. Identify at least three content-level and three relational-level messages in the encounter. How were the relational-level messages conveyed? What role did culture and prior experiences play in the encounter? Were you mostly satisfied with communication during this encounter? Why or why not?
3. What do you think of the case studies about St. Jude Hospital (Box 1.6) and the baseball player's physical rehabilitation (Box 1.8)? Have your experiences been mostly similar to these or different? How?
4. Divide a sheet of paper into three columns. Label them "biomedical," "biopsychosocial," and "socio-cultural." Under each heading, list aspects of your health well described by that perspective. Reflect on how these factors influence the way you think about and communicate about your health.

CHAPTER 2

The Landscape for Health Communication

Julian is in class one day when he begins to feel queasy. "That's weird," he thinks. "It's probably that late-night pizza catching up with me. Or maybe it's the stress of final exams in a few weeks." He rubs his stomach and tries to concentrate on the class.

Health issues, both large and small, arise nearly daily in our lives. They are often resolved with a good night's sleep or an Internet search. At other times, they require that we navigate the health care system. Either way, one thing is certain: We will all be involved in health care in one way or another—as patients, loved ones, community members, professionals, researchers, and/or policy-makers. This chapter provides a foundation for understanding some of the most pressing issues in health care.

As you may remember from Chapter 1, one tenet of transactional communication is that we are influenced by the larger contexts and systems in which we live. Therefore, before we launch an in-depth exploration of health communication issues, it's important to understand the landscape in which they occur. We will delve further into many of these issues throughout the book. For now, it is enough to speak knowledgeably about issues related to cost-effectiveness, communication technology, and health care reform. These issues affect us as participants in health-related endeavors. They also prepare us, as scholars, to better appreciate how and why people communicate as they do about health.

Current Issues in Health Care

When Julian's stomach is still bothering him several days later, his friends urge him to see a doctor. Julian knows it is good advice. If this is something serious, he'd like to stop it before it gets worse. On the other hand, he has a number of reservations: He would hate to miss school or work right now. The last time he tried to get a doctor's appointment, he had to wait a week and then sit in the waiting room for more than an hour. He's not sure he can afford a doctor's visit. And even if he had the time and money, he doesn't quite know whom to call. For now, he decides, he will look up his symptoms online and see what he can learn that way.

Julian's internal dialogue reflects many of the important issues in health care and health communication today—preventive care, cost and efficiency, treatment approaches, and patient empowerment.

PREVENTIVE CARE

It is healthier, and ultimately less costly, to prevent illnesses and injuries than to treat them once they become serious. If Julian is developing appendicitis, for example, early care might prevent surgery, permanent damage to his health, and even death. This is true of health concerns across the board. When conditions such as diabetes, cancer, obesity, and asthma are not well managed, they typically cause serious complications that are costly and difficult to treat (Mahon & Weymouth, 2012).

The value of early and preventive care is evident in countries that make it a priority. Japan spends less than $3,000 per citizen on health care annually, whereas the United States spends about $8,000 ("Health Expenditures," 2009; Mahon & Weymouth, 2012). Unlike the United States, however, Japan invests its much smaller budget heavily in prevention, regular care, and early detection of disease. Partly as a result, Japanese citizens live an average of five years longer than Americans and outperform the United States on many other health indicators as well (WHO, 2012c).

Clearly, it is in everyone's best interest to keep people healthy, but providing preventive care is not simple. It requires a different orientation and infrastructure than reactive care, and it relies on the concerted efforts of everyday citizens and a diverse array of professionals. A large part of the effort involves communication. As we discuss in Chapters 12 through 14, public health involves mass-communicated messages, one-on-one communication, partnerships and community resources, crisis management, and more. And since prevention usually involves ongoing attention to a complex array of factors, the most effective efforts are led by diverse groups of community members, public health professionals, physicians, nurses, dietitians, pharmacists, social workers, health campaign designers, and others. In Chapter 5, we talk about the rewards and challenges of communication in multidisciplinary teams such as these.

COST EFFICIENCY

Part of Julian's dilemma involves the time and costs involved in receiving care. These issues are serious concerns among health leaders and policy-makers as well. The United States spends 11 times more on health care now than it did in 1980 ("National Health Care Expenditure," 2014) and far more, per citizen, than any other nation. However it lags behind other industrialized nations in terms of equitable care for all citizens. The upshot is that, despite large budgets, treatment delays are common and many people receive almost no care at all. Nearly everyone agrees that the system must become more efficient.

IN YOUR EXPERIENCE

- Have you ever witnessed treatment duplications or health care practices that wasted time or money? If so, explain how.

Part of the financial crisis is a reflection of health care's success. Worldwide, the average lifespan is more than twice as long as it was in 1900, mostly because of better living conditions and health care, at least in some regions (Roser, 2015). During that same time, health costs have increased dramatically as medicine has becoming increasingly high tech and specialized.

In the United States, a chasm has emerged between people who can keep up with the rising costs of health care and those who cannot. The government created Medicare and Medicaid in 1965 to provide health insurance to impoverished children, pregnant women, people with disabilities, and individuals who are 65 and older. Even so, by the year 2010, nearly 50 million Americans (about 1 in 6 people) were uninsured, reflecting the reality that insurance premiums rose 10 times faster than wages between 2001 and 2008 (How, Fryer, McCarthy, Schoen, & Schor, 2011; Robert Wood Johnson Foundation, 2008).

As you might predict, people without insurance tend to forego regular checkups and health screenings and to seek care only when they are seriously ill or injured. It might seem that this would save the system money. But as we just discussed, the opposite is true, since prevention is more cost effective than treatment. In states with the largest number of uninsured residents, health care costs are higher—as much as five times higher—than in well-insured states (Cantor, Schoen, Belloff, How, & McCarthy, 2007).

CAN YOU GUESS? PART 1

1. What percentage of Americans who go bankrupt do so because of medical bills?
2. What percentage of Americans who go bankrupt because of medical bills were insured when their health crises began?
3. What is the average medical debt that drives people into bankruptcy?

Answers appear at the end of the chapter.

Wasteful practices also contribute to high costs. Analysts estimate that the United States could save more than $100 billion a year by curbing excessive insurance administration costs (The Commonwealth Fund, 2011). Waste also results from hospital visits and other care that could be avoided with more effective communication. Americans are five times more likely than residents of other countries to report that their doctors order duplicate tests and do not have test results when they show up for appointments (The Commonwealth Fund, 2011). In Chapter 10, we discuss ways that people in many health organizations are striving to design more cost-effective systems.

Managed care, launched in the late 1980s, was a wide-scale effort to increase efficiency and make health more affordable. More recently, the Affordable Care Act offers incentives for health organizations that cut costs without sacrificing patient outcomes. Later in the chapter, we talk more about these two initiatives and their impact on health communication.

CAN YOU GUESS? PART 2

1. What percentage of U.S. residents age 65 and older are uninsured?
2. Prior to the Affordable Care Act, passed in 2010, the number of uninsured residents in the United States was equal to the population of which state?
   a. Maine
   b. Alabama
   c. Oklahoma

Answers appear at the end of the chapter.

TREATMENT APPROACHES

Julian is unsure whether his symptoms are the result of stress, a common virus, or something more serious. As he considers what to do next, he wonders whether he should call the campus counseling center or a physician.

The question of whether to seek mental or physical care stems largely from a philosophy made popular by philosopher René Descartes in the 1600s. In this section we briefly contrast Descartes' dualistic model with holistic medicine.

Mind-Body Dualism

A powerful idea emerged in Europe as the Middle Ages gave way to the Renaissance. Health care during the Middle Ages had been offered mostly through the Catholic Church. Although the church recognized physical and emotional manifestations of health, it focused on spiritualism as the main cause and cure of these maladies. The church went so far as to ban surgery, based on the belief that the soul inhabits a person's entire body; therefore the body should not be altered (A. D. White, 1896/1925). Partly in response to the church's dominance, Renaissance philosopher and mathematician René Descartes (1596–1650) proposed a radically different way of thinking about the soul, mind, and body. His ideas continue to influence conventional Western medicine today.

Descartes proposed that the soul dwells only temporarily in the human body and lives on after the body dies. He also theorized that the soul is seated in the human brain (other animals being presumably soulless). Based on **Cartesian dualism**, the body and soul are separate entities, and the soul is most closely associated with the mind, not spread throughout the body (Cottingham, 1992).

WHAT DO YOU THINK?

- In what ways do you consider the mind and body to be separate? In what ways intertwined?
- Have you ever experienced a health concern that could not easily be verified?

The medical implications of Cartesian dualism are profound, including the separation of conventional Western medicine into two branches, one for the mind and one for the body. From this perspective, disease (a physical condition) is distinguishable from illness (the condition as it is experienced). Of course, this distinction goes only so far. Few people would argue that the mind and the body have no influence on each other. Nevertheless, dualism was, and still is, accepted as a general principle. For the most part, medical doctors (e.g., internists, cardiologists, neurologists) consider it their primary function to treat physical ailments. Mental health is more the domain of psychiatrists, psychologists, social workers, and the like.

Cartesian dualism has heavily influenced conventional Western medicine, but it is only one of many models. A contrast is available in holistic medicine, which we discuss next.

Holistic Approach

One of the most influential holistic approaches is Traditional Chinese Medicine (TCM), which dates to 1766 B.C. TCM is based on the idea that health is a reflection of energy that flows within the body and between the body and one's external environment. Optimal health results when these forms of energy are balanced and their flow unimpeded.

Communication within this tradition involves using the senses—observing, touching, and smelling—to assess a person's health status and the best remedies for him or her (Xutian, Cao, Wozniak, Junion, & Boisvert, 2012). TCM practitioners are trained to sense and to visualize energy circulation within people and within the patterns of their life, with special attention to energy deficiencies, excesses, and obstructions (Xutian et al., 2012).

Even in health systems that adhere largely to a conventional Western approach, holistic medicine has gained popularity in recent years. Nearly 4 in 10 Americans now use therapies such as chiropractic, acupuncture, and relaxation therapy—and worldwide, 8 in 10 people use these therapies (National Center for Complementary, 2012). These methods are relatively inexpensive and are geared toward prevention and long-term health maintenance.

From the perspective of conventional Western medicine, it's easy to see why Julian might wonder if he should see a mental health counselor or a medical doctor. However, that distinction is often less relevant to holistic care.

This brief overview may stimulate your thinking in the next section of the book, in which we explore research about patient–caregiver communication. In Chapter 7, we talk more about these and other ways of conceptualizing health and health care.

PATIENT EMPOWERMENT

Julian notices that, in addition to an upset stomach, he has begun to feel a dull pain in the region of his belly button. He pulls out his phone to look up those symptoms online.

It is easier than ever to be knowledgeable about health. It is the subject of television channels, magazines, books, news programs, advertisements, and extensive computer databases. News media in the United States release more than 3,500 health-related stories in a typical 18-month period (Kaiser Family Foundation, 2008). The current Information Age coincides with a move toward **patient empowerment** (Hardey, 2008). Empowerment means that lay persons have considerable knowledge and influence concerning their own health.

If Julian visits a care provider, he may approach the encounter with knowledge he has gained online and with the increasingly common idea that, as a patient, he will take an active role in the experience. Empowered patients tend to ask questions and state preferences. And, compared to previous generations of patients, they are more likely to seek health consultations, not because they are ill, but because they would like information or feedback on a health issue.

These factors may reduce the status difference between patients and their caregivers. As Tom Ferguson (1997) puts it:

> *As we move farther into the Information Age, health professionals will do more than just*

treat their patients' ills—they will increasingly serve as their coaches, teachers, and colleagues, working side-by-side with empowered consumers in a high-quality system of computer-supported, low-cost, self-managed care. (para. 34)

It will be interesting to see how patients and caregivers adapt to the idea that they are well-informed partners working toward common goals. On the one hand, patient empowerment relieves some of the pressure on caregivers to "fix" people who do very little to maintain their own health (R. M. Kaplan, 1997). On the other, patient empowerment dispels the notion that people should simply follow health professionals' orders. It's no longer enough (if ever it was) simply to tell patients what to do. Empowered patients want information and the right to make their own decisions. Changing expectations require new communication skills and different styles of interaction on the part of patients and caregivers.

So far, we have taken an introductory look at four issues foremost on the minds of health care professionals and scholars: prevention, cost efficiency, treatment modalities, and patient empowerment. In the next section, we broaden the scope to consider three macro-level influences on health care—global health issues, population shifts, and technology use.

Impact of Social Changes

When Julian looks up "pain near the belly button" he notices a news story about a pandemic that has killed or sickened people in 20 countries. He notes with relief that his symptoms are nothing like theirs, but it reminds him to take precautions before his study-abroad experience just months away.

Changes in the world around us have profound influences on health care. Here we examine three of those changes in terms of global health, population shifts, and technological advances.

GLOBAL HEALTH

Travel, immigration, and the international exchange of food and products mean that diseases today are continually carried across national borders. The outbreak of Ebola in 2014 provided a striking example of how quickly a communicable disease can spread. Ebola killed more than 10,000 people in three West African countries and sickened or killed about 50 people in five other countries (WHO, 2015, "Ebola Situation").

The number of new Ebola cases had dropped dramatically, as of press time. However, the AIDS epidemic has been far more global and persistent. The number of new HIV/AIDS cases has leveled off since 2000, partly because of aggressive health promotion efforts. Slower spread of the virus is an intermediate victory for health educators, but the situation remains critical. In Chapter 12 we focus on international teamwork and the intercultural competence necessary to deal effectively with Ebola, SARS, AIDS, avian flu, and other public health concerns.

CHANGING POPULATIONS

Population shifts are also changing health care needs in the United States. One shift is toward an older society. About 1 in 5 Americans soon will be 65 or older (Ortman, Velkoff, & Hogan, 2014). Although many older adults are healthy, they are more likely than others to have chronic diseases, which will increase the need for medical care, assisted living facilities, social services, and home care.

The racial and cultural mix of American society is also changing. By 2042, people from current minority racial and ethnic groups will comprise the majority of the U.S. population (U.S. Census Bureau News, 2008). This presents an unprecedented richness of diversity. Unfortunately, it is anticipated that people from minority groups will still have disproportionately fewer educational and professional opportunities than others, meaning that the number of underprivileged individuals in the United Sates will probably rise.

People with limited education and income are typically most in need of health care but are least likely to be informed about health issues and to utilize health services. Health literacy challenges often cause harmful misunderstandings, treatment failures, avoidable suffering and hospitalization, and even premature death. It is not yet clear whether technology will help bridge literacy gaps (by presenting information in clear, visual terms and in multiple languages) or whether people already at a disadvantage will fall further behind because they do not have equal access to information-rich resources such as the Internet. (We return to these topics in Chapters 6 and 9.)

Complicating the issue even further, diversity among health care workers is not expected to keep pace with the overall population. Currently, minorities comprise about 12% of physicians and 18.5% of registered nurses in the United States, which is far smaller than their representation (nearly 30%) in the population (U.S. Bureau of Labor Statistics, 2015; U.S. Census Bureau, 2014). As a result, the odds are that patients will be treated by caregivers who differ markedly from them in terms of knowledge, needs, and cultural beliefs. Communication is a valuable tool for meeting this challenge (Chapters 6 and 7).

CAN YOU GUESS? PART 3

1. Does the United States spend more on national defense or on health care?
2. Order the following countries, from the one that spends the least on health care, per capita (dollars divided by the number of citizens), to the one that spends the most: Australia ______, Iceland ______, the United Kingdom ______, China ______, USA ______, France ______
3. Which, if any, of the following countries outranks the United States on the World Health Organization's evaluation of national health systems? France, Japan, Cyprus, Saudi Arabia, Morocco, Chile, Costa Rica, Cuba, Colombia, Malta

Answers appear at the end of the chapter.

TECHNOLOGY USE

When Julian visits the doctor, she confirms that his appendix is slightly enlarged. She prescribes antibiotics and asks Julian to check in with her daily via email so they can closely monitor his symptoms, since appendicitis can be life threatening. "If you don't feel better in the next few days, call the phone number on this card," she says. "A nurse is available around the clock to answer questions and make arrangements for emergency care, if necessary. Or, if you prefer, use our online chat service to communicate with a member of our care team any time."

As Julian's experience illustrates, new options in technology are expanding the opportunities for health communication. Telemedicine, the ability to offer care from a distance, now avails many people with medical care, information, and social support they would not otherwise receive.

In addition, new eHealth options, which convey information via computers and mobile devices, are emerging everyday. eHealth involves information of general interest as well as personalized messages tailored to individuals' goals. New mobile apps allow people to measure, record, and reflect on health indicators that are important to them, and if they wish, to share that data with health professionals.

Another promising eHealth option involves multimedia storytelling, in which people are not only consumers of information but are actively (and interactively) involved in sharing health-related narratives that they create themselves (Cozma, 2009). The process can be rich, therapeutic, and informative. At the same time, it sometimes diverts attention from scientific information, which is typically more complex and less emotionally immediate than personal stories (Cozma). We explore issues related to telemedicine, eHealth, media storytelling, and more in Chapter 9 and in *Health and Communication Technology* segments throughout the book.

Technology may also improve the affordability and quality of health care. Used effectively, electronic medical records (EMRs) can save time, prevent

The information age affords people who are technology literate with the chance to be proactive consumers of health-related information.

mistakes, and help coordinate patient care. EMRs are similar to traditional patient records. However, because they can be viewed and shared by a number of health professionals in different locations, they allow caregivers to more easily avoid treatment overlaps and drug interactions and to track patients' overall progress. EMRs are also invaluable in emergencies, when paper records might be unavailable or when waiting for them would waste precious time.

In contrast to countries such as the Netherlands and New Zealand, in which nearly all physicians use electronic medical records, only about 46% of U.S. physicians utilize them (The Commonwealth Fund, 2011). As we discuss in Chapter 9, this is partly because EMR systems can be cumbersome to use and clogged with unorganized information.

If these challenges can be overcome, EMRs may represent a way to improve communicate and save money and lives.

In closing this section, although it may seem that the average person is not directly affected by shifts in the health industry, that is far from the case. Changes influence the type of caregivers people are likely to see, what services are available, and what role individuals play in maintaining their own health. People who work in the health industry are likely to experience the stress and promise of change, the pressure to save money, the opportunity to use new technology, and the need to communicate effectively with a variety of people and include them as partners in their own care.

In the next two sections, we take a closer look at two efforts to make health care more affordable, less wasteful, and more accessible—managed care and health care reform.

Managed Care

Let's back up a bit in Julian's story. . . . Before he called a doctor, he phoned his parents to check on his insurance status, remembering that his older sister was uninsured her last year in college because, like him, she was a part-time student. Julian's parents assure him that the rules have changed since then and he is indeed covered on their health insurance policy. On that encouraging note, they tell him how to access a website that lists care providers included on their plan.

Julian's conversation with his parents reflects elements of managed care and the Affordable Care Act, which we will talk about next.

Managed care organizations coordinate the costs and delivery of health services. Whereas health decisions were once made almost entirely by caregivers and patients, managed care organizations now recruit patients, match them up with caregivers and facilities, and monitor expenses. As such, managed care represents the influence of people (or entities) other than patients and caregivers. By managing resources such as money, labor, technology, and facilities, people in managed care organizations seek to make health care more efficient and affordable. Since managed care took root in the 1980s, it has expanded to include 99% of U.S. residents with employer-sponsored health plans and nearly 90% of physicians (Boukus, Cassil, & O'Malley, 2009; Henry J. Kaiser, 2014). To understand the variety of managed care organizations, let's fast forward a year or so and pretend that Julian is choosing between health insurance options, which he is likely to do when he gets a full-time job. Here is a description of his main options and the implications of each in terms of health communication.

CONVENTIONAL INSURANCE

At one point, nearly everyone who had health insurance in the United States had conventional (also known as *indemnity*) insurance. Now, less than 1% of employee-sponsored plans meet this description (Henry J. Kaiser, 2014). But let's imagine that Julian's employer is one of the few that offers this option.

As a conventional insurance subscriber, Julian will pay a set monthly amount (**insurance premium**) and the first $500 or so of his annual medical expenses (his **deductible**). If his expenses exceed this deductible, insurance will pay most of the remaining costs (usually about 80%) and he will pay the rest. To prevent him from going into overwhelming debt, there is an upper limit, called a **catastrophic cap**, on the amount of out-of-pocket money he will be required to pay each year. Beyond that limit, insurance will pay 100%.

On the downside, premiums for conventional insurance are usually higher than in other plans. However, subscribers have more freedom than in other plans to choose their own doctors and other providers. From a communication perspective, this means

Reimbursement rates based on diagnosis-related groups (DRGs) encourage hospitals to treat and discharge patients quickly. This can create a dilemma for health professionals when they feel a patient would benefit from more care but his or her ability to pay for it has ended.

Julian will have the chance to choose care providers with whom he feels most comfortable.

Conventional insurance is classified as **fee-for-service** because providers are paid (reimbursed) for specific care they provide. In other words, doctors, hospitals, physical therapists, and so on, make money only if people use their services. One implication is that care providers may overprescribe tests and treatments. Another is that wellness is not highly rewarded in the fee-for-service model. Traditionally, conventional insurance policies have not covered routine checkups.

Conventional insurance represents a **third-party payer** system because, as you can see, there are three parties involved—the provider, the patient, and the payer (insurance company). Over time, the balance of power between these parties has shifted. For example, insurance companies used to pay hospitals based on the costs they incurred while providing care. Beginning in the early 1980s, however, the U.S. government and insurance companies began establishing flat-rate reimbursement amounts for inpatient hospital procedures. Because the rates were classified within general types of care (e.g., cardiac, oncology), they came to be known as **diagnosis-related groups (DRGs)**. This is known as a **prospective payment structure** because reimbursement is established in advance rather than after care has been provided. This payment structure has made communication between care providers and funding agencies particularly important. If they are not on the same page in terms of what care a patient needs, it is unlikely that the provider will receive full payment.

DRGs are meant to reward hospitals for cutting costs and expediting care. They probably have, to some extent. A hospital whose expenses fall below the reimbursement rate can keep the difference as profit. A few other things have happened as well. For one, hospital stays have become dramatically shorter and available only to people with serious illnesses and injuries. Some hospitals have also begun to limit or discontinue procedures with low reimbursement rates.

DRGs sometimes put health professionals in the uncomfortable position of telling patients that they have reached the limit of what their insurance will cover. Said a health professional in one study, "Little grandma with a broken hip can't get but 20 feet in her walker. It's tough for her to get around but [under DRGs] she doesn't belong in the hospital . . . so you sign them out. And it's terribly cruel!" (Geist & Hardesty, 1992, p. x).

DRGs are not only a factor in traditional insurance, but also in managed care. Let's consider Julian's options in that arena. The averages presented here are based on the Henry J. Kaiser Family Foundation's 2014 employee health benefits survey.

HEALTH MAINTENANCE ORGANIZATION

A **health maintenance organization (HMO)** is designed to be more or less a one-stop shop for members' health needs. An HMO hires physicians and other care providers, who work directly for the HMO. Their salaries are covered by the premiums that members pay each month. If Julian chooses an HMO, he will pay a monthly premium and a **copay** every time he visits a doctor.[1] This includes checkups and preventive care visits. Most HMOs do not have deductibles, but about a third of them do.

Knowing that he will probably never pay more than $25 a visit, Julian might be more willing to have annual checkups and to seek care for minor health

[1]For now, let's leave prescription drugs, outpatient surgery, and hospital care out of the mix. With managed care, separate copays and deductibles usually apply to those services.

concerns than if he had conventional insurance. This is meant to save money in the long run, both for members and for HMOs.

Among managed care options, HMOs present the smallest set of provider options. Julian may only see care providers who work for the HMO, and he may not always have a choice about whom he sees among them.

As an HMO member, Julian cannot see specialists unless such care is recommended by a primary care physician in the HMO. This is designed to avoid unnecessary visits and costs, but the approval process and limitations can be frustrating.

You guessed it: HMOs are not third-party payer systems. In their case, it's as if the insurance company and the medical center had merged into one. And they are not based on fee-for-service. Instead, HMOs are **capitated systems**. They receive a set (capitated) amount, in the form of premiums (plus minor copays), no matter what care they provide. It is the job of HMOs to manage both the budget and the care.

Some people (including many care providers) worry that combining the insurance company with the medical center presents a conflict of interest. We'll talk more about that shortly. First, let's continue the tour of managed care options.

PREFERRED PROVIDER ORGANIZATION

A **preferred provider organization (PPO)**, also in the managed care family, works a little differently. If Julian joins a PPO, his premium will probably be about the same as if he joined an HMO, but he will have an annual deductible, and his copay will vary by procedure.

Here's how it works. Rather than hiring care providers outright, as HMOs do, PPOs contract with independent care providers. The PPO agrees to put the provider on a "preferred" list if the provider offers services at agreed-on discount rates to the PPO's members. Julian's copay will be a percentage of this discounted fee. This means he will pay different amounts for different services. It also means he can choose any care providers he wishes, with one caveat: As the name implies, providers on the "preferred" list cost less than those who are not. There are often higher copays and/or separate deductibles for providers not on the list. But unlike HMO members, Julian will receive *some* financial coverage no matter which caregivers he chooses.

If Julian requires a lot of care or if he sees non-preferred providers, he is likely to pay more as a PPO member than as an HMO member. But he will have more freedom of choice in a PPO, which can be a bonus in terms of relationship building. He may also encounter less conflict of interest because (1) PPO providers do not work directly for the managed care organization, so they may be spared some of the pressure to cut costs and speed up patient visits, and (2) they operate on a fee-for-service basis that gives them more incentive to prescribe (rather than avoid) tests and treatment. These advantages may be why the majority of people with employee health plans choose PPOs (58% compared to 13% in HMOs).

HIGH-DEDUCTIBLE HEALTH PLAN

Perhaps Julian is in excellent health and almost never seeks medical care. He may wonder, "Why should I pay such high premiums when I never meet the deductible anyway? My money goes in, but it doesn't come out—at least it doesn't come to me." And if he is really thinking long-term, he might also wonder, "Rather than paying high premiums, why can't I save that money for the future, when my medical bills are likely to be higher?"

These are the basic concepts behind **high-deductible health plans (HDHPs)**. Members pay relatively low monthly premiums. In exchange, their deductibles are two to three times more than for other plans and the catastrophic cap is several thousand dollars higher.

HDHP members qualify to invest in tax-deferred **health savings accounts (HSA)** that they can use to pay for current and future medical expenses. This is meant to encourage people to control their own health costs. After all, if Julian has a high deductible and is

WHAT DO YOU THINK?

- Which type of health insurance do you prefer as a consumer? Why?
- What type would you prefer as a health professional? Why?
- Less than half of Americans fully understand their health insurance plans. Do you feel confident that you understand yours?
- Do you worry that your doctor might not prescribe tests or treatments because he or she is being pressured to cut costs? Why or why not?

paying medical bills from his own account, he might think twice before seeing a doctor.

Unfortunately, this is also the downside of HDHPs. Some people buy into them because they can afford the lower premiums only to find that they cannot afford the out-of-pocket costs that lie ahead. Reports abound of people who are insured but still cannot afford to buy prescription drugs or see a doctor. Even if Julian has not needed much medical care in years past, one accident or major illness can wreck his finances.

As you can see, managed care has given rise to its own vocabulary, and the system and terms continue to evolve. For a handy synopsis of relevant terms, see Box 2.1.

Managed care also affects hospitals, medical centers, treatment and diagnostic centers, and other organizations. Their budgets and decisions are heavily influenced by budget constraints, paperwork, and capitation, as you will see in the following synopsis of the pros and cons of managed care.

BOX 2.1

Managed Care at a Glance

MANAGED CARE: A health care system in which income, resources, and health services are supervised by a managing body such as a health maintenance organization or preferred provider organization. Patients pay the organization a set fee each month to receive health services.

HEALTH MAINTENANCE ORGANIZATION (HMO): A managed care organization that offers enrollees a variety of health services for a set monthly fee and copays. Caregivers are usually employed directly by the HMO and provide services only to HMO members.

PREFERRED PROVIDER ORGANIZATION (PPO): A managed care organization that pays independent caregivers a discounted fee for each service they provide to PPO members. Patients may visit providers not on the preferred list, but they pay higher fees to do so.

HIGH-DEDUCTIBLE HEALTH PLAN (HDHP): A managed care plan with lower-than-normal premiums but higher deductibles and out-of-pocket spending caps. Most HDHPs qualify members to establish tax-exempt health savings accounts.

HEALTH SAVINGS ACCOUNT (HSA): A tax-exempt savings plan (a lot like an IRA) in which people can set aside money to pay future medical bills. U.S. taxpayers qualify for HSAs if they are part of high-deductible health plans. Money saved can be used over many years' time.

HEALTH REIMBURSEMENT ACCOUNT (HRA): Not to be confused with an HSA, a health reimbursement account (HRA) is a temporary fund in which an employee can set aside tax-exempt money for health care costs incurred within the plan year. For example, you might have $100 set aside from each paycheck before taxes. Your employer will use this money to reimburse you for medical expenses during the year. Typically, if you do not use the money in an HRA by year's end, you forfeit the balance.

PREMIUM: A membership fee paid by subscribers in a conventional insurance or managed care plan. Usually deducted from one's paycheck.

CAPITATION: A set fee paid to cover a person's health needs, regardless of the care actually required.

CATASTROPHIC CAP: An upper limit on the amount of out-of-pocket expense a subscriber is required to pay each year.

COPAY: The portion of a health care bill the patient is required to pay when services are rendered.

DEDUCTIBLE: The amount of out-of-pocket medical expense an insured individual is required to pay before receiving financial assistance from the insurer. For example, you might pay the first $500 of your emergency room bill, and insurance will pay 80% of the remaining cost.

FEE-FOR-SERVICE: The practice of being paid for specific care provided.

PROS AND CONS OF MANAGED CARE

Overall, there are upsides and downsides to managed care. Following are a few considerations both ways. One note before we begin: In the parlance of health care, *insurers* include both conventional insurance companies and managed care organizations. However, as you have seen, 99% of insurance policies are now managed care memberships. So when people talk about "insurers" these days, they mostly mean managed care organizations.

Advantages

Following are some factors in favor of managed care.

PREDICTIVE BUDGETING The beauty of capitation is that it offers predictable, steady income based on members' contributions. Although the budget under managed care is typically smaller than before, advance planning is more feasible. "Capitation gave us the flexibility to use our budget with creativity limited only by our imaginations and habits," recall physicians Joseph Dorsey and Donald Berwick (2008, p. A9) of Harvard Pilgrim Health Care. They invested in innovative and patient-friendly services such as reminder calls, after-hours phone access, extended clinic hours, time-saving technology, and more. As a result, in the early days of managed care, their patient/members made half as many visits to emergency rooms as the state average.

INCENTIVE TO REDUCE COSTS Managed care rewards health care organizations for streamlining processes and eliminating wasteful practices. With capitation and DRGs, only organizations that operate in a cost-effective way make money.

MORE AFFORDABLE CARE A related benefit is that managed care is designed to make health care more affordable. In a global sense, the system is oriented toward making the most of every health care dollar. At an individual level, patients pay set or reduced fees, even if they need a lot of care. This can be especially valuable to people with chronic illnesses who benefit from regular treatment (Nussbaum, Ragan, & Whaley, 2003).

WELLNESS The expectation early on was that managed care organizations would invest in disease prevention and education because, with capitation, well patients would cost them less than sick or injured ones. (As you will soon see, this potential has not been well realized so far.)

ADMINISTRATIVE ASSISTANCE AND TEAMWORK Individual health professionals may also benefit from managed care. One physician says that managed care gave him his life back. He does not make as much money as before, but as an HMO employee he does not have as many administrative responsibilities. He is only on call one day a week, and he can schedule days off—all luxuries he did not have as a physician entrepreneur.

CAREER JUMP START Managed care organizations can also offer the advantages of a ready-made caseload. Signing on as an HMO employee or a preferred provider means built-in advertising among hundreds or thousands of available patients.

ADVANTAGES OF MANAGED CARE

- The potential for predictive budgeting and teamwork
- Goal of making health care more affordable
- Incentive to keep patients well
- Less administrative load for practitioners
- Ready-made caseload for practitioners

Disadvantages

Unfortunately, as the system has evolved, the disadvantages of managed care have become numerous. It may help as you read the following list of drawbacks to keep in mind that *something* had to be done. It is conceivable that we would be in even worse shape without the managed care revolution. But clearly, we still have a long way to go.

COSTS CONTINUE TO RISE One disappointment is that, overall, the goal of cutting costs has not been realized. Managed care may have slowed spiraling costs to some extent, but premiums have climbed steadily. During the 1990s, health insurance premiums rose by 53%, far outpacing inflation and wage increases (Economic Research Initiative, 2005). The upward spiral has moderated somewhat since 2009—rising only by 26% in five years (Henry J. Kaiser, 2014). However, it still outstrips wage increases and inflation.

Some spokespersons for managed care say that premium hikes are necessary because health expenses are rising and the population is getting older. However, critics charge that managed care organizations are making profits while patients and providers lose money. The average salary of managed care executives is about $200,000 a year (Economic Research Institute, 2012), a figure that has been rising even as industry spokespeople say premium hikes are necessary.

PREVENTION STILL NOT A PRIORITY It is sometimes said that the United States does not have a health care system, it has an illness care system. Managed care was supposed to change that by shifting the focus to cost-saving prevention. That has not happened on the scale many people had hoped. This is mostly because prevention efforts cost in the short run but save in the long run. "The managed care plans don't think it's worthwhile to invest in prevention programs when people change their plans frequently, trying to get lower costs," said a managed care executive on an anonymous survey ("Health Economics," 2003, p. 56). In other words, predictably enough, managed care organizations are often reluctant to invest in the long-term health of short-term members.

INCENTIVE TO LIMIT CARE Critics are also troubled that managed care organizations sometimes pressure providers to limit care and speed up patient visits. Journalists coined the phrase "death by HMO" to refer to instances in which people's health was hurt or destroyed when decision makers in managed care organizations refused to authorize expensive treatments or delayed approval until it was too late.

Some people worry that these incentives will interfere with caregivers' professional judgment. It is common for HMOs to withhold a portion of physicians' pay, to be awarded only if the treatment they prescribe comes in under budget and only if they see a specified (usually large) number of patients per day.

Equally as worrisome are so-called **gag rules** that prohibit physicians from telling patients about costly treatment options. For example, if the doctor believes that a cancer patient might benefit from a certain treatment, but the treatment is expensive or not covered by the health plan, the doctor would be disciplined for even mentioning it to the patient. Although the American Medical Association and the federal government have banned the use of gag rules, many say they are at least implicitly enforced. About 31% of managed care physicians surveyed said they had avoided mentioning useful medical procedures to patients because those procedures were not covered by the health plan (Wynia, VanGeest, Cummins, & Wilson, 2003).

Overall, many health professionals worry that patients' mistrust is damaging their professional reputations and diminishing how much patients trust them (Gorawara-Bhat, Gallagher, & Levinson, 2003).

LIMITED CHOICES As mentioned, patients in managed care lose some of the ability to choose or switch caregivers. Even with PPOs, there is a strong financial incentive to see providers on the short list. To receive full benefits, members are limited to providers who participate in their care plans, and they may be forced to switch providers if they change employers or if their employers change managed care affiliations. Such disruptions may compromise the quality of patient–caregiver relationships. Some people are more worried than others. Less than half (44%) of older adults surveyed said they would switch doctors to save money (Tu, 2005). However, people ages 18 to 34 felt differently. A large majority (70%) of them would choose a lower-priced plan, even if it required them to change doctors (Tu).

CONFIDENTIALITY JEOPARDIZED Medical information becomes less confidential when patient records and caregiving decisions are scrutinized by members of a managed care organization. Of the 51 hospital patients interviewed by Maria Brann and Marifran Mattson (2004), 81% were concerned that their confidential medical information would be inappropriately shared by people within the health care organization. In an earlier study, 80% of physicians surveyed said they might divulge sensitive information (such as drug abuse) to other members of a health maintenance organization, even if patients asked them not to tell (Eastman, Eastman, & Tolson, 1997).

DISADVANTAGES OF MANAGED CARE

- Health care costs continue to rise
- Prevention goals still not realized
- Pressure to control costs and speed up visits
- Patients' choice of caregivers is often limited
- Patient privacy is at risk
- Red tape is time consuming and frustrating

RED TAPE OVERLOAD Finally, a great deal of energy in managed care is diverted to bureaucracy. Many caregivers say that it is nearly impossible to do their jobs well and meet the increased demand for paperwork. When Locum Tenens, a physician staffing agency, surveyed 2,400 physicians across the United States, only 3% were satisfied with the current health system. The most common complaint was frustration about the hassles and delays of managed care ("Physicians Report," 2008).

Of a similar mind, Bhupinder Singh, a New York general practitioner, told the *New York Times:*

> *Thirty percent of my hospital admissions are being denied. There's a 45-day limit on the appeal. You don't bill in time, you lose everything. You're discussing this with a managed care rep on the phone and you think: "You're sitting there, I'm sitting here. How do you know anything about this patient?" (quoted by Jauhar, 2008a, p. 5)*

Likewise, Texas physicians surveyed about managed care gave the system a resounding thumbs-down (Greene, 2008). The majority said they have had to hire extra staff to deal with managed care procedures that are needlessly complex and time consuming. (See Figure 2.1 for more.)

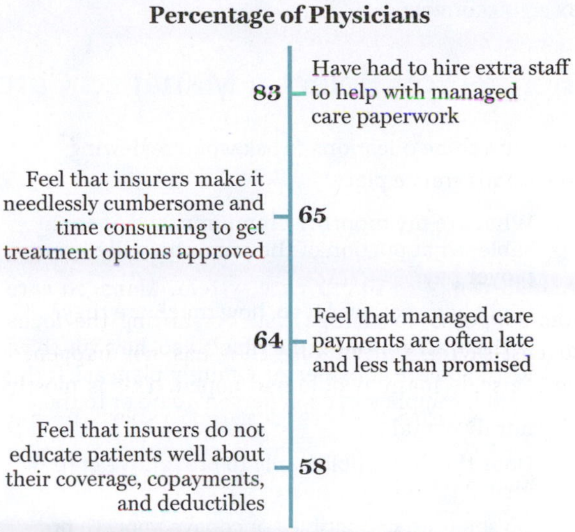

FIGURE 2.1 The majority of Texas physicians surveyed about managed care felt the system wastes money and time.

Source: Greene, J. (2008, February 25). Turning the tables: Insurers win low marks in doc-satisfaction survey. *Modern Healthcare,* 38(8), 58.

The discontent begins even before many physicians enter practice. Of more than 2,000 medical students surveyed, 35% strongly agreed (and only 5% disagreed) with the statement that "physicians have a responsibility to take care of patients regardless of their ability to pay" (E. Frank, Modi, Elon, & Coughlin, 2008, p. 140). Only 1 in 10 agreed that managed care, as it is currently implemented, does a good job at providing that care.

The extra paperwork translates to less time with patients. An extensive study of hospital nurses revealed that the nurses spent less than one-fifth of their time (just shy of 2 hours per 10-hour shift) providing direct patient care (Hendrich, Chow, Skierczynski, & Lu, 2008). They spent the most time (nearly 4 hours per shift) doing required paperwork. (The rest was spent communicating with other care team members, getting supplies, moving between rooms, and so on.) Patients are frustrated by the red tape as well. Says one managed care Medicaid patient:

> *It's hard to get a doctor who takes Medicaid. They send out a list of doctors who'll see us, but they don't tell you that only a few'll take new patients. Nobody wants Medicaid patients. The doctors hate dealing with us, the insurance is such a pain in the butt. (Gillespie, 2001, p. 109)*

All in all, the managed care landscape is pretty unsatisfying and even downright frightening. It has changed significantly from the early days when, as physicians Dorsey and Berwick (2008) recall, "neither of us can recall a single instance of being told by management to withhold from a patient any care that we thought, based on evidence, could help" (p. A9). Dorsey and Berwick's initial optimism has turned to disillusionment. Now, they charge, managed care has been "hijacked by insurance companies" such that physicians are "handcuffed" to procedures and limitations meant to save money today rather than provide high-quality care that will pay off in the long run (p. A9).

For some questions to ask as you consider various managed care plans, see Box 2.2.

BOX 2.2 RESOURCES

Before You Select a Managed Care Plan

Here are some questions to ask when reviewing health insurance plans.

1. What are my monthly premiums, and, if applicable, what portion of the premium will my employer pay?
2. Will I have copays? If so, how much are they?
3. Is there an annual deductible? If so, how much is it? (If you are considering a family plan, ask if this amount applies to each person's care or to the family overall.)
4. Does the deductible apply to preventive care visits?
5. Do separate deductibles or copays apply to preventive care, prescription drugs, outpatient surgery, hospital stays, or visits to nonpreferred providers?
6. Is there an annual catastrophic cap (a limit on my out-of-pocket) on expenses? If so, what is it? What expenses count toward this amount?
7. How many (and which) physicians and specialists are on the plan or the preferred provider list? (It's a good idea to call a few of these before you sign on, to see if they are accepting new patients and to gauge how long patients typically wait to get an appointment. Just because a provider appears on the list doesn't mean he or she has time for more patients.)
8. Are there conditions or treatments not covered by this plan? (Managed care has not been particularly good about funding care for mental health and some other concerns. Ask in advance what's covered and what is not.)
9. Is it required that I establish a primary care physician? If so, who are my options? If an HMO, will I be able to see the same physician every time, or will I be required to see whoever is available?
10. To what extent will the plan restrict the prescription drugs I am able to buy with benefits? (Every plan has formularies, which are lists of approved drugs that the plan covers. Some plans have long lists, and some have short ones. Particularly if you know which drugs you prefer or need to take, it is wise to ask in advance if they are covered.)
11. Which hospitals are included in this plan? If more than one, can I choose from among them?

Health Care Reform

If health equaled wealth, U.S. citizens would live longer than anyone else. The United States spends eight times the worldwide average, per capita, on health care. Yet 28 countries have longer life expectancies (WHO, 2008b). This surprises many people who assume that the U.S. health care system is the best in the world. In reality, it *is* the best in many respects, but only for people who are rich enough to afford it and who live in regions with abundant health resources. Americans who are health poor experience a different reality.

"There are often two Americas," conclude analysts for The Commonwealth Fund, a private agency that monitors health care performance (2013, p. 1). One America is populated by people in states such as Massachusetts, Hawaii, Vermont, Minnesota, and Connecticut that lead the nation in terms of insured residents, access to care, preventive care, and other health indicators. Even low-income residents of these states typically fare better than members of the middle class in "second America" states—such as Texas, Mississippi, Florida, and Nevada—where barriers to care and premature death rates can be four times as high.

Overall, the U.S. health care system does not make the Top 5 list among industrialized nations. It's not even in the top 20. It comes in thirty-seventh, according to the World Health Organization ("World Health Report," 2000), which has conducted the latest—and, for most purposes, the only—worldwide ranking of health systems. And WHO is not alone in its assessment. Researchers at The Commonwealth Fund give the United States a D (64%) on overall health, quality of care, access to care, efficiency, and equity (Commonwealth Fund, 2011).

The United States scores so poorly overall because some people receive no or little care while others receive a disproportionate share of the pie. That imbalance drives up costs for everyone and adversely affects health, even for people who are well insured. In this section, we discuss issues related to health care reform and aspects of the Affordable Care Act. As you will see, the concepts covered here are relevant to the issues of cost, efficiency, and access we discussed at the beginning of the chapter.

CAN YOU GUESS? PART 4

1. Which state in the United States has the largest percentage of insured residents?
2. Which state has the lowest percentage?

Answers appear at the end of the chapter.

UNIVERSAL COVERAGE

Imagine knowing that, from the moment you are born until you die, you can get health care any time you need it. **Universal coverage** means that all citizens (and, in some countries, all temporary residents and visitors as well) are assured of health care. Universal coverage is based on a commitment to offer health services to everyone who needs them, regardless of age, ability to pay, or any other factor. For example, Italy has universal coverage. A few years ago, when the Vidrines (an American family) were visiting Rome, one of them got food poisoning. Local residents escorted the family to the emergency room of a Roman hospital. "They immediately gave Joshua a stretcher," recalls Andrea Vidrine of her son's care. "He had two rounds of antibiotics, several liters of IV fluids, an ultrasound, and three blood tests, and he spent a night in the ER." There was no charge for the visit.

In this section we review the rationale for universal coverage as well as different ways of providing and paying for it.

Rationale

Some people oppose universal coverage on the grounds that individuals should take personal responsibility for their health and health care expenses. They worry that the wealthy will end up paying for care of the poor. Another argument is that people may overuse the health system if they have unlimited access to care ("Should the Government," n.d.).

People who support universal coverage argue that poor health costs everyone, in terms of unnecessary suffering, lost productivity, the spread of contagious diseases left untreated, and high medical bills that ultimately cost taxpayers more than preventive care would. Another argument is that providing care for all citizens is an ethical and moral responsibility. Some argue, as well, that healthy citizens add to a nation's prosperity and productivity. Physician Joseph Swedish (2008) puts it this way:

> *We know firsthand what happens when an uninsured diabetic postpones treatment and ends up in the emergency room, or is hospitalized for a preventable complication. We treat the cancer patient who convinced himself to ignore early warning signs, fearing the expense associated with the lack of insurance coverage. These are human tragedies as well as avoidable costs.* (p. 22)

Next, we look at two models for universal coverage—single- and multi-payer systems.

PERSPECTIVES

"When I came to the U.S.A., it took two to three years for me to use the health system because I didn't understand it."

—*Mexican immigrant*

Single- and Multi-Payer Systems

As the name suggests, in a **single-payer system,** one source pays the bills for all essential care. The funding source may be a government agency or a national health insurance company. By contrast, in **multi-payer systems**, health insurance is provided by a variety of sources, usually including both private companies and government programs.

Exceptions exist, of course. Residents of single-payer systems can typically buy supplemental insurance, if they wish. And even the U.S. system, which is primarily multi-payer, has single-payer components. Medicare, for example, is the main provider of coverage for people 65 and older.

There are several advantages of a single-payer system. For one, because people pay into the same system throughout their lives, the dividends they contribute when they are healthy offset the costs they incur when they are not. For another, system administrators know they will care for a person all of his or her life, so they have a vested interest in maintaining that person's health. In multi-payer systems, knowing that subscribers may change insurers at any time, there is less incentive to invest in their long-term health. Proponents of single-payer systems argue that they provide consistent and streamlined processes, continuity of care, clearer member benefits, and lower administrative costs (Hsiao, Knight, Kappel, & Done, 2011).

Multi-payer systems present different advantages. First, the overall tax burden is usually lower than in single-payer systems, since individuals typically pay out of pocket in multi-payer systems. Second, some people favor multi-payer systems because they involve more marketplace competition and less government involvement than single-payer systems. Third, if everyone's care is funded at the same level, some of the amenities (opulent hospital lobbies and so on) designed to entice affluent clientele may be scaled back. And finally, if one entity sets reimbursement rates, the amount it pays to health providers may be lower than it would otherwise be. One way that Japan limits health care spending is by paying doctors and hospitals less than they are paid in the United States (Arnquist, 2009).

Funding

One way to fund health care for everyone is through taxes. Another is to require everyone to buy health insurance. A third model is to make employers partly responsible for employees' insurance options and premiums. Of course, these options are not mutually exclusive. The United States relies on a combination of all three.

Since it is uncommon to find employer-sponsored health care in countries with universal coverage, the United States is on fairly uncertain terrain in this regard. Let's look more closely at the issues involved.

Employers in the United States originally began cosponsoring health insurance during the industrial revolution of the 1800s. Without universal coverage, employers found it in their best interest to subsidize care so their employees could remain as healthy and productive as possible. Health benefits became even more popular during World War II, as a perk to attract applicants when workers were scarce (U. Reinhardt, 2014).

Fast-forward to today. As we will discuss in a moment, the Affordable Care Act requires large businesses in the United States (which comprise about 4% of total businesses) to offer full-time employees affordable health coverage that meets minimum standards. Some employers object to this mandate, and some have refused to offer coverage for health products (most notably contraceptives) that they find morally objectionable.

Debate is ongoing about the role of employers in funding—and defining—the care that U.S. workers receive. Some fear what will happen if employers stop offering health insurance. Others say it might be better for employers to spend the money, instead, on higher wages or on health care vouchers and let people choose and pay for insurance options on their own. For better or worse, employee-sponsored health care has been on the decline since 2001, to the point that only about 53% of children and working-age adults now have insurance through their employers (Abelson, 2012).

WHAT DO YOU THINK?

- Are you in favor of universal coverage? Why or why not?
- As you see them, what are the pros and cons of employee-sponsored health insurance?

THE AFFORDABLE CARE ACT

As you may notice in Table 2.1, nearly all of the top 40 health systems offer universal coverage. In fact, until recent years, the United States was the only wealthy industrialized nation that did not.

Incorporating universal coverage is not a new idea in the United States. Proposals to implement it date as far back as 1915 (Dranove, 2008). It became an

Public discourse over health care reform has been passionate in recent years. Joining the debate means becoming familiar with the vocabulary and issues involved in universal coverage and other reform elements.

TABLE 2.1 World Health Systems Performance Ranking

RANKING AMONG WORLD HEALTH SYSTEMS	TYPE OF HEALTH COVERAGE
1 France	Universal
2 Italy	Universal
3 San Marino	Universal
4 Andorra	Universal
5 Malta	Universal
6 Singapore	Universal
7 Spain	Universal
8 Oman	Universal
9 Austria	Universal
10 Japan	Universal
11 Norway	Universal
12 Portugal	Universal
13 Monaco	Universal
14 Greece	Universal
15 Iceland	Universal
16 Luxembourg	Universal
17 Netherlands	Universal
18 United Kingdom	Universal
19 Ireland	Universal
20 Switzerland	Universal
21 Belgium	Universal
22 Colombia	Universal
23 Sweden	Universal
24 Cyprus	Universal
25 Germany	Universal
26 Saudi Arabia	Universal
27 United Arab Emirates	Universal
28 Israel	Universal
29 Morocco	
30 Canada	Universal
31 Finland	Universal
32 Australia	Universal
33 Chile	Universal
34 Denmark	Universal
36 Costa Rica	Universal
37 United States	*
38 Slovenia	Universal
39 Cuba	Universal
40 Brunei	Universal

Source: World Health Organization World Health Report, 2000

**The United States did not have universal coverage when this report was issued but has since passed legislation to implement it, leaving Morocco as the only country studied without universal coverage.*

especially hot topic, however, as the twentieth century closed on a record-breaking number of uninsured residents and skyrocketing health costs. In 2008, most physicians (63%) and Americans (81%) said they were in favor of reforms that would allow everyone to have health coverage (Commonwealth Fund, 2008b; Keyhani & Federman, 2009). By that time, San Francisco, Massachusetts, and Vermont had adopted universal coverage plans of their own.

The United States adopted universal coverage in 2010, with a plan similar to the one adopted by Massachusetts three years earlier. The Patient Protection and Affordable Care Act (the Affordable Care Act, ACA, or Obamacare for short) established dramatic changes in health care. We review the main provisions here and then consider the pros and cons.

Provisions

Here are the main provisions of the Affordable Care Act.

- *Multi-payer model.* People who like their current insurance can keep it, provided that it meets national and state standards.
- *Health benefit exchange.* The health exchange is an online marketplace for health insurance. People may log onto HealthCare.gov during the open enrollment period (November 15 through February 15) to see if they qualify for financial assistance and to select from a range of insurance plans that meet designated standards for coverage. Under some circumstances, people can sign up for coverage outside the open enrollment period or deal directly with private insurers at any time during the year.
- *Coverage of the "essential 10."* The ACA stipulates that, at a minimum, health insurance policies must cover services in 10 essential categories,

including emergency care, outpatient care, inpatient hospitalization, maternity and newborn care, mental health services, prescription drugs, rehabilitation for injury and disease recovery, labwork, pediatric care, and preventive care.

- *Parental coverage until age 26.* Under the new provisions, insurance companies must allow sons and daughters up to age 26 to be included on their parents' plans. (This is why Julian was eligible to be covered by his parents' insurance plan although his sister, a few years earlier, was not.)
- *Free prevention and wellness exams.* Insurance subscribers are entitled to receive immunizations, annual checkups, and 15 to 26 types of health screening without incurring copays or deductibles.
- *Individual mandate.* The Affordable Care Act includes an individual mandate, meaning that all U.S. residents (with a few exceptions for religious reasons and other factors) are required to maintain health insurance. People must either submit proof of insurance with their annual income tax returns or pay a fine for every month during the year in which they did not have insurance. The fines vary by income level.
- *Employer mandate.* Employers with the equivalent of at least 50 full-time employees (defined as 30 hours a week) must offer them affordable health insurance or pay fines. (This is also known as a *pay or play* policy.) Tax incentives are provided for medium- and small-sized employers' businesses who, although they are not required to offer health coverage, choose to do so.
- *Insurance policy reform.* Insurance companies are required to (1) accept subscribers regardless of preexisting conditions, (2) submit rate-hike proposals for review and judgment, (3) abolish lifetime and annual limits on coverage, and (4) spend at least 80% of what they collect in premiums to pay for health benefits and quality improvements.
- *Health care resources.* The Affordable Care Act designates funding for scholarships and student-loan-forgiveness programs for people who wish to become health professionals, for free and low-cost preventive care and early detection procedures, and for the creation of new public health centers.
- *State partnerships.* The Affordable Care Act also provides federal funds to help states expand their Medicaid rosters, compensate primary care doctors, and fund children's health insurance programs.

Other provisions are designed to improve quality of care, spur innovation and efficiency, reduce fraud, and so on.

Since health care reform affects everyone, it is important that you are able to participate in discussions about it. As with any issue, there are both advantages and disadvantages to the Affordable Care Act.

Potential and Advantages

The most obvious advantage of the Affordable Care Act is that it has increased the number of insured U.S. residents. Researchers at the Robert Wood Johnson Foundation predicted that, without reform measures, the number of uninsured Americans would have risen to an unprecedented 66 million, but that with reform, it should drop to 26 million (Blavin, Buettgens, & Roth, 2012; Robert Wood Johnson Foundation, 2010).

Although Black and Latino Americans are still less likely than other citizens to be insured, for the first time in 15 years, the number of insured Americans rose rather than fell. The following numbers reflect

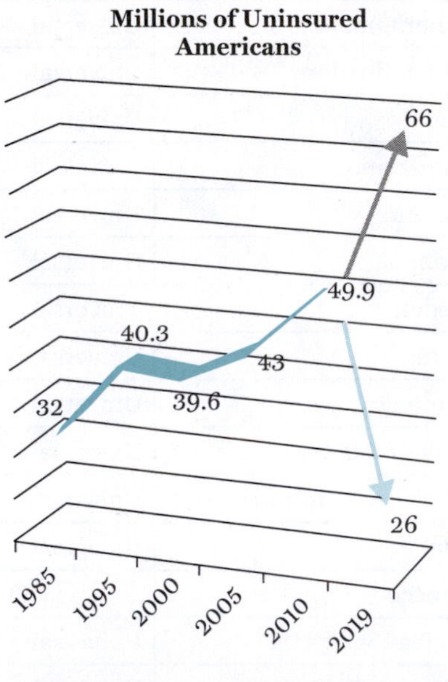

FIGURE 2.2 Researchers for the Robert Wood Johnson Foundation predicted that the number of uninsured Americans would rise to a record 66 million without health care reform but should drop to 26 million with implementation of the Affordable Care Act.

Sources: Blavin, Buettgens, & Roth, 2012; Collins, Garber, & Davis, 2011; Holohan & Chen, 2011; Robert Wood Johnson Foundation, 2010; "Uninsured in America," 2000.

changes between 2012 and 2014 (Collins, Rasmussen, Doty, & Beutel, 2015b).

- The total number of uninsured Americans dropped from 37 million to 29 million.
- The number of adults who went without needed medical care dropped from 80 million (43%) to 66 million (36%).
- The number of Americans who have trouble paying their medical bills dropped from 75 million to 64 million.

Based on provisions of the Affordable Care Act, people who are insured can be confident that their policies will cover essential services and preventive care.

A second advantage involves continuity of care. Under provisions of the ACA, people are less likely to go without health care because they change jobs or have existing health concerns.

Third, the system is designed with costs in mind. Requiring everyone to pay into health care should ultimately provide more coverage and ease the demand on services funded solely through taxpayer contributions. Where business is concerned, the ACA provides tax breaks for medium- and small-sized businesses (which comprise 96% of American companies) if they choose to offer health insurance to employees.

A fourth advantage involves a boost to the economy and labor force. The need for qualified health professionals and health care administrative personnel is expected to rise precipitously (U.S. Bureau of Labor Statistics, 2012a, 2012b).

Finally, as pointed out earlier, many feel that the most important reason to implement universal coverage is to boost quality of life and the nation's health.

Challenges and Disadvantages

On the flip side, offering care to tens of millions of people who have largely gone without it is likely to challenge the current infrastructure. Although the Affordable Care Act includes funding to build new community health centers and to train additional health professionals, some people are worried that the costs will be hard to bear (Murdock, 2012).

A second concern involves the cost of ramping up health care.

- The initial cost of expanding health services will be about $1.1 trillion nationwide (Congressional Budget Office [CBO], 2012).
- Income taxes have increased by about 1.2% for individuals who earn $200,000 or more a year and for couples who earn at least $250,000 (CBO, 2012).
- Large businesses may incur added expense if the coverage they previously offered did not cover the "essential 10" or if they are required to lower employees' premiums to make them affordable. The ACA defines affordable as 9.5% or less of an employee's household income. For some businesses, the added cost is expected to be about $5,000 a year per employee (Troy & Wilson, 2014).

Some large employers have opted out of health coverage and decided to pay the fines instead.

Third, some insurance policies have been canceled or become more expensive as a result of the new standards for coverage. So far, rate increases vary widely—from 1.7% (for the same coverage) to 21% (for enhanced coverage) (Gruber, 2014). The norm before the Affordable Care Act was an increase of about 10% per year.

Fourth, although more people than before are insured, many of them are underinsured. One way that employers and insurance companies are lowering premiums is by raising deductibles. As a consequence, about 1 in 4 people under age 65 who have insurance say they still cannot afford to seek care when they need it (The Commonwealth Fund, 2015). Although these people are protected from catastrophic medical bills, the care that might keep their illnesses from worsening may still be out of reach.

Finally, some people feel that the Affordable Care Act does not go far enough. Documented immigrants are required to have health insurance, but they do not qualify for Medicaid or similar services for as many as five years. Undocumented immigrants are not eligible for public-option insurance (Siskin, 2011). And some analysts charge that the ACA does not do enough to eliminate fraud and waste, two of the biggest causes of high medical bills.

Table 2.2 presents a more thorough list of the strengths and weaknesses of the Affordable Care Act. So far, it is a tough call whether to put "cost" in the plus or minus column. On the one hand, it will be costly, at least in the short run. On the other hand, the Affordable Care Act is designed to stop runaway expenditures, reward efficiency, and put greater emphasis on cost-saving prevention and early intervention. The Congressional Budget Office (an independent, nonpartisan agency) estimates that improved care will decrease the national deficit by $138 billion by 2021. Keep watching to see how it plays out.

In closing, we are living in a historic time. The future of health care is being crafted now, and it is safe to say that you will be involved in it, one way or

TABLE 2.2 Pros and Cons of the Affordable Care Act

<table>
<tr><th>PROVISION</th><th>THE UPSIDE</th><th>THE DOWNSIDE</th></tr>
<tr><td>Health benefit exchange.</td><td>• Citizens can determine if they qualify for subsidies and can compare insurance options.
• Insurance companies can present their policies in a competitive, comparative environment.</td><td>• Some people choose insurance policies based on low premiums, only to find that they cannot afford the high deductibles.</td></tr>
<tr><td>Individual mandate.</td><td>• About 30 million previously uninsured Americans are expected to have coverage (CBO, 2014).</td><td>• Even paying moderate and subsidized insurance premiums is a hardship for some.
• Those who do not enroll (about 1% of the population) will be fined (CBO, 2014).</td></tr>
<tr><td>Insurance is required to cover 10 essential benefits.</td><td>• Subscribers are less likely to find that their insurance does not cover essential services such as having a baby, undergoing surgery, or going to the emergency room.</td><td rowspan="4">• Insurance premiums for the same policy, which grew about 10% a year before the ACA, have risen an average of 11.7% since (Gruber, 2014).
• Policies that previously excluded essential services have risen by 3% to 21% (Gruber).
• Some insurers have canceled policies that no longer meet minimum standards.
• Two in three employers now, or may soon, offer only high-deductible plans ("Medical Cost," 2015).</td></tr>
<tr><td>Insurance companies are required to accept subscribers with preexisting conditions and to abolish lifetime and annual limits on coverage.</td><td>• People no longer have to worry that losing their job will mean losing health insurance.
• The risk of incurring catastrophic medical bills is reduced.</td></tr>
<tr><td>Insurance companies are required to spend at least 80% of premiums on coverage and quality enhancements.</td><td>• Consumers saw a benefit of $5 billion in benefits and rebates in the first two years ("New Report," 2015).</td></tr>
<tr><td>Insurance companies must allow sons and daughters to be covered on their parents' plans through age 26.</td><td>• The percentage of 19- to 34-year-olds without insurance has dropped from 27% to 19% (Collins et al., 2015a).</td></tr>
<tr><td>Employer mandate.</td><td>• Small- and medium-sized companies that choose to offer health plans qualify for tax breaks and assistance.</td><td>• For large businesses, the cost of offering health coverage that meets minimum standards is expected to rise.
• Some companies are expected to cancel health plans and pay the fines instead, referring 3 to 5 million Americans to the exchange for coverage (CBO, 2012).</td></tr>
<tr><td>Greater access to care.</td><td>• Revenue is up at many for-profit health care organizations, who are seeing more patients and a greater percentage of insured patients than before (e.g., Stynes, 2014).</td><td>• Health care costs may rise in the short run, as people who have gone without care are able to get it.</td></tr>
<tr><td>Subsidized care for low-income citizens.</td><td>• About 5% of the population will receive financial assistance to pay for health insurance (CBO, 2014).
• Changes are expected to decrease the national deficit by $138 billion by 2021 (CBO, 2012).</td><td>• The initial cost of ramping up health care will be about $1.1 trillion (CBO, 2012).
• Taxes will be about 1.2% higher on the nation's wealthiest individuals.</td></tr>
</table>

BOX 2.3 ETHICAL CONSIDERATIONS

Classroom Debate on Health Care Reform

The Affordable Care Act is currently the most controversial issue in health care. You have already been exposed to numerous viewpoints about it. Look up recent events and changes (provisions continue to evolve) and develop your own viewpoints.

Hold a classroom debate. Divide the class into two groups: (1) those in favor of the Affordable Care Act and (2) those who oppose it. Or hold a series of smaller debates on key aspects, such as (a) multi- versus single-payer systems, (b) coverage of the "essential 10" services, (c) parental coverage of adult children up to age 26, (d) the individual mandate, and (e) the employer mandate.

Appoint team captains or have the instructor moderate. One group at a time should present its arguments, with time after each argument for questions and challenges. (Make sure talking time is divided fairly among the participants.)

As the debate progresses, people may change their minds. If so, they should get up and move to the group that best represents their viewpoints.

another. To communicate competently about any aspect of health care, it is important to know the terminology and the basic issues. Hopefully what you have learned here will make you a more active participant in the process, whatever role you play.

Summary

The current health care system is quickly evolving, making health communication a dynamic and important consideration. Professionals and community members are attempting to make prevention a priority, design a more efficient and affordable health system, and empower patients. Although Cartesian dualism is still highly influential, more holistic models of health care are gaining attention as well, partly because they focus on prevention and are often less costly than biomedicine.

Health communication is a powerful means of creating partnerships with people in different parts of the world, responding to the needs of changing populations, and making the most of technology. It remains to be seen whether innovations will improve or worsen the plight of people with health literacy challenges.

The United States is renowned for its scientific, high-tech medical system. However, spiraling costs and overutilization have made it necessary to allocate health resources with care. Managed care, which developed from the need to rein in medical costs, has spawned new concerns about the quality of care Americans will receive from organizations that have a vested interest in saving money. Few are satisfied that managed care has lived up to its potential to cut costs, promote wellness, stimulate teamwork, and trim waste. Instead, managed care is often criticized for creating hassles and roadblocks, increasing paperwork, second-guessing doctors' judgments, and restricting patients' options.

Health care reform efforts are designed to create structures and processes that nurture good health among the population. The United States—despite spending more than other countries and despite its reputation for offering highly skilled, high-tech care—has not led the world on most health indicators, mostly because tens of millions of people have gone largely without health care. The Affordable Care Act, passed in 2010, has established universal coverage in the United States and reformed insurance. However, the issue is still evolving. Follow the developments in the years to come.

The need to provide people with high-quality, affordable health care is a challenge worthy of our best efforts. Throughout the rest of the book, we will examine health care from multiple perspectives—both personal and global—to better understand the needs and opportunities that lie before us.

Key Terms and Theories

Cartesian dualism
patient empowerment
managed care organizations
insurance premium
insurance deductible
catastrophic cap
fee-for-service

third-party payer
diagnosis-related groups (DRGs)
prospective payment structure
health maintenance organization (HMO)
copay
capitated system
preferred provider organization (PPO)
high-deductible health plan (HDHP)
health savings account (HSA)
health reimbursement account (HRA)
gag rules
universal coverage
single-payer system
multi-payer system
individual mandate

Discussion Questions

1. In your opinion, under what circumstances is mind-body dualism an effective approach to health care? In what situations does a holistic approach seem more effective? Which model better explains communication in the health care encounters you have experienced? Describe that communication.
2. Under what circumstances, if any, do you feel like an empowered patient? Under what circumstances, if any, do you feel disempowered? Create hypothetical examples that illustrate (a) how an empowered patient might communicate and (b) how a disempowered patient might communicate.
3. With what social groups do you identify in terms of age, education, race, ethnicity, or any other terms? Do you feel these groups are well served by health care? Why or why not? What health communication advantages do you have as a member of these groups? What disadvantages?
4. Do you think managed care is mostly good or mostly detrimental? Why? What pros and cons are most important to you? If you were able to change managed care for the better, what might you do?
5. Are you more in favor of a single-payer or a multi-payer system? Why?
6. Do you support or oppose the idea of an individual mandate? Why? What role, if any, do you think employers should play in defining and paying for employees' health insurance?
7. Which provisions of the Affordable Care Act do you support? Which do you oppose? Why?

Answers to *Can You Guess?*

Part 1

1. About 50% of Americans who go bankrupt do so because of medical bills.
2. About 75% of Americans who go bankrupt because of medical bills were insured when their health crises began.
3. The average out-of-pocket medical debt for those who go bankrupt is $11,854.

Source: *Himmelstein, Warren, Thorne, & Woolhandler, 2005*

Part 2

1. Only about 1% of Americans over age 65 are not insured. This is largely because 90% of older adults in the United States qualify for Medicare benefits. Keep in mind, however, that unregistered immigrants, homeless individuals, and some other populations do not show up much on the statistical radar. And being insured does not mean that older adults are fully covered. Many still pay large amounts for prescription drugs and long-term care.
2. It was a trick question. The number of uninsured Americans in 2012 was equal to the population of Maine, Alabama, Oklahoma, *and* Alaska, Arizona, Colorado, Connecticut, Delaware, Hawaii, Idaho, Iowa, Kansas, Montana, New Mexico, North Dakota, Oregon, South Carolina, Vermont, West Virginia, and Wyoming combined.

Part 3

1. The United States spends about one and a half times as much on health care as it does on national defense (Center on Budget and Policy Priorities, 2015).
2. From least to most dollars spent, per capita: China ($274), UK ($3,064), Iceland ($4,051), France ($4,968), Australia ($5,991), United States ($8,467) (WHO, 2014b).
3. The only country on the list that does not outrank the United States is Cuba ("World Health Report," 2000).

Part 4

1. Massachusetts has the greatest percentage (99%) of insured residents (Bebinger, 2014). Delaware is next with 93% ("Health Insurance," 2013).
2. Texas has the lowest percentage (80%) of uninsured residents ("Health Insurance," 2013).

The Roles of Patients and Professional Caregivers

PART II

It is fitting that we begin our in-depth exploration of health communication at the most personal level—those moments when we look another person in the eye and seek to offer comfort and care, or, as patients, open ourselves to receive what another can do to help us. There is something remarkable about the patient–caregiver relationship that makes it far more than a business transaction. In this section we will explore common patterns of patient–caregiver communication—from brusque, rushed encounters that may leave us feeling exposed and disappointed, to moments of true connection and compassion that, whether or not they heal our bodies, comfort our souls. In Chapter 3, we explore the communication patterns that characterize patient–caregiver communication—who talks, who listens, what stories are shared, and so on. Then, in Chapters 4 and 5, we immerse ourselves, first, in what it means to be a patient, and next, in what it feels like to be a professional caregiver, including the hopes, fears, joys, and frustrations of both roles. Hopefully, you will finish the section with an enhanced respect and appreciation for everyone involved.

Each patient ought to feel somewhat the better after the physician's visit, irrespective of the nature of the illness.

—WARFIELD THEOBALD LONGCOPE

CHAPTER 3

Patient–Caregiver Communication

Ben noticed a lump in his breast just after his fifty-eighth birthday. Embarrassed about the problem, he avoided mentioning it to his wife for several months, thinking it would probably go away on its own. When she learned about it, his wife encouraged, then begged Ben to see a doctor. In the next few months other family members joined her entreaties. Finally, Ben made a doctor's appointment. On the day of the appointment the family was anxious to hear what the doctor said. Imagine their surprise when Ben returned and said the visit went "just fine," but he didn't tell the doctor about the lump. When the shocked family asked why, Ben shrugged and said, "He didn't ask me."

This true story illustrates some of the complex factors that affect patient–caregiver communication. Although it may sound foolish not to tell a physician about our health concerns, research suggests that episodes like Ben's occur quite frequently. In a classic study of 800 visits to a pediatric emergency clinic, 26% of the parents said they did *not* tell the doctor what concerned them most (Korsch & Negrete, 1972). In this case, Ben felt that the doctor did not encourage him or even give him a chance to share the information. Health professionals may see the matter differently, wondering why patients seem to play guessing games with them rather than coming to the point.

The issue is even more complicated when language barriers are an issue. Hispanic women interviewed for one study described a discouraging cycle in which they struggled to express themselves in English, which seemed to frustrate their doctors, which in turn made the women feel even more tongue tied (Julliard et al., 2008). Especially when the women's concerns involved sensitive issues such as genital health, domestic violence, or sexual orientation, they were most likely to stay silent about them, even though they wanted their doctors to know. Most of the women said they could overcome their hesitancy when doctors seemed compassionate and interested and when they use skilled interpreters as needed.

This chapter examines what happens during medical transactions—who talks, who listens, and how people behave. As you will see, communicating well is important for a number of reasons. Patient–caregiver communication has an impact on how well patients recover, how they tolerate pain, how much stress they experience, and whether people follow medical advice.

Moreover, health professionals are less likely to be sued for malpractice if they communicate effectively with patients. Physicians and dentists who have never been sued are observed to spend more time with patients, use more humor, and solicit patients' participation more often than doctors who have been sued (Dym, 2008). By some accounts, disappointing communication is at the root of most patient complaints and at least one in four malpractice suits (Watson, 2014).

Because patient–caregiver communication is so important, researchers and others tend to judge it by high standards. As you read about (and experience) patient–caregiver communication, you may be tempted to blame one party or another if the communication seems insensitive or ineffective. A student asked to sum up health communication literature once declared, "What I get is that doctors are mean and patients are dumb." Though most people might not be so blunt, experts and students alike are often guilty of similar assumptions.

Resist the urge to draw simplistic conclusions. Keep in mind that patients and caregivers work together to shape their communication patterns. As we discussed in Chapter 1, communication is a transactional process, meaning that communicators exert mutual influence on each other such that the approach one participant takes suggests how the other should respond (Rawlins, 1989, 1992; Watzlawick, Beavin, & Jackson, 1967). For instance, if a health professional acts like a parent, the patient is encouraged to behave in the complementary role of a child (and the other way around). Patients sometimes become frustrated with their caregivers' parent-like behavior, unmindful that they may have encouraged it by adopting meek and submissive roles themselves (R. Adams, Price, Tucker, Nguyen, & Wilson, 2012). Stephen Bochner (1983) urges people not to consider patients and caregivers as adversaries but as "reasonable people of good will, trying to exchange views with other reasonable people of equally good will" (p. 128) in circumstances that are sometimes very challenging.

The chapter is divided into four sections. The first describes a lopsided power dynamic that has characterized many medical encounters since the Industrial Revolution. The second contrasts that pattern with a more collaborative model of patient–caregiver communication that is gaining favor. The third presents communication skill builders involving motivational interviewing, dialogue, narrative medicine, and tips for patients. The final section looks at efforts to create communication-friendly, healing environments. (To further explore the ideas in this chapter and throughout the book, see Box 3.1 for a list of relevant journals.)

BOX 3.1 RESOURCES

Journals That Feature Health Communication Research

Health Communication
Journal of Health Communication
Communication & Medicine
Social Science & Medicine
Journal of Applied Communication Research
Journal of Communication in Healthcare
Journal of Qualitative Health Research
Journal of the American Medical Association
Australian Journal of Communication
New England Journal of Health
American Journal of Public Health
Journal of Health and Social Behavior
Communication Monographs
Communication Quarterly
Communication Research
Communication Studies
Communication Yearbook
Critical Studies in Mass Communication
Critical Studies in Media
Developmental Psychology
Discourse and Society
Discourse Analysis
Human Communication Research
Journal of Communication
Journal of Personality and Social Psychology
Journal of Sociology
Language and Social Interaction
Medical Education
Medical Economics
Patient Care
Patient Education and Counseling
Annals of Internal Medicine
Annals of Family Medicine
Academic Medicine
Health Psychology

Before we begin, here are a few notes about what appears in this chapter and what doesn't. First, content is guided in large part by published research, the majority of which focuses on physician communication. However, the field is gradually broadening to include more research about nurses, pharmacists, paramedics, physical therapists, technicians, and others. Therefore you will see references to communication with a broader range of caregivers than in years past. You will also notice that this chapter focuses on interactions with professional caregivers. This excludes the more than 60 million family caregivers who care for ill or injured loved ones at home. Since the challenges and rewards of family caregivers deserve special attention, we will focus on them separately, in Chapter 8. Finally, this chapter focuses mostly on face-to-face communication, which, as you know, is now only part of the picture. We look more closely at the impact of technology-mediated communication in Chapter 9. The impact of such technology has become so powerful that it merits a chapter of its own. All the same, keep in mind that communication in its many forms functions as an integrated whole.

Medical Talk and Power Differentials

When a psychiatrist responds to friendly emails from a child she counsels regularly, some of her colleagues say she should keep a greater distance. Elsewhere, a fellow psychiatrist grapples with how to respond when a patient who is mentally ill refuses to undergo testing for a serious disease that can be treated if doctors can confirm that he has it.

These real-life scenarios were shared by participants in a Swedish study of ethical considerations that psychiatrists regularly encounter[1] (Pelto-Piri, Engström, & Engström, 2013). Both situations concern issues of power. In the first, the physician's colleagues believe she is too involved with her young patient. She feels otherwise—that being "happy and friendly" is natural and that it supports a sense of shared power between her and the patient. In the second scenario, the psychiatrist grapples with whether to give the patient power (by complying with his wishes) or to exert power on his behalf by insisting that he be tested.

In some ways, it makes sense to give health professionals power. They have the benefit of advanced education, access to technology, and high social status. Moreover, the very definition of patienthood suggests someone who requires assistance. As a consequence, we often speak in terms of *doctor's orders, patient compliance,* and the like. This language suggests that health professionals have authority that patients do not.

However, patients are in the driver's seat in some ways. For the most part, health professionals cannot treat them without their permission, nor can they require patients to follow medical advice. They cannot even require people to show up for exams. All the same, patients may not perceive that they have much choice in these matters. In this section, we look at traditional communication patterns in patient–caregiver communication in terms of who does most of the talking, listening, questioning, and topic selection.

WHAT DO YOU THINK?

- In your opinion, should health professionals engage in friendly email exchanges with patients, or should they maintain a greater interpersonal distance than that? Why?
- What would you do as a health professional if a patient refused medical tests that might lead to better care? Would the patient's state of mind make a difference in your decision? If so, how?

KNOWLEDGE AND POWER

One aspect of caregiver-centered communication involves unequal access to information. Jay Katz (1984) reflects on the long-standing belief that physicians should act on their own authority "without consulting their patients about the decisions that need to be made" (p. 2). For many decades, doctors felt it was unkind to "confuse" patients with medical details or to "burden" them with making medical decisions (Katz, 1984). They might go so far as to avoid telling patients their diagnosis or their chances of recovery, if they thought the patient incapable of coping with that information or understanding it.

[1] In these examples, gendered pronouns have been assigned randomly to the participants, solely for the purpose of talking about them. The article is not specific about their sex.

Some people still feel there are times when health professionals should withhold information from patients. Others feel that patients should be guaranteed full disclosure and the power to make their own decisions. (See Box 3.2 for an ethical consideration of both perspectives.)

The equation is also complicated for nonphysician caregivers, who are usually expected not to divulge sensitive information to patients, but to allow physicians to make those disclosures. For example, an ultrasound technician who detects a mass that appears to be cancerous will not usually say anything about it to the patient. Instead, the tech will bring it to the attention of radiologists and other physicians, who will evaluate the information and convey their conclusions to the patient. This system can save patients from hearing speculative and potentially contradictory information from multiple caregivers. However, it can be problematic when a member of the care team who is expected to stay silent has reservations, or knows of wrongdoing, concerning a patient's care (DuBois et al., 2012).

BOX 3.2 ETHICAL CONSIDERATIONS

Therapeutic Privilege

Although Anna (age 68) is seriously ill, she feels relatively well and her spirits seem high. She often remarks to those around her that she is feeling much better and she is eager to talk of future plans. However, it is obvious to her care providers and to her family that she will not live more than a few months. The family has asked Anna's physician not to tell her she is dying. They argue that she probably knows she's dying but that her behavior implies a request that people not bring up the issue. They feel that Anna's current happiness is what really matters at this point, and they are reluctant to impose bad news on her, particularly when there is nothing that can be done about it.

Therapeutic privilege is the prerogative sometimes granted to physicians to withhold information from patients if they feel that disclosing the information would do more harm than good (Katz, 1984). Robert Veatch (1991) argues that therapeutic privilege is indefensible because it runs counter to the goal of making patients informed partners in their own care. Charles Lund (1995) takes a more moderate view. He asserts that physicians should almost always tell patients the truth, but he warns that blunt honesty is not always the kindest method of disclosure.

In some cultures, people prefer to shield family members from distressing news about their health. In Japan, for instance, although people typically want to know the truth about their own health, they often insist that physicians shield family members from distressing diagnoses (Kakai, 2002). Based on cultural ideas about illness and death, they are afraid of destroying their loved one's hope and are fearful that talking about adverse outcomes might lead to their occurrence (Kakai, 2002).

What Do You Think?

1. If you were Anna's physician, would you tell her that she does not have long to live? Why or why not?
2. If physicians withhold information, should they go so far as to lie if patients ask outright about their prognosis?
3. How do you respond to the argument that physicians can never be sure about patients' odds of recovery, so it's sometimes better to withhold information that might diminish their hope?
4. What if you were a physician and a patient told you, "If this condition is terminal, don't tell me"? Would you withhold information even if it meant making treatment decisions on the patient's behalf?
5. What if patients do not say "Don't tell me" outright, but their actions seem to suggest that they don't want to know if the news is bad? Would you tell them?
6. Is it ever permissible to give a patient's family information without telling the patient? If so, under what circumstances?
7. If you were the patient, are there any circumstances in which you would wish information to be withheld from you?

WHO TALKS AND WHO LISTENS

An asymmetrical pattern in which physicians do most of the talking is common. When researchers observed physicians at the beginning of medical exams, the doctors typically asked patients to describe their concerns, but then interrupted the patients within 16 to 18 seconds (Beckman & Frankel, 1984; Dyche & Swiderski, 2005). A similar pattern characterizes the speech of medical residents. Among those studied, more than one-third began medical exams *without* asking patients about their concerns. Presumably, the residents felt they already knew what was on the patients' minds. But those who didn't ask, and therefore didn't listen, were 24% less likely than their peers to identify and address patients' main concerns (Dyche & Swiderski).

Sometimes, the wording that professionals use influences patients' responses more than they realize. Close study reveals that patients give more detailed responses when physicians ask open-ended questions (such as *What can I do for you today?*) than when they ask yes-or-no questions (*So you're sick, huh?*) or comment on a patient's symptoms (*You're having body aches.*) (Heritage & Robinson, 2006). Closed-ended questions and comments may give patients the impression that health professionals do not want details or that they already know them. This may be lost on caregivers who assume that patients will speak up if they have concerns, regardless of how the conversation begins. (See Box 3.3 for more on this.)

The tenets of transactional communication remind us that health communication is a collaborative enterprise. Therefore it may not surprise you that patients often support an unequal balance of power in

Traditionally, health professionals have been expected to do most of the talking—mostly asking questions and giving advice.

BOX 3.3

Doorknob Disclosures

The instant intimacy demanded in medical situations is tricky to manage. The caregiver may wish to get right to the point, but the patient may consider it extremely risky (or even rude) to disclose information in the first few seconds of the conversation. However, delaying disclosures or beating around the bush can waste valuable time, often at the expense of other people.

Based on the norms of everyday conversation, patients often began with small concerns, not their main worries. For example, a patient might say initially that she is suffering from fatigue or a sore throat, and then disclose later that depression is actually her biggest problem. It often happens that patients blurt out their main concerns just as a physician is leaving the room. These so-called **doorknob disclosures** occur at what seems to be the last instant of the medical visit. The health professional in such a situation can postpone the main concern until another time or, as more often happens, launch what is in effect *another* medical interview with the patient. All in all, it may be worthwhile for health professionals to earn patients' trust, so they feel comfortable raising sensitive issues right away, and for patients to be forthcoming early on in medical encounters.

their own ways. For example, they typically yield the floor to doctors. In one study, patients went silent 94% of the time when physicians began talking, and the patients rarely finished what they had been saying before the interruption (Li, Krysko, Desroches, & Deagle, 2004). In one study, a woman told her doctor that she was sure she had a kidney infection, based on her experience with kidney infections in the past. But when the physician responded, "Let me take a look. Since I am the doctor here . . ." the woman quickly relinquished her claim to know what was going on and was submissive during the remainder of the medical visit (K. Walker, Arnold, Miller-Day, & Webb, 2002, p. 52).

This inequitable pattern of talking and listening may occur because health professionals feel rushed and because they have been trained to zero in on specific causes of illness. At the same time, patients may consider it rude to be assertive with health professionals. However, when patients do not speak up, their caregivers may have inadequate information with which to make diagnoses and suggest acceptable treatment options, and the patients may feel belittled and frustrated that they did not express what was chief on their minds. In the end, not listening may waste more time and energy than it saves.

QUESTIONS AND DIRECTIVES

Health professionals traditionally have used talking time mostly to ask questions and to issue **directives** (instructions or commands). For example, physical therapists usually talk about twice as much as their patients, mostly asking about past health concerns and giving instructions (Roberts & Bucksey, 2007). We should not assume that health professionals do this as a matter of personal preference, however. Like everyone else, they operate within organizational structures that impose their own guidelines and limitations. As evidence of this, a Canadian study showed that medical residents, although assertive, were less so than physicians. In the episodes studied, residents asked 80% of the questions during medical exams (compared to physicians' 89%) and spent twice as long (about 19.7 minutes) with patients as did the physicians (Pahal, 2006). The researcher concluded that the residents were more comfortable extending exams and entertaining patients' questions because they were not under the same time constraints as doctors and because, unlike doctors, the residents were not paid based on the number of patients they saw.

BLOCKING

When a distressed patient asked her doctor, "You know how you get sorta scared?" researchers observed the physician's response. Rather than addressing the woman's emotional reference, the doctor simply asked, "How long were you on the estrogen?" (Suchman, Markakis, Beckman, & Frankel, 1997, p. 679).

Blocking is a process by which people steer talk away from certain subjects. Health professionals sometimes use topic shifts and questions to block patients' complaints and to avoid their emotional disclosures. For example, when Diane Morse and colleagues (2008) analyzed medical visits involving people with lung cancer, they identified 384 opportunities for the physicians involved to display empathy. However, the doctors expressed empathy only about 10% of those times, usually at the conclusion of the interviews. The researchers concluded that the physicians' task orientation often blinded them to emotional aspects of the experience for patients (Morse, Edwardsen, & Gordon, 2008).

Caregivers' approach may seem callous, but sometimes they are at a loss for how to respond. Medical students, for example, often avoid emotional topics because they do not feel qualified or comfortable talking about them (Lumma-Sellenthin, 2009). Lenore Buckley (2008) remembers a student struggling to comfort a patient with HIV who had lost his job and his family and wasn't sure life was still worth living. The medical student told Buckley, "I just don't feel that I know enough to offer him any advice. I can't imagine how difficult this is for him" (p. xii). Buckley, a physician herself, reflects that the student did not lack empathy. Instead, he feared, as anyone might, that saying the wrong thing might make the patient feel worse.

PATRONIZING BEHAVIOR

Critical theorists point out ways in which some health professionals **patronize** patients (treat them as if they are inferior) by withholding information, speaking down to them, and shrugging off their feelings as childish or inconsequential. Some behavior is clearly patronizing. But much of it involves a judgment call. For example, is it patronizing when a nursing home staff member talks to an older adult in a high, singsong voice using simple words? When researchers

Mary Lee Hummert and Debra Mazloff (2001) asked older adults to view a video simulation of such an encounter, some participants felt the staff member was condescending. One said that she treated the older woman "like she was a 4-year-old," and several observed that the staff member did most of the talking and did not listen (Hummert & Mazloff, 2001, p. 174). However, some others in the focus group thought the staff member was being kind or that she inadvertently sounded patronizing, although she probably meant well (Hummert & Mazloff, 2001).

One challenge of health communication is that the same behavior may be interpreted differently depending on people's perspective. Another is that, even when people are well versed in communication techniques, cultural and situational factors may inhibit them from open expression (more on this in Chapters 6 and 7). Health communication scholar Christina Beck describes her panic and frustration when a doctor refused to take her seriously (Beck, Ragan, & du Pré, 1997). Previously diagnosed with a hormone deficiency that had already caused one miscarriage, Beck pleaded with her new doctor to begin hormone replacement therapy at the beginning of her next pregnancy. Calling her "honey" and telling her "don't worry," the doctor declined to do so. Within weeks Beck suffered another miscarriage. Writing of the experience, Beck expresses regret that she, "a normally assertive, intelligent, and well-educated woman," did not take a firmer stand or switch doctors.

Of course, patients sometimes behave badly as well. See Box 3.4 for tips on handling problematic behavior by both patients and professionals.

BOX 3.4

Stepping Over the Line

It's sometimes difficult to establish what behaviors are appropriate between a patient and a caregiver. Touch, personal disclosures, and body exposure usually reserved for intimate relationships are often required in medical settings.

Usually both parties recognize the boundary between intimacy (a unique sense of closeness, interdependence, and trust) and detached concern (the effort to understand another person, but with restricted emotional involvement). However, patients and caregivers sometimes cross the line. Farber et al. (1997) call actions that cross the line between intimacy and professionalism **transgressions**, from the Latin phrase meaning "to step across".

Transgressions frequently have painful and confusing results. Feelings of heartache, disappointment, guilt, and loss of reputation may result. Patients, typically in positions of lesser power, may feel violated or forced into behaving against their wishes. Professionals may feel harassed or embarrassed and may face legal action and loss of professional privileges.

Sexual contact is an obvious transgression, but other behavior can be inappropriate as well. Doctors say that patients sometimes transgress by demanding more time than the caregiver can give, asking for money or favors, being overly flirtatious or seductive, giving frequent or expensive gifts, and even being verbally abusive, bringing or threatening to bring weapons, and shouting. Nurses and others are sometimes harassed by patients who grab them and make suggestive comments (Zook, 1997). Caregivers may transgress by making sexual advances, asking unnecessary personal questions, insulting patients, or sharing confidential information with others.

Researchers propose that transgressions may result from patients' vulnerability, their need for assurance, and the trust they place in their caregivers. Caregivers, too, may experience strong feelings (either positive or negative) in relation to patients, feelings that may be heightened by a sense of isolation from family and friends.

Following are some steps for addressing transgressions based on work by Pateet, Fremonta, and Miovic (2011), Farber, Novack, and O'Brien (1997), and R. Zook (1997).

- Take stock of personal needs and social expectations that may motivate a transgression (loneliness, need for approval, etc.).

continued

- Establish clear boundaries for touch and talk, perhaps by creating and distributing a list of prohibited behaviors.
- Be careful not to send ambiguous or mixed messages.
- Seek the counsel of support groups, friends, and colleagues.
- Enlist the help of mental health professionals if it seems warranted.
- If possible, have others present during problematic transactions.
- Acknowledge transgression attempts and discuss them in a calm way with the other person.
- If inappropriate behavior does not stop, let the other person know you intend to take formal action. If it still does not stop, contact a health care supervisor or the local medical society.

WHY DO WE DO IT?

Patterns such as those just described point to power inequities between patients and health professionals. Power is not inherently negative. It can be used to help others, as when a caregiver uses her influence to advocate on a patient's behalf or guide her toward healthy behaviors. However, you may feel frustrated by examples that suggest an unfair or abusive use of power. The reality is that patients do not usually like a lopsided power dynamic, but neither do most health professionals. So, if neither side typically likes it, why do we engage in it?

Our reason is that we may not feel we have a choice. We may underestimate our options, concluding that "I *have* to take control because many patients either don't speak up or they talk too much," or "The nurse practitioner didn't give me a chance to say much."

Another lies with the power of social expectations. Accepted rules of politeness and professionalism may guide our actions, even if we do not particularly like them. In the current political climate in which doctors are criticized for being domineering, it is easy to forget that for many generations, society expected them to be dominant and patients to be submissive. Changing such deeply ingrained ideas is usually a slow and cautious process. Indeed, professionals who want patients to be forthcoming may find some who are still uncomfortable doing so. Kathryn Greene's (2009) **disclosure decision-making model (DD-MM)** proposes that patients do not simply say what is on their minds. Instead, they weigh three key factors first:

- *What outcomes can I predict if I share this information?* Patients are most likely to share information if they believe they will not be judged negatively because of it, if the information seems relevant, and if they think it will lead to better care. However, if they do not feel ready to hear what might result, they may still remain silent.
- *How is the other person likely to respond?* Patients who trust their caregivers and feel they can predict how they will respond may feel safer disclosing private information.
- *Can I share this information effectively?* Even if the information is important, patients who worry that they will sound stupid or awkward sharing it might shy away from doing so.

As this list suggests, trust is important, particularly when sharing serious or embarrassing concerns that people are unlikely to know about otherwise (Greene, 2009; Greene et al., 2012).

Third, as mentioned, institutional routines and rules play a role. Open communication is discouraged when patients and professionals feel rushed, lack privacy, and/or do not have a chance to interact regularly. (For an example of this, see Box 3.5.)

Fourth, health professionals who wish to share power may find themselves in an ethical bind. As the examples that open this section illustrate, it is not always easy to decide when to be assertive and when to be accepting. A course in Turkey was useful in helping nursing students manage that tricky balance. The students studied communication techniques related to both empathy and assertiveness and then coached each other during experiential activities (Ünal, 2012). A majority of the students finished the course significantly more assertive and more self-aware than when they began, suggesting that they were better prepared both to empower patients and to express their own viewpoints.

BOX 3.5 PERSPECTIVES

Tyranny of the Urgent

A father whose young daughter fell and bloodied her nose waits anxiously for her to be seen in the emergency room. After 20 minutes, he approaches the window and tells a triage nurse of his concerns. She replies that they are seeing people with more serious concerns first. When the man says his daughter now has a headache, and her case may be serious as well, the nurse retorts, "Well, if she fell on her nose, she's going to have a headache." (Eisenberg, Baglia, & Pynes, 2006, p. 201). The researchers who describe this scenario reflect that, in this instance and others like it, "patients are expected to play a 'sick role' in which they passively and cooperatively submit to the expert opinion of the professionals" (p. 205).

For their part, health professionals are sometimes "ruled by the tyranny of the urgent," in the words of nursing professor Kenneth Walsh and colleagues (2009, p. 176). "Not only are we short on time to speak, we are short on time to listen," they say (p. 168).

It should also be said that, although asymmetrical power has long been the norm, many caregivers are quite responsive and patient centered. Michelle G. Greene and coauthors (1996) describe an encounter in which a physician responded compassionately after a distraught 84-year-old patient said her family was pressuring her to provide care for a mentally ill family member. The doctor earned the patient's gratitude by writing a letter to her family saying that they should respect her wishes for the sake of her health. The researchers observe that the caregiver acknowledged the woman's feelings, reassured her that he was concerned, and offered specific assistance (Greene, Adelman, & Majerovitz, 1996).

In the following section, we explore a trend toward more equal footing between patients and professionals.

WHAT DO YOU THINK?

- In your opinion, should health professionals and patients work toward greater equity in medical conversations?
- If so, what could patients do to help accomplish this?
- What could professionals do?
- In your experience, in what ways do the rules and routines of medical settings encourage open communication? In what ways do they discourage it? What would you change if you could?

Collaborative Communication Model

Dr. Price has just confirmed that Victor, a teenage boy in her care, has type 2 diabetes. Significantly overweight, Victor has often been teased at school, although he is a good student. Dr. Price must decide how to share the life-changing news that Victor will need immediate and long-term treatment for diabetes (Edgar, Satterfield, & Whaley, 2005).

Health professionals regularly experience pivotal points such as this. One option is to present the information in an authoritarian way, with strict instructions about what Victor must do to protect his health. Another is to involve him as an active and well-informed participant in the process. **Collaborative medical communication** involves participants' proactive desire to treat each other as peers who openly discuss health options and make mutually satisfying decisions (Balint & Shelton, 1996; Laine & Davidoff, 1996). Whereas traditional communication often supports a power differential, collaborative communication signals an explicit desire to be equal partners. It is neither entirely patient centered nor caregiver centered. Instead, participants work together. To illustrate, let's return to Dr. Price and Victor, as Timothy Edgar and colleagues (2005) tell the story.

Rather than use medical terminology that most people do not understand, Dr. Price helps Victor understand his condition by comparing it to a logjam on a river. "Picture for a minute your bloodstream as a river and the sugar as logs," she says (p. 99). If workers downstream do not get the logs out of the river, they cause a logjam. In your case, she explains to Victor, your pancreas does its job by getting sugar into your blood, but the receptor sites "downstream" do not absorb it effectively. Because of that, she points out, Victor probably feels hungry and tired a lot, but eating the wrong things just makes him feel worse (Edgar et al., 2005). During a conversation in which Dr. Price shares information and invites Victor and his family to ask questions, he comes to realize that he will feel better once he puts fewer logs (less starch and carbohydrates) into his system and starts an exercise program to help "open" the receptor sites that will turn the sugar into energy he can use. At the end of the visit, Dr. Price gives Victor a blank notepad on which he can write questions as they occur to him before their next visit (Edgar et al., 2005).

Health care interactions in which the participants function as collaborators—rather than boss and subordinate—are becoming more popular. We consider why next.

REASONS FOR A SHIFT

There are two main motivations behind the shift toward more collaborative patient–caregiver communication: knowledge and outcomes.

First, if knowledge is power, everyday people have more of it. As the public becomes more educated about health matters, many people are no longer content answering closed-ended questions and following orders. They wish to discuss options and participate in medical decision-making. This can be challenging. Self-educated patients sometimes frustrate health professionals, especially when they interpret the patients' assertiveness as disrespect and feel they must "de-educate" patients about unreliable information. A patient in Alex Broom's (2008) study overheard his physician call him "difficult and overinformed" after he asked the doctor about information he had learned online (p. 101). However, many professionals feel that well-educated and active patients are a bonus. Says Gail Weiss (2008), "It's the rare physician who doesn't acknowledge that now, more than ever, physicians learn from their patients" (para. 3).

IN YOUR EXPERIENCE

- Have you ever had to make a difficult decision about whether to share a health concern with someone else?
- If so, what factors did you consider?
- Did you reveal your concern or not?
- What happened as a result?

Second, many people realize that, although caregiver-dominated communication seems efficient in the short run, it is often counterproductive. For example, patients who perceive their physicians to be domineering talk less than others and are less likely to share information with them (Schmid Mast, Hall, & Roter, 2008). In contrast, patients who perceive their doctors to be caring are more at ease than other patients and share their feelings more easily (Schmid Mast et al., 2008). Patients who are actively involved in medical encounters are also likely to remember more than others about treatment recommendations (Dillon, 2012).

When patients are forthcoming about their concerns, health professionals have an easier time understanding what is wrong. It is also a plus when patients are actively engaged in designing in treatment plans that they can and will carry out. It's no wonder that both patients and caregivers enjoy these encounters.

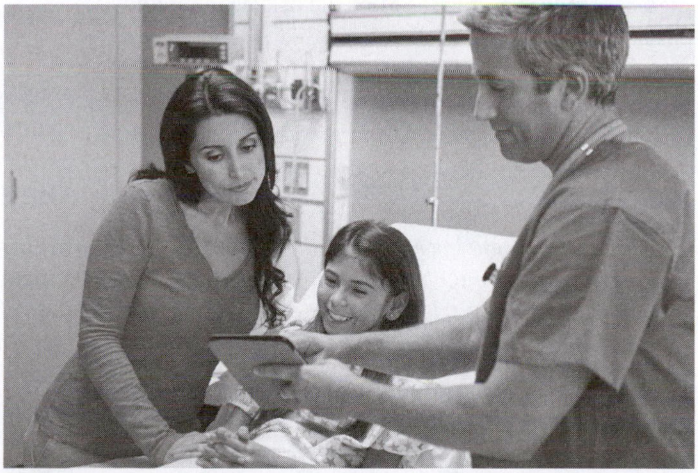

Health professionals who share information with patients and their loved ones and invite their input embody a collaborative communication style.

Physicians, nurses, and genetic counselors (particularly female caregivers) who feel they are highly engaged with patients usually consider their work more meaningful and are less likely to experience burnout than other caregivers (Geller, Bernhardt, Carrese, Rushton, & Kolodner, 2008).

All in all, caregiver-centered communication is not a thing of the past, and collaborative communication is not entirely new. Some health professionals have always been careful to empower and listen to patients. But we do have a better understanding now of the benefits and techniques involved. Next we consider a theory of collaborative engagement and explore some practical ways to encourage partnerships between patients and caregivers.

THEORETICAL FOUNDATIONS

> *Michelle, a 15-year-old caring for her 5-month-old daughter, seeks emergency care for excessive menstrual bleeding. Although Michelle was hospitalized two weeks earlier for asthma and she suspects that the asthma and her current problem are the result of stress, she does not mention either the hospitalization or the stress to her doctors.*

This true story, described by Amanda Young and Linda Flower (2002), illustrates what they call a *rhetoric of passivity*, based on participants' assumption that patients should go along with what caregivers say and do. Back in the emergency department, the medical student caring for Michelle asks leading and closed-ended questions that do not encourage her to share her concerns. For her part, Michelle makes only brief replies and is not assertive about sharing what is on her mind. Consequently, Young and Flower report:

> *Michelle leaves the hospital with a referral to see a gynecologist with no discussion of what she thinks is causing her problem—a list of stressors that would boggle the mind of a middle-class adult, let alone a 15-year-old single mother in the inner city.* (*p. 82*)

Young and Flower (2002) propose an alternative model of communication based on a *rhetoric of agency* that recognizes patients as co-agents in health encounters. Their **model of collaborative interpretation (CI)** proposes that health communication is most effective when patients actualize the roles of decision makers and problem solvers and when caregivers function as counselors or friends who work alongside patients to help them achieve shared goals. This rhetorical shift relies on the mutual efforts of everyone involved. It cannot work if patients are unwilling to share their stories and take an active role in health care transactions. Nor will it work if caregivers embody a paternalist notion that they know what is best for patients. With the CI model, patients and caregivers, together, establish shared goals and work collaboratively to pursue them.

Importantly, the CI model does not privilege either patients or caregivers. Instead, as Young and Flower (2002) describe it, the goal is "an experience that validates the expertise of both patient and provider and that dignifies the patient's needs" (p. 89). Such a model can be difficult to create, especially since it is a new idea for many people. As a guide, Young and Flower describe communicative acts that support collaborative interpretations. They include the following:

- Draw on each other's expertise by asking for details about past experiences with the health concern;
- Consider how the patient feels the health concern influences his or her lifestyle and physical, mental, and emotional health;
- Explicitly discuss both parties' interpretations of the health concern;
- Encourage both parties to share their goals and expectations; and
- Develop a mutual sense of control by identifying strategies that you both feel are beneficial, practical, and acceptable.

Now let's take a closer look at research about the collaborative model.

THE EMERGING MODEL

In an issue of *Health Communication* devoted to "The Patient as a Central Construct," Robert Kaplan (1997, p. 75) forecast a move away from the "find it—fix it" biomedical model to an "outcomes model" that emphasizes long-term quality of life. The goal of the outcomes model is to minimize people's reliance on medicine and to maximize the importance of their everyday health and fulfillment. Oncologist Jamie Van Roen believes in this. She says:

> *The first thing I do to try to make the relationship real is teach them [patients] to complain.*

> *I tell them I don't know what it's like to be the patient, to have cancer. It's a matter of control. Patients often feel like they have lost control of everything. I try to give it back.* (quoted by Magee & D'Antonio, 2003, p. 202)

Significantly, this model requires a wide-angle focus that extends far beyond organic indications of illness. Diet, exercise, emotional health, attitude, and similar factors become issues of immediate concern. Caregivers such as nutritionists, exercise physiologists, counselors, and others are in a good position to help.

As health becomes a way of life, not just an occasional excursion to the doctor's office, many people feel it is insensible to treat patients as passive or incidental components of the process. Patricia Geist and Jennifer Dreyer (1993) apply Eisenberg and Goodall's concept of dialogue to medical encounters. A **dialogue** is a conversation in which both people participate fully and equitably, each influencing the encounter in ways that make it a unique creation. When conversational partners engage in dialogue, they do not simply adopt ready-made roles; they create them to suit their own situations and preferences.

In the book *On Call: A Doctor's Days and Nights in Residency,* Emily Transue (2004) describes her first conversation with a patient she knew to have terminal cancer. Aware that he had been experiencing depression, Transue asked the man, "How are your spirits?" and he replied, "As good as you could expect them to be, I guess. . . . Not that I don't have my moments." Rather than brushing his words aside, Transue said, "Tell me about the moments" (p. 13). The patient shared with her that he sometimes considered taking his own life, but he stuck around to have more time with his beloved dog. Transue says that such details helped her understand the man better and provide the care he needed. Together, she says, they learned about dying and all the steps along the way.

Researchers suggest that patients and their families are typically more satisfied with an equal give and take than with one-sided conversations (Benjamin et al., 2015). For example, even people who are highly frightened about dental care respond well when dentists and dental assistants show a genuine interest in them, engage them in conversation, and work hard to earn their trust (Kulich, Berggren, & Hallberg, 2003).

CAN YOU GUESS?

- Between 2007 and 2012, how many states saw improvements in patient-centered hospital care?
- In how many states did patient-centered care stay the same?
- In how many did it worsen?

Answers appear at the end of the chapter.

John Suchwalko remembers a doctor's visit that changed his life and that illustrates a patient's perspective on collaborative communication. "My blood pressure was off the charts, but I didn't feel anything," Suchwalko says (quoted by Magee & D'Antonio, 2003, p. 49). He was also overweight, seldom exercised, was a smoker, and had high cholesterol. It's easy to imagine that a physician might convey disapproval. But Suchwalko's doctor, George Hanna, didn't. As Suchwalko describes it:

> *The thing that impressed me about Dr. Hanna was that he didn't come down on me real hard. I didn't feel like I had been sent to the vice principal's office and he was wagging a finger in my face saying, "You better do this" or "You better do that." Instead he came across like he was a very knowledgeable friend. . . . From then on, I was on a diet, I started walking every day, and I came into his office every two weeks. He would talk to me, encourage me, keep me going. That helped a lot.* (p. 49)

The collaborative model involves more than just doctors. For example, medical technicians and therapists also spend a great deal of time with patients and often form individualized ways of interacting with them. In the context of well-developed relationships, being collaborative means responding to the unique preferences of each person. Laura Ellingson (2011) describes dialysis technicians' commitment to "figuring out" patients and treating them in ways that they appreciate, even though it means adopting a different interaction style with each patient. Ellingson presents the technicians' remarks in poetic form. Here is an example of a statement by one technician in her study.

> . . . he was—well to me still *is*—
> a grumpy old man. . . .
> It took me a week or so until I figured
> him out.
> Give him a bad time, argue with him
> and it makes him happy. That's him.
> I hate to say it.
> You got to be, kind of like,
> disrespectful towards him
> and speak to him in his own language
> in order for him to be happy. . . .
> Oh I love that old man.
> He's one of those patients that when it's time
> for him to go—it's gonna hurt.
>
> *—Dialysis technician quoted in poetic form by Laura Ellingson (2011, p. 7)*

Patient-centered care has been shown to enhance satisfaction, help overcome racial and ethnic discrimination, lower costs, and improve medical outcomes (Epstein, Fiscella, Lesser, & Stange, 2010). As a result, some funding agencies and health care advocates have begun to measure caregivers' proficiency at it. Care providers earn highest marks if they engage in rapport-building behaviors, are nonverbally attentive, encourage patients to tell their stories, ask follow-up questions, are tactful and respectful, present information clearly, and show empathy and support (van Zanten, Boulet, & McKinley, 2007).

There are several reasons that health professionals may be reluctant to engage fully in collaborative communication, however. They may feel that the treatment is so straightforward as not to require collaboration. (Patients may or may not share this sense of routine.) The caregiver may worry that negotiating the decision will take too long, or that the process of shared decision making may feel uncomfortable, either because it is likely to be emotional or because there do not seem to be a lot of good options. Or they may be untrained in this communication approach (Légaré & Witteman, 2013).

Paramedics in one study say that it is fairly easy to communicate about facts and procedures, but it is often very difficult to talk about uncertainty and potential outcomes, particularly when there is no easy solution to a patient's problem or when the prognosis is poor (Nordby & Nøhr, 2011). For that reason, they say, they sometimes keep a bit of distance so they don't "put a foot in it" or invite requests they will be unable to fulfill. At the same time, the paramedics describe episodes in which patients are deeply grateful for personal attention. For example, one paramedic was able to arrange for a patient in the final stages of cancer to go straight into a hospital room rather than wait in the hospital reception area first. The paramedic said of the experience:

> *We tried to make everything as comfortable as we could, and when we were finished, I said, "I cannot say have a good recovery, but I hope we have contributed to making this journey as pain free as possible for you." The patient had tears in his eyes, and said that if there were angels on earth, then they had to be us. (Nordby & Nøhr, 2011, p. 220)*

Health professionals are regularly involved in the types of highly charged conversations most other people experience only occasionally. In an essay about the "problematic art of conversation," three New Zealand nursing scholars propose that it may help to consider that conversations need not be about finding definitive answers, but instead about exploring ideas and reactions to them (Walsh, Jordan, & Apolloni, 2009). Conversation, they say, can be a form of "talking aloud" that improves the quality of relationships and, ultimately, the decisions that participants reach. Approached this way, conversations are nonadversarial. Parties do not square off for debates. Instead, they engage in an exploration as partners with perhaps different but equally valid perspectives. Walsh and coauthors suggest that "puzzle" is a better conceptualization than "problem" when it comes to exploring new ideas, and that focusing on "purpose" (*What are we trying to achieve and why?*) is often more fruitful than focusing immediately on solutions (*Here's what I think we should do . . .*).

All in all, collaborative communication can be rewarding for everyone involved. But it is not always easy. To help, here is a collection of communication approaches that may be useful in initiating and taking part in medical dialogues: motivational interviewing, dialogue, narrative medicine, and tips for patients. The chapter concludes with a discussion of communication-friendly healing environments.

Communication Skill Builders

This section presents tips for patients and professionals on adapting a collaborative perspective.

MOTIVATIONAL INTERVIEWING

We may as well admit it: Most of us *know* about healthy behaviors, but we don't always do them. We are aware that we should work out more, eat less fast food, drink more water, get more sleep, and so forth. But sometimes other options seem more appealing or important. Even when we have the healthiest of intentions, once the day starts, a hamburger is a quick meal on the way to school, it is too hot or too cold to jog, and so on. A whole range of factors seems to keep us from doing what we intended. Theorist Brenda Dervin calls these *gaps*.

Dervin and colleagues propose that life is an enterprise in sense making (Dervin, 1999; Dervin & Frenette, 2001). They use the terms *nouning* and *verbing* to illustrate the point. **Nouning** implies that things are static and predictable. From this perspective, we decide to drink more water, and we do, as simple as that. But more often, life feels more like **verbing**, a process in which we continually make sense of changing circumstances because new information becomes available to us, our perspective changes, circumstances transform, or the like. As this occurs, gaps emerge in what we believe and in the actions available to us.

To employ a simple example, perhaps you are determined to drink more water today, but the vending machine is out, a friend surprises you with a latte, or you run out of change. Now there is an unforeseen gap. To visualize what Dervin and colleagues call *gappiness*, imagine walking down a sidewalk, fairly certain about where you are going, and then finding that a significant section of the pavement ahead of you is missing. It may be an easy matter to bridge the gap, or it may not. But if you are to keep going in the original direction, you must bridge it in some way. In our example, bridging might mean finding a different vending machine, refusing the latte, or getting change. If you foresaw the gap, perhaps you planned ahead and brought a water bottle with you. Conversely, you might abandon the gappy path for now and resolve to try again tomorrow. This is a simple example. As you might imagine, it is often a lot more complicated. The main point is that life is inherently gappy. We continually adjust our goals and behaviors in light of changing circumstances. It is no wonder health professionals want to throw up their hands sometimes. Health (a noun) *is* really important. Yet for a wide range of reasons, people's actions (the verbs) do not always support that ideal.

This leads us to another concept that recognizes the verbing side of life—**motivational interviewing (MI)**. Stephen Rollnick and William Miller (1995) conceptualized MI as "a directive, client-centered counseling style for eliciting behavior change by helping clients to explore and resolve ambivalence" (para. 3). Let's break that definition down. As the wording suggests, MI was originally designed for use in psychotherapy, but it has since found utility in a variety of settings. It is most frequently applied to health-related behavior choices, but the basic premises of MI work in nearly every setting, including a casual conversation with a friend or an internal dialogue.

MI is appealing to many because it is patient centered and nonconfrontational. The counselor/interviewer does not play a coercive or prescriptive role. That is, he or she does not tell the client what to do. In fact, although the interviewer may be knowledgeable about options, he or she does not presume to know what is best for the other person. Instead, the interviewer respects that people weigh a variety of factors when making decisions, so they almost always have mixed feelings (ambivalence) about change. The interviewer's job is respectfully and nonjudgmentally to ask questions about (elicit) a person's feelings, to help clarify those feelings, and to support the person in making choices (resolving the ambivalence).

In one study, nurses used MI to help people experiencing cancer-related pain examine their feelings about various treatment options (Fahey et al., 2008). From a distance it may seem that a person in pain would naturally seek pain relievers, but as you probably know from personal experience (even considering a headache or sore muscle), the decision is more complicated than that. For one thing, there is no one right way to respond to pain. We might consider it weak to seek relief, or we may be afraid that we will mute our body's natural warning signs. We might fear that we will become addicted to painkillers, that they will make us groggy, and so on. (See Box 3.6 for more on the link between communication and pain.)

BOX 3.6

Ouch!

Sitting in a quiet reception room you read an article while waiting for your appointment. With little or no warning, a woman walks up to you, extends her hand, and abruptly hits you on the arm. Instantly your blood pressure rises as you become angry and confused. . . . Here's a second scenario. Same setting, but this time, as the woman approaches, she says, "There is a mosquito on your arm, hold still!" Then using the same motion, she gently hits your arm. Is your reaction the same? Most likely not.

This scenario, presented by Niki Henson (2007, p. 32), reminds dental assistants to tell patients exactly what to expect, even if it will hurt. Her words are right on target. Research is consistent that effective communication can modify people's experience of pain. For one thing, people with realistic expectations about pain are usually better able to cope, and they typically consider the pain less severe than others (Adams & Field, 2001).

Another factor is people's reluctance to ask for pain relief. Although 98% of people with abdominal distress in an emergency department were in pain, only one-third of them asked for pain medication (Yee, Puntillo, Miaskowski, & Neighbor, 2006). The most common explanation was that they were afraid of inconveniencing the staff or of appearing weak. However, unresolved pain often slows recovery and is stressful for patients, their loved ones, and caregivers. Caregivers can help by educating people about what to expect and encouraging them to ask for relief when they are in pain.

It's hard to imagine a more challenging scenario than managing the pain of people who cannot express themselves clearly. In an attempt to help, nurses who care for people with dementia implemented a pain-assessment checklist to help gauge patients' comfort levels even when the patients could not articulate their feelings. Over three months' time the patients showed reduced signs of unresolved pain, and the nurses rated themselves less stressed and less likely to experience burnout than before (Fuchs-Lacelle, Hadjistavropoulos, & Lix, 2008).

MI practitioners respect this natural ambivalence and try to help people sort through it on their own terms. MI is a true partnership. As Rollnick and Miller (1995) write, "The therapist respects the client's autonomy and freedom of choice (and consequences) regarding his or her own behaviour" (para. 4).

Following are some common techniques and assumptions of MI, illustrated with questions adapted from Miller & Rollnick (2002) and Fahey and colleagues' (2008) work with people experiencing pain and from Gerry Welch and colleagues' (2006) work with diabetes patients.[2]

- *Set a respectful tone.* Explain the basic ideas of MI, and express a sincere commitment to listen to and learn from the other person.
- *Let the decision maker set the agenda.* Ask initial questions to help identify what is important to him or her: *Are you happy with the way things are?... What is going well?... Is there anything that could be better?... Do you have concerns about pain?... Why do you think you have pain?*
- *Gauge the decision maker's interest.* Keep in mind that change is self-motivated. If the issue is not important to the decision maker, it is probably not fruitful to focus on it. You might ask: *On a scale of 1 to 10, how important is it to you to reduce your pain?*
- *Explore ambivalence.* Remember that people almost always have mixed feelings about change, based on values, experiences, confidence level, perceived alternatives, and so on. It is often useful to invite discussion of these factors: *It sounds like eating sweets makes you feel unwell, yet you crave them. Is that how it feels?... What would change in your life if you had less*

[2]Our vocabulary is as yet inadequate to describe the partnering roles that people play in health scenarios. For clarity's sake, I refer to the people involved as *interviewer* and *decision maker.* You could insert a variety of terms in place of *decision maker—client, patient, friend, self.*

pain?... What factors might prevent you from eating a healthy diet?

- *Listen.* Let the decision maker do most of the talking.
- *Elicit–provide–elicit.* Ask a question, reflect your understanding of the answer, and then ask questions to get a deeper understanding of the issue, as in: *I hear you saying that you would enjoy being around loved ones more if you were in less pain, but you're worried that you might become addicted to the medication. Why does that worry you?*
- *Identify multiple options (including doing nothing) and weigh their merits.* Some questions to ask include: *What options are you aware of?... What are the advantages of your current diet? What are the disadvantages?... What are the advantages of changing your diet? What are the disadvantages?*
- *Partner; don't persuade.* If you would like to suggest options or information, make sure they do not sound like prescriptions. For example, you might say: *If you'd like, I'll tell you a bit more about...* or *Here are a few things that work for some people...*
- *Roll with resistance.* Avoid arguing or convincing. Instead, try to understand thoroughly the decision maker's reluctance to change: *It sounds like you're interested in biofeedback, but you're not confident that it will work.*
- *Gauge the decision maker's sense of confidence and self-efficacy.* You might ask: *On a 1-to-10 scale, how confident are you that you can manage the pain by... ?* Keep in mind that confidence, in this case, is not simply a matter of positive attitude. Someone may be unconfident that she can engage in speech therapy twice a week because she does not have regular transportation.
- *Focus on small, incremental changes.* Often, we are not confident that we can make drastic changes, but small ones seem doable. Focus on baby steps: *You indicated that your pain level is usually an 8 out of 10. What do you think it would take to get it down to a 6?*
- *Collaborate and empower.* Emphasize that you are partners in the process and that you will work together and adjust the strategy as you go: *I hear you saying that you would like to try sugar-free snacks. Would you like to try that for two weeks, then come back and we'll see how it's going?... What can I or other people do to help you reach your goal?*

This is but a brief overview of MI. Research supports its efficacy at helping people cope with and continue dialysis (McCarley, 2009), quit smoking (Bock et al., 2008), lose weight (Riiser et al., 2014), seek help when considering suicide (Britton, Williams, & Conner, 2008), and more.

MOTIVATIONAL INTERVIEWING TOOLBOX

Imagine that a friend is concerned because work commitments keep him from working out as much as he would like. Following are some 1-to-10 questions you might ask.

- On a scale of 1 to 10, how concerned are you about this?
- If 10 represents working out as much as you would like and 1 is not working out at all, where are you?
- What would it take to move 1 or 2 points closer to your ideal?

Experts encourage people to use a full range of resources where health is concerned. For example, pharmacists are among the most knowledgeable but underutilized health experts.

DIALOGUE

Following are some other techniques for encouraging collaborative communication. Although patients as well as caregivers may use these, the majority of the literature is addressed to caregivers, recognizing perhaps that patients are traditionally more likely to follow their caregivers' cues than the other way around.

Nonverbal Encouragement

Researchers have noted several ways that caregivers can nonverbally encourage patients to take a more active role in medical encounters.

- *Look interested.* Patients respond well when caregivers show interest in what they are saying, and they gauge caregivers' interest primarily based on their nonverbal cues (Nicolai, Demmel, & Farsch, 2010). For example, the parents of pediatric patients are more satisfied with nurses, doctors, and other health professionals when they show attentive listening behaviors (e.g., eye contact, body orientation, encouraging nods) and seem friendly, open, and approachable (Wanzer, Booth-Butterfield, & Gruber, 2004).
- *Touch (cautiously).* People may interpret touch in a number of ways. Subjected to physical contact and proximity usually reserved for intimate relationships, some patients may feel defensive or violated. However, patients undergoing stressful procedures often say they are comforted when a trusted nurse touches them or holds their hand (Bundgaard, Sørensen, & Nielsen, 2011).
- *Allow silence.* Physician Frederic Platt, the author of numerous books and articles on patient–caregiver communication, says that asking the right questions is only half the challenge. The rest is waiting for the answers. "Pausing long enough to allow the patient to find that answer is hard," Platt acknowledges. "Nature and doctors abhor a vacuum; we rush to fill the silences. It works better if we can trust the silence to do its work" (Platt, 1995, p. 13).
- *Pay attention to nonverbal displays.* Partly because patients are so nonassertive verbally, health professionals may use nonverbal cues to gauge patients' feelings as well as the severity of their symptoms (Mast, 2007). Patients tend to be more satisfied with providers who are skillful at understanding body language and are able to display their own emotions nonverbally (Mast, 2007).

Verbal Encouragement

The challenge has sometimes been to get patients to open up and share concerns. Suchman and colleagues (1997) lament lost opportunities for sharing emotions, asserting that "the feeling of being understood by another person is intrinsically therapeutic" (p. 678). However, many patients feel inhibited, fearing that it is inappropriate for them to share feelings. Some caregivers have overcome patients' inhibitions by using open-ended questions, treating people as equals, encouraging self-disclosure, coaching patients, and using humor. Here are a few tips.

- *Start on a friendly note.* When researcher Gretchen Norling (2005) asked people to describe an experience in which they felt a high degree of rapport with a physician, many said that the first few moments of a medical visit set the tone. They were most likely to feel rapport with the doctor if he or she shook hands with them, smiled, and engaged in a polite greeting and introduction.
- *Remember that small talk is no small matter.* Courteous comments such as "How are you doing?" and "What do you do for work?" have a significant impact on patient satisfaction and may enhance trust and rapport in ways that ultimately save time and improve medical care (Koermer & Kilbane, 2008, p. 75).
- *Use open questions.* Branch and Malik (1993) propose that skillful communicators can address patients' concerns in intense but brief discussions. They observed five physicians who invited patients to expand the scope of medical talk with open questions such as "What else?" By listening attentively, the physicians were able to hear the patients' concerns in 3 to 7 minutes. The patients were satisfied, and the doctors won accolades as some of Massachusetts's most outstanding general physicians.
- *Determine the real issue(s)* before *conducting the exam.* Keep in mind that patients often work up to their main concerns. Do not launch into a physical exam until you are sure what the main point of the visit is. Some experts suggest asking "Is anything else on your mind today?" and then asking "What else?" at least three times or until the patient says he or she has no other concerns. Only then should you collaboratively establish an agenda for the encounter—which may not include all concerns, but should focus on the most important of them.

- *Don't rush.* Give patients a reasonable amount of time to express their concerns.
- *Avoid abrupt topic shifts.* If you suddenly change the subject, patients may wonder if they have offended you or if you have really been listening. To reduce misunderstandings, strive for smooth transitions, such as "I appreciate your sharing these things; we're going to have to shift gears now and I'll ask you some different types of questions about your symptoms" (suggested by Smith & Hoppe, 1991, p. 464).
- *Listen to the patient's stories.* People typically experience health on many levels. Listen for what Ashley Hesson and colleagues call a patient's three stories: a *physical story* that involves bodily symptoms, a *personal story* that situates the person's experiences within a personal and psychosocial context, and an *emotional story* that describes how he or she feels about the health issue and its effects (Hesson, Sarinopoulos, Frankel, & Smith, 2012).
- *Pay attention to distress markers.* Remember that patients often stutter and stammer when they are working up to important disclosures. Do not change the subject before you know what is on their minds. Your reassurance may help them speak openly.
- *Ask for the patient's feedback.* Most people will not interrupt you to let you know they cannot follow your advice. You must ask, as in, "How do you feel about this option?" and "Is there anything that would make this hard for you to do?"
- *Reassure patients.* Keep in mind that people seek medical attention for many reasons—to be reassured, forgiven, comforted, cured. Words mean a lot ("You needn't feel embarrassed about this." "It's not your fault." "I understand.") Patients typically consider that providers who are open and reassuring understand them better than those who seem controlling (Silvester, Patterson, Koczwara, & Ferguson, 2007). Annette Harres (2008) found that caregivers can show empathy and invite response by using friendly tag questions such as, "You're in pain, aren't you?" (p. 49).
- *Treat people as equals.* Status differences often inhibit open communication. For example, some health professionals earn patients' trust (and gratitude) by disclosing some of their own feelings and reassuring patients who seem nervous or unsure (du Pré, 2002; Smith-du Pré & Beck, 1996).
- *Coach patients.* After researchers trained physicians and the parents of pediatric patients using the PACE model (present information, ask questions, check your understanding, express any concerns), the parents shared more information with the doctors, expressed their concerns more freely, and were more likely than other patients to verify the information the doctors gave them by asking additional questions and restating what they understood (Harrington, Norling, Witte, Taylor, & Andrews, 2007). Physicians trained in the model were more likely than before to encourage parents' questions and to engage them in collaborative decision making. And they accomplished all of this without significantly adding to the length of exams.
- *Consider using humor.* The use of mild, respectful humor seems to be a particularly effective means of minimizing status differences between patients and caregivers (du Pré, 1998; McCreaddie & Payne, 2012) and helping family caregivers relieve stress (Bethea, Travis, & Pecchioni, 2000). Conversational humor can help participants speak candidly without seeming like "bad patients" and can help people in health care situations develop a sense of immediacy and friendliness (Scholl, 2007).
- *Minimize distractions.* James Price Dillard and associates studied medical visits during which parents of newborns who were suspected of having cystic fibrosis found out for sure if their babies were ill (Dillard, Carson, Bernard, Laxova, & Farrell, 2004; Dillard, Shen, Laxova, & Farrell, 2008). Even during such important meetings, distractions often made it difficult for the parents to concentrate. The most common distractions were the infants themselves, followed by siblings who were also present. Other distractions included noises from children in nearby rooms, staff and equipment, phone calls, and announcements over the public address system (J. Dillard et al., 2008). The researchers suggest meeting in a quiet office, outside the hospital or clinic if necessary, and providing follow-up information that parents can take with them.

For an example of especially pleasing patient–caregiver communication, read the mother's story in Box 3.7.

BOX 3.7 PERSPECTIVES

A Mother's Experience at the Dentist

When I first took Kathryn to the dentist, she was very apprehensive. She had never been before due to lack of dental insurance and money, and she only went to the doctor when she was really sick, which was once every 2 years or so. Most illnesses we handled at home, and the idea of preventive care was foreign to her. I knew she needed to go. I knew she wasn't brushing as good as she should, and I also knew that sometimes she lied to me about brushing at all. I couldn't watch her every minute.

When I remarried last year, we were finally fortunate enough to have dental insurance, only we found out there was a 1-year waiting period for anything other than cleanings. So I waited.

Finally, the year was up, and in July I took Kathryn to the dentist for the first time in her life. I tried in advance to make her understand that it was all right to be scared, but that did not mean that it was all right to whine, cry, and generally throw a fit. I told her again and again that I would never take her to anyone I didn't trust or anyone I thought would harm or hurt her unnecessarily.

On a Saturday morning we drove 40 miles to the dental center. Right away, the staff tried to make Kathryn feel at home. The receptionist greeted me and Kathryn by name and asked Kathryn if she was tired from getting up so early on a Saturday. But as I filled out the forms, Kathryn hid behind me, and she spent a lot of time trying to hug me and kiss my cheek. She always does this when she is nervous.

I found I was nervous as well. Not only could I not ease Kathryn's fears, but I found myself feeling like I was a bad parent for not bringing her to the dentist until she was 8. I wasn't sure, as nice as the receptionist was, if she would understand things like no money and no insurance. So we didn't talk about the fact that Kathryn should have been to the dentist years ago; we just talked about easy things, like the nice weather and my wedding pictures.

Soon it was time for Kathryn to go back. After taking X-rays the hygienist led us back to an examination room and found me a small stool to sit on so that I could stay in the same room. She was very friendly and made me feel comfortable. She was also nice to Kathryn and didn't put us down for not coming in sooner.

The cleaning was a little nerve racking, since it was a bit uncomfortable, and Kathryn has a wonderful gag reflex. But the hygienist never seemed to get upset, and she even talked to Kathryn as though she understood, asking her questions like "It's a little scary at first, isn't it?" and "Are you okay? We can wait a minute if you want to, but if we go ahead, we'll be done sooner." It was great that she was so understanding.

By this time, Kathryn was less apprehensive about me leaving the room for a few minutes. The dentist and I walked to the other end of the hall, where he explained that Kathryn had a lot of cavities. He recommended a series of four brief appointments to help Kathryn become more at ease as they repaired her teeth. He made me feel at ease, telling me what a pretty girl Kathryn was. Then he got serious and let me know he understood my concerns about not bringing her in sooner, but not to worry. The cavities were not severe, they were all in baby teeth, and although there were several, they would be easy to fix.

I collected Kathryn and stopped by the front desk, where the receptionist pulled out a surprise box and let Kathryn pick out what she wanted. The next visits were not as bad as Kathryn thought they would be. Every time she was a little happier and not so apprehensive about what would happen. Once she had been through the routine, she knew what to expect, and that helped. She said she liked everyone at the dentist's office. Once I brought a newspaper article I had written about Kathryn's school with her picture in it. The staff insisted on reading the whole thing and remarked what a good writer I was and how pretty Kathryn was. They also insisted on seeing my wedding pictures. It wasn't just something to be nice; they really wanted to see them.

I feel good taking Kathryn there because I know, no matter what, we will get the best treatment. Not only that, but we have established friendships with these people that will last. They truly believe they are there to serve, and they show that in everything they do. Just ask Kathryn. She'll tell you.

—DONNA

NARRATIVE MEDICINE

Anne had seen a lot of doctors over the years, but Dr. Falchuk was different. She could barely believe her ears as he sat before her

> *Falchuk offered a gentle smile. "I want to hear your story in your own words." Anne glanced at the clock on the wall, the steady sweep of the second hand ticking off precious time. Her internist had told her that Dr. Falchuk was a prominent specialist, that there was a long line waiting to see him. Her problem was hardly urgent, and she got an appointment in less than two months only because of a cancellation in his Christmas-week schedule. But she detected no hint of rush or impatience in the doctor. His calm made it seem as if he had all the time in the world.* (Groopman, 2007, p. 12)

Actually, Anne's condition *was* urgent. As Groopman relates her story, although she was eating 3,000 calories a day, she was unable to keep food down and she had become critically underweight. The problem had persisted for 15 years, and although Anne was only in her thirties, her body's systems were crashing. Of the 30 or so doctors she had consulted before Dr. Falchuk, none had asked to hear her whole story, as he did. Instead, most doctors had asked only brief, closed-ended questions. Their subsequent diagnoses ranged from depression to bulimia, to irritable bowel syndrome, and more. Some felt that the illness was "all in her head." Most urged her to eat a high-carbohydrate diet of cereals and breads to gain weight. But her health kept deteriorating.

After listening carefully to Anne's story from beginning to end, Falchuk was the first to identify her disease correctly. He suspected—and confirmed—that she had celiac disease, a severe allergy to the gluten found in many grain products (notably the same products that other doctors were urging Anne to eat). Falchuk's diagnosis and the subsequent diet change saved Anne's life. When Groopman (2007) interviewed Falchuk about the episode, he denied doing anything extraordinary. Listening to patients' stories *should* be a doctor's first priority, Falchuk said, avowing that "once you remove yourself from the patient's story, you are no longer truly a doctor" (quoted by Groopman, p. 2007).

Narrative medicine is an approach championed most notably by physician and medical school professor Rita Charon. It involves respect for people's stories and the awareness that storytelling unites both the teller and the listener in a unique and shared experience with profound implications for life and for healing (Charon, 2006). Charon proposes that narrative medicine is both an ideal and a method. It involves a commitment to deep and sincere listening, a belief in the power of stories to heal and to reveal what needs healing, and the courage to, as Charon puts it, "inhabit" another person's point of view for a while.

Charon (2009b) presents narrative medicine as a means of bridging the "chasms and divisions and discontinuities" of health care and the experience of being ill (p. 197). The disconnect may have blinded Anne's previous caregivers to the true problem. Falchuk was different from them in that he attentively listened to her. In doing so, he was able to identify what all the others had missed. Charon shares his belief that medicine, at its best, bridges the gaps between people. Genuine engagement, she says, requires the courage to face raw and uncomfortable emotions. But it also offers revelations and connections beyond imagining. Here are a few of the key principles involved.

Narrative medicine embraces the idea that storytelling is a natural way of making sense of the world. Any time people gather, even for a few moments, they tell stories. One person tells another what it was like to undergo surgery, have a baby, go on a blind date, or so on. Communication scholar William Rawlins (2009) proclaims, from personal experience and many years researching the topic, that "making stories with friends is good for the heart and the soul" (p. 168). This is especially true when we are trying to make sense of a serious occurrence such as a health event that interrupts the storyline we imagined for ourselves. "Sickness summons stories," writes narrative theorist Lynn Harter (2009, p. 141).

Moreover, people tell stories for some very compelling reasons. At a surface level, narratives are informative. They tell people of specific goings-on and perhaps prepare them to take part in similar circumstances.

WHAT DO YOU THINK?

- What's your opinion of Dr. Falchuk's approach?
- Why do you think more doctors do not behave as he did?

But at an even deeper level, narratives shape interpretations and viewpoints—some would say that they shape reality. In Charon's words, through the events of life and our stories about them "we become who we are, discover who we are, accept who we are, rage or pleasure toward who we are" (2009a, p. 120).

Narrative medicine involves compassionate engagement and a respect for the uniqueness and wholeness of each individual. Here is a powerful example told by Charon:

> *My first gesture after hearing out a woman with muscular dystrophy and impending respiratory failure was to sit as close to the patient as I could, thigh to thigh, my hands in my lap, trying to inhabit her climate of panicky despair so as not to leave her alone in it. And so we were on a search together right from the beginning. (2009a, p. 123)*

Charon begins conversations with new patients by saying, "I will be your doctor, so I must learn a great deal about your body and your health and life. Please tell me what you think I should know about your situation" (2009a, p. 122). Then she listens, without writing or typing or any other activity that might distract.

Far from being a waste of time, Charon says that listening without interrupting has enabled her to learn things that might have taken years to discover otherwise. "Having hastened the development of genuine listening and learning about the patient, I found myself able to do things that mattered right from the beginning" (2009a, p. 122). But the process is not only for her benefit. Telling one's story has a value even more inherent. "The patient's body talks with the patient's self, in an odd and powerful way, while I, the witness, listen," Charon says, observing that we often come to understand and integrate facets of ourselves through storytelling (p. 122).

Narrative medicine embraces the idea that health professionals are not, and cannot be, all knowing and all powerful. Indeed, many would argue that the expectation that they should be omnipotent and infallible fosters a sense of distance and authority that is at odds with true engagement. From the perspective of narrative medicine, even when there is nothing a professional can do to cure a patient, the act of being present with that person is therapeutic and affirming. As Charon puts it, "one knows, one feels, one responds, and one *joins with* the one who suffers" (2006, p. 12).

Harter (2009) tells of a physician who includes in patient charts notes about what and whom they love and what they dream of doing. In the chart of Anna, a young woman with bone cancer, he included her prom and graduation photos, two life events he knew were important to her. Later, in a poignant meeting in which he had to tell Anna that her cancer had spread to her lungs, he asked, "What other chapters in your life do you want to write, Anna? How can I help you write those?" (quoted by Harter, 2009, p. 141). Rather than talking, he listened.

Narratives are important to health communication in several ways. As mentioned, patients naturally speak in narrative form, describing their concerns within a sequence of events that they consider relevant. Narratives often address a sophisticated array of factors simultaneously, and they may be a means of conveying what we would not otherwise blurt out. Timothy Halkowski (2006) observed that patients often present a "sequence of noticings" that involve emerging indications of a potential health problem and what the patient did about them at each step. These narrative details may seem superfluous to caregivers, who may wonder, as one doctor puts it, why patients don't just come to the point and "bottom-line it." But for patients, Halkowski says, these narratives allow them to manage the dilemma of simultaneously impressing doctors that their concerns are legitimate while avoiding being typified as melodramatic or overly self-concerned. The patient is able to present a number of indicators that are demonstrated as being relevant to the current concern, underscoring its status as real rather than imagined. Patients can also share useful information about what has or has not worked so far. This sequential narrative, Halkowski says, gives patients a mechanism for presenting their concerns in an informative and identity-supporting way.

This leads to another reason that narratives are important: They are loaded with information. A sensitive listener can detect cues to a person's hopes, fears, doubts, future intentions, and more. Particularly since patients are often nonassertive about expressing these feelings, caregivers may find that narratives offer valuable insights. Subtle cues may be the only indications that a person is dissatisfied, in despair, reluctant to cooperate, overly anxious to please, or so on. All of these feelings can be directly relevant to the success of medical care.

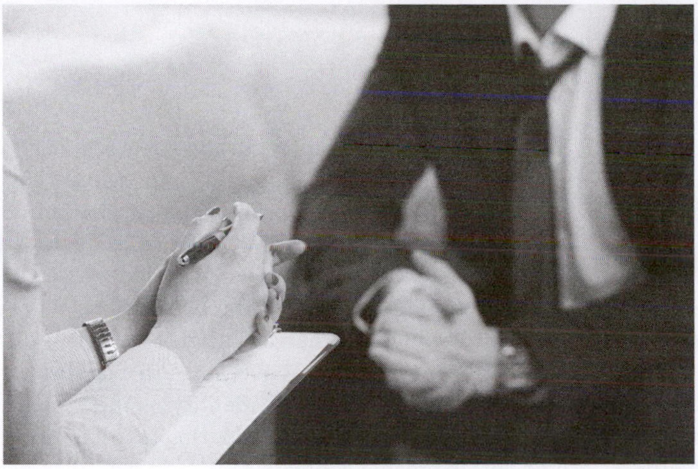

Narrative medicine is based on a commitment to hearing patients' stories, both for the information they convey and for the therapeutic value of expressing one's self and being understood.

Janice Brown and Julia Addington-Hall (2007) identified four types of narratives in the stories told by people with motor neuron disease (MND), a neurological disorder that gradually diminishes people's ability to move and speak. Most people with MND die in 3 to 5 years.

- ***Sustaining narratives*** emphasize hope and positive thinking. For example, one mother of two young children said she was grateful for what she could still do, even though her ability to walk and talk were ebbing. "I mean, I still feel I could be a lot worse off. I mean I know everything's hard work, but there's no pain in it" (p. 204).
- ***Enduring narratives*** describe a process of stoically living through one's suffering, ambivalent about whether it would be better to live or to die. One man in the study, who could no longer move his hands or arms, said, "They say there's not much they can do about it, you have just got to take it" (p. 205). He said he had instructed caregivers not to resuscitate him if he had a heart attack because dying would be better than "sitting here like this" (p. 205).
- In ***preserving narratives,*** people describe illness as something to be conquered, with varying levels of confidence in their ability to do so. One participant in the study had turned to holistic therapies in addition to pharmaceutical prescriptions, changed his diet, and eliminated chemicals from his home. "I am just willing to try anything," he said (p. 205).
- ***Fracturing narratives*** describe fear, loss, denial, and threats to self-concept. Said one woman with MND: "I try and remain optimistic and fear that if the day comes when I have to fully embrace this illness, possibly because of increasing symptoms, then I will totally fall apart. I am trying to postpone that moment" (p. 206).

The researchers reflect that caregivers can better understand people by listening to their narratives and appreciating that those narratives are likely to evolve over time.

Finally, there is something more to narratives—something less easily measured, but unquestionably powerful in the act of bearing witness to another person's story. As Richard Zaner (2009) expresses it, there is, in narrative, something between people "that does not belong exclusively to either person" (p. 170) but lives in the "terrain where wonder holds sway" (p. 170). Within that terrain, says Charon (2006), caregivers connect with others through a sense of genuine curiosity and concern, and they learn a great deal about themselves in the process.

If the move toward patient empowerment continues, narratives are likely to become more influential components of patient–caregiver communication. Geist and Gates (1996) describe the process as "movement from biology to biography" (p. 221). When caregivers listen and ask open-ended questions, they can learn a great deal, not only about patients' physical conditions, but also about their expectations and values (Eggly, 2002). How relevant are such factors to personal health? Very relevant, according to the integrative health theory (Box 3.8), which proposes that health is not an isolated condition, but an alignment between multiple factors.

Narrative medicine represents a move away from the historical divide between mind and body that we discussed in Chapter 2. Charon reminds us that narratives help to bridge the gap between people and between what she calls "the unstable gap between the body and the self" (2009a, p. 122), facilitating reconciliation between a person's body and his or her "totality of being" (p. 124).

BOX 3.8 THEORETICAL FOUNDATIONS

Integrative Health Model

Health cannot accurately be reduced to a failure of body, identity, or behavior, say the creators of integrative health theory (Lambert et al., 1997). Instead, **integrative health theory** proposes that health is the alignment between interpretive accounts (assumptions and explanations), performance (activities and behaviors), and self-image (understanding of one's own identity).

Ideally, alignment is stable and enduring (the person is healthy), but a change in any one force can upset the alignment. Lambert and colleagues (1997) present the example of a man who feels healthy despite undiagnosed high blood pressure. However, once his condition is diagnosed and he begins taking medication for it, the man experiences a side effect (impotence). His interpretive account—that, as a healthy male and husband (his self-image), he should have a sexual relationship with his wife—is threatened by his inability to engage in sexual intercourse (performance). In short, "the impotence is a resistance that destabilizes his healthy alignment," write Lambert and associates. "When he realizes he is impotent, he no longer feels healthy" (p. 34).

Lambert and colleagues (1997) use the term **resistance** to describe factors that threaten alignment. The effects of resistance are not predictable or universal. The man in the previous example might respond by altering his self-image, redefining his ideas about being a good husband, or resuming sexual activity by ceasing the medication (Lambert et al.).

People may have a difficult time adjusting to resistance factors that seem small to others. By the same token, over time, people sometimes achieve alignment that others would not think possible. Marianne Brady and David Cella (1995) described the resiliency with which some cancer patients ultimately adapt to their illness: "Many even say they are strengthened by the experience and note an improved outlook on life, enhanced interpersonal relationships and a deepened sense of personal strength" (para. 13). Although their physical abilities may be compromised by the disease, these people apparently adjust other factors to achieve a new (even an improved) sense of alignment.

The integrative health model presents several implications for health communication. For one, it sets aside the centuries-old question of whether health is fundamentally a matter of mind or body. By rejecting reductionist notions, it provides an inclusive definition of health that relies more on alignment between factors than isolation of any one element. From this perspective, a health examination would not be focused on identifying the "cause" of a health concern but in considering how it is situated within broader contexts.

Another implication is that restoring alignment may be simple or complex. Sometimes there is primarily one form of resistance. Lambert and coauthors (1997) give the example of an appendectomy that restores a young woman to full health. In her case, alignment is disrupted but quickly restored. In other situations, however, focusing on one resistance point may not help (or may even worsen) overall alignment. For example, amputating a limb may remove physical danger but plunge the patient into personal crisis. Considering this, the biomedical model may be appropriate for some medical encounters but woefully insufficient for others.

A third implication is that outcomes are neither static nor definitive. Lambert and colleagues (1997) write, "It is never known in advance which accommodations will be successful, nor is it known whether accommodations will themselves lead to the emergence of new resistances" (p. 35). Even when alignment is present, there is no guarantee it will stay that way. In fact, it almost certainly will be challenged. Because of this, health is viewed more productively as a process, as a temporal emergence, than as an outcome.

Finally, in the midst of this complexity, Lambert and colleagues (1997) argue that there is one constant: *The patient is always central in the process.* As an individual involved in the ongoing work of balancing identity and performance, a "patient is at the center of the aligned elements" and is "also the one doing the work of interactive stabilization" (p. 31).

continued

What Do You Think?

1. In what ways do your daily activities support your self-image? How would you feel if you lost the ability to perform these activities?
2. Think of the last time you felt unhealthy. What resistance factors were involved? Was alignment restored? If so, how?

Suggested Sources

Integrative health is based on the collective ideas of a number of theorists. For the rich background behind this theory, see the following:

Charmaz, K. (1987). Struggling for a self: Identity levels of the chronically ill. In J. Roth & P. Conrad (Eds.), *Research in the sociology of health care* (pp. 283–321). Greenwich, CT: JAI Press.

Corbin, J., & Strauss, A. L. (1988). Experiencing body failure and a disrupted self image. In J. Corbin & A. L. Strauss (Eds.), *Unending work and care: Managing chronic illness at home* (pp. 49–67). San Francisco: Jossey-Bass.

Goffman, E. (1974). *Frame analysis: An essay on the organization of experience*. New York: Harper Colophon.

Lambert, B. L., Street, R. L., Cegala, D. J., Smith, D. H., Kurtz, S., & Schofield, T. (1997). Provider–patient communication, patient-centered care, and the mangle of practice. *Health Communication, 9*, 27–43.

Pickering, A. (1995). *The mangle of practice: Time, agency, and science*. Chicago: University of Chicago Press.

In this section, we have focused a great deal on what caregivers can do to encourage effective communication. See Box 3.9 for communication tips designed specifically for patients and Box 3.10 for career opportunities in health communication research.

Ever mindful that communication is influenced by the environment in which it occurs, we next look at efforts to create physical environments that are conducive to healing and open communication.

BOX 3.9

Communication Tips for Patients

Here are some suggestions from the experts.

- *Take stock.* Consider Rita Charon's question: "Please tell me what you think I should know about your situation." You need not memorize or rehearse an answer, but do give some thought to what you want caregivers to know, as well as your goals for the visit and your concerns at a physical, emotional, and social level.
- *Create a one-page health history.* In an easy-to-read format, present information about your health (medications, illnesses, hospitalizations, allergies, surgeries) and any diseases diagnosed in your immediate family. Bring a copy to all doctor visits and hospital stays.
- *Write down and rank-order your concerns.* Doctors like a list—*if* it helps them get a succinct overview of all your concerns and *if* the list identifies what you consider most important. (Keep in mind that you may not have time to go through all the items on the list in one visit. Bring an extra copy to share and to include in your chart.)
- *Prepare for the standard questions.* Be ready with answers to such questions as, *What does it feel like? When? Where? For how long?*

continued

continued

- *Choose health care providers carefully.* Find professionals who are well respected by their peers and who listen well and make you feel comfortable. Your feelings are as legitimate as your medications and health history. Find someone who pays attention to both.
- *Don't overlook valuable resources.* There are probably more people available to help you than you realize. For example, pharmacists can offer advice about prescription and nonprescription medications, address concerns, and serve as ongoing advisors and guides (Gade, 2007). Likewise, dieticians, athletic trainers, and others can help with health-related behaviors.
- *Know what treatment you are supposed to get, and make sure your caregivers know it, too.* As we will discuss in Chapter 5, medical mistakes happen. Tell caregivers why you are at the clinic or hospital, and make sure everyone agrees. This might prevent a wrong-side surgery or medication error.
- *Help set the agenda.* Be as clear as possible when making an appointment so that the caregiver knows your concerns and expectations. ("I'm experiencing sharp abdominal pains" and "I'd like an overall physical and a chance to ask some questions.")
- *Talk to the nurse.* Odds are you will speak with a nurse before you speak with a doctor. Let the nurse know your concerns. He or she can help facilitate your visit.
- *Don't abuse the clock.* The reality is that caregivers must budget their time. Most are willing to listen when they appreciate that what you are saying is relevant to your concern. For your part, speak freely, but emphasize the relevance of what you want to share and avoid going off on tangents.
- *Take an active role.* Doctors usually understand patients' goals more clearly and share more information when patients ask questions and state their concerns, preferences, and opinions (Cegala, Street, & Clinch, 2007). Leana Wen reflects on a frustrating year in which her mother's doctors repeatedly misdiagnosed and overlooked her cancer. She wishes she could rewrite history and insist that her mother tell her doctors earlier on: "All these tests we've done are negative but I know there's something wrong. Let's start from the beginning and let me tell you my story again" (quoted by Al-Samarrie, 2014, p. 25).
- *Acknowledge reservations.* If something prevents you from speaking frankly with a caregiver, let that person know ("I'm embarrassed" or "I'm afraid" or "I can't afford that").
- *Be assertive.* If your questions have not been answered or if you do not agree with the advice given, state your feelings in a clear and respectful way. Walking away dissatisfied helps no one.

BOX 3.10 CAREER OPPORTUNITIES

Health Communication Research

Professor
Researcher
Consultant

Career Resources and Job Listings

- Association of American Medical Colleges: www.aamc.org
- *Chronicle of Higher Education*: chronicle.com
- European Association for Communication in Health Care: www.each.eu
- International Communication Association: www.icahdq.org
- National Communication Association: www.natcom.org
- Society of Behavioral Medicine: www.sbm.org
- Society of Teachers of Family Medicine: www.stfm.org
- U.S. Bureau of Labor Statistics: www.bls.gov

Healing Environments

> *I wanted to design a building where the healing process begins the moment a patient enters in the front door.*—CÉSAR PELLI

Pelli, a design consultant to the Mayo Clinic, describes the careful attention he and others devote to the clinic's physical environment (Berry & Seltman, 2008, p. 41). Traditionally, medical settings come across as intimidating and sterile. The rooms are usually cramped and the furnishings austere. Some medical centers, such as Mayo, instead have committed to creating a different atmosphere. The idea is that environments that soothe and uplift can lower stress, reduce pain, keep people's spirits up, and facilitate better communication.

Mayo designers go so far as personally to examine each sheet of marble to be incorporated in floors and staircases to make sure that no unpleasant designs are suggested in the natural color variations. Their goal is to inspire confidence and health from the ground up. The clinic is famous for its art (much of it donated by grateful patients), soaring architecture, large windows, and live music. A grand piano is available in the main lobby of each Mayo campus. James Hodge, who chairs the clinic's art committee, says:

> *It is rare that someone is not playing the piano in the Gonda lobby. I've seen patients and visitors join in a sing-along—once patients and visitors were dancing. Another time a diva of opera paused and spontaneously sang. On another occasion, a well-known pop musician sang while a volunteer accompanied him on the piano.* (quoted by Berry & Seltman, p. 42)

Even supposed luxuries are considered part of the healing experience. When Serena Fleischaker donated chandeliers for a Mayo grand lobby, she explained that she wanted to provide a beautiful, soothing presence for people coping with hardship. "I want the Chihuly glass chandeliers to pleasantly distract people, to cause them to raise their eyes toward the heavens, to pause in the anxious interludes between appointments, to have a tiny respite from their suffering," she said (quoted by Berry & Seltman, p. 41). The clinic also features large windows, grand staircases, gardens, fountains, and quiet sitting areas.

With the goal of improving communication and emotional well-being, some health practitioners and researchers are examining—and in many cases reshaping—the environments in which patients and caregivers communicate. Research supports that physical environments have a significant influence on health-related communication. Hospital patients tend to fare better whey they can view nature out of a window or in serene artwork, listen to music they enjoy, control the lighting and temperature in their rooms, and have peace and quiet (Salonen et al., 2013).

PERSPECTIVES

"Normal hospitals aren't this relaxing, I thought, when I entered the birthing center where my nephew Jacob was born. There were lush, green plants in every corner and ocean paintings on the walls. The staff was friendly and seemed excited to share the experience with us. Each time a baby was born, the sound of 'Lullaby and Goodnight' softly flowed from overhead speakers. Finally my brother came out and announced with a grin, '8 pounds, 9 ounces, and 21 inches long.' My family jumped from their seats to hug him. It was Italian-family-overload at its best."

—*Nicole Yeakos*

SOOTHING SURROUNDINGS

One effort to restructure medical environments is led by **Planetree**, a nonprofit organization that helps medical centers establish pleasing and empowering surroundings. Planetree was founded in California in 1978 by Angelica Thieriot, who was dismayed by how "cold, impersonal, and lonely" she found U.S. hospitals compared to those of her native Argentina (Schwade, 1994, para. 23). (Planetree is named after the type of tree under which Hippocrates is said to have mentored medical students.)

Hospitals influenced by the Planetree model usually offer hotel-style rooms with accommodations for overnight visitors. Patients are encouraged to wear their own clothing, and soothing colors and adjustable lighting help to reduce the cold sterility common to clinical settings ("Patient Satisfaction," 2007). Rooms are equipped with thermostats so that patients can control the temperature. Treatment areas allow patients to gaze at colored glass, gardens, or soothing displays as they undergo procedures.

Large windows are a key Planetree feature, allowing access to sunlight and a view of plants, flowers, and fountains. At some hospitals, "healing gardens" provide living displays of plants honored through the centuries for their curative properties, complete with labels describing the significance of each.

"We may not be able to cure every patient, but we can help them heal," says registered nurse Diane Ball of Delnor Hospital in Illinois (quoted by Rocha, 2010, para. 9). When Delnor adopted the Planetree model team, the staff designed more spacious patient rooms with large windows and balconies. They also created comfortable sleeping space for patients' loved ones and abolished "visiting hours" so they could visit any time and for as long as they liked. "Cookie ladies" now distribute sweet and nutritious treats to people throughout the hospital. Patients can also request free massages and visits by trained companion dogs. They are invited to bring their own music, check out selections from an in-house library, or request that therapeutic music be played live in their rooms (Rocha).

WHAT DO YOU THINK?

- In your experience, does one's physical environment affect healing and communication? Why or why not?
- If so, what elements would you find most appealing?

Summary

The traditional power difference between patients and caregivers is manifested in conversations in which patients tend to acquiesce and professionals to dominate. The practice has long been for care providers to do the majority of the talking and ask most of the questions (questions that usually stipulate brief responses). Unwittingly or not, patients often collaborate in the lopsided nature of these medical conversations by speaking hesitantly and abandoning topics when interrupted.

Although it may seem expedient for caregivers to keep a tight rein on medical interviews, ineffective patient–caregiver communication is hurtful for everyone involved. Some scholars argue that health practitioners should strike a balance between being assertive and honoring patients' rights to express themselves as well. People who do not feel rapport with their caregivers are more likely than others to sue for malpractice, to experience heightened pain, to withhold information that may be important to an accurate diagnosis, to switch caregivers or avoid medical care altogether, and to distrust medical advice. Evidence suggests that good communication is not merely a nicety; it is good medicine. Good communication (open, trusting, clear, and thorough) can help participants in medical encounters arrive at accurate diagnoses, mutually acceptable treatment plans, clear expectations, a shared sense of support and solidarity, and proactive strategies for health maintenance. What's more, effective communication can help ease patients' anxiety and pain and assist them in navigating the complexities of the health care system.

Many caregivers, far from being anxious to abuse the power granted them, are frustrated by the barriers it creates. They attempt to empower patients through the use of encouraging words and nonverbal gestures, touch, and humor. Collaborative communication is neither caregiver centered nor patient centered, but instead is dedicated to active partnerships.

Motivational interviewing is one technique for involving people as active participants in health-related decisions. The interviewer issues no orders or commands and makes no judgments. Instead, he or she asks questions to help decision makers explore the perceived advantages and disadvantages of various options.

Likewise, narratives are a key component of patient talk and may reveal much more than factual details. Storytelling usually reflects how people view the world, how they see themselves in relation to others, and what events are most significant to them. Information of this sort can give caregivers valuable insight and can provide a therapeutic way for them to authentically engage with patients.

Patients may respond to illness in many ways—from relief to terror—and may experience changes in their personal identity as a result of illness. Integrative health theory describes the importance of alignment and resistance in maintaining good health.

No matter what the medium or setting, communication between patients and caregivers is most effective when both sides are sensitive to each other's goals. For their part, patients can strive to communicate more clearly and assertively. Caregivers can show that they are sensitive to the challenges people face in communicating about issues that are often personal, fearsome, and uncertain.

Recognizing that the physical environment affects how people feel and how they communicate, some medical centers are redesigning facilities to include beautiful views, peaceful settings, amenities for family members, soothing music, and artwork.

Key Terms and Theories

therapeutic privilege
doorknob disclosures
directives
blocking
patronize
transgressions
disclosure decision-making model (DD-MM)
collaborative medical communication
model of collaborative interpretation (CI)
dialogue
nouning
verbing
motivational interviewing (MI)
narrative medicine
sustaining narratives
enduring narratives
preserving narratives
fracturing narratives
integrative health theory
resistance
Planetree

Discussion Questions

1. What is the significance of regarding patient–caregiver communication as transactional?
2. Traditionally, health professionals have had more control over medical conversations than patients have had. What factors contribute to the prevalence of provider-centered communication? Describe some of the communication patterns involved. How do patients' behaviors contribute to these dynamics? How do caregivers' behaviors contribute?
3. What is therapeutic privilege? What guidelines would you suggest for using this privilege?
4. Why might patients and caregivers commit transgressions? What are some methods for handling transgression attempts? Provide a few examples.
5. How could patients and caregivers lessen the likelihood of doorknob disclosures?
6. According to the disclosure decision-making model, what three considerations affect whether people disclose nonvisible health concerns to someone else?
7. Compare a "rhetoric of passivity" with a "rhetoric of agency." What are some communication strategies caregivers and patients can use to accomplish collaborative interpretation? Apply these to an example of your own.
8. Compare the assumptions of physician-centered and collaborative communication. How is the caregiver's role different in each model? How is the patient's role different? What are some of the reasons that many people are shifting from provider-centered to collaborative communication?
9. What are the assumptions and techniques of motivational interviewing? Would you enjoy being part of such an interview? Why or why not?
10. Think of a health concern you have experienced personally. When asked about it, what does your narrative include? What elements of the narrative are most important in terms of your feelings about it and its importance in your life? Now analyze the experience in terms of integrative health theory. In what ways did you experience *alignment? Resistance?*

11. Look around the room where you are now. In what ways is it a "healthy" or "healing" environment? Conversely, in what ways does it increase your stress level and sense of discomfort?

Answers to *Can You Guess?*

The news is good. Patient-centered hospital care improved in 48 states and stayed the same in the other two (Radley, McCarthy, Lippa, Hayes, & Schoen, 2014). It did not worsen in any of them. Although medical care did not improve in all respects, analysts think the gain in patient-centeredness is probably a reflection of combined state and federal attention to quality care (Radley et al.).

CHAPTER 4

Patient Perspectives

I remember, as a child, the distinct smell of the doctor's office. It's different than any other odor, and it leaves a lasting impression. The smell of rubbing alcohol, the smell of medicines, and the smell of antibacterial soap on the doctor's hands. As a child, you don't know what to make of it.

These musings by a college student evoke vivid images of patienthood. Whatever else we remember of childhood, most of us will never forget the sensory alert of waiting anxiously to be seen by a doctor.

Being a patient can be a frightening experience, even as an adult. Uncertainty is guaranteed, and pain is a strong possibility. At the same time, though, there is the promise of relief, a cure, or a reassuring health assessment. (See Box 4.1 for a true story about one patient's experience managing uncertainty.)

In this chapter we look at health care situations through patients' eyes. We investigate the informal socialization process that helps people learn how to behave in that role, what patients generally like and dislike, and what motivates people to follow (and, just as often, to ignore) medical advice. The chapter concludes with a discussion of illness and personal identity.

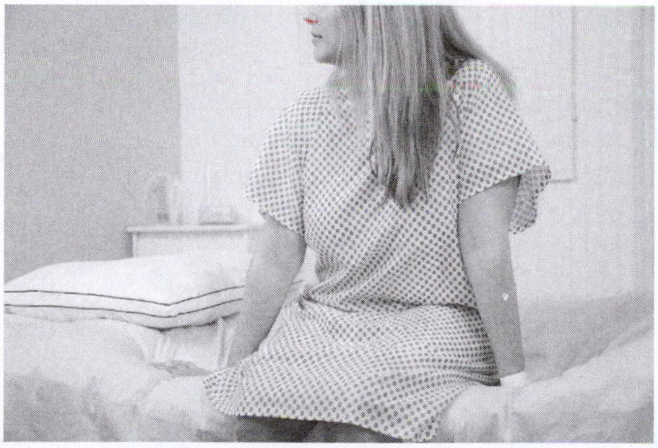

A great deal rides on how effectively patients communicate with care providers. However, there is typically little instruction on how to do that well. All in all, patients may feel that they are trying to play a role without knowing the script.

As we explore these topics, bear in mind that, although there are facets of patienthood (such as embarrassment, anxiety, hope, and gratitude) that we are all likely to experience at some point, the experience of being a patient is also highly personal and cultural. Examples throughout this chapter highlight some of that diversity, and Chapters 6 and 7 are devoted to diverse perspectives, including the intersection of health and culture, race, gender, age, and many other factors.

BOX 4.1 PERSPECTIVES

The Agony of Uncertainty

It all began one day when I was in eighth-grade physical education class. As the class began to warm up and stretch, I noticed a knot on my knee. A month passed and the knot did not go away. In fact it grew from the size of a pencil eraser to the size of a quarter. My mother made an appointment with our family doctor, and I began to panic. I personally gave myself one year to live.

During my appointment the doctor asked questions like, "Have you fallen down recently?" I was so distraught I felt like screaming, "I did not come in here for a bump and scrape!" But I just said no.

After ordering X-rays, the doctor said he could not tell if the knot was a cyst or a tumor and referred us to a bone and joint specialist. I was beyond scared. I was only 13 and had never had anything worse than the flu. I had so many questions, but there wasn't much chance to ask them. Every question I asked got a brief response, when what I really wanted was a full explanation and, above all, reassurance. The conversation went something like this:

DOCTOR: It looks like you have a cyst or a tumor. I'm going to refer you to a specialist.

ME: What does that mean?

DOCTOR: It means he will look at your knee and figure out what is going on.

ME: Is it serious?

DOCTOR: That's what he'll be able to determine.

ME: Well, OK.

I wasn't sure about the difference between a cyst and a tumor, and both sounded horrible. I was afraid the doctor would laugh if I said I was afraid of having cancer. Or had he just told me I *did* have cancer? I left not knowing, and I had to wait a month to see the specialist.

On the day of the appointment with the specialist, Dr. Benze, we waited 2½ hours to see him. However, his personality and gentle manner made up for the wait. Dr. Benze compassionately and carefully told me the lump (now the size of a small orange) was a tumor. When I began to cry, he explained that not all tumors are cancerous. He arranged to surgically remove the tumor in 2 days, and he promised to tell me everything about the surgery in advance and to share the lab results with me as soon as he received them.

On the day before surgery my mother and I visited the hospital to make arrangements. The admitting attendant was detached and unfriendly, but the nurses and doctors were wonderful. They tried to make me feel comfortable and relaxed. An outpatient nurse sat down with us and described in detail what would happen before, during, and after the surgery. I felt comfortable asking every question I did not feel safe asking the first doctor.

Suffice it to say that the surgery went well. The tumor was not cancerous, and I have had no more tumors. Overall, the experience was a positive one. The worst part was leaving the first doctor's office with so many fears and questions I never got to voice. Although the surgery was frightening, I felt better once people started telling me what was going on.

—SARAH

What Do You Think?

1. Do you think the first doctor could have communicated more effectively with Sarah? If so, how?
2. Do you think Sarah could have communicated more effectively? If so, how?
3. Sometimes doctors feel they will alarm or confuse patients (especially young patients) by giving them medical details. Do you agree?
4. How can patients help ensure that they get the information they want?

Patient Socialization

Being a patient often means suspending the rules of everyday interaction. For example, the touch and physical exposure usually reserved for intimate relationships occurs under bright lights in the company of strangers. In emergencies or intense circumstances such as childbirth, modesty may not be on anyone's mind. During routine exams, however, participants tend to display in subtle ways that the body-as-examined is more an object than an intimate landscape. Christian Heath (2006) observed that patients typically lower their eyelids, turn their heads aside, and gaze into the middle distance during potentially embarrassing or painful examinations. At the same time, health professionals typically avoid direct eye contact, focusing instead on particular parts of the patient's body. This "body work," as Heath calls it, involves a sophisticated, collaborative performance in which participants display that they are not involved in an intimate or callous infringement of personal space, but in a clinically approved interaction with its own rules of appropriateness.

Verbal interactions can be equally as challenging. Although patients are unlikely to agree with everything their caregivers say, they may fear that speaking up will make them seem difficult or disrespectful (Frosch, May, Rendle, Tietbohl, & Elwyn, 2012). Most patients who disagree with their doctors either stay quiet or hint at their disagreement by asking questions or talking about their preferences. In one study, only 1 in 7 patients said that they tell their doctors outright when they disagree with them (Adams, Elwyn, Légaré, & Frosch, 2012). It is easy to imagine the misunderstandings that occur as a result.

Considering the challenges, how do people learn to embody a patient role? Unlike health professionals, patients are usually in medical situations only briefly and occasionally. Moreover, whereas caregivers-in-training are usually required to observe experienced professionals, everyday people seldom get to observe other patients. Thus, socialization into the role of patient requires a good deal of guesswork and experimentation. People apply their everyday knowledge to the role and generally display all the hesitancy you might expect. This section describes the Voice of Lifeworld, the typical power difference between patients and professionals, and the dilemmas people face when they disagree with their caregivers.

Voice of Lifeworld

When 25-year-old Jessica Tar told her dentist her tongue had been hurting, she didn't expect it to be anything serious. But when tests revealed cancer, the prescribed treatment was nearly as frightening as the diagnosis. Doctors would have to remove a portion of her tongue. As an aspiring singer and actress, Tar was devastated to realize that her speech might be affected. "I was crying that day like I had never cried before," she remembers ("Jessica's Story," n.d.).

Actress Jessica Tar's ambitions were threatened when doctors had to remove a small portion of her tongue because of a tumor. Oral surgeon Jatin Shah took her lifeworld concerns seriously and worked with her to devise a treatment plan that saved her life and helped her resume life as usual.

We follow Tar's experiences in this section, in which we explore the role of communication in making sense of health care experiences. Patients typically speak with what Elliot Mishler (1984) calls the **Voice of Lifeworld**, which is primarily concerned with health and illness as they relate to everyday experiences. Whereas a health professional may understand back pain in terms of specific discs and muscles, from a lifeworld perspective, the main issue may be that the pain interferes with a person's ability to pick up a child or perform tasks at work. When asked what is wrong, patients typically describe sensations and events, as in, "I get a horrible pain behind my eyes when I try to read the newspaper. It really scares me."

In contrast to the Voice of Medicine—which is primarily oriented to evidence, measurement, and precision—the Voice of Lifeworld is more oriented to feelings and contexts. From this perspective, it is natural that Tar was worried, not only about her physical condition, but about how treatment would affect her daily life and her career.

FEELINGS VERSUS EVIDENCE

Patients typically gauge whether they are sick or healthy based on personal experience, comparisons with others, and gut instinct (Mishler, 1981, 1984). Health professionals, however, are typically taught to rely on empirical verification. Therefore, they may put more faith in their own observations and in diagnostic tests than in patients' descriptions of what is wrong.

Put another way, as a general principle, patients typically trust feelings, whereas health professionals trust evidence. This disconnect can lead patients to feel that they are not being heard and that health professionals are unsympathetic to their feelings (Cousin, Mast, Roter, & Hall, 2012).

WHAT DO YOU THINK?

- Have you ever found yourself reluctant or unable to tell a health professional what you wanted to say?
- If so, what held you back?
- What factors would make it easier for you to communicate openly?

Health professionals may have many reasons for diverting talk away from lifeworld issues. They may consider them irrelevant to the patient's medical condition or outside of their control. Or they may be uncomfortable discussing issues because they lack experience with them or they have not been trained to engage in those types of conversations (Waitzkin, 1991). "Under these circumstances doctors typically interject questions, interrupt, or otherwise change the topic, to return to the voice of medicine," says medical theorist Howard Waitzkin (1991, p. 25).

Although the contrast between the Voice of Lifeworld and the Voice of Medicine can lead to misunderstandings, it is possible to bridge the gap. Tar was treated by oral surgeon Jatin Shah, who reviewed laboratory reports about her condition but realized that Tar's emotional health was as important as her physical recovery. In the midst of her distress, Dr. Shah asked her, "Other than the cancer you have, what is bothering you?" ("Jessica's Story," n.d.).

SPECIFIC VERSUS DIFFUSE

One result of disparate philosophies is that health professionals are often precise, whereas patients are diffuse. To illustrate, a care provider may hear "pain behind the eyes" and want to know exactly where, how strong, how long. Patients, however, may be concerned with surrounding issues (*Will I die? Can I still be a good parent? Am I going blind? Do I have a tumor? What have I done to deserve this?*). Although both mean well, health professionals may be frustrated when patients "go on and on," and patients may feel rebuffed when caregivers seem uninterested in their stories.

Patients also tend to be diffuse in their perception of what gives rise to illness. Unlike conventional medicine practitioners, who typically strive to find specific causes, patients often perceive that an illness has multiple causes, common among them stress and relationship issues. Consequently, scientific specificity may seem sorely deficient in explaining illnesses as patients perceive them. People may leave exams wondering if their caregivers really understood their problems at all.

Patients may also have numerous goals that take precedence over purely physical healing. They may wish to vent emotions, confess, or be reassured, forgiven, or comforted during a medical visit. These goals may pose a challenge to some professionals' efforts to set aside what they consider extraneous factors and focus on measurable ones.

All in all, patients tend to interpret illnesses in the broad context of everyday life, whereas many professionals are taught to reduce diseases to their simplest, most measurable parts. As we saw in Chapter 3, however, some patients and health professionals adopt a collaborative approach that integrates medical and lifeworld voices. Working together, Tar and Dr. Shah determined to preserve her verbal abilities and self-image as much as possible, without compromising her chances of physical recovery. The surgery was successful in removing the cancer, and after months of therapy to help her eat, talk, and swallow effectively, Tar found her voice again. She has since become a mother of two and a professional actress. (You can catch her as Christine Benash in *The Meat Puppet* and as a nurse in *Zombies vs. Joe Alien*.) Tar says she feels lucky to have found a collaborator in Dr. Shah, who listened to her and was "invested in my life" ("Jessica's Story," n.d.).

BRIDGING THE GAP

An American physician is put on the spot when a Russian family in his care complains that physical therapy sessions in the United States are briefer and more superficial than those in their homeland. The physician might spring to the defense of American health care. Instead, he says, "Maybe it's not as good, but that's all we can afford. You know?" (Lo, 2010, p. 491).

In this real-life episode, the doctor bridges the gap between his experiences and his patients' by acknowledging that, indeed, theirs may be a better model. The physician later reflected that his nondefensive response seemed to help the family accept the different care model and cooperate in making the most of it (Lo, 2010).

This is one example of how patients and caregivers might meet in the middle. The trend toward preventive care might also narrow the divide between medical and lifeworld voices. Prevention is, by nature, a diffuse topic involving an array of risk factors and lifestyle decisions. Furthermore, talking about prevention is usually not as emotionally intense as talking about existing illness. Some speculate that a third voice will emerge that feels natural to both patients and professionals.

PERSPECTIVES

"I have been to two different clinics for the same concern. At one, I saw a doctor within 15 minutes. The staff was extremely friendly and helpful. At the other clinic, I was not met by a staff member, but rather by a sign-in sheet and a number. I immediately felt insignificant. After a long wait I finally was called back to my own room, where I sat for another hour and a half. The doctor was unfriendly and said, 'There is not much I can do,' even when I told her what treatment had worked last time. That visit made me feel as if no one cared."

—*Dustin*

Next we turn to some factors that define particular patient experiences, including the nature of the health concern, the personalities involved, and participants' communication skills.

WHAT DO YOU THINK?

The term *patient* connotes a person in ill health who seeks the services of a care provider. Some theorists suggest that the terms *health citizen*, *health decision maker*, and *health client* are preferable because they acknowledge that people are involved in health care all the time, not just when they seek professional assistance (Neuberger, 1999; Rimal, Ratzan, Arnston, & Freimuth, 1997).

- Do you feel the term *patient* is accurate when describing well people seeking to maintain their own health?
- Brainstorm some other terms we might use. Which is your favorite?

Patient Characteristics

Patients face a number of dilemmas in terms of open communication. For one, although they have an incentive to maintain health professionals' positive regard, they might doubt the validity of a diagnosis or may wish to reiterate information that the care provider has dismissed as unimportant. In this case, patients may perceive two unappealing options: risk causing offense or remain silent. In other situations, patients may wish to ask questions and be assertive, but they may not feel well enough informed to do so. In this section, we explore challenging situations such as these from patients' perspective.

NATURE OF THE ILLNESS

People with conditions that are chronic or hard to define may have a difficult time navigating those issues with professionals. In some cases, the challenge is to establish what is most important. For example, a patient with depression may feel that other concerns are brushed aside as psychosomatic even when they are legitimate. After studying low-income patients experiencing depression and chronic health problems, Renée Gillespie (2001) concluded that many of them "resented feeling as though they had to prove or stress how sick they 'really' were" to doctors (p. 109).

Their frustration was compounded by the fear that doctors would consider them "neurotic" if they became emotional about their health concerns and frustration.

Another challenge is keeping people with chronic conditions well informed and involved in their care (Wright Nunes et al., 2011). Some health organizations pair these patients with nurses, who communicate with them regularly, help monitor their health, and support them in making healthy lifestyle choices. Patients often say that the nurses are able to spend more time with them than doctors can, and they are well qualified to monitor their health when nothing out of the ordinary is worrying them (Mahomed, St. John, & Patterson, 2012). Said one patient: "[The nurse] really listens to you, which is important. Quite often now people look at computers and you feel like saying 'Hey I'm over here.' But no, she's not like that. She gives you good quality time" (Mahomed et al., p. 2544). (See Box 4.2 for more on the presence of technology in the exam room.)

PATIENT DISPOSITION

Individuals' backgrounds and personalities also influence how they communicate as patients. After reviewing the literature, Jeffery Robinson (2003) concluded that a number of factors may cause patients to be unassertive during health care visits:

- They may think it is appropriate to be passive.
- They may be too fearful or anxious to be assertive.
- They may not know or understand enough to participate in medical discussions.
- They may be discouraged by health professionals' communication styles.
- Socioeconomic factors, such as education level, may influence their willingness to participate.
- The nature of the medical visit (routine or symptom specific) may affect their behavior.
- The length of the visit and the people present may temper their involvement.

A number of studies support these ideas. In general, patients are more likely to be **self-advocates**—actively seeking health information, comfortable talking about health concerns, and assertive about seeking care—if they are well educated (Street, Gordon, Ward, Krupat, & Kravitz, 2005) and if they are confident they can make a difference in their own health (Curtin et al., 2008).

BOX 4.2 HEALTH AND COMMUNICATION TECHNOLOGY

Computer in the Room

By Christopher Elkins

These days a third party is often present in the examination room—one with a shiny face and a keyboard. Computers are playing an increasingly prevalent role in conversations between patients and health professionals (Pearce, Arnold, Phillips, Trumble, & Dwan, 2012). Summary screens and online prompts direct caregivers to ask particular questions and to type in information during the visit. This can prevent professionals from overlooking important points. However, it may also distract them from what patients are saying, since computer software has a sequence of its own and a preference for standardized medical jargon.

Some people worry that a computer in the room will sway conversations toward the Voice of Medicine rather than the Voice of Lifeworld and make health professionals less attentive and present with patients. That is a serious concern considering that patients are less likely to follow medical advice when they believe their voices have not been heard (Solomon, Knapp, Raynor, & Atkin, 2013).

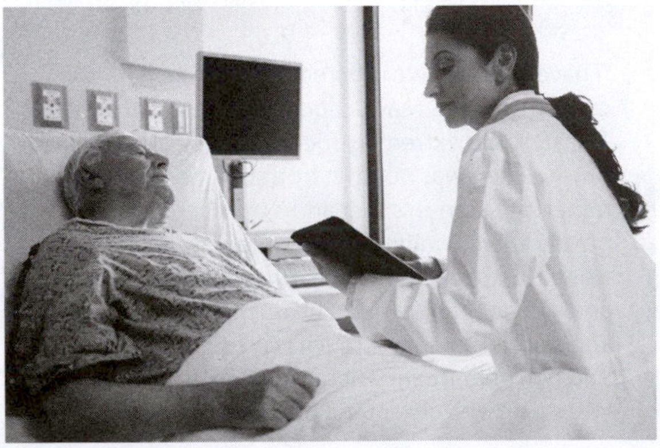

COMMUNICATION SKILLS

It is probably obvious by now that a great deal hinges on patient–caregiver communication. Patients who are at ease and confident about their ability to communicate effectively are usually more satisfied than other patients with the care they receive (Chou, Wang, Finney Rutten, Moser, & Hesse, 2010). What's more, patients who are involved in decisions about their own care typically feel significantly more confident in those decisions than patients who are simply given advice (Zikmund-Fisher et al., 2010).

Even well-educated patients with good communication skills may find themselves out of their depth conversing about medical topics. Communication training programs for patients are scarce, but even modest efforts have had some success. Some involve quick coaching sessions in medical office waiting rooms, during which patients are usually encouraged to ask questions during the visit, provide information, and verify their understanding of information (Bylund, D'Agostino, Ho, & Chewning, 2010; Cegala & Broz, 2003). The larger challenge, however, is that even if people are trained *how* to pose questions, they may not know *what* to ask. Donald Cegala and Stefne Broz (2003) reflect:

> *Most patients do not formulate questions until they have had time to process what the physician has said or do not realize their lack of understanding until they try to follow the recommended treatment or explain their illness to someone.* (p. 10)

The lesson for health professionals is to provide take-home information and opportunities for follow-up questions whenever possible.

One program with merit involved the use of a patient information form (Figure 4.1). Mary Talen and colleagues invited random patients in a physician's waiting room to fill out the form and bring it with them into the exam room. Most patients felt the forms allowed them to do a better job communicating their concerns, understanding their doctors, and actively participating in the encounters. Physicians reported that patients who used the forms demonstrated better organizational skills and attitudes than patients who did not use them (Talen, Muller-Held, Eshleman, & Stephens, 2011).

In his book *How Doctors Think,* Jerome Groopman (2007) offers behind-the-scenes insights for patients so they can more actively collaborate with their doctors. A physician himself, Groopman attests, "Doctors desperately need patients and their families and friends to help them think. Without their help, physicians are denied key clues to what is really wrong" (pp. 7–8). Following are some of his suggestions.

Keep in mind that doctors' emotions may sometimes influence their judgment. As Groopman (2007) puts it, "Patients and their loved ones swim together with physicians in a sea of feelings" (p. 58). Sometimes, he says, patients can help doctors put things in perspective. He shares an example during which a patient told his doctor, "Don't save me from an unpleasant [medical] test just because we're friends" (p. 58). His gentle remark helped the doctor realize that she had been tempted to do just that. In another case, a middle-aged woman whose previous doctors had written off her symptoms to menopause helped her new doctor see beyond that stereotype by saying:

> *I know I'm in menopause, and all five doctors have told me that's the cause of my problems. And two told me that I'm crazy. And, frankly, I am a little crazy. . . . But I think this is something else, that what I'm feeling is more than just menopause.* (Groopman, 2007, p. 56)

Her doctor listened, and the patient was right. She had a rare tumor that, if left untreated, might have threatened her life. Groopman concludes that patients can help doctors by acknowledging emotions out loud rather than leaving them unspoken.

Recognize the limits of emergency medicine. An assessment in the ER is typically only a snapshot attempt to find a problem. ER doctors do not usually have the benefit of long-standing relationships with patients or full access to their medical records. Thus, their evaluation is incomplete at best. Groopman declares, "The last thing I want is a patient to leave the ER and say, 'The doctor said there is nothing wrong with me'" (p. 74). If the concern is serious, follow-up care and further assessment are essential.

PERSPECTIVES

"My grandmother is the most selfless person I have ever met. She will do anything to help anyone, even if it means sacrificing something for herself. She drives several hours a day to help people as a hospice nurse. But when it comes to her own health, we have to beg her to see a doctor."

—Brittany

Name____________________________ **Date of Birth:** ________________

Address:____________________________
(Circle Preferred method of contact)

Phone:______________ **Cell:** __________________ **Email:** ____________

Type of Visit: (Check one)

______Recent Health Problem: (e.g. accidents, fevers, sudden pain)

______Prevention or Routine Care (physicals, paps, screening, exams, well-child care)

______Check up for Disease (e.g. high blood pressure, diabetes, asthma)

______New Patient

Please write down your reason for seeing your Doctor today.

Problems	**When did the problem start**	**What have you tried?**	**Rank Which Problem is the most important Today?** **1 = Most Important** **2 = 2nd Important** **3 = 3rd Important**

FIGURE 4-1 A research team led by Mary Talen (2011) coached patients to fill out an information form similar to this one and use it as the basis for communicating during a doctor's office visit. Both patients and physicians considered those conversations to be more effective and better organized than normal. The full form also included a drawing of a male and a female body on which patients could make notes, a place to list changes in their health, a chart of medications with dosage and purpose, and an option to request a private conversation with the doctor.

Beware of your own stereotypes. Caregivers are sensitive to discrimination, just as patients are. Groopman tells of episodes in which patients take one look at a doctor, and based solely on his or her skin color, demand to be seen by someone else. Judy-Ann Bigby, an African American physician who oversees residents, recommends that residents who are female or from minority cultures always wear their lab coats and name badges and keep their stethoscopes visible. Even so, she says, "they will sometimes be asked if they have come to take the meal tray" (p. 96). Patients are responsible for showing health professionals the same respect they wish to be shown themselves.

Accept medical uncertainty. Patients may find comfort in believing that health professionals know exactly what is wrong with them, but that is not always the case. Sometimes the underlying causes of an illness are revealed only gradually with persistent investigation over time. A false sense of certainty can blind both professionals and patients to the real or multiple causes of an illness. Groopman encourages patients not to criticize care providers for uncertainty or pressure them into acting more certain than they feel.

Ask questions. Caregivers are subject to cognitive errors and limitations, just like everyone else. Groopman admits, "Sometimes I come to the end of my thinking and am not sure what to do next" (p. 264). He encourages patients to stimulate health professionals' thinking and communication by asking such questions as, *What else could this be? What's the worst-case scenario? What should I expect next? Is it possible I have more than one problem?* and *Is there any evidence that doesn't fit?*

In the next two sections we look at factors that contribute to patient satisfaction and patient–caregiver cooperation.

Satisfaction

Patients in the United States have many grievances about medical care, but they consider themselves moderately satisfied overall. About 77% of adults in the United States are satisfied with the care they receive (Gamble, 2012). Yet patients have a number of serious complaints. Slightly more than half say they are unhappy with doctors' level of caring, rude staff members, and cumbersome check-in and check-out procedures (Feldman, 2008). Lengthy wait times are one of the strongest predictors of patient dissatisfaction (McMullen & Netland, 2013). (Chapter 5 features a cancer center that reduced wait times by 50% and made better use of caregivers' time in the process.)

What do most patients do when they feel their goals have not been met? Evidence suggests that they usually abandon their goals, at least for the time being, rather than challenge their caregivers (Dyche & Swiderski, 2005). This may be because a damaged identity is hard to mend, whereas specific goals can usually be pursued at a later date. Dissatisfied patients tend to switch caregivers or go back to them again and again, perhaps hoping for the right conditions in which to accomplish their goals. All the while, caregivers may be unaware of their dissatisfaction.

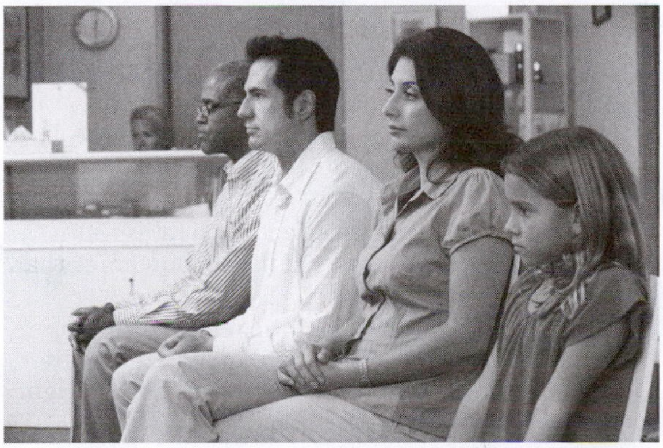

Two of the main sources of patient dissatisfaction involve lengthy wait times and a sense that the health professional is rushed and inattentive.

CAN YOU GUESS?

?

Which of the following countries offers the most effective and patient-centered health care—the United States, Germany, New Zealand, Australia, Canada, or the United Kingdom?

The answers appear at the end of the chapter.

On the other hand, patients appreciate receiving plenty of information, taking part in decisions, and being heard and respected (Jangland, Gunningberg, & Carlsson, 2009). They want to know they can speak freely and that their doctors will not turn against them if they seek second opinions (Jadad & Rizo, 2003). Another strong predictor of patient satisfaction is the sense that caregivers are concerned about them and have empathy for what they are feeling (Cousin et al., 2012). In operational terms, patients like health professionals who listen, ask questions, keep them well informed, and encourage them (Jadad & Rizo, 2003). In the next section, we take a closer look at what patients like and dislike about health care experiences.

ATTENTIVENESS AND RESPECT

Patient satisfaction is more closely linked to caregivers' communication than to their technical skills (Tarrant, Windridge, Boulton, Baker, & Freeman, 2003). This may be because it is difficult to judge technical skills and because people tend to assume that caregivers are technically competent. It may also reflect how important communication skills are to diagnosis and treatment. In the article "I Am a Good Patient Believe it or Not," Alejandro Jadad and Carlos Rizo (2003) conclude, after interviewing patients: "In most cases it would not take fancy technology, extra time, or increased costs to satisfy what patients 'want.' It would take only an assertive patient and a confident health-care provider who is willing to listen" (para. 6).

It is no surprise that, whatever their age, people like health professionals who seem to take them seriously and like them back (Grant, Cissna, & Rosenfeld, 2000). That impression is enhanced when caregivers are courteous and nonverbally expressive, maintain eye contact, ask about patients' coping strategies, and encourage them and their families to participate in medical decision making (Hart, Kelleher, Drotar, & Scholle, 2007; Koermer & Kilbane, 2008). (See Box 4.3 for a discussion about patient satisfaction and whether we put too much stock in it.)

Caregivers also get high marks for listening attentively and acknowledging patients' emotions without trying to control them (Grant et al., 2000). In contrast, patients are displeased when they feel their dignity has been compromised (Milika & Trorey, 2008). Some of the most commonly perceived threats to dignity include the following (from Milika & Trorey):

- *Invasions of privacy.* Patients surveyed say they feel dishonored when staff members allow them to be physically exposed to others or carelessly allow others to read or overhear their confidential information. Before he retired, physician John Egerton (2007) had a rule for his front-office staff: "Avoid mentioning the patient's name and diagnosis in the same sentence" (Milika & Trorey, 2008, para. 6.) For instance, never say, "John Smith has prostatitis again" or "Helen Will has head lice" (para. 6). Naturally, caregivers must discuss patients and their conditions, but they should do so in private. Making statements where others might overhear them threatens patients' privacy and portrays them as symptoms rather than as complete persons.
- *Curt, discourteous, or disrespectful communication.* Patients say they resent it when caregivers neglect to introduce themselves or when they ignore them, seem disinterested, or talk down to them. Some patients also prefer not to be addressed by first name.
- *Compromised appearance.* Patients typically report feeling most dignified when they are allowed to wear their own clothing and jewelry.

Satisfaction may vary by health concern. Overall, the least satisfied patients are those with chronic, hard-to-cure conditions such as headaches and back pain (Tan, Jensen, Thornby, & Anderson, 2006). In contrast, obstetric, cancer, and heart patients are more satisfied than average, perhaps because these conditions are typically treated as more serious and legitimate.

PERSPECTIVES

A physician committed to empowering patients was initially confounded when an immigrant patient wanted him to simply tell her what to do, even after he laid out the pros and cons of various treatment options. Then he arrived upon a solution. He said to the patient, "I'm going to tell you what I would advise for my own mother . . . But in America we don't make you do things. So now you have to adjust to the fact that we don't make you do things" (Lo, 2010, p. 491). The physician later reflected that this "hybridization" of paternalism and empowerment made them both feel comfortable with the patient's decision.

BOX 4.3

Is Satisfaction Overrated?

In a *New York Times* editorial, oncology nurse Theresa Brown (2012) proposes that a focus on patient satisfaction might diminish the quality of medical care. She worries that health professionals might cut back on painful, but important, procedures and overinvest in pleasing amenities that do not improve health outcomes. "Evaluating hospital care in terms of its ability to offer positive experiences could easily put pressure on the system to do things it can't, at the expense of what it should," says Brown (para. 11).

What Do You Think?

1. Are patients likely to rate medical care more favorably if it's pleasant? If so, are there ways to help them better understand?
2. Do you think it is more effective to rate health care centers on the basis of health outcomes than on patient satisfaction?
3. What do you say to those who feel that ratings based on health outcomes will penalize health care centers and professionals who take on high-risk and end-of-life cases?
4. In your opinion, what is the best way to rate the effectiveness of health care?

CONVENIENCE

Patients also like it when things run smoothly. Satisfaction is enhanced when the wait is not long and when their health plans cover the costs (Bleustein, Valaitis, & Jones, 2010; Fenton, Jerant, Bertakis, & Franks, 2012). Hospitals in recent years have begun efforts to streamline paperwork and admitting procedures (Huvane, 2008). Convenience is also a factor in the creation of retail clinics in drugstores and department stores across the country (Lowes, 2008). To date, little research has been done about health communication in those settings.

PATIENTS' WISH LIST

- Attentiveness
- Respect
- Convenience
- Privacy
- Empathy
- Sense of control
- Genuine caring

A SENSE OF CONTROL

Patients appreciate being well informed and actively involved in their care. Although people appreciate doctors' advice, only about 20% of patients want their caregivers to make decisions without them (Deloitte, 2008b). This applies to everyday decisions as well as major treatment options. One hospital patient interviewed said he appreciates it when nurses who bathe him wash body areas he cannot reach and then ask, "Would you like to do the rest for yourself?" (quoted in Milika & Trorey, 2008, p. 2713). He says he feels respected when he is given choices, and this one allows him to maintain dignity and take care of private needs himself as much as possible.

Other patients echo the same sentiment. A man with diabetes in Ciechanowski and Katon's (2006) study describes his favorite doctor this way:

> *He doesn't just come in, do your treatment and leave. He kind of talks, you know, "How are things going? Tell me about yourself," and he has a fabulous memory. He remembers about those things that you tell him. . . . I don't know if it's just a really good memory, or he puts notes in the chart, or whatever, but it's just . . . he makes you feel comfortable coming in. (p. 3074)*

Conversely, patients often feel sidelined when health professionals use words they do not understand and when they seemed rushed. One medical professional interviewed said that, when she is rushed, she tends to use medical jargon to save time, even when she knows patients will not understand it (Dahm, 2012, p. 684). Patients in the same study said they pick up on the urgency and tend to stay quiet about their questions. As one patient put it: "There is just a whole line of people . . . You don't wanna keep the doctor up in saying 'oh what does this mean?'" (p. 685).

Cooperation and Consent

Let's go back to a summer day in 2008 when Tiger Woods limped up the sloping hill of Torrey Pines golf course. He made the final shot to finish one stroke ahead of his nearest competitor after a grueling playoff in a golf tournament that included 91 holes. Woods won the U.S. Open that year, thrilling fans but confounding his doctors, who had urged him not to play because of a knee injury.

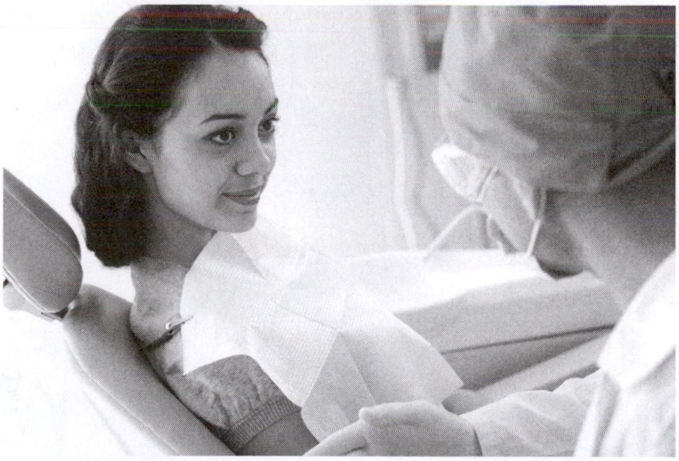

Many patients report that dental professionals are their main source of information about oral health, which makes it essential that they spend time with patients and be good communicators (Horowitz, Wang, & Kleinman, 2012).

In this respect Woods is not so different from the majority of us. Although we are unlikely to challenge our doctors' advice in person, only 50% to 60% of us follow medical advice completely or most of the time (Martin, Williams, Haskard, & Dimatteo, 2005). Some of the advice we are prone to ignore involves avoiding dangerous and unhealthy behaviors, undergoing recommended health screenings, seeing specialists, making regular doctors' appointments, taking prescribed drugs as directed, exercising often, eating healthy foods, and so on.

As Michael Burgoon and Judee Burgoon (1990) observe, it is curious that we do not follow medical advice more closely, considering that we pay for the advice, presumably stand to benefit from it, and typically revere the expertise of medical professionals. In the next section we explore some of the reasons why we may not follow through. Then we examine health professionals' stake in treatment outcomes and policies concerning informed consent.

CAREERS IN PATIENT ADVOCACY

Patient navigators help individual patients and their families locate providers, make appointments, and handle insurance, language and communication, and transportation challenges. The nonprofit Harold P. Freeman Patient Navigation Institute in New York City offers career training, as do the Center to Reduce Cancer Health Disparities, the National Cancer Institute, and others. National salary and job outlook data are not yet available.

See Box 4.4 for more resources about related careers.

REASONS FOR NONCOOPERATION

If patients don't follow medical advice, it does not necessarily mean they are lazy or indifferent about their health. A number of more legitimate concerns may affect their decisions.

For one, medical recommendations may be impossible or impractical to carry out. A patient may be unable to afford prescribed medications or may be physically incapable of performing suggested routines. For example, people who miss dialysis treatments often report that no one is available to drive them to and from appointments (Gordon, Leon, & Sehgal, 2003). Likewise, low-income patients may have little choice concerning their exposure to "avoidable" health threats. As Gillespie (2001) describes it:

> *Low-income families live in older homes filled with lifetimes of dust and molding timber. They breathe the air polluted by factories that never cease production and by the cars of daily downtown professionals who sleep in clean, suburban air each night. Often depressed, they are more likely to smoke and less likely to eat well. Many sleep on the floor, knowing that the asthma this triggers could kill them, but afraid that a stray bullet shot through the window will do so sooner.* (p. 114)

BOX 4.4 CAREER OPPORTUNITIES

Patient Advocacy

Patient advocate
Patient navigator
Social worker
Case manager
Patient care coordinator or consultant

Career Resources and Job Listings

- Patient Advocate Foundation: www.patientadvocate.org
- National Patient Advocate Foundation: www.npaf.org
- Patient Navigator Outreach and Chronic Disease Prevention Demonstration Program: http://bhpr.hrsa.gov/nursing/grants/patientnavigator.html
- National Association of Social Workers: www.socialworkers .org
- Council on Social Work Education: www.cswe.org
- Case Management Society of America: www.cmsa.org
- National Organization for Human Services: www.nationalhumanservices.org
- U.S. Bureau of Labor Statistics Occupational Outlook Handbook: www.bls.gov/ooh

In other situations, recommended regimens may be so foreign to people that they cannot easily integrate them into their lifestyles. For instance, it may seem inconceivable to remove red meat completely from one's diet. Or, like Tiger Woods, people may feel that some goals and obligations are too important to miss, even if it means risking a personal illness or injury.

HURDLES TO COOPERATION

Patients may not follow medical advice for any of the following reasons:

- Impossible or impractical
- Unaffordable
- Unclear understanding
- Culturally or personally unacceptable
- Diagnosis seems incorrect
- Treatment seems unneeded or unhelpful
- Unpleasant side effects

Second, people may not agree with health professionals' assessments or treatment recommendations. Research suggests that people are likely to distrust diagnoses and ignore medical advice if they are not able to describe their concerns during medical visits (Frankel & Beckman, 1989). People may also deny diagnoses that threaten their self-image. It may be difficult to admit obesity, hearing loss, depression, sexually transmitted diseases, and the like.

Third, people may stop medical routines prematurely if they perceive that they have no effect or if their symptoms cease (Forrest, Shadmi, Nutting, & Starfield, 2007). For example, it is difficult to get people to continue treatment for conditions such as high blood pressure because they cannot directly perceive that the medicine has a positive effect.

Finally, patients may stop taking medication if they experience unpleasant side effects (Penn, Watermeyer, & Evans, 2011) or if they do not believe it will help (Makarem, Smith, Mudambi, & Hunt, 2014). Under those circumstances, they may try other methods or conclude that the cure is worse than the disease.

These factors are exacerbated when care providers do not encourage patients to express their concerns and reservations at the time they give medical advice. Evidence suggests that many people leave their doctors' offices knowing they cannot or will not follow through with the advice given, but they do not feel free to say so. Doctors who assume that patients should follow orders regardless of their circumstances may be discouraged when treatment outcomes are less than optimal. And, if people do not feel comfortable talking with a caregiver, they may not fess up later that they did not follow his or her advice.

CARE PROVIDERS' INVESTMENT

It may be tempting to assume that, if patients do not follow medical advice, they have only themselves to blame. But health professionals may be blamed as well. Lack of patient–caregiver cooperation often results in harmful health outcomes. Nonadherence is linked to diabetes treatment failures (Joy, 2008), increased hospitalization for heart failure (Fonarow et al., 2008), and asthma-related complications and deaths (Gillisen, 2007), to name just a few. These are not just patients' problems.

Care providers' careers may be damaged by excessive treatment failures. With capitation and restricted reimbursements, health care organizations lose money on patients who do not improve as expected. Consequently, hospitals may refuse to grant physicians privileges if their treatment outcomes are below par, and medical groups may deny them employment for the same reason. Health professionals' reputations among patients may suffer as well. Physician Wesley Sugai says he does not treat patients who chronically ignore medical advice without explanation:

> *As a rural solo pediatrician, I have neither the time nor the desire to try to convince parents about the importance of childhood immunizations, follow-up with specialists, or medications. . . . I tell parents that I have to be able to trust them to carry out the treatment plan, just as they must trust me to prescribe the proper therapy. If neither of us trusts the other, then the patient–doctor relationship is nonexistent and we must go our separate ways.* (Sugai, 2008, p. 14)

Sugai says that he does work with patients who are up front about reservations or limitations that affect their health behaviors. All in all, it is important for everyone that patients who cannot follow treatment advice or who do not agree with it feel comfortable admitting that and negotiating more suitable options.

WE'RE IN THIS TOGETHER

When patients and health professionals do not see eye to eye, the following adverse effects are likely:

- Treatment failures
- Frustration
- Wasted time
- Avoidable expenses
- Loss of professional reputation or privileges
- Risks to public health

Public health is at stake as well. Good communication and healthy behaviors can avert pandemics and reduce the incidence of avoidable illnesses and injuries. In the United States, the cost of preventable hospitalizations is about $25 billion per year, equal to nearly 10% of total health costs (United Health Foundation, 2015). Analyst Bill Clements (1996) advises, "Make no mistake about it: Bad communication costs you money" (para. 3).

Considering these factors, how far should health professionals go to gain patients' cooperation? Some doctors are trying cash rewards (see Box 4.5). Others are trying to involve patients more in medical decision making. As the next section illustrates, over time, public policy has changed concerning patients' role in medical decisions.

INFORMED CONSENT

For centuries, physicians considered it wise to tell patients only as much as they could understand (in the doctors' opinion) and nothing that might dissuade them from following medical advice. For example, if a doctor judged that the potential advantages of a drug outweighed its possible side effects, the doctor might not tell the patient about side effects, for fear the

Videos about treatment options can help patients become well informed about risks and benefits before they decide whether to consent to treatment.

BOX 4.5

Cash for Cooperation?

Communication is important, but can it stack up to cold, hard cash? Maybe not. Some medical centers have had success with innovative cash-for-compliance programs that reward patients for healthy behavior. Incentives include cash or cash coupons (usually $4 or $5 or a chance to win from $25 to $100) for keeping appointments, maintaining healthy blood pressure (for hypertensive patients), reaching weight-loss goals, immunizing children, or abstaining from drug abuse.

Program sponsors say it is less expensive to offer cash prizes than to pay staff to work overtime or call patients, and everyone stands to gain if incentives reduce unnecessary care and keep serious health concerns from escalating. It's not clear, however, if patients will develop the motivation to continue the behaviors without the rewards.

What Do You Think?

1. Would you be more likely to engage in healthy behaviors if you might receive a cash award or prize for doing so?
2. If you said yes, would you be likely to cease those behaviors if the reward were no longer available?
3. Do you think reward systems are a good idea? Why or why not?

patient would not take the drug (J. Katz, 1995). Likewise, although doctors have always been required to get patients' permission before they operated on them, they have not been required to tell patients about the risks involved.

In most cases physicians were presumably following their best judgment. In some cases, however, patients were subjected to risks, even to deadly medical experiments and exploitation, without their knowledge. At particular risk have been members of racial minorities and financially impoverished members of society. One example is the **Tuskegee Syphilis Study** conducted in Alabama (Box 4.6). Another famous case involves Henrietta Lacks, an African American

BOX 4.6 ETHICAL CONSIDERATIONS

Patients' Right to Informed Consent

During the infamous Tuskegee Syphilis Study, which began in 1932, some 600 African American men were enrolled without their knowledge in a medical experiment. They were patients of the Public Health Service in Macon County, Alabama, and the experiment was conducted by the U.S. government through the Tuskegee Institute in Alabama.

Although medical researchers knew that 399 of the men had syphilis, the men were not told. Doctors simply told all the men they had "bad blood" and provided them with medicine, meals, and burial expenses. However, the medicine was not really medicine at all. It was a harmless but ineffectual placebo.

The study was designed to help medical researchers learn more about the effects of syphilis among African Americans. Syphilis is a sexually transmitted disease that affects the bones, liver, heart, and central nervous system. In advanced stages, it can cause open sores, heart damage, tumors, blindness, insanity, and death. When the study was begun, there was no effective treatment for syphilis. However, by 1940, penicillin was known to be effective at treating and even curing it.

The syphilis patients in the Tuskegee experiment were not given penicillin. Instead, researchers continued to watch the disease progress until the experiment was called off in 1972, some 40 years after it began.

When details of the Tuskegee study were made public, there was an angry outcry. Some likened it to the Nazis' medical experiments on Jewish prisoners during World War II. The courts eventually ordered the federal government to pay the men and their families a total of $10 million for the injury and indignity they had suffered. Twenty-five years after the end of the experiment, President Bill Clinton publicly apologized for the government's behavior in May 1997.

Now, before patients are given medical treatment (experimental or otherwise), they must be fully informed, give consent, and be aware that they can cease treatment at any time. It is hoped that informed consent will prevent atrocities such as the Tuskegee Syphilis Study. But informed consent is sometimes hard to apply. Jauhar (2008b) describes the ethical challenges of informed consent in some instances:

> *[An] issue I continue to struggle with today is how to balance patient autonomy with the physician's obligation to do the best for his patient. As a doctor, when do you let your patient make a bad decision: When, if ever, do you draw the line? What if a decision could cost your patient's life? How hard do you push him to change his mind? At the same time, it's his life. Who are you to tell him how to live? (p. 233)*

Jauhar (2008b) describes a particularly difficult case when a hospital patient, Mr. Smith, began to cough up blood and have trouble breathing. His condition quickly deteriorated, and doctors knew they would have to act quickly to save his life. Their only hope was to insert a temporary breathing tube. But the patient adamantly refused. In his mind, being intubated seemed a worse fate than death. Mr. Smith's fear seemed irrational, yet he was coherent and capable of communicating—thus he was capable of giving (or refusing) informed consent. As the doctor responsible for Mr. Smith's care, Jauhar faced a dilemma. He could honor the patient's wishes and allow him to die,

continued

continued

or he could overrule the patient and insert the breathing tube by force. What would you have done?

Jauhar chose to insert the breathing tube, although the staff had to restrain Mr. Smith physically to do it. During the procedure Jauhar worried that the patient would hate him for disobeying his wishes. "'If you live through this,' I whispered to Mr. Smith, 'I hope you can forgive me'" (Jauhar, 2008b, pp. 236–237). Two weeks later, as Mr. Smith neared recovery, Jauhar stopped by his room and told the patient he was responsible for the decision. The patient considered his response for a moment. "I've been through a lot," he finally said, his voice still hoarse from two weeks of intubation. . . . But thank you" (p. 237). This is an extreme case, but it illustrates some of the ethical dilemmas involved in informed consent.

What Do You Think?

1. Do you agree with Jauhar's decision? Why or why not? What would you have done in his place?
2. Sometimes medical information is difficult to understand fully. How should we establish if the consenting person is informed enough to give consent?
3. Some people, such as those with terminal illnesses, are willing (even anxious) to try untested therapies. Researchers may not know what results to expect, and they may even anticipate negative outcomes. Who should decide whether the patient undergoes untested therapies? Should public money be used in these cases?
4. In medical research, is it ever justified to deceive people (as in giving placebos) to make sure they are not just responding to the power of suggestion? If so, under what conditions?
5. Sometimes it is in the best interest of society or health care workers to know if a person has a contagious disease (such as AIDS). If the person doesn't consent to a test for that disease, do you think it should be permissible to perform the test without the person's knowledge? (A vial of blood may be used for a variety of tests without the patient knowing it.)
6. On what grounds, if any, should health professionals judge whether a patient is emotionally capable of making a life-or-death judgment about emergency treatment?

mother of five who died of cervical cancer in 1951. But "not all of Henrietta Lacks died that day," explains her family ("Lacks Family," 2012, para. 1). Lacks's cancer cells had the unprecedented ability to live and multiply in a laboratory environment. Without Lacks's consent, medical researchers kept some of her cells, multiplied and cloned them, and shared them with colleagues worldwide. To date, scientists have grown 50 million metric tons of Lacks' cells (known by the code name HeLa) and have used them as the basis for some of the most transformational medical breakthroughs in history, including a vaccine for polio, and treatments for cancer, herpes, leukemia, Parkinson's disease, AIDS, and more (Margonelli, 2010; Silver, 2013). The Lacks family was not informed about the use of her cells for more than 20 years, and they have never received proceeds from the sale of her organic material (worth tens of millions of dollars and counting). The upshot is that the Lacks family is still unable to "afford access to the health care advances their mother's cells made possible" (Henrietta Lacks Foundation, 2015, para. 3).

Public outrage over the Tuskegee Syphilis Study and others like it led the U.S. government to pass informed-consent laws. **Informed consent** means that patients must (a) be made fully aware of known treatment risks, benefits, and options; (b) be deemed capable of understanding such information and making a responsible judgment; and (c) be aware that they may refuse to participate or may cease treatment at any time (Ashley & O'Rourke, 1997). When patients are children or are otherwise unable to make decisions, close family members may be allowed to consent on their behalf.

Informed-consent requirements are designed to allow patients enough information so that they can make knowledgeable judgments about their own care. Some theorists believe that health care should go even further toward including patients in treatment decisions. As early as 1973, medical analyst Harold Walker predicted that doctors would become less authoritarian and more persuasive. The difference is subtle but important. From an authoritarian perspective, patients are expected to *comply* with doctors' orders. From a persuasive perspective, however, they take an active role in decision making as patients. They *cooperate* in the process as informed and influential participants.

If people are included in decision making as patients, it may be possible to overcome or accommodate many of the factors that have kept them from following medical advice. The health professional who is aware of a patient's financial and physical limitations, cultural reservations, denial, or discouragement is better able to negotiate acceptable options with him or her. At the very least, patients and caregivers can establish outright what each is willing to do. This may ultimately be less frustrating than allowing their differences to go unspoken.

Informed consent is a victory for patient empowerment. However, the terms are sometimes hard to apply, even when people try hard to do so. For example, a long list of complications (many of them extremely unlikely) might result from a simple procedure. It may be impractical or impossible to list every possible outcome. However, physicians may be accused of negligence if an unlikely outcome results and the patient was not warned about it in advance. Language differences also present challenges. It is sometimes difficult to understand medical and legal terminology. In focus groups, Spanish speakers in the United States with literacy challenges said that consent and privacy forms that had been translated into Spanish were too long and wordy, the fine print aroused their suspicious, and they felt rushed to comply without fully understanding the forms or discussing them with family members (Cortés, Drainoni, Henault, & Paasche-Orlow, 2010). (We talk more about health literacy challenges in Chapter 6.)

On the bright side, when they are available, multimedia presentations about medical procedures often increase understanding prior to informed consent. Melissa Wanzer and colleagues invited the parents and guardians of children who were recommended for endoscopies to view a four-minute video about hospital procedures and an interactive presentation about informed consent, including optional voice-over and a true-false quiz they could take as many times as they liked at their own pace. Compared to parents and guardians who simply reviewed informed consent forms with a physician, those who took part in the multimedia presentation understood more about the procedure and were subsequently less anxious about it and more satisfied with the care their children received (Wanzer et al., 2010).

Partly because complete disclosure is so difficult to define, the courts have been reluctant to hold physicians responsible for informed-consent violations except in clear-cut cases. Review Box 4.6 for ethical implications concerning informed consent.

Illness and Personal Identity

"The old story goes, 'When life gives you lemons, make lemonade.' But what do you do when life gives you cancer?" So begins a video by Stephen Sutton (2014), a teenage boy with incurable, advanced-stage cancer. His next words are, "This is not a sob story. This is Stephen's story."

Stephen's Story attracted worldwide attention when, soon after his diagnosis, Sutton uploaded to Facebook a bucket list of 46 experiences he wished to enjoy. In the 4 years before his death, Sutton accomplished

People respond to illness and dying in different ways. When Stephen Sutton, shown here, was diagnosed with terminal cancer as a teenager, he went public with a bucket list of what we hoped to experience in his final years and a captivating social media chronicle of his adventures.

nearly everything on his list and then some. He set out to raise 10,000 pounds for teens with cancer, and eventually raised 469 times that much (the equivalent of more than $7 million in the United States). He organized charity events, spoke to audiences about his life journey, recruited more than 500 people to help him set a Guinness World Record, and more. Even since Sutton's death, people have continued to raise millions in his name.

Sutton's story is not an ideal or typical illness experience. There *is* no ideal or typical experience. Although people with long-term illnesses tend to experience recognizable phases of identity management, the way they cope and define themselves is as unique as people themselves. To understand the effects of illness on personal identity, consider for a moment who you are. A few words might come to mind: student, son, daughter, parent, athlete, kind, smart, energetic, and the like. To the extent that you and the people around you agree on these roles and descriptions, they make up your identity. They define who you are, and you are not likely to change in unforeseen, significant ways. **Personal identity** is a relatively enduring set of characteristics that define a person.

At first consideration, having an identity may seem easy. You simply are who you are. However, the deeper reality is that you work hard to "be" who you are. People generally want to be viewed favorably and to feel good about themselves. Therefore, they act in ways that are consistent with the positive image they wish to portray (Goffman, 1967). Like other people, you are probably invested in maintaining the qualities and talents that make you unique. Very often, this requires a great deal of work (studying, listening, practicing, rehearsing, exercising, etc.). These behaviors are not "you," but they do support the identity that helps you and others understand you.

Communication is the primary means by which people negotiate their identities. What if your appearance or your ability to talk changed substantially? What if people began treating you differently, as in speaking loudly and slowly to you or avoiding eye contact with you? Even minor illnesses and injuries can interfere with your ability to "be" who you are. If the effects are short lived, you may not experience a serious transformation. However, long-term effects can change how you see yourself and how others treat you.

Michael Arrington (2003) interviewed men with prostate cancer, the treatment of which may render men impotent and incontinent. One man in the study, Walsh, describes his struggle to reconcile his sense of self and manhood with his inability to have an erection:

> *And the final thing was to know myself. Do I know what's happening to me? Do I understand, in my own anxieties, how important, as I look back on it, the whole sexual experience of my own sexuality has been to me? Have I overloaded myself with that or not? Have I given it too much value in life? Are there things in life that are maybe more important to me personally than that? I think that evaluation and that process is one that I have given a lot of time and attention to, being the kind of a person I am.* (p. 35)

Some men in the study chose various methods (pumps, injections, pills) for simulating erections, but others felt that such solutions were phony and inauthentic. Said one man:

> *Come on. That's not sex. That's, forget that stuff; that's not gonna cut it with me. I'm just done with it, that's all. . . . It's not a natural thing when you do that. I just don't, uh, want to be an artificial man.* (p. 38)

Thus, the men either found new ways to achieve or define sexual performance or they redefined its importance in their lives. For example, one participant in the study said that men who cannot find other ways to please their partners sexually are "piss-poor lovers" anyway (Arrington, 2003, p. 39).

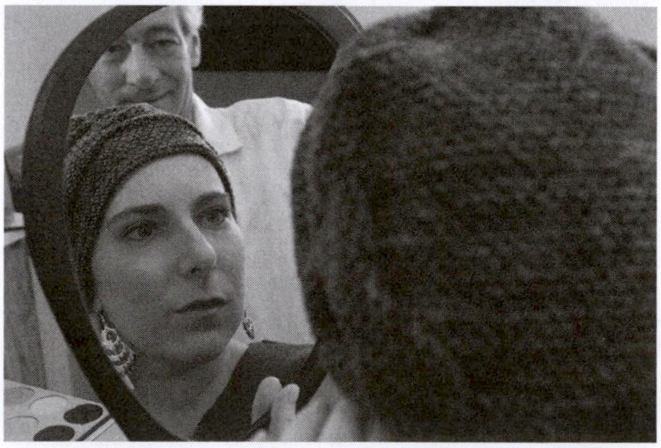

It can be difficult to reconcile one's sense of self with the physical effects of some illnesses and treatments, but even conditions that are invisible to others can impact personal identity.

In addition to personal identities, you probably have a collection of **social identities**, characterized by perceived membership in societal groups such as "teenagers," "Hispanic Americans," and "retired persons" (Harwood & Sparks, 2003). Based on the groups with which you identify, you may expect yourself (and others like you) to think and behave in particular ways. For example, you may be surprised when a youthful friend reveals that she has a serious heart condition, and you may thereafter view her as "older" than her peers (Kundrat & Nussbaum, 2003). Dilemmas are also presented for people with conditions such as inflammatory bowel disease that are highly personal (Defenbaugh, 2013) and for those undergoing treatments such as chemotherapy that cause visible changes in their appearance. A woman in one study who lost her hair during cancer treatments describes looking in the mirror and alternating between two reactions: "*The reflection is not me* . . . It's me . . . It's not me" (quoted by Koszalinski & Williams, 2012, p. 119).

When people are diagnosed with identity-threatening illnesses, their health status may become part of their identity as well. Jake Harwood and Lisa Sparks (2003) call this a **tertiary identity**—a label that defines simultaneously the illness and a person's alignment toward it. For example, a participant in a leadership retreat introduces herself as, among other things, a "breast cancer survivor." The group responds with applause and hugs. Surviving cancer is treated as courageous and admirable, and group members feel a sense of intimacy that she has shared this news with them. Harwood and Sparks propose that a number of tertiary identities are available to people with the same health conditions. For example, the woman in this example might have said, "I'm a cancer victim" rather than a "survivor." It is likely that the group's reaction (and their image of her) would have been somewhat different. Perhaps even more important, different wording might reflect something important about the way she viewed her *own* circumstances.

This section examines how people tend to manage their identities in the life-altering circumstances of ill health.

REACTIONS TO ILLNESS

Individuals' reactions to illness may be surprising, even to themselves. Kathy Charmaz has studied the way that people with long-term illnesses seek to reconcile their previous identities with the changed circumstances in which they find themselves. She has identified four stages common to the process. First, people typically take on a **supernormal identity**, determined not to let the illness stop them from being better than ever. This stage is usually followed by a sense of **restored self**, in which people are not quite as optimistic but typically deny that the illness has changed them. The third stage is **contingent personal identity**, in which people admit that they may not be able to do everything they could previously do and they begin to confront the consequences of a changed identity. The final stage, **salvaged self**, represents the development of a transformed identity that integrates former aspects of self with current limitations (Charmaz, 1987). Stephen Sutton, whose story begins this section, ultimately said that his goal was to show people "what it's like to have something go wrong with your life but not to be defined by it" (Sutton, n.d.). Not everyone goes through every stage or spends the same amount of time in each stage. However, Charmaz's model illustrates that illness and identity are sometimes intertwined and that people actively try to manage their identity when illness threatens their ability to behave as they normally would.

A SENSE OF CONTROL

Cancer patients who are allowed to decide for themselves whom to tell about their condition, how much to tell them, when, and how often experience a sense of control that enhances their coping ability. On the other hand, people who are discouraged from communicating and those who feel that others are controlling the flow of information often perceive a damaging loss of control (Donovan-Kicken, Tollison, & Goins, 2011).

In the case study "I Want You to Put Me in the Grave With All My Limbs" (Sharf, Haidet, & Kroll, 2005), a woman with a family history of diabetes says she would rather die at age 60 than experience amputation. Many people may shudder at such a choice, but for her, the devastation of losing a limb is familiar and distinctly identity threatening. She explains:

> *My grandfather had no legs; my dad has no legs, and part of his chest is missing, and*

> *part of one hand is missing, and he can only see out of one eye, but not very good. Also, my dad's brother has one hand missing, and one leg missing and so forth. And so it goes in the family.* (*Sharf et al., p. 43*)

Sometimes people's abilities are not substantially altered by their health conditions, but they may be surprised or dismayed to have conditions that seem to clash with their established beliefs. For instance, an unmarried high school teacher may be horrified to learn that she is pregnant and may wonder if her pregnancy will affect students' image of her or cost her job.

It can be useful to ascertain whether people consider their health conditions to be identity threatening and how they react to that possibility. Patients may feel determined, ashamed, victimized, or even relieved by diagnoses. Some respond to illness with a zealous determination to "beat" it, as if it were an enemy. Others interpret illness as punishment. For others, it is comforting to have a name for the illness and perhaps a plan for dealing with it.

Leigh Ford and Brigitte Christmon (2005) illustrate this diversity well with narratives from women who have had breast cancer or feared that they might. One woman, Helen, described the nausea and fatigue of undergoing chemotherapy while doing her best as a wife and mother. She says, "It was a terrible time for us, but when I look back at it now, I feel nothing but pride in our resilience as a family and in the love that allowed us to make this work" (p. 160). Another woman said she put her faith in God when she did not know what lay ahead. A third challenged the "corporatization of breast cancer," saying:

> *Breast cancer is now part of the market economy. We have pink ribbons and scarves and bears and T-shirts and coffee mugs and wind chimes and breast cancer candles and tchotchkes galore. There is something offensive about this. Most of these items advertise that "part of the proceeds go to breast cancer research." I wonder how much—and to what end? I prefer a straight business transaction—at least the motives and agenda are clear.* (*p. 165*)

She also questioned the pink-ribbon movement's emphasis on feminine beauty, optimism, and survival—to the extent of ignoring the deadly and devastating aspects of breast cancer. "If you refuse to enact the role of the noble survivor," she said, "you are invisible and marginalized, not just by mainstream society but also by most other women who have experienced this disease" (p. 163). Samantha King (2010) agrees, calling the pink campaign largely a "tyranny of cheerfulness" depicting breast cancer survivors as "youthful, ultrafeminine, slim, light-skinned if not white, radiant with health, joyful and proud" (p. 287).

These diverse reactions can be informative. We may assume that people who are upbeat are "taking it well" or are "strong." But in some instances, they are hiding deeper feelings or harboring unrealistic expectations. Others may feel their illness is degrading or unfair. People who seem relieved may have expected something worse (it might be helpful to know what), or they may simply be glad to escape part of the dread and uncertainty of not knowing. In the case of extended illnesses, reactions are likely to vary considerably even within one person.

Following are a few implications for communication concerning illness and personal identity:

- Narratives can be a means to convey, establish, and negotiate self-identity. There is often value in the listening and in the telling.
- Avoid preconceived notions about how people will or should respond to health crises. Instead, ask questions and listen without judgment.
- Recognize that personal identity is a fluid concept that changes over time and in different situations. A person's identity at one stage of an illness may be quite different than at another. Be attentive to these changes.
- When physical treatment goals are at odds with identity goals, as they often are, communicate openly and collaboratively about the differences. Honor the importance of multiple perspectives.
- Do not overestimate the accuracy of superficial cues. People who seem to be taking things "well" may be avoiding the issue, and people who are taking them "poorly" may be in a natural stage of adjustment.
- Be careful about the words you use. *Survivor* supports a different identity than *victim*, and so on. Also pay attention to the words other people use. These may present openings for conversation, as in, "You refer to yourself as 'a crip' since the accident. Do you feel that people treat you that way?"

In the context of a health crisis, the process of identity management is likely to be varied, uncertain, and effortful. Sometimes the best thing we can do is be receptive listeners as the process unfolds.

Summary

In contrast to the well-established ways in which caregivers are socialized, people learn how to be patients mostly through life experience and watching others. Patients often communicate in hesitant and nonassertive ways because they are uncertain what is expected of them and afraid to seem rude or ignorant.

Although a professional may conceive of health as a biological phenomenon to be identified by its physical manifestations, patients are more likely to interpret illnesses in light of their effects on everyday activities. The Voice of Lifeworld is concerned with feelings and events. Patients' communication and their willingness to self-advocate are influenced by a variety of factors, including the nature of their illnesses, their personalities, and their communication skills. Throughout this chapter, we have examined suggestions by experts on how patients can be more active participants in medical encounters.

Patient satisfaction is often based more on how caregivers listen and empathize than on patients' perception of their technical competency. People typically prefer care providers who seem interested, caring, and sympathetic. They also appreciate having a sense of control and being treated with dignity. As a whole, people in the United States tend to have serious complaints but still consider themselves satisfied with health care overall.

People's adherence to medical advice is notoriously low for a range of reasons, including limited money and resources, mistrust of the diagnosis or treatment plan, a sense that the illness is cured, and a perception that the treatment is worse than the disease. Although patients may have good reasons for not following medical advice, the results can be disastrous for them, for health professionals, and for the public. Many health advocates urge patients and professionals to be more explicit about negotiating treatment options that are practical and acceptable.

Ethical principles and U.S. laws stipulate that patients be well informed about health choices and allowed to decide for themselves what care they will and will not receive. Informed-consent laws protect people from atrocities such as the Tuskegee Syphilis Study, but some cases fall within a gray zone in which it is difficult to determine when patients are too distraught or fearful to make informed choices.

Illness can affect people's very identity. Evidence suggests that people work to maintain their identities, even when illness changes their patterns of behavior.

Now that we have considered patients' perspectives, we will explore how health communication looks through professional caregivers' eyes.

Key Terms and Theories

Voice of Lifeworld
self-advocates
Tuskegee Syphilis Study
informed consent
personal identity
social identities
tertiary identity
supernormal identity
restored self
contingent personal identity
salvaged self

Discussion Questions

1. Write a paragraph about a health concern you or someone you know has experienced. Does your description mostly reflect the Voice of Lifeworld or the Voice of Medicine? How?
2. If you were a health professional and a patient felt the treatment advice you gave her was unlikely to work, would you want to know about her reservations? Why or why not? What is the best way the patient might express her disagreement?
3. Imagine a scenario in which someone you love has been having agonizing headaches and doctors cannot figure out what is wrong. Write down several communication options that incorporate Jerome Groopman's (2007) advice to patients.
4. Think of the most dissatisfying health experience you have ever experienced. Create two columns on a sheet of paper. On the left side, write down what happened. On the right side, rewrite the experience to be more satisfying. What would you change? Why?
5. Have you ever stopped taking prescription medicine before you were supposed to or missed a dosage? Have you engaged in unhealthy habits you would rather not admit to your doctor? If so, what factors affected your decision? Do any of the factors covered in this chapter apply to your situation? If so, which ones?

6. Imagine that someone close to you is diagnosed with diabetes and will have to radically alter his diet and take insulin injections every day. How might this affect his personal identity? His tertiary identity? If he perceives this to be a serious threat to his identity, what phases might he experience, as reflected in Charmaz's (1987) model of identity management?

Answer to *Can You Guess?*

Of the countries listed, the United Kingdom ranks highest in terms of patient-centered care and effective care (The Commonwealth Fund, 2014). Out of 11 industrialized countries, the United States ranks sixth and fifth on these indicators, respectively.

CHAPTER 5

Caregiver Perspectives

Healthcare executive Fred Lee remembers a moment when a nurse's comment made the difference between hope and despair. His mother had just been badly injured in an automobile accident in which his father was killed. As Lee rushed to be with his mother in the hospital he was already frantic, thinking that the intensive care team might forbid him from remaining with her:

> *As I walked into the unit, I was a time-bomb ready to go off if anybody tried to limit my time with my mother. When I entered her room, it was a shock to see her on the ventilator. Her head was in a steel halo with rods running from the rim into her skull. Her face was swollen beyond recognition. . . . Not knowing if she was awake or not, I said softly, "Mother, this is Fred and I am here now to be with you." . . . The nurse turned around and looked at me. I thought, Here it comes. Give it your best shot, lady. But instead, the nurse smiled and said, "My, my, my, you should see what your touch just did to your mother's vital signs. It's amazing. We need you here all of the time!"* (Lee, 2004, pp. 61–62)

This story illustrates many of the facets of modern-day medicine. Health care is a mix of life-saving technology, institutional rules and guidelines, and, at its best, a deep appreciation for the role that compassion, love, and touch play as well. The example also points to the powerful role of communication. Lee reflects: "Could she [the nurse] have come up with a more perfectly timed thing to say? It was as if she had read my mind and in one gracious comment had made me feel needed and welcome, an essential part of the healing team" (p. 62).

Lee's experience brings to mind the privileges and challenges of working every day with human life. Health professionals—whether they are technicians, physical therapists, dentists, pharmacists, physicians, or another of the many professionals we will discuss in this chapter—experience many of the same challenges and rewards while communicating with people who need their help. (See Box 5.1 for career options in patient care.)

In this chapter we look at health care from the diverse perspectives of professional caregivers. We begin at the beginning, with the factors that lead people to careers in caregiving and how candidates are selected, educated, and socialized. Then we follow the path of caregivers-in-training through initial clinical experiences and into the professional domain. Along the way we focus on issues related to time, maturity, mindfulness, confidence, and satisfaction. Then we zero in on three issues: medical mistakes, stress and burnout, and interdisciplinary teamwork. Teamwork is a promising, but not always easy, opportunity to maximize effectiveness and reduce the stress of caregiving.

WHAT DO YOU THINK?

What is the best term to describe professionals who assist others in maintaining and restoring health? A few options are *clinicians, health providers, health care providers, health professionals,* and *caregivers*. You may have other ideas. Which do you prefer and why?

BOX 5.1 CAREER OPPORTUNITIES

Dentists, Hygienists, and Assistants

Dental specializations include oral and maxillofacial surgery, orthodontics, and prosthodontics.

- *Dentists* make an average of $149,310 a year. The job market is expected to increase 16% between 2012 and 2022.
- *Dental hygienists* with associate's degrees earn an average of $70,210 a year, and the job outlook is much better than average, with need expected to increase 33%.
- *Dental assistants* make an average of $34,500 per year. The number of positions is expected to increase 25%.

Emergency Personnel

Emergency medical technicians (EMTs) and paramedics make about $31,020 a year. The job outlook is good, with the need expected to rise 23% between 2012 and 2022.

Midlevel Providers

Two types of midlevel providers are nurse practitioners (NPs) and physician assistants (PAs), both of whom are specially trained and state licensed.

- NPs and PAs are of equal status, about midway between that of doctors and nurses.
- For minor health concerns, they function much like doctors, performing routines exams and minor biopsies, suturing cuts, and so on.
- Annual salaries range from $90,930 to $96,460.
- The need for midlevel providers is expected to rise at least 31% between 2012 and 2022.

Mental Health Professionals

- *Psychologists* earn about $69,280 a year. The need is expected to rise 12%. Requirements typically include a doctorate degree and state license.
- *Psychiatrists* have medical degrees. They typically make about $200,000 a year.
- Most *social workers* have bachelor's or master's degrees. The number of positions is growing at the faster-than-average rate of 19%. Social workers make an average of $44,200 per year.
- *Mental health counselors* and *marriage and family therapists* have master's degrees and state licenses. They make about $41,500 per year. The need is expected to increase 29% between 2012 and 2022.

Nurses

- *Registered nurses* (RNs) are the largest segment of health professionals, and 61% of them work in general medicine hospitals. Most of the others work in doctors' offices, specialized hospitals, nursing homes, and home health agencies. RNs have associate's or bachelor's degrees in nursing and are state licensed. Annual salaries average $65,470. The number of jobs for RNs is expected to grow 19% between 2012 and 2022.
- *Licensed practical nurse* (LPN) and *licensed vocational nurse* (LVN) positions usually require a year or so of specialized training after high school. Annual salaries average $41,540, and demand is expected to increase by 25%.

Physical Rehabilitation Professionals

- *Physical, occupational, and speech-language therapy* positions typically require a graduate degree and state licensing. Salaries range from $69,870 to

continued

$79,860 a year, and the need is expected to rise between 19% and 39% between 2012 and 2022.

- *Recreational therapists* usually have a bachelor's degree and make about $42,280 a year. The job outlook is average, with a 13% increase in positions expected.
- *Respiratory therapists* are typically required to have at least an associate's degree. They make about $55,870 a year, and a 19% increase in positions is expected.
- *Assistants* in the fields mentioned above with specialized associate's degrees make about $49,000 a year and *aides* with high school diplomas about $23,700.

Physical Fitness and Diet Specialists

- *Dieticians* and *nutritionists* have a bachelor's degree or higher in the field, and the average salary is $55,240. Higher-than-average job growth of 21% is expected.
- *Athletic trainers* are required to hold a bachelor's degree or master's degree in the field. The average salary is $42,690 a year, and demand is expected to increase 19%.
- *Massage therapists* complete training after high school and certification or licensure requirements. They earn about $35,970 a year, and job growth is higher than average.
- *Fitness trainers* and *instructors* with high school diplomas work mostly in fitness and recreation centers. They typically make about $31,720 a year. Demand is expected to increase 13%.

Osteopaths

Doctors of osteopathic medicine (DOs) go to medical school, complete internship and residency requirements, and function as physicians. Their focus is on holistic health and enhancing the body's ability to heal itself through physical strength and skeletal alignment, accomplished, in part, through physical manipulation of the body (American Association of Colleges of Osteopathic Medicine [AACOM], 2012). They make up 7% of physicians in the United States (AACOM).

Pharmacists and Pharmacy Technicians

- *Pharmacists* work in retail establishments, clinics, and hospitals. They dispense medications and counsel people about side effects, diet and stress, treatment of minor health concerns, and other health issues. They make an average of $116,670 a year. A doctoral or professional degree is required. The job outlook is average, with a 14% increase in positions expected between 2012 and 2022.
- *Pharmacy technicians* usually make about $29,320 a year. A training program after high school may be required. Demand is expected to increase 20%.

Physicians and Surgeons

Physicians and *surgeons* work in medical practices, hospitals, universities, and other organizations caring for patients, serving in leadership roles, and sometimes teaching and conducting research.

- Shortages are expected in general and family practice, internal medicine, and obstetrics/gynecology, particularly in rural areas of the country ("Physicians and Surgeons," 2008).
- Annual salaries range from $407,300 a year for anesthesiologists to $205,400 for internal medicine specialists and $189,000 for family practitioners.
- The job outlook is better than average, with a 24% increase in the number of positions expected between 2012 and 2022.

Technicians and Technologists

- *Medical records* and *health information technicians* with an associate's or bachelor's degree earn about $42,160 a year. The need is expected to increase 22% between 2012 and 2022.
- *Psychiatric technicians* and *aides* with on-the-job training make about $27,440 a year. Demand is expected to rise 5%.
- *Surgical technologists* with an associate's or bachelor's degree earn about $41,790 a year. Jobs are expected to increase 30%.
- *Occupational health and safety technicians* with a high school diploma or associate's degree earn an average of $47,440 per year. The job outlook is about average, with an 11% increase expected.
- *Radiology technologists* with an associate's degree earn about $55,910 a year. The job outlook is better than average, with an increase of 21% expected.
- *Clinical laboratory technicians* with a bachelor's degree usually earn $47,829 a year. The number of positions is expected to rise by 22%.

Source: *U.S. Bureau of Labor Statistics, 2014b*

Caregiver Preparation

Let's start with the reality that not everyone is allowed to become a professional caregiver. Only about 39% of the people who apply to U.S. nursing schools and 43.6% of those who apply to medical schools are accepted (American Association of Colleges of Nursing [AACN], 2012, 2015; Association of American Medical Colleges, 2014). The acceptance rates are lower (10% or less) at the country's most sought-after physician assistant programs ("Physician Assistant," 2015). The main reason is lack of resources. For instance, nursing schools in the United States turn down nearly 80,000 qualified applicants in a typical year because they do not have the faculty or facilities to accommodate them (AACN, 2012).

Qualifications to enter professional fields differ widely. Technicians typically complete specialized training and apprenticeships before being licensed. The requirements to become a physician, psychologist, pharmacist, dentist, or rehabilitation therapist (e.g., respiratory, speech, recreation, physical, occupational) involve graduate-level coursework, internships, and sometimes, postgraduate residencies and fellowships.

EMPHASIS ON SCIENCE

Health care in the United States is typically distinguished as being either conventional (also called orthodox) or complementary and alternative (also called holistic). As the terms *alternative* and *complementary* imply, for the last 100 years or so, holistic therapies have been treated largely as peripheral to biomedicine. In keeping with a biomedical perspective, conventional caregivers are often chosen for their aptitude in science. Here is a brief overview of how these ideas have evolved.

Campaign of Orthodox Medicine

In *The Silent World of Doctor and Patient*, Jay Katz (1984) makes a case that conventional practitioners in the early 1900s sought to distinguish themselves as the legitimate guardians of people's health. In Katz's view, this campaign was not entirely self-serving. Many people believed that scientific knowledge and technology could be used to eradicate disease. Whether conventional medicine was more concerned with this goal or with attaining professional dominance, the effect was the same. Folk medicine was largely discredited as quackery, and orthodox medicine gained a virtual monopoly over health care. As Katz describes it, this monopoly seemed to eliminate the need for health professionals, particularly physicians, to explain or justify their actions:

> *Since they no longer had to defend themselves against the criticism of rival groups, doctors asserted more adamantly, and now without fear of contradiction, that laymen could not judge medical practices and had to comply with medical orders.* (p. 39)

Soon, the authority of health professionals (physicians, especially) was considered unquestionable. They were not expected to express doubts or uncertainties, and they were not to be influenced by the opinions of people (including patients) less educated than themselves.

The image of professional caregivers as all-knowing authorities inspired public trust. But defining medical professionalism in terms of certainty and scientific expertise discouraged care providers from showing emotions or admitting doubts or mistakes (Katz, 1984). At the same time, patients and their loved ones were often silenced into submission. Soon, many patients were too trusting or intimidated to speak freely to health professionals (Katz, 1984).

In the early 1900s, medicine came to be viewed mostly in terms of science. Folk methods were largely pushed aside, not to gain widespread popularity again for about 100 years.

The Flexner Report

One part of the campaign to promote scientific medicine took the form of medical school reform. Prior to 1900, most medical schools in the United States were run as private businesses, oriented more toward profit than rigorous education (Cassedy, 1991). Such schools produced thousands of physicians with little knowledge of biology or physiology.

Disturbed by the low scientific standards in these schools, the American Medical Association commissioned Abraham Flexner of the Carnegie Foundation to evaluate U.S. medical schools and make recommendations. The **Flexner Report**, published in 1910, was a stinging indictment. It charged that all but a few medical schools in the country—the notable exceptions were Harvard, Johns Hopkins, and Western Reserve—were lax in their coverage of biology and other sciences. The report also criticized medical schools for not offering more supervised, hands-on experience with patients.

WHAT DO YOU THINK?

The Flexner Report led medical schools to focus intensely on science. In your opinion, what is lost and what is gained by this focus?

Nearly two-thirds of U.S. medical schools did close, unable to meet the reform standards that Flexner proposed (Twaddle & Hessler, 1987). Most of the schools that remained open were incorporated within universities, where the curricula focused on organic aspects of disease and on clinical and laboratory experience supporting a biomedical perspective. An emphasis on science took root in nursing and many other caregiver education programs as well.

Decline of Holistic and Folk Medicine

For the most part, holistic and folk healers were not prepared to fight the emerging dominance of conventional medicine. Americans were enamored with science and technology—both of which were firmly rooted in the camp of conventional medicine by the early 1900s. Moreover, there was little to unite diverse healers, and because their treatments promised gradual and long-term effects, outcomes were hard to isolate and measure (Cassedy, 1991).

Osteopathy and chiropractic were among the only sects to maintain popularity. Other forms of therapy, such as acupuncture and herbal remedies, faded from significance for several decades, at least in the United States. Interestingly, the very reasons that led to their decline—long-term results, low-tech methods—are now contributing to a resurgence of popularity as people seek to reduce costs and to prevent ill health. We focus more on that in Chapter 7.

Science-Based Curricula

Few people question the value of scientific inquiry, biology, and physiology in caregiver education programs. However, as you will see, some feel that they should be equally concerned about ethics and social skills.

It is said that the average medical student learns 10,000 words that are not in general use outside medicine. Other medical careers also involve extensive, specialized vocabularies. Although the terms are useful among health professionals, they can create a semantic barrier between care providers and their patients.

Sometimes the compassionate elements of caregiving are overshadowed by a curricular emphasis on the body as a mechanism. Analysts often point to the use of cadavers in this regard. Students preparing to become physicians, rehabilitation therapists, and dentists typically dissect cadavers to learn about the body. That can be a great learning experience. But Alan Bonsteel (1997) argues that an overreliance on cadavers encourages students to regard the body as an inanimate object. There is no need to communicate with a cadaver, treat it gently, or wonder about its feelings, he says. Bonsteel urges educators not to portray people as impersonal "biological systems," but as individuals with feelings and emotions. He maintains that "cold, clinical" professionals result from programs that concentrate on science but neglect interpersonal communication, social issues, and ethics.

Another issue is that, under pressure, students may memorize information without understanding it, a process called **rote learning**. In this situation, they may perform well on multiple-choice exams but may be incapable of applying the information to actual situations. When researchers compared two medical curricula in the United Kingdom, they found that students in the traditional lecture-based curriculum were less confident in their knowledge than students who took part in small-group discussions of actual medical clients (A. Grant, Kinnersley, & Field, 2012). Said one student, reflecting on the challenge of a lecture-based curriculum, "There is a lot of written information that you have to get down and quite often it goes in this ear and straight out onto the paper rather than actually going into your head at all" (p. 3).

WHAT DO YOU THINK?

- Which do you prefer as a student—rote learning or problem-based learning (PBL)? Why?
- Would you rather have a caregiver who learned via rote or PBL?

In curricula that utilize **problem-based learning (PBL)**, students apply information to actual scenarios rather than simply memorizing it. For instance, they might be presented with a case study and asked to analyze the patient's condition and identify factors relevant to his or her health. PBL is positively correlated with improved performance and knowledge among pharmacology students (Dube, Ghadlinge, Mungal, Saleem, & Kulkarni, 2014) and with health professionals' competence after graduation, particularly in terms of their ability to communicate about complex health matters (Koh, Khoo, Wong, & Koh, 2008).

Another PBL technique involves interactions with so-called standardized patients, that is, people who are trained to play the part of patients, with realistic symptoms and emotional concerns. These interactions are usually videotaped so that students can review them later, with feedback from their professors and the mock patients who were involved.

Evolving Models

One model of caregiver training that is gaining popularity is interprofessional education (IPE), in which health science students develop expertise in two or more fields such as medicine, pharmacology, nursing, physical therapy, social work, midwifery, and so on. The idea is that well-rounded practitioners will be better prepared to fill multiple roles, address complex health needs, and collaborate with diverse colleagues (WHO, 2013). IPE graduates often take a more active role than others in multidisciplinary teamwork and are usually more open and respectful toward colleagues with diverse backgrounds (D. Morris & Matthews, 2014). They also tend to be particularly adaptive and confident when communicating with patients (Defenbaugh & Chikotas, 2015; Hagemeier, Hess, Hagen, & Sorah, 2014).

COMMUNICATION TRAINING

Traditionally, communication skill training was a minimal part of caregiver training. However, it is emerging as a priority, supported by evidence that communication can be instrumental in making good decisions, reducing costs, improving health outcomes, raising patient satisfaction, and minimizing mistakes and misunderstandings (Epstein, Fiscella, Lesser, & Stange, 2010).

Spokespersons for the Accreditation Council on Graduate Medical Education (ACGME) have proclaimed that "effective communication skills are at the heart of quality patient care" (p. 20) and are essential to leadership and teamwork. The council defines communication competence as the ability to interact effectively with patients, family members, community members, and colleagues from a wide range of socioeconomic and cultural backgrounds. Guidelines stress interpersonal communication, teamwork, and leadership (ACGME, 2015). We focus on these skills in this chapter and throughout the book.

PERSPECTIVES

"The artist knows when the patient needs a warm smile, reassuring words, or a gentle hug. It's the artists who make every patient feel welcome, comfortable, secure, hopeful. The artist sees the anxiety and reassures the new mother that her baby's fever is nothing to worry about. . . . The artist knows when there's nothing more the engineer can do and helps the patient and family cope at the end of life. What the artist does is why I became a physician."

—*Denis Cortese, MD, President and CEO, Mayo Clinic*

Research about the impact of communication skills training is promising. Patient satisfaction scores often rise when physicians take part in such training, probably because those doctors tend to give more information, show more sensitivity, and address a greater variety of patients' lifestyle behaviors than others (Haskard et al., 2008). Likewise, nurses are typically more confident about their ability to interact effectively with patients after communication skills training (Wilkinson, Perry, Blanchard, & Linsell, 2008).

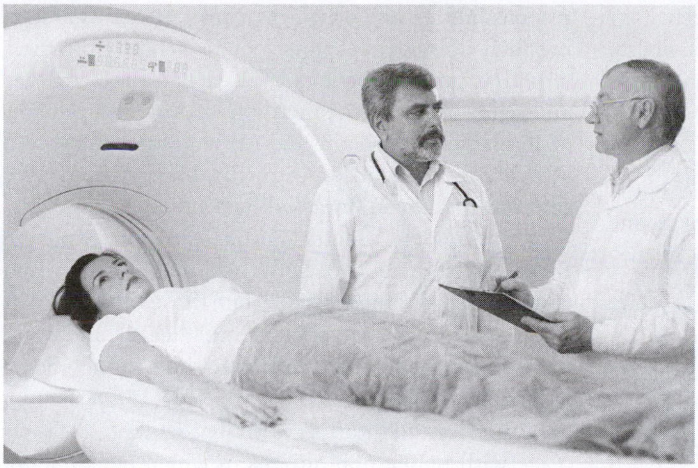

One limitation of the Voice of Medicine is that it does not provide caregivers with much of a vehicle for sharing their emotions or focusing on patients' unique experiences.

Communication training is most effective under three conditions. One is involvement by a diverse array of caregivers, such as physical therapists, nurses, doctors, and health educators (Ammentorp, Kofoed, & Laulund, 2011; Parry, 2008). Another is the use of experiential activities, including role-playing, observations, and discussions (Lundine, Buckley, Hutchinson, & Lockyer, 2008). A third essential element is an integration of theory and goal-based performance (Street & De Haes, 2013). All in all, students who understand the theory and research behind effective communication and have ample opportunities to practice seem to get the most out of communication training programs.

With the evidence mounting, many advocates call for even more communication training on topics such as delivering bad news (Zakrzewski, Ho, & Braga-Mele, 2008) and collaborating with patients (Rodriguez et al., 2008).

SOCIALIZATION

We have discussed the coursework, but becoming a health professional is not strictly a matter of studying hard. It is also a process of **socialization**—learning to behave appropriately within a specific community. School is often the first place people begin to learn what it means to act and talk like a professional caregiver. Few other experiences are so extensive and life altering. The intensity, uniqueness, and isolation make high-intensity caregiver education programs especially hospitable arenas for socialization.

One impact of socialization into a specialized community such as health care is that members, once socialized, may have expectations and practices that differ substantially from other peoples'. In Chapter 3 we talked about the Voicc of Lifeworld that is typically spoken by patients. In contrast, caregivers in the United States are expected to be proficient in what Elliot Mishler (1984) calls the **Voice of Medicine**. As the vocabulary of traditional biomedicine, this voice is characterized by carefully controlled compassion and a concern for accuracy and expediency.

The Voice of Medicine is designed to help people. One limitation, however, is that it is not designed to facilitate emotional expression. Instead, it focuses mostly on medical terminology and physical details. For the most part, patients' individuality is treated as less important than their bodily conditions. However impersonal it may sound, the Voice of Medicine answers to the extraordinary demands of time and emotion exacted from health professionals and suits society's image of them as stoically objective and in control. As you read this section, consider the pros and cons of the Voice of Medicine.

Let's trace some of the factors that influence the socialization process as we move out of the classroom and into clinical environments. As you will see, this going-public phase is an important step in donning the identity of a health professional.

Hidden Curriculum

Socialization occurs partly as a result of the **hidden curriculum**; that is, the attitudes and practices that others model, even though they do not explicitly teach them. As medical professor Michael Wilkes says:

> *We can teach extensively about the appropriateness of respecting different cultures, different beliefs and different health practices, but when the student hears a resident dissing a patient's mistaken notions of disease, or hears them making fun of a patient's body, the lesson is clear—to be a part of the "club," this is the expected behavior.* (*quoted by Lauer, 2008, p. 50*)

Wilkes and others warn that, very often, seeing is doing when it comes to shaping new professionals. True change comes through modeling the behaviors that we want others to adopt.

Isolation

Intense caregiver programs typically involve both physical and experiential isolation. Long hours mean less time in the company of family and friends. At the same time, the uniqueness of students' experiences can make them feel different from others.

Emily Transue (2004) recalls the initial shock of clinical work. "I had woken up that morning having never seen a death, and by lunchtime I had been part of one," she says. "Nothing in medical school or in life had prepared me for that moment. . . . I felt wrenchingly and terribly alone" (p. 1). As she felt herself being transformed by the experience, Transue wondered if the people she loved could still relate to her. "Would they understand what I had just seen and done? Would I be inevitably separated from them by this experience and those that would follow it?" (p. 1).

Being different from others can be a special feeling. It can also interfere with relationships and with communication, particularly when people are still figuring out the roles they should play.

Identity in Limbo

The process of framing a new identity typically involves a phase during which people experience a sense of limbo. Caregivers-in-training are no longer laypersons, but they are not yet full-fledged professionals either.

As in the military, health care typically observes a strict hierarchy, and those at the lowest levels are reminded in many ways of their lowly status. Medical interns are sometimes referred to as "the dirt on which the ladder stands" (Hirschmann, 2008, p. 59) and as those who get "pimped first, blamed first, and thanked last" (Jauhar, 2008b, p. 201). Dietitian students in a Canadian study described a dynamic in which preceptors asserted that they had superior power by withholding information and demoralizing the students (MacLellan & Lordly, 2008). Said one student in the study, "Sometimes it feels as though interns, we are put at the bottom of the priority list. . . . I sometimes feel as though my ideas and input are disregarded without any consideration" (p. E87).

Role theory explains such behavior by proposing that social roles are defined by unique sets of rights, responsibilities, and privileges (Mead, 1934). By asserting their power, preceptors may be sending the message that initiates have not yet earned the privileges and rights of bona fide practitioners. Among graduates of 16 medical schools in the United States, 84% said they had been belittled in medical school, and 42% said they had been harassed by professors, residents, classmates, or patients (Frank, Carrera, Stratton, Bickel, & Nora, 2006). Only 13% of those surveyed considered the abuse severe, but those who did suffered significant losses in mental health and were more likely than others to regret choosing medicine as a career.

Students and interns are further reminded of their place with public pop quizzes in which personnel of higher status can publicly challenge them to answer questions and make diagnoses. They may also be called on to do **scut work**, menial chores that no one else wants to do. It is commonly accepted that some of these chores are assigned mainly to punish or humiliate the newcomers.

Although students often have immense responsibility, they have less experience than the professionals around them. In the midst of this, there is usually little time for students to get their bearings. The expectation that they will move expeditiously from observers to participants is reflected in the traditional clinical battle cry, "Watch one, do one, teach one" (Conrad, 1988, p. 326). Learning on the job can be a frightening experience when human lives (including one's own) are at stake.

But, gradually, even as they are being cast as peons within the system, students may begin to see themselves as different, even superior, to those *outside* it.

Privileges

It can be exhilarating to be part of the action and learning at a rapid pace. Medical interns sometimes say that, as much as they long for a day off, when it comes they feel adrift and left out. When things got really tough, Transue (2004) reminded herself, "I will never learn as much in any year of my life as I will in this one. I may never have the same intensity of experience. I intend to make the most of it" (p. 34).

To be granted access to wonders seldom witnessed can also be a heady experience. Perri Klass (1987) recalls a sense of wonder dissecting cadavers, reflecting that she was doing something "normal people never do" (p. 37). Klass compared the sensation to initiation into a priesthood.

In these ways and others, students get an early dose of the responsibilities, but also the privileges, that go along with professional status. Sometimes, as they begin to feel more like professionals and less like students, the emotional distance between them and their patients widens, as we discuss next.

Resentment

The rigors of clinical experience can lead to darker aspects of socialization. Confronted by overwhelming demands, it is not surprising that students sometimes begin to regard patients as adversaries. Phillip Reilly (1987) remembers the extreme exhaustion during his residency that led him to resent the neediness of a comatose patient: "He was an enemy, part of the plot to deprive me of sleep. If he died, I could sleep for another hour. If he lived, I would be up all night" (p. 226).

> **WHAT DO YOU THINK?**
>
> - What is your reaction to residents' admission that they sometimes yearn for a declining patient to go ahead and die so that they can finally get some rest?
> - Can you imagine feeling a similar way under the same sort of pressure?

Medical professionals sometimes refer to patients in derogatory terms, such as *drain circlers* and *gomers*. The first is a reference to patients who are expected to die (go down the drain) soon. The second, an acronym for "get out of my emergency room," generally refers to older patients who have little chance of recovering and are seen as wasting valuable time and space.

During medical school, students' empathy for patients typically decreases, especially among male students who are in so called *high-tech* specializations, such as surgery, rather than *high-touch* fields, such as psychiatry (Dehning et al., 2014). Empathy typically plummets even more during their internships (Rosen, Gimotty, Shea, & Bellini, 2006). Many medical school graduates report that, by the end of their intern year, they are less overwhelmed than before, but also less compassionate and less emotionally available.

If students are persuaded by the curriculum and mentors that disease is best understood in physical terms, depersonalizing patients begins to feel acceptable. Focusing on specific, organic concerns is more familiar and less emotionally exhausting than thinking in terms of unique individuals.

Nursing and midwifery students have typically not experienced the same level of empathy-loss as medical students. Analysts speculate that this is because the former are typically engaged in closer, ongoing relationships with individual patients and because a large percentage of nursing and midwifery students are women (Williams et al., 2014). Women's empathy scores tend to be higher than men's across medical disciplines, probably because women are more often socialized to provide care for others in daily life.

Some schools have made empathy a part of the curriculum. The Northeastern University School of Pharmacy in Boston implemented a program in which pharmacy students learn about nutrition and weight management and then, for a week, model the behaviors they would recommend to an obese or diabetic person (Trujillo & Hardy, 2009). The students are asked to calculate what portion of a limited family budget would be available for food purchases after subtracting medical costs, and then design a grocery list and shop for the recommended foods. Five months after the exercise, the students reported that the experience was still with them. They felt more confident counseling people about dietary matters and more sympathetic toward people with weight problems, especially those trying to buy healthy foods with limited financial means. Said one student, "This activity really made me realize how important it is to understand someone's culture and income level before recommending lifestyle changes" (p. 6).

Implications

It is natural to feel a mixture of awe and outrage over what some people go through on the way to becoming professional caregivers. Abuse and resentment can seem antithetical to a caregiver role. Indeed, efforts are under way at some universities and medical centers to redesign how things are done. (See Box 5.2.)

> **WHAT DO YOU THINK?**
>
> - Have you seen evidence of caregivers who come to resent the demands of their patients or to depersonalize them?
> - If so, what have you observed?
> - Why do you think it happened?

BOX 5.2

Medical School Reform

Juggling 8 courses with 35 hours of lecture per week, Audrey Young takes a deep breath and looks at her desk, which is stacked 2 feet high with papers. It's her second year of medical school, which she recalls as "the hardest stress" of an arduous process.

In this and other reflections in her book *What Patients Taught Me: A Medical Student's Journey*, Young (2004) describes a medical school experience that began with two years of intense studying and lectures. Regrettably, she says, she "didn't set foot in a real clinic or talk with a practicing doctor for months" during that time (p. 39).

Traditionally, medical students have been required to learn enormous amounts of scientific material in their first two years, followed by two years focused on clinical experience. Within that model, students have only a delayed opportunity to apply what they are learning. And when they do face actual patients, they may find themselves at a loss to remember everything they crammed to learn. One intern describes what happened when a pulmonologist asked her, "What do you think of when you see a nodulorecticular pattern?"

> You want an honest answer? *I think to myself.* When I see a nodulorecticular pattern on a chest x-ray, I think: nothing. *I know we learned about this in med school, but my mind is drawing a complete blank. Worse, I'm panicking, thinking:* What am I doing here? How am I supposed to succeed as an intern if I can't even remember the differential diagnosis of a nodulorecticular chest x-ray? *(Transue, 2004, p. 16)*

This is not unusual. In fact, some people maintain that separating science and application interferes with learning. Moreover, linking the medical school curriculum with actual patient care may humanize the process by continually reminding medical students of the interpersonal dynamics involved. Here are a few examples of medical schools that have broken the mold.

Some schools, such as the University of California at San Francisco, are experimenting with integrated medical curricula in which information from various disciplines is woven together, along with clinical experiences. This method may help students to develop integrated knowledge and to apply it immediately in natural contexts. The new method is not without challenges, of course. Faculty who are accustomed to structuring their own classroom experiences are challenged to work, instead, as part of multidisciplinary teams. Students sometimes feel the information is less organized than in the traditional one-subject-per-course curricula, and they are apprehensive about being immersed in complex concepts before they have mastered the fundamentals (Muller, Jain, Loeser, & Irby, 2008). After studying the program, Muller and colleagues suggest that faculty can overcome these challenges by providing an overall "conceptual scaffolding" for students at every step.

A program at Harvard Medical School requires students to participate in a three-year course on doctor–patient relationships. The program is designed to create "humanistic physicians" who appreciate social and psychological aspects of illness and embody ethics, warmth, and sensitivity. The course makes use of small-group discussions to help students explore their own feelings and philosophies and work together to develop communication skills.

Pediatric residents at the University of California (UC), Davis, do not just train in hospitals and clinics. They also work as advocates in the community, actively partnering with various groups to improve the overall health of children. "Physicians have a greater responsibility to their patients beyond telling them what will keep them healthy," says Richard Pan, a UC physician who developed the program. "We need to be in our patients' communities and neighborhoods working with families" ("Getting Doctors Out," 2002, para. 3). The program has won numerous awards, and research shows that physicians tend to maintain their community-oriented focus after they transition into licensed medical practice (Paterniti, Pan, Smith, Horan, & West, 2006).

Whether justified or not, intense demands and demoralizing rituals endure partly because they serve several functions. For one, the high-pressure environment may prepare students for the actual demands of practice, which require great patience, endurance, and emotional control. One school of thought is that students put to the test early on will be better prepared to handle pressure later.

Second, a clearly established chain of command (power differential) may help health care teams make quick decisions and carry them out. Decisive, centralized decision making reduces the likelihood that caregivers' efforts will be disorganized and uncoordinated.

Third, the hardships may strengthen group membership. Students often say they feel a bond with people who went through the process alongside them. The result is often an enduring sense of camaraderie.

Fourth, the hardships serve collectively as a **rite of passage,** a challenge that qualifies students for advancement. Graduates may feel an extraordinary sense of accomplishment as they qualify for higher rank by surviving the harsh years as an initiate.

On the downside, caregivers may come to identify with each other more than they identify with their patients. They may also feel that, based on their experiences, others are in no position to question their judgment. For example, after they are licensed, physicians may chafe at questions and comments that seem to challenge their authority, reasoning that they have now earned the right to call the shots. Such assumptions may cause patients and coworkers to consider them arrogant and bossy. Another danger is that harsh conditions early on imply that people should be stoic and self-sacrificing as professionals. With excessive work and minimal opportunities to relax or vent emotions, they may end up in worse shape than their patients. We talk more about burnout later in the chapter.

Compassion Rebound

On a positive note, there is evidence that caregivers typically bounce back and regain at least a portion of their idealism and compassion once they are in the field. One medical resident who was quite candid about the callousness he and others developed as interns remembers a house call later on when he forgot his stethoscope, blood pressure cuff, prescription pad, and all the rest. "Without my tools, I couldn't follow my usual procedures, so I just sat at [the patient's] bedside, stroking his hand. Afterward, in the kitchen, I sat with his wife and had a cup of tea," he remembers (Jauhar, 2008b, p. 177). On his way home, he reflected on the sense of peace and satisfaction the encounter had given him. And his kindness was not forgotten. Two years later, the patient's wife wrote to thank him again and say she would never forget his thoughtfulness.

Next, let's move from the education phase to professional practice to examine other factors that influence the way health professionals communicate.

Systems-Level Influences on Caregivers

Once they join the ranks of health professionals, caregivers are influenced by a range of factors, including organizational protocols and time constraints. These factors can be both enabling and frustrating. On the good side, most care providers say the frustrations are tempered by unforgettable moments in which they connect with people and know they are making a difference. Real-life examples throughout this chapter highlight the impact that health professionals have on peoples' lives.

Let's start our discussion of system theory with an example.

ORGANIZATIONAL CULTURE

The cancer center administrators were stunned. A Japanese sensei (master or teacher) with Toyota had handed them a map of their medical center and asked them to illustrate, with blue yarn, the path patients usually took in the process of receiving care there. By the time they were done, representatives from the Virginia Mason Cancer Center in Seattle had created a maze-like web of yarn that went back and forth, up and down various floors, circled back over itself, and demonstrated clearly that the staff was putting patients under ridiculous emotional and physical stress just to get treatment (Mars, 2011).

Charles Kenny, who wrote a book about the Virginia Mason experience, observes that the team members were horrified to realize that "they were taking these patients, for whom time is absolutely the most precious thing in their lives, and they were wasting huge amounts of it" (quoted by Weinberg, 2011, para. 6).

Systems theory awakens us to the presence of **organizational processes**, which are habitual or prescribed ways of doing things, and **organizational culture**, which comprises members' basic beliefs and assumptions about an organization, its members, and the organization's place in the larger environment (Schein, 1986). To the extent that these behaviors and assumptions become part of everyday thinking, they contribute to the culture of an organization and the socially constructed identities of people within it.

Familiar routines and structures often have a taken-for-granted quality that blinds people to alternatives. Organizational members become, as systems theorist Peter Senge (2006) puts it, "prisoners of systems" that they themselves create. No one at Virginia Mason wanted patients to exhaust themselves traversing the large facility, but they had probably never questioned the necessity of it. Once awakened to the problem, they realized that individual action would not be enough to solve it. A more productive option would be to redesign the system itself.

The staff of Virginia Mason did just that. They converted the perimeter of the building into a sunny pathway with waterfront views that patients can follow in a logical progression when it is necessary for them to move from one area to another. They also created a central corridor that allows care providers to easily move from one treatment room to another so that patients don't have to. These and other changes have reduced the average time that patients spend in the medical center by 50% and made it possible to eliminate waiting rooms. Because of the changes, Virginia Mason skyrocketed to the top 1% in the nation in terms of safety and efficiency and earned a 37% reduction in insurance premiums (Kenney, 2010; Weinberg, 2011). The system continues to evolve, but it is both kinder and more efficient than it used to be. The staff now treats more patients in less time, which is good for patients and for the bottom line. Profits are up, but the greatest satisfaction, say team members, is doing what is right for their patients.

Although people often assume that health professionals call the shots, in reality, they are constrained in many ways by the systems in which they operate. Many of the conditions that influence what happens in patient–provider communication are established at a systemic, not an individual, level. The Virginia Mason example demonstrates this and perhaps offers some encouragement that, if people are not happy with a system, they may be able to improve it. After all, as Senge (2006) points out, even small changes to a system can have potent implications.

Next, let's examine some of the systems-level factors that influence care providers' communication and satisfaction.

TIME

Sharon Spalding, an avid runner and cyclist, felt like an unlikely candidate for breast cancer. "I was in the best shape of my life and had just run a marathon," she says ("Pushing the Limits," n.d., para. 3). In the months following her diagnosis, chemotherapy made Spalding feel tired, yet she yearned for physical activity. Fortunately, her caregivers had time to get to know her.

Spalding's care team designed a treatment plan specific to her needs and lifestyle, including consultations with a certified cancer exercise trainer. The trainer helped her develop light workout routines that eased her lethargy when she was sickest, and then as she improved, more vigorous regimens so she could resume running and biking as she had before.

A critical element in this real-life scenario is time—time to listen and time to respond effectively. When time is short, health professionals may seem rushed and impatient. Although it is tempting to blame them for this less-than-hospitable demeanor, care providers usually dislike time constraints as much as patients do. Like patients, they typically feel most satisfied when they have time to develop trust and share information unhurriedly (Bell, Bringman, Bush, & Phillips, 2006; Kisa, Kawabata, Itou, Nishimoto, & Maezawa, 2011; Tellis-Nayak, 2005).

Health professionals who are worried about time constraints may limit talk to specific physical indicators—perhaps reasoning that friends, family members, clergy, counselors, and others are available to offer emotional support, but they are uniquely qualified to diagnose physical conditions and prescribe treatments. They may also reason that a fast pace is the only alternative to turning away people in need. As a nurse in one study explained it, although it is rewarding to spend time with individual patients, doing so may mean less time for other patients and more work for one's colleagues (Chan, Jones, & Wong, 2013). However, rushing may be counterproductive in that it often results in follow-up visits that might have been avoided, poorly developed relationships, misunderstandings, and other time-intensive outcomes.

WHAT DO YOU THINK?

- How do you respond to some health professionals' argument that they must limit patients' input so that they can keep visits within a particular time limit?
- In your opinion, how can patients collaborate with care providers to manage time effectively?

One option is to make the most of caregivers at every level. For example, midlevel providers such as nurse practitioners (NPs) and physician assistants (PAs) now handle routine and minor concerns in some medical offices, which frees physicians to spend more time with seriously ill patients. Patients are typically satisfied with NPs and PAs because they are often less rushed than doctors and they tend to focus on social and personal concerns in addition to biomedical matters (Budzi, Lurie, Singh, & Hooker, 2010; Charlton, Dearing, Berry, & Johnson, 2008).

Researcher and psychologist Jeffrey Rudolph (2008) offers the following tips for bonding with patients when time is limited:

- *Start strong.* Shake hands, look the patient in the eye, inspire trust from the beginning.
- *Do not interrupt, and do not multitask.* Give the patient your full attention.
- *Empower patients.* Provide information, web links, follow-up phone calls, and other means of encouraging the patient's active involvement during and after the encounter.
- *Do not end the visit before you ask if the patient has other questions or concerns.* You are not actually saving time if the patient leaves without knowing what to do next. And even if you make a note to address some of the concerns on the next visit, it is ultimately more efficient to encourage full disclosure than to remain in the dark about what a patient wants and needs.

Now that we have looked at some of the external factors that influence caregivers, let's shift our focus to the emotional health of caregivers.

BOX 5.3 ETHICAL CONSIDERATIONS

Privacy Regulations Incite Controversy

In recent years some people have been outraged to learn that health care providers have sold or carelessly leaked their "confidential" medical information to others. For example, a Florida state worker was able to download the names of people diagnosed with AIDS (Barnard, 2003). Companies, including Eli Lilly pharmaceuticals and CVS Pharmacy, have been charged with selling the names of patients on Prozac and other drugs (Ho, 2002; "Medical Records," 2001). The problem has grown since the advent of computer databases that make it easy to transmit medical data that was once stored only in doctors' filing cabinets (Conan, 2002).

New federal regulations went into effect in 2003 to prevent these types of privacy violations. The Health Insurance Portability and Accountability Act, better known as HIPAA, provides patients increased access to their own medical records and regulates who else may see them. The regulations—which present a number of implications for health communication—have provoked a good deal of controversy.

One area of controversy involves the mandate to inform patients of privacy regulations. HIPAA requires health care providers to give every client a written copy of the organization's privacy policies. As a consumer, you have probably encountered this in the form of *HIPAA Alert* or *Patient Privacy* statements that doctors, pharmacists, health plans, dentists, and others ask you to sign. On the surface, this seems like a positive measure. Patients are informed up front about the measures being taken to protect their privacy and their right to file a grievance if the rules are not upheld. However, the process is less than perfect.

continued

continued

For one thing, the forms can be lengthy and difficult to understand, especially for people with limited reading skills. Compounding this is the implied or explicit demand that patients sign the forms whether they understand them or not. According to the U.S. Department of Health and Human Services, it is not necessary for patients to sign this form to receive care or services (Health Privacy Project, 2003). However, based on confusion about HIPAA standards (the act is about 400 pages long) and fear of incurring costly fines for noncompliance, a number of health care providers have refused to treat patients who do not sign the privacy notices.

The most serious complaint about the privacy notices is that they do not give patients a choice about how their medical information will be used. Early on, legislators envisioned the forms as consent letters. Patients could say yes or no to receiving information about the latest drugs or treatment options associated with their medical needs. For example, if you are on a drug commonly used to treat AIDS, you might appreciate receiving updates and promotional information about related drugs. However, you might feel that putting such information in the mail is a violation of your privacy. Says one physician, "When my postman knows what diseases my wife has, that's not appropriate" (Barnard, 2003, para. 19). Others worry that, if these mailing lists are in circulation, the information will be used to discriminate unfairly against them. One man, who mistakenly receives information meant for people with hepatitis C, wonders:

> *What happens now with—my wife and I are going to be refinancing our house, and what if somehow the erroneous information that I have hepatitis C finds its way from an insurance company or a pharmacy, a manufacturer, something like that, into someone's financial database and they say, "Well, jeez, we don't want to lend money to someone who has hepatitis C"? (Conan, 2002, transcript p. 7)*

Under HIPAA regulations, health care providers cannot sell their mailing lists to others. However, they can accept money to send information to patients themselves as long as the information is health related. Either way, the information is in the mail. Janlori Goldman, director of the Health Privacy Project, says, "They don't have to tell the customer they're doing it, and they don't have to give the customer the chance to opt out" (quoted by Conan, 2002, transcript p. 6).

Despite HIPAA's shortcomings, it does emphasize providers' legal responsibility to maintain privacy. In 2008, Lawanda Jackson, an administrative specialist who had previously worked for the UCLA Medical Center, was indicted for selling celebrities' medical information to the media. Jackson pled guilty, but she died before the trial began. If she had been convicted, she faced a maximum 10-year jail sentence and $250,000 fine ("Former UCLA," 2008). Less obvious breaches of confidentiality are harder to identify and eliminate. Perhaps the most common breaches involve overheard conversations about patient care and leaving patient paperwork (such as registration forms) where others can see it (Brann, 2007). In one study, 81% of patients interviewed expressed concern that their medical information would be inappropriately shared with people in the organization not responsible for their care (Brann & Mattson, 2004).

There isn't room enough to outline all the provisions of HIPAA or to describe the pros and cons of each, but here are a few of the mandates.

- Health care clients must be assured of confidential environments.
- Health care clients around the country have the right to see their medical records and suggest changes.
- People who believe their medical privacy has been violated can register a complaint with the U.S. Department of Health and Human Services. Some people feel that this regulation should have included the provision for patients to sue for breaches of confidentiality. That right is not guaranteed under HIPAA.
- HIPAA requires that health care providers adopt a standardized set of codes, train staff about privacy regulations, and appoint a staff member to oversee implementation of HIPAA. The benefits are that medical information will be easier to share and compare, and privacy will be a top-agenda item. However, some medical

continued

professionals say the regulations allow even less time for patient care in already short-staffed medical units.

What Do You Think?

1. Have you been asked to sign a HIPAA Alert? Did you understand the information provided? Did you feel that you had to sign?
2. Under what circumstances, if any, would you like to receive health-related information through the mail? Do you feel it is important that people have an opportunity to opt out of such mailing lists?
3. Have you ever felt that you had to discuss confidential medical information within earshot of others (e.g., at a pharmacy counter or during a medical visit)? Do you feel this is a serious problem? If so, what would you do to fix it?
4. Some people believe the private-environment regulations are too strict. For example, an orthodontist who previously encouraged patients and families to move throughout the clinic and get to know staff members issued an HIPAA Alert saying, "We must now regretfully restrict all patients and friends to the reception seating areas only." What is your opinion of this?
5. How far do you think the federal government should go to enforce privacy regulations? Do you agree with adding staff members, more paperwork, and oversight committees? Would you suggest other or additional measures?

Psychological Influences on Caregivers

Health care can be emotionally challenging. Care providers may act in ways that puzzle or wound others, even as they are themselves reeling under the pressure. In this section, we discuss how caregivers are affected by emotional preparedness, mindfulness, confidence, and satisfaction.

EMOTIONAL PREPAREDNESS

Patients look to health professionals not only for technical advice but also for wisdom and understanding. However, they sometimes have less everyday life experience than the patients who turn to them for guidance. As Weston and Lipkin put it, we "may know precise drug treatment but stand empty-handed and mute before the patient who desperately needs counsel and support" (1989, p. 45).

As a result, providers may avoid emotional matters or offer stiff platitudes, such as "I'm sure it will all be fine." Patients are likely to sense the insincerity and may feel that their concerns have been brushed aside as unimportant. Seldom do patients realize that caregivers may not *know* how to respond, having never experienced or been prepared for the situation at hand.

At the same time, we all have emotional hot buttons. When one of these sore spots is touched, the emotional response can surprise the care provider and the patient, although neither may understand it (Novack et al., 1997). For example, a health professional may feel resentment, disgust, or sexual attraction for a patient, may become overly protective, or may wish to have nothing to do with him or her. Novack and coauthors point out that personal biases are unavoidable, but professionals will have a hard time putting their feelings in perspective if they do not take time to acknowledge and understand them. We consider ways to do that at the end of this section.

WHAT DO YOU THINK?

- Even if you did not show it outwardly, have you ever been surprised by your emotional reaction in a health care experience?
- If so, what caused you to feel that way?
- What are some of your emotional hot buttons, and how might they influence you as a patient or a caregiver?

MINDFULNESS

When negative feelings start to creep in, says a first-year nursing and midwifery student, "I acknowledge that and I go: Oh no, stop . . . try and be positive.

I think that has helped me more than anything" (quoted by van der Riet, Rossiter, Kirby, Dluzewska, & Harmon, 2015, p. 46). The student developed this response in a seven-week program to cultivate **mindfulness**, which is defined as awareness of one's self and others and a nonjudgmental respect for diversity (Epstein, 1999).

Research about the effects of mindful health communication is encouraging. Nurses in the program just described reported that the mindful techniques they learned helped them focus, manage stress, sleep better, and be more fully present with people (van der Riet et al., 2015). In a similar way, physicians who took part in small-group interactions to increase mindfulness experienced an increased sense of empowerment and engagement (West et al., 2014). The positive effects go both ways. Patients report feeling satisfied with highly mindful health professionals and say that mindful caregivers seem more patient centered and affiliative than others (Beach et al., 2013).

Marleah Dean and Richard Street, Jr. (2014) presented a three-part model to guide health professionals in being mindful with people in distress. The model involves, first, *recognizing* the person's feelings with a statement such as, "It sounds like you are overwhelmed with all the possible options for treatment" (Dean & Street, Table 1). The second stage is *exploring* those feelings together by actively listening and encouraging the distressed person to describe how he or she feels. The final stage involves *therapeutic action* in which the people involved collaborate to determine the most helpful course of action. This stage may involve statements such as, "We will figure this out together," "Would you like to . . . ?" and "We are here to help you" (Dean & Street, Table 1). Dean and Street emphasize that this model is not simply about what professionals say to people who are distressed, but about developing genuine awareness and compassion for peoples' feelings.

CONFIDENCE

"What gives me the right to be here?" wondered a psychology doctorate student about his first encounters with patients (Weir, 2013, para. 3). It is natural to feel like an imposter when one adopts a new role. Health professionals say they sometimes doubt their capacity to cure and understand the people they treat, and they wonder what gives them the right to make decisions and know others' most intimate secrets. Their confidence may also be shaken by mistakes, a topic we cover later in the chapter.

Socialized to be confident and in control, health professionals may hide their self-doubt behind a protective gruffness or arrogance. The message is, "Don't get too close," not because they dislike people but because they are at a loss or are intimidated by people's appraisals of them. Patients may misinterpret this behavior as cold and distant.

Caregivers' self-doubt may be more of an issue as patients become more knowledgeable and assertive. While it was once assumed that patients could not understand the details of their conditions, today patients may know more than their caregivers about particular experimental procedures or the latest research. Professionals cannot be expected to know offhand the latest details of every medical condition. Still, they may feel defensive or inadequate when they do not.

SATISFACTION

Most people seem to take it for granted that health professionals' satisfaction is either guaranteed or irrelevant. However, dissatisfaction among professionals correlates with stress, burnout, and high employee turnover rates. For these reasons, scholars such as Ashley Duggan (2006) urge researchers to give more attention to caregivers' emotional well-being.

Care providers' satisfaction is bolstered when patients are friendly and up front about their needs

Like patients, health professionals are most satisfied when they have time to make personal connections with patients.

(J. Halbesleben, 2006), when the providers are confident about their communication skills (McKinley & Perino, 2013), and when they feel appreciated and proud of the work they do (Brett, Branstetter, & Wagner, 2014). Health professionals are also sensitive to issues of autonomy and respect. For example, nurses are most likely to stay in the profession if they feel that people recognize and honor their efforts and involve them in decision making (Tourangeau & Cranley, 2005).

A common frustration involves the nonmedical aspects of health care. Of 2,400 physicians surveyed, only 3% said that they are *not* frustrated by the "business" aspects of being doctors ("Physicians Report," 2008). Their frustrations involve hassles over reimbursement, medical liability issues, being overworked, and feeling overwhelmed by regulations and policies (Terrell, 2007). One implication is that, if health professionals seem tired and rushed, it may be more because of bureaucratic demands than the challenges of patient care.

Despite the challenges inherent in being a professional caregiver, the majority of providers say they would choose medicine all over again, knowing what they know now. The most rewarding aspects of the job, they say, are the satisfaction of making a difference and the thrill of solving health-related problems ("Physicians Report," 2008).

We focus now on two issues that can be distressing to caregivers—burnout and mistakes—and one that holds promise for improving the first two: interdisciplinary teamwork.

CAN YOU GUESS?

- What percentage of Americans worked in health care prior to 1960?
- What percentage work in health care now?
- Who has the highest average salary—registered nurses, pharmacists, or physical therapists?

Answers appear at the end of the chapter.

Stress and Burnout

"Helping people can be extremely hazardous to your physical and mental health," attests psychiatrist James Gill (quoted by Wicks, 2008, p. 21). Burnout is higher in health care than in other fields, and it may manifest in harmful ways, such as depression and substance abuse. (See Box 5.4 for a true story about one physician's substance abuse.)

Burnout is a combination of factors, including emotional exhaustion, depersonalization, and a reduced sense of personal accomplishment (Maslach, 1982). **Emotional exhaustion** is the feeling of being "drained and used up" (Maslach, p. 3). People experiencing emotional exhaustion feel that they can no longer summon motivation or compassion. **Depersonalization** is the tendency to treat people in an unfeeling, impersonal way. From this perspective, people may seem contemptible and weak, and the individual experiencing burnout may resent their requests. A **reduced sense of personal accomplishment** involves feeling like a failure. People who feel this way may become depressed, experience low self-esteem, and leave their jobs or avoid certain tasks.

People experiencing burnout are at elevated risk for heart disease, depression, and accidents. They are also more likely than others to be apathetic, to miss work, and to leave the profession (Paris & Hoge, 2010). What's more, burnout is linked to poor patient outcomes. In one study, patients of high-burnout physicians recovered more slowly and left the hospital later than the patients of physicians who were not burned out, apparently because the emotionally exhausted physicians were less attentive to details and because their relationships with patients were not as open

PERSPECTIVES

"The summer after my freshman year I volunteered at a small outpatient surgery center. I changed bed sheets, shredded old patient files, and even observed surgeries with patients' permission. Most of my time was in pre-op, where patients were prepped for surgery. I noticed how nervous most patients were. They often cried and sought comfort from family and staff members. The staff was friendly and personable with every patient. They even joked or told funny stories to calm people's nerves. That made an impact on me."

—*Vickie*

BOX 5.4 PERSPECTIVES

Blowing the Whistle on an Impaired Physician

As manager of a small community clinic, having to identify an impaired physician was not on my agenda. Clinic operations were going smoothly and patients seemed to like the clinic and the physician, Dr. Havard (not his real name). I knew things about Dr. Havard, such as his turbulent relationship with his ex-wife and his constant financial difficulties. However, he seemed to be a caring and sensitive doctor. Several months into his employment at the clinic, I started noticing strange behavioral changes in Dr. Havard, such as being chronically late for work and his inability to account for missing narcotic samples.

I thought Dr. Havard's actions were suspicious, but I did not know they were signs of an impending problem until I received a phone call from a representative of an Internet pharmaceutical company. The woman on the other end of the phone explained to me that large quantities of a prescription narcotic had been ordered for the clinic. I explained to her that the physician does not dispense narcotics on the premises because of the potential of robbery. After several similar phone calls from various companies, I approached Dr. Havard with the information. He said, "It's all a mistake. I'll take care of it."

I knew that he was not going to resolve the situation, and the phone calls became more frequent, demanding payment in excess of $20,000. I notified the clinic administrator, whose office is in a neighboring city. When I originally reported the problem, the administrator told me to "watch and listen." A week later, while working in my office, I received a phone call from a local pharmacist, who explained to me that a clinic patient presented a prescription for the same narcotic with authorization for three refills from Dr. Havard. She called because she knew it was rare for Dr. Havard to write prescriptions for such a large quantity of narcotics. When I asked for a description of the patient, she described Dr. Havard to a "T." After my initial shock, I called the administrator back and explained the situation. The next day, the administrator confronted Dr. Havard and asked if he had written the prescription. He denied it and said he didn't know who the patient was. I was given the "go-ahead" to treat the prescription as stolen and contact the Sheriff's Department.

Soon after the incident, Dr. Havard was drug tested and suspended from employment because he tested positive for narcotics and could not produce a legitimate prescription. When sheriff's deputies caught up with him, he confessed to writing the prescription for a "relative." He was offered assistance through the state's impaired-practitioners program. The program offers confidential counseling and assistance and the chance to resume practice.

I felt that I was ruining Dr. Havard's career by turning him in. However, I had an ethical and moral obligation to report him to protect his patients.

—DENISE

What Do You Think?

1. If you discovered that your doctor was abusing narcotics, would it change your opinion of him or her?
2. Would you want the doctor to undergo counseling and have a second chance to practice medicine? Why or why not?

and trusting as they could have been (Halbesleben & Rathert, 2008).

CAUSES

Some of the most common causes of stress and burnout among health professionals involve conflict, emotional fatigue, and excessive workload. We discuss those factors here, and then review communication tips for maintaining one's sense of enthusiasm and purpose, even when the job is challenging.

Conflict

Caregivers of all types can probably relate to the nurses in one study, who said they feel stressed when they are faced with conflicting demands, such as

PERSPECTIVES

"I'm not a cancer survivor," declares Mathew, a rambunctious 11-year-old, "I'm more than that; I'm a thriver" ("Mathew," n.d., para. 4). When he was diagnosed at age 6 with lymphoma, the medical jargon went over Mathew's head. He was more concerned with whether he could have a treat. "I was also totally excited that I would get to ride in an ambulance," he remembers (para. 4). Although the days ahead were not always easy, Mathew's infectious enthusiasm inspired the people around him, and he did indeed survive and thrive. Research shows that caring for patients who have good attitudes and are actively engaged with them can stave off burnout for health professionals (Halbesleben, 2006).

responding to multiple requests at the same time or interrupting patient care to answer phones or fill out paperwork (Happell et al., 2013; Rosenstein & O'Daniel, 2008). The frustration is exacerbated, the nurses say, if supervisors and colleagues do not appreciate their efforts.

Another stressor arises when care providers are required to carry out treatment decisions they believe to be inappropriate or harmful to patients (Catlin et al., 2008). These situations place them in a **double bind**, meaning there are negative consequences no matter which option they choose. They may feel that it is unacceptable to challenge the orders they have been given. At the same time, it may seem insupportable to put patients in danger.

Emotions

Intense emotions can cause stress and lead to emotional exhaustion. Although caregivers work in emotionally charged situations, they are required to remain calm (Pincus, 1995). (See Box 5.5 for tips on dealing with difficult patients.) In the same vein, they are expected to be caring and compassionate yet keep their emotions in check. To cope with these challenges, health professionals often develop what Harold Lief and Renée Fox (1963) call **detached concern**, a sense of caring about other people without becoming emotionally involved in the process. Some degree of detachment is useful to keep from feeling overwhelmed. However, the expectation that health professionals will squelch or avoid their own emotions may lead them to become apathetic, cynical, and confused.

Workload

An excessive workload or a highly monotonous one can cause stress. Because of funding structures and limited resources, hospital patients are said to be "quicker and sicker" than in the past, meaning that overnight stays are now limited to people who are very sick or badly hurt. As a consequence, hospital personnel are likely to be involved in difficult, intense situations most of the time.

At the other end of the spectrum, some caregivers must cope with monotonous, repetitive tasks. Laura Ellingson (2007) studied staff members at a dialysis care center, where they are required to perform the same routines over and over. Many of the caregivers said they break the monotony by focusing on the unique qualities of each patient. As one put it: "Our job is repetitious, but the patients are not. Yeah, they all have the same illness, they have kidney failure, but each person is different, so that's what makes it different every day" (p. 109).

HEALTHY STRATEGIES

Ironically, the very qualities that draw people to careers in health care make them especially prone to burnout. The **empathic communication model of burnout** suggests that health care is appealing to

PERSPECTIVES

Since retirement, every day is Saturday for Virgil Jernigan, especially since an attentive care provider suggested that he be evaluated for heart problems. While Jernigan was in the hospital to have foot surgery, he mentioned to a nurse practitioner that he had been feeling tired and out of breath (Weiss, 2013). She took his concerns seriously and ordered cardiac tests, which revealed a leaking valve in his heart. As it turned out, Jernigan had two surgeries—one on his foot and one to repair his heart valve. The first eased his pain. The second saved his life. Now, Jernigan says, he is back to playing golf every "Saturday," grateful to the medical professionals who made it possible.

BOX 5.5 COMMUNICATION SKILL BUILDER

Dealing with Difficult Patients

Some patients bring out the best in their caregivers. Others—a small percentage but powerful nonetheless—evoke defensiveness and anger. Experts offer the following tips for communicating effectively with people who are stressed, tired, and worried, without becoming too frustrated yourself.

- *Treat complaints as opportunities*. Frustrated patients and family members may want or need something they are afraid to ask for outright. Their emotion can be a signpost calling your attention to it. Physician Calvin Martin recalls an aggressive patient who threw things at the staff and yelled at everyone around him. "He knew he was dying, but everyone else was denying it," he says. Once the doctor learned the problem and was honest with the patient, his entire demeanor changed. "He was wonderful after that," Martin recalls (quoted by Magee & D'Antonio, 2003, p. 163). He says, "In medical school they tell you that 75% of the people you are going to see have nothing really wrong with them. That's not true. I think they all have something real, but we are just not finding it" (p. 164).
- *Empower team members to handle problems before they grow*. Most nonclinical problems start as minor annoyances—a phone call not returned, an appointment mix-up. A quick and thoughtful response (even if the patient has not complained) may save a great deal of time and stress down the line.
- *Invest in patient relationships*. In *The Field Guide to the Difficult Patient Interview*, Platt and Gordon (2004) propose that "engaging our patients in a partnership with us" and "enlisting them in following our recommendations" are the hallmarks of effective communication (p. 3). They encourage caregivers to take the time to know patients and establish mutual trust and rapport. "Spending more time early in our patient encounters saves time in the long run," they maintain (p. 3).
- *Show empathy*. Demonstrate through words and nonverbal cues that you understand what the patient is experiencing. Listen attentively, paraphrase to check your understanding, and ask for clarification until the patient confirms that you understand what he or she is trying to express (Platt & Gordon, 2004).
- *Display curiosity*. If a patient hints at a grievance or a concern that she or he is reluctant to share, show a gentle and encouraging interest in hearing more. Platt and Gordon (2004) use the example of a patient who refuses to say how much she smokes. They propose saying, "That is really interesting! Of course you don't have to tell me. But I am enormously curious to understand why you don't want to tell me. Can you help me understand that?" (p. 118).
- *Try a little humor*. If the patient shows an inclination toward it, you can sometimes use gentle humor to clear the air. Transue (2004) recalls a hospital patient who did nothing but complain about the food, the service, and the interruptions. She recalls thinking to herself, "I'm pretty sure there's humor under his crabbiness, but I can never quite pin it down" (p. 100). One day the man declared that he wouldn't leave the hospital until the food there improved. Several days later, after checking his lab results and vital signs, Transue was prepared to discharge him, but she asked first, "Has the food gotten any better?" She recalls:

> *He stares at me for a long moment. Finally he bursts out laughing. "How do you think I'll answer that . . . Has the food gotten any better. You get out of here—" . . . I wave and walk away, listening to him laugh." (p. 101)*

people who are concerned about others and are able to imagine others' joy and pain (Miller, Birkholt, Scott, & Stage, 1995; Miller, Stiff, & Ellis, 1988). These people are typically responsive communicators (able to communicate well with people in distress), but they may easily feel overwhelmed by constant exposure to emotional situations.

Regrettably, caregivers usually receive little instruction on how to care for themselves, and the symptoms of burnout may creep up on them before they know it. "The causes of burnout are often so quiet and insidious that we fail to notice them until they have caused a great deal of harm," observes Robert Wicks (2008, p. 18). Here are some suggestions for avoiding burnout, mostly drawn from Wicks's (2008) book *The Resilient Clinician.*

- *Hold daily debriefings with yourself.* Honestly assess your own emotions and hot buttons. Reflect on such questions as: What made me sad? Overwhelmed me? Sexually aroused me? Made me extremely happy or even confused me? (Wicks, 2008, p. 31).
- *Resist the urge to put off the "good stuff."* Wicks (2008) recommends making time for quiet walks, meditation, laughter, listening to enjoyable music, having friends over for dinner, daydreaming, being in nature, making love, and journaling.
- *Be mindful about what makes you happy.* Frequently consider your answers to the following questions: What is my heart's desire? What is truly important to me? How do I most want to live? (Wicks, 2008).
- *Invest in gratifying relationships.* The **Relational Health Communication Competence Model** observes that communication, social support, and emotional resilience are positively associated with each other (Kreps, 1988; Query & Kreps, 1996). Research bears out that providers' stress is eased when patients and colleagues are supportive of one another (Fiabane, Giorgi, Sguazzin, & Argentero, 2013; Gelsema et al., 2006).
- *Design your own time pie.* What amount of your time do you (or would you like) to devote to each of the following—being with loved ones, working, learning new things, spending time alone, being creative?
- *Seek the company of people whose presence replenishes you.* A good friend who listens without judgment or who helps you find the humor in a tense situation can ward off burnout. Transue (2004) remembers a playful conversation with a fellow intern who asked her, "Do you really want to be a doctor for the rest of your life?" Transue joked, "I don't even want to be a doctor for the rest of the week, especially" (p. 75).

Let's turn, now, to a topic of particular stress for caregivers—one that often boils down to an issue of communication.

PERSPECTIVES

"His gruff, Irish exterior belied his sweet nature," remembers nurse Sarah Horstmann (2013) of a patient she will never forget. The man arrived in the hospital in the final days of his life, and all he asked for was oatmeal. "When his tray came, he found cream of wheat instead," Horstmann recalls. To ease his disappointment, she rummaged through the unit's kitchen and found a rare package of oatmeal. When she brought it to the patient, "he was delighted and blew me a kiss and gave me a wink," she says. Although his chart indicated that he needed assistance to eat, "he dug right in" on his own that day. Horstmann recalls with gratitude the pleasure it gave her to care for him and meet his family. "I became a nurse because I want to care for people and make a difference," she says. "Being touched in return is an added bonus."

Medical Mistakes

"Doctor Amputates Wrong Leg"

The headlines told a shocking story. A Tampa surgeon, Rolando Sanchez, had mistakenly removed Willie King's left leg rather than his right one. It is easy to imagine the anguish of a patient with one good leg and one bad leg, awakening to realize the good leg is gone. "Now he'll be without any legs at all," mourned the patient's brother ("Florida Hospital," 1995, para. 4).

WHY MISTAKES HAPPEN

The Willie King case is horrifying. But the public did not hear the whole story. In his book *Medical Errors and Medical Narcissism,* clinical ethicist John Banja (2005) relates the behind-the-scenes facts of the case. First, King did not have one good leg and one bad leg. He suffered from diabetes and related vascular diseases to such an extent that open sores on both legs had developed gangrene, his skin was cold to the touch, and it was nearly impossible to detect a pulse in either leg. The left leg (which was mistakenly amputated) was actually worse than the right, and King was aware that he would lose both legs before long. He chose to have the right leg amputated first because it was the more painful of the two. So it was not an easy choice between good leg and bad leg. But a cascade of communication errors contributed to the mistake as well.

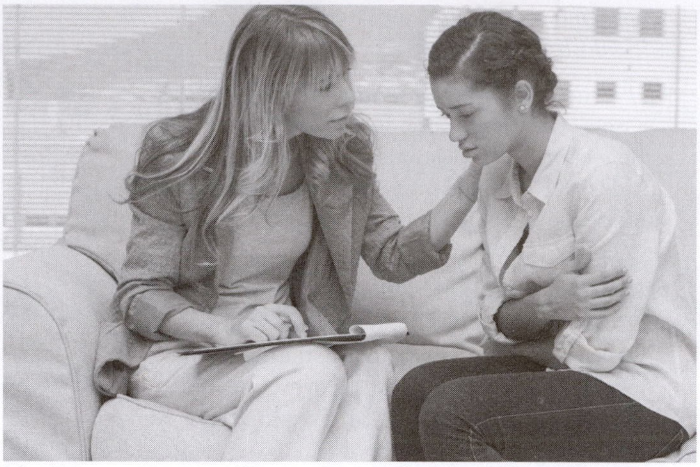

Caregivers often experience grief and withdrawal after serious mistakes, many of which stem from miscommunication in the context of time pressures.

Someone dropped the ball. Who? There's no easy answer, says Banja (2005). The public might imagine a distracted, careless, or bumbling surgeon. However, Dr. Sanchez was anything but. He was "at the height of a sterling medical career" (Banja, 2005, p. 9), having served as chief resident among his colleagues at New York University School of Medicine and professor at Albert Einstein College of Medicine before returning to practice in his native Tampa. The mistake ended with him, but it began much earlier.

Because of a miscommunication between Dr. Sanchez's office staff and the surgery department at the hospital, the surgical staff incorrectly listed the procedure as a left-leg amputation. A hospital nurse detected the error and told another nurse about it. That nurse put a surgery-schedule correction notice on a clipboard, which she gave to another nurse. Each nurse began a sequence of remedial events. But the sequence was somehow interrupted. The correction never made it to the official surgical log or to the blackboard in the surgery unit.

Yet another correction opportunity arose just prior to surgery, when King told a nurse that his right leg was to be amputated. She noted this on his record but prepared his left leg. When the surgeon entered the room, King's body was draped, except for the left leg, which was braced and ready for the operation. Sanchez confirmed, by looking at the blackboard, that this was the intended leg, and he was nearly done with the surgery before the medical team realized the error.

It is easy to see, in retrospect, that the mistake might not have happened if people had communicated more clearly with each other or if the surgical team had consulted King's consent form (which correctly indicated his right leg) rather than relying on the blackboard or surgery schedule. But at the time, people were following standard procedure, and the error occurred because of system and communication breakdowns that were beyond any one person's control (Banja, 2005).

Banja (2005) points out the systemic nature of this mistake and others like it. "Well-trained, well-motivated people make errors all the time," he says (p. 11). By some experts' reckoning, medical errors are the third leading cause of death in the United States, accounting for about 400,000 premature deaths per year (James, 2013). Medical mistakes are often the result of ineffective communication—sloppy handwriting, forgotten or delayed instructions, busy shift changes in which there is not time to talk about everything in a patient's chart, and so on (Pham et al., 2011; Ross et al., 2013). Small omissions and misunderstandings can quickly lead to critical breakdowns.

PERSPECTIVES

Caregivers sometimes grapple with mistakes made long before they began caring for a patient. For example, an African American woman with diabetes who felt she had been treated "like a dog" by an ophthalmologist in the past was reluctant to undergo another eye exam. Rather than shrugging off the grievance, her current doctor said, "You know, this may be coming very late, and it may not come from the person who needs to apologize, but . . . let me apologize to you, and let me say that this is not the way we want to practice medicine" (Lo, 2010, p. 492). After that, the woman felt better about trying again and was pleased with the care she received.

WHAT HAPPENS AFTER A MISTAKE?

People who are hurt by medical mistakes often say they just want an apology, to feel that they are getting the full story, and reassurance that the organization is taking steps to avoid similar errors in the future. It can be agonizing not to know exactly what caused a loved one's death or suffering. Dale Ann Micalizzi (2008) recalls her own bewildered grief when her 11-year-old son died following a relatively minor surgery to treat an infected cut on his ankle.

Micalizzi says her family did not want to sue. She works for an HMO herself and understands the intricacies of medical settings. But otherwise, no one would tell them what happened. "We were owed the truth," she says. "Money wasn't an issue for us" (2008, para. 12). Micalizzi describes sitting in a courtroom three years later, seeing the defense team consult a 6-inch-thick binder containing her son's medical records and reports from the hospital investigation. "This was information that I had begged to see for such a long time and have still never seen," she says. "In the intervening time I had searched for the truth, only to hit my head against walls of silence" (para. 8).

Errors can happen in any organization, in or out of health care. But medical mistakes are particularly hard to handle because the stakes are so high and because caregivers are not expected to commit errors. When health professionals' mistakes are brought to light, they may suffer more than people in other occupations from feelings of guilt and inadequacy, recriminations from others, and legal action. Even if others are involved in medical mistakes, it is typically physicians who are sued. And they may feel personally responsible, even when events were out of their control.

On the one hand, it is hard to deal with guilt and self-blame in isolation. Ethical guidelines and a sense of fair play encourage health professionals to make full disclosure to patients and their loved ones, to apologize, and to take corrective action. Likewise, hospitals' contracts with insurers typically stipulate that the hospital will promptly report medical errors when they occur. However, caregivers may be discouraged from admitting mistakes by their own sense of distress, by fears about their reputation, by ego needs that make them reluctant to admit fallibility, and by reluctance either to blame others or to accept blame for what is often a systemic chain of events involving numerous people (Banja, 2005).

Banja (2005) proposes that health professionals may rationalize not saying anything because they believe no permanent harm was done, the error probably did not change the outcome (e.g., "the patient would have died anyway"), knowing about the mistake would only make the family feel worse, or the mistake was not anyone's fault, just something that happened.

> ### IN YOUR EXPERIENCE ?
>
> Many people hurt by medical errors say they just want an apology, the full story, and assurance that future errors will be prevented.
>
> - If a family member of yours nearly died from a medical error, do you think these factors would influence your desire to sue for malpractice? Why or why not?
> - What other factors might influence how you felt?

Added to people's natural reluctance to admit mistakes are more tangible considerations, such as *Who will be held responsible?* and *Who will pay?* Malpractice insurance policies often include a clause that revokes coverage if the physician admits culpability (Banja, 2005, p. 22). Thus, although patients yearn for apologies and explanations, and health professionals may want to provide them, they may feel that, if they own up to mistakes, they are on their own if lawsuits ensue.

The issue is not only who will pay for a malpractice judgment, it is also who will pay for remedial care. For example, if a hospital stay is extended or a patient is transferred to an intensive care unit because of a medical error, who pays for the extra care? In recent years, many insurance companies have declared that they will not pay costs associated with what they call *never events*. **Never events** are loosely defined as clear, preventable errors with serious consequences. "Think wrong-side surgery," says Dennis Murray (2007, p. 18). The idea is that hospitals with a strong financial incentive to avoid never events will be more diligent about preventing them, identifying their root causes if they do occur, and avoiding future tragedies.

But the issue is not clear cut. A gray zone surrounds less obvious avoidable outcomes, such as infections. If a patient contracts an infection in the hospital, was the staff negligent? In many cases it is hard to say what constitutes negligence versus a reasonable (but imperfect) standard of care. David Burda (2008) worries that insurers may become so stringent that medical professionals will be afraid to try new procedures. Even if the standard options are not working, professionals may feel they cannot step out of bounds for fear of being either sued or refused payment. And Burda warns that caregivers who are terrified of making mistakes will not learn very much, and they will probably order so many precautionary tests that precious medical resources will be squandered.

Medical mistakes (and perceived mistakes) are not only expensive; they can be demoralizing and humiliating. Although many new residents consider that doctors are likely to be sued at least once (Noland & Walter, 2006), it can be devastating when it happens. Family physician Steven Erickson (2008) remembers being sued over a difficult birth that resulted in the baby's having brain damage. In the courtroom, he weathered aggressive questioning by the plaintiff's attorney, all the while worrying that his colleagues, family, and friends would think less of him and doubt his judgment. Erickson won the case, but embarrassment and fear of future lawsuits shadowed him for a year, until he met a new patient, Roger. Roger had just moved to town, and he and his wife had chosen Erickson to be their doctor based on their son's recommendation. A year earlier, their son had served on the jury that heard the malpractice case against Erickson. Roger said that, as a farmer, his son had explained to fellow jurors that births do not always go perfectly even when the doctor is honest, competent, and doing his or her best. Writes Erickson:

> *I thanked him for his candor and finished up the visit, all the while fighting to maintain my composure. But as I walked back to my office, my eyes welled up and I was crying. After all the embarrassment and self-doubt my malpractice case had engendered in me, there was a juror who not only believed my defense, but trusted me enough to refer his elderly father and mother to me.* (p. 33)

Erickson's words remind us that while we should guard citizens' right to reasonable legal recourse if they have been badly treated, lawsuits have many costs, emotional and financial. Very often, patients wish to avoid lawsuits just as much as medical professionals do, but a variety of human and systemic restraints may stand between them. When it comes down to it, the factors that lead to mistakes—and the factors that determine what will happen afterward if mistakes are made—involve mostly one thing: communication. Effective communication has the potential to save lives and prevent some of the anguish that bereaved families and guilt-ridden professionals feel as a result of errors.

COMMUNICATION SKILL BUILDER: MANAGING MEDICAL MISTAKES

A research team led by Margaret Plews-Ogan identified five stages common among health professionals coping with serious medical mistakes. The first stage is *acceptance*, which involves recognizing a mistake and its effects. The second stage, *stepping in*, involves taking responsibility for the mistake, often by telling colleagues, patients, and their loved ones about the error and apologizing. Said one physician, "I felt like the right thing to do was to go talk to them and tell them and if they felt like they needed to sue me then you know we would just have to deal with that" (Plews-Ogan, Owens, & May, 2013, p. 238). Although difficult, this stage was a turning point for many care providers in the study, who felt they could cope more effectively afterward.

In the third stage, *integration*, health professionals assimilate what they have learned from the mistake and take stock of a revised identity in which they admit to themselves that they are capable of making errors that have tragic consequences. Some physicians interviewed by Plews-Ogan and colleagues (2013) left medicine temporarily in the wake of mistakes. From that process often emerges a *new narrative* stage, in which professionals typically emerge as more humble and cautious than before.

The final stage, *wisdom*, involves knowledge mixed with compassion and understanding. As one doctor put it, "I certainly am absolutely more understanding and forgiving of the frailties of others, whether my coworkers or the nurses" (Plews-Ogan et al., p. 240).

Following are some tips from the experts on how to avoid misunderstandings, disappointments, and lawsuits, and how to respond when mistakes occur.

From the Beginning

- *Establish trust.* Invest in open and trusting relationships with patients from the very beginning. Be sincere, polite, friendly, and engaging. Patients are less likely to sue doctors whom they like and trust (Boodman, 1997), and it is easier to share decisions and to admit mistakes with people one knows and trusts.

- *Invite feedback.* Patients who play an active role in deciding on treatment options are more likely to consider them worthwhile, even if things do not work out perfectly.
- *Respond to complaints and requests as quickly as possible.* Patients who perceive that you do not care or are not paying attention are more likely to assume you have neglected other aspects of their care. When you are unavoidably delayed, apologize, explain why, and express your sincere concern.
- *Show that you care.* Do not assume that patients know you care. Be explicit, as in "I don't know if we can eliminate 100% of your pain. But I think, if we work together, we can do a lot. It would make me happy to see you smiling and walking again."
- *Create realistic expectations.* Brushing aside patients' concerns, as in saying, "There's nothing to worry about," may set them up to be disappointed and even to file lawsuits down the line. Attorney S. Allan Adelman (2008) suggests, "You can't always prevent undesirable outcomes, but you can help create realistic expectations" (p. 14).
- *Put it in writing.* "Document, ad nauseam," recommends Ralph Caldroney (2008), a family physician who has never been sued in 30 years of practice.
- *Do not be shy about giving referrals.* If another doctor can help, or the patient wants a second opinion, be supportive. Do not cast yourself as the roadblock that kept the patient from exploring all avenues (Caldroney, 2008).
- *Do not forget the family.* Keep in mind that family members often have opinions and fears of their own. Invite their input, and nurture those relationships.
- *Own up to small mistakes.* Showing that you have nothing to hide can engender trust.

Some organizations are also using technology to improve communication and minimize communication breakdowns (see Box 5.6).

If an Error Does Occur

John Banja and Geri Amori (2005, p. 178) recommend the following five-step guide to telling a patient or his or her loved ones about a medical mistake:

1. Rehearse how you will disclose the information.
2. Deliver it as simply, truthfully, and clearly as possible.
3. Stop talking and listen.
4. Assess how the news is being received.
5. Respond empathically.

Banja and Amori recommend using the word *error* or *mistake* rather than blurring the issue with terms such as *unintended outcome* or *unexpected occurrence.* They also coach health professionals to tell the people affected: (1) when and where the error occurred, (2) what harm resulted, (3) what actions have been taken to offset the harm, (4) actions being taken to

BOX 5.6 HEALTH AND COMMUNICATION TECHNOLOGY

Mobile App Helps Save Time and Prevent Errors

Some health care organizations are using mobile applications to avoid communication gaps, delays, and medical errors. For example, a New Jersey hospital invested in a secure smartphone app that lets members of the care team know instantly when patients have a request or question and when test results are ready (Leventhal, 2014).

Prior to adopting the new technology, patient care involved "a cascade of phone calls . . . that are meant to connect the treating physician with the patient's primary care physician, consulting specialists, nurse practitioners, nurses and therapists," says an industry analyst (Leventhal, 2014). That process might take hours or days, and information was often lost or distorted along the way, contributing to errors and oversights.

With the use of an app to keep everyone on the same page, the hospital has reduced patient wait times, the length of hospital stays, and the number of errors. The savings amount to more than $1 million a year, not to mention the suffering avoided with effective communication.

prevent future errors, (5) who will be caring for the patient and how, (6) a description of systemic factors that contributed to the error, (7) the costs of responding to the error and how they will be handled, and (8) information about counseling and support resources. They also recommend that the speaker "apologize profusely" and mean it (p. 185).

Finally, do not let doubt and remorse cripple your confidence. It is easy to obsess about what might have happened—if only you had stopped by one more time, ordered one more test, put a request in writing rather than called it in, and so on. These are not necessarily errors, just limitations in the amount a person can do.

The advantages of multidisciplinary teamwork in health care are powerful, but so are the communication challenges.

The chapter concludes with a communication strategy that has the potential to ease some of the pressure on health care professionals.

Multidisciplinary Teamwork

Mr. S, age 65, is retired from the automotive industry. Although he lives alone, he joins close friends for breakfast out twice a week, a tradition they have maintained for 15 years. In the last two weeks, however, his health has deteriorated to the point where he can barely walk and it is difficult for him to talk. He is a smoker and has been treated in the past for heart disease and emphysema, but he has never felt this sick, tired, or discouraged. He worries that he will no longer be able to spend time with his friends.*

What is the best approach for optimizing Mr. S's health? A team of students at the University of Utah addressed this question in a program designed to prepare them for multidisciplinary teamwork as health professionals (Barnett, Hollister, & Hall, 2011). Mr. S is a hypothetical patient created by medical school professor Caroline Milne, complete with vital signs, health history, socioeconomic profile, and more. The students—preparing for careers in pharmacology, nursing, medicine, audiology, nutrition, physical therapy, and occupational therapy—formed multidisciplinary teams to meet with a trained actor who portrayed Mr. S and to devise a plan for his care.

Students who participated in the program gave it high marks. Most said that it impressed upon them the benefits of involving diverse perspectives in patient care. They also said that the experience made them more comfortable interacting with people in other medical disciplines. This is important, since a common barrier to teamwork is lack of trust and communication between people in different fields (Bindler, Richardson, Daratha, & Wordell, 2012).

There is a move toward more multidisciplinary teamwork in health care, both to meet patients' diverse needs and to make the most of health resources. Teams may include social workers, recreational therapy, psychologists, dieticians, pain specialists, and people in many other fields. In this section we look at the rewards and challenges of multidisciplinary teamwork.

Simply defined, a **team** is "a set of individuals who work together to achieve common objectives" (Unsworth, 1996, p. 483). Teamwork is nothing new to health care, but the rules and reasons for teamwork are changing. To apply the terminology of management guru Peter Drucker, health care teams used to function like baseball teams, but now they must act like doubles tennis partners. Drucker (1993) writes that (managerially speaking) a doubles tennis game is different from a baseball game. In baseball, each player is assigned a position, with a specific set of tasks

*I assigned the patient this name simply to make him easier to discuss. The research report itself does not name him.

to perform. The pitcher pitches, the catcher catches, the batter bats, and so on. The game is specialized and precise. Doubles tennis is different—faster, less precise. Players have basic positions but must always be poised to help each other, and there is scarcely time to stand still.

Health professionals used to play their positions with little overlap (like baseball players). A patient might see a physical therapist, a nurse, a doctor, and a laboratory technician—but one at a time, never all together. Technically, the caregivers were working toward the same goal, but they contributed in specialized ways, independently. The problem is that team members who do not communicate with each other are likely to drop the ball. Lack of communication can lead to duplicated efforts, costly (and sometimes life-threatening) delays, frustration, and wasted time. Teamwork can minimize the waste and frustration. However, teamwork is not always easy to accomplish.

An organization famous for teamwork is Mayo Clinic. There's a saying at Mayo that "teamwork is not an option," it's the rule (Berry & Seltman, 2008, p. 51). The medical center is unusual in that, although it is one of the largest in the world, it is a truly integrated system. To appreciate how, let's consider a patient-care scenario somewhere else. Typically, a patient with a serious health concern schedules an appointment with a primary care physician, who refers her to a separate facility for diagnostic tests, where the staff sends her back to the doctor for results, who refers her to a specialist in a different location, who might recommend surgery at still a different place, and so on. The patient probably has to make appointments with each provider separately, supply her health history and insurance information at each office, and perhaps wait weeks or months between appointments. The physicians involved with the patient's care probably do not work directly for the hospital, nor are they likely to have an easy or quick way to communicate with each other or to review an overall medical chart for the patient. (In many cases, there is no overall patient chart. Instead, each doctor maintains a separate chart detailing his or her work with the patient.)

In contrast, Mayo Clinic is a fully integrated system of doctors, specialists, therapists, hospitals, laboratories, and everyone and everything else needed to provide comprehensive medical care. Everyone involved—including the physicians—works for the clinic. They are linked with sophisticated communication technology and, very often, close enough proximity to allow face-to-face conversations about patients. The Mayo team practices what they call "destination medicine." When patients go there for serious health concerns, they should be prepared to stay in town for a few days. In that time, they will probably be seen by several specialists, have diagnostic tests done, and undergo treatment—all on the same campus. Even surgeries are typically scheduled on a next-day basis. The whole process from the initial consultation, through visits with specialists, diagnostic tests, and even surgery and recovery—might take three to five days, compared to weeks or months elsewhere.

Mayo's streamlined efficiency is supported by an organizational culture that values and rewards teamwork as well as a carefully designed infrastructure. All appointments are made through one centralized system. This saves time and energy and allows the staff to coordinate the timing and sequence of tests and treatments. Pathologists and radiologists immediately evaluate diagnostic test data, usually before the patient leaves the office, in case more data is required. The results are immediately posted in the patient's electronic medical record. Every caregiver has instant, online access to the patient's comprehensive medical record, including all test results and other physicians' notes. This makes it feasible for everyone to get the full picture, to avoid delays or duplications, and to work effectively as a team. All the while, physicians are free to collaborate and to refer patients to each other without loss of income because they are all on salaries and are all part of the same team. "It's like you are working in an organism; you are not a single cell out there practicing," says Mayo physician Nina Schwenk. "I have access to the best minds on any topic, any disease or problem I come up with and they're one phone call away" (quoted by Berry & Seltman, 2008, p. 53).

ADVANTAGES

One advantage of teamwork is that members are able to apply multiple perspectives to a problem, enhancing innovation and creativity. This applies to overarching issues, such as new cost-cutting measures and service lines, and to everyday dilemmas.

Another advantage is that interdisciplinary teamwork blurs the lines between departments and presents new opportunities for diverse employees to take part in decision making, which is linked to job satisfaction and retention. One result is that doctors and nurses are again playing a major role in health care management.

Third, teamwork reduces costly oversights that may occur when people are devoted to highly specialized tasks. Health care organizations can no longer afford, if ever they could, the oversights that result when team members do not communicate well with each other. Ask any hospital employee about patients who have gotten "lost in the system." Usually the story is that the patient is scheduled for a series of treatments or tests, but somewhere along the way everyone assumes that the patient is with someone else—until they realize the poor soul has spent hours lying on a gurney in the hallway.

Bureaucracies are especially vulnerable to these kinds of oversights because many tasks do not fall squarely within the boundaries of any job description. Teamwork encourages people to look at the larger picture and pitch in, even with tasks that are not specifically assigned to them. For example, nurses who notice that lab results have not arrived on time may take the initiative to find out if tests were run and why results are delayed. This extra effort can save time and money in the long run.

Fourth, teamwork is well suited to biopsychosocial care. Members of some organizations have concluded that the best way to keep patients healthy is to pay attention to their broad range of concerns. As physician Alan R. Zwerner advises:

> *The dog ate a 100-year-old patient's glasses, and she's not eligible for a covered pair for another year? Give her a pair. Free. It could prevent a fall that would break her hip. There is a reward for quality care, patient satisfaction, and doing the right thing at the right time. (quoted by Azevedo, 1996, para. 22)*

Teams can help provide care that simultaneously addresses a variety of issues such as patients' personal resources, nutrition, exercise, psychological well-being, and more.

Finally, team members may benefit from their involvement with coworkers. Teamwork allows professionals to share the immense responsibilities of health care, provide mutual support, and learn from each other.

ADVANTAGES OF INTERDISCIPLINARY TEAMWORK

- Multiple perspectives enhance innovation and creativity
- Team members may be gratified to have input
- Reduces costly oversights
- Enhances biopsychosocial care
- Responsibilities and learning are shared

DIFFICULTIES AND DRAWBACKS

None of this means that teamwork is easy. Although it presents many advantages, there are potential disadvantages as well.

For one thing, teamwork takes time. If a quick decision is needed, an individual may be better qualified to make it. Some nurses in Julie Apker's (2001) study appreciated opportunities to be part of shared-governance teams. Others felt overwhelmed. Said one nurse, "I don't feel it's fair to give someone a project if they don't have time" (quoted by Apker, 2001, p. 125).

Second, especially if they are rushed or intimidated, team members may resort to **groupthink**; that is, going along with ideas they would not normally support (Janis, 1972). Third, busy schedules make it hard to schedule meetings, especially if the organization is not supportive in allowing time for teamwork.

Finally, teamwork can also be particularly difficult because health professionals from different disciplines often have very different ideas about health, which creates the potential for competition and conflict. Status differences can cause rifts and intolerance. Health care is often characterized by what Kreps (1990) calls **professional prejudice**. Some professions are considered more prestigious than others, which means that people without impressive titles (including patients) may be excluded from discussions even though they have valuable information and ideas to share.

CHALLENGES OF INTERDISCIPLINARY TEAMWORK

- Can be time consuming
- Danger of groupthink
- Scheduling difficulties
- Can involve competition and conflict

COMMUNICATION SKILL BUILDER: WORKING IN TEAMS

Following are some of experts' tips for working through the tricky communication dilemmas just described.

- *Honor the contributions of every individual.* Few organizations honor this ideal more than Mayo Clinic. Denis Cortese remembers his early experiences as a physician at the clinic (related by Berry & Seltman, 2008, p. 44). "I was unaccustomed to have a desk attendant tell me, a physician, that I needed to adjust my schedule to see a patient right away," Cortese says. But then another physician pulled him aside. "He explained that at Mayo Clinic, the focus is always on the patient. And whichever member of the staff is interacting with the patient deserves our full support," Cortese recalls. "I've never forgotten that lesson." Cortese is now CEO of Mayo Clinic.
- *Take time to build trust and camaraderie.* When quick or important decisions are needed, the investment will pay off.
- *Conduct team meetings with the goal of involving everyone.* Minimize distractions and sit so that all members can easily see each other. Establish ground rules for attendance, discussions, and decision making. Before trying to solve a problem, make sure group members agree on the nature, importance, and cause of the problem. Encourage all group members to contribute ideas, and strive to find creative options that meet numerous goals simultaneously. Summarize group discussions and decisions out loud to clarify the group's viewpoints and perspectives.
- *Develop a deep understanding of what each team member has to offer.* People bring unique talents and perspectives as well as professional backgrounds.
- *Be aware that conflict is a natural part of group work.* Group members who remain committed to the task often work through the conflict to achieve a mutual sense of accomplishment.
- *Monitor the health of the team.* "Diagnose communication errors as you would any illness," recommend Eduardo Salas and colleagues (2008, p. 333), adding, "Examine the team and look for symptoms, then treat the symptoms through team learning and self-correction."

Summary

We have looked at health care through the eyes of caregivers, including the joys and challenges involved in such a role. Becoming a health professional typically involves a socialization process.

Training programs and clinical experiences serve a powerful role in preparing people, helping them accept the immense privileges and responsibilities of practice, and in suggesting what communication strategies are helpful and appropriate. As students become professionals, they typically adopt the communication styles, logic, and attitudes of their mentors, for better or worse. Emerging guidelines establish communication as a core competency for caregivers, recognizing that it can help save time and money, improve medical outcomes, and prevent much of the frustration that patients and caregivers feel. Reform efforts are underway that focus on knowledge, communication skills training, and clinical experience integrated with science education.

The way caregivers communicate also reflects professional pressures. Patients may be quick to assume that caregivers do not want to spend time with them, when caregivers may have little say in the matter themselves. Indeed, time constraints are often as frustrating to professionals as they are to patients.

Caregivers are expected to be quick but thorough, strong but emotionally accessible, always available but never tired, and honest but infallible. Understanding these conflicting demands may help people understand why caregivers communicate as they do and identify healthy ways to help avoid burnout. Mindfulness is one way to help patients feel valued and appreciated, and at the same time, help health professionals manage stress.

Systems theory encourages us that we can change customary ways of doing things and avoid simplistic assumptions and shortsighted solutions. Well-designed systems can save time and improve the health care experience for everyone involved. They can also help to minimize the number and severity of medical mistakes, which typically result from miscommunication.

A great deal of evidence suggests that health professionals are least likely to be sued if they build strong and trusting relationships with patients, take time to discuss treatment options and consequences carefully, and thoroughly describe their decision processes in writing. When mistakes do occur, disclosing them compassionately and fully can prevent lawsuits, provide comfort to those affected, and relieve some of the guilt that caregivers feel.

Interdisciplinary teamwork is not always easy, but it offers extraordinary rewards in terms of quality decision making, shared responsibility, and holistic perspectives of people's health.

As stressful as it is, health care can also be richly rewarding, and most caregivers consider it immensely gratifying to help patients. As any caregiver will attest, there is no such thing as a routine day. In the next unit, we will look at diversity among people and in cultural ideas about health and healing.

Key Terms and Theories

Flexner Report
rote learning
problem-based learning (PBL)
socialization
Voice of Medicine
hidden curriculum
role theory
scut work
rite of passage
organizational processes
organizational culture
mindfulness
burnout
emotional exhaustion
depersonalization
reduced sense of personal accomplishment
double bind
detached concern
empathic communication model of burnout
Relational Health Communication Competence Model
never events
team
groupthink
professional prejudice

Discussion Questions

1. Create a hypothetical scenario that illustrates role theory in the context of a health care interaction.
2. Considering the transformation at Virginia Mason Cancer Center, what might medical staff members do to improve the environment and reduce wait times? Be creative.
3. Describe how time constraints may affect patient–caregiver communication and influence caregiver satisfaction. How do you respond to some health professionals' argument that they must limit patient's input so they can keep exams within a particular time limit? How might organizational leaders help with this? How might patients help?
4. Describe the provisions of the Health Insurance Portability and Accountability Act (HIPAA). What would you change about the act, if you could, to make it more effective in terms of communicating about health?
5. What do you think of the "Blowing the Whistle" case study? Why do you think substance abuse is higher than normal among health care providers?
6. Name some strategies for avoiding burnout as a caregiver. Which of these do you, or might you, incorporate into your own life whether you are a caregiver or not?
7. In the case of Willie King, whom do you believe should be held responsible for amputating the wrong leg? Why? Whom, if anyone, should be sued? Who should pay the extra medical bills?
8. What do you say to health professionals who are devastated by a mistake and want to apologize, yet are afraid that doing so will invalidate their malpractice coverage and possibly destroy their careers?
9. Imagine that your grandfather is the hypothetical patient described in the chapter as Mr. S. What types of professionals would you choose to be on his care team? What factors would you like them to focus on mostly? Why?

Answers to *Can You Guess?*

- About 3% of Americans in the private sector worked in the health care prior to 1960 (U.S. Bureau of Labor Statistics, 2009).
- Since 1960, the percentage of Americans with health-related careers has nearly quadrupled to 11% and continues to grow (U.S. Bureau of Labor Statistics, 2009).
- On average, pharmacists are the highest paid health professionals on the list. Physical therapists are the second, following by registered nurses (U.S. Bureau of Labor Statistics, 2014b).

PART III

Sociocultural Issues

We can become so caught up in our own view of health and healing that we forget that these are largely cultural constructs. In some cultures, *healing* evokes images of science and technology, in others, the power of Mother Nature and meditation. Bernie Siegel has taught us that love and laughter should be part of the mix as well. Sadly, diversity sometimes becomes the basis for discrimination and exclusion, such that the color of our skin is a factor in how long we are likely to live, not because we are born with different genetic blueprints, but because inequitable resources and discrimination affect our health. In this section, we sample a rich variety of cultural perspectives about health and healing. We also look at the link between health and race, socioeconomic status, literacy, and other factors. As you will see, effective communication is our most promising means of learning about, celebrating, and integrating diverse ideas.

> If you watch how nature deals with adversity, continually renewing itself, you can't help but learn.
>
> —BERNIE SEIGEL, MD

CHAPTER 6

Diversity in Health Care

She was in a motorized wheelchair that she controlled with her only usable finger. I could not understand her guttural speech or her facial contortions. She could not consistently hold her head up or control her drooling. After a few desperate moments, I asked her if she knew how to use a typewriter. She managed to make me understand a "yes" answer, and I ran out of the room to locate a typewriter on a movable stand. Pleased with my ingenuity, I stood next to her expecting some limited request. My smugness gave way to sheer awe as she painstakingly, letter by letter, tapped out with her left fourth finger the question: "What are the risks for me taking the birth control pill?"

In this account, Lucy Candib (1994, p. 139) recalls a young woman who taught her anew to respect each patient as an individual. It may be tempting to group people within impersonal categories. However, there is extraordinary diversity among the people who seek health care.

Since diversity among health professionals still does not reflect the diversity in the population overall, people are likely to see caregivers whose experiences are different than their own. This can be an opportunity for growth and connection. It can also be an occasion for misunderstandings. The difference often lies in the quality of communication they share.

In this chapter we explore diversity among both patients and caregivers in terms of socioeconomic status and literacy, sexual orientation, race and ethnicity, language, disabilities, and age. As you will see, factors such as these interconnect in unique ways to influence health and the way we communicate about it.

Intersectionality Theory

"Human lives cannot be reduced to single characteristics," writes theorist Olena Hankivsky (2012, p. 1713). No one is simply a man or a woman, heterosexual or gay, rich or poor, or so on. Instead, individuals are influenced by how these identities (and many others) intersect within the context of larger environments. These points are central to **intersectionality theory,** which proposes that a person's social position emerges within the interface of micro-level personal identities and macro-level sociocultural patterns (Bauer, 2014). Each of these levels is dynamic and complex. Personal identity may reflect age, race, sexual orientation, physical ability, and education, to name just a few. Sociocultural variables may include sexism, racism, power, resources, public policies, and so on (Crenshaw, 1989, 1991).

One implication of intersectionality theory is that social position is not simply the sum total of different identities. Lisa Bowleg (2008) offers the example that "Black + Lesbian + Woman ≠ Black Lesbian Woman" (p. 312). Indeed, the theory emerged in the late 1980s, when Kimberlé Crenshaw (1989) made a similar observation—that issues facing Black women were not well represented in either the civil rights movement, which focused mostly on Black men, or the women's movement, which focused mostly on White women.

Another implication it that it is infeasible to rank-order the variables that influence social position. This becomes obvious if you try to answer the question, "Which influences your life more—your sex or your race?" You would probably say, "I can't compare them" or "It depends." As Bowleg (2012) points out, "no social category or form of social inequality is more salient than another from an intersectionality perspective" (p. 1271). In the end, the *intersection* of complex micro- and macro-level factors is different and more impactful than any factor on its own.

When applied to health communication, intersectionality theory reminds us that categorizations such as *older adults*, *persons with disabilities*, and *the poor* mean very little by themselves. The theory also draws attention to people who are exceptionally disadvantaged by the multiplicity of factors that influence them. For example, Hispanic immigrants in a New Mexico community say they are aware that diabetes may kill them one day, but many of them struggle daily just to feed their families, do not have health insurance, and feel that health professionals resent it when they use the community clinic. In the context of all these factors, many of the immigrants believe, or at least hope, that they can manage diabetes on their own with folk remedies (Page-Reeves et al., 2013). A health campaign that addresses only one of these issues is unlikely to change their circumstances very much.

Intersectionality theory also emphasizes that guesses and generalizations often have harmful consequences. There is no substitute for getting to know people (be they coworkers, patients, members of at-risk communities, or anyone else) in terms of the overlapping identities and social structures that define life as they experience it. Achieving this level of localized knowledge may seem like a daunting challenge, but evidence suggests that it can be both rewarding and effective in terms of carrying out research, creating high-impact health campaigns, and developing effective health policies (Hankivsky, 2012; Hankivksy et al., 2014; Turpin, 2013).

The remainder of this chapter explores aspects of personal identity most often referenced in intersectionality theory. (Chapter 8 broadens the scope to explore more macro-level considerations.) As you read, keep in mind that, although it is most manageable to talk about these dimensions of identity one at a time, they are not experienced that way and their effects are not the same for everyone.

Socioeconomic Status

Zoe, a part-time home care aide, helps to dress and bathe people with limited physical abilities. She likes her job, but the pay is minimal and she is frightened by the neighborhoods where some of her clients live. It's not much help to talk to her boss, whose main complaint is all the overtime she must put in. By contrast, Zoe wishes she could work enough hours a week to qualify for health insurance. Without a high school diploma, she wonders if things will ever get easier.

Many aspects of Zoe's life reflect elements of **socioeconomic status (SES)**, an overarching term that factors in education, income, employment level, and similar variables. Education is such a powerful predictor of health in the United States that a 25-year-old woman who did not graduate from high school is likely to die 8.6 years sooner than a woman the same age with a college degree. The lifespan differential among men is even larger, at 9.3 years (National Center for Health Statistics, 2012).

The issue is not entirely about education, but about the larger reality that people with limited education often (although not always) experience poor living conditions, financial strain, stress, and other disadvantages. Partly because of these factors, people of low SES are more likely than the general population to suffer from depression, to have attention-deficit/hyperactivity disorder, be obese, to smoke, to have poor oral health, to have various forms of cancer, and more (Cruz, 2014; National Center for Health Statistics, 2012; Peretti-Watel et al., 2014).

Many factors play into the link between health and SES. We will focus here on the powerful role of communication. Zoe has an advantage because she is fairly comfortable communicating in health care environments. But as you will see, many people of low socioeconomic status are not.

One reason many individuals of low SES suffer from poor health is that they typically receive less health and dental care than other people. This is partly because they have limited financial resources and partly because they tend to be dissatisfied with the care they receive; thus they may avoid it (Becker & Newsom, 2003; Horowitz et al., 2012). The dissatisfaction may arise from disparate expectations.

For the most part, physicians in the United States consider patients to be proactive if they are assertive, ask questions, and engage actively in conversations (Verlinde, De Laender, De Maesschalck, Deveugele, & Willems, 2012). However, people of low SES are typically less assertive than other patients. They tend to ask fewer questions and reveal less about their health concerns (Fowler, 2006). This may be because they are not highly knowledgeable about health issues, they are intimidated by health professionals, and/or they consider it disrespectful to question or challenge them (Bao, Fox, & Escarce, 2007).

Whatever the reasons, it's easy to predict the downward spiral that can result from these mismatched expectations. Health professionals may perceive that low-SES patients are uninterested or apathetic. As a result, they themselves may come off as less attentive and less immediate than they normally would, which can further heighten patients' anxiety and reticence, and so on.

IN YOUR EXPERIENCE

- Have you ever felt that you were regarded as having lower social status than a caregiver who was treating you?
- If so, what cues gave you this impression?
- How did that dynamic influence the communication between you?
- What might have improved the situation?

HEALTH AND COMMUNICATION TECHNOLOGY

Free mHealth services, such as text4baby, send text messages (in English or Spanish) about pregnancy and parenting to people who sign up. Since more people now have mobile devices than computers, such services may help narrow the information gap. A text4baby subscriber in Avery Holton and Bard Love's (2013) study said, "You don't feel so lonely when the information comes to you on your own terms. You have the power to do something about your health and the health of others" (pp. 531–532).

A second factor is that health professionals tend to offer less information and guidance to patients of low SES than to others. In nearly 6,000 patient interactions studied, physicians were twice as likely to discuss cancer screening with patients who were college graduates as with patients who had not finished high school (Bao et al., 2007). (The only exception was talk about mammograms, which was mostly the same regardless of SES.) Information deficits such as these are particularly unfortunate because people of low SES are typically more fearful about their health than most people and are often less able to judge the severity of their illnesses themselves (James et al., 2008).

Third, low-SES patients are less likely than others to feel confident reading health information and understanding health statistics (Smith, Wolf, & Wagner, 2010). They are also less likely to seek out health information online (Hovick, Liang, & Kahlor, 2014; Lee, Ramírez, Lewis, Gray, & Hornik, 2012). As a result, they tend to rely mostly on television and people they know for health information, which contributes to a knowledge gap since those sources do not offer as much information as the Web (Seo & Matsaganis, 2013). On the bright side, some health promoters are using mobile devices to convey information to people who might not otherwise get it. As you will see in Chapter 9, mobile technology is now prevalent, even among people who don't have computers. (See the Health and Communication Technology box for more.)

Fourth, it may be especially tricky to negotiate treatment decisions when patients have limited means.

Physicians surveyed by Susannah Bernheim and associates (2008) said that, ideally, SES should not be a factor when making treatment decisions, but practically speaking it often *is*. That's because patients of low SES may lack reliable transportation, have rigid or unpredictable work schedules, be incapable of paying for medications, or experience difficulty finding specialists or therapists who will take them on as clients. Said one doctor in the study:

> *He [a patient] was a trucker . . . we really had to tailor the medication. He did not have any proper time to eat, and you know, he did not have time to come to his appointments. We have to tailor his appointments according to his travel schedule. It is not optimal, but we do the best we can.* (p. 56)

In this and other ways, physicians surveyed said they try hard, but they are often constrained by factors outside their control (Bernheim, Ross, Krumholz, & Bradley, 2008).

Finally, preconceived notions can be a stumbling block to communication between health professionals and patients of low SES. Many of the general practitioners Sara Willems and colleagues (2005) interviewed consider that people are impoverished mostly because they do not try hard enough to overcome their circumstances. Said one doctor, "They don't want to change their situation . . . they are used to it. They no longer have the courage to change it" (p. 179). Another one said, "They are not interested in their health. They don't see the advantage of, for example, healthy food" (p. 180). Although these were common viewpoints, some doctors in the study *were* vigorous advocates of seeking care for impoverished patients and actively tried to help them improve their neighborhoods and living conditions (Willems, Swinnen, & De Maeseneer, 2005).

Although we have been talking in generalities, keep in mind that there is enormous diversity among people who fall into the category of low SES. For example, some people have low-income jobs but are highly educated. Evidence suggests that these individuals are even more dissatisfied than others when they feel rushed or belittled during health care encounters (Jensen, King, Guntzviller, & Davis, 2010).

Issues of socioeconomic status point to the dangers of stereotyping and categorizing. As you will see next, people who suffer from health literacy challenges also work hard to avoid feeling judged and alienated.

Health Literacy

The hospital staff uses an orange to teach a patient how to give himself daily insulin shots for diabetes. Later, when his blood sugar is worse than ever, the staff realizes the communication breakdown: The man has been injecting insulin into oranges at home and then eating them (Boodman, 2011).

...

A tired mother misunderstands the instructions "3 tsps" on a cough syrup bottle. She uses tablespoons rather than teaspoons, thereby giving her child the equivalent of 9 teaspoons of medicine.

...

When a man sees that the results of his biopsy for prostate cancer are "positive," he is relieved. He doesn't realize that "positive" means he has cancer.

...

Health literacy refers to individuals' ability to access health information, to understand it, and to apply it in ways that promote good health (WHO, 1998). The conventional idea of literacy as the ability to read is part of the equation. But health literacy involves a great deal more than that. To be health literate, people must also:

- understand the language in which information is conveyed (be it English, Spanish, statistical jargon, legal talk, or some other language variant),
- have access to reliable and relevant information,
- be interested in health-related information,
- have the social skills to discuss health matters with others,
- have adequate hearing and/or vision to get the information,
- understand how to apply the information, and
- be willing and able to put health information to effective use.

Regarded in this way, it's clear that being health literate is no simple matter. Medical information is often baffling, even to well-educated individuals. The man who thought "positive" meant he was cancer free was attorney and former New York mayor Rudy Giuliani (Boodman, 2011). Such a misunderstanding could happen to anyone.

To the 32 million adults in the United States with serious health literacy challenges, misunderstandings can have tragic consequences (U.S. Department of Education, 2015). They are less likely than other people to get flu shots and undergo cancer screenings, and they are more likely to miss appointments, to misuse medication, to prepare improperly for procedures, to be hospitalized, and to die prematurely (Berkman et al., 2011).

Part of the problem is that health tends to have a language of its own, and health professionals may forget how foreign it is to most people. For example, "Why do hospitals have signs for the 'nephrology department' when patients with kidney disease who need that department's services are unlikely to know what the word nephrology means?" asks a representative of Harvard University's school of public health ("Improving Americans'," 2011, para. 1). (See Table 6.1 for a list of other words that can easily baffle people, and suggestions for expressing the same ideas more clearly.)

Of course, people who are not strong readers are at a distinct disadvantage. About 22%

This page from *What To Do When Your Child Gets Sick* (Mayer & Kuklierus, 1999) is an example of the easy-to-understand advice the book provides for parents about children's minor health concerns. Use of the book in diverse communities resulted in 58% fewer emergency room visits, 42% fewer doctor visits, 29% fewer school-day absences, and 42% fewer work days missed by primary caregivers (Herman & Jackson, 2010). The researchers estimate that each family in the study saved about $450 per year in health care expenses, and since more than 9,000 families were involved, the total savings were more than $5 million.

TABLE 6.1 Words That Can Baffle

Following are some of the "words to watch" in the American Medical Association's free Ask Me 3 health literacy toolkit, along with suggestions for being more easily understood.

COULD BE CONFUSING	A CLEARER ALTERNATIVE
Adverse (reaction)	Bad
Ailment	Sickness, illness, problem with your health
Benign	Will not cause harm; is not cancer
Cognitive	Learning; thinking
Excessive	Too much
Intake	What you eat or drink; what goes into your body
Lesion	Wound; sore; infected patch of skin
Noncancerous	Not cancer
Oral	By mouth
Progressive	Gets worse
Referral	Ask you to see another doctor; get a second opinion

For more, visit the National Patient Safety Foundation website at www.npsf.org.

of adults in the United States read below a fifth-grade level ("National Assessment of Adult Literacy," 2014). However, most health information is written at a much higher level (Ryan et al., 2014). That includes instructions on prescription bottles and medical consent forms.

In the United States, literacy is a special challenge for people who do not speak English well. Researchers in California found that residents with limited English were more than three times more likely than others to have health literacy challenges and poor health status as a result (Sentell & Braun, 2012). (We talk more about language barriers later in the chapter.)

Emotions play a role as well. People who are otherwise highly literate may feel so overwhelmed by medical information that they cannot pay close attention to it. For example, imagine that a health professional is teaching you to provide care at home for a loved one with a ventricular assist device, which involves a wire extending from inside your loved one's chest to a bank of complicated electronics, says patient advocate Diana Dilger (2013):

> *You're in charge of making sure the wire stays clean. It if doesn't, it could mean infection and possible death. . . . You might pay an obscene amount of attention every time she shows you how to do it. But maybe the enormity of this responsibility blocks you from really remembering every step.* (para. 2 and 4)

Dilger recommends that health professionals acknowledge the emotional intensity of encounters such as these, provide written or online instructions, and schedule follow-up conversations to make sure people have a chance to ask questions when they are thinking more clearly.

HEALTH AND COMMUNICATION TECHNOLOGY

Medical consent forms can be confusing, but online computer modules and videos can help people with literacy challenges better understand the risks and benefits of treatment options. Because these formats present information both visually and verbally, they help overcome many communication barriers (Bickmore et al., 2010; Shue, O'Hara, Marini, McKenzie, & Schreiner, 2010).

Literacy challenges may be masked by embarrassment. People are often too ashamed to admit they cannot read or understand medical information (Mackert, Donovan, Mabry, Guadagno, & Stout, 2014). Even friends and family members may not realize it. At a briefing to launch the American Medical Association's (AMA) new health literacy initiative, physician David W. Baker said:

> *We find that a lot of people have gone through their lives and listen to the radio, watch television and don't read their newspapers too often but can get by pretty well with minimal reading skills. . . . They come into the health care setting and they are all of a sudden faced with medications and instructions and all of this information written at too high a level for easy comprehension.* (AMA, 2003, para. 7)

People in this situation may be mortified to admit that they do not understand. As a result, they are more likely than others to avoid medical care, to take medicine incorrectly, to overlook health risk factors, and to miss out on important information. Avoidable health care costs attributed to health literacy are estimated at $106 billion to $238 billion a year in the United States—enough money to insure more than 40 million people (Vernon, Trujillo, Rosenbaum, & DeBuono, 2007).

Communication Skill Builder: Surmounting Status and Literacy Barriers

The unfortunate result of status- and literacy-related communication barriers is that the neediest people often receive the least amount of information and attention. In an effort to overcome that, experts offer the following tips for public health professionals, caregivers, and patients.

SUGGESTIONS FOR PUBLIC HEALTH CARE PROFESSIONALS

1. *Watch your language.* Words such as *pandemic*, *influenza*, and *prevalence* can frighten and confuse rather than inform. Use everyday language instead (CDC, 2014b).

2. *Use multiple formats.* A combination of words, diagrams, and videos helps to appeal to people with diverse learning styles and literacy resources.
3. *Evaluate messages for effectiveness and cultural appropriateness.* Audience reaction is the ultimate gauge of how effective messages are. Pilot health messages with target audience members before disseminating them, and then assess their impact afterwards.
4. *Focus on action.* Specific suggestions for health behavior can be more valuable than lengthy explanations.

SUGGESTIONS FOR HEALTH CARE PROVIDERS

1. *Create shame-free environments.* Make it easy for patients who do not understand information to get assistance without embarrassment. For example, routinely offer to help patients fill out intake paperwork rather than simply handing it to them. A statement such as, "These forms can be confusing. The nurse will help you, if you like," signals that it is okay and normal to need assistance.
2. *Gauge literacy levels.* Although it is difficult for most people to admit literacy challenges aloud, about 90% of patients say it would be helpful if their doctors understood their limitations (Wolf et al., 2007). Most are in favor of simple questionnaires that allow them to disclose reading and math challenges in a face-saving way (Ferguson, Lowman, & DeWalt, 2011; Vangeest, Welch, & Weiner, 2010).
3. *Be attentive and respectful.* Try to identify patients' needs and respect their contributions. Do not assume they are uninterested if they are quiet.
4. *Let patients know what is expected.* Patients may be tongue tied by intimidation or simply be unaware of what is expected of them. Explain routines and encourage them to participate in discussions.
5. *Use metaphors and pictures to help explain complex ideas.* Remember that words and concepts you consider familiar may be baffling to nonprofessionals. Comparing pneumonia to a saturated sponge or arthritis to creaky hinges can help bridge the gap between health information and concepts that people already understand.
6. *Use the teach-back method to make sure patients understand.* Physician Howard J. Zeitz describes his approach: "The way I do it is to ask, 'When you get home tonight, your husband or wife will probably want to know what happened. What are you going to tell him or her about what you and I agreed to in the office today?'" (quoted by O'Reilly, 2012, section 3). Unless patients can explain aloud what you have told them, you cannot be sure they understand. (Asking "Do you understand?" or "Do you have any questions?" is notoriously ineffective. Most people will simply say "yes" and "no" to avoid sounding foolish.)

SUGGESTIONS FOR PATIENTS

1. *Be explicit about your feelings.* Do not assume that health professionals understand your concerns. Statements such as, "I'm embarrassed to say this but . . ." or "I feel scared about . . ." will help them know how you feel.
2. *Ask three key questions.* The American Medical Association and cosponsors of the Ask Me 3 program encourage patients to ask the following questions: *What is my main problem? What do I need to do?* and *Why is it important for me to do this?* (Ask Me 3, n.d.).
3. *Admit it if you don't understand.* "You are not alone if you find things confusing at times," says a spokesperson for Ask Me 3. You might say, "This is new to me. Will you please explain that one more time?" (Ask Me 3, n.d.).

WHAT DO YOU THINK?

Experts point out that we all have health literacy challenges to some extent.

- Can you think of a time when you didn't understand health-related information? If so, what did you do?
- What factors might affect your ability to understand complex medical information in the future?

Gender Identities

In the article "Do Ask, Do Tell," physician Jennifer E. Potter (2002) asserts that individuals who do not identify as heterosexual often receive substandard care because doctors are not aware of, or misunderstand, their sexual identity and behaviors. Potter recalls her own experience as a teenager when, after she told her family physician that she was attracted to girls, he laughed it off as a "phase a lot of girls go through" (p. 341). Even later, as a student at Harvard Medical School, Potter says she was encouraged to keep her lesbianism secret.

Fear of social rejection can rob people of needed comfort, acceptance, and information when it comes to health. In this section, we examine a diverse array of gender identities and the implications for health communication. The acronym **LGBTQQIAAP** represents some of these identities. (See Box 6.1 for an explanation of what each letter represents.) The length of the acronym is evidence of the immense diversity of gender identities. However, it is only a partial list, and many people identify with more than one identity, highlighting the reality that gender is an evolving and fluid construct. (Some of the following passages use the more common acronym LGBTQ, simply as an abbreviation.)

The fluidity of gender is well captured by **queer theory**, which challenges the notion of static identities and rigid social categories (Butler, 1999). The queer theory perspective holds that labels such as *man* and *woman* underrepresent the multitude and complexity of gender identities that people actually experience.

Former Olympic athlete Bruce Jenner made news in 2015 when he transitioned to a female identity as Caitlyn (Derschowitz, 2015). Members of so-called gender minorities often face a dilemma: It may feel disingenuous to remain quiet about the identity they want for themselves, but socially risky to divulge it.

BOX 6.1

Nuanced Gender Identities

Following are a few of the gender identities people may use to describe themselves, as represented in the acronym LGBTQQIAAP.

Lesbian typically describes women who are sexually attracted to women.

Gay can be used to describe people who are attracted to members of their same sex.

Bisexual individuals are attracted to people of both sexes.

Transgender individuals do not feel that their biological sex is a good description of who they are. For example, people who were born with male physical characteristics may identify more with a feminine identity, and vice versa.

Queer is purposefully ambiguous. People typically describe themselves as queer if they do not feel that other gender adjectives describe them well or if they dislike the idea of gender categorizations in general.

Questioning illustrates that gender is not always a fixed or static construct.

Intersex individuals have some combination of both male and female genitalia, either externally or internally (testes and ovaries).

Asexual individuals are not interested in sex.

Allies are people who are heterosexual but support the idea of nuanced gender identities.

Pansexual individuals are attracted to people based on qualities that are not gender specific.

As a participant in one study quipped, labels are "for pickle jars, not people" (Adams, Braun, & McCreanor, 2014, p. 461).

ASSUMPTIONS

One challenge in health care is that institutional notions of gender are still largely heteronormative. For example, Elizabeth Goins and Danee Pye (2013) point out the quandary that begins with intake paperwork at a doctor's office. How should a lesbian woman answer the question "Have you ever had sexual intercourse?" If she says yes, her doctor may assume that she has sex with men, thus she should consider contraceptives and so on. If she says no, the doctor may assume she is not sexually active, thus not at risk for sexually transmitted diseases and other concerns (Goins & Pyee).

Jennifer Potter, whose story begins this section, describes how a psychiatrist tried to "cure" her of homosexuality and how doctors urged her to use birth control, never considering that she might be sexually active with women rather than men. Although Potter regarded the prescription for the pill "absurd," previous experience had taught her to maintain the charade of accepting it rather than being honest and possibly inciting her doctor's disapproval (Potter, 2002). Research tells of many patients who regularly face the same dilemma.

Transgender and intersex individuals face similar challenges. It may be inaccurate or problematic for them to declare only one biological sex, yet written forms seldom acknowledge options other than male *or* female (Redfern & Sinclair, 2014). The implication is that anything else is invalid or abnormal. Negative reactions by health professionals can be especially hurtful for members of so-called gender minorities, for one, because they may have specialized health needs, and for another, because they frequently face the pain of social censure and rejection.

Lane Dziengel describes himself as "transcending gender." He was considered a female at birth, but all his life he has identified mostly as a male, and people have typically assumed he is male based on his appearance and behavior. Dziengel, who is now a social worker, describes the response of many medical personnel when, as an adult, he wished to have a double mastectomy:

> *When I called surgical clinics, I was often met with terse or dismissive responses to questions, skepticism, and insistence that insurance would not pay for the surgery. Frontline staff would not schedule an appointment once they heard I did not have a cancer diagnosis. The range of questions, tone of voice, and adamant opinion that surgery could not happen was discouraging and disempowering.* (*Dziengel, 2014, p. 108*)

Dziengel eventually had the surgery with the support of a physician sympathetic to his wishes. Close friends and his romantic partner provided encouragement. However, Dziengel reflects that many people in his position are not so lucky. They may not have supportive health providers or loved ones, and they may not understand the health care system as well as he does.

RISKS OF SILENCE

Members of gender minorities often say that they feel vulnerable about disclosing their identity in the margins (literally) of health history questionnaires or during medical visits when they don't know how people will react (Redfern & Sinclair, 2014). On the other hand, they have numerous reasons for wanting people to know.

For one, staying quiet may rob people of valuable health information and guidance. When researchers surveyed African American men who have sex with men, they found that those who communicated openly with their caregivers were more likely than others to be aware of their hepatitis risk and to be vaccinated for it. However, their numbers were small. Only 34% of the men in the study had been vaccinated (Rhodes, Yee, & Hergenrather, 2003).

Although the Internet may be one way for LGBTQ individuals to find information they are not comfortable asking about in person, accurate online sources are still fairly scarce (Rose & Friedman, 2013). A study of websites about lesbian sexual health revealed that they were often difficult for the average person to understand and they focused mostly on HIV and AIDS and very little on family planning or preventive measures such as mammograms and gynecological care (Lindley, Friedman, & Struble, 2012).

Another risk of staying quiet is that it deprives people of opportunities to feel valued for who they are. Potter (2002) says she has sometimes passed as heterosexual. "On the face of it, maintaining silence makes almost everyone happy," she reflects—everyone, that is, except herself and her closest friends (p. 342). In periods in which she allowed people to believe she was heterosexual, Potter says she felt she was lying by omission. Pretending to be straight eroded her self-respect and put her in cahoots with people who wished to ignore and invalidate multiple gender identities. It also isolated her socially. She could not introduce her long-term partner to friends or invite her to professional and social gatherings. Now, although Potter is open with her close friends and associates, some people still presume she is heterosexual. "Coming out is a process that never ends," she says. "Every time I meet someone new I must decide if, how, and when I will reveal my sexual orientation" (p. 342).

A third danger is that, if partners are not acknowledged or if they are not married, they may be denied visiting privileges and information when one of them is sick or injured. This point hit home with internist Suzanne Koven when she had shoulder surgery. "My husband of 30 years did all the things a loving spouse would be expected to do: He fluffed my pillows and put toothpaste on my toothbrush (try doing that with one arm!) and overlooked my crankiness," she remembers. It saddens her, she says, to think of "lesbian and gay couples who are as deeply committed as my husband and I are" but who are not allowed the same opportunity to support their loved ones during health crises (Koven, 2012, para. 1–3).

In summary, like everyone else, LGBTQQIAAP individuals are adversely affected when they feel they cannot be open with their caregivers. For their part, caregivers who avoid talking about sexuality are not necessarily prejudiced. They may be embarrassed or uncomfortable with the subject or feel that it lies outside their expertise, especially because their training probably did not address issues of diverse gender identity (Levine, 2013). Following are some suggestions to make the subject easier to talk about.

COMMUNICATION SKILL BUILDER: TALKING ABOUT GENDER

Experts offer the following suggestions for health professionals.

1. *Practice aloud.* People who rehearse conversations about sex and gender with friends and colleagues may feel more comfortable conversing about these topics with patients. Caregivers who are comfortable with the topic are more likely to help patients feel at ease as well (Gamlin, 1999).
2. *Change your paperwork.* Include an option for patients to indicate sexual identity on health profile questionnaires, if they wish, and to indicate if they have sex with men, women, or both (Goins & Pye, 2013). (It is probably most useful to let people describe themselves rather than providing a fixed number of gender identities.)
3. *Do not ignore the issue.* Research suggests that most LGBTQ individuals would like health professionals to know about their sexual identity, but they tend to wait (often in vain) for them to ask about it directly.
4. *Avoid judgment.* Even subtle signs of disapproval can discourage patients from sharing information and concerns that are integral to their care (Redfern & Sinclair, 2014).

As you will see in the next sections, a similar fear of discrimination influences people of different races.

Race and Ethnicity

Racism can make you sick. That is the conclusion of studies linking race to well-being, medical care, and life expectancy. As this section shows, people of nondominant races and ethnicities are often at a disadvantage where health and longevity are concerned. We will look at those patterns and then consider how racism has influenced health professionals.

Racism is discrimination based on a person's race. Race is an imprecise term, loosely defined in terms of social identity and hereditary background. Practically speaking, people often judge race by visible characteristics, such as skin color, although appearance is not a reliable indication of race.

IN YOUR EXPERIENCE

Have you ever felt unfairly discriminated against because of your sex, sexual orientation, appearance, race, gender, ability, or ethnicity in a health care setting or other situation? If so, how?

In the United States, race is associated with life expectancy. The average life span of an African American male is 72.3 years, which is more than 4 years shorter than the overall male average in the United States (CDC, 2014a). Likewise, African American women live an average of 78 years, which is nearly 3 years shorter than the American average for women. The good news is that the disparity has shrunk in recent years. The bad news is that, overall, members of racial and ethnic minorities in the United States still have poorer health than other groups, regardless of gains in terms of education, income, and other factors (McKnight, 2004).

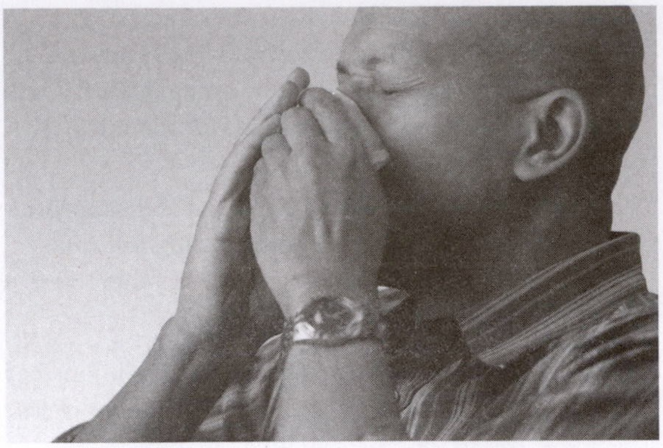

Recent research shows that, when their doctors recommend a flu shot, only about 62% of Black Americans follow through, compared to 93% of White Americans and 84% of Asian Americans. The difference seems to rely on trust and communication. Patients in the study who trusted their doctors were far more likely than others to follow their advice ("A Doctor's Advice," 2015).

Research shows that the link between health and race is social rather than biological. In other words, people of minority status do not suffer ill health because of the genes they are born with but because of what occurs during their lifetimes (Bhopal, 1998).

DIFFERENT CARE AND OUTCOMES

Race and ethnicity are linked to health. Hispanic Americans are twice as likely as others to die from diabetes, and African Americans are significantly more likely than others to die from cancer, heart disease, and AIDS (Smedley, Stith, & Nelson, 2003). Part of the reason is that they receive different care. For example, Black Americans are less likely than White Americans to receive advanced cardiac therapy while they recover from heart attacks (Peterson et al., 2008). Similarly, in an extensive study of more than 20,000 people with cancer in the head or neck, Molina and colleagues (2008) found that White patients lived an average of 40 months, compared to 21 months for Black patients. The difference was significant even when researchers controlled for age, income, and other health concerns.

EXPLANATIONS

There are several reasons why people of different races may receive different medical care and respond to it differently. Overall, the differences seem rooted in distrust, high risk, lack of knowledge, limited access, and ineffective patient–caregiver communication.

Distrust

Some people steer clear of health care because they distrust the medical establishment based on historic patterns of discrimination such as the Tuskegee Syphilis Study described in Chapter 4 (Meredith, Eisenman, Rhodes, Ryan, & Long, 2007). In the United States, members of racial and ethnic minorities are more likely than others to feel that their doctors fail to listen, to show respect, and to explain things clearly (Commonwealth Fund, 2008a). About 14% of Asian Americans, 12% of Hispanic Americans, and 11% of African Americans feel this way—compared to 9% of non-Hispanic White Americans.

Distrust may cause people to underutilize health services and to doubt the validity of medical advice (Armstrong et al., 2013). This could contribute to the comparatively low number of medical interventions among African Americans and Hispanics. They may be approved for prescriptions they never fill and may decline to undergo medical procedures if they distrust health professionals. Or they may avoid seeking care at all.

High Risk, Low Knowledge

Members of some minority groups are not well informed about health issues even though they are at high risk for them. One risk factor is the daily stress of social discrimination. Medical research shows higher than average incidence of hypertension and heart disease among people are subjected to everyday discrimination, such as poor service, insults, and being treated as inferior or stupid (Szanton et al, 2012).

Minorities may also be at high risk because a disproportionate number of them are of low socioeconomic status. With limited resources, they may suffer from poor living conditions, stress, unhealthy diets, and insufficient access to health information and health services (Dinwiddie, Zambrana, & Garza, 2014).

Despite their high-risk status, members of minority races may be relatively unaware of health issues because, on average, they do not use or trust mainstream media as much as White audiences and because many health messages are not designed to appeal to minority audiences. In the United States, Black men are twice as likely to die of prostate cancer as White men are, but Black men are significantly less knowledgeable about the warning signs (Weinrich et al., 2007).

Individuals who are not well informed about health services and disease warning signs are more likely than others to become seriously ill before they seek medical attention (Ginossar, 2014). If people are sicker than others when they seek medical care, that might explain, in part, why they do not respond to treatment as well and why they do not undergo the same procedures as other patients.

Limited Access

A third explanation is that members of minority groups have comparatively low access to advanced medical facilities. In the United States, people without health insurance are about half as likely as others to be screened for cancer (Collins, Rasmussen, Doty, & Beutel, 2015a). They are also less likely to qualify for care in medical centers that offer high-tech and advanced-care treatment (Govindarajan & Schull, 2003), and they are more likely to go without needed care and to be financially devastated by medical bills (Chung, 2008).

There is some room for optimism. As you may remember from Chapter 2, the percentage of Americans with health insurance has gone up among all races since passage of the Affordable Care Act (Collins et al., 2015a, 2015b). There is still a race and ethnicity gap. About 1 in 5 Black Americans and 1 in 3 Latino Americans are still uninsured (compared to 1 in 10 non-Hispanic White Americans), and some people with insurance are hampered by high deductibles and copays. However, the numbers are rising.

Patient–Caregiver Communication

Access to health care is an important step. But what happens during care matters as well. Members of racial and ethnic minorities sometimes perceive that medical personnel are reluctant to implement costly procedures they might use to treat other patients. An African American participant in Meredith Grady and Tim Edgar's (2003) study remembers being diagnosed with diabetes and the diagnosing physician's reaction:

> *He said, "I need to write this prescription for these pills, but you'll never take them and you'll come back and tell me you're still eating pig's feet and everything. . . . Then why do I still need to write this prescription?" And I'm like, "I don't eat pig's feet."* (p. 393)

The patient was left to wonder how the doctor's prejudicial assumptions affected other decisions as well.

The idea that stereotypes affect physicians' judgment is supported by research. Some 55% of doctors surveyed say they believe White patients receive better care than minority patients, and nearly 2 out of 3 have personally witnessed such episodes (American Medical Association, 2005). When Clara Manfredi and colleagues (2010) studied nearly 500 American cancer patients, they found that, all else being equal, the Black patients were less often referred to cancer specialists than the White patients were (Manfredi, Kaiser, Matthews, & Johnson, 2010).

It's a familiar theme. A decade earlier, Schulman and colleagues (1999) videotaped actor/patients describing chest pains using the same words and gestures, wearing identical clothing (hospital gowns), in the same setting. The patients differed only in terms of age, sex, and race. Doctors who viewed the patients' videotaped presentations of symptoms were significantly more likely to recommend heart catheterization for White male patients than for female or Black patients. (See Box 6.2 for a discussion of ethical principles when allocating health resources.)

In the context of overcoming health disparities, it is notable that the racial and ethnic diversity of America is underrepresented in the health professions. Although African Americans and Hispanic Americans together make up about 30% of the U.S. population, only 16% of the country's dentists, 14% of pharmacists, 12% of physicians, and 18.5% of registered nurses are from these groups (U.S. Census Bureau, 2014; U.S. Bureau of Labor Statistics, 2014a).

Although patients and health professionals can establish trust even if they come from different backgrounds, rapport often seems easiest when people have a good deal in common. In a study of pediatricians and parents, when parents and doctors were of the same race, they shared more laughter during the exam. When they were of the same gender, the parents asked more biomedical questions than other patients. And when doctors and parents were both highly educated, they shared more laughter, more expressions of concern, more self-disclosure, and more biomedical information (Brown, Ueno, Smith, Austin, & Bickman, 2007). The researchers speculate that similarities increased the participants' sense of comfort and affinity.

Other evidence suggests that care providers from underserved groups are more willing than their peers

BOX 6.2 ETHICAL CONSIDERATIONS

Who Gets What Care?

Doctor, do everything you can!

Is it ever justified for a doctor to do less than everything possible? Conventional American wisdom says no. Americans have come to expect that professionals will provide the best possible care, cost notwithstanding. However, it has become too expensive to do everything possible for every person.

One of the highest-profile cases was that of 7-year-old Coby Howard in 1987, whose life depended on a $100,000 bone marrow transplant. Oregon officials had previously decided to remove organ transplants from the list of procedures covered by Medicaid, meaning the family would have to come up with the money themselves. They were able to collect $700,000 in donations, but not soon enough. Coby died without having received a transplant. Floyd McCay, a spokesperson for the Oregon governor's office at the time, said:

> *We are rationing health care on the basis of price. The state shouldn't have to pay for these things to begin with. But as long as they are forced to make decisions, you will have children with names and faces that will die or have severe difficulties. (quoted by Egan, 1988, para. 10)*

An Oregon physician explained that, for the price of one organ transplant, the state could fund prenatal care for about 25 pregnant women, an investment with broader implications and the potential to avoid expensive care for premature and unhealthy newborns.

Many people feel that if the U.S. health system is to survive, it is necessary to make judgments about who gets what care. Health care leaders are being called on to eliminate excessive and unnecessary procedures. The question is: *Where is the line between necessary and unnecessary?*

One option is to provide care to those people who can afford it. This option places underprivileged persons at a disadvantage and may create a deeper schism between people of high and low socioeconomic status. All in all, few people are willing to allow low-income citizens to suffer in ill health.

Another option is to give priority to procedures that are known to have high success rates. For instance, a procedure that gives patients a 30% chance of survival may be granted priority over one with a 20% survival rate. This seems logical, but it's difficult to allow patients to go untreated when there is even a 1 in 5 chance of saving their lives. As Norman Levinsky (1995) points out, statistics are merely generalizations, and every patient is unique. There is no guarantee that a risky procedure will fail or that a tried-and-true one will succeed. Moreover, statistics vary, and sticking with well-established procedures diminishes the chances of developing new, better ones.

Still another option is to provide care for people who are likely to enjoy the highest quality of life as a result. From that perspective, it might be more important to fund expensive treatment to help a young child walk than to help an 85-year-old use his legs again following a stroke. Levinsky (1995) warns that such judgment calls are likely to lead to unfair discrimination. He wonders how it is possible to judge people's quality of life, and warns that such judgments are likely to be biased against people who hold values different from those of the medical decision maker.

As you can see, deciding how health resources will be allocated is no simple matter. To get an idea of how difficult it is, try answering the following questions.

What Do You Think?

1. If one person can afford expensive treatment but another cannot, is it okay to refuse care to the less affluent person?
2. If there is a slight chance that an expensive experimental drug will prolong a dying person's life, should the insurance company or health organization pay for use of the drug?
3. If two patients suffer from the same condition, should they be treated differently? What if one is a child and one is very old? What if one is famous and the other is unknown? What if one is homeless and the other is a community leader?

continued

4. If you could fund only two of the following procedures, which would you choose? On what criteria would you base your choices?
   a. Surgery to help an infertile couple conceive a child
   b. Plastic surgery to improve the appearance of a person born with a facial deformity
   c. Chemotherapy for a very sick person
   d. Drug therapy that might prevent a person from getting AIDS
5. Who should decide which care will be funded? Doctors? Funding agencies? Community members? Patients? Legislators?
6. If research is able to develop improved treatment options but the cost of the research significantly raises health care costs, should the system continue to fund research? What if higher costs mean some people will lose their insurance?
7. Doctors say one reason they overtreat patients is because they may be sued for malpractice if they don't do everything possible. How would you resolve this dilemma?

to provide care for underprivileged patients. About 49% of minority medical students say they will provide care for the underserved, compared to 19% of White students, and 16% of students from non-White minority groups who are already well represented in medicine (mostly Asian Americans and Americans with ancestry from India, Pakistan, and the Pacific Islands) (Saha, Guiton, Wimmers, & Wilkerson, 2008). Contact with diverse classmates seems to help others become more sensitive to cultural differences as well. Medical students whose classmates are highly diverse are 33% more likely than others to feel confident in their ability to care for minority patients and 44% more likely to advocate equitable care for everyone (Saha et al., 2008).

Based on evidence such as this, some people feel that recruiting more minority health professionals should be a priority. See Box 6.3 for a discussion of

BOX 6.3 ETHICAL CONSIDERATIONS

Is Affirmative Action Justified or Not?

Everyone wants the best doctor possible. The question is whether race and ethnicity have a place in that equation. Based on civil rights legislation passed in the 1960s, state **affirmative action** laws require publicly funded universities to give preference to minority applicants who meet admission requirements.

Affirmative action is meant to offset historic patterns of discrimination that have limited opportunities for women and minorities and have resulted in them being significantly underrepresented in professional positions.

Affirmative action does not require acceptance of unqualified persons, nor does it set quotas requiring a certain number or percentage of minority members. Institutions are under no obligation to accept individuals who do not meet qualifications. However, if minority applicants meet the established criteria for admittance, they may be chosen even if nonminority applicants also meet or exceed the criteria.

Controversy sometimes arises when nonminority applicants who meet (or exceed) the minimum requirements for medical school admission are passed over in favor of minority candidates. Opponents of

continued

continued

affirmative action argue that prospective doctors should be chosen only on the basis of their academic qualifications. On the other hand, people who favor affirmative action argue that the public is poorly served by physicians who do not reflect the diversity of the overall population.

What Do You Think?

1. Do you feel medical schools should consider sex, race, and ethnicity when reviewing applicants? Why or why not?
2. How do you respond to the argument that affirmative action sometimes allows people to be accepted into medical school even though others' credentials are higher?
3. How do you respond to the argument that affirmative action is needed to help the medical profession more closely reflect the concerns and backgrounds of patients?

the pros and cons of making diversity a criterion in admissions decisions.

We have spoken a good deal in this section about racial and ethnic identities. But, of course, people differ on an even deeper level as well. A new type of discrimination—based on health conditions that have not even surfaced yet—may loom ahead. See Box 6.4 for information about the pros and cons of genetic profiling.

BOX 6.4

Genetic Profiling: A View Into Your Health Future

> *"The crystal ball says you will live a long and healthy life."*

It's hard to put much stock in such a prediction. But scientists have come up with something better. They did it by unlocking the codes that make up individuals' genetic blueprints ("Human Genome," 2008).

These days you might have genetic testing done to find out if you are predisposed to various forms of cancer, liver disease, Alzheimer's disease, or other conditions known to have a genetic link. Being predisposed to these diseases doesn't mean you'll necessarily get them. In fact, one promise of genetic testing is that you might find out in time to lower your odds. For example, you might engage in more preventive behaviors if you know you are at high risk. Your doctor might start screening you for the identified conditions earlier than usual and, in some cases, begin preventive therapies. Focusing on genes might also help medical scientists design new ways of treating and preventing diseases.

One reservation concerning genetic testing is people's fear that the results will be used against them or their family members. The Genetic Information Nondiscrimination Act of 2008 (better known as GINA) stipulates that health insurance companies cannot refuse health coverage on the basis of genetic test results, nor can they require people to undergo genetic testing. By extension, GINA rules out informal genetic profiling, such as basing a person's insurance rates on a family history of heart disease. In the past, health insurance companies could figure family history into the price of your coverage. GINA now forbids that practice.

GINA also stipulates that employers cannot judge job applicants or current employees on the basis of genetic profiles. That is, they cannot hire, fire, promote, or refuse to promote anyone because of genetic

continued

propensities. Nor can employers require, request, or purchase genetic test results on any employee. (This does not apply to tests designed to monitor the effects of workplace exposure to dangerous materials. Those are still allowed.)

It is important to note what GINA does not cover, however. The stipulations don't apply to life insurance, long-term care insurance, or disability insurance. And GINA doesn't apply to the U.S. military, the Veterans Administration, or the Indian Health Service, because they are governed by a different set of laws.

What Do You Think?

1. If it were affordable, would you undergo genetic testing? Why or why not?
2. Are you worried that genetic test results may be used to discriminate unfairly against individuals or groups of people? Why or why not?
3. Suppose your test results show a genetic propensity for a disease that, so far, we don't know how to prevent. Would you want to know? Why or why not?
4. Do you think genetic test results would strengthen your resolve to engage in healthy behaviors?

Language Differences

Physician Harold Jenkins set a goal for himself to learn at least un poquito (a little bit) of Spanish. He began writing several new Spanish words on index cards every day and studying them. While driving to work, he challenged himself to read traffic signs and license plate numbers aloud in Spanish. "I even rolled my Rs," he recalls (Jenkins, 2008, p. 42).

Spanish-speaking nurses who work with Jenkins have encouraged him. They aren't put off that he can only speak Spanish in present tense or that his pronunciation is sometimes a bit off. (One nurse was amused when he asked a patient to "vacuum deeply" instead of inhaling.) They give Jenkins a thumbs-up for trying. His patients appreciate the effort as well. Jenkins says he feels like a better doctor when he can understand and speak at least a bit of the patients' language. He's right. It's hard to offer quality care across a language gap. And that gap is likely to grow. Between 1980 and 2010, the number of U.S. residents who speak a language other than English at home (most often Spanish) more than doubled (Ryan, 2013).

A physician at Maimonides Medical Center in New York asserts that language differences increase a patient's risk factor by about 25%. "When you walk up to a person from another country who speaks another language, that is a risk—period. It's as much of a risk factor as diabetes or anything else," says the doctor (quoted by Salamon, 2008, para. 5).

Cognizant of the risk, Maimonides Medical Center employs more than 30 patient representatives who help families and interpret when needed. The medical center's president and CEO Pamela Brier has implemented a "Code of Mutual Respect," complete with staff training sessions on communication

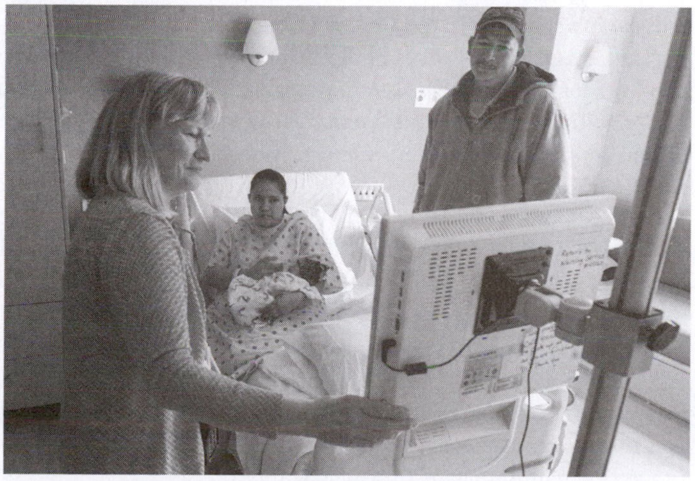

A social worker communicates with a Spanish-speaking family with the help of a remote interpreter available in the hospital via video technology.

and diversity appreciation. The extra effort is worth it, says Brier:

> *Communication problems are what cause mishaps that can harm patients. I mean communications between doctor and nurse, nurse and clerk, housekeeper to nurse or doctor, everybody. The idea of the "Code of Mutual Respect" for me was to make the place safer and medical care better. (quoted by Salamon, para. 9)*

It is her conviction that good communication is good medicine and good business.

Language barriers can be challenging for patients and caregivers for many reasons. It is difficult to make an accurate diagnosis if the caregiver cannot fully understand what the patient is experiencing. And even if the diagnosis is correct, it's hard to ensure that patients are fully informed concerning their medical options. (Box 6.5 describes the experiences of a Spanish-speaking woman in a U.S. hospital.)

For the most part, the U.S. health system has not kept pace with the rising number of Spanish-speaking residents. At one urban children's hospital, 68% of residents speak little or no Spanish, yet most say they care for patients with limited English proficiency "often" or "every day" (O'Leary, Federico, & Hampers, 2003). Most of the residents feel that Spanish-speaking families understand the diagnosis only "sometimes" or "never," and 80% of the residents say they avoid caring for these patients whenever possible.

BOX 6.5 PERSPECTIVES

Language Barriers in a Health Care Emergency

Picture yourself in Mexico at a hospital trying to get someone, anyone, to help make a terrible pain in your stomach go away. You hear: "Tú no hablas español, y nadie te puede entender." In other words, "You don't speak Spanish, and no one can understand you." Finally, you find a first-year English student, a schoolboy, who attempts to translate. Next, you find yourself in a room, half-clothed, wearing a hospital robe, wondering: Did the boy understand me? Did the doctors understand him? What is wrong with me? What is happening?

Perhaps this will give you some idea what it's like for Spanish speakers in the United States health care system. This is a true story about my mother, Maria, and her mother, Consuelo, Cuban Americans trying to deal with the frustrations, anxieties, and fears of communicating with medical professionals who speak a different language.

The Story

Consuelo had been showing symptoms for some time before finally agreeing to see a doctor. Now that she had moved to a new city with little to no Hispanic culture, she wondered fearfully if she would be able to communicate with doctors. But this time the pain was intense, and at least she had her daughter, Maria, to help her communicate. Consuelo wanted very much to be understood, and maybe this time she would be. That thought finally gave her the courage to see a doctor.

At the doctor's office Consuelo could tell something was wrong. She was now in her early sixties and knew her diabetes was not getting any better. She understood enough of the conversations between the doctors and her daughter to gather that she needed a heart catheterization. Maria was not giving her all the details, but Consuelo could sense from her body language that the procedure was serious. She was right. A few moments later she found herself being wheeled off to the operating room for an emergency catheterization—without Maria. Now she felt more scared and afraid, knowing she had no means of communicating with the people around her and unsure what they were doing or why.

Before the procedure, the surgeon needed Consuelo to understand the process and answer some questions. This was no easy task. Once again, as Consuelo had feared, she was unable to communicate. By this time, she began feeling extremely anxious and frustrated that neither the surgeon nor any of his assistants could understand what she was saying. Finally, after what seemed decades, the surgeon summoned Maria to the operating room after finding no one else who could translate.

For Maria, the experience involved mixed emotions. She had accompanied her mother many times

continued

before to the hospital but had never been allowed inside the operating room. Now that she was there, she felt more anxious than ever. First, she wanted to do a good job because she felt that her mother's life depended on it. Second, she felt uneasy being in the room because she was unfamiliar with the environment. Consequently, Maria did not know how she should act, what she should say, or what was expected of her. She also had to fight her emotional reactions at seeing her mother on the operating table. However, Maria was relieved to be able to be with her mother and decided to concentrate on positive feelings to get them both through the experience.

When Consuelo was back in a hospital room after the procedure, the doctor broke the news that Consuelo needed open-heart surgery and would soon be transferred to a larger hospital. Once again, Consuelo could tell something negative was being conveyed, but knew she would have to wait until the conversation was over to get the full story from Maria. Waiting only added to her anxiety. A few times, Consuelo tried to interrupt, but was only chastised by Maria for interfering with her efforts to understand the implications of what the doctor was trying to tell her.

Unfortunately, although the larger hospital was located within a predominantly Hispanic community, few doctors and nurses there could speak Spanish. That meant that Maria and her husband, Jesús, would have to take turns staying at the hospital to translate for Consuelo. But the difference in Consuelo's outlook was remarkable. After only a few hours in the new hospital, she started to feel better about herself and less depressed. This was because the new physicians, regardless of whether they spoke Spanish well or not, attempted to speak to her in Spanish and to understand what she was saying. Consuelo recalled one young physician who would walk into her room saying, "Buenos días," bringing a smile to her face, and then leave saying, "Buenas noches," despite the time of day, making her laugh. These small gestures made all the difference to Consuelo.

Maria noticed that her mother began to light up whenever a doctor entered the room. She also noted that the doctors were no longer looking at her but talking directly to her mother instead. Maria was still translating, but she was no longer the focus of their conversation. In return, she noticed that her mother seemed more attentive and willing to follow the doctors' advice. A few times, Consuelo even answered the physicians in English with responses such as "Yes" when she understood what they were saying. This in turn would make them laugh and rub her hand as a sign of acceptance and reward. And if this were not enough, Consuelo was introduced to a Spanish-speaking nurse at the hospital who would occasionally visit, making her feel even more at home.

The surgery went well, but following it, Consuelo was paired with a therapist who could not speak Spanish and made no effort to communicate with her. She began to feel depressed and frustrated again. But she learned to get over this new obstacle quickly after talking about her feelings with her family. They found a way to make her realize that her good experiences at the new hospital far outweighed the bad ones, and soon Consuelo was able to ignore the therapist's behavior and move on with her treatment.

Consuelo was in the hospital for about a month. In that time she learned a lot about what she liked and did not like. As a result, she asked Maria to help her look for doctors who would be as attentive with her as the hospital doctors had been. Now Consuelo has at least one doctor she likes very much who speaks Spanish.

—MARIE

What Do You Think?

1. How might you have acted if you were Consuelo? If you were Maria?
2. Do you think hospitals should do more to accommodate non-English speakers? Why or why not?
3. How could Consuelo have eliminated some of her anxiety?
4. What could the first surgeon have done to help both Maria and Consuelo feel more at ease?
5. Researchers have found that people are more fearful about medical visits if they feel socially alienated and disconnected from their environments. What might we do to ease these feelings?
6. Have you ever been in a situation in which you have had to communicate with someone who did not speak the same language as you? How did you handle the situation?

In many medical settings, family members and bilingual employees fill in as untrained interpreters. It's common for members of the housekeeping staff to serve as interpreters even if they speak English poorly themselves and have little knowledge of medical terminology. Medical interpreting is difficult. Even interpreters who are fluent in both languages may have a hard time fully conveying the speakers' tone and intent. Sometimes a direct translation is not easy or possible. For example, exclamations such as "okey dokey," "geez," and "oh boy" are used to convey more than their literal meaning. They may be meant to express sympathy, claim or relinquish a turn at talk, encourage the other person to go on, call attention to something, or so on, but their intended meaning can easily be lost in translation (Vickers & Goble, 2011).

Medical center managers may be hesitant to incur the expense of professional interpreters because guidelines for reimbursement are unclear in many states. California has led the nation in this regard. Based on the Medical Interpreter Law passed in 2009, health insurers there are now responsible for making sure that patients have adequate language assistance.

Other efforts are underway as well. Wake Forest University School of Medicine has piloted a training program to help physician assistants work effectively with interpreters and Spanish-speaking patients. After a four-hour training session, 94% to 97% of students were able to demonstrate proficiency in role-play scenarios that involved interpreters and non-English-speaking patients (Marion, Hildebrandt, Davis, Marin, & Crandall, 2008). Members of other organizations report success using trained interpreters who are either present in the exam room or linked via telephone or videoconference technology (Jones, Gill, Harrison, Meakin, & Wallace, 2003). (For more about careers related to diversity in health care, see Box 6.6.)

Disabilities

Joanne had time for a cup of coffee and a chance to read the newspaper. Friday was the day that the personal ads ran in the paper. Joanna read these ads without fail, trying to picture what kind of man would write advertisements to find dates. Although she sometimes thought about answering one of these ads, she never did. What would she say? "Woman, 28 years old, math whiz, attractive, red hair, green eyes, likes movies, jazz, loves to cook, uses a wheelchair to get around." No, she just couldn't picture it. (*Braithwaite & Japp, 2005, p. 175*)

Individuals with disabilities are often confronted with frustrating dichotomies. For one, people tend either to treat their disabilities as the most important thing about them or self-consciously to avoid the issue entirely. Health professionals have typically not received much training on how to communicate with people who have disabilities. Consequently, when treating these individuals, physicians often focus on the disability and ignore medical concerns that are not directly related to it (Braithwaite & Thompson, 2000).

On the other hand, well-meaning acquaintances may consider it taboo to talk about the disability. A woman described by Dawn Braithwaite and Lynn Harter (2000) said she initially appreciated it when her future husband did not make a big deal about her disability when they met. But after several months of

BOX 6.6 CAREER OPPORTUNITIES

Diversity Awareness

Diversity officer
Health care interpreter
Equal Employment Opportunity (EEO) officer

Career Resources and Job Listings

- American Hospital Association's Institute for Diversity in Health Management: www.diversityconnection.org
- National Council on Interpreting in Health Care: www.ncihc.org
- Registry of Interpreters for the Deaf: www.rid.org
- U.S. Equal Employment Opportunity Commission: www.eeoc.gov
- U.S. Bureau of Labor Statistics Occupational Outlook Handbook: www.bls.gov/oco

getting to know each other, she was exasperated that he never even mentioned the subject. Eventually she brought it up to end the awkward silence about it.

Another dichotomy concerns the way persons with disabilities are regarded by society. Sally Nemeth, a health communication scholar who is blind, reflects that people with disabilities are often cast "either as heroic super crips or as tragic, usually embittered and angry, unfortunates worthy only of pity and charity" (Nemeth, 2000, p. 40). The reality is that people with disabilities are much like anyone else.

It's frustrating to be treated as helpless or unsophisticated. Health professionals (and others) tend to treat individuals with disabilities as if they are childlike—speaking slowly and loudly to them even when that is not necessary and giving instructions rather than asking for their opinions. People may avoid talking to people with disabilities about sensitive subjects such as sex.

People whose disabilities are invisible to others may encounter unique difficulties. Some individuals may be loath to admit disabilities they think will make them seem dependent or pitiful (Moore & Miller, 2003). A study of people with heart disease revealed that they often consider themselves older than their same-age peers, largely because of physical limitations and attention to end-of-life issues typically associated with older people (Kundrat & Nussbaum, 2003). (For more about the frustration of invisible disabilities, see Box 6.7.)

These challenges have an effect on health communication. Individuals with disabilities are typically less satisfied with managed care providers than with doctors they choose themselves, mostly because doctors

BOX 6.7 PERSPECTIVES

My Disability Doesn't Show

Dear Editor,

Since receiving my handicapped hangtag two years ago, I have been rudely approached by so many people that I've lost count.

I am a 44-year-old female, tall, thin, and do not walk with a cane, nor am I in need of a wheelchair. My handicap is internal, from two major back surgeries, and although I do have pain while walking, I walk with confidence. By simply looking at me, one would not know that I have a handicap.

Since using my handicapped hangtag, I have been rudely approached by, not only people off campus, but from just as many students on campus. I have heard it all, from "You sure look handicapped" or "You must really be handicapped from driving a car like that (a 1992 Firebird)," to "How can I get one of those (a handicapped hangtag)?" These comments not only hurt my feelings but are truly insulting, especially since I received my back injuries from serving my country while in the military, and the scar on my back extends from my neck to my buttocks.

I would like to educate everyone on campus, as well as people off campus, that not all handicaps are visible. Not everyone with a handicap is over 60, nor do they have to walk with a cane, nor do they have to be in a wheelchair.

In order to receive a handicapped hangtag, the Department of Motor Vehicles requires that one must have limitations of walking because of arthritic, neurological or orthopedic (which I have) conditions, and one must have a disability rating of 50% or greater. My disability rating is 80% and is permanent.

The last comment came January 28th by a student getting into his blue truck, which was parked next to me in front of the campus police station. The young man made the normal comment that I did not look handicapped. Normally I usually just tell people if they have a problem with me to take my license plate number and report me, but this time, I lost it and told this guy to mind his own business, and added a few explicit words to boot.

I would like to see people stop stereotyping others based on their looks and think before they inadvertently insult someone, because it really does make me feel bad, and I have every right to use my handicapped tag.

—BEVERLY DAVIS

on a provider list may not be knowledgeable about or comfortable dealing with disabilities (Kroll, Beatty, & Bingham, 2003). And because of the need for trust and familiarity, it may be particularly stressful for persons with disabilities to change doctors (O'Connell, Bailey, & Pearce, 2003). Physicians admit that they *do* often feel uncomfortable caring for people with disabilities, particularly if they involve mental impairments (Aulagnier et al., 2005).

On the bright side, even brief training sessions tend to help caregivers interact more confidently and sensitively (Tuffrey-Wijne, Hollins, & Curfs, 2005). In a training program piloted by Ashley Duggan and colleagues (2009), medical students interacted with trained standardized-patient educators with disabilities, then took part in interactive feedback sessions about the experience. The medical students acknowledged that the patients' disabilities and appliances sometimes made them feel awkward and uncomfortable, they were unsure whether to talk about the disability or ignore it, and their advice was sometimes off the mark, as when one medical student advised a wheelchair user to ease the symptoms of her tendonitis by not using her shoulder. The student later told the mock patient, with chagrin: "Your arms are your mobility and independence, and I'm telling you to stop you using them" (Duggan, Bradshaw, Carroll, Rattigan, & Altman, 2009, p. 804).

Following are some tips from the experts.

COMMUNICATION SKILL BUILDER: INTERACTING WITH PEOPLE WHO HAVE DISABILITIES

1. Talk to people with disabilities directly, not to their interpreters or companions.
2. Remember to identify yourself to sight-impaired persons.
3. Treat adults with disabilities as adults.
4. When a person with a disability is difficult to understand, listen attentively, and then paraphrase to make sure you heard correctly.
5. Whenever possible, sit down when speaking to people in wheelchairs so that you can communicate at eye level.
6. Relax! For example, don't be embarrassed if you accidentally say "See you later" to a blind person.
7. Don't insist on helping people with disabilities. If they don't ask for help or if they decline your offer of assistance, respect their wishes (Soule & Roloff, 2000). (It's okay to extend the same common courtesies you would offer an able-bodied friend, such as holding a door open.)
8. Heed the wisdom of Thuy-Phuong Do and Patricia Geist (2000), who remind us: "Everyone is othered to some extent; we all possess disabilities, whether visible or invisible" (p. 60).

As you are probably gathering by now, the concept of being "othered," or treated as if you do not belong, is demoralizing in everyday life and particularly in medical transactions. As the following section shows, age can be a source of "othering" as well.

Age

Aging alone is rarely viewed in a positive light and thus has led many to depict aging as a time of great loss and decline. —JON NUSSBAUM (2007, P. 1)

In his presidential address to members of the International Communication Association, Nussbaum (2007) challenged scholars to reconsider social assumptions about aging. "Aging alone has also been a favorite of the great poets, playwrights, and novelists, who love to make us feel the 'horribleness' of our lonely human existence," he said (p. 1). But that idea, he argued, is more cultural myth than objective reality: "My mission is to spread the news that we are not purely or even remotely organisms that exist only within our own skins" (p. 1). Nussbaum proposed that it is possible to age happily and that the nexus of sustained quality of life is effective communication, as evidenced by people's ability to manage interpersonal conflict, develop relationships, manage uncertainty, share thoughts and ideas, and more.

In this section we examine the communication practices that affect people throughout their lives. We focus first on children and then more extensively on older adults. As you will see, both groups use health care services a great deal, and their communication is profoundly affected by the assumptions of people around them.

CHILDREN

She gots bad monsters inside her tummy that try to eat her up. —4-YEAR-OLD SOPHIA EXPLAINING HER MOTHER'S BREAST CANCER

This quote, from Jenifer Kopfman and Eileen Berlin Ray's (2005) case study "Talking to Children About Illness" (p. 113), helps to illustrate the way children make sense of illness. Although their conceptualizations may seem naive, children are often remarkably attuned to the ramifications of illness experiences. When Sophia's young friend Ethan asked her what color the monsters were, she said, "I think they're orange 'cause orange's a gross color" (p. 113). She went on to explain what happened when her mother received chemotherapy:

> *She always gives me lots of hugs and kisses before she gets her medicine from the doctor 'cause she says it makes her throw up and be tired after she takes it, and I hafta be quiet and let her sleep and not ask for too many hugs and kisses until she feels better again. (p. 113)*

After that, Ethan showed Sophia his "scary monster face" and they dashed off to play.

Communicating with children can be challenging because their perceptions are often different from those of adults. For example, children may perceive that painful medical treatments are a means of punishment (Ryan-Wenger & Gardner, 2012). Moreover, children may be unsure how to express their feelings or may be afraid to speak freely in front of people they don't know.

Bryan Whaley and Tim Edgar (2008) outline the phases of development in which children conceptualize illness with increasing degrees of sophistication. In the **prelogical conceptualization** phase (roughly ages 2–6), children define illness as something caused by a tangible, external agent, such as a monster or the sun. In the **concrete-logical conceptualization** phase (ages 7–10), children begin to differentiate between external causes, such as wind and cold, and internal manifestations, such as sneezing and talking funny. In the **formal-logical conceptualization** phase (ages 11 and older), children are remarkably adept at envisioning the complex influence of agents they cannot readily see. Whaley and Edgar share the following example of formal-logical conceptualizing from Bibace and Walsh's (1981) study, in which they asked children older than 11 to explain various illnesses:

> *Have you ever been sick? "Yes." What was wrong? "My platelet count was down." What's that? "In the bloodstream they are like white blood cells. They help kill germs." Why did you get sick? "There were more germs than platelets. They killed the platelets off."* (*Bibace & Walsh, p. 37*)

This is clearly a far more sophisticated explanation than Sophia's concept of orange monsters, which is a good reminder that children's ideas typically evolve over time.

> **PERSPECTIVES**
>
> When researchers asked 200 children being seen in an emergency department if they would prefer a male or female doctor, 78% of the boys and 80% of the girls expressed a preference for a female (Waseem & Ryan, 2005). In contrast, 60% of the parents preferred a male doctor. None of the children and only 21% of the parents said they would like "the best" physician, regardless of gender.

Parents' Role in Children's Care

Parents can be both a help and a hindrance in caring for young patients. Many times, parents have valuable information about their children's conditions and are able to comfort them as no one else could. Parents may become especially frustrated if their concerns are not taken seriously or if they do not feel well informed about their children's health needs (Haskell, Mannix, James, & Mayer, 2012). And rightly so. Parents are the children's principal caregivers, and their responsibility does not end at the doctor's office or hospital. However, it can be difficult for caregivers to attend to young children *and* manage the complex emotions of their parents. Parents tend to be especially anxious, guilty, and uncertain where their children's health is concerned.

When children are hospitalized, parents and professional caregivers may have conflicting ideas about what care each of them should provide. It may be unclear who is to feed the child, change bandages, and perform other tasks. With nurses' input, Rebecca Adams and Roxanne Parrott (1994) drafted a list of tasks parents should perform for their hospitalized children. By sharing the list with parents (orally and in writing), the nurses were able to reduce parents' uncertainty and their own. As a result, the nurses were more satisfied with their jobs, and the parents were more confident in the care their children received.

Communication Skill Builder: Talking With Children About Illness

Bryan Whaley, who has conducted extensive research about children in health situations, and colleagues offer the following advice for explaining illnesses to children.

1. *Let children set the tone.* Determine what the child wants and needs to know before launching into explanations the child may find incomprehensible, distressing, or irrelevant to his or her concerns (Nussbaum, Ragan, & Whaley, 2003; Whaley, 1999; Whaley & Edgar, 2008).
2. *Pay attention.* Notice how the child conceives of illness and medical care. Ask questions and invite the child to describe (and perhaps to draw) his or her images of medical care and illness (Whaley, 2000).
3. *Go easy on medical terminology.* Usually, children are more interested in how an illness will influence their lives and activities than in the precise germs, tests, and scientific names involved. As Whaley (1999) puts it, "Disease and etiology appear inconsequential or of negligible concern to children," at least when they are young (p. 190).
4. *Talk about illness as something normal.* Children are typically reassured to know that their illnesses are normal and manageable. Speaking of an illness as a crisis or mystery may interfere with the child's coping ability (Whaley, 1999).

Buchholz (1992) adds that children benefit from honesty. Like adults, children usually cope better if they have a realistic idea of what to expect from health care experiences. Adults should also keep in mind that prior experience with medical procedures may not diminish children's fear and anxiety (Buchholz, 1992). Experienced youngsters may be all too aware of how frightening and painful procedures can be.

OLDER ADULTS

When a physician told James McCague's 85-year-old aunt that she was not a candidate for bypass surgery because she was "quite functional" for her age, she objected. "I am the sole caretaker of my 90-year-old sister," she said. "I can't be just 'functional.' I want to be as healthy as I can be" (McCague, 2001, p. 104). Her doctor saw her point and performed the procedure.

A physician himself, McCague reflects on changes among elderly patients:

> *The elderly patient does not report symptoms with resignation; the questions ask for a solution. The elderly patient does not want his [or her] questions taken within the context of his age and, more important, is angry when the physician does so. (p. 104)*

McCague advises fellow health professionals to consider that, while it may sometimes be necessary to shape and moderate expectations, people's desire to be healthy whatever their age is real and laudable. "We must never ignore or ridicule it," he says. "And my aunt? She had her revascularization several years ago. I called her last week to say hello, but she wasn't home; she was in town getting her passport photo" (p. 104).

Experts predict that about 1 in 5 Americans will be 65 or older by the year 2050 (Ortman, Velkoff, & Hogan, 2014). Population shifts will likely change health care needs and transform our understanding of the aging process. As with all stereotypes, the belief that all members of a group are alike in some way (e.g., sad, fun, weak, jovial) never holds water. **Ageism** is discrimination based on a person's age. It occurs when people judge others by preconceived notions about their age group, as when managers refuse to hire people over 65 because they believe employees of that age are not productive.

CAN YOU GUESS?

1. Around the world, in which country do people have the longest average life expectancy?
2. In which country are people's lives the shortest?
3. How does the average life span for men and women in the United States compare?

Answers appear at the end of the chapter.

Ageism results largely from negative stereotypes of older adults. Health personnel sometimes reinforce these stereotypes by referring to older patients in such derogatory terms as "coffin dodgers" and "digging for worms" (Fowler & Nussbaum, 2008). Older adults are often portrayed in the media as unhealthy, lonely, unhappy, and irritable (Robinson, Callister, Magoffin, & Moore,

2006). Of 84 Facebook groups that talked about older adults, only one presented them in a positive light. Most described older adults as annoying, grouchy, and incompetent (Levy, Chung, Bedford, & Navrazhina, 2014).

People with ageist beliefs are unlikely to regard older adults as unique individuals who can change, learn, react, and grow physically stronger. Instead, they tend to patronize older adults by speaking very slowly to them, using baby talk, and restricting conversations to happy subjects (Hummert & Shaner, 1994). They may even avoid communicating with older adults (Giles, Ballard, & McCann, 2002).

Social beliefs about growing older often have profound implications for people's identity. When Laura Hurd Clarke and Meredith Griffin (2008) interviewed women ages 50 to 70, many of them said they actively engage in beauty work to maintain a youthful appearance because they believe that, if they do not, they will become "invisible" in society's eyes. As one woman in the study put it: "Be young or you're not counted" (p. 660). Another expounded:

> *We won't love women if they're not lovely. . . . And as you get older, you get less and less okay, and people look at you less and less. . . . It gets down to "Well, you're old. You can't look good anyway." So, I think it's about trying to look young, youthful, perky, and put on this "See I'm lovely, you can love me" kind of thing. (pp. 660–661)*

Women in the study said they feel immense pressure, both from the idea that women's worth is inherent in their appearance, and from the notion that feminine beauty is inherently youthful.

Based on the idea that getting older is a process of decline, people often assume that natural signs of aging (hearing loss, vocal changes) indicate cognitive deficits. Young adults tend to underestimate the cognitive abilities of older adults with known hearing loss, although they score them highly on wisdom and visual memory (Ryan, Anas, & Vuckovich, 2007).

Despite Western society's cynical views about aging, many older adults enjoy good health, rewarding relationships, and a positive outlook on life (Nussbaum, Ragan, & Whaley, 2003). When Laurie Schur and Lisa Thompson interviewed women 80 and older for the video documentaries *Greedy for Life* (2008) and *The Beauty of Aging* (2012), they found that some of the women were frustrated with the effects of aging, but most said they were having the time of their lives. A 97-year-old woman in the video said, "A few years ago someone asked me what time of my life did I like best and I said 'now.'" Another one said, "I see women 50 and 60 decide to give up on life and go sit down somewhere, don't look forward to a future. Even at 82 years old I've still got things that I want to do."

Helen Mirren is challenging the notion that women can only be sexy if they are young. When she was in her 60s Mirren starred as a sexy action hero in *Red* and *Red 2*, and she continues to play femme fatales in her 70s. Some people predict that she and other baby boomers will transform society's view of aging.

The baby boomers may change popular notions about aging. Actress Helen Mirren, for one, is defying the adage that women above a certain age cannot be sexy or adventurous. Now in her seventies, Mirren continues to play action roles and allow herself to be depicted in the nude or partially clothed. What's more, she insists that the images be portrayed realistically, not computer enhanced to make her appear younger than she is (Overton, du Pré, & Pecchioni, 2015).

WHAT DO YOU THINK?

- Do you think people typically become less attractive as they age? Why or why not?
- What are the implications for older adults' social status and their appeal as relationship partners and community members?

Communication Accommodation Theory

Despite changing trends, reconciling Western society's negative view of aging with new ideas about getting older is still a challenging enterprise with numerous implications for health communication. When people believe, rightly or wrongly, that older adults have diminished capacities, they tend to change their behavior toward them. For instance, people may speak more loudly to accommodate a hearing loss or move closer to accommodate an older adult's shortsightedness. To **accommodate** is to adapt to another person's style or needs.

In some cases, accommodation is useful and appreciated. According to **communication accommodation theory**, people tend to mirror each other's communication styles to display liking and respect (Coupland, Coupland, & Giles, 1991). **Convergence** occurs when partners use similar gestures, tone of voice, vocabulary, and so on. On the other hand, **divergence** involves acting differently from the other person, as in whispering when the other shouts. Divergence implies that the partners are socially distant. They may be asserting uniqueness, pursuing different goals, or displaying that they don't understand or don't like each other.

To illustrate, patients who are baffled by their doctors' rapid explanations may converge by speaking rapidly themselves or by being silent to accommodate the physicians' speech. However, patients may diverge by paraphrasing the explanations more slowly to make sure they understand them. Socially speaking, divergence is risky, in that it shows the participants to be somewhat out of sync. Extreme divergence may seem disrespectful or rude.

People often mirror the behaviors of their conversational partners without really thinking about it, especially if they like each other. Accommodation can spiral, however, so that feedback encourages people to escalate their behaviors toward each other. For instance, when a dear friend speaks loudly and slowly to an older adult, the older person may respond in a similar way, which may reinforce the friend's belief that he or she is a bit slow and hard of hearing. In turn, the friend may accommodate even more, and so on. Thus, what was intended to be accommodation has become **overaccommodation**, an exaggerated response to a perceived need.

Especially if the overaccommodation is pervasive (everybody seems to do it), older individuals may begin to believe that they are indeed of diminished capacity, and they may behave in line with that expectation (Ryan & Butler, 1996). In short, they start to "do" being old, as society has defined it.

Older adults usually have no control over the cues that suggest to others that they are aging. An older-sounding voice is one example. In one study, people whose voices sounded old were perceived by others to be older than their contemporaries and even perceived *themselves* to be older (Mulac & Giles, 1996). An "old" voice is quivery and breathy, with prolonged vowel sounds and extended pauses between words. These characteristics are certainly not signs that the speaker is less intelligent or is physically impaired in any significant way, but they may be enough to spur accommodation and overaccommodation.

Ironically, a great number of accommodating behaviors are unnecessary. Contrary to the assumption that older people are worse communicators than others, they are sometimes better. Mark Bergstrom and Jon Nussbaum (1996) found that respondents over age 50 handled conflict more cooperatively and productively than young adults, who were more apt to be confrontational and judgmental. There is also evidence that older adults compensate for deficiencies in some areas by becoming stronger in others. For example, many become especially good at reading nonverbal cues if their hearing diminishes (Fowler & Nussbaum, 2008).

Older adults are not as helpless as many people think. "What's important to remember about people over age 65 is that while many begin to experience some physical limitations, they learn to live with them and lead happy and productive lives," says a spokesperson for the American Psychological Association ("Older Adults' Health," n.d., p. 1). According to the most recent U.S. census, today's older adults are better educated, healthier, and more affluent than any generation before them. They are also socially engaged. Indeed, they are more likely to vote than younger people are. And only 4.5% of people ages 75 to 84 live in nursing homes. The reality is that accommodating behaviors are usually unnecessary (U.S. Census Bureau, 2011).

TRY IT OUT

- To test the effects of communication accommodation, try altering your speech and observing how a conversational partner reacts. Does he or she converge (e.g., whisper if you whisper) or diverge?
- How would you react if everyone started speaking unusually slowly or loudly to you?
- Start to notice how you communicate with older adults. Do you behave differently than you would with other people. If so, how?

Implications of Ageism and Overaccommodation

Ageism and overaccommodation present several implications for health communication. For one, older adults are usually treated by caregivers who are significantly younger than they are. If they are unfamiliar with the diversity of the older generation, young people tend to rely on stereotypes. They may lump older adults into simplistic categories, such as frail, mild-mannered grandparents, or worse, cantankerous grumps.

Second, people may not try very hard to maintain or restore older people's health. Research indicates that people expect older adults to be ill and confused. As a result, they tend to shrug off older adults' illnesses and emotional distress as unavoidable and untreatable. In short, if they do not believe older people can change, people don't try very hard to help them.

Third, studies support that treating people as if they are helpless encourages them to believe it. Margaret Baltes and Hans-Werner Wahl (1996) found that, in one nursing home, caregivers encouraged older adults to be dependent by being attentive and supportive when the residents needed help but discouraging or ignoring them when they seemed independent. By contrast, researchers in another nursing home coached residents to take an active role in their health and encouraged the staff to support those efforts. The older adults in that setting experienced significantly higher levels of self-efficacy and perceived health benefits (Yeon-Hwan & HeeKyung, 2014).

Fourth, caregivers tend to underestimate older adults' desire for information. Caregivers may assume they are not interested in medical details, are incapable of understanding them, or will be unduly frightened by risk factors. However, research suggests that most older adults are interested in and capable of understanding and assessing risks. In fact, because of long-standing experience, older adults often have more extensive medical vocabularies than younger people. Reflecting this, older adults' satisfaction with medical care is most closely linked to how well health professionals listen, how concerned and attentive they are, and how actively they include patients in decision making (Atherly, Kane, & Smith, 2004).

WHAT DO YOU THINK?

- Ask older people you know which term(s) they prefer from the following list and why: elders, seniors, elderly, older adults, senior citizen.
- What did you learn about their preferences?
- It's common for people in their eighties and nineties to say they do not feel old or consider themselves "seniors" or "elderly" at all. Did any of the people you talked to feel that way? What do you learn from that?

Communication Patterns

Although older and younger adults are not as different from one another as people may think, it's worth noting several communication patterns that distinguish older adults' behavior in medical contexts. For example, because they may have been taught to respect authority figures by not interrupting, older adults may be reluctant to ask questions and assert themselves with health professionals, despite their desire to participate and be well informed (Nussbaum, Ragan, & Whaley, 2003).

Conversely, some older adults become what Fowler and Nussbaum (2008) call *extreme talkers*, chatting incessantly about topics that may seem irrelevant to their health concerns. Given time constraints in medical organizations, "it is quite easy to imagine communication with patients who have a tendency to stray from the matter at hand being quite frustrating" to doctors and others (Fowler & Nussbaum, p. 165).

Third, caregivers may be put off by the presence of loved ones who often accompany older adults to medical visits. According to Nussbaum, Ragan, and Whaley (2003), very often "the companion will ask more questions, will cause the medical encounter to last significantly longer, and will expect more information regarding the health of the older patient than the older patient normally seeks" (p. 192).

Finally, the fast pace of medical contexts may be incompatible with older adults' health needs, which (although they are not necessarily debilitating) are likely to be more numerous and chronic than those of younger patients, making it infeasible to cover them during quick visits (Nussbaum, Pecchioni, Grant, & Folwell, 2000).

Promising Options

Even brief training sessions have been effective in dispelling ageist assumptions among medical students and health professionals (Christmas, Park, Schmaltz, Gozu, & Durso, 2008). Although not yet widespread, such educational programs may help change the way older adults are treated in medical situations.

Technology provides another resource. The next section discusses communication technology as it affects older adults.

Communication Technology and Older Adults

Advanced technology can be a benefit or a liability for older adults. From one perspective, access to online health information and interaction expands opportunities for adults with limited mobility. On the other hand, older adults who do not keep up with technology may have difficulty finding and keeping jobs and staying in the mainstream of a technology-savvy society. There is some evidence that older adults are rising to the challenge.

"It's clear that older adults, like their younger counterparts, don't want to be left behind on the information highway," writes Donald Lindberg (2002, p. 13). About half of people age 65 and older now use the Internet, and about two-thirds of those who do log on daily (Zickuhr & Madden, 2012).

Evidence suggests that many older adults who are proficient at using online resources benefit from a sense of control over their environment and personal fate. They also feel less isolated and more informed about choices and options than they might otherwise. Based on these ideals, Douglas McConatha (2002) proposed what he called the **e-quality theory of aging**, which posits that older adults benefit as both teachers and learners when they "use, contribute to, influence, and express themselves" in electronic environments (p. 38).

Based on experience working with older adults in an assisted living facility, David Lansdale (2002) notes that residents experienced a new sense of freedom when they learned to use an online computer made available to them. Lansdale applies the metaphors of "driving" and "going back to school." He writes:

> *Driving is the antidote to helplessness. One of the most exciting events in adolescence comes with access to the keys to the car, and the freedom it promises. At the other end of life's continuum, an elder is often forced to relinquish the keys, often one of the more trying transitions of a lifetime.* (p. 135)

Lansdale says that older adults who begin using the computer are free again to "go" where they please and choose their own paths and experiences. At the same time, they can relieve boredom and feel that they are participating in life beyond the facility's borders. Similarly, by "going back to school" via the Internet, many older adults find pleasure in expanding their knowledge and skills. This provides a striking contrast to the view of aging as a steady decline in intellect and abilities.

The Internet may even serve as a modern equivalent to a house call. In their study of Internet use among people ages 63 to 83, Wendy Macias and Sally McMillan (2008) report that many older adults are "bringing the physician and health information into their homes through the Internet" (p. 38). The Web allows them to take their time, learning as much or as little as they like about a health concern without being constrained by someone else's timetable. One woman in the study said:

> *When my husband had his shoulder replacement, he could not get in to therapy right away, and that's when I went in to the websites and was able to print actual diagrams and information about what . . . to do, so then when we finally got in to the therapy and back to the doctor, he said this was very good.* (p. 38)

Although participants in the study sometimes felt overwhelmed by the volume of online information and unsure what information to trust, they generally appreciated the opportunity to research their own concerns and issues affecting their friends and family members.

Summary

As we consider diversity in health care, intersectionality theory reminds us that a person's social position reflects a dynamic, multidimensional interface between factors at both a micro and a macro level. The most powerful implication of this for health communication is that, since some people experience life at the intersection of many factors that put them at a disadvantage, it is more effective for policy-makers and health professionals to become acquainted with people than to make assumptions based on nebulous or isolated categories.

Patients of low socioeconomic status are typically more fearful and less informed than others, but they typically talk less during medical exams and are likely to be treated within a strictly biomedical model. In addition to the communication challenges, practical considerations such as financial constraints, inflexible working schedules, and lack of transportation may limit the care they are able to receive.

Health literacy challenges affect 1 in 7 adults in the United States and hundreds of millions of people worldwide. Adverse effects include unnecessary suffering, frequent misunderstandings, reduced productivity, shame, premature death, and billions spent on avoidable health needs. Better communication is the solution. Patients and caregivers can most effectively bridge literacy gaps if they develop trust, acknowledge and reconsider stereotypes, make the most of face-to-face communication, and encourage questions and open dialogue.

Medical training and health care routines have traditionally overlooked gender diversity in the population. Health professionals may feel out of their depth discussing sexual issues, although ignoring them may compromise medical care because some health risks are related to sex and because close relationships are crucial to coping. For their part, patients may be reluctant to bring up the issue for fear of being negatively judged. Experts offer tips for bridging the gap.

Although members of racial and ethnic minorities are often at high risk for health concerns, their health may suffer because they don't trust doctors and because they have limited access to medical facilities and health information. Some evidence suggests that doctors treat African Americans and Hispanics differently from White patients. We have yet to fully transcend decades of racist and segregationist thinking in the United States, and the impact is realized in worse health and shorter lives for members of racial and ethnic minorities.

A new source of health information (and potential discrimination) looms ahead in the form of genetic profiling. Already, people who understand their genetic predisposition for various diseases may be able to offset their risks and take part in early screening procedures. The Genetic Information Nondiscrimination Act of 2008 is designed to minimize the risk that genetic risk factors will be used to penalize people in terms of employment and health insurance.

Some risk factors are not genetic, but social and linguistic. People in the United States who do not speak English well are at a disadvantage as patients. Patients baffled by language differences may agree to procedures they don't understand or may be so frustrated that they don't return for further care. Caregivers can be frustrated also and may be held liable if adverse outcomes result. The good news is that community interpreters and long-distance interpretation services have mostly pleasing results if they are used. Still, people who are not proficient in English may wish to bring a friend or relative along, since interpreters are sometimes not available.

Many people treat individuals with disabilities as if they are childlike or incapable of contributing to conversations and decisions. These assumptions may seriously limit communication between them and their caregivers. Moreover, the same attitudes can make it difficult to cope on a daily basis. Although people mean well, their actions may stigmatize and isolate individuals with disabilities. Suggestions are presented to make communication more equitable and respectful.

Children frequently undergo routine exams and emergency care, but they may have a difficult time dealing with the foreign atmosphere, strangers, and threat of pain that medical care poses. Parents can help, but their role is somewhat ambiguous. Caregivers may feel that parents are either too demanding or not helpful enough.

Finally, older adults may be typecast in ways that affect their personal identities and the health care they receive. Ageist assumptions that older people are less healthy and less intelligent than others may cause people to write off legitimate health concerns as unavoidable signs of old age. Communication accommodation behaviors are often unnecessary and can be stigmatizing, especially if carried to extremes.

Key Terms and Theories

intersectionality theory
socioeconomic status
health literacy
LGBTQQIAAP
queer theory
racism
affirmative action
prelogical conceptualization
concrete-logical conceptualization
formal-logical conceptualization
ageism
accommodate
communication accommodation theory
convergence
divergence
overaccommodation
e-quality theory of aging

Discussion Questions

1. Consider the brief scenario described by Lucy Candib at the beginning of the chapter. What elements of intersectionality theory can you apply to the patient she describes? What micro- and macro-level factors intersect to define your own social position?
2. How might you apply the factors relevant to socioeconomic status to yourself? In what ways are you privileged? In what ways are you disadvantaged? How do these affect your health and the way you communicate about it?
3. We are all more literate in some ways than others. What types of information do you find it easy to understand? What types are difficult for you? How might someone best help you understand information you find challenging?
4. List at least 10 words that describe your gender identity. Do you relate to any of the identities represented in the acronym LGBTQQIAAP? Does your gender identity influence your health and the way you communicate about it? If so, how?
5. What are some explanations of why people of different races seem to achieve different health outcomes? Have you ever witnessed or experienced any of these factors? If so, which ones?
6. Are you interested in knowing your genetic profile? Why or why not? Are you concerned that, if you have a genetic profile, the information might be used against you? Why or why not?
7. Do you think affirmative action should be maintained or abolished as a factor when selecting students for caregiver education programs (Box 6.3). Why do you feel that way?
8. What did you learn from the case study "Language Barriers in a Health Care Emergency" (Box 6.5)? Have you ever been in a situation in which it was difficult to understand or convey important information? If so, what happened?
9. Researchers make the point that we all have abilities and disabilities of different sorts. What do you consider your greatest abilities? Your greatest challenges? Do these influence your identity and the way people treat you? If so, how?
10. Imagine that you must explain to a child what it means to have cancer. What language and metaphors might you use? How would you change the way you communicate based on the child's age and ability to conceptualize illness?
11. Think carefully about the way you communicate with older adults? Does your communication exhibit accommodation in any way? If so, how? Do you think the accommodation is necessary or might you be overaccommodating?

Answers to *Can You Guess?*

1. The longest-living people in the world are women in Japan, who live an average of 87 years.
2. The shortest average life span occurs among men in Sierra Leone (West Africa), who live an average of 45 years.
3. In the United States, men live an average of 74 years and women 80 years.

Source: *World Health Organization, 2012a*

CHAPTER 7

Cultural Conceptions of Health and Illness

Ella, a labor and delivery nurse, is puzzled when a woman who has just given birth refuses an ice pack to ease her swelling and leaves a glass of cold water untouched, even though she is very thirsty.

Logan, a hospice volunteer, arrives at a client's home to find it crowded with friends and family members. They are welcoming and polite, but they are firm in insisting that Logan not speak with the ill person.

Devorah keeps her breast cancer diagnosis a secret, even from her close friends. However, she suspects that some people have found out because they avoid talking to her or making eye contact when they pass on the street.

Each of these episodes illustrates a cultural view of health and healing. In the first, the new mother is a Caribbean immigrant. Based on traditional beliefs, she considers it unhealthy to touch anything cold just after a birth. However, if the nurse offers hot tea, she would gratefully accept it to soothe her thirst (Winkelman, 2009).

Logan has arrived at the home of a Hispanic family whose members pride themselves on caring for loved ones personally. They fear that the presence of a hospice volunteer will make their loved one think they feel burdened by his care (Evans & Ume, 2012).

Devorah is a member of a charedi Jewish community in which it is considered immodest to speak about breasts, even to close friends. Members of this community may also consider her unappealing as a wife or mother, because they believe her children will be genetically predisposed to cancer (Coleman, 2009).

In this chapter we examine the impact of culture on health and healing. We explore cultures associated with Asian, Hispanic, Arab, Native American, African American, Cambodian, and Canadian communities, among others. The list seems long, but it barely scratches the surface. Entire books are dedicated to the topic of health and diverse cultural perspectives. (Box 7.1 suggests a few of them.) As you read, bear in mind that this review can offer only

BOX 7.1 RESOURCES

More About Culture and Health

- Dutta, M. J. (2008). *Communicating health: A culture-centered approach*. Cambridge, MA: Polity Press.
- Galanti, G.-A. (2014). *Caring for patients from different cultures* (5th ed.). Philadelphia, PA: University of Pennsylvania Press.
- Zoller, H. M., & Dutta, M. J. (Eds.). (2008). *Emerging perspectives in health communication: Meaning, culture, and power*. New York: Routledge.
- Transcultural Nursing Society and the *Journal of Transcultural Nursing*: www.tcns.org
- Ethnomed: www.ethnomed.org (includes multilingual health information)
- Robert Wood Johnson Foundation on Vulnerable Populations: http://www.rwjf.org/en/library/research/2015/05/vulnerable-populations-research-and-policy-briefs.html
- *Journal of Multicultural Counseling and Development*: http://www.jmcdonline.org/
- Guide to Choosing and Adapting Culturally and Linguistically Competent Health Promotion Materials: http://nccc.georgetown.edu/documents/Materials_Guide.pdf

a broad look at cultural customs. People vary widely from each other, even within the same culture.

The chapter begins with a discussion of culture and cultural competence. It then describes the influence of sex roles and family involvement on health, followed by cultural perspectives on what it means to be healthy, to be sick, and to help others. The chapter concludes with a focus on holistic medicine.

Culture and Cultural Competence

Culture refers to a set of beliefs, rules, and practices that are shared by a group of people. Cultural assumptions suggest how members should behave, what roles they are expected to play, and how various events and actions should be interpreted (Samovar & Porter, 2007). As the opening examples illustrate, cultural assumptions can affect what people consider acceptable, admirable, and shameful regarding health. In a deeper sense, culture may even define what it means to be healthy, as you will see later in the chapter.

Cultural beliefs often have a taken-for-granted quality that makes it difficult to imagine or accept alternatives. **Ethnocentrism** is the attitude that one's own culture is better than others. Even when people mean well, it's easy to feel slighted by the implication that others hold a different view. After an administrator at a Canadian hospital suggested that staff members not wish patients "Merry Christmas," one nurse fumed, "Why should we worry that it offends someone of a non-Christian culture? That really is too bad. I think the administrator was hoping to be politically correct, but it happened to offend a lot of people" (Kirkham, 2003, p. 768). The nurse felt that Canada was a "Christian country" and people should honor that perspective.

Contrast that with the anguish of a Cambodian family in an American hospital where the staff insists on cutting off silk threads that encircle the patient's wrist. The threads were tied on by a holy person in a traditional *Baci* ceremony as a way to "tie in the soul." To the family, cutting these threads renders a person vulnerable and invites bad luck (Galanti, 2014). Although that view is not the dominant perspective in the United States, it is immensely important to the family.

THE CHALLENGE OF MULTICULTURALISM

It is difficult to discuss diversity and health responsibly. For one thing, culture is not a fixed construct, but an evolving and complex one. Even within the same culture, what is considered appropriate for one person, in one situation, may be unacceptable for another. No amount of cultural knowledge allows us to predict accurately how an individual will think or behave. Furthermore, speaking in terms of people's differences can overshadow the ways in which they are alike, and it can inadvertently distance the people being described. As David Napier and colleagues

(2014) observe, talking about diversity can feel divisive rather than inclusive. At the same time, it is negligent and insensitive to ignore the influence of culture. The tenets of cultural competence can help us navigate this tricky landscape.

Cultural Competence in Health Care

As manager of a community health center in Australia, Jeffery Fuller puzzled over how to interact respectfully with a diverse array of clients. He worried that staff members would be insensitive to patients' wishes. But he also worried that they would clam up around diverse patients or abandon important medical goals so as not to offend. After studying research about the issue and trying different approaches, Fuller and his team decided to avoid assumptions as much as possible, and instead, to communicate openly with patients about their cultural and personal viewpoints. He subsequently published a model of cultural competence in health care that reflects that perspective.

Fuller's **reflective negotiation model** involves two enacted commitments and an end goal (Fuller, 2003). The commitments involve sensitivity to cultural differences and to self-awareness. The goal is that, together, these will foster a collaborative "space for negotiation," in which patients and professionals can respectfully exchange ideas without feeling constrained by status or cultural differences.

Sensitivity to cultural differences involves knowledge, which emerges to varying extents when people seek out information and when they interact with people from different cultures. Knowledge is helpful, but it is an insufficient measure of cultural competence for three main reasons (Fuller, 2003). For one, health professionals cannot know the ins and outs of every culture with which they come in contact. For another, people operate within complex webs of cultural significance, and it is impossible to know which of them are most salient in a particular situation: *Is it more germane that a patient is female or that she is Himalayan? Does it matter more that she is a CEO now or that she grew up in a low-income housing project?* Of course, it is impossible to say. Third, as we have already established, people differ from one another, even within the same culture.

This presents a rather daunting prospect for cultural competence: If knowledge isn't enough, what else is there? Fuller (2003) proposes that cultural competence involves inquisitiveness. In other words, it *embraces* ambiguity. Rather than making presumptions, culturally competent health professionals attentively observe and inquire. Toward that end, Geri-Ann Galanti (2014) recommends that caregivers ask patients three critical questions: *What do you think is wrong? What do you think caused your problem?* and *How do you cope with your condition?* The answers, she says, reveal a great deal about how patients define their conditions and the impact of those conditions on their lives.

At the same time, culturally competent individuals look inward to become aware of their own emotional hot buttons and ego threats. For example, a nurse in Fuller's (2003) study said:

> *I'm a white male in a society that's increasingly worried about diversity, feminism, and respecting homeless people. I'm none of those things, and I think it's an area where it would be easy for me to be fearful if I wanted to be.* (p. 788)

The nurse said he listens to his inner voice so he can recognize when he feels threatened or bothered. He finds that this awareness allows him to make conscious choices rather than isolating himself or being judgmental. Thus, in the same way that being sensitive to others involves asking questions, self-awareness involves honest introspection: *What am I feeling? What am I afraid of? Are my feelings rational? What are my options?*

It is important to note that cultural competence does not privilege one perspective over another. Consider the experience of a health professional prepping a Sikh child for surgery. Religious edicts prohibit cutting or shaving one's hair, which is considered a gift from God. On the other hand, medical experts recommend that surgical sites be shaved to reduce the risk of infection. Sensitive to the parents' distress, the caregiver tells the parents that she understands the rule about not cutting hair. If she has their permission, she will shave only a small area at the surgical site to protect the child's health. The parents consent, and both sides are comfortable moving forward (Galanti, 2014).

From Fuller's (2003) perspective, cultural competence involves respect for one another's viewpoints. However, especially when the stakes are high, it also involves a process of reflective negotiation. For example, physicians find themselves in a difficult position when patients seem chronically depressed but feel that it would be shameful to admit those feelings.

One option is to campaign for a mutually acceptable interpretation, as when one doctor said to a patient: "If you had diabetes, you would say to me, 'Please help me fix this.' And this is no different. It's just chemicals in your brain instead of chemicals in your liver or your kidney" (Patel, Schnall, Little, Lewis-Fernández, & Pincus, 2014, p. 1265).

All in all, Fuller's (2003) reflective negotiation model recognizes that health care occurs within an intricate constellation of beliefs. The model presents cultural competence as an ongoing process in which we must be both introspective and interested in other people. Fuller recognizes that diversity can stir up powerful emotions but proposes that the mutual benefits of negotiation are worth the effort.

With these commitments in mind, we next examine two sociocultural factors that help to shape our identities and influence the nature of health communication: gender and family.

PERSPECTIVES

A 16-year-old girl in Belize leaves the local clinic before having a Pap smear because she is confused by a nursing student's description of the procedure. However, she returns to the clinic after her mother tells her that a Pap smear is "part of the journey of being a woman" (p. 130). Researchers Joy Hart and Kandi Walker (2008) reflect that the mother's explanation calmed the girl's fears because it was more culturally familiar than the nurse's medical explanation.

Cultural Conceptions of Health

A patient describes a perplexing set of symptoms, including a sense of heaviness and insomnia. Physical tests can detect nothing wrong. The patient attributes his illness to "too much wind" and "not enough blood" as a result of his past immoral behavior. A folk healer has been treating him with meditation and herbal therapies (Kleinman, Eisenberg, & Good, 1978).

A health professional might conclude that the man is delusional or uneducated. However, if she is familiar with traditional Chinese medicine, she may discern that "too much wind" and "not enough blood" refer to a sense of being tired, dull, and out of sorts (Dharmananda, 2010). Considering the man's reference to "heaviness" and "insomnia," his account may be a face-saving way of implying that he is depressed.

Examples such as this one highlight that well-meaning people can trip over cultural gaps, sometimes with harmful consequences. This section describes two cultural perspectives on health—one that conceives of health in mostly organic terms and one that interprets health as harmony between many factors.

HEALTH AS ORGANIC

In the mid-1800s, a chemistry professor in France developed a new procedure to stop wine from souring before consumers could enjoy it. A few years later, the same professor helped to keep the silk industry alive by discovering what was killing off silkworms (Swazey & Reeds, 1978). He couldn't know it at the time, but these efforts would lead the professor, Louis Pasteur, to revolutionize medicine.

Pasteur realized that the wine was souring and the silkworms were dying because of tiny organisms called germs. He didn't discover germs. A Dutch biologist had done that nearly 200 years earlier. But Pasteur was the first to recognize that germs could be killed and, with effort, be kept out of sterile environments. (His discovery would lead him to *pasteurize* milk, among other things.) Prior to Pasteur's discovery, scientists believed that germs spontaneously generated and could not be contained or avoided (Zimmerman & Zimmerman, 2002).

Simply put, **germ theory** states that disease is caused by microscopic organisms, such as bacteria and viruses (Twaddle & Hessler, 1987). Pasteur's breakthrough helped hospitals and medical centers become safer than in the past. Health professionals began to sterilize medical instruments and environments and to separate people with contagious diseases from others (Marwick, 1997).

PERSPECTIVES

An American medical student studying in Sri Lanka was surprised when the surgical team entered the operating room barefoot. They explained to her that they could sterilize their feet more effectively than they could sterilize footwear (Nicholas, 2014).

Pasteur's ideas seeped into popular culture, as well. An **organic model** of health took root, based on the assumption that health can be understood in terms of the presence (or absence) of physical indicators. Caregivers and researchers began to rely heavily on scientific tests to diagnose patients and to conduct medical research (Raffel & Raffel, 1989). At the core of the organic approach is the conviction that, if health professionals are vigilant enough, they can minimize or eradicate most illnesses. Indeed, an awareness of microscopic agents has allowed communities to remove the threat of many contagious diseases, reduce the incidence of infection, and develop inoculations against smallpox, measles, polio, and many other harmful conditions.

If you grew up in an environment that reveres biomedicine, it may seem strange to consider the organic perspective a matter of culture. One quality of cultural assumptions is that, over time, they tend to assume the authority of universal truth. That's not to say that biomedicine is wrong or false. But it is certainly not the only perspective on health, and it does have limitations.

One limitation is the model's inability to account for conditions that cannot be physically verified. People with undetectable conditions, such as chronic fatigue syndrome, sometimes say the worst part is that so many people regard their condition as "not real" (Komaroff & Fagioli, 1996). A similar phenomenon affects people with mental illness. In the United States, mental illness has long been regarded as less authentic than physical illness—an assumption that changed (at least somewhat) only when researchers identified a chemical basis for some mental disorders (Byck, 1986). Objectively speaking, mental illness did not become any more *real*, at that point. It simply became more culturally acceptable.

Another limitation is that the organic approach largely excludes social, spiritual, and psychological factors that may be relevant to the lived experience of health and illness. Since the Industrial Revolution, many doctors in the United States have been reluctant to bring up spiritual concerns during medical visits, perhaps because they are uncomfortable with them or they seem irrelevant. This is understandable to some people, but it can seem cold and impersonal to those who are accustomed to a different style of care. Members of some African American and Latino communities, for example, are often dissatisfied with health care because they perceive that caregivers are distant and uninterested compared to the close sense of community they value (Mead et al., 2013).

A third limitation is that, although classifying people as either healthy or sick feels logical in a binary way, it is an oversimplification. As Charles Rossiter (1975) points out, *sick* and *healthy* are inadequate to describe all aspects of the human condition. There are varying levels of sickness and varying levels of health. Moreover, some people are unhealthy although they do not have specific diseases.

IN YOUR EXPERIENCE

- Do you have experience interacting with people from diverse cultures? If so, what are the most important things you have learned?
- Have you ever experienced health care in a different culture? If so, what was your experience like? How was it similar to the health care you experience at home? How was it different?

HEALTH AS HARMONIC BALANCE

As you may remember from Chapter 1, the World Health Organization defines health as "a state of complete physical, mental, and social well-being and not merely the absence of disease or infirmity" (WHO, 1948, p. 1). From this perspective, health exists at the nexus of many factors, including personal beliefs, contact with other people, aspects of the environment, physical strength, and many more. From the **harmonic balance perspective**, health is not simply the absence of physical signs of disease. Rather, it is a sense of overall well-being and equilibrium. This perspective is in keeping with the biopsychosocial and sociocultural perspectives introduced in Chapter 1. Following are a few examples that illustrate cultural perspectives on health as a harmonic balance.

Physical, Emotional, and Spiritual

Members of many cultures do not perceive the mind/body dualism popular in Western thought (see Chapter 2). Instead, they regard the mind and body as an interwoven whole and perceive that one affects the other.

The Hispanic concepts of *susto* and *coraje* are examples. Both refer to emotionally intense and unpleasant episodes. The idea is that a traumatizing experience can diminish one's spiritual vitality and upset the link between body and soul (Durà-Vilà & Hodes, 2012). In most Mexican cultures, ***susto*** (SOO-sto) means *fright* and ***coraje*** (core-AH-hey) means *anger.* In one study of Mexican American immigrants, the majority felt their diabetes was at least partly caused by either *susto* or *coraje* (Mendenhall, Fernandez, Adler, & Jacobs, 2012).

Members of some traditional Navajo cultures also honor a connection between mind, body, and soul. They believe that the best way to remain healthy is to balance physical strength, social interactions, and spiritual beliefs ("Native American," 2010). Concentrating on only one factor can upset the delicate balance between them. For example, striving for physical strength without also seeking spiritual growth is not healthy, and a person may become ill because of the imbalance. This is not to say that Navajo deny the existence of germs. They accept that germs cause some diseases. But they also observe that some people are less vulnerable than others to them. If several people are exposed to a contagious disease, some of them are likely to get sick, but others may not. Based on Navajo beliefs, people who live balanced lives are more likely to remain well, even when they are exposed to physical threats.

Harmony With Nature

> *[Mother Earth] is something that heals you if you let it. You don't always feel it. You have to be thinking about it. You can't just go out for a walk and feel it. You have to be spiritually connected to feel her.* (*Wilson, 2003, third section, para. 8*)

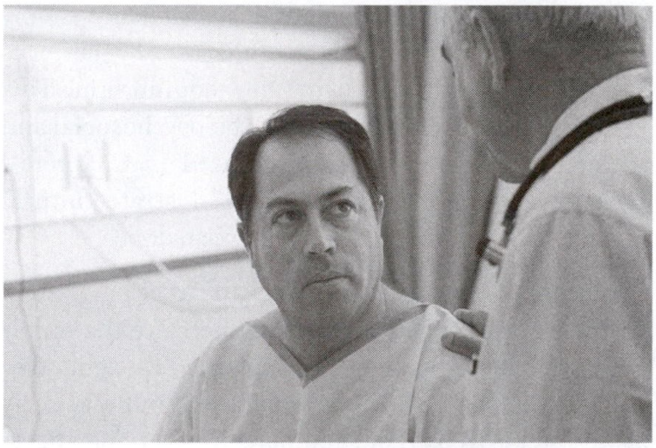

Based on their own personal and cultural preferences, patients may feel that health professionals are either overly familiar or aloof. Negotiating expectations requires that people communicate well with each other and pay attention to their own reactions.

This statement, by a member of the Odawa aboriginal community in Canada, emphasizes the therapeutic value of living in harmony with nature. Similar beliefs are common in Caribbean communities and many others.

Illustrative of this idea, the renowned biologist Edward O. Wilson proposed the **biophilia hypothesis** that people have an inherent affinity for nature and often derive a sense of well-being from contact with it. A good deal of research suggests that people typically do experience decreased stress, elevated moods, and other positive benefits from activities such as gardening, dog walking, and hiking (Chen, Tu, & Ho, 2013; McCune, Beck, & Johnson, 2011). Based on this evidence, urban planning coalitions such as Eco advocate for at least a 20% increase in parks, public gardens, and other green spaces to bolster community health (Hall, 2014).

Hot and Cold

In one of the examples that opens this chapter, a new mother refuses an ice pack and cold water because she has just given birth. In many traditional Caribbean, Chinese, and Latin American cultures, health is considered in terms of "hot" and "cold" (Sobo & Loustaunau, 2010; Winkelman, 2009). Bodily conditions are associated with different temperatures, as are foods, drinks, and other elements of the environment. For example, childbirth is considered hot. To counteract it with something cold might interfere with the body's natural healing process. In other circumstances—such as when a person feels lethargic (a cold condition)—hot substances such as coffee and chocolate can counter that and help restore a healthy balance.

"Hot" and "cold" are not always literal temperatures (coffee is hot, but so are chocolate, cinnamon, and tobacco). The real determinant is a substance's effect on the body, which can also be metaphoric. Hot foods are energizing. By contrast, low-calorie foods, such as fruits and vegetables, are cold. Health professionals sensitive to this perspective can recommend remedies that are both helpful and culturally suitable. For instance, cold juice might be regarded as inappropriate to counteract the flu (which is considered cold), but hot tea may be a useful and appealing alternative (Winkelman, 2009).

Heat and cold are interwoven with the Chinese conception of *Qi*, which we will discuss next. But before moving on, it's worth noting that even people not raised in the cultures mentioned here may rely on thermal metaphors. For example, people in the United

States may describe a personable caregiver as *warm* and friendly, bemoan the misery of catching a *cold*, and long for the healing value of *hot* chicken soup.

PERSPECTIVES

Deeply committed to the healing power of positive thinking, a Navajo man becomes upset when his doctor describes the negative outcomes that may result from an upcoming surgery (Indian Health Service, n.d.).

Energy

Around the world, members of many cultures conceive of health primarily in terms of energy. For example, a traditional Hindu individual from Asian India may believe that accidents are caused by **karma**—energy that results from either good or bad deeds in the past. From this viewpoint, a disabling injury may be regarded as the inevitable consequence of bad karma. Recovery may involve not only physical healing, but a resolve to be more altruistic in the future (Gupta, 2010).

According to the Chinese Tao, **yin** and **yang** are polar energies whose cyclical forces define all living things (Uba, 1992). *Yin* is associated with coolness and reflection, and *yang* with brightness and warmth. Cycles and combinations of yin and yang define human life and unite all forms of existence.

Within this belief, one's central life energy is called ***Qi*** (pronounced *chee,* sometimes spelled "chi"). Illness and even death may result if *Qi* is wasted or if yin and yang are not balanced. Life energy is sustained and balanced by awareness, rhythmic breathing, physical regimens, and meditation.

Qi is often difficult to grasp and study from an empirical perspective because it is invisible. *Qi* is sensed rather than measured or directly observed (Ho, 2006). Unlike in organic medicine, in which the practitioner and the patient are treated as distinctly separate entities, *Qi* is a force that flows through them both. As one practitioner described it, an acupuncturist is "the conduit between the heavenly and the earthly *Qi* and it comes through you and through your hands and into the needle and the point" (Ho, 2006, p. 426). Some highly experienced people are said to know what is wrong with a person by sensing the person's *Qi* visually or through touch.

IN YOUR EXPERIENCE

- Describe a situation in which your health was affected by organic factors.
- Describe a time when multiple factors, together, influenced your well-being.

In closing, although there is explanatory value in contrasting the organic and harmonic balance approaches, in reality they overlap and coexist. Physical health is a significant component of both perspectives. Moreover, each model may be appropriate in different situations, and sometimes they are useful together. Amos Deinard, a pediatrician at the University of Minnesota Hospital, says, "Our attitude is, you bring your shaman and we'll bring our surgeon and let's see if we can work on this problem together" (quoted by Goode, 1993, para. 7).

Making Sense of Health Experiences

Two friends, one Jamaican and one American, watch a woman cross the street. The American thinks, "Look how slender she is. She must have a healthy diet." The Jamaican thinks, "I wonder what sort of stress has caused her to be so thin. She is unwell" (adapted from Sobo & Loustaunau, 2010, p. 86).

As mentioned, one function of culture is to make sense of the world. In this example, a slender physique is interpreted as healthy to one friend and unhealthy to another. In a similar way, depending on one's culture and circumstances, death might be interpreted as a glorious ascension to the afterlife or as a tragic and regrettable occurrence. An illness may be regarded as an unfair and random affliction or as a valuable opportunity for renewed awareness. (See Box 7.2 for more about that idea.)

This section explores how members of various cultures make sense of health conditions.

HEALTH CONDITION AS SOCIAL ASSET

By now it should be clear that interpretations of illness and health are not absolute. What members of one culture consider tragic, others may revere.

BOX 7.2 THEORETICAL FOUNDATIONS

Theory of Health as Expanded Consciousness

The majority of us spend our lives trying to stay healthy, and when we get sick we want nothing more than to be well again. We may be missing the point. According to Margaret Newman's **theory of health as expanded consciousness**, a health crisis is not necessarily negative or undesirable (Newman, 2000). Instead, health events are integral parts of life that provide opportunities for growth and change.

Newman is inspired by David Bohm's (1980) concept that our everyday life is influenced by underlying patterns that characterize who we are and what we experience. Bohm conceived of two types of order—the **explicate order**, made up of the tangible elements of our existence, and the **implicate order**, comprising patterns beneath the surface. Although the tangible elements of our lives may seem like the "real thing" because we can see, hear, taste, and feel them, the meaning of what we do often lies within the underlying, implicate order. Bohm compares the dual nature of life to waves on the ocean. We can see the waves, but we won't really understand what causes them unless we explore the underwater currents that give rise to them.

Within this metaphor, a health event makes waves. It disrupts what might otherwise seem to be a peaceful, unremarkable existence. As nurse and nurse educator, Newman (2000) observes:

> *The thing that brings people to the attention of a nurse is a situation that they do not know how to handle. They are at a choice point. Each of us at some time in our lives is brought to a point when the "old rules" do not work anymore, when what we have considered progress does not work anymore. We have done everything "right" but things still do not work. (p. 99)*

You might ask: And this is a *good* thing? According to Newman, yes. In her view, life is a process of attaining greater levels of understanding and awareness. When things stop working well, we experience a sense of chaos. But, she says, if we "hang in there," the uncertainty and ambiguity of a health crisis may become a means of seeing underlying patterns and transcending previous limitations. This can be a richly rewarding and liberating experience (Newman, 2000).

Imagine a person who has worked throughout her life to support others. She has devoted her energy and time to doing well at work, caring for her family, running errands, serving on committees, cleaning the house and yard, and so on. She is lauded with thanks and awards. Meanwhile, she appears less physically fit than she used to be. Her hair and clothing are not carefully groomed and tended. But this is nothing compared to what is happening within her. In fulfilling so many outward "obligations," she neglects her own spiritual and emotional growth. Although she interacts frequently with people, she doesn't share much of herself or appreciate the uniqueness of the people around her.

Suddenly (or what appears to be suddenly), the woman comes down with the flu and must cancel her commitments for several days. Faced with this prospect, she might put all her energy into fighting the illness, frustrated that it has interrupted her life. Or she might look for a deeper level of meaning. What does the illness (an outward manifestation) suggest about what is happening within her? And at an even deeper level, what does this disruption signal about the underlying pattern of her life? Perhaps this is an opportunity to reevaluate a pattern that appears virtuous on the surface but is harmful to her and others in the larger scheme of things. Perhaps understanding the pattern will allow her to restructure her life in a way that is more functional and adaptive, allowing her to develop her inner self as well as perform helpful tasks in the tangible world. Or perhaps she will ignore the underlying currents until they give rise to a much bigger, harder-to-ignore "wave," such as a stroke or a heart attack.

Seen this way, health events are opportunities for developing higher levels of understanding and more effective interactions with our environments. Greater harmony between inner and outer levels of existence provides the means for seeing beyond one's self and transcending old habits and assumptions. As Newman learned from her mentor, Martha Rogers, "health and illness should be viewed equally

continued

as expressions of the life process in its totality" (Newman, 2000, p. 7).

Newman (2000) coaches nurses to help people find the meanings and patterns revealed by their health experiences, whether or not their diseases are eradicated. She writes:

> *Transcendence of the limitations of the disease does not necessarily mean more freedom from the disease; it does mean more meaningful relationships and greater freedom in a spiritual sense. These factors are considered an expansion of consciousness.* (p. 65)

Furthermore, a health crisis is not merely a senseless or regrettable circumstance. Newman (1986) writes that, since she began to regard health as the expansion of consciousness,

> *illness and disease have lost their demoralizing power. . . . The expansion of consciousness never ends. In this way aging has lost its power. Death has lost its power. There is peace and meaning in suffering. We are free from the things we have feared—loss, death, dependency. We can let go of fear.* (p. 3)

What Do You Think?

1. Have you ever learned something valuable about yourself as the result of a health crisis?
2. What can caregivers and loved ones do to help people evaluate their life circumstances when an illness occurs?
3. In what ways are your health and outward, everyday life (explicate order) influenced by underlying factors (implicate order)?

Suggested Sources

Bohm, D. (1980). *Wholeness and the implicate order.* London: Routledge & Kegan Paul.

Coward, D. D. (1990, Fall). The lived experience of self-transcendence in women with advanced breast cancer. *Nursing Science Quarterly, 3*(3), 162–169.

du Pré, A., & Ray, E. B. (2008). Comforting episodes: Transcendent experiences of cancer survivors. In L. Sparks, H. D. O'Hair, & G. L. Kreps (Eds.), *Cancer, communication and aging* (pp. 99–114). Cresskill, NJ: Hampton Press.

Malinski, V. M. (Ed.). (1986). *Explorations on Martha Rogers' science of unitary human beings.* Norwalk, CT: Appleton-Century-Crofts.

Newman, M. A. (1995). *A developing discipline: Selected works of Margaret Newman.* New York: National League for Nursing Press.

Newman, M. A. (2000). *Health as expanding consciousness* (2nd ed.). Boston: Jones & Bartlett.

Rogers, M. E. (1986). Science of unitary human beings. In V. M. Malinski (Ed.), *Explorations on Martha Rogers' science of unitary human beings* (pp. 3–14). Norwalk, CT: Appleton-Century-Crofts.

For example, Native American folklore is rich with examples of spirit leaders who fall into sleep-like trances that last for several days (Neihardt, 1932). A biomedical practitioner might classify these episodes as comas, but in some Native American cultures they are regarded as sacred opportunities for the person to leave the body and experience the spiritual realm. The person's dreams in this state are often carefully noted and used as the basis for ceremonial dances and rituals.

Another famous example is described in the book *The Spirit Catches You and You Fall Down,* which describes the life of Lia, a young Hmong girl in California who has frequent seizures (Fadiman, 1997). Her family considers Lia special because the episodes allow her to have contact with the divine. However, biomedical practitioners diagnose her with epilepsy and charge the parents with negligence for not keeping Lia on antiseizure medication. The book chronicles the intercultural struggle to define what is healthy, what is holy, and what is best for Lia.

Less extreme examples of the illness-or-asset dilemma involve people whose "deformities" and "diseases" make them especially good at what they do. For example, doctors believe that the legendary violinist Niccolò Paganini probably had a genetic disorder that affected collagen in his body (S. Kean, 2012). As a result, his health was always fragile, but Paganini was able to hyperextend his thumbs in ways that other violinists couldn't. Likewise, some professional basketball players probably have gigantism, a condition that results in the overproduction of growth hormone (Caba, 2016). Evidence also suggests that many fashion models have eating disorders that benefit them professionally but damage their health (Murgatroyd, 2015; National Eating Disorders, 2015).

On the flip side are health conditions that society regards with fear or revulsion. We discuss those next.

PERSPECTIVES

About 10 million Hispanic residents of the United States who did not have health insurance prior to passage of the Affordable Care Act now qualify for it (Fox, 2014). The opportunity and challenge for health professionals is to negotiate ideas about health and healing with a patient population that is increasingly diverse.

HEALTH CONDITION AS SOCIAL LIABILITY

At different times in history, epilepsy, cancer, tuberculosis, mental illness, AIDS, and other ailments have been viewed so negatively that people with these conditions were shunned or even imprisoned (H. Friedman & DiMatteo, 1979). Sick people may be regarded as a threat to the moral order because behaviors associated with their conditions are considered immoral or because their conditions seem contagious or frightening.

Many times, public reaction is not based on facts but on fears or cultural assumptions. Prior to 1950, people were so fearful of cancer that they typically avoided telling anyone outside the family if a loved one was diagnosed with it (Holland & Zittoun, 1990). They often chose not to tell the patient either. As more accurate information about the disease surfaced, namely that it is not contagious, public opinion and communication about it changed as well.

As you will see here, ill health often has negative social connotations in that the affected person may be treated as cursed, unappealing, negligent, or victimized.

PERSPECTIVES

During the Middle Ages in England, mentally ill individuals were incarcerated as criminals and thereafter denied the right to marry or own property (MacDonald, 1981). Still today, in many areas of the world, mental illness is considered God's punishment, and people make great efforts to deny and conceal it (Purnell, 2008).

Disease as Curse

When other explanatory models fail, people may reason that illness is caused by God or witches. As White (1896/1925) puts it, "In those periods when man sees everywhere miracle and nowhere law . . . he naturally ascribes his diseases either to the wrath of a good being or to the malice of an evil being" (p. 1).

During the bubonic plague of the fourteenth century, more than one-third of the European population died (Slack, 1991). Struggling to make sense of this devastating epidemic, people killed tens of thousands of women, accusing them of using witchcraft to make their neighbors ill (Nelkin & Gilman, 1991). Others attributed the plague to God's wrath over women's fashions, blasphemy, drunkenness, improper religious observances, and other behaviors (Slack, 1991).

If people believe illness is a curse, they may try to keep their health condition secret, and they may write off efforts at prevention and treatment. In Europe in the late 1700s, some people refused the smallpox vaccination because it was regarded as interference with God's way (Nelkin & Gilman, 1991). For similar reasons, some Kashmiri men in India, although at high risk for diabetes, frequently decline treatment or lifestyle changes because they feel that the disease is Allah's will and they should enjoy life (including eating what they want) until it is their fate to die (Naeem, 2003).

Stigma

For those whose conditions stir society's fears and prejudices, disease is clearly more than a physical phenomenon. People may be considered frightening, corrupt, or immoral on the basis of health-related factors. As Erving Goffman (1963) uses the term, **stigma** refers to social rejection in which a person is treated as dishonorable or is ignored altogether. A striking example of this involves mental illness. A meta-analysis of research on the topic revealed that people with mental illness are stigmatized in regions as far-reaching and diverse as Finland, Africa, Japan, the United States, and Estonia (Boyd, Adler, Otilingam, & Peters, 2014). So great is the stigma that many people with mental illness internalize the harsh judgments and suffer reduced self-esteem and a sense of helplessness as a result (Boyd et al.).

Likewise, numerous studies tell of HIV and AIDS survivors who have been fired from their jobs and abandoned by their families and friends (e.g., Ugarte, Högberg, Valladares, & Essén, 2013). Stigmatized in this way, people with HIV or AIDS must often choose between two forms of isolation. Either they keep the diagnosis a secret (eschewing potential support), or they tell others and risk being shunned and avoided by them.

Stacy Bias, self-proclaimed fat activist and educator, has taken a stand against stigmatizing behaviors and bullying. She founded FatGirl Speaks, a conference featuring performances and fashion shows that celebrate women of all sizes, as well as the BelliesAreBeautiful.com website at which she invites people to post photos in celebration of size diversity.

One effect of social stigma is that people's individuality, even their humanity, is overshadowed by a particular characteristic. Activist and educator Stacy Bias (2015) wrote about a shaming episode (one of many) on a public train during which a passenger goaded her by loudly lambasting what he called "fat slobs" as being "lazy" and "irresponsible" and "like drunks." Bias considered saying to him, "Hi! I'm a real live fat person. . . . I'm up here in front of you being an actual human being" (para. 7). In the end, Bias's efforts to inspire the man's understanding and compassion only resulted in him bullying her more aggressively. She reflects that "stigma kills people. It make us sick, silent, and afraid to advocate for ourselves. It isolates us, turns us against ourselves, and breaks down our mental health" (para. 26). Because the issue of weight is so socially sensitive, people who are considered obese may find that health professionals either focus mostly on their weight, avoid the issue, or address it awkwardly (Knight-Agarwal, Kaur, Williams, Davey, & Davis, 2014). That is especially regrettable since people who have been subjected to ridicule may feel that there are few trustworthy confidants to whom they can talk openly (Puhl & Heuer, 2010). Stacy Bias is challenging the stigma, however, with blog posts, speaking engagements, and events designed to shed the shame and challenge the notion that beauty and health equate to being "thin, beautiful, white, and heterosexual" (Bias, 2014). (Read more about her work at stacybias.net/blog).

PERSPECTIVES

Nisha, a native of India, caught HIV at age 19 from the man her parents had arranged for her to marry (de Souza, 2009). When her husband became seriously ill, Nisha was beaten and disowned by her husband's family, who blamed her for his misfortune. Nisha returned to live with her parents and younger sisters, but when they found out she was HIV positive, they shunned her as well. Nisha now works for a nonprofit organization that provides care for people with HIV and AIDS and educates the public about these conditions.

The Morality of Prevention

It seemed for a time that reframing disease in scientific terms would shield sufferers from moral judgment. Ironically, Western society has attributed a moral quality to science, with the effect that people who get sick are often considered to be lazy or ignorant.

The news is filled with health warnings and risk factors. Such information enables people to make healthy choices, enhancing their own well-being and assuring themselves of long, healthy lives. At least that's one implication: Take care of yourself and there is no reason you should become ill. But taken too far, the same idea can lead to prejudice against ill persons.

One backlash of the prevention movement is the presumption that, if illness can be avoided, ill people have not tried very hard to stay healthy. "Why isn't it possible to just get sick without it also being your fault?" asks physician/essayist Paul Marantz (1990, p. 1186). Marantz describes the smug comments surrounding a young friend's unexpected death from heart failure. A medical resident minimized the man's death by dubbing him "a real couch potato" (Marantz, 1990, p. 1186). Marantz was angry that onlookers would judge his friend, even to the extent of making his premature death seem okay or deserved.

The fallacy that only the lazy or indifferent get sick compounds the hardship of being ill. People fall ill for reasons that are hard to explain, even though they have worked hard to stay healthy. Marantz (1990) and others propose that suffering is often made worse by the assumption that ill persons engineer their own misfortunes.

One alternative to blaming ill persons is to see them as victims of circumstances beyond their control. As you will see, however, there are also social implications to playing the victim role.

WHAT DO YOU THINK?

- Why might members of a society stigmatize ill individuals?
- Some people feel that smoking and obesity have become stigmatized in the United States. Do you agree or disagree? Why?

Victim Role

As the average life span has increased, so has the duration of chronic diseases. These days, many people with serious diseases survive and lead relatively normal lives. This has created a semantic dilemma. These people are not accurately described as "patients."

So what do you call a person with AIDS or cancer or emphysema? A common practice is to call them victims, as in "AIDS victims" or "cancer victims." However, many people so described resent the implications of that characterization. When Laura Barnes, a life coach in Arizona, posted her original poem "I Am Not a Victim of Breast Cancer" online, it went viral, apparently striking a chord with many people. Here are a few lines from the poem:

> I am not a victim of breast cancer.
>
> I am experiencing breast cancer.
>
> I am not dying.
>
> I am living. . . .
>
> I am not weak or diminished.
>
> I am strong and whole and complete. . . .
>
> I am not powerless.
>
> I am powerful beyond measure.

You can read the entire poem by searching for "Laura Barnes" and "I Am Not a Victim" online (Barnes, n.d.).

In closing, this section offers a powerful reminder that serious health concerns have social and cultural implications. In some cases, a person enjoys social benefits as a result of the condition. More often, however, serious health issues—particularly if they are frightening or baffling—are interpreted as a punishment, a sign of depravity, or as bad luck. As the next section illustrates, culture not only helps to conceptualize what health and illness mean, but how we should behave in the context of social structures.

Social Roles and Health

The hospital staff was offended by the behavior of a 25-year-old male patient. As one of them describes it:

> *He was very uncooperative and refused to do anything for himself. He would ring for the nurses and demand, "You get here right now and do this." He would not, however, accept anything he had not specifically requested, including lunch trays and medication. He posted a sign on his door that read, "Do not enter without knocking, including the nurses."* (Sobo & Loustaunau, 2010, p. 32)

Eventually, a relative of one of the nurses provided an explanation. The patient was a wealthy man from Iran, accustomed to having servants and not accustomed to having women (such as female nurses) tell him what to do. Most of the staff came from a different background. They took it as a given that women be treated as equals and that patients accept the rituals and products of medical care as they knew it. Some of them may also have felt slighted about being "bossed around" by someone younger than them. The staff felt badly treated, but so did the patient, who interpreted the staff's behavior toward him as disrespectful and belittling.

As this episode illustrates, health communication is influenced by the social roles that people play in a larger sense. Some of the most powerful influences on social identity, and therefore on health communication, involve gender and family.

SEX, GENDER, AND HEALTH

It is oversimplified to consider *male* and *female* an either-or dichotomy. As we discussed in Chapter 6, intersex individuals embody physical characteristics of both, and most of us identify with traits culturally defined as feminine and those considered masculine. As you read the following section, keep in mind that the real issue is not one's biological sex, but rather cultural constructs about what it means to be masculine, feminine, or some mixture of both.

Female Identity and Health

In many cultures, women are economically dependent on men and are considered to be subordinate to them. Partly because of this, women worldwide are less likely than men to have regular access to health care, and the gap is even greater if the women are economically impoverished (Gustavo et al., 2013). The perception that women are less powerful than men sometimes fosters a patriarchal pattern in which women are treated as less active agents than men in making health-related decisions. For example, a Canadian study showed that physicians discussed a patient's preferences for knee surgery 57% of the time when the patient was male but only 15% of the time when the patient was female (Borkhoff et al., 2013).

There is also a tendency in some cultures to consider women's primary role to be childbearing and childrearing. In the United States, breast cancer gets more attention than other women's health topics, although heart disease is actually the number-one cause of death among women, just as it is among men (CDC, 2015c).

A cultural focus on motherhood puts women at a disadvantage in some ways, but privileges them in others. Among some members of the Muslim faith, female fertility is revered to such an extent that a woman's inability to bear children, and even the onset of menopause, can be seen as shameful (Douki, Zineb, Nacef, & Halbreich, 2007). On the other hand, a Jordanian man interviewed about his wife's health said, "She is the one who nurtures the young generation while the man is busy outside the home. . . . her health is a higher priority than my health" (Taha, Al-Qutob, Nyström, Wahlström, & Berggren, 2013, p. 9).

Ironically, although women are often valued in terms of their reproductive capacity, expectations about female modesty and chastity may shield them from gynecological health information. Women may avoid or dread "shameful" and "embarrassing" medical examinations. In some African American and Appalachian cultures, talk about reproductive health and sexually transmitted diseases is considered so taboo that girls do not learn much about these issues from their parents (Studts, Tarasenko, & Schoenberg, 2013; Warren-Jeanpiere, Miller, & Warren, 2010).

Women also suffer disproportionately from domestic violence. About 12 million women a year in the United States, and 1 in 3 women worldwide, are physically assaulted by intimate partners or raped by others (CDC, 2014c; WHO, 2014b). As a consequence, women in the United States are two to three times more likely than men to experience the recurring nightmares, fear, and emotional agitation of posttraumatic stress disorder (PTSD) (Vogt, 2013).

Because intimate-partner violence is a difficult issue to talk about, health professionals may not ask about it and may not even realize that women wish they would. A study of Lebanese women revealed that they would rather talk about abuse with health professionals than with friends or neighbors, if the professionals are nonjudgmental and keep the information confidential. The women suggested that doctors and social workers ask them directly if they are experiencing violence at home. Said one woman in the study, "I trust my doctor more than I trust my neighbor, I talk to him and he usually guides me what is best for me to do" (Usta, Antoun, Ambuel, & Khawaja, 2012, p. 216).

Chris Kyle, shown here with Dean Cain during a taping of *Stars Earn Stripes*, was the inspiration for the movie *American Sniper*. Kyle was killed by a veteran reported to be suffering from post-traumatic stress disorder. In the United States, men are four times more likely than women to be murdered and four times more likely to commit suicide, partly because of cultural expectations that they fight for honor and that they keep quiet about depression.

Male Identity and Health

In many cultures, men are expected to be strong, stoic, and virile. This can be empowering, as when they are considered active agents in making decisions about their health. However, it can also shame men who feel that their health concerns are signs of weakness. The expectation that they be "strong" and "protective" can also put them in harm's way.

In some traditional Latin American and Arab communities, among many others, men's worth is defined largely in terms of their career success and how well they provide for their families (Kumar, Warnke, & Karabenick, 2014; Rubenstein & Macías-González, 2012). A downward emotional spiral can result when men perceive that they do not measure up to these expectations. However, few people may know it. Admitting to others that they feel ashamed or depressed can make men feel even weaker and more vulnerable. Rico, a middle-aged man of Mexican descent, admitted in counseling that he felt constantly criticized and belittled, imagining his father saying he should be "working harder," his boss saying he was "not working fast enough," and his own self-critical voice saying, "I am stupid and everyone might find out if I don't hide it" (Shepard & Rabinowitz, 2013, p. 456). Rico reflected on how difficult it was to voice those feelings aloud, even in a group therapy session with other men.

The social implications of ill health can be especially hard on men who consider their conditions to be emasculating. For example, men experiencing erectile dysfunction, incontinence, sexually transmitted diseases, and eating disorders may have a hard time admitting their concerns to loved ones or seeking treatment (respectively, Peate, 2012; Hrisanfow & Hägglund, 2013; Morris et al., 2014; Dalgliesh & Nutt, 2013).

Whereas women are more likely than men to experience violence in the home, men more often encounter it in social settings and in battle. In the United States, men are nearly four times more likely than women to be murdered, most often by firearms (CDC, 2013). This is partly because men in some cultures are expected to fight. For example, in parts of the southern and western United States, men feel duty bound to respond aggressively and even violently if they perceive that someone has insulted their honor or that of their family or religion (Crowder & Kemmelmeier, 2014). Homicide rates tend to be higher than normal in these communities, but so do suicides, especially among men who feel they have been publicly shamed (Crowder & Kemmelmeier). In the United States, men are four times more likely to commit suicide than women (CDC, 2012).

Men are also more likely than women to be in formal combat. Of the roughly 7,000 American troops killed in Iraq and Afghanistan to date, 98% have been men ("Faces of the Fallen," 2015). What many people don't realize is that an even larger number of American service members—about 25 a month—die by their own hand while on active duty (T. Williams, 2012). Suicide has outpaced combat as the leading cause of death in those war zones. Additionally, at least 150,000 members of the American military are expected to return from war with posttraumatic stress disorder (Mayo Clinic, 2015; Ramchand, Karney, Osilla, Burns, & Caldarone, 2008).

In summary, the importance of health communication is underscored by patterns that cast women and men in narrowly defined roles and discourage them from talking about some health concerns. The issue is not so much that some cultural expectations are wrong, as that they can be very restrictive. Some people observe that gender roles are becoming less rigid in some regions of the world, as evidenced by the increasing visibility of women as educated professionals and the relatively small but growing number of men who are stay-at-home fathers (Krajewski & Beach Slatten, 2013; Rampell, 2014).

Next we discuss another type of social identity that affects nearly everyone: the roles we play as family members.

FAMILY ROLES AND HEALTH COMMUNICATION

Family members are often involved in caring for one another on a daily basis. But it is sometimes unclear how, and to what extent, loved ones should be involved in health care rituals and decisions when health professionals are involved.

Since family is particularly important in many Hispanic and Latino communities, misunderstandings can occur when loved ones' presence clashes with health professionals' notions of efficiency and privacy. A hospital nurse in one study expressed frustration that some families insist on being always present, saying, "The patient is perfectly fine, they don't need to have anybody stay in overnight, but they will insist and make a big fuss" (Kirkham, 2003, p. 771).

The very notion of family is open to interpretation. It is common for a traditional Arab household to include several generations as well as uncles, cousins, and others. Men are largely expected to provide for the family and women to raise the children and perform domestic tasks. In this collectivistic culture, a dishonorable action by one member may bring shame on the entire family. This means that some health conditions, such as mental illness and out-of-marriage pregnancies, may have powerful implications for the entire family. Health care professionals are encouraged to approach these matters delicately. Even when the issue is not a shameful one, many traditional Arabs prefer that doctors not tell the patient directly about a serious and terminal illness, but instead give the news to the nearest relative or the male head of the family, who, in turn, will share it with the others (N. Ahmad, 2004).

For individuals, such as immigrants, who may not have extensive family nearby, even the presence of caring strangers can be comforting in a health crisis. Part of the Muslim creed involves caring for people in need (Padela, Killawi, Forman, DeMonner, & Heisler, 2012). Therefore caregivers may wish to be at the bedside of Muslim community members, even if they did not previously know them.

All in all, experts encourage health professionals to honor patients' wishes about family involvement as much as possible, since loved ones may be crucial to healing, coping, and decision making (Zoucha & Broome, 2008). We talk more about family caregivers in Chapter 8. (See Box 7.3 for more about a Thai family providing caring for a loved one.)

BOX 7.3 PERSPECTIVES

Thai Customs and a Son's Duty

Absolutely nothing in Thai culture is as important as a son's duty to take care of his elderly parents. My paternal grandmother came to live with my family when I was 15 years old. She left Chonburi, a small city in the eastern part of Thailand, and moved to Bangkok after my grandfather died of a heart attack. Grandmother Kim had been paralyzed for 20 years because of a bad fall, so my father insisted she must come to live with us so we could take proper care of her and so she wouldn't be lonely.

Grandmother Kim was 91 years old then, but she still had a great memory, especially about finances. Even though she had no expenses of her own, she insisted that my father give her a monthly allowance. She kept perfect mental notes on the status of her money so that she could distribute it as she pleased. For example, every day before I left for school, Grandmother gave me some money to give to the monk she watched on television each day. She was looking after her future by buying merit enough to go to heaven when she died. Grandmother also gave me money for myself each morning, and she gave other people money as well.

Although she required a lot of care and assistance, Grandmother was not depressed. Instead, she seemed happy and content with her financial projects and with providing advice to our family. Still, my mother and I watched over her constantly and we hired a private nurse to help take care of her. My mother was a very skillful and competent caregiver since she had taken classes at the hospital to prepare her to take care of Grandmother Kim.

continued

continued

After I graduated from high school, I pursued a bachelor's degree at a university far from home. I would go back every weekend, however. When she was 95, Grandmother began to get weak. The doctor said she might have lung cancer. I didn't think she had any diseases; instead, I believed it was her time to go to heaven. My father didn't think she had lung cancer, either. He was convinced her lungs were perfect because she had no symptoms of any lung problem. No matter how strongly my father opposed the doctor's opinion, the doctor insisted on a lung biopsy as soon as possible. We agreed not to tell my grandmother about any suspicion of cancer, since we thought it might be too hard for her to know. We agreed only to tell her she had suffered a stroke. As we waited during the surgery, my father confided in me that he was unsure he had made the right decision to let the doctor do a biopsy.

When the results came back, my grandmother didn't have cancer. After she came home, everyone expected her to feel better. Unfortunately, Grandmother got worse. We took her to another doctor, who said that, since a biopsy could make an elderly patient weaker, it had been inappropriate to do the procedure. My father asked the doctor how much time his mother had left in this world. He told us that Grandmother could not be expected to live longer than one year. She died within several weeks.

Although I was away at the university when Grandmother died, I quickly returned. It is Thai custom that kin and family have to see the dead person before the body is placed in the coffin. Therefore I had a chance to see her for the last time in the mortuary. As my mother and I got her dressed and cut her hair, I noticed that Grandmother's body was small and cold. I told my mother that Grandmother had kissed me and told me to be a good girl the last time I saw her. Up to this day, I still remember every single word she told me. I think she knew her time to go was close. However, she didn't show any signs that she was afraid of death.

My father blamed the first doctor for his mother's death, but he blamed himself most of all. He thought that if he had insisted the doctor not perform the biopsy, she would have stayed with us longer. My mother and I both tried to comfort Father. I thought the best way to relieve him of some of his sorrow was to tell him that it was time for Grandmother to go. She had stayed longer than most other people could; also she had suffered from a stroke and had been paralyzed for a long time. However, I do understand my father's feeling because he is a son, and his responsibility is to do everything to keep his mother alive and healthy.

—PEM

Illness and Coping Metaphors

When Robin Williams died by suicide in 2014, CNN explained that the star "was battling depression" and *People* magazine proposed that he "fought, and lost, his battles with addiction and depression" (respectively, Duke, 2014; Tauber, 2014, headline). In many cultures, military metaphors such as these are common. They imply that "fighting" is the most effective and admirable way to respond to illness. In other cultures, however, responding to illness more closely resembles a peace initiative. We explore both perspectives here.

"FIGHT FOR YOUR LIFE"

The battle metaphor of ill health is bolstered by an organic, scientific perspective. The body, especially when ill, is regarded as a complex and unpredictable space vulnerable to invasion by enemy forces (bacteria, viruses, allergens) beyond most people's understanding. An analysis of media coverage conducted by

Many in the media described Robin Williams's death as a lost battle. From that perspective, illness is an enemy to be fought, and ideally, to be defeated.

Juanne Nancarrow Clarke and Jeannine Binns (2006) helps to illustrate this idea.

A sense that the human body is on the verge of war or disaster is evident in terms such as *heart attack, asthma attack,* and *risk factors* (Clarke & Binns, 2006). From that perspective, it is recommended that people be vigilant (*watch for warning signs*) and ready to engage in combat (*fight* disease). When illness does occur, it is often portrayed as an invader that has attacked the body-as-fortress (Clarke & Binns, 2006). Ill individuals are encouraged to *be strong* and to *fight for their lives.* Within this metaphoric landscape, medical care is described as *life-saving, state of the art,* and *tried, tested, and true.* Some medications (such as Viagra) are even heralded as "miracle drugs" (Baglia, 2005, p. 28).

If people recover, they are said to *triumph* over disease. Otherwise, they *lose their battle* with heart disease, cancer, or any number of other conditions. The implication is clear: Death represents defeat.

CAN YOU GUESS?

Who wrote the book *Illness as Metaphor* (1978) that challenged the idea (popular at that time) that conditions such as cancer and tuberculosis were most common among people with certain types of personalities?

a. Ursula K. Le Guin

b. Hunter S. Thompson

c. Susan Sontag

The answer appears at the end of the chapter.

"STRIVE FOR PEACE AND FLEXIBILITY"

In contrast to the military metaphor, members of some cultures in Korea and China, for example, believe in making peace with the body, especially when a serious health concern emerges.

They may engage in meditation and yoga to bring the mind and body into harmony and to evoke a sense of calm (Woodyard, 2011). These activities are consistent with other cultural customs, such as taking part in tai chi, qigong, karate, and tae kwon do—all designed to enhance spiritual and bodily awareness, flexibility, and fluid strength.

This perspective portrays the body not as a battlefield, but as a place of natural harmony. It follows that the best way to maintain good health is to honor the body and follow its rhythms.

In traditional Chinese medicine, for example, interventions are typically mild and designed to enhance the body's natural functioning. Aggressive interventions, such as surgery and strong drugs, may be viewed suspiciously as interfering with the body's natural rhythms. Some people depict traditional Eastern medicine as *health from within* and Western medicine as a *cure from without.*

Of course, the dichotomy between military and peace metaphors is not absolute. There is evidence to support both. People may embrace harmony-enhancing activities *and* the stance of a warrior. Still, it is helpful to highlight the essential differences between these perspectives so we can better understand the shades between them.

WHAT DO YOU THINK?

- Are there ways in which the military metaphor is appealing to you? If so, how?
- Are there ways in which the peace and flexibility perspective is appealing to you? If so, how?
- On balance, which feels more familiar to you? More appealing?

Sick Roles and Healer Roles

Culturally speaking, there are right and wrong ways to "do" being ill and providing assistance. For example, members of some Arab cultures expect women to cry out in pain during labor and delivery (Ahmad, 2004), whereas members of some Hispanic cultures believe that pain should be endured stoically because it is God's wish (Duggleby, 2003). Likewise, people might be expected to remain "respectfully" quiet in medical encounters or to take a "responsible" role by sharing their thoughts. The rules for being a good patient and a good caregiver may be contradictory and confusing. Nevertheless, with people's health hanging in the balance, participants may fervently wish to behave correctly.

A **role** is a set of expectations that applies to people performing various functions in the culture. For example, people may play the roles of patient, doctor, sister, friend, employee, and parent. Each role is guided by a set of culturally approved rules. Typically, one role exists in relation to another: patient–caregiver, student–teacher, parent–child, and so on. A role may lose meaning without its counterpart (e.g., a teacher is not a teacher without students). Therefore, role-playing is a collaborative endeavor, and people usually adjust their performances to form meaningful combinations. This can be so compelling that people sometimes feel forced into roles they would rather not assume. For example, if your conversational partner adopts a parental role, you may feel like a child, and you may act that way even if you would rather not. To do otherwise might seem uncooperative and rude.

As you will see in this section, patients and caregivers often play complementary roles—as mechanics and machines, providers and consumers, parents and children, and so on. Keep in mind that these roles are collaborative achievements, supported by participants' mutual efforts. This does not mean the participants always like the roles they assume. They may be motivated by a sense of cultural appropriateness or the perceived need to "play the scene" as the other person is playing it.

PERSPECTIVES

The traditional Muslim diet forbids the consumption of pork or alcohol. This can make hospital food, including foods fried in animal lard, unacceptable and can be an issue with medications, such as some forms of insulin that are derived from pigs, and cough syrups that include alcohol.

MECHANICS AND MACHINES

From one perspective, caregivers are similar to mechanics and patients to machines. The implication is that patients are relatively passive and care providers are expected to be analytical and capable of fixing the problems that are presented.

This perspective does not encourage emotional communication between patients and health professionals. The focus is more on identifying physical abnormalities and fixing them. When providers take on a mechanic role, they are typically more concerned with what they can observe and change than what a patient might be feeling.

Some people feel that scientific medicine is relatively mechanistic. That is, when health professionals take on the role of scientists, they are much like mechanics—concerned with the orderly physical functioning of the human body. As mechanics or scientists, care providers are expected to be objective, value neutral, and capable of collecting information, diagnosing a problem, and fixing it. It may seem inappropriate for them to display emotions or to call into play such intangible notions as faith and spirituality. Eric Cassell (1991) puts it this way: "Adjectives like warm, tall, swollen, or painful exist only for persons but, ideally, science deals only with measurable quantities like temperature, vertical dimensions, diameters" (p. 18).

One advantage of the mechanic-scientist role is that it reduces the emotional drain on health professionals. If patients are like machines who simply need fixing, emotions need not become part of the process

(Bonsteel, 1997). At the same time, the confidence that people *can* be fixed may seem comforting and neat.

Of course, patients may not appreciate being treated like machines. Some argue that ignoring patients' descriptions and considering them passive in their own care casts them as little more than a set of parts. In Richard Swiderski's (1976) analysis of medicine through the ages, he concludes that doctors have often considered patients less relevant than their pulse rates, blood, and urine. This is an image the public has embraced as well, as evidenced by patients' disappointment when their physicians do not run tests or prescribe medications. One reason for overuse of antibiotics is patients' insistence that treatment be embodied in some physical form, even when pharmacology suggests it will have no effect (Fisher, 1994). Moreover, the unrealistic belief that doctors can fix anything may lead to disappointment and even lawsuits.

PERSPECTIVES

> *"Your patient has no more right to all the truth you know than he has to all the medicine in your saddlebags. . . . He should only get so much as is good for him."*

That was the message from revered physician Oliver Wendell Holmes at the 1871 commencement address at Bellevue Hospital College. Holmes also advised the graduates to adopt the habit of "shrewd old doctors" who keep a few stock phrases to quiet "patients who insist on knowing the pathology of their complaints without the slightest capacity of understanding their scientific explanation" (Holmes, 1891, p. 389).

PARENTS AND CHILDREN

The popular expression "doctor's orders" suggests a relationship in which physicians issue directions that patients are expected to obey. This approach is consistent with **paternalism**, the idea that patients are like children and caregivers are like parents.

The dynamic that "health providers know best" may be enacted in cultures common in Japan, India, and Venezuela that honor a **high power distance**—that is, the degree to which they defer to people of greater power or status (Hofstede, 2001). Members of these cultures may consider it rude to disagree with or question an authority figure such as a health professional. In these cultures, patients have traditionally declined to take part in treatment decisions, preferring that professionals make decisions on their behalf ("Reducing Health Disparities," 2005). It is risky to assume that this is always the case, though. When Dana Lathan Alden and colleagues (2010) interviewed urban Vietnamese women, most of them indicated that they would like a say in choices regarding their contraception use, even though it is common in their culture to honor the judgment of physicians without question (Alden, Merz, & Thi, 2010).

One challenge of the paternalistic model is that professionals may misunderstand how much patients understand and agree with them. For example, Japanese individuals may use the word "yes" to signal politely that they understand the speaker, not as a sign that they agree. If they have questions, they may not ask them, for this might be seen as criticism.

Another challenge is that health professionals may be expected to know what is best for their patients. Some theorists believe this is a dubious assumption because patients may have many feelings and desires unknown to their care providers (Bealieu-Volk, 2014). Expecting providers to anticipate and act on patients' wishes may place an unrealistic burden on them and unfairly rob patients of opportunities to make their own decisions. (See Box 7.4 for more on this issue.)

SPIRITUALISTS AND BELIEVERS

Caregivers may be cast as spiritualists who use their powers on behalf of faithful patients. The image of caregivers as spiritual figures (and even as gods) was established thousands of years ago. Jesus has been called "the great physician" and is revered for legendary acts of curing the sick (Moore, Van Arsdale, Glittenberg, & Aldrich, 1987). Throughout history, physicians have been described as "little gods," a celestial metaphor that extends to nurses, often portrayed as "angels of mercy" (Moore et al., 1987, p. 232).

Anthropologists have compared the physician's role to that of a priest, a powerful and somewhat mysterious authority figure. This awe-inspiring image may be strengthened by patients' reverence and physicians' displays of power. Pendleton and colleagues (1984) point to doctors' laboratory coats, specialized vocabulary, and honorific titles as supporting props in this image. They also suggest that the image is bolstered by an information imbalance that makes

BOX 7.4 ETHICAL CONSIDERATIONS

Physician as Parent or Partner?

Medical ethicist Robert Veatch (1983) reflects that physicians are often criticized as being "aloof and unconcerned" rather than concerned and attentive, as people would like them to be. In short, physicians often act like strangers when patients wish they would act like friends or family members.

Paternalism (the idea that doctors are like parents) is a long-standing tradition. The Hippocratic oath, written approximately 2,500 years ago, beseeches physicians to use their best "ability and judgment" on each patient's behalf. This presumes that physicians are well acquainted with medicine *and* with the particular needs and preferences of each patient. Paternalism is also based on the belief that physicians are more capable of making medical decisions than patients are.

Some people feel that paternalism is outdated. Veatch (1983) points out that it is difficult to know patients well in the current age of large patient loads, specialization, and emergency and outpatient care. These factors make it unlikely that doctors will understand the unique needs and preferences of each patient. The paternalistic model is also criticized as inconsistent with patient empowerment, which presumes that patients are knowledgeable and active agents in their own health care (Emanuel & Emanuel, 1995).

What Do You Think?

1. Do you feel it is realistic or preferable for health caregivers to know their patients' feelings and values? If so, how might they accomplish this? If not, what alternatives would you suggest?
2. Can you think of circumstances in which you would want your physician to know your feelings and life circumstances?
3. Can you think of circumstances in which you would rather your physician did not know you well?
4. Do you feel patients are capable of making decisions about their own care?

physicians' knowledge seem all the more marvelous: "Powerful rituals, such as examining and prescribing, are the more charismatic in the absence of adequate explanations" (p. 9).

By contrast, folk healing is typically oriented toward lifeworld concerns (Chapter 4). Usually, a folk healer's role is to integrate social support with spiritual faith and physical treatment. Among the most well-known healers and spiritualists are the shamans and hand-tremblers of Native American cultures and the *curanderos* (coo-ran-DARE-ohs) of Mexican American cultures. These folk healers are usually well-known members of their communities. As such, they are familiar and accessible, without institutional boundaries or technical jargon.

A shaman is believed to coax a patient's disease into his or her own body and then expel it through strength of will (Hutch, 2013). The assumption is that illness is an invasion of magical or supernatural forces. The faithful believe shamans can communicate with beings beyond the physical world, an ability that gives them magical abilities and healing powers.

Folk medicine's focus on sense-making and social support addresses the distinction between healing and curing. McWhinney (1989, p. 29) calls *healing* a "restoration of wholeness," which includes spiritual and moral consideration, as opposed to purely physical *curing*, which he says may still leave a patient in "anguish of spirit" about the causes, effects, and fears associated with the illness.

Another spiritualist group is the Christian Science Church. Some members of this religion believe that conventional medicine is anti-Christian and that illness is an illusion and can be cured only through prayer (Christian Science, n.d.). Thus, they may refuse biomedical therapies, including surgery. This has raised controversy across the nation, especially when children's lives are involved. Currently, the church's website presents examples of people who were cured by prayer and mind control but says health-related decisions are up to individual members.

A belief in the supernatural also characterizes the health beliefs of some southern Appalachians. In that culture, spiritual ceremonies involving faith healing and glossolalia (speaking in tongues) are believed to restore health. **Faith healers** are expected to channel the curative power of the Holy Spirit, which they pass to believers through ceremonies known as the laying on of hands. **Glossolalia** involves a trancelike state during which a worshipper seems to speak in a foreign language. It is believed that the language is known only to God, or that it is a foreign tongue known to some but unknown to the worshipper, except through divine inspiration.

The success of a spiritual ceremony is often said to rely on the patient's faith in the healer and the greater spiritual force that has accepted the healer as a medium. One result of this assumption is that failure to recover may be construed as an indication of the patient's insufficient faith (Kearney, 1978). For this reason, patients may be particularly trusting and may benefit from the power of positive thinking. However, if their conditions do not improve, they may be loath to admit it.

Even scientists acknowledge the power of faith, although they are not likely to regard it as the central focus of their work. Evidence supports that people who expect to be cured sometimes are, even when the "treatment" is an inactive **placebo** such as flavored water or sugar. Placebo effects are so common that medical researchers routinely give some research participants an actual treatment and give other people a placebo. If the treatment group does not experience greater effects than the placebo group, the researchers cannot be sure they are measuring anything more than the power of suggestion. The reverse is sometimes true as well. People who have no confidence in a treatment may be unaffected by it. These examples do not prove that all disease can be reduced to the effects of faith and emotions. However, they demonstrate that there is more to disease than meets the (microscopic) eye.

A religious-like faith in caregivers serves multiple goals. It inspires confidence on the part of patient and caregiver, which may be an important part of healing. It also honors the extraordinary role health professionals play in managing life and health. There is a downside, though, in dashed hopes and exorbitant malpractice claims. With the expectation that medicine can work miracles if done correctly, people may feel particularly angry when things do not go well, and they may rightly or wrongly charge that their caregivers are incompetent (Kreps, 1990).

PROVIDERS AND CONSUMERS

It has become popular to describe health care in terms of consumerism. Patients are regarded as shoppers or clients who pay caregivers primarily to provide information and carry out the patients' wishes. Consumerism is fueled in part by Internet resources. People can now look up extensive health information for themselves. Websites such as ConsumerReportsHealth.org, DoctorScorecard.com, and AngiesList.com now offer reviews of hospitals, treatments, products, and professionals—including consumer reviews of doctors' bedside manner, perceived quality of care, price, the cleanliness of their offices, the courteousness of their staff members, and more.

Competitiveness has made many care providers especially mindful of patient satisfaction. However, some who see themselves as serving a higher purpose than profit margins find the marketplace metaphors disturbing. Analysts warn that consumer websites can have a backlash. For one, anyone can file comments online but most people don't. As a result, the comments that appear may not represent most patients' opinions. For another, physicians who are worried about their stats may be dissuaded from taking high-risk cases, which are more likely than others to result in lawsuits and disappointing outcomes. Thus, consumer reviews can inadvertently punish doctors for going out on a limb for patients with critical or rare conditions.

Years ago, Howard Friedman and M. Robin DiMatteo (1979) cautioned that consumerism may be a risky conceptualization for all involved. If the customer is always right, they wondered, will medical centers that respect patients' treatment decisions later be held liable if adverse outcomes result? Friedman and DiMatteo also worried that pleasing patients may sometimes be at odds with helping them. Considering that the most effective medical options are sometimes the most unpleasant, how far will caregivers go to avoid upsetting their patients?

Similarly, consumerism seems to place cost as a top priority. Richard Glass (1996) is concerned that physicians may choose less aggressive treatment options if they are forced to be more mindful of cost than care. A physician himself, Glass maintains that patients "rightly expect something different from their doctors than from consumer goods salespersons" (p. 148). He argues that a marketplace mentality may have "perverse effects" on medical care, and he beseeches health care managers not to interfere unduly in medical decision making.

There is some evidence that people who are well informed about health information do not view their doctors in quite the same way as before. Unlike

BOX 7.5 PERSPECTIVES

Partners in Care

Tina, a middle-aged mother of two, has been referred to a hemodialysis center for treatment. When she arrives for her first visit, an advanced nurse practitioner notices that she is upset and takes the time to speak with her. Tina says she has long had diabetes, but she does not understand why her doctor wants her to undergo dialysis. She feels fine and her family relies on her to work full time.

Recognizing that Tina needs to be an active agent in making decisions about her own care, the nurse practitioner listens attentively to her concerns and helps her better understand her medical condition, which involves kidney disease that might kill her without treatment. Together, they devise a regimen in which Tina is able to undergo dialysis for about a year until she receives a donor kidney.

Debra Hain and Dainne Sandy (2013) write about Tina in an article on the value of being a partner, rather than a parent, when it comes to patients. They reflect that a paternalistic model probably would not have helped Tina understand the need for dialysis or coordinate her care in light of her other responsibilities.

"Tina is forever grateful for the support she received at a time she desperately needed it," the authors write, reflecting that, when the nurse practitioner asked Tina what had made her start dialysis, she replied warmly, "It's the way you spoke to me" (Hain & Sandy, 2013. p. 156).

What Do You Think?

1. In what circumstances, if any, might you follow a doctor's advice without question?
2. In what circumstances, if any, would you rather be treated as a partner in making decisions about your care?

generations past, people are unlikely to believe that doctors have all the answers (Lowrey & Anderson, 2006). This may diminish physicians' professional status. Or it may simply fuel a different kind of relationship, such as the one we will discuss next.

PARTNERS

Only as partners do patients and caregivers assume roles of roughly equal power. Of course, they each bring something different to the encounter in terms of experiences and expertise. But as partners, they orient themselves to identifying mutually satisfying solutions, acting as peers in the process. The partner role is consistent with collaborative medical talk (Chapter 5).

The success of health care managed in this way hinges largely on the quality of patient–caregiver relationships. In 1996, the *Journal of the American Medical Association* introduced a column called "The Patient–Physician Relationship." In an article launching the new feature, Richard Glass (1996) proclaimed the doctor–patient link to be the "center of medicine," a covenant not to be compromised by impersonal reliance on technology or profit-oriented decisions. This emphasis underscores the importance of trusting communication between patients and caregivers.

Some people find the partnership model appealing because it allows both patients and health professionals to have influence over medical decisions, as opposed to being strictly patient centered or caregiver centered. Hufford (1997) attests that patients have important and relevant statements to make about their own health: "Sick people, it turns out, often do know exactly what has been happening to them, what it feels like, and when it happens, and there is nothing fictional about it" (p. 118). (See Box 7.5 for an example.)

One way to encourage patients' active participation is to follow the lead of Myra Skluth (2007) and create patient to-do lists. She and patients negotiate the terms of the to-do lists, and then each keeps a copy. "This approach works very well," she says (p. 16). Because the to-do lists are in patients' charts, "if they call with questions, the nurses know exactly what I told them. I can also review the items with them at the beginning of the next visit—what they accomplished, and what they didn't and why. I find my patients really appreciate this" (p. 16).

Few people criticize the idea of patients and health professionals as partners. However, this may be a difficult transition to make. Both sides have traditionally upheld the expectation that professionals will guide medical discussions and patients will be relatively quiet and passive in their presence. A shift is possible, and indeed we see some evidence of it, but it will require continued change and cooperation on both sides.

In closing this section, these interaction models characterize various aspects of medical discourse, yet they are not as simple as they appear. Transactions often, perhaps always, involve elements of several models, even if one is dominant. The following discussion of holistic medicine involves a treatment model that draws upon many of the ideas we have discussed about health as harmonic balance and can employ, at times, any of the relationship types described here (Ho & Bylund, 2008).

IN YOUR EXPERIENCE

- Which of the roles described in this section have you played as either a patient or a caregiver?
- Which appeal to you most and why?

Holistic Care

Lisa immediately notices the differences between this setting and her doctor's office. Soft music is playing, and the lights and colors are soothing. She lies on a massage table and Jing, an acupuncturist, encourages her to relax. Despite her fear of needles, Lisa finds the experience mostly painless. "I could barely feel the needles go in," she says. "There was the slightest of sensations, followed by a feeling of energy flowing."

This story, adapted from Lisa Rosenthal's blog ("Fertility," 2012), describes an initial experience with holistic care. In the United States, options such as acupuncture, meditation, and chiropractic—once derided as quackery—are gaining acceptance. There are a number of reasons for this, including their emphasis on open communication. The following section describes holistic forms of medicine, factors fueling recent interest in them, and their advantages and drawbacks.

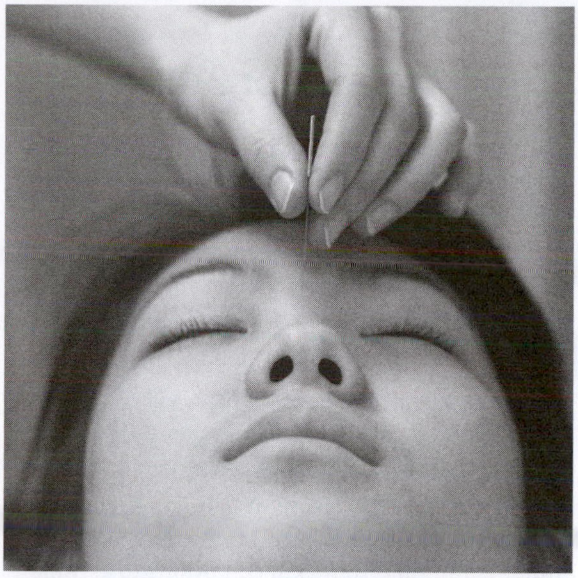

Holistic therapies such as acupuncture have gained acceptance in recent years, partly because they are typically less expensive and invasive than many biomedical procedures.

TERMINOLOGY

The term *alternative medicine* has traditionally been applied to therapies that have not been scientifically researched and consequently approved by professional associations such as the American Medical Association. However, "alternative" is not a particularly accurate description of these therapies. As Lisa Schreiber (2005) points out, it is not an either/or proposition. Many people use "alternative" therapies in conjunction with other treatments. For example, meditation, prayer, and yoga are not biomedical means of treating cancer, but most oncologists agree that, if they are useful in promoting emotional well-being, they are valuable components of a treatment regimen.

Some people have adopted the term *complementary medicine* or *complementary and alternative medicine (CAM)*. These are somewhat problematic as well, in that they define these therapies not by what they *are* but simply in terms of their (implicitly peripheral) relation to biomedicine. Another semantic alternative is the term *traditional medicine,* used in parts of the world such as Africa, Asia, and Latin America. However, this term seems to exclude recent innovations. For lack of a better term, this section follows Schreiber's suggestion and uses the term *holistic medicine.* Some make a good point that not all methods

BOX 7.6

Holistic Medicine at a Glance

ACUPUNCTURE is believed to stimulate and balance the body's energy flow (Qi) through the use of tiny needles inserted in the skin.

AYURVEDA is based on ancient Indian practices, including yoga, diet, and meditation.

BIOFEEDBACK involves learning to recognize the body's physiological states (such as tension) and to control them.

CHIROPRACTIC MEDICINE focuses on the physical alignment of the spine, muscles, and nerves.

HERBAL THERAPIES use plant extracts such as chamomile, licorice, and St. John's wort to treat ailments ranging from skin conditions to asthma and depression.

HOLISTIC CARE emphasizes overall well-being (physical and emotional), with an emphasis on maintaining health, not just curing ailments.

INTEGRATIVE MEDICINE combines biomedical and naturopathic therapies.

HOMEOPATHIC MEDICINE uses very small doses to escalate symptoms in an effort to stimulate the body's immune system. (In contrast, most mainstream medical care is *allopathic*, relying on remedies that counteract symptoms.) *Homeo* is derived from the Greek word meaning "same," and *allo* comes from the Greek word for "other."

NATUROPATHIC MEDICINE focuses on diet and the use of herbal therapies to help people maintain good health.

OSTEOPATHIC MEDICINE is taught in traditional medical schools. This branch of medicine focuses on the muscular and skeletal system, treating the body as an integrated unit.

REIKI (pronounced RAY-kee) is based on the Japanese tradition of channeling energy through the healer's hands to increase the patient's spiritual strength.

TRADITIONAL ASIAN MEDICINE includes therapies such as herbal remedies, acupuncture, and massage. It is based on establishing a healthy flow of energy through the body and achieving harmony between mind, body, spirit, and surroundings.

that fall within this rubric are holistic. However, for the most part, their approach is more holistic than biomedical therapies, which are grounded to a large extent in identifying specific causes and cures of illness. A brief glossary that explains the wide variety of holistic therapies is available in Box 7.6.

IN YOUR EXPERIENCE

- Have you ever taken part in holistic treatment (e.g., meditation, herbal supplements, acupuncture, chiropractic)?
- If so, what was your experience?
- Have you told your doctor about these activities? Why or why not?

POPULARITY

There are several reasons for the recent popularity of holistic medicine. For one, an increasing number of people are receptive to the idea. About 38% of adults in the United States and 12% of children use holistic therapies such as acupuncture, chiropractic, Ayurveda, meditation, massage, yoga, and hypnosis (National Center for Complementary, 2012). Acceptance is even greater in some areas of the world. According to the latest statistics, in some parts of Asia and Africa, 80% of citizens rely primarily on holistic care (WHO, 2008a).

Second, well-trained caregivers are becoming more plentiful. In the United States, chiropractic is one of the fastest-growing occupations. There are currently about 44,400 chiropractors in the United States, and the number is expected to rise 15% between 2012 and 2022 (U.S. Bureau of Labor Statistics, 2014b).

Third, research dollars are more available than in the past. In 1997, the U.S. Congress voted to fund an Office of Alternative Medicine as part of the National Institutes of Health (NIH). This new NIH office offers funding for researchers interested in testing the efficacy of diverse therapies. For example, acupuncture has been shown in clinical trials to help some people lose weight, relieve chronic depression, diminish some forms of pain, and meet a range of other treatment goals, particularly when combined with other forms of care (Cho, Lee, Thabane, & Lee, 2009; Tough & White, 2011; Zhang, Chen, Yip, Ng, & Wong, 2010).

Finally, many insurance companies and physicians are now giving the go-ahead to nonbiomedical treatments, and Medicare and workers' compensation plans in all 50 states reimburse chiropractic care. (For more about careers in holistic medicine, see Box 7.7.)

ADVANTAGES

There are several reasons for the growing popularity of holistic care. For one, such care typically involves low-cost and low-tech methods. If these are useful, they stand to reduce health care costs. That is good news for insurance companies and managed care, if people simultaneously maintain their involvement in conventional care, which they seem inclined to do. The World Health Organization is supporting research to see if low-cost herbal remedies can effectively treat malaria, AIDS, diabetes, and other conditions in impoverished areas of the world.

Second, holistic methods are usually based on simple principles that may be more understandable and less frightening to patients than conventional medicine. People who use holistic therapies often do so with the goal of maintaining health in everyday ways (National Institute of Medicine, 2005). For the most part, these people also see biomedical practitioners, although they tend not to tell doctors about holistic methods they are also using.

Third, holistic practitioners often spend more time with their patients and develop closer relationships with them than do biomedical practitioners. This may suit people who feel that most medical settings are too impersonal. As a holistic practitioner in Geist-Martin and Bell's (2009) study expressed it, "The most important thing is to listen. If I listen to the patient I am able to know what worries him, what he needs, what bothers him, and from there I can better maneuver the process" (p. 636).

BOX 7.7 CAREER OPPORTUNITIES

Holistic Medicine

Acupuncturist
Chiropractor
Holistic nurse
Massage therapist
Midwife
Naturopathic physician
Nutritionist/dietician
Reiki practitioner
Yoga instructor

Career Resources and Job Listings

- Academy of Nutrition and Dietetics: http://www.eatright.org
- Accrediting Bureau of Health Education Schools: http://www.abhes.org
- American Association of Naturopathic Physicians: http://naturopathic.org/content.asp?contentid=60
- American Chiropractic Association: http://www.acatoday.org
- American College of Nurse Midwives: http://www.midwife.org
- American Council on Exercise: http://www.acefitness.org
- American Massage Therapy Association: http://www.amtamassage.org/index.html
- Associated Bodywork and Massage Professionals: http://www.abmp.com/home
- Association of Chiropractic Colleges: http://www.chirocolleges.org
- Commission on Dietetic Registration: http://www.cdrnet.org
- International Association of Reiki Professionals: http://www.iarp.org
- U.S. Bureau of Labor Statistics Occupational Outlook Handbook: http://www.bls.gov/ooh

Fourth, holistic therapies are usually more directed to health maintenance than biomedicine, which has traditionally focused on curing and treating. The new imperative to conserve health care resources and money makes prevention appealing.

Finally, people may turn to holistic therapies if other methods offer little or no help. For example, symptoms of anxiety that are not alleviated by medication may sometimes be managed with relaxation and biofeedback.

DRAWBACKS

Many holistic therapies are nonthreatening. Energy work, relaxation, and minute traces of natural substances (as in homeopathy) are unlikely to hurt anyone. However, some therapies involve the use of herbs and other natural products. Because they are considered dietary supplements rather than drugs, the U.S. Food and Drug Administration (FDA) does not require manufacturers to register them or prove their safety before they go on the market. Consequently, many supplements are not thoroughly researched. This is worrisome, first, because significant health risks are associated with some natural therapies. Taken by the wrong person or in the wrong amount, they can be deadly. Some natural remedies have caused lead poisoning, hepatitis, and renal failure. The herb germander, often included in herbal teas and tablets, has been linked to acute nonviral hepatitis. Before it was banned, the herb ephedra, sold as an enhancement for bodybuilding, was linked to at least 17 deaths (Capriotti, 1999; WHO, 2003, Update 83).

Another concern is that people may be swindled into buying useless products. Cancer patients, for instance, are vulnerable to advertisers who claim to provide the latest life-saving serums. The FDA cautions consumers to beware of wording such as "treats all forms of cancer," "skin cancers disappear," and "shrinks malignant tumors" (U.S. FDA, 2008). Such claims signal a scam, not a bona fide product. Consumers should also realize that "actual patients" and spokespersons who appear to be physicians actually may be actors hired to sell the product.

Third, endangered plant species may be wiped out in the zeal to provide health benefits (and reap the financial awards) associated with high-demand herbal remedies. Already, harvesters have endangered rain forests in Malaysia, Africa, and the Amazon. Environmentalists urge world citizens to consider regulations, herbal farming, and ocean-based cultivation to protect the planet's wildlife.

A final drawback involves a lack of communication. Only about one-third of Americans who use holistic therapies tell their physicians about them (Kennedy, Chi-Chuan, & Wu, 2007). One woman in the United Kingdom described her doctors' reaction to acupuncture: "They didn't actually ridicule it, but they said, 'hmmm' [frowns]. I felt like they didn't really want to talk about it" (Tovey & Broom, 2007, p. 2556). All the same, when doctors do not know about other treatments, they may prescribe medications that interact with them in dangerous ways.

In summary, considering both the potential advantages and drawbacks of holistic therapies, it is important that people become comfortable talking about them. Lisa's experience, which began this section, was a positive one. Once the needles were in place, Jing wrapped her in a warm blanket and said she should close her eyes and relax. "The best way that I can describe the experience is to relate it to twinkling lights," Lisa recalls. "It was a lovely, subtle feeling. . . . The rest of the day I felt relaxed, calm, and as serene as I feel after a restorative yoga class" ("Fertility," 2012).

Summary

As we strive to become better communicators, it is important to understand diverse perspectives and to appreciate that, to some extent, health and healing are cultural constructs. Although it can be tempting to ignore or devalue ideas that differ radically from one's own, ethnocentrism undermines cultural competence.

Fuller's reflective negotiation model of cultural competence in health care reminds us that certainty is not the goal. Knowledge of different cultures helps to some extent, but we cannot know all there is to know. Neither should we assume that people all act the same or are influenced by only one culture. True cultural competence involves a continual process of asking and listening—both to others and to oneself. The goal is not to privilege any one perspective, but to negotiate for respectful and mutually appealing options.

The way that we think about health influences how we think and talk about it. From one perspective, disease is an organic phenomenon, and what shows up under a microscope may be more to the point than a patient's subjective experiences. Consistent with the biomedical model, this perspective considers undetectable conditions less real than physically verifiable ones. From another perspective, some people believe health is affected by harmonic balance among such factors as relationships, spiritual forces, the environment, behavior, and energy fields within the body.

The theory of health as expanded consciousness proposes that a health disruption can be a valuable opportunity for reflection and change. Whether a health condition is an asset or a liability relies partly on social interpretation. It may be considered fortunate or tragic that a person has seizures, is very tall, extremely thin, or so on. Even members of cultures steeped in organic definitions of disease may stigmatize people with some disorders. Especially when a condition is threatening or difficult to understand, it is common to blame ill persons for their conditions or to see them as cursed or lazy.

Cultural beliefs and customs often have a profound influence on men and women's health behaviors. In many cultures, women are encouraged to be dependent and to focus mostly on motherhood. Whereas women are more likely than men to experience violent assaults from intimate partners, men are more likely to die in fights or battles. Partly because men are often expected to be aggressive and to avoid showing emotional distress, they are more likely than women to feel shamed by emotional concerns and to avoid communicating about them.

People in certain cultures will be distressed if family members are not allowed to participate in their care. This may or may not be consistent with the routines and beliefs of health professionals.

In some cultures, a military metaphor of health characterizes "fighting" as the most effective and admirable way to respond to illness. In other cultures, people are encouraged to pursue peace and flexibility, and illnesses are seen as a valuable opportunity for reflection and change.

Cultural values and assumptions are embodied in the roles that patients and caregivers play. How one interprets illness has an effect on the type of healing process preferred. If disease is regarded as a physical phenomenon, patients may be like passive machines and caregivers like mechanics or scientists. Patients may be considered incapable if they are cast as children seeking the guidance of parent-like caregivers who know what is best.

Caregivers have been deified to varying extents. Even orthodox practitioners who pride themselves on science-based care are regarded with awe for their extraordinary ability to understand and treat illness. In some cultures, healers are spiritual leaders, expected to channel supernatural powers for the benefit of faithful patients. Considering patients and caregivers to be consumers and providers is more enabling for patients, but some people worry that medical care may suffer if it is forced to uphold the rules of the marketplace. Finally, as partners, patients and caregivers work to build mutually satisfying relationships and care plans.

Holistic care specialists focus primarily on lifestyle changes and natural remedies. These diverse therapies are gaining popularity based on public interest, an increase in trained care providers, new research, and increased acceptance by health plans and biomedical practitioners.

Some people seek holistic care when they are not satisfied with the results or nature of biomedicine. In the majority of cases, however, people continue to see physicians and other practitioners as well. The downsides are that some products are not well researched before they go on the market, people may be tricked into buying useless products, and large-scale harvest of natural remedies threatens the environment. Although individuals may assume that natural products are not harmful, they can be deadly. All in all, it is a good idea to become knowledgeable about herbs and supplements before trying them.

Key Terms and Theories

culture
ethnocentrism
reflective negotiation model
germ theory
organic model
harmonic balance perspective
susto
coraje
biophilia hypothesis
karma
yin and yang
Qi
theory of health as expanded consciousness
explicate order
implicate order
stigma
role

paternalism
high power distance
faith healers
glossolalia
placebo

Discussion Questions

1. Consider the quote on page 154 by the nurse who was offended by the suggestion that staff members avoid telling patients "Merry Christmas." If she were to follow the principles of Fuller's reflective negotiation model, what questions might she ask other people? What questions might she ask herself? What might be a good outcome in that situation?
2. What aspects of your health are well explained by an organic approach? By a harmonic approach? If you made a list of healthy behaviors you would like to adopt, what, if anything, would you list in terms of organic factors? What, if anything, would reflect the desire for balance? Why?
3. If you were to schedule a day's worth of activities in which you would experience a balance of yin and yang energy, what might that day include? Do you think living that way on a consistent basis would influence your health? Why or why not?
4. Think of a health episode you or someone you know has experienced. In what way did explicate-level factors play a role? In what way did implicate-level factors influence what happened? Do you think these factors have a significant impact on health overall?
5. Reread the "I Am Not a Victim of Breast Cancer" poem on page 164 or go online and read the entire poem. In what ways does the author seem to be addressing the stigma of disease? What do her words suggest about the notion that people with cancer are "victims?"
6. In what ways is your life affected by your gender? By your role as a family member? Do any of these factors influence your health or the way you communicate about health? If so, how?
7. Are you more inclined to respond to illness as a "fighter" or as a "peacekeeper" or as a bit of both? What behaviors reflect your approach? Do you believe they are effective? Why or why not?
8. Which of the patient–caregiver role sets best describes your health care experiences? Which do you prefer? Why?
9. Have you participated in holistic care, either as a patient or a practitioner? If so, describe the role of communication in your experience. What were the potential advantages and disadvantages, in your opinion?

Answer to *Can You Guess?*

If you answered Susan Sontag, you are correct. In *Illness as Metaphor*, Sontag (1978), who underwent extensive treatment for breast cancer herself, delivered scathing criticism of a medical model that seemed to blame people for their own diseases through references to a so-called cancer personality and the supposed (unsupported) link between artistic temperament and susceptibility to tuberculosis.

PART IV

Coping and Health Resources

We all need each other.

—LEO BUSCAGLIA

Two of the most powerful means we have for staying healthy and happy have little in common with each other on the surface.

One is the love and support of people around us. Research is overwhelming that people who have close and supportive relationships with others consider themselves healthier, cope with adversity better, and tend to live longer than others. Communication is the means through which we foster and maintain those ties. In Chapter 8, we will talk about the role of social support, including how we can be effective listeners and good friends and what it means to cope, together, with health crises and end-of-life experiences. We will also look at a few social-support disasters, when efforts that are meant to be helpful turn out to be hurtful instead. The lessons from those experiences can help us avoid the same outcomes.

The second resource is communication technology. At first glance, technology feels far removed from the warmth of companionship and social support. But we find that it can help us to establish and maintain supportive relationships, become well informed, and feel that we have the resources to cope with health issues. The possibilities are expanding faster than we ever imagined, as you will see in Chapter 9.

This unlikely combination of health resources reminds us that—in its many forms—communication is a powerful part of what allows us to be happy in good times and in the midst of life's great challenges.

CHAPTER 8

Social Support, Family Caregiving, and End of Life

Struggling to be strong after the death of his young daughter, Alonzo is hurt and mystified when friends' first question is, "How is your wife?"

Margie misses the normal times, when people talked to her about the weather, boys, and school. Now they just hold doors for her and try not to stare at her wheelchair.

Everyone knows Drew's illness is very serious, but no one speaks of it to him. Drew wonders how he is supposed to cope with such an emotional topic in silence.

Lucy spends two hours each morning and three hours each evening caring for her three children and her elderly mother. In between, she maintains a full-time job outside the home. Lucy is glad she can help, but she wonders how many years it will be before she can take a vacation or spend a quiet day alone. Such thoughts make her feel sad and guilty.

Mario is pleased with life and himself. Things have not been easy, but he appreciates the pleasures of life like never before. Friends and loved ones are closer, and he is at peace with himself. He marvels that dying has brought about some of the best days of his life.

As these scenarios suggest, the majority of communication about health does not occur in a doctor's office or hospital. It occurs at home, at the grocery store, on the telephone, and in other settings of everyday life. Spouses, children, friends, and coworkers often have as much influence as doctors and nurses.

Social support includes a broad range of activities, from comforting a friend after a romantic disappointment, to listening while a grieving father tells and retells his story, to performing an Internet data search, to acknowledging that a handicapped individual is a normal person.

Most people perform more supportive behaviors than they realize and, as a consequence, have positive effects on people's health and moods. Research shows that supportive communication can help speed healing, reduce loneliness, reduce symptoms and stress, lessen pain, and build self-esteem (see, e.g., Chia, 2009; Segrin & Domschke, 2011; Thomtén, Soares, & Sundin, 2011). And the benefits go both ways. People who provide social support often feel an enhanced sense of well-being themselves (Robinson & Tian, 2009).

This chapter begins with a conceptual overview of coping and social support, including the role that communication plays as we demonstrate caring for others, strive for a sense of control, and negotiate uncertainties. We will talk about the benefits of social support, but also what happens when well intentioned efforts hurt more than they help. Then we briefly explore the role of animal companions and the idea of health crises as transformative experiences before we examine social support in two contexts—family caregiving and end-of-life experiences.

CULTURE AND HEALTH

A paradox puzzles researchers: Hispanic Americans are more likely than average to suffer from unfair discrimination, low incomes, poor living conditions, and limited education—factors that typically contribute to poor health. However, they tend to live several years longer than Black and non-Hispanic White Americans. One explanation involves social support. Some researchers feel that a cultural emphasis on family relationships and close-knit communities accounts, in part, for Hispanic Americans' comparative good health and longer lives (Scommegna, 2013).

Conceptual Overview

In the simplest sense, support involves people helping people. Melanie Barnes and Steve Duck (1994) define **social support** as "behaviors that, whether directly or indirectly, communicate to an individual that she or he is valued and cared for by others" (p. 176). Some theorists (e.g., Albrecht & Adelman, 1987) consider that the central function of social support is increasing a person's sense of control. Their viewpoint is substantiated by research (covered in this chapter) that people cope best when they feel well informed and actively involved. This section describes different coping mechanisms and the role social support plays in helping people through crisis situations.

THEORETICAL PERSPECTIVES

The **buffering hypothesis** holds that social support is most important when we encounter potentially stressful experiences, in which case knowing that other people are there for us can cushion (buffer) us from feeling overwhelmed or helpless (Cohen & Wills, 1985). For example, your ability to cope with bad news may be strengthened by the conviction that loved ones will stick by you no matter what, will be understanding listeners, will help with information and assistance, and so on. The buffering process is likely to be especially meaningful if the support offered matches the support you feel you need. One college student said that, when he tore the anterior cruciate ligament (ACL) in his knee on vacation, he was relatively calm about it because his girlfriend, a physical therapy assistant, was by his side, telling him what to expect in terms of pain, treatment, and recovery. He says her presence and knowledge made the experience feel "doable."

In another sense, social support is like money in the bank. It is nice to know it is there, even if we don't spend it. The **direct-effect** or **main-effect model** proposes that social support is beneficial even when we are not encountering notable stressors. A strong social network helps us feel valued every day and is a reassuring reminder that friends' support is always available (Barnes & Duck, 1994). Joann Reinhardt and colleagues (2006) found that adults age 65 and older who were experiencing vision loss were least likely to be depressed and most likely to adapt well to lifestyle changes if they perceived that they had strong emotional support. For them, actually receiving support was less important than knowing it was there if they needed it (Reinhardt, Boerner, & Horowitz, 2006).

Indeed, the main-effect model suggests that we may encounter fewer stressful episodes and enjoy greater overall health if we have strong social networks (Cohen & Wills, 1985). Older adults who are

Evidence suggests that older adults with active social networks may outlive their least socially active peers as many as 10 years.

unsatisfied with the amount of emotional support they received from friends and family members are twice as likely to rate their health only "fair" or "poor" as their peers who feel emotionally supported (White, Philogene, Fine, & Sinha, 2009). They may even live longer. In an Australian study of people 70 and older, those with the most active social networks (in the top third as compared to their peers) were 22% more likely to live another 10 years than those with the least active networks (Giles, Glonek, Luszcz, & Andrews, 2005). This is no surprise to older adults who have experienced the death of a spouse. They typically say that the best coping strategy is to keep busy and interact with others, and the worst coping strategy is to isolate oneself at home (Bergstrom & Holmes, 2000).

There are several reasons for the link between social ties and good health. One is that we learn from others and develop confidence through interactions. Teens are most likely to negotiate safer-sex options with their partners (Troth & Peterson, 2000) and avoid eating disorders (Botta & Dumlao, 2002; Miller-Day & Marks, 2006) if they come from families that display a collaborative problem-solving orientation rather than a distant or conflict-avoidant orientation. Others' actions are informative guides to behavior, especially in intense and uncertain times. For example, when news broke that Patrick Swayze had pancreatic cancer at about the same time health communication scholar Barbara Sharf learned that her childhood friend Rita had been diagnosed with the disease, Sharf says that Swayze's narrative became part of their experience as well. Sharf (2010) writes that she scanned newsstands for tidbits, enthralled by Swayze's resolve to keep working and his frank descriptions about both the tolerable and the "hellish" aspects of the disease. When she heard news of Swayze's death four months after Rita's, she says that the news brought fresh waves of grief.

Second, physical benefits are associated with strong social ties. Resting blood pressure and blood glucose levels are lower (healthier) among people who express a great deal of affection compared to those who do not (Floyd, Hesse, & Haynes, 2007), and shared humor tends to reduce tension, enhance mood, and boost immunity (Alston, 2007; Lockwood & Yoshimura, 2014; Wanzer, Sparks, & Frymier, 2009). In contrast, lonely individuals are more likely than others to sleep poorly, to feel stressed, and to have poor health (Hawkley, Masi, Berry, & Cacioppo, 2006; Segrin & Passalacqua, 2010).

Third, loved ones may support us in making healthy decisions. Teenagers are most likely to be effective when confronting their peers about alcohol abuse if both parties perceive that they are good friends and that the concern is legitimate (Malis & Roloff, 2007). Likewise, romantic partners with whom we share a high sense of intimacy are more likely than others to convince us to improve our diets and engage in other healthy behaviors (Dennis, 2006).

It is important to note that the quality of our relationships is more important than the quantity. Having a few close friends and loved ones is typically healthier than an active social life without much intimacy (Segrin & Passalacqua, 2010). And it matters why people support us. Friends' attention is flattering partly because it is freely given, whereas family members are more obliged. When individuals studied by Metts and Manns (1996) told loved ones they had HIV or AIDS, friends were typically more supportive than family, perhaps because the family members were more overwhelmed by their own emotions.

Friendship quality is especially important in later life. After age 70 or so, we are likely to put stock in a small number of very close friends and family members (Nussbaum, Baringer, Fisher, & Kundrat, 2008). These smaller, more intimate networks are well suited to situations in which we may have limited mobility, when close friends are likely to rely extensively on

BOX 8.1

When Communication Ability is Compromised

Unfortunately, health concerns can interfere with social interaction and friendships, particularly when an individual's ability to communicate is affected. When researchers led by Jennifer Bute (2007) interviewed friends and loved ones of people with compromised communication abilities, they found that some of them continued to feel an easy and even improved camaraderie despite communication limits. But many experienced it as a profound loss, particularly if dementia was involved (Bute, Donovan-Kicken, & Martins, 2007). Said one woman in the study, "It is a different relationship. . . . I have lost the friend I used to have before" (p. 239).

What Do You Think?

1. Have you ever experienced difficulty communicating with someone because of a disability? If so, how did you handle the situation?
2. Has your ability to communicate ever been compromised, even temporarily? Did people respond to you differently? If so, how?
3. What would you do if a loved one could no longer communicate easily with you? Do you think it would change your relationship? If so, how?

each other, and when changes in hearing and vision may impact our communication abilities (Nussbaum et al., 2008). (See Box 8.1 for more about the effects of communication impairments.)

In short, the buffering hypothesis and main-effects model suggest that social support is helpful both during major life events and the challenges of everyday life. For many reasons, in ways that change throughout our lives, having strong social ties is good for our health. Later in the chapter, we will discuss other theoretical perspectives, including dialectics and problematic integration theory. But to establish a basis for those, let us first shift to the more specific topic of coping.

COPING

To understand social support, it is useful to consider what it means to cope. As Sandra Metts and Heather Manns (1996) define it, **coping** is "the process of managing stressful situations" (p. 356) that range from everyday hassles to life-threatening occurrences.

Coping usually involves two efforts: changing what can be changed (**problem solving**) and adapting to what cannot be changed (**emotional adjustment**) (Tardy, 1994). Of course, it is not always easy to know when to solve a problem and when to adjust to it. The options vary according to the people and the circumstances involved. Often, coping strategies depend on how much control people believe they have over their situations.

Sometimes attaining a sense of control requires reevaluating ideas about one's body. Canadian researchers Jennifer English and colleagues (2008) interviewed women about the strategies they used to heal emotionally and physically from the effects of breast cancer. From the respondents' stories, the researchers conceptualized the body as a "therapeutic landscape." Often, they say, that term is used to describe places and physical environments such as spas, gardens, and nature that foster a sense of peace and well-being. In this case, English and colleagues applied the same idea to the body, regarding it as a place of illness but also of healing and recovery.

Breast cancer is particularly relevant to the landscape image, of course, because mastectomies represent a physical redefinition of the body-physical. Although the women interviewed were unaware of the landscape concept, their stories naturally illustrated it. For example, one woman described her body as a damaged object:

> *It was feeling like I had been broken. . . . My body was cut up and I took all these chemical drugs and I was radiated, and you know what I mean. I just sort of in my mind felt like I was coming from a not very good physical place.* (p. 71)

Another described the realization that radiation was permeating the very cells of her body. She felt the experience was simultaneously taking her into the depths of her unconscious. The women also spoke of the physical changes in their bodies—hair loss, weight gain, and their new awareness of the food, air, and other elements around them. In a therapeutic sense, they spoke about the healing properties of time spent with friends, exercising, and enjoying nature. Many said such pleasures were more intense because life had lost some of the taken-for-granted quality it used to have. The authors conclude:

> *The body, being the smallest and most personal landscape, represents the embodiment of illness for women living with breast cancer. In other words, the body is both an everyday site of illness but also an everyday landscape of healing.* (*English, Wilson, & Keller-Olaman, 2008, p. 76*)

In this way and many others, illness, coping, and healing occupy the same spaces in human experience.

SENSE OF CONTROL

When people believe they can manage their health successfully, they are said to have **health self-efficacy** (Bandura, 1986). Efficacy is derived from the Latin term for "change-producing." People with high self-efficacy are more likely than others to maintain healthy lifestyles because they are confident in their ability to make changes that have positive consequences. A sense of self-efficacy may be fostered by positive experiences in the past, encouragement from others, and an **internal locus of control**, which is the belief that people control their own destinies. Locus of control is more general than health self-efficacy, although the two are often related. Many North Americans have an internal locus of control. As a result, they tend to be change oriented and hard working, but they may be frustrated by failure and may feel baffled and betrayed when things do not work out as they had planned. People who believe they control their own fate may be reluctant to ask for help and may believe they are responsible for what happens—both good and bad. Faced with ill health, they might ask, "What did I do to cause this?" Even assured that no one is to blame, these people may feel guilty and ineffectual.

WHAT DO YOU THINK?

- In what ways do you perceive that you control your health?
- What factors do you consider to be out of your control?
- What has led you to these beliefs?

Sometimes making sense of a health event involves comparing it to something familiar. In a study of American and Puerto Rican male veterans recovering from strokes, many of the men compared having a stroke to a crash or a hurricane because it was unexpected and destructive (Boylstein, Rittman, & Hinojosa, 2007). However, the men typically chose a different metaphor—war—to describe their recovery. Like war, they said, recovery requires immense courage, determination, and active engagement. "I've always been a fighter," said one man (p. 284). Another said, "You quit, they're gonna win. Now where's the fight in you?" (p. 284). The researchers note that, in the men's stories, the "enemy" was typically a body part (an arm, a leg, or a hand) that no longer worked like it did before and that required diligent therapy and exercise. The men's explanations revealed that, although their strokes seemed to have come from out of the blue, they considered themselves active agents in getting well again.

In contrast, people who do not believe they can change their health for the better have low health self-efficacy. This is common in cultures in which people have an **external locus of control**, that is, the belief that events are controlled mostly by outside forces. Because of their belief in fate, these people are sometimes characterized as **fatalistic**. They are likely to regard events as God's will or the natural order of things.

People with low health self-efficacy may not be motivated to take personal action regarding health matters. For example, even if they are aware of healthy dietary recommendations, they may not change their diets because they do not feel they have control over their health (Rimal, 2000). In fatalistic cultures, people may reason, "It makes no sense to change my lifestyle. I will die when it's my time, no sooner or later," or "I am sick because God willed it. Therefore, it's not right to seek a medical cure."

People with a fatalistic worldview are significantly more likely than others to feel that cancer is unpreventable and to avoid seeking information about the subject (Ramanadhan & Viswanath, 2006). And, as you might expect, adolescents with an external locus of control are more apt to "follow the crowd" and smoke if their friends do (Booth-Butterfield, Anderson, & Booth-Butterfield, 2000).

Our locus of control may also influence how we interpret other people's actions and health. For example, do people become overweight because of behavioral choices or because of factors beyond their control? As information surfaces about a genetic tendency toward obesity in some people, the public is likely to feel more sympathetic toward overweight people (Jeong, 2007). But at the same time, people may become more lax about health behaviors, concluding that obesity either is or is not their genetic destiny and there's not much they can do about it (Jeong, 2007).

As with most things, the extremes are typically dysfunctional. People at either end of the internal/external locus-of-control scale are likely to have trouble coping. One moderating effect, at least for fatalists, is a healthy dose of confidence. Some researchers have found that people are less likely to avoid threatening health messages if they are well informed and confident about prevention methods (Fry & Prentice-Dunn, 2005).

People with high self-efficacy are typically problem solvers, highly motivated to protect their own health. However, they may be at a loss when illness reduces their sense of control. In some situations, people are powerless to change their health status or to repay their caregivers' kindness. One man adapting to physical limitations after a stroke described his frustration this way: "It's hard to depend on other people to take you places. Because, you know, they have things they have to do, and they need to get done, and you don't want to interfere with their schedule" (Egbert, Koch, Coeling, & Ayers, 2006, p. 49). Forced dependence may be especially demoralizing for people who have always believed they can control their health. In these situations, a belief in fate may help people accept what they cannot change. All in all, effective coping seems to combine elements of both problem solving and acceptance.

DIALECTICS

Of course, no one perceives an entirely internal or external local of control. We occupy a perspective somewhere between the two, and we may shift perspectives over time. This is an observation well explained by **dialectics**, which describes the ongoing tension of meaning between coexisting but contradictory constructs such as hopeless and hopeful (Baxter, 1988; Rawlins, 1989).

We continually navigate meaning within dialectic continua based on our circumstances, beliefs, and interactions with others. For example, family caregivers often describe ongoing efforts to balance the dialectic between attending to their own needs and sacrificing themselves to care for loved ones (Brann, Himes, Dillow, & Weber, 2010). In a similar way, hospice nurses say they strive for a balance between being honest with families and at least temporarily shielding them from information that would overwhelm them (Gilstrap & White, 2015).

IN YOUR EXPERIENCE

Meaning is not a one-way destination.
Based on the principles of dialectics, we continually navigate a place between opposites, such as keeping our emotions to ourselves and sharing them openly with others. Can you identify examples in your own experience in which you have managed the dialectics between being hopeful and realistic, attending to self and sacrificing self, and expressing emotions and suppressing emotional displays?

People also manage the dialectic between being hopeful and realistic. Many people consider it adaptive to be optimistic, and it sometimes is. But the dialectic perspective challenges the notion that there is one right or static way to think. Instead, meaning is adaptive and changing. For example, a man caring for his wife following a stroke said that, after several years of determined optimism, they began to accept that she would never use her arm and leg again. As he put it, "We backed off . . . We're not expecting miracles anymore" (Brann et al., 2010, p. 327). That sense of acceptance can sometimes bring peace and can lead to more effective, realistic coping strategies.

We cope with some degree of stress every day. But crises test our limits. Next we take a closer look at what is involved when that happens.

CRISIS

At every crisis in one's life, it is absolute salvation to have some sympathetic friend to whom you can think aloud without restraint or misgiving. —Woodrow Wilson

A **crisis** is an occurrence that exceeds a person's normal coping ability. The first sign of crisis is usually a sense that events are out of control. This may give rise to panic or denial. For example, the parent of a seriously ill child remembers, "I didn't want to talk about it because it was something I wanted to shut in the back of my mind and have go away" (Chesler & Barbarin, 1984, p. 123).

People in crisis are likely to feel that things have changed, perhaps forever. During difficult times, people often yearn for the simple routines that characterized everyday life. It may seem that things will never be the same again. Following a death, for example, grieving loved ones may wonder how they will ever resume daily activities when they feel so sad and disconnected to the things that used to seem normal. It is common for people in intense grief to forget momentarily how to perform simple routines or drive familiar routes.

One of the most distressing aspects of a crisis can be the sense that one is helpless and not in control. Health professionals can help by actively involving patients in making decisions and expressing their preferences. Patients who feel that they can ask questions and be assertive tend to experience less anxiety and more optimism than those who feel that their input is not valued (Venetis, Robinson, & Kearney, 2015).

IN YOUR EXPERIENCE

- Have you ever experienced a crisis?
- If so, did it feel that things might never be the same again?
- What coping strategies did you use?
- What types of support from others were most helpful?

A major crisis may serve as a turning point or dividing line. People affected by serious illnesses often feel their life has two parts, before the diagnosis and after it (Tiedtke, de Rijk, Donceel, Christiaens, & Dierckx de Casterl, 2012). Circumstances are so radically altered that nothing seems the same. The change is not always negative. People who learn to cope with terminal illnesses or near-death experiences sometimes say they are happier than before, appreciating pleasures they used to disregard. A cancer survivor interviewed by Jennifer Anderson and Patricia Geist Martin (2003) reflects on the strength and courage she has discovered while undergoing surgery and radiation treatments:

> *I wear my scar as a badge of courage but I've never thought of myself as a courageous person. But I am, I am a courageous person. People notice the scar. But you know, I don't mind the scar. Years ago, I decided that I wanted to change my name, to pick out who I wanted to be. Ivy came to mind because I liked the plant. It's a vine, it is strong, you can cut it down and it comes back. There's a lot of strength in Ivy.* (p. 138)

We'll talk more about transformative health experiences later in the chapter.

NORMALCY

A sense of crisis does not usually abate until it seems that life is normal again. **Normalcy** is essentially the sense that things are comfortable, predictable, and familiar. Being normal is not always as easy as it sounds. It requires the cooperation of other people,

Following an automobile accident that left her paralyzed from the neck down, Samantha Rodzwicz was eager to return to college and her philanthropic efforts as soon as possible. During college, she helped to raise more than $40,000 to help others. Rodzwicz is shown here at her college graduation in 2010 with her sister Veronica. She went on to earn a master's degree in communication.

even strangers (Barnes & Duck, 1994). Consider the dilemma of individuals with physical disabilities. Often, their toughest challenge is not learning to use wheelchairs or other appliances. It is resuming a sense of life as usual. Without this, they are trapped in a crisis-like state, excluded from the comfortable give and take of everyday transactions with people (Braithwaite, 1996). Persons with disabilities may be inundated with people willing to help them but with very few who engage them in casual conversation or friendly debates over politics or sports. When people behave as if individuals with disabilities are unlike other people (even by being unusually kind or helpful toward them), they perpetuate a sense of crisis and alienation (Braithwaite, 1996).

We have talked about the value of social support and personal coping strategies. But how do the two intersect? Here are some of the communication strategies involved.

Coping and Communication

Coping strategies and social support often look very much alike in that they tend to fall into two main categories: **action-facilitating,** performing tasks and collecting information; and **nurturing,** building self-esteem, acknowledging and expressing emotions, and providing companionship (Cutrona & Suhr, 1994). Here is an overview of communication strategies based on these categories.

ACTION-FACILITATING SUPPORT

Two types of action-facilitating support are performing tasks and favors and providing information. For instance, people might support someone trying to lose weight by sharing fitness information, buying healthy foods, and serving as exercise companions.

Tasks and favors are called **instrumental support** (Cutrona & Suhr, 1994). Instrumental support is usually most appreciated when care receivers feel they are active participants in the process and are involved in decision making (Forsythe et al., 2014). **Informational support** might involve performing an Internet data search, sharing personal experiences, passing along news clips, and so on. Information can help people increase their understanding and make wise decisions. A cancer survivor in one study said she worries about every change in her body, so she appreciates her physicians' willingness to run tests to be sure nothing is wrong. "Otherwise, I'm going to sit here freaking out all the time," reflects the woman (Miller, 2014, p. 236).

Even when people cannot change their circumstances, those who are knowledgeable about what is happening usually feel more in control, experience less pain, and recover more quickly than others. Margo Charchuk describes the sense of hopelessness and impotence she felt as the mother of a seriously ill child (Connor) in a neonatal intensive care unit (NICU). "I felt that I was an outsider looking in with no voice in the care of my child," she writes (Charchuk & Simpson, 2005, p. 198). While uninformed, she felt hopeless. Charchuk urges health providers to foster hope, even when the outcome is uncertain:

> *In my experience, health care providers can help parents to enjoy their child and find hope in the moment even if the child will not ultimately survive. . . . I hoped that he would live, but I also had hope that I was being a good mother and that I was doing all that I could to ensure his health and safety. When I was involved in his care, my hopes increased, as this enabled me to feel I was being a good parent. I did not lose hope when the information was bad; I only lost hope when I was given no information at all.* (pp. 194–195)

Charchuk describes a dilemma that many people feel in health situations. She sensed that, if she showed emotion, health professionals would consider that she was incapable of hearing the hard truths and making important decisions, but if she did not show emotion, they might overlook her fervent concern and desire to know more. One of the most hope-enhancing events of Charchuk's account occurred when a NICU nurse invited her to rub the baby's back to soothe him. "The importance of this small amount of control that I was able to take helped restore my hope," she remembers (p. 199).

Although most people, like Charchuk, say it feels better to be well informed, sometimes too much information can feel overwhelming and compromise our coping ability (L. Miller, 2014). The theory of problematic integration (see Box 8.2) describes how and why we manage ambiguous, contradictory, and complex information.

BOX 8.2

Theory of Problematic Integration

Imagine that you will go through life knowing with relative certainty what to expect and how to feel. Perhaps you will graduate, establish a rewarding career, stay healthy and fit until retirement, and enjoy your later years with the money you have wisely saved along the way. At least this is what you expect and what you hope will happen.

The **theory of problematic integration** is based on the idea that we orient to life in terms of *expectations* (what we think will probably happen) and *evaluations* (whether occurrences are good or bad) (Babrow, 2001). However, our expectations and values are challenged almost constantly in large and small ways. (Although this sounds regrettable, the challenges are actually opportunities for greater development, a point to be discussed presently.)

As defined by Austin Babrow and colleagues, the theory of problematic integration describes a process in which communication serves to establish a relatively stable orientation to the world but also to challenge and transform that orientation (Babrow, 1992; Brashers & Babrow, 1996; Ford, Babrow, & Stohl, 1996; Russell & Babrow, 2011). *Problematic integration* (PI) occurs when expectations and evaluations are at odds, uncertain, changing, or impossible to fulfill. The disruption may be relatively minor (perhaps a setback that delays graduation) or major (someone close to you is diagnosed with a life-changing illness). Whatever the case, communication will play a pivotal role at every stage of your experience. As Babrow (2001) puts it:

> *Communication shapes conceptions of our world—both its composition and meaning, particularly its values. [Problematic integration theory] also suggests that communication shapes and reflects problematic formulations of these conceptions and orientations to experience. (p. 556)*

In recognizing that communication helps to define, challenge, and transform our experiences, Babrow (2001) makes the point that uncertainty is not inherently bad or good, and we are not always able to extinguish uncertainty by dousing it with information. Sometimes uncertainty exists because we have too little or too much information or because we are not sure what to make of the information presented to us.

We make sense of the world partly through the stories we tell and partly through our efforts to achieve coherence between our narratives and other accounts, or what Russell and Babrow (2011) call "preexisting narrative frames," such as media depictions of environmental hazards and terrorism. As we both construct and confront narrative themes, we assess risk by selectively evaluating, bracketing, integrating, and comparing information from many sources within what philosophers call the blooming, buzzing confusion of experience (Russell & Babrow, 2011).

Uncertainty and ambivalence may also be inherent in the information we receive about our health and threats to it. Scientific findings change, and every promise of relief is accompanied by some degree of risk and side affects (Gill & Babrow, 2007; Russell & Babrow, 2011). Furthermore, resolving one uncertainty may produce others. Babrow writes that "PI permeates human experience" (p. 564), although it is difficult to predict when and how uncertainties will arise. Going back to Babrow's first point, the notion of uncertainty is not necessarily undesirable. Indeed, he suggests that uncertainty presents an "opportunity for self-exploration" (p. 563).

Consider the example of advance-care planning provided by Stephen Hines (2001). Medical professionals have typically been disappointed by patients' disinclination to specify what care they wish to have (or forgo) should they become too ill to express their wishes. Hines suggests that people shy away from the issue because health care professionals, in their desire to reduce their own uncertainty in end-of-life situations, have not been very sensitive to the uncertainties experienced by prospective patients and their loved ones. In short, people may neglect to file advance-care directives, not because they are indifferent or stubborn, but because the uncertainty surrounding them feels unmanageable.

This brief review does not encompass all the facets of problematic integration theory, but hopefully it does illustrate something about the ways in which people constitute, challenge, and transform their understandings, particularly in health-related crises.

NURTURING SUPPORT

Nurturing typically involves three types of support: esteem support, emotional support, and social network support. These are not directly oriented to task goals but, rather, to helping people feel better about themselves and their situations.

Esteem support involves efforts to make another person feel valued and competent. Here is an example from a study by Maria Carpiac-Claver and Lené Levy-Storms (2007) in a long-term care facility:

> *A nurse aide stands next to the resident after delivering her tray of food and says in a soft and moderately pitched voice,* Hi [resident's name]. Okay. Want a spoon? *The resident, with laughter in her voice, says,* Thank you *and smiles broadly at the nurse aide. The nurse aide gives the resident a spoon and says,* Here you go. *The resident thanks the nurse aide while shaking her head and pulling the nurse aide down to give her a kiss on the cheek. (p. 61)*

When a family coping with cancer donated seven hours of recorded telephone conversations to researcher Wayne Beach, he teamed up with colleagues to create *The Cancer Play*, a theatrical production based on those real-life conversations. Most cancer patients and their loved ones who have seen the play say that it validates their need to communicate with each other and to share compassion and emotional support (Beach, Buller, Dozier, Buller, & Gutzmer, 2014). For more about the play, visit "The Cancer Play" on Facebook.

The researchers observed other nurse aides laughing and singing with residents and helping those with cognitive impairments keep their memories active. Carpiac-Claver and Levy-Storms identified four themes of the nurse aides' affective communication: *personal conversation*, pleasantries and talk not directed to any particular task; *addressing the resident*, using the person's name or a term of endearment; *checking in*, asking and looking to see if the resident is feeling okay or needs anything; and *emotional support/praise*, as in saying, "You look beautiful today!" or "Congratulations!"

Encouraging words may ease feelings of helplessness and despair. People often report that unconditional approval is the most helpful form of support. Statements such as "We're behind you no matter what you decide" are comforting reminders that loved ones will not leave if the situation is difficult to handle. Listening is also important. Studies show that most distressed individuals are not looking for advice; they just want to talk and be heard (Lehman, Ellard, & Wortman, 1986). Following are some tips from the experts on listening well.

Communication Skill Builder: Supportive Listening

Brant Burleson, a leading authority on social support, offered the following tips for being a supportive listener (based on Burleson, 1990, 1994).

- *Focus on the other person.* Give the person a chance to talk freely. Focus on what he or she is saying rather than on your own feelings and experiences.
- *Remain neutral.* Resist the urge to label people and experiences as good or bad. Likewise, encourage the speaker to describe experiences rather than label them.
- *Concentrate on feelings.* Focus on feelings rather than events. It is usually more supportive to explore why someone feels a certain way than to focus on events themselves.
- *Legitimize the other person's emotions.* Statements such as "I understand how you

might feel that way" are typically more helpful than telling the other person how to feel or how not to feel.

- *Summarize what you hear.* Calmly summarizing the speaker's statements can help clarify the situation and help the distressed individual understand what he or she is feeling. As Burleson (1994) explained, "Due to the intensity and immediacy of their feelings, distressed persons may lack understanding of these feelings" (p. 13).

Emotional support includes efforts to acknowledge and understand what another person is feeling. This support is particularly valuable when people must adapt to what they cannot change. In a health crisis it is common to feel angry, baffled, afraid, depressed, or even unexpectedly relieved or giddy.

Emotions are a natural part of coping with health crises, yet many people are uncomfortable with emotional displays—theirs or others people's. They may be afraid to appear weak or may be reluctant to upset others. The result is that people tend to present the appearance that things are going well, even when they are not. In interviews with grieving parents, fathers were more likely than mothers to use work as a distractive coping mechanism, whereas the women were more likely than the men to talk about their feelings and stay close to family members. Partly as a result, the women reported feeling more in control of their grieving process than the men did six months after the loss of a child (Alam, Barrera, D'Agostino, Nicholas, & Schneiderman, 2012). Although it was probably not obvious to others, the men probably needed support as much as their wives did.

Problems may arise when people find themselves feigning a cheerfulness they do not feel or avoiding subjects they actually wish to discuss. Suppressing emotions commonly leads to depression, especially among men (Flynn, Hollenstein, & Mackey, 2010). When asked, people (patients, caregivers, and others) often say they avoid sensitive topics because they do not wish to distress the people around them (Bevan, Rogers, Andrews, & Sparks, 2012). However, when interviewed individually, people usually express the private wish that subjects such as death be brought into the open. In the long run, it is usually easier to cope when emotions can be expressed and discussed without trepidation. Following are some tips for accomplishing this.

Communication Skill Builder: Allowing Emotional Expression

- *Look for "affective moments."* Physician Frederic Platt (1995) encourages caregivers to stay tuned for signs of strong feelings such as anger, sadness, fear, and helplessness. These are opportunities to understand something important about the other person and his or her coping status, he says.
- *When necessary, give yourself a moment.* Emotions often flood out other thoughts, making it difficult to respond effectively. A helpful strategy is to say, "Let me stop and think about what you've been telling me for a moment" (Platt, 1995, p. 25).
- *Keep in mind that people usually benefit from opportunities to talk openly and honestly.* People with advanced cancer who feel they can talk about subjects like death and pain with their loved ones typically cope better than people who consider those topics taboo (Thomsen, Rydahl-Hansen, & Wagner, 2010).
- *People in grief often find it insensitive and unhelpful when others try to minimize their losses or get them to cheer up.* One cancer survivor put it this way: "The emotions went up and down, up and down. I talked to Jack and he listened. There was a point where Jack's optimism got to me. It was like stop, you're not listening to me. I could die, stop" (Anderson & Geist-Martin, 2003, p. 137).
- *Acknowledge and respect emotions.* Branch, Levinson, and Platt (1996, para. 15) suggest the following communication tools for responding to emotions: (1) Acknowledge the emotion: "I can understand how upsetting it must be"; (2) show respect: "You've been doing your best to cope"; (3) reflect: "It sounds as though you are really feeling overwhelmed"; and (4) support and partner: "Maybe we can work together on these things."

All in all, it is important to remember that emotions are a natural part of the coping process and that the person who displays strong and even conflicting emotions may be coping more effectively than the one who keeps a stiff upper lip.

Social Networks

Common sources of social-network support include family members, friends, professionals, support groups, virtual communities, and self-help literature. Each source is likely to provide a somewhat different form of assistance. Since we have said a good deal already about the value of social networks, we will focus here on support groups.

Support groups are made up of people with similar concerns who meet regularly to discuss their feelings and experiences. They range from informal self-help groups to treatment groups facilitated by trained professionals and from groups that meet in person to virtual groups conducted entirely online.

> **HEALTH AND COMMUNICATION TECHNOLOGY**
>
> Online support groups may be particularly valuable for people with physical disabilities and their loved ones. In a study of people coping with amyotrophic lateral sclerosis (ALS, also called Lou Gehrig's disease), participants reported using online forums mostly to request and share information (Loane & D'Alessandro, 2013). In one instance, a woman without insurance who was worried that her husband might have ALS logged on to see if his symptoms were similar to those of ALS patients. Respondents sympathized with her situation and suggested affordable options for having him tested.

In their various forms, support groups are popular around the world. More than 24,000 Al-Anon/Alateen group meetings are conducted in 30 languages in 130 countries (Al-Anon.org). There are also support groups for people dealing with grief, codependence, an enormous variety of illnesses and addictions, and other concerns. The effort may be justified. Support group members tend to experience fewer symptoms and less stress, and they may even live longer than similar people who are not members ("Living With Cancer," 1997; Wright, 2002).

Support groups have several advantages. Communicating with similar others may help people feel that they are not alone or abnormal. People going through similar experiences can also give firsthand information on what to expect and how to behave. At the same time, support group members may feel better about themselves because they are able to both express empathy with others and receive empathic messages themselves (Han et al., 2011). Another advantage is the convenience and low cost of support groups. Because they are made up mostly of laypersons, there are few or no fees, and for the most part, members can schedule meetings where and when they wish, even online. One advantage of online support groups is the option to interact with people on a weak-tie basis—that is, to engage in relationships that do not require a great of time or emotional investment (Han, Hou, Kim, & Gustafson, 2014). Members of computer-mediated support communities often perceive that there is less risk of a judgment response in these relationships and that the information gleaned from them is more objective than loved ones would be able to provide (Wright & Rains, 2014). (We'll talk more about strong and weak social ties in Chapter 9.)

The greatest dangers are that support groups will become counterproductive gripe sessions or that members will develop an us-versus-them viewpoint. They may begin to feel that no one outside the group understands them as well as they understand each other, a form of oversupport we will discuss next.

When Social Support Goes Wrong

Lucinda has seemed depressed for weeks. Some of her friends are attentive and sympathetic. Others are frustrated because they think Lucinda is not trying very hard to improve her outlook and is exaggerating her distress to get attention.

Interpretations such as these are personal and cultural. When people in one study were asked to consider a hypothetical case in which a person close to them was depressed, Hispanic respondents were likely to be sympathetic if they felt the person was helpless and was trying to get attention, whereas other respondents more often reacted negatively to the idea that a person might play up her symptoms to gain the spotlight (Siegel et al., 2012).

Although it is often difficult to know when social support will be helpful and when it might make a problem worse, following are some scenarios in which ineffective social support seems to hurt more than it helps.

FRIENDS DISAPPEAR

When Suleika Jaouad was diagnosed with leukemia at age 22, everything in her life changed. She was forced to give up her new job in Paris and return to the United States to move back in with her parents, spend months in the hospital, and cope with treatments that were painful and frightening and will make it difficult for her to conceive children in the future. In the midst of all of this, she says, she was shocked that many of her friends suddenly disappeared from her life. She explains:

> *I think another aspect of being a young adult with cancer is that most of your friends, hopefully, you know, have never had to experience life-threatening illnesses themselves. . . . So a lot of my friends had no idea how to respond and found it really difficult not just to find the right words, but sometimes to find any words at all. ("Life Interrupted," "On the 'Social Awkwardness' of Cancer," 2012, para. 1)*

Jaouad said she was hurt and mystified by her friends' absence when she really needed them.

HURTFUL JESTS

Here is another example, shared by Sherianne Shuler, who learned a great deal about effective and ineffective social support efforts when her 15-month-old daughter Lily was hospitalized with a rare, life-threatening infection. For example, an acquaintance who visited her in the hospital joked insensitively: "Nice hair, Shuler! . . . That's what you've got to love about Sheri Shuler, you don't care about things like that! If it were me, I'd be worried about my hair. But you just don't care!" Hurt, Shuler replied, "I think if you had a daughter in a coma and on a ventilator you wouldn't care." Inwardly, she says, she was silently screaming, "SHE'S SERIOUSLY STILL TALKING ABOUT HOW SHITTY I LOOK?" (Shuler, 2011, p. 200). The comments made her self-conscious at a time when she already felt vulnerable and overwhelmed.

Shuler also remembers feeling overwhelmed by the number of phone calls and emails she received and grateful that she could post information on a blog since the process was therapeutic and took less energy than talking to everyone separately. Phone messages

When Suleika Jaouad was diagnosed with leukemia at age 22, she says that many of her friends were at a loss for what do say or do around her.

Sheri Shuler enjoys time with daughter Lily, shown here at age 6. A health scare when Lily was a toddler taught her a great deal about social support efforts that are helpful and those that are not.

with offers such as "Call if you need . . ." were also unhelpful. Although people meant well, the energy and temerity it took to make such requests during a difficult time were prohibitive. Shuler observes, "As we learned, there are plenty of ways to offer well-meaning but ineffective support" (p. 199).

On the other hand, Shuler says it was immensely comforting when friends sent cards, letters, snacks, and healthy meals without being asked and without expecting anything in return. And she was grateful for people who took turns being present with her in the hospital waiting room without expecting her to talk or play hostess in any way. Says Shuler, "I was floored by this thoughtful support my friends were providing. It was the gift of space and company simultaneously" (p. 199). Fortunately, Lily made a full recovery.

TOO MUCH SUPPORT

Especially if "supportive" efforts are offered inappropriately or profusely, they can impair people's coping abilities. **Oversupport** is defined as excessive and unnecessary help (Edwards & Noller, 1998). Following is a discussion of three types of oversupport: overhelping, overinforming, and overempathizing.

Overhelping is providing too much instrumental assistance. This can make people feel like children or shield them from life experiences. People who are overhelped may perceive a loss of control, especially if others take on tasks for them without their consent (Morgan & Brazda, 2013).

> **IN YOUR EXPERIENCE**
>
> - Have you ever felt babied into a sick role?
> - Have you ever felt confused or overwhelmed by information?
> - If so, how did you cope?

Forcing information on people when they are too distraught to understand it or accept it (**overinforming**) may only heighten their stress. Philip Muskin (1998) calls this "truth dumping" and warns people against it. Health-related information can be confusing and frightening. Facts change and outlooks vary. People may shy away from the truth, preferring to preserve hope or minimize their confusion.

Overempathizing is actually something of a misnomer, because it applies only to a particular type of empathy, called *emotional contagion*. In a general sense, **empathy** is the ability to show that you understand how someone else is feeling. Katherine Miller and colleagues (1995) identified two components of empathy: **empathic concern**, which is an intellectual appreciation of someone's feelings; and **emotional contagion**, which involves actually feeling emotions similar to the other person's. Research shows that the second kind, emotional contagion, can be overdone (Miller, Birkholt, Scott, & Stage, 1995).

Taken to extremes, emotional contagion can be detrimental to both support providers and recipients. For example, support groups members sometimes empathize so much with each other that they distance themselves from others (Vilhauer, 2011). Another danger is that people may hesitate to express themselves to listeners who are likely to become upset. In Eric Zook's (1993) case study, a man who cared for his dying partner at home remembers, "As long as I was kind of detached and logical about it, he would take it [his declining health] very well" (p. 117).

Finally, some people find emotional empathy overwhelming or belittling. They may avoid scenes in which others seem to pity them. Wayne Beach (2002) describes the "stoic orientation" adopted by a father and son discussing the news that the mother was diagnosed with cancer. The son received the news calmly. Rather than reacting emotionally, he initially responded with a series of "OKs" and technical questions such as, "That's the one above her kidney?" (p. 279). Beach speculates that this factual, stoic orientation saved the father and son from immediately "flooding out." In this way, they were able both to maintain composure and to display that they were knowledgeable and capable of coping with the news.

> **IN YOUR EXPERIENCE**
>
> - Have you ever felt at a loss when trying to comfort someone? If so, what did you do? What happened?
> - Have you ever felt that people abandoned you when you needed social support?

A NOTE OF ENCOURAGEMENT

Before you become too self-conscious about offering social support, consider that, although some of these examples were hurtful, the lessons behind them are fairly simple.

- *Do not overwhelm the distressed individual with requests for information.* If it is important for people to stay informed, appoint one person to convey news to the others.
- *Be careful with humor, and avoid making jokes at others' expense.* People may not feel like laughing during a tense situation, and joking put-downs can be devastating when people are already feeling vulnerable.
- *"Call me if you need me" is usually not helpful.* It puts the onus for action on the distressed individual at a time when he or she is probably not up to the effort.
- *It's okay if you do not know what to say. Just say something gentle or be available to listen.*
- *Adopt a no-strings-attached approach.* When uncertain what to do, provide a quiet favor such as mowing the lawn, leaving a casserole, or simply being present without requiring anything from the distressed individual.

Here is a follow-up to the story about Suleika Jaouad, who was initially hurt by her friends' silence. Jaouad says their dilemma began to dawn on her when she remembered how she felt, just a few years before, when a friend phoned her to say that he had testicular cancer. She says:

> *I remembered feeling so afraid when he called me and shared his diagnosis with me. And following that phone call, I, you know, I sat down and tried to compose an email, and I just didn't feel like I had the right words. I couldn't find the perfect words, so I said nothing. And I wasn't there for him at all during his cancer treatment. And I tried to remember that, and it's helped me forgive and understand the reactions of certain friends in my life and to realize that generally it's not that people don't care. It's that they're afraid or that they don't know what to say. (para. 3)*

Jaouad's advice to people who want to offer comfort but are not sure what to say is to forget about finding "the perfect words" and just say something. For her part, she says a highlight of her year was apologizing to the friend she had been unable to comfort several years before. "He understood, and he said, 'I know that you understand now,'" she says (para. 4).

On that note, we turn to a form of love and comfort that communicates a great deal but requires no words at all.

Animal Companions

> *At Sunrise Hospital in Las Vegas, Nevada, care sometimes comes with four legs and floppy ears. About 12 dogs visit the hospital every few days through Pet Partners (formerly the Delta Society), a nonprofit organization that provides training and coordination for more than 10,000 carefully trained animal–volunteer teams throughout the world. The animals serve as therapeutic companions to people with health concerns.*

Pet Partners leaders say the animals (mostly dogs and cats, but also a few horses) provide stress relief, a break from boredom, inspiration, and health benefits. The furry friends have been known to inspire people to keep up difficult physical therapy routines and to distract and calm children undergoing medical procedures. The staff at Sunrise Hospital reports that the animals are some patients' only visitors and they are a fun pick-me-up for people who choose to take part. "Often time, you'll see a patient who is really down in the dumps, and the dogs will show up in the room and their eyes light up," says Tracy Netherton, the hospital's volunteer coordinator (quoted by DeLucia, 2011, para. 4).

IN YOUR EXPERIENCE

- Have you ever felt that an animal was a good friend? Why or why not?
- Do you think animal companionship affects your coping ability?

There is evidence that animal companions often have positive effects on people's anxiety levels (Barker & Dawson, 1998), blood pressure (Allen, Blascovich, & Mendes, 2002), recovery time (Allen et al., 2002), and survival rates after heart attacks (Friedmann & Thomas, 1995); and even that trained dogs can help with the diagnosis and treatment of conditions such as diabetes, cancer, and epilepsy (Wells, 2009).

Oncologist Edward Creagan of Mayo Clinic is a believer. He includes the names of people's pets in their medical history notes. In his experience, pets can be people's reason for living, and talking about pets is often calming for staff members as well as patients. Creagan attests, "None of us can speak about their pets without smiling" (Pet Partners video, n.d.).

We turn now to a type of experience that may occur when you least expect it and may have profound consequences for coping.

Transformative Experiences

Carol Bishop Mills remembers the day her daughter Maren was born:

> *Dr. Jacobs, the NICU doctor, approached my bed about 15 minutes later and handed me a gorgeous baby girl. He was very pleasant and smiled when he told us all about her. "Mr. and Mrs. Mills, your daughter is quite healthy. She seems to have a strong heart, and her kidneys will be fine. There was some fluid pooled, but it will eliminate itself naturally. Her APGAR scores [used to measure a newborn's health] were 8 and 9 [out of a possible 10]. She's a beautiful little girl. There are some preliminary indicators in her features that she might have trisomy 21, Down syndrome, but we need to run some blood work to confirm that."* (Mills, 2005, p. 198)

The Mills were not surprised. They suspected that their baby might have special needs. But they *were* deeply grateful—grateful that the doctor had not said "I'm sorry" or labeled their daughter "abnormal." Instead he saw, as they did, a unique, perfect little girl in radiant good health with a condition not all children have.

Good health is often defined in terms of what is "normal" or "expected." A deviation from that can feel like a tragedy—meaningless and unfair. In reality, however, what looks on the surface like a "bad outcome" can turn out to be one of life's most valuable and important gifts. Mills (2005) attests that, although no one hopes to have a child with Down syndrome, "it is simply a gift we were given that we would have never known to ask for and probably would never have understood before our Little Miss Magic captivated our hearts" (p. 196).

Maren dressed as a fairy at her fifth birthday party.

In this section we explore instances in which, in the midst of what might seem to be great hardship, people discover unexpected rewards. From the perspective of social constructivism (e.g., Berger & Luckmann, 1966), life is defined largely by a quest for meaning that is shaped both by our own experiences and by our interactions with others. To illustrate the powerful effect of social interaction, let's return to Mills's (2005) case study, but this time we will look through the eyes of Kate, another mother, who has just given birth to Joshua:

> *We heard a cry, we saw our boy, and then heard the following from Dr. Lee, "I am so sorry to tell you this. This baby looks like a Down's. I'm so sorry. . . . In 20 years, I've never delivered a Down's. Didn't you have tests? . . . I'm sure it's a Down's. I am so, so sorry."* (quoted by Mills, p. 199)

As you might imagine, Kate's experience was much different from the Millses'. "In my heart, I knew the Down syndrome was my fault, and it was clear the doctor was angry," Kate remembers thinking. "I didn't have a boy, in my mind, I had an 'it,' a Down's, one of those short, funny, retarded kids that work at grocery stores. My mind flooded with thoughts of drooling, retardation, the little yellow buses, the teasing, and the problems" (quoted by Mills, p. 199).

Mills (2005) reports that Kate and her husband Chris have come to realize that Down syndrome is only one feature—a relatively insignificant one—in the myriad qualities that make their son Joshua wonderful. But they have often had to overcome health professionals' hurtful comments in the process. Considering what people may learn from her experiences, Mills says, "I really hope that students realize that, often, it is not the diagnosis that is so scary, but the language we use to talk about it . . . is so embedded in cultural disdain that [it] taints our view."

We may all sometimes fall into the hurtful trap of believing, as Kate and Chris's doctor did, that there is a norm—a normal way to look, a normal life span, a normal reaction, and so on—and that what is "normal" is the "good" or "right" way to be. Most people who experience a crisis initially feel the same way, wondering: *Is this my fault? What did I do to deserve this? Why did this happen? Can I make it okay again?* In short, if the norm is right, a deviation means something has gone wrong. This is a common assumption because the unknown is often frightening and because, as humans, we are continually involved in sense-making, and an unexpected occurrence can rob us of our sense of safety and meaning. For this reason, it is especially important to learn more about diverse ways of being (in other words, shrink our distrust of the unknown) and to remind ourselves continually that, although it takes courage to embrace them, some of life's most enriching gifts lie beyond the status quo.

You might be surprised how frequently people who have been part of health crises (even to the extent of learning that they do not have long to live) ultimately consider themselves grateful for the experience. Athena du Pré and Eileen Berlin Ray (2008) examined such episodes in a study of **transcendent experiences**, which they define as episodes in which people come to perceive an overarching meaning, or supra-meaning, within experiences that might otherwise seem senseless or unthinkable (p. 103). The term *supra-meaning* comes from psychologist Victor Frankl's (1959) reflections about life in a Nazi concentration camp during World War II. In the midst of suffering more horrific than most of us can imagine, Frankl observed that some of his fellow prisoners still found a reason to value life and to be optimistic about the future, largely because they perceived a meaning in life that was not bounded by the barbed-wire fences that kept them physically captive. Frankl came to believe that a quest for meaning is the primary motivation of human nature. From his perspective, write du Pré and Ray, "transcendence is not denial of one's circumstances, but an awareness that those circumstances exist within the framework of something more meaningful than one might previously have imagined" (p. 103).

In a similar way, people who do not have long to live sometimes say life takes on a new, larger meaning that makes everyday concerns seem trivial. As one cancer survivor put it:

> *I am no longer concerned that someone might see me in the same outfit and I no longer have to have the same sweater in every color. I can now not finish a book if I don't like it. Every day is a guessing game. But that's okay. I'm still here to talk about it.* (*Brett, 2003, p. B1*).

Others say they have been able to lay old grievances to rest and have developed a heightened appreciation for nature and loved ones. Many people facing life-altering circumstances say they have found larger meaning in a spiritual quest that involves helping others, dedicating themselves to a cause larger than themselves, allowing themselves to be creative and have fun, and seeking to live up to their full awareness and potential (Egbert, Sparks, Kreps, & du Pré, 2008). Some people say the loss of a loved one was relieved in part by the knowledge that his or her organs helped save lives. (See Box 8.3 for more on this topic.)

This is not an easy or guaranteed process. Transcendence often happens when we least expect it. Being aware that what appears tragic on the surface may eventually yield something beautiful is a good start toward coping when things seem their darkest.

We turn next to two contexts with powerful implications for social support and coping: family caregiving and end of life.

Friends and Family as Caregivers

> *Carol Green rushes into the caregiver support group with her hair partly in curlers, her sweater buttoned crookedly, a smudge on her face, two different shoes, and a panicked look on her face. "I can't find my keys! We have an appointment, we're late, and I CAN'T FIND MY KEYS!" she exclaims, wildly tossing items from her overflowing handbag.*

"The audience roars," Green says. "They recognize the situation. They are family caregivers." The scenario is a skit, but it is only partly satirical. The sense of being in disarray, trying to manage constantly changing situations involving medications, appointments, finances, companionship, insurance claims,

BOX 8.3

Organ Donations: The Nicholas Effect

Recently I strolled through a park in Rome with Andrea Mongiardo, a 23-year-old Italian whose heart once belonged to my own son.

With this comment, Reg Green (2003) introduces the Nicholas Green Foundation website, named in honor of 7-year-old Nicholas, who was killed near Naples by robbers who mistook the Greens' car for their own and fired into the vehicle. Even in their shock and grief over the sudden attack, Reg Green recalls, he and his wife agreed that Nicholas's organs should be donated to others. The family has since befriended the seven people whose lives were changed as a result. Reg Green remembers when he and his wife met these organ recipients for the first time:

> *Our grief was still agonizingly raw. But that meeting, which both of us had to steel ourselves to attend, was explosive. A door opened and in came this mass of humanity, some smiling, some tearful, some ebullient, some bashful, a stunning demonstration of the momentous consequences every donation can have. We now think of them as an extended family. We've watched the children grow and leave school and get their driver's licenses and the adults go back to work. One of them, 19-year-old Maria Pia Pedala, in a coma with liver failure on the day Nicholas died, bounced back to good health, married and has since had a baby boy. And, yes, they have called him Nicholas.* (para. 11)

Reg Green's (1999) book *The Nicholas Effect: A Boy's Gift to the World* and a video of the same title tell the family's story.

In the United States, an average of 19 people a day die waiting for organ transplants (OrganDonor.gov, 2008). The waiting list is more than 100,000 people long, and the greatest need is for kidneys (accounting for 76% of all transplants).

The issue of organ donation is an emotional one. Based on sensationalized accounts on TV and in the movies, people may fear that medical professionals will allow them to die so they can have their organs, or that their organs will be sold on the underground market (Frates, Bohrer, & Thomas, 2006; Morgan, Harrison, Afifi, Long, & Stephenson, 2008).

In reality, physicians who care for a patient are not involved in decisions about his or her organ donation. That is handled by an entirely different staff and medical team. Moreover, strict U.S. laws prohibit the sale or purchase of organs as well as bribery for desired organs ("Organ Donation," 2008, para. 3). Another common myth is that organ donation will mar a deceased person's appearance such that the family cannot have an open casket at the funeral. This is not true. Physicians are able to maintain the person's appearance so that people cannot tell the difference ("Organ Donation," 2008).

What Do You Think?

1. What factors make you more (or less) inclined to register as an organ donor?
2. What is most fearful about the prospect? What is most appealing?
3. Unlike the Greens, who live in Italy, people in the United States are not usually given the opportunity to meet the people who receive a loved one's organs. Would you want to meet them? Why or why not?
4. Have you seen TV programs or movies in which people's organs are misused? Were the depictions realistic, in your opinion? Do you think such depictions affect people's attitudes about organ donation?

Suggested Resources

- *Journal of the American Medical Association* on Organ Donation: http://jama.ama-assn.org/cgi/reprint/299/2/244.pdf
- U.S. Department of Health and Human Services: OrganDonor.gov
- National Kidney Foundation Facts About Organ Donation and Transplant: www.kidney.org/news/newsroom/fs_new/25factsorgdon&trans.cfm
- Mayo Clinic: "Organ Donation: Don't Let These 10 Myths Confuse You": www.mayoclinic.com/health/organ-donation/FL00077
- The Nicholas Green Foundation: www.nicholasgreen.org

bathing, dressing, food preparation, transportation, emotional support, organizing and apprising others, and so on, is real, she says.

Green facilitates a family caregiver support group through her local Council on Aging. At similar group meetings around the country, anyone interested may learn skills, share concerns, socialize, and take a breather from the everyday demands of family caregiving.

"At meetings, after we cover the essential information, I always say to people, 'If this is your only chance to get out this week, go now! Catch a movie, read a book, take some time for yourself,'" Green says. "Sometimes we need that permission to get away for a little while. My dream is I want to give something back to these people who give so much."

Green draws upon her years as a nurse and her personal experience caring long distance for a parent who has dementia. She is among the 13% of family caregivers in the United States who coordinate services and travel frequently to take care of loved ones who live more than an hour's drive away ("Caregiving in the U.S.," 2009).

The need for integrated support is rising along with the need for family caregivers. Reasons for the increase are manifold. For one, the number of people age 65 and older is expected to triple worldwide between 2009 and 2050 (U.S. Census Bureau, 2009). Already, 13% of Americans are at least 65, and experts predict the proportion to reach 20% by the year 2050 (Ortman, Velkoff, & Hogan (2014). The same trend is occurring in more than 100 other countries, notable among them Germany, Italy, China, and Japan (U.S. Census Bureau, 2009).

IN YOUR EXPERIENCE

- Have you ever been involved in caring for a loved one at home?
- If so, what did you find rewarding about the experience?
- What was difficult about it? What might make it easier?

Another factor is that hospital stays are shorter than they used to be. As Donna Laframboise (1998) put it, "Good news! You can go home from the hospital tomorrow. Bad news! You'll have to do everything yourself, even though you're still on crutches or full of stitches" (p. 26).

The average family caregiver in the United States is a 49-year-old woman. To be a better caregiver, she has probably cut back on hours at work and has seen her income and savings decrease as a result. The challenges are immense, but most family caregivers say the process is rewarding as well.

As we review the rewards and challenges of family caregiving, keep in mind that loved ones are an important source of social support, but they also need support themselves. While the rewards of caregiving can be immensely gratifying, family caregivers experience grief, uncertainty, and exhaustion as well, and their needs are frequently overlooked in concern over the ill individuals. This section focuses on people who provide ongoing care for loved ones at home. Before we begin, note that we often speak in terms of *family caregivers*, and the vast majority (86%) are indeed family members, but the rest are actually honorary family members—friends and neighbors who pitch in as well ("Caregiving in the U.S.," 2009).

PROFILE OF THE FAMILY CAREGIVER

About 66 million people in the United States provide some amount of at-home care for a loved one ("Caregiving in the U.S.," 2009). The average age of family caregivers is 49, and about two-thirds of them are women. At least 37% of people who care for an older adult also have children or grandchildren living with them ("Caregiving in the U.S.," 2009).

CAN YOU GUESS?

What percentage of family caregivers say that dementia is their main concern?

The answer appears at the end of the chapter.

The challenge for family caregivers is to balance many factors at once, including the costs involved. Nearly half of families in the United States who provide full-time care for a loved one at home have drained all or most of their savings to make ends meet ("Evercare Study," 2009). On the bright side, 76% say that these sacrifices have allowed them to maintain a steady quality of care for their loved ones ("Evercare Study," 2009).

STRESS AND BURNOUT

Caregiving is no simple task. By some estimates, adults today will spend more time caring for their parents than they will raising their own children. In addition to providing medical care and assistance, family caregivers are frequently responsible for maintaining households and budgets, working at careers outside the home, and providing information and support to others.

Legislation passed in the 1990s helps career people provide care for needy family members. The **Family and Medical Leave Act of 1993** guarantees that people can take up to 12 weeks off work to care for ailing family members, seek medical care themselves, or bring new children into their families (through birth, adoption, or foster parenting). However, the act does not require that employers pay workers while they are on leave, and it does not apply to all companies or all employees. To be eligible, employees must have worked at the company at least one year for an average of 25 hours or more per week. Only companies with at least 50 employees are obligated to provide medical and family leave.

Although most people juggling careers and caregiving say they feel good about what they do overall, it is easy to feel stressed, exhausted, and resentful at times. Said a woman caring for her 94-year-old grandmother, "It is hard to get out and just get my hair done or go to a doctor's appointment for myself, so I go without. But I feel so guilty if I ask for help" (Potter, n.d., para. 2).

Part of the strain is emotional. Caregivers may grieve over future plans that no longer seem possible. A 76-year-old woman caring for her ailing husband lamented, "This isn't how we planned to spend our retirement years.... Why did this happen to us?" (quoted by Ruppert, 1996, p. 40).

It is also painful to see a loved one suffer or change. The progression of Alzheimer's disease is particularly heart wrenching. Caregivers may watch sadly as the individual's personality and awareness gradually change. Sometimes Alzheimer's patients become belligerent or unable to recognize the people around them (see Box 8.4). To make matters worse, caregivers may feel guilty about their own frustration and resentment. It may seem wrong to be angry with a person who is ill and needy.

Family caregivers may also feel unprepared to perform the tasks delegated to them. Although they now perform many services once carried out by health professionals, they often receive only minimal instruction on what to do and what to expect. As a result, they may feel overwhelmed and may worry that they will do something wrong or will miss important warning signs. When a loved one's life is at stake, the pressure can be as exhausting as the physical demands of caregiving.

Family caregivers may jeopardize their own health if they overextend themselves. People are like elastic, says Geila Bar-David of the Caregiver Support Project in Toronto (Laframboise, 1998). If they are stretched too thin for too long, they will lose strength and may even snap. Caregivers who are reluctant to leave their posts may need reminding that they will be of no use unless they remain healthy (emotionally and physically) themselves.

CARING FOR CAREGIVERS

We began this unit with information about a caregivers' support group. Family caregivers need time for themselves as well as assistance and education. They also need a break from the social isolation that can come with at-home caregiving. Friends and other family members are a promising source of support. In a meta-analysis of 50 studies about family caregiving, a prominent theme was that caregivers missed opportunities to socialize with others (Al-Janabi, Coast, & Flynn, 2008).

Caregivers often say that a word of encouragement or thanks is their greatest reward. Said one man who cares for his wife at home:

> *Sometimes she'll look up to me and give me such a priceless lovely smile, which says it all, and then the other morning she laid down for a bit and looked up to me and said, "You're lovely. I love you." It came out clear as a bell. Well, you can't put a price on that, can you?* (*Al-Janabi et al., 2008, pp. 116–117*)

All in all, supportive communication can sweeten the rewards of caregiving and lessen the demands. For a list of resources for family caregivers, see the *Check it Out!* box.

BOX 8.4 PERSPECTIVES

A Long Goodbye to Grandmother

A few years ago, I lost my grandmother to Alzheimer's disease. Until she died, I saw my grandmother every week of my life. We had a very close relationship.

Alzheimer's is not a disease that just appears one day and kills you. It causes gradual deterioration of a person's memory and sense of being. Minutes and days and years all seem the same or don't exist at all. My grandmother's condition started about one year before her death.

Before Grandma got Alzheimer's, our extended family was fairly close. No one wanted to put Grandma in a nursing home, but caring for her was not going to be easy. Her three daughters (including my mother) decided Grandma would stay with each of them for one week at a time.

Grandma and I had always enjoyed playing Scrabble and working crossword puzzles together. She always tried to get me to use my thinking skills. My favorite times were when she would tell me stories about when she was a young girl or a teenager. She was a very flirty girl, although she had a prissy attitude as an elderly person.

As Grandma's forgetfulness worsened, she often forgot what year it was. She would also forget to eat. Soon she could no longer remember conversations we had had. I could answer a question and five minutes later, she'd ask it again. I would tell her every week why and where I was going to school. We would talk about the world now compared to the world in her day. Sometimes she would talk out loud to her parents, who had been dead 50 or 60 years.

Her worst times were at night. She stayed up most of the night talking to people she thought were there. As much as I loved Grandma, I would get aggravated with her during those nights of constant talking. Several times a night, we'd go into her room to comfort her. She'd whine and cry like a child. It was difficult for me to deal with this. I started distancing myself from her during the day because she made me angry with the things she did at night. Even though I knew she had no idea what she was doing, it still aggravated me.

The stress started wearing on other family relationships as well. The daughters started finding fault with each other. No one said anything out loud, but the frustration was there under the surface. I was sad to see relationships start to disintegrate. I asked my grandmother to forgive me even if she didn't quite understand why.

Over the months, Grandma's condition deteriorated. She lost touch with reality and she lost trust in her family. One day she and I were home by ourselves and I got her a glass of water. When I gave it to her, she smelled it. Then she looked at me and said, "I never thought you would do this." I asked what she meant, and she said, "Of all people, I didn't think you would poison me. I expected the others, but not you." This hurt me very much. I took the glass of water and poured it down the sink and let her watch me pour a new glass. But she continued to believe I was trying to kill her.

By the time she died, Grandma weighed less than 95 pounds. The times that I could talk with her were over. She stayed with us for the last month of her life. She was in such bad condition we didn't want to move her. The night of her death my mom and dad left for church and I stayed behind. I read her the Bible and sang her some songs while I played my guitar. As I did this she began to cry a little. I didn't expect her to respond, but that was a special moment. About five hours later, she died in her bed, with her family in the room with her.

—NICHOLAS

CHECK IT OUT!

For more resources and data about family caregivers, see the following websites:

- AARP Planning Guide for Families: http://assets.aarp.org/www.aarp.org_/articles/foundation/aa66r2_care.pdf
- Family Caregiver Alliance: http://www.caregiver.org/caregiver/jsp/home.jsp
- National Alliance for Caregiving: http://www.caregiving.org
- National Association of Area Agencies on Aging: http://www.n4a.org
- National Caregivers Library: http://www.caregiverslibrary.org/home.aspx
- National Council on Aging: http://www.ncoa.org
- National Family Caregivers Association: http://www.nfcacares.org
- U.S. Administration on Aging National Family Caregiver Support Program: http://www.aoa.gov/AoA_programs/HCLTC/Caregiver/index.aspx
- U.S. Department of Health and Human Services Caregiver Resources: http://www.adsa.dshs.wa.gov/caregiving

In the words of Lori Roscoe and colleagues (2013), health professionals often adopt a "GPS-style" of communication with critically ill patients, focusing on where they are at the moment and what the next step will be. They suggest that a broader "Google Earth" perspective would also be valuable, so patients can more easily see where they are in the context of their disease progression and what lies beyond the next turn in the road (Roscoe, Tullis, Reich, & McCaffrey, 2013).

End-Of-Life Experiences

> *It was not my first time at the Cleveland Clinic—I had visited my sister-in-law, Annie, there before. But as I walked in this time, I knew that things were going to be different. I knew that Annie was dying of ovarian cancer that she had been fighting for the past 2½ years and that we were going to be facing a whole host of new issues this time.* (*Teresa Thompson, 2011, p. 177*)

With this statement, Thompson begins an examination of what she calls "a delicate balance" between hope and information at the end of life. She describes Annie's experiences managing the need for both hope and frank information. When the two seemed contradictory, Thompson says, the warmth of the caregiver's demeanor often made the difference in Annie's ability to cope effectively with the information. Thompson concludes that "hope is best engendered by a combination of honesty and empathy" that encompasses faith, dignity, peace, humor, and meaning, as well as treatment goals (p. 185).

In this section we explore the role of communication and social support at the end of life.

Death is an unpleasant topic to people in many Western cultures. "Death is un-American. It doesn't square with our philosophy of optimism, of progress," wrote Herbert Kramer, a terminally ill cancer patient (Kramer & Kramer, 1993, para. 21). Nevertheless, dying is inevitable, and it marks a stage of life during which social support is crucial. End-of-life experiences also can be more meaningful and beautiful than many people realize.

To some people, the phrase "a good death" seems like an oxymoron. They do not believe there is such a thing. However, many people argue that dying can be a special (albeit emotional) experience with many positive aspects. This section analyzes these two perspectives, which are characterized as "life at all costs" and "death with dignity." It also explains advance-care directives and offers experts' advice for dealing with death.

WHAT DO YOU THINK?

Cultural concepts of death vary widely, from the idea of a popping gently like a soap bubble, as in the Japanese concept of *pokkuri shinu*, to the ancient Greek depiction of Thanatos as the grim reaper. In your opinion, is there such a thing as a good death? If so, how would you describe it?

LIFE AT ALL COSTS

Have you ever walked past a hospital morgue? Probably not. Most hospitals locate the morgue in an out-of-the-way area where people will not chance upon it. Morgue staff members may be regarded as somewhat weird and eccentric based on their choice of occupation. This may seem perfectly understandable if you grew up in a society in which death was regarded as gross and ghoulish.

Today's Grim Reaper is a modern-day version of Thanatos, the merciless and malicious Greek god born of "darkness" and "sleep." In Greek mythology, Thanatos is often depicted as a rival of Bios (Greek for "life"). The lessons of such tales are easy to divine: Death is the enemy of life. Life is victory, death a merciless and permanent defeat. In modern terms, medicine is associated with Bios. Health professionals are considered, quite literally, to be in *mortal* combat with the enemy, death. Hence we entertain such notions as "battling cancer" and "fighting for one's life." These conceptualizations thrive in an atmosphere in which death is considered taboo and unknown, and medicine the ultimate savior.

If you are a caregiver pledged to maintain life, death may be more than creepy. It may represent failure. Caregivers have several incentives to keep patients from dying. For one, they are typically trained to preserve life, not allow it to end. Most physicians approach medicine as detectives and problem solvers—endeavors that are successful only if they solve the mystery and fix the problem (Ragan & Goldsmith, 2008). Moreover, death is frightening, even to professionals who have encountered it before (Hegedus, Zana, & Szabó, 2008). Saving a life is usually a rewarding experience, whereas a patient's death may bring feelings of guilt and grief. Finally, caregivers (doctors especially) may be harshly criticized or sued if a patient dies. Physicians' decisions are often intensely scrutinized by family members, lawyers, insurance companies, quality assurance and risk management personnel, administrators, and others. Jack McCue (1995) attests, "It is little wonder that physicians engage in inappropriately heroic battles against dying and death, even when it may be apparent to physician, patient, and family that a rapid, good death is the best outcome" (para. 2).

Medicine's dedication to preserving life has many benefits. Caregivers' devotion and talent, along with their access to medical technology, has helped to increase the average American's life expectancy from 47.3 to 78.3 years since 1900 (U.S. Census Bureau, 2012). But a "life at all costs" approach can rob people of the opportunity for a good death. Susan Block (2001) calls a good death "The Art of the Possible." The means of realizing this possibility, she says, lie in making people physically comfortable and helping them nurture caring relationships, maintain a sense of self, find meaning, feel a sense of control, and prepare for death. One man at the end of his life asserted, "What this last year has provided me with is the occasion to be deliberately open to receiving other people's love and care . . . and I'm delighted when it happens" (quoted by Block, p. 2902).

Many caregivers who become comfortable with death say it is a privilege to be with people at the end of their lives. A physician Block (2001) interviewed said of one dying patient:

> *I really like seeing him because no matter how distraught I am about that particular day or feeling overwhelmed . . . I feel so much better after each visit with him. It's almost like he's a doctor to me.* (*p. 2903*)

Loved ones often feel the same way, that they have learned something precious by being present at the end of a cherished individual's life.

Conventional wisdom says we are likely to lose faith or be angry at God when someone close to us dies. However, this occurs mostly when death is sudden or when people have not accepted its inevitability. Participants in Maureen Keeley's (2004) study of "final conversations" say their loss was tempered by a renewed sense of comfort, meaning, and spirituality. Said one, "You can't go through this . . . witnessing death, without that awe of what life is. Where it comes from and where it goes" (quoted by Keeley, 2004, p. 95). In another episode, a survivor remembers asking a loved one, "When you get to heaven, you know, keep an eye out on my girls," and her reply, "I will, you know. I'll be their guardian angel" (p. 97). In these episodes, the dying individual was able to help others find peace and comfort.

CULTURE AND HEALTH

It is traditional among the Māori of New Zealand to sing to loved ones who are dying. Said one woman of her brother: "Even though you could see the pain on his face, but you know when his song was sung to him, it soothed him a lot" (Oetzel, Simpson, Berryman, Iti, & Reddy, 2015, p. 354).

Proponents of a good death remind us that it might not involve preserving life as long as possible. As McCue (1995) proposes, "a rapid, good death" is sometimes preferable to a prolonged, painful end. Prolonging life sometimes means prolonging death.

Caregivers and others who perceive death to be a frightening enemy are not well equipped to help with end-of-life care. Dying individuals sometimes feel forgotten and ignored because their caregivers are uncomfortable with death, reluctant to become emotionally involved with them, and uncertain how to act around dying people.

Unfortunately, the opportunity to die peacefully among loved ones is sometimes lost in a confusion of tubes, wires, monitors, and hospital restrictions. It may be comforting to have professionals on hand, but it is hard for loved ones to be present and difficult to maintain a sense of intimacy and individuality in an institutional setting such as a hospital. Communication scholar Sandra Ragan reflects on the difference between her father's death and her sister's:

> *Dad's death was a conflicted one: He died in a hospital, connected to various machines, and in constant fear, until his last 48 hours, when he entered a morphine-induced semi-consciousness, that his doctors would not give him adequate medication.* (*Ragan, Wittenberg, & Hall, 2003, p. 219*)

In contrast, her sister died at home under hospice care:

> *Sherry died peacefully in her own home with no medical intervention other than oxygen, a catheter, and the blessing of morphine and Ativan. Her family and loved ones surrounded her, and throughout her last night, she was cradled by her daughter and her beloved cocker spaniel.* (*Ragan et al., 2003, pp. 219–220*)

DEATH WITH DIGNITY

In Japan, a metaphor for the ideal death is *pokkuri shinu*, which translates roughly into "popping like a bubble." People in many cultures share the same wish, of living fully and then dying without languishing slowly away. In the United States, a good death is often described as one in which people maintain dignity and die surrounded by loved ones and familiar, comforting surroundings.

The motto of death with dignity is attributable mostly to **hospice**, an organization that provides support and care for dying individuals and their families. Hospice provides **palliative care**, which is designed to keep a person as comfortable and fulfilled as possible at the end of life but not designed to cure the main illness once it has been determined that medical care will not improve it. More than 4 in 10 of all dying patients in the United States now receive hospice care, mostly at home during the last three weeks of their lives, and of those, 86.6% consider their care to be "excellent" ("Hospice Care," 2012).

Central to hospice's philosophy is the belief that death is a natural part of life, thus personal and unique. People are encouraged to die as they have lived, surrounded by the people and things they love most. Hospice volunteers and professional caregivers visit with terminally ill individuals and their loved ones to talk with them about death (if they wish), to make sure the dying person is not in pain, to encourage spiritual exploration (if they wish), and to provide many forms of assistance. In this effort, hospice is more oriented toward personal expression, emotions, spirituality, and social concerns than is conventional Western medicine. Loved ones are considered important participants in the dying process.

Beth Perry, a hospice nurse, recalls an especially rewarding experience helping a dying patient. "Roman, a handsome man in his mid-50s, seemed too well to be a patient on a palliative care unit," she remembers (Perry, 2002, para. 5). But Roman *was* dying, and he was bored and tired of the process—ready for the tedium to end. Although Roman's caregivers knew his death was near, they sought a way to rekindle his sense of purpose. Someone remembered that he and his wife had bought a new home just before he became ill, and the grounds were not yet landscaped. They suggested that the couple plan the garden and grounds together. "The result was amazing," writes Perry:

> *The next time we visited the pair, gone was the stony silence, the painful watching of time tick by. Instead, we found the two of them with their noses in the same magazine, eagerly debating annuals versus perennials, tulips versus delphiniums. (para. 7)*

Although Roman did not live to plant the garden, his last days were filled with enthusiasm rather than boredom. Julie, another nurse caring for Roman, says, "People can take almost anything, but they can't take being forgotten. They want to know that something they have done will live on after they die, and sometimes it is part of my role to help them" (quoted by Perry, 2002, para. 8).

Sometimes it is difficult to know what to say during end-of-life experiences. Sandra Sanchez-Reilly, MD, coauthor of *Communication as Comfort: Multiple Voices in Palliative Care,* told a dying patient in her care, "There are five things I tell my patients to say to everyone in their last day of their lives. Please forgive me; I forgive you; I love you; I will miss you. Goodbye." When a patient told her he was not scared and wiped away a tear, Sanchez-Reilly said to him, "You have taught the team many things today, Mr. ______. The team is here to learn. What else would you like to teach them?" (Ragan, Wittenberg-Lyles, Goldsmith, & Sanchez-Reilly, 2008, p. 80).

In another instance described in the same book, a husband helped his wife accept the need for hospice. Elaine Wittenberg-Lyles describes the hospital-room interaction, which she witnessed as a researcher. The patient expressed her fears about enrolling in hospice to a nurse who suggested the idea, until the patient's husband took his wife's hand in his and said to her through his tears, "I've been married to you for almost twenty-five years. I have never cheated on you. I have never lied to you. I'm not lying to you now. You need hospice. I need hospice. We need hospice" (Ragan et al., 2008, p. 146). Then the two leaned toward each other and cried.

Hospice volunteers also play a vital role in end-of-life communication. A beautiful account of this is available in Elissa Foster's (2007) book *Communicating at the End of Life: Finding Magic in the Mundane.* In the book, Foster chronicles her year as a hospice volunteer and shares the stories of other volunteers and the patients she meets along the way. Threaded throughout the narrative is Foster's relationship with Dorothy, a petite, energetic woman with "lively blue-green" eyes and white, close-cropped hair. Dorothy is under hospice care because doctors recognize that she is in the final stages of chronic obstructive pulmonary disease (COPD). Foster captures the confusion and concern she feels as Dorothy's condition seems, alternately, to deteriorate and to improve over time. She also reveals the mutuality of their relationship. Dorothy is not simply the recipient of Foster's care. The caring goes both ways. When Dorothy dies, Foster visits her family, shares hugs and tears with them, and thanks them for "sharing" their mother with her. She later reflects, "My relationship with Dorothy taught me that I could connect with someone whom I hardly know, simply by being there and being willing to let it happen" (p. 210).

Advance-Care Directives

Advance-care directives describe in advance the medical care a person wishes to receive (or not receive) if he or she becomes too ill to communicate. These directives take some of the pressure off caregivers and loved ones who might otherwise be forced to make those decisions on their own.

Despite the advantages, only about 1 in 4 adults in the United States has completed an advance-care directive (Rao, Anderson, Lin, & Laux, 2014). That leaves an overwhelming number of people without written instructions about their end-of-life care, even though communicating one's preferences is central to the idea of a good death (Borreani et al., 2008). Confusion about advance directives is particularly prevalent among people with literacy challenges (Sudore, Schillinger, Knight, & Fried, 2010).

Advance-care directives have become more specific through the years. When they were first conceptualized as "living wills" in the 1960s, they typically referred in vague terms to "heroic" life-saving measures (Emanuel & Emanuel, 1998). This presented obvious difficulties in interpretation (e.g., *Is a feeding tube heroic? Is intravenous therapy heroic?*). It is now common for advance-care directives to include a person's preferences regarding specific procedures and circumstances, to endow someone with decision-making authority, and to describe the person's philosophy of life and death to help guide decisions during unanticipated circumstances. (See Box 8.5 for a discussion of the right-to-die issue.)

BOX 8.5 ETHICAL CONSIDERATIONS

Do People Have a Right to Die?

Oregon made history in 1997 by legalizing physician-assisted suicide for terminally ill patients. Under the law, a physician may help a person commit suicide if at least two physicians verify that the person has less than six months to live and the patient requests help with suicide at least once in writing and twice verbally, with at least 15 days between requests.

Physician-assisted suicide refers to instances in which, at the request of a terminally ill person, a doctor provides the means for that person to end his or her own life (Krug, 1998). The doctor does not actually kill the patient. This is different from **euthanasia** (also called *mercy killing*), in which a physician or family member intentionally kills the patient to end his or her suffering. The distinction lies in who does the killing—the patient or another person.

The person most commonly associated with physician-assisted suicide was Jack Kevorkian, a physician who, by his own estimate, assisted in the suicides of 130 people. Kevorkian was tried for murder five times, but he was not convicted until the fifth trial, which concluded in April 1999. Kevorkian was declared guilty of second-degree murder by a Michigan jury and sentenced to 10 to 25 years in prison. The conviction was based on an assisted suicide that Kevorkian videotaped and allowed to be broadcast on *60 Minutes* (Willing, 1999). Kevorkian, who was released on parole in 2007 and died in 2011, argued that he was motivated by compassion for people dying slow, painful deaths. His opponents charged that he was a medical "hitman" operating outside the law (Robertson, 1999).

Controversy over physician-assisted suicide is likely to continue for quite some time, with people vigorously arguing both sides of the issue. Proponents of physician-assisted suicide include Dax Cowart, who was badly burned in an explosion in 1973 (Cowart & Burt, 1998). Two-thirds of Cowart's body was burned in the accident, and he lost his eyesight and his fingers. For more than a year Cowart begged doctors to let him die. Despite his pleas, medical teams continued to treat his burns. The treatment kept Cowart alive and eventually helped him regain the ability to walk. But during that time he was in nearly unbearable agony. He recalls, "The pain was excruciating, it was so far beyond any pain that I ever knew was possible, that I simply could not endure it" (para. 21). Cowart supports physician-assisted suicide. However, even if a law such as Oregon's had been in place when his accident occurred, he would not have qualified for lawful physician-assisted suicide because he was not dying.

Cowart is now an attorney in Corpus Christi, Texas, and describes himself as "happier than most people." But he maintains his conviction that people should not be forced to undergo treatment they do not wish, even if that treatment is needed to keep them alive (Cowart & Burt, 1998). Faced with the same ordeal again, he feels he would wish to die and should be allowed to do so. Cowart's views are captured in his videos *Please Let Me Die* and *Dax's Case*.

On the other side of the issue, some argue that people in intense pain and grief may not see things clearly enough to make life-ending decisions. They point out that Cowart has changed his mind about living with his disabilities. Although he initially felt life would be empty, he now is happy and successful (Cowart & Burt, 1998). Other critics say ill (even terminally ill) patients may request death for the wrong reasons. They may be afraid about the future, feel out of control and scared, or believe they are a burden to loved ones (Muskin, 1998). For these reasons, they feel it is wrong to help someone commit suicide, even if the person requests it.

What Do You Think?

1. Under what circumstances, if any, do you feel patients should be assisted in killing themselves?
2. Should it make a difference whether a patient is terminally ill or not?
3. If you were in Dax Cowart's place, do you feel you would want to die? What would you have done if you were Cowart's caregivers and loved ones?
4. What do you think of the argument that people who are scared and in pain may be not thinking clearly enough to make life-or-death decisions?
5. What do you think of the counterargument—that people should not second-guess the patient's wishes because they cannot fully understand the extent of his or her personal suffering?

BOX 8.6 CAREER OPPORTUNITIES

Social Services and Mental Health

Mental health counselor
Social worker
Psychologist
Social service manager
Hospice/palliative care provider
Home health aide
Senior citizen services providers

Career Resources and Job Listings

- American Mental Health Counselors Association: www.amhca.org
- American Psychological Association: www.apa.org
- National Association of School Psychologists: www.nasponline.org
- American Board of Professional Psychology: www.abpp.org
- National Organization for Human Services: www.nationalhumanservices.org
- Hospice: www.hospicenet.org
- Hospice careers: hospicechoices.com
- National Association for Home Care and Hospice: www.nahc.org

Communication Skill Builder: Delivering Bad News

One of the most difficult communication challenges that anyone faces is sharing devastating news with another. Bad news is never easy to give or to receive. But there are a number of communication strategies that help optimize people's coping ability. Here are some suggestions from the experts on how to share bad news compassionately.

- *Build caring relationships from the beginning.* In a study of recently diagnosed cancer patients, Pär Salander (2002) found that patients did not describe one distinct event during which they learned of their diagnosis. They considered that it occurred within the context of ongoing relationships with the medical staff. Said one woman, "The kindness, the support, and the help I received from the entire staff when treatment started is what I appreciate the most" (p. 724).
- *Foreshadow the disclosure.* A simple statement such as "The news isn't as good as we hoped" may help prepare people for what is to come.
- *Invite the recipient to bring along supportive others.*
- *Talk in a quiet, private place.* Resist the temptation to deliver bad news in a hallway or semiprivate space. Likewise, avoid delivering bad news over the phone whenever possible (Sparks, Villagran, Parker-Raley, & Cunningham, 2007).
- *Tell the truth.* People typically cope better when they know what is happening and what to expect. This is true even when death is expected. A participant in Thomas McCormick and Becky Conley's (1995) study said, "That's one of the things that I like my doctor for, because he was plain with me that I was incurable" (para. 38). She explained that people who do not know they are dying cannot prepare for it emotionally or practically. They lose the chance to settle financial affairs, communicate with loved ones, set new priorities for their limited time, and adjust emotionally to what is occurring.
- *Be clear about your meaning.* Patients often interpret hedge terms such as "possible" to mean that the news giver is attempting to soften the blow of bad news rather than convey actual uncertainty (Pighin & Bonnefon, 2011). Asked to interpret comments such as "It is possible the pain will increase," most patients felt the caregiver was really saying that the pain would probably or certainly increase (Pighin & Bonnefon, 2011, p. 171).
- *Avoid medical jargon.*
- *Acknowledge and legitimize emotions.* Emotions are a natural part of the coping process. Ignoring

them may make the news recipient feel foolish or inappropriate. Instead, acknowledge emotions with statements such as "I know this is very hard to hear," "I understand this can feel overwhelming," and "It's natural to feel a range of emotions when you learn something like this."

- *Take your cues from the recipient.* Do not be surprised if people seem stoic or distant on hearing bad news, whereas others are tearful or even angry. It is hard for any of us to say how we will react in such circumstances. Patients typically say it is unhelpful when someone attempts to impose a particular agenda or set of emotions on them (Maynard & Frankel, 2006). One patient whom Salander (2002) interviewed wondered, "Why did they have to be so dramatic? Suddenly, everybody looked so grave and became so low-voiced. It gave me a feeling of unreality" (p. 725).
- *Show genuine caring.* As one woman put it, "A hug or supportive word in passing worked miracles" (quoted by Salander, 2002, p. 727).
- *Inform and empathize.* Research shows that, no matter how bad the news, patients want both high-quality information and empathy, and one does not compensate for the other. In other words, lots of information does not make up for a lack of emotional supportiveness or visa versa. People typically want both (Sastre, Sorum, & Mullet, 2011).
- *Be aware of personal and cultural preferences for bad-news delivery.* Some people, such as members of traditional Native American cultures, prefer that bad news be delivered indirectly through metaphors and storytelling (T. Thompson & Gillotti, 2005). In some other cultures, speaking bad news aloud is considered unlucky.
- *Offer support.* Indicate your own support and offer other resources to help people learn, adjust, and cope.
- *Be ready with options and a plan of action.* Although some people may need time to take in the bad news before they make decisions, most say that having a specified next step helped them funnel their energy and emotion in positive ways and feel less like helpless victims.
- *Schedule an information follow-up.* Keep in mind that few people can absorb and remember many details when they are feeling intense emotions. Written materials may help, as will a follow-up visit to talk about the details once the news has sunk in.

For career resources relevant to mental health and coping, see Box 8.6.

Communication Skill Builder: Coping With Death

One positive aspect of death is that it draws people together. Loved ones who may not have seen each other in years unite again with a common concern. Death also provides an occasion for contemplating life and the purpose of living. A sense of insight and spirituality often surrounds death (McCormick & Conley, 1995). Moreover, by sharing in loved ones' deaths, people may become less fearful of death themselves. Joyce Dyer, who wrote *In a Tangled Wood* (1996) about her mother's nine-year experience with Alzheimer's disease, reflected after her death:

> *I want to remember every moment I had with my mother, including every second of the last nine years. I want to remember her toothless grin, her screams, her growing fondness for sweets and then for nothing at all, the bouquets of uprooted flowers she picked for me from her unit's patio, the way she tried to fold her bib, the rare pats on my cheek that meant everything, her last words, her last party, her last dance. And I want to remember what I learned from aides and nurses, from volunteers and cleaning staff, from my mother's own sick friends. I don't want to forget a single thing.* (Dyer, 1996, p. 136)

People may be surprised by the mixture of emotions they feel about death. Most of us are not sure what to expect, and consequently we are often uncertain how to act around dying individuals. Based on news reports and movies, people typically imagine death as violent and scary. However, the majority of deaths are nothing like that. Colin Parkes (1998) describes the typical death as a "quiet slipping away" without pain or horror.

One nurse described her initial discomfort when a young man in her care joked that he had to live quickly because he would not live long (Erdman, 1993). The nurse was eventually able to laugh with the young man when he quipped that he was watching movies on fast-forward and bathing his dog in the drive-through carwash to save time. Writes Erdman, "The nurse was at first caught off guard by the patient's comments, but the humor opened the door to further communication about death" (p. 59).

Three themes emerge in the narratives of older adults reflecting on the death of loved ones: loss, feelings, coping. The feelings are mixed, but not as negative as you might expect. In Caplan, Haslett, and Burleson's (2005) study of older adult bereavement narratives, 36% of the feelings were negative (fear, loneliness, sadness), but 43% were positive (optimism, thankfulness for time spent together, and so on). Said one woman, whose husband died in 1993, "I don't dwell on the sickness and problems of what happened then, but my thoughts and memories instead, think of all the good and wonderful life we had together with the six children" (p. 244).

In her book *On Death and Dying,* Elisabeth Kübler-Ross (1969) describes the process of coping with death in five stages: denial and isolation, anger, bargaining, depression, and acceptance. Not everyone experiences all five stages or in the order given, but dying individuals and the people around them are likely to experience many of these phases. Although with enough time and support many people eventually feel peaceful about death, they may at times refuse to believe what is told them, or they may feel angry, overwhelmed, sad, or hopeless. Often, people feel their God has let them down, and they react by showing anger or attempting to bargain for mercy. It may be reassuring to remember that these stages are common and legitimate components of the coping process.

Summary

A diverse number of behaviors make up social support. Support is useful in everyday life and in times of crisis. What is most supportive depends on the nature of the situation, the people involved, and their perception of health self-efficacy. Sometimes problem solving is the most effective coping strategy. In those instances, instrumental and informative support are likely to be appreciated. When the situation calls for emotional adjustment, nurturing support may be a useful way to help people feel better about themselves, express their emotions, and feel that others will stand by them in times of trouble.

Even a relatively minor health event can constitute a crisis if the people involved do not have adequate skills or resources to cope with it. Often, the difference between thriving and declining involves the amount of social support that we perceive is available to us.

Being normal sounds easy, but to members of society viewed as abnormal, achieving a sense of normalcy can seem as impossible as it is desirable. People do well to remember that individuals who have disabilities or are ill do not usually benefit from being treated as if they are childlike or helpless.

People usually cope more effectively when they can discuss sensitive topics than when they feel compelled to feign cheerfulness. Do not assume that individuals are coping well because they are quiet or do not display much emotion. Research suggests that these people often receive less support than others, although they probably need it just as much. Communication is most supportive when it allows distressed individuals to express themselves as they wish and to set the pace for talk and action. Supportive listeners are attentive, nonjudgmental, and able to help people understand their own emotions.

Information is often useful in coping, but as the theory of problematic integration points out, information sometimes creates as many uncertainties and contradictions as it does certainties. Sometimes it can be overwhelming.

The quality of our relationships (with family members, friends, and even animals) has a powerful effect on our health. Strong networks, including social support group membership, are often life enhancing. Likewise, what seems like a crisis is sometimes revealed as a transcendent experience in which people come to perceive an overarching meaning that makes sense of situations that initially seemed tragic or pointless.

Although social support is invaluable, inappropriate or excessive amounts of it can be counterproductive. Too little assistance can make people feel abandoned. Too much can cause a sense of helplessness and dependence. Likewise, too much information or ill-timed disclosures can tax people's coping ability, and emotional contagion can be exhausting and can discourage people from describing their feelings. A few simple guidelines can help to ensure that supportive efforts are comforting rather than hurtful.

As the need for family caregivers has risen, the demands on their time have increased as well. Loved ones are an important source of social support, but they, too, need support. Support groups, skills-training programs, and the assistance of family and friends are key.

Medicine has traditionally considered death a failure, to be avoided at all costs, but groups such as hospice promote the philosophy that there is such a thing as a good death. For the most part, a good death unites people in a sense of peace and comfort. When people are able to cope effectively, death may bring people together and help them overcome their fears.

Key Terms and Theories

social support
buffering hypothesis
direct-effect or main-effect model
coping
problem solving
emotional adjustment
health self-efficacy
internal locus of control
external locus of control
fatalistic
dialectics
crisis
normalcy
action-facilitating support
nurturing support
instrumental support
informational support
theory of problematic integration
esteem support
emotional support
support groups
oversupport
overhelping
overinforming
overempathizing
empathy
empathic concern
emotional contagion
transcendent experiences
Family and Medical Leave Act of 1993
hospice
palliative care
advance-care directives
physician-assisted suicide
euthanasia

Discussion Questions

1. On a scale of 1 to 10, how would you rate your social support network in terms of the number of people you know? In terms of the quality of your interactions? Do you think relationships have an impact on your health? If so, how? Is the quantity or quality of your social ties more important to your well-being? Why?
2. Describe an instance in which you offered someone action-facilitating support and an instance in which you offered someone nurturing support. Now describe instances in which you received these forms of support. What was the outcome in each instance? Were the supportive efforts mostly effective or ineffective? Why?
3. Divide a paper into two columns. In the left hand, write specific expectations for your future. In the right column, evaluate each expectation in terms of whether it is likely to be good or bad, easy or difficult, likely or unlikely. The theory of problematic integration suggests that some of these expectations are likely to come true and some are not. What role is communication likely to play in pursuing the expectations you value? In coping with unforeseen circumstances along the way?
4. In what ways can people be oversupportive? What are the likely outcomes of different types of oversupport? Name five tips for assuring that sure social support efforts are effective.
5. Have you ever felt that an animal was a good friend? Why or why not? Do you think animal companionship affects your coping ability?
6. Compare the birth experiences of Carol Bishop Mills and her husband with those of Kate and Chris. What do you learn from these examples?
7. What does the term *transcendent experience* mean? Can you think of examples from movies or your own experiences?

8. In your opinion, is there such a thing as a good death? If so, how would you describe it?
9. Do you have an advance-care directive? Why or why not?
10. What is your opinion of the right-to-die issue (Box 8.5)? Why?

Answer to *Can You Guess?*

The percentage of family caregivers who say dementia is their main concern doubled (from 6% to 12%) between 2004 and 2009 ("Caregiving in the U.S.," 2009).

CHAPTER 9

eHealth, mHealth, and Telehealth

"Is there a doctor on board?" If anyone is carrying a smartphone, the answer might as well be yes. That's the message from Eric Topol in his book *The Patient Will See You Now* (2015).

As an airplane passenger, Topol has diagnosed numerous passengers in distress using applications on his smartphone. In one case, he used a mobile app to monitor the electrical signals of a woman's heart when she began feeling unwell. The data indicated that she was having a heart attack, and Topol alerted the crew to make an emergency landing. Another time, when a passenger fainted, Topol used his phone to measure the man's heart activity, blood pressure, and blood oxygen level, and even to see an ultrasound image of his heart. The data pointed to a nonthreatening drop in blood pressure and the flight continued (Topol, 2015).

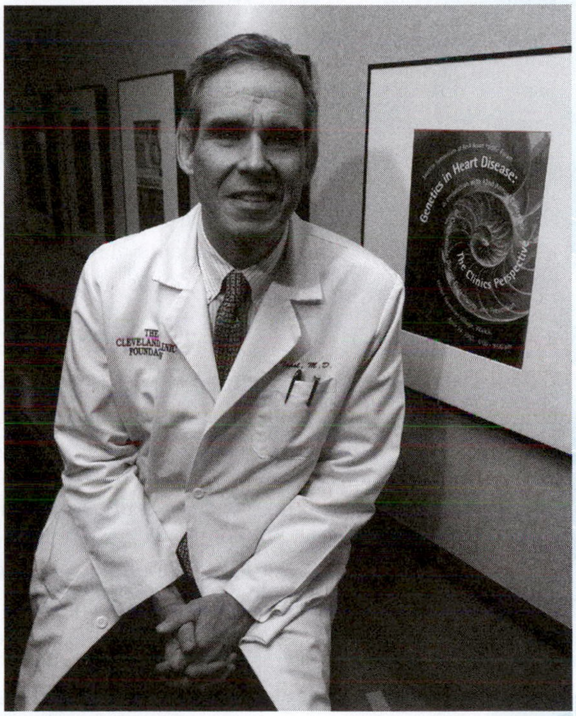

Cardiologist Eric Topol, author of *The Patient Will See You Now* (2015), predicts a time in the near future when people will use smartphone apps to diagnose ailments and digitally capture data, such as heart rhythms and blood oxygen levels, that they can transmit instantly to their doctors.

Here's the kicker: Although Topol is a cardiologist, he proposes that anyone with a smartphone could have done what he did and reached the same conclusions. Mobile apps are already available that use computer algorithms to diagnose conditions and offer recommendations in minutes. For example, a person with a suspicious mole or an irregular heartbeat can find out what is going on right away and receive immediate advice on what to do next. The process is typically as easy as uploading a photo or placing the device against one's chest or fingertips, and most results are written so that even children can

Worried about a skin rash or a suspicious mole? Smartphone apps such as SkinVision now allow you to take a picture of it and submit it for computer analysis. Within minutes, you will receive a diagnosis and suggestions about what to do next, whether that involves treating a minor condition yourself or seeing a professional for a more serious concern.

understand them (Topol, 2015). The result, Topol says, is a rise not only in smartphones, but of increasingly smart *patients*.

In the future, Topol (2015) predicts, technology will promote people to the executive boardroom in terms of their own health. Whereas they were previously treated as low-level employees at best, patients may function more as chief operating officers (COOs). "The COO monitors *all* the operations of the body. He [or she] is fully in charge," Topol says (p. 12). If people function as COOs of their own health, then smartphones are their crackerjack information technology departments that provide up-to-the-minute, easy-to-understand data and visuals so they can make well-informed decisions. Topol compares that process to the traditional medical model in which people have often waited weeks for medical appointments, seen doctors for only about 10 minutes at a time, waited even longer for diagnostic tests and analysis, and then rarely had full access to their own medical charts or test results.

Within the model that Topol (2015) envisions, technology does not replace communication with one's physician; it *enhances* it. Physicians will function as chief executive officers, meaning they will not try to do everything themselves. Instead, they will help prepare patients and other members of the care team to manage day-to-day operations, which will free doctors to spend more time with patients when serious issues emerge.

Not everyone is optimistic about the move toward more virtual interactions and patient autonomy. As you will see later in the chapter, some fear that it will undermine patient–caregiver relationships and result in superficial diagnoses and advice. But for his part, Topol (2015) is excited about a possible future in which patients understand very well what is wrong with them and know when to manage issues on their own and when to seek help. He got a taste of that recently, when a patient emailed him an electrocardiogram (heart activity) pattern with the message, "I'm in atrial fib, now what do I do?" Topol reflects:

> *I knew the world had changed. The patient's phone hadn't just recorded the data—it had interpreted it! A smart algorithm was now trumping my skills as a cardiologist. Putting this power in everyone's pocket could preempt an emergency room visit or an urgent clinic appointment.* (*p. 6*)

Whereas some health professionals might be threatened by this sea change, Topol considers it to be a "democratization of medicine" that may support good health and lower health care costs. (See Box 9.1 for more on the issue.)

In this chapter we explore **eHealth**, which involves the use of technology to transcend geographical distance in promoting good health. A number of efforts fall within the rubric of eHealth. **mHealth** involves

HEALTH AND COMMUNICATION TECHNOLOGY

One promise of eHealth is assistance to regions of the world in which conventional care is scarce. The following websites provide information about the use of medical technology in remote regions of Africa:

- Praekelt Foundation: http://www.praekeltfoundation.org/
- Health eVillages (Pronounced Healthy Villages): http://www.healthevillages.org/
- mHealth Alliance: http://mhealthknowledge.org/
- Medic Mobile: http://medicmobile.org/

BOX 9.1 ETHICAL CONSIDERATIONS

The Pros and Cons of Telemedicine

So far in this chapter you have read about the views of Eric Topol (2015), who envisions a medical system in which everyday people use technology to assess their health and learn about their options. In what he calls "the democratization of medicine," patients are empowered to manage their health and to consult health professionals when they need assistance.

Topol proposes that doctor visits and hospital stays will be less necessary in the future because patients and caregivers will be able to communicate in real time via video/audio technology and because a great deal of diagnostic data will be collected and shared electronically. As Topol puts it:

> *Since 2600 bc, doctors ruled the roost. Now patients increasingly will be generating their own data—by doing the physical exam through smart phone sensors, for example—and driving their own care. They'll be able to video chat with a doctor at any moment, 24/7, for the same costs as a co-pay to see a doctor in person (quoted by Larkin, 2014, para. 4).*

A contrasting view is presented by people who fear that eHealth will compromise doctor–patient relationships and lead physicians to offer medical advice to patients they have not met or examined but have only communicated with via phone calls, emails, online chats, or text messages. In 2015, Texas set some of the strictest limits on telemedicine to date, requiring that patients who consult with a health professional via telemedicine must be physically present at a satellite medical center at the time (Definitive Healthcare. 2015). Physicians who would like to communicate with local patients via technology must meet with them in person before offering them advice over a phone, computer, or mobile device. As one doctor puts it, "What can the quality of service be when it's sight unseen and you have no relationship to the patient?" (quoted by E. Walters, 2015, para. 14).

What Do You Think?

1. Are there situations in which you would prefer to consult with a health professional on the phone or via a video chat rather than visiting a doctor's office or emergency room? If so, when?
2. Are there circumstances in which a virtual medical visit or hospital stay would be inferior to an in-person interaction? If so, when?
3. Consider Topol's scenario in which a patient notices an unusual mole and is able to upload a photo of the mole via a smartphone app and find out in minutes (based on computer algorithms) if it appears to be harmless or if he or she should seek medical attention for it. What are the advantages of quick access to medical information of this nature? What are the disadvantages?
4. How might your life and health be affected by easy-to-use mobile health evaluators that could instantly tell you your blood alcohol level, heart rate`a, blood sugar level, sleeping patterns, and so on, and provide advice on responding effectively?
5. How might your life be affected if medical visits more often occur via telemedicine than in person?

the use of devices such as mobile phones, tablet computers, and personal digital assistants. **Telehealth** utilizes technology to facilitate long-distance health care, education, administrative teamwork, and disaster responses (WHO, 2010a, 2011b). **Telemedicine** is a subset of telehealth that specifically involves offering clinical services to patients at a distance, usually through the use of teleconference exams and shared diagnostic data, but also via phone and computer-mediated conversations. The overarching category of eHealth also includes a variety of other activities, such as communication between everyday people via blogs, tweets, text messages, and other electronic means. Our increasing reliance on these technologies as both health citizens and professionals underscores the central role communication plays in health.

eHealth

I had a question, you know? I didn't really feel comfortable asking my mom, 'cause she was the only one around. You know, I was like, I went on the Internet and I was like, "Can a girl get pregnant during her period?"

This statement by a 17-year-old high school student in Rachel Jones and Ann Biddlecom's (2011, p. 115) study of teens' online communication illustrates one role the Internet plays in health-related behavior. Sometimes eHealth is an alternative to talking about topics that are embarrassing to discuss with another person. As you will see in this section, people have this and numerous other goals in mind when they utilize electronic health resources. We will explore these goals as we pursue answers to questions such as, *Why and under what circumstances do people seek electronic health information? Is online health information mostly helpful or not?* and *How has technology influenced the nature of health communication?*

THEORETICAL FOUNDATIONS

Before we begin, let's clarify the role that eHealth plays in shaping public discourse and establishing social ties.

The Three Spheres

As social actors, we recognize that different rules of engagement apply to our interactions depending on the circumstances. G. Thomas Goodnight (1982) and Robert Cox (2010) have identified **three spheres** with powerful influence on the way we communicate with others: the personal, technical, and public.

The **personal sphere** involves communication between a small number of people that is usually not made part of the public record (Goodnight, 1982). The most common example is a casual conversation between friends or acquaintances. In today's environment, texts and emails to close friends also fall within this sphere. If, in personal communication, we seek to debate an issue, we usually do so with few formal rules of argumentation, and we may be swayed by the personalities of the people involved to either overstate or understate our claims (Goodnight, 1982).

In contrast, the **technical sphere** is governed by strict rules, such as agreed-upon standards for what constitutes evidence and causality (Goodnight, 1982). Rather than a conversation between two friends, think of a debate between scientists or trial attorneys. Scientific journals are replete with technical information that is carefully vetted based on a strict set of standards. This information may or may not have a presence in everyday discourse.

The **public sphere** is more inclusive than the other two. It is created through "conversation, argument, debate, or questioning" about issues that concern people at a community or global level (Cox, 2010, p. 26). As Cox puts it, active discourse about subjects of mutual interest brings the public sphere into being. One way this occurs is when concerns previously treated as private become topics of shared interest with others. Cox asserts that the public sphere is not confined to official spaces, such as courtrooms or Senate chambers, but occurs as well in restaurants and supermarkets, on radio call-in shows, and in any other space in which people engage with each other. It also occurs via Facebook, Twitter feeds, blogs, websites, and other electronic venues. In short, the public sphere involves a diversity of perspectives in a discursive climate that invites participation.

Here is a health-related example. When Candace and Steve Lightner's 13-year-old daughter was killed by a drunk driver in 1980, people might have treated it as a personal tragedy. Their other two children previously had been injured by impaired drivers, but had survived. In all three cases, the drivers received little or no punishment. But by the third incident, this one even more tragic than the others, Candy Lightner had had enough. She felt that the issue of drunk driving was not a personal issue but a public one, and she launched a grassroots campaign that gave rise to Mothers Against Drunk Driving (MADD) and new levels of public awareness and legislation.

As you can see in this example, the spheres are not always clearly distinct from one another at a glance. However, Goodnight (1982) maintained that an important difference is present beneath the surface, namely the discursive standards that establish what is appropriate and admissible within each sphere. Goodnight worried that the public sphere might be "eroded" by overreliance on personal evidence, which is subject to distortion by personality and other factors, and technical evidence, whose parameters are sometimes inadequate to admit diverse forms of reason and evidence.

CULTURE AND HEALTH

For many people, going to a doctor's office or hospital feels like visiting an alien land. Medicine has a culture, look, smell, and set of rules that are largely different from everyday life. However, some analysts predict that the cultural gap between everyday life and health care will blur as mHealth becomes more pervasive. Patients who can monitor their conditions and receive advice specific to their concerns 24 hours a day may drive a movement toward more conversational, multidimensional interactions with health care providers (Gur-Arie, 2014).

Empathic posts by people we do not know well (weak-tie relationships) can be powerful sources of support, especially when our close friends feel as overwhelmed as we do.

We have only scratched the surface concerning the theoretical implications of spheres, but a basic understanding will do for now in that it highlights a fascinating aspect of emerging communication technology—the widespread potential for people to introduce issues into the public sphere. As in the MADD case and many others, powerful implications emerge when health, often a deeply personal concern, becomes the topic of public communication. That has always been true, and grassroots efforts have always existed. What is changing is the ease and access with which people can place information in the public sphere. **Web 2.0**, a term used to describe Internet users' ability to create and share information online (via YouTube, blogs, wikis, and so on), has made it possible for everyday citizens to step beyond the role of information consumer into the shoes of message creators and publishers.

Now, with a bit of basic training and access to a computer, everyday people can create messages and make them available worldwide. The extent to which those messages are adopted as topics of public discourse varies. The point is that the widespread ability to do this is unprecedented in history. This changes the nature of our relationships with others.

Weak and Strong Ties

It is now relatively easy to communicate about personal matters with people you are never likely to meet in person. Rather than keeping a personal journal, you might create a blog or Twitter feed on which you post ideas and reflections that anyone can see. You might expect your friends to visit your blog, but be surprised by postings from people you do not know who say your words moved them or they relate to what you are experiencing. In some ways, we are not as alone as we used to be. Our potential for social interaction and connection with diverse others (at least as far as we can take that electronically) is nearly infinite.

Relevant to this idea is Mark Granovetter's **social network theory**, which proposes that we experience **strong ties** with people whose social networks overlap ours a great deal (close friends and members of our inner circle) and **weak ties** (acquaintanceships) with people whose social networks do not overlap much with our own (Granovetter, 1973, 1983). We tend to interact with our good friends in what Granovetter (1983) refers to as a "closely knit clump" (p. 202). There are advantages to this in terms of stability, loyalty, and comfort. However, weak ties are also important in that they help us avoid an isolated and insular perspective on the world.

It is often through weak ties that we learn new ideas, are exposed to opportunities beyond our current circumstances, and experience the flexibility of being different from the expectations of our close friends. In addition, people to whom we have strong ties tend to experience the same stressors that we do, so weak ties can be sources of support when our close friends feel as overwhelmed as we do. And the ties that bind sometimes change. If, for example, you learn that you have diabetes, you may feel that you suddenly have less in common with your old friends (who still engage in their customary ways of thinking, eating, and behaving) and more in common with people you do not know well but who have the same lifestyle/health concerns as you. For these reasons, Granovetter (1973, 1983) titled his seminal essays "The Strength of Weak Ties."

Health blogs make it possible to create a sense of community among people with weak ties. Bloggers with chronic health conditions often perceive that their well-being is enhanced when people post supportive comments, even when they do not know those people personally (Rains & Keating, 2011).

Blog coordinators at Wego Health, a social media company that encourages collaboration among health care activists, propose a question each month and invite people to post their thoughts about it. In April 2012, the question was, "If you had a superpower—what would it be? How would you use it?"

Tiffany Marie Peterson (2012), who identifies herself as a lupus ePatient, responded to the superpower question with her version of the Miranda rights that police in the United States recite to crime suspects. Her version, the Miranda Health Rights, is for a different sort of offender, those guilty of offering "ridiculous uneducated notions" such as:

> *It's my fault I have lupus . . . a miracle herb can cure my disease . . . if only I just ate 10 vegetables a day lupus would disappear . . . how I should just quit while I'm ahead because there's no cure and so on. (para. 9)*

Peterson's Miranda Health Rights include the following:

> *I have the right to remain silent and refuse to comply shall you inflict any harm upon my health . . . You have the right to consult Dr. Google before speaking/approaching me with ignorance about my condition/and or health. If need be I can refer you to an ePatient advocate and have them present during questioning now or in the future . . . If you cannot conduct a Google search, information will be selected for you before any uneducated responses or questioning. (para. 8)*

She concludes, "These Miranda Health rights are my superpowers!" (para. 10). Peterson's post displays her experience with eHealth. She refers to herself as an ePatient and sees "Dr. Google" and ePatient advocates as antidotes to the harm caused by people who offer uninformed advice. In her case, the Internet is a way to vent, share stories with others, and alleviate ignorance about a condition that many people do not understand. (For more on ePatients, see Box 9.2.)

A few lessons emerge from considering eHealth communication from the perspective of spheres and

BOX 9.2

Profile of an ePatientces

In the broadest sense, ePatients are "Internet-savvy" people who "meet their own health needs using the Internet and other information and communication technology" (K. Kim & Kwon, 2010, p. 712). They typically find health-related information, share it with others, investigate treatment options and more, online. They tend to be comparatively young, well educated, and affluent, meaning they are probably already information rich (Koch-Weser et al., 2010). Even though ePatients use online resources more than other people, most of them say doctors are still their favorite source of health information. They just yearn for more detail than their physicians typically provide (K. Kim & Kwon, 2010).

The term *ePatient* is still evolving. Many people who look up health information online and share it with others are not patients at all. For example, nearly 7 in 10 people who seek cancer information online do not have cancer (K. Kim & Kwon, 2010). Kyunghye Kim and Nahyun Kwon (2010) advocate a finer distinction by defining **ePatients** as "people with illness seeking information or help from the Internet to make informed health decisions" (p. 712).

No matter how you define the concept, electronic health information and ePatients are certainly here to stay in some form.

social ties. One is that the options for health-related expression and social support (a topic we discussed in Chapter 8) are expansive at both the personal and public levels. Another is that, with a proliferation of messages in the public sphere, there is some danger that people will mistake narratives, and even misconceptions, for scientific truths. Raluca Cozma (2009), for one, worries that inaccuracies may be perpetuated if people rely on folk wisdom rather than facts. She found knowledge differences between, on the one hand, people who rely heavily on personal-sphere sources such as blogs and, on the other, people who rely more on health organization websites (public sphere sources) and health news sites (technical sphere sources). People whose information comes mostly from the personal sphere are more likely than others to believe health myths, such as the common but unsupported notions that carrots improve eyesight, filtered cigarettes prevent cancer, and calcium-rich foods prevent tooth decay. Just as Goodnight (1982) worried that the public sphere would be eroded, others feel we have a great deal to lose if the technical sphere loses status as a source of reliable information.

With these issues in mind, let's take a closer look at people's motivation for using communication technology.

Why and When Do People Seek ehealth Information?

> *My alarm clock went off hours before the sun began rising. I silenced it, slowly got out of bed and began getting ready for my morning gym session. Sill half-asleep, I turned on the bright lights of the bathroom and began brushing my teeth. What happened next is something I never imagined could happen and something I will remember for the rest of my life.*

Health events, such as this one described by a university student, sometimes sneak up on us when expert care is not readily available. Here, in her words, is what happened next:

> *I had somehow managed to open my mouth too wide while brushing my teeth and it was stuck open. My poor jaw was stuck open with toothpaste dripping from the corners of my lips. At that moment, panic set in. Tears were rolling down my cheeks. I felt so helpless. I franticallly got online and tried to find solutions.*

In this case, the woman's first impulse was to seek information online. "It was so early I didn't want to wake up my roommate," she explains. "So I'm standing there with my mouth hanging open trying to Google 'how to fix your jaw' in my cell phone."

In this section we examine the reasons people seek health information electronically. Earlier in the chapter we heard the perspective of a teenager who searched for sex education online because she didn't want to ask her mother. The woman with the dislocated jaw was motivated by different goals—namely, to find information quickly, to avoid inconveniencing others, and hopefully, to solve an unexpected and urgent dilemma. As we explore theories of eHealth information seeking, consider how well they describe your experiences.

One perspective is that uncertainty motivates information seeking, especially if individuals perceive an urgent need or risk. Theorists call it **information sufficiency threshold**—the amount of information a person needs in order to feel capable of coping with and understanding a threatening issue (Chaiken, 1980; Chaiken, Giner-Sorolla, & Chen, 1996; Griffin, Dunwoody, & Neuwirth, 1999). In the story of the dislocated jaw, the young woman said her first reaction was to think, "I don't know what to do!" That sent her scrambling for information in the quickest way she could think of—an Internet search on her phone. It was a clear case of information *in*sufficiency, and she was highly motivated to learn quickly.

Availability is not everything. We are likely to avoid or ignore eHealth information we perceive to be overwhelming, irrelevant, or untrustworthy.

However, uncertainty is not always the singular or deciding factor. For a variety of reasons, people might *not* seek information, even if they acknowledge that they do not know much about an important issue. Maybe they do not believe more knowledge will make a difference. The **health information acquisition model** established the basis for many theories that have followed it. The model proposes that people are motivated to seek information when something calls their attention to a concern, they do not perceive that they are well informed about it, it seems important to find out soon, and they think they will be able to find trustworthy and useful information (Freimuth, Stein, & Kean, 1989). Central to this theory is the idea that people first consider how much they already know and then weigh the costs and rewards of seeking additional information. The woman with the dislocated jaw said she felt sure she could fix the problem if she learned how to do it online. She had high self-efficacy (a term you may remember from Chapter 8 that describes the belief that we can make a difference in managing our own health).

Let's add some additional dimensions to the information-seeking equation. The **Theory of Motivated Information Management** (TMIM) by Walid Afifi and Judith Weiner (2004) has several aspects in common with the health information acquisition model in that both presume that people seek information when they are anxious about something and feel it would be helpful to learn more about it. TMIM, however, also addresses coping confidence (*Am I ready to deal with what I might learn?*) and people's choice of information channels (*How might I get this information?*). According to TMIM, the likelihood that people will seek information depends on their perceived need for it, their coping ability, and the way in which the information is conveyed. Regarding information channels, TMIM addresses not just why people want information and what they hope to learn, but *how* they pursue that information. Afifi and Weiner propose that people seek information most readily from sources they believe to be relevant, accurate, and trustworthy.

Most people prefer that sensitive and important information be conveyed in emotionally immediate, information-rich ways—for example, in person rather than via a text or phone call (Brown, Parker, Furber, & Thomas, 2011). Especially when the stakes are high, people typically appreciate the presence of both verbal and nonverbal cues and indications that the other person cares and is willing to listen. (The exception is that some people prefer to receive emotional news at a distance so that they can avoid "flooding out" emotionally in front of other people [Beach, 2002].) Most people also prefer to hear serious news directly from an expert. In short, the source matters, and it affects how likely people are to believe what they read and hear.

WHAT DO YOU THINK?

How would you like to receive bad news about your health? Would an email or an instant message be as effective as a phone call? Would a phone call be as effective as a face-to-face conversation? Why?

It follows from TMIM that, when the stakes are high, people typically prefer interpersonal communication with individuals they trust. Partly for this reason, people who do not feel that health professionals are empathic and patient centered are more likely than satisfied patients to seek health information on the Internet (Tustin, 2010). Satisfied patients may already feel their needs have been met, whereas the others do not.

Yet another dimension is added by the **Integrative Model of Online Health Information Seeking**, which posits that social structures and inequities manifest in individual differences that, in turn, influence how able and motivated people are to seek eHealth information (Dutta, Bodie, & Basu, 2008). As you may remember from Chapters 1 and 6, 14% of adults in the United States have difficulty reading or understanding English, and the percentages are even higher in many parts of the world. An increased reliance on computer-mediated information may create an even larger gap between them and people who are already rich in health information. (We will return to this topic in a moment.) Literacy is not the only factor. If individuals believe health authorities do not care about people like them, they are unlikely to put much stock in their advice or to actively seek health information from them. Other barriers include limited access to technology and the perception that other concerns—such as hunger or day-to-day survival in a violent neighborhood—are higher priorities than long-term health. An important aspect of this theory is that it focuses on individual differences, but it recognizes that they do not happen by chance. Discrimination, education, hunger, violence, and other factors are often rooted in macro-level issues such that some groups of people have advantages that others do not. Dutta, Bodie, and Basu (2008) explain:

> *In the absence of health-enhancing structures within the minority community, young people are less likely to learn about the relevance of health behaviors, to have role models promoting health behaviors, and to value health-promoting behaviors owing to the lack of resources that would support such behaviors. As a consequence, they are more likely to focus on the daily struggles of survival.* (p. 184)

From this perspective, eHealth is not simply a matter of making information available. On a deeper level, issues such as trust and access influence how likely people are to seek and to believe that information.

In contrast to the youth whom Dutta and colleagues describe, people who feel they are proficient at finding health information online are more likely than others to be active Internet users (Duplaga, 2015). In this way, one set of advantages (skill and confidence) heightens others (knowledge and its benefits). This is noteworthy because, compared to television, Internet navigation requires a higher level of confidence and a more sophisticated set of skills. There is also a degree of social expectation. The chance of going online is heightened when people perceive that (a) loved ones expect to them do so and (b) online information is valued by one's peers as useful and appropriate (Smith-McLallen, Fishbein, & Hornik, 2011). This points to another factor that may be lacking in underprivileged populations—the social expectation that people can use technology to improve their lives.

As you can see, theories about information seeking naturally overlap because they reflect similar phenomena, but theorists add various nuances to the picture. Most scholars suggest (and research supports) that people are most likely to seek health information if they are confident that they can find it and use it affectively, they feel emotionally capable of dealing with what they find, and they expect that the results will be worth the effort. The Theory of Motivated Information Management focuses a great deal on interpersonal sources of information and reminds us that the source and channel sometimes matter as much as the content. As one of the first models to focus specifically on electronic modalities, the Integrative Model of Online Health Information Seeking calls attention to social structures and opportunities that constrain individual action. Unlike information that people may glean incidentally from TV or billboards, eHealth information usually comes to their attention because they actively seek it. One exception is information in pop-up advertisements or tangential hits that can sometimes be different from what people are seeking and can even contradict healthy advice. We discuss this topic in more detail later in this chapter.

Is Online Health Information Useful?

As you might imagine, there are advantages and disadvantages to using eHealth resources. Let's start with the good news.

ADVANTAGES

Online sources offer plentiful opportunities to learn and to connect with others.

Rich Array of Information

The Internet is typically engaging and in-depth, which gives it a leg up on TV news. For example, people who rely on newspapers and Internet for cancer information are typically better informed than people who rely on local TV news, probably because information in writing is usually more detailed and precise than television content (Kealey & Berkman, 2010). Furthermore, people who rely on TV news for cancer information often underestimate their cancer risk because such programming often focuses on ways to prevent cancer, which makes it seem an avoidable outcome (Kealey & Berkman, 2010).

Practical Advice

The Internet offers health-related guidance 24 hours a day. Some evidence indicates that Internet searches are most satisfying when they help people meet specific goals—such as choosing what foods to eat, treating a minor injury, or curing a headache—rather than simply providing general information (Y. Lee, Park, & Widdows, 2009). Of course, online advice is only useful if it is trustworthy. As we will discuss in a moment, that is sometimes a shaky supposition.

Social Support

Online resources offer a means to share information and social support with other people (see Chapter 8 for more). This opportunity is particularly beneficial for people who are short on time or transportation, have disabilities or responsibilities that prevent them from leaving home, or who find comfort in the relative anonymity of technology-mediated conversations. Evidence suggests that peers' online advice is often quite helpful. More than 6 out of 10 people who signed on to an online suicide-survivors support group said they found the experience comforting (Kramer et al., 2015).

DISADVANTAGES

Despite the potential advantages of online communication, eHealth attempts fall short in some ways.

Unreliable Information

Online information is not always dependable. For example, only 1 in 5 weight loss websites studied provided consistently accurate information (Modave, Shokar, Peñaranda, & Nguyen, 2014). Even when information is inaccurate or incomplete, it tends to circulate quickly through social media.

Researchers led by Brittany Seymour studied the way information about fluoride proliferated among members of an online community who oppose adding it to public water supplies. The researchers traced thousands of online engagements to two highly influential Facebook posts presented as summaries of scientific research. The original posts were viewed, liked, shared, and/or commented on 4,500 times, representing what Seymour and colleagues call a "digital pandemic" of information. In this case, it was equally a pandemic of misinformation. About half of the posts misrepresented the research they purported to summarize. The discrepancies were difficult to detect, however, because 60% of hyperlinks to the original studies required viewers to sift through multiple web layers to find them, and about 12% of the links were dead ends. The researchers reflect that rampant transfer of misinformation is fed by the ease of social media use compared to in-depth data searches and by our tendency to follow and "friend" people whose attitudes are similar to our own (Seymour, Getman, Saraf, Zhang, & Kalenderian, 2015).

Although people over age 60 are more likely than young adults to have health concerns, they are only one-third as likely to learn about health online (D. Smith, 2011).

In light of how much unreliable information is available, media literacy is critical. However, when researchers asked university students to rate the quality of medical information from two different sources—the U.S. National Institutes of Health and a pharmaceutical company—the students rated information from both sources about the same, although one was an independent, science-based source and the other a commercial enterprise with an interest in selling products (J. Kim, 2011). On the other hand, Twitter users in another study trusted original tweets from health experts more than they trusted tweets from nonprofessionals (Lee & Sundar, 2013). Clearly, the issue is a complex one. As you will see in Chapter 11, one of the keys to media literacy is considering the sender's motive and whether the sponsor is likely to be biased.

One aspect of media literacy involves the type and amount of information people seek and remember. Jeff Niederdeppe and colleagues (2007) differentiate between **health information seeking,** which involves an active search for information, and **health information scanning**, which includes information that comes up in conversation or in the media and sticks in the memory. They have found that information gained while health *seeking* is usually of greater depth and of more direct assistance in making medical decisions. However, people are exposed to far more information incidentally than purposefully, making health *scanning* important as well.

Conflicting Information

A second drawback concerns information that is contradictory or counterproductive. Jones and Biddlecom (2011) point out that the Internet is not great at providing sex education. As one teenager in their study put it, you can find information about safer sex and abstinence online if you look for it, but along the way you are likely to find a lot more information leading you in the opposite direction:

> *The Internet, it's pretty much just like a giant billboard for sex. It's really, it's not a good place to go if you are young, because being on Internet, because all the pop ups and things you could type in kind of makes you want to have sex. So it really doesn't enforce the abstinence rule and birth control, safe sex anything.* (*quoted by Jones & Biddlecom, 2011, p. 118*)

Like this teen, most of those in Jones and Biddlecom's study felt that the Internet was not a helpful source of information about abstinence or contraception.

Overwhelming Amounts of Information

A third drawback is the sheer volume of information provided online, which can be especially baffling when it is new to the reader, complex, or far outside the realm of common knowledge. A recent Google search for "breast cancer" yielded more than 94 million hits.

In a study of online resources for people with HIV or AIDS, Keith J. Horvath and colleagues (2010) found an extensive but potentially bewildering amount of information. Information overload can be especially distressing for people who are newly diagnosed and may not yet have a good idea what to expect or how to judge the timeliness and quality of the information they find. Horvath and his team suggest that website developers create a framework that begins with a general overview and allows readers to move in stages to more complex and varied information. Otherwise, they say, rather than serving as a source of comfort, online information can be frightening, confusing, and overwhelming.

Digital Divide

The irony is that people most in need of health information—older adults and those with lower-than-average income and education levels—are least likely to have access to the Internet, where such information is most plentiful. In the United States:

- Individuals ages 18 to 29 are three times more likely than those 60 and older to learn about health online (Smith, 2011)
- High-speed Internet access is nearly twice as prevalent in households that make at least $50,000 as in others (File & Ryan, 2014).
- College graduates are nearly 2½ times more likely to use the Internet for health information than people who did not graduate from high school (Smith, 2011).

All of these factors point to a digital divide that privileges some people and systematically excludes others.

A digital disability divide also separates people who can easily use online resources from those for who cannot. Imagine trying to navigate the Web without using a mouse or a keyboard or without seeing the screen. Try operating a smartphone without using your hands or with your eyes closed. These challenges quickly reveal why people with physical challenges and visual impairments are less likely than others to own computers or find online information accessible (Sachdeva, Tuikka, Kimppa, & Suomi, 2015).

Software has been available for some time to convert text into audio messages and to allow people to speak rather than type messages. However, funding and training for these systems has lagged. Closed captioning, when it is available, is often inaccurate. And programmers still struggle to capture the visually complex and nonlinear character of web information (Hong, Kim, Trimi, & Hyun, 2015). John Hermann, who is blind, describes the dilemma. If you are a sighted person using the Web, he says,

> *your eyes fly around, sometimes randomly and sometimes in response to cues onscreen. You hunt for links and cherrypick from galleries. The word you're looking for catches your eye, so you click it. Consciously or subconsciously, you usually know where to look.* (*Hermann, 2010, para. 8*)

By contrast, for people with visual impairments, "there is no 'looking'" (Hermann, para. 9). Hearing the content, instead, means listening to a lot of information you would not have chosen and trying to mentally organize information that was designed to be seen as a whole rather than heard in a linear fashion. Hermann and others applaud emerging software that not only narrates information but describes the screen ("three menu buttons at the top that read . . . four vertical columns have the headings . . ." and so on). However, everyone agrees there is a long way to go. Around the globe, the World Wide Web Consortium brings together people who hope eventually to make online resources accessible to everyone, regardless of reading ability, native language, physical limitations, and other factors. You can follow their efforts at www.w3.org.

Another crucial element is **health information efficacy**, how confident a person is that he or she can find and understand health information. Health information efficacy is highest among people who are well educated and who have experience in health care situations (Hall, Bernhardt, Dodd, & Vollrath, 2015). Women are typically more likely than men—and older adults more likely than younger ones—to have high health information efficacy and to actively seek health and prevention information (Basu & Dutta, 2008). These comparisons are important because confidence and health information seeking can help people more effectively cope with health concerns and make decisions about them.

COMMUNICATION SKILL BUILDER: USING THE INTERNET EFFECTIVELY

To distinguish between trustworthy and unreliable information online, experts offer the following suggestions:

- Do not trust information if there is no author or sponsor or if the source given is not well known.
- Look for another source if the sponsors are trying to sell a product rather than offer free information. Plenty of websites make reliable health information available free.
- Do not rely on information if it is dated, references are missing, or references do not seem legitimate.
- Keep in mind that legitimate health practitioners do not speak in terms of "secret formulas" or "miraculous cures." Only con artists use such language (Kowalski, 1997). Other red-flag claims include such wording as "Treats all forms of cancer," "Cancer disappears," and "Nontoxic" (U.S. Food & Drug Administration, 2008).
- Do not be convinced by case studies of "actual" satisfied customers. An isolated case does not prove a product's effectiveness, and this may not be an actual customer.
- Do your own research. Read medical journal articles. Ask health professionals.
- Read the fine print carefully. Look for disclaimers and vague wording.
- Report suspicious claims to the Federal Trade Commission, Better Business Bureau, or state attorney general's office.

In case you are wondering what happened to the student whose jaw got stuck open, here is the rest of the story. She eventually woke her roommate and the two of them conducted a more thorough search on their computer. "I had to put a wash cloth in my mouth because I was drooling," the student now says, laughing. "We *had* to fix it!" But when nothing they read online worked, they went to a hospital emergency room, where a doctor was able to get her jaw in place again.

Interestingly, when the same thing happened to the student several weeks later, she did not go online. Instead, she went straight to the ER. Her sense of self-efficacy had vanished during the first experience. "I tried. It's too hard," she says. Her experience bears out the conclusion that online information can be immensely valuable, but it is not always enough.

How Has Technology Influenced Health Communication?

> *With the best will in the world, unless your friends and family have been through it they just won't get it. . . . They won't understand the raw pain of not being able to have your own children. The only people who will understand that are other people who are in your place. And now the Internet is here, I mean what people did before the Internet I don't know.*

This statement by a participant in Lisa Hinton and colleagues' (2010, p. 439) study of people undergoing fertility treatment brings up a good question: *How are things different since the Internet?*

CAN YOU GUESS? PART 1

?

Which group is most likely to get health information on television? From family and friends? From health care providers?

A. Black Americans

B. Hispanic Americans

C. Non-Hispanic White Americans

Answers appear at the end of the chapter.

Some analysts worry that, whereas before the Internet people relied almost exclusively on health professionals and loved ones for medical information and advice, they may now rely on Internet sources instead. So far, the evidence is reassuring. People do not seem to pick only one source of information. In fact, cancer survivors who seek information both online and from health professionals often find that one source reinforces the other, adding a sense of depth and validity to what they learn in both places (Moldovan-Johnson, Tan, & Hornik, 2014).

Overall, evidence suggests that people use online and interpersonal communication to varying degrees based on how accessible each form of communication is and how well it meets their needs. In some ways, the Internet has become a means to meet social and informational needs that are not satisfied in face-to-face communication (Hou & Shim, 2010). This phenomenon is well expressed in **uses and gratifications theory**, which suggests that people engage with mediated messages in an active, goal-oriented way. The implication is that, far from being passive recipients of whatever comes their way, people are motivated to engage with media when doing so satisfies their need for information, cognitive exercise, social stimulation, escape, entertainment, or some other need (Katz, Blumler, & Gurevitch, 1974).

Consider the reasons you turn on the TV or boot up your computer after a long day. Maybe you hope to catch up on the day's news (information needs), relax and forget about your worries (escape and entertainment), watch a show about the history of the solar system (cognitive exercise), enjoy the familiar personalities of characters in your favorite sitcom (social stimulation), or catch up with friends via Facebook or other social media (social interaction).

As media have changed, so have people's habits. About 60% of college students say they probably qualify as addicted to their cell phones (J. Roberts, Luc Honore Petnji, & Manolis, 2014). Experts agree, considering that college students spend an average of 7 to 10 hours a day on their phones (sometimes while doing other things), mostly interfacing with friends via texts, emails, and Facebook (Roberts et al., 2014).

College students in the United States spend an average of 7 to 10 hours a day using their phones, often in conjunction with other activities (J. Roberts et al., 2014). Uses and gratifications theory suggests that they use mobile media to meet social, information, and cognitive needs.

Conversely, perhaps you had a great day and just want to sit outside and watch the sun set in peace and quiet. This may be a sign that, today at least, you do not need electronic media to satisfy needs. They have been met in other ways.

The same premises apply to health needs. As mentioned, people use the Internet to expand their knowledge. They also use it to meet needs they have not been able to fulfill otherwise. For example, women newly diagnosed with breast cancer who have unmet needs for information or emotional support are more likely than others to use Internet sources and to gravitate to the type of online information that best meets their needs (Lee & Hawkins, 2010).

By the same token, online interactions may help people satisfy their need for comfort and belonging. When Hinton and colleagues (2010) interviewed people undergoing treatment for infertility, they discovered a pervasive sense of social isolation among them. Because conceiving a baby is an intimate and emotional matter and people sometimes feel they have personally failed when they cannot conceive, many of those interviewed felt separate from the people around them—as if they were the "odd one out" or even a "leper" or "pariah" (Hinton, Kurinczuk, & Ziebland, 2010, p. 438). Many said the Internet was a "friend," a "lifeline," or their "only friend" during the experience (p. 438). One woman interviewed for the study described her experience with an online forum this way:

> *And you suddenly feel normal. You feel accepted. You can go on the forum and say, you know, "I've just walked past a pregnant woman in Sainsbury's and I found myself standing in the fruit and veg aisle bawling my eyes out." And everyone else would think, "Oh, that's a bit of an overreaction." The girls in the forum were just like, "No I'm with you, I've done that, I've been there."* (p. 438)

In this way, Internet conversations were often a source of simultaneously personal and anonymous (weak-tie) support. This was true when people merely "lurked" (read without commenting) on sites and when they took an active role.

There is another link between eHealth and patient–caregiver relationships in that patients do not always disclose to their doctors that they use online resources, which can lead to misunderstandings and confusion. Rebecca Imes and colleagues (2008) found that patients are likely to stay quiet about online searches if (a) they feel confident that they can judge the quality of online information for themselves, (b) they are afraid their caregivers would think less of them, (c) they do not feel there is enough time to work the topic into a conversation, and/or (d) they do not want to give the impression of encroaching on the care provider's "turf" (p. 545). Imes's team cautions that patient satisfaction and quality of care may be compromised if patients do not feel comfortable disclosing what they are thinking to their doctors or checking the veracity of information they have seen online (Imes, Bylund, Sabee, Routsong, & Sanford, 2008).

All in all, it seems that the Internet has provided people with another option in terms of serving their information and relational needs. Like most options, it can be taken too far. However, for the most part, online information is used as a complement to, not a substitute for, face-to-face health communication. Let's shift now to a particular type of eHealth that relies on mobile technology.

CAN YOU GUESS? PART 2

Who relies on the Internet for health information more—people who are healthy or people who are not?

The answer appears at the end of the chapter.

mHealth

Imagine using your mobile phone to monitor the heart rate of an unborn child and transmit that information instantly to a database so medical professionals can monitor pregnancy and labor even when they cannot be there in person. Mercy Hospital Mount Lawley in Western Australia is experimenting with equipment that does just that, with hopes that it will one day be used all over the world (WHO, 2011a). Computer scientists invented the mobile phone app to serve as an easy-to-use, low-cost version of equipment usually found only in hospitals. They hope it will facilitate prenatal care for women in remote regions and for those with high-risk pregnancies.

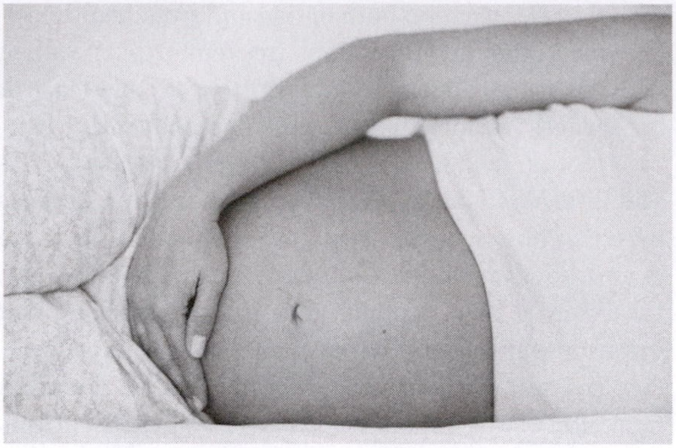

With new smartphone apps and attachments, pregnant women can now monitor the movement and heart rate of their unborn babies and send the information instantly to a monitored database if they wish.

As a whole, health-related apps are easy to use. Many involve little more than the camera in a smartphone, with which you might instantly submit photos or video to learn, for example, if the bite on your arm is from a poisonous spider or if a person is exhibiting signs of a stroke (WHO, 2011a). Or you might use an app to measure your blood alcohol level before driving; get instant guidance on how to perform CPR or help someone who is choking; or track depression, weight changes, drug reactions, and other health issues.

The revolution made possible by mobile technology has worldwide implications. About 2.2 billion people around the world access the Internet through desktop or laptop computers ("Information," 2011). By contrast, more than twice that many—a whopping 5 billion people worldwide—use mobile devices such as phones and tablet computers, and more than 7 in 10 of them live in countries with low or middle incomes (WHO, 2011b; see Figure 9.1). Wireless signals now cover 85% of the world. Indeed, more people now have mobile devices than have electricity in their homes. It is easy to see why mHealth has emerged as a particularly powerful means of sharing and recording health information.

A variety of **social entrepreneurs** (people who apply business principles to societal needs) are focused on health. Health-related mobile apps are expected to become a $26 billion-per-year industry within the next few years (Jahns, 2013). Communication technology experts working to develop mHealth resources have found that the best systems do not

FIGURE 9.1 Worldwide, mobile technology is more than twice as prevalent as computer-based Internet usage, especially in developing countries, where people are more likely to have mobile technology than electricity in their homes.

replace existing health services, but rather extend them beyond their current reach.

mHealth is not without challenges, however. One is the lack of a standard operating platform among mobile devices. Currently, people who wish to use most health apps must choose between Android and Apple, who are competitors rather than collaborators in the mHealth arena (J. Kim, 2014). Other challenges involve the cost of technology, the need for public education about mHealth, and privacy concerns.

One area of mobile health with few barriers is the use of **short message services (SMS)**, such as texts and tweets. Since health involves everyday choices, SMS options are emerging that offer regular tips and encouragement about diet, weight control, mental health, and more.

Marketed in the right way, consumers seem receptive to these mHealth services. For example, when health promoters in San Francisco offered a free text-message service about sexual health for 15- to 19-year-olds, more than 4,500 people expressed an interest in signing up (Lefebvre, 2009).

Another program, Text2Quit, sends free emails and texts to people who are trying to quit smoking. In a study of university students who signed up for the program, 3 in 4 said they read all or most of every text (emails were less popular), and many used an online component of the program that allowed them to track how many cigarettes they smoked per day (Abroms et al., 2012). Far from being passive recipients, each student interfaced with the program an average of 12 times over three months, responding to text questions such as "Please be honest, did you quit today?" and requesting specialized messages, as when they texted CRAVE for help avoiding temptation. (See the *Check It Out!* inset for more about free text-message reminders.)

CHECK IT OUT!

Free text-message services provide health-related tips and reminders as frequently as you want them about issues you choose. Here are a few to consider:

- StickK: http://www.stickk.com
- Remember it Now: http://www.rememberit now.com
- My Fitness Pal: https://www.myfitnesspal.com/
- HassleMe: http://www.hassleme.co.uk/

So far we have talked mostly about the interface between information consumers and creators. Let's move to a different component of eHealth.

Telehealth

It's common for residents in rural areas of Mississippi to drive 40 minutes or more to be seen by medical specialists. But a telehealth program offered through the University of Mississippi Medical Center has brought medicine closer to home. Since it was launched in 2003, the program has offered long-distance care, health education, disaster response, and other services to more than 500,000 residents of the state via more than 100 health centers ("Health Care Delivery," 2015).

The university's telehealth program allows patients and caregivers to interact in real time via two-way teleconferencing (Barnes, 2015). Medical personnel at the university work with staff members at medical centers throughout the state to conduct exams and discuss medical information. Digital cameras and stethoscopes transmit detailed information to everyone involved. The program was recognized by the American Telehealth Association as one of the best in the country.

Telemedicine and the broader term telehealth are derived from the Greek work *tele*, which means "far." As the World Health Organization puts it, telemedicine is "healing at a distance" (WHO, 2010a, p. 8). Here are a few examples of how telehealth works, as well as the advantages and challenges it presents.

TELEMEDICINE

Elsebeth and Ian have chronic obstructive pulmonary disease (COPD), a lung condition that affects about 65 million people around the world, making it difficult for them to breathe (COPD Foundation, n.d.). When they both experience a flare-up of symptoms, Elsebeth is hospitalized in the conventional sense, whereas Ian is admitted to a virtual hospital. Both see their doctors during daily rounds, but Elsebeth sees them in person, whereas Ian communicates via a two-way video chat. In addition, a care team visits Ian's home to provide medication, monitoring equipment, and a mobile tablet with which he can contact health professionals 24 hours a day to communicate with them in real time. Which situation would you prefer?

A team of researchers in Denmark addressed that question based on the impressions of actual COPD patients admitted to physical and virtual hospitals (Emme et al., 2014). They found that patients' impressions varied depending on the severity of their symptoms. Those who were frightened and felt their symptoms were out of control appreciated being in a conventional medical setting. However, those who were able to manage their symptoms fairly well valued the sense of being more in control of their care at home. Because patients of the virtual hospital were trained to use the medical equipment themselves, they were able to monitor their conditions and make minor adjustments to treatment regimens without asking for help or permission. Indeed, many of them were reluctant to return medical and communication equipment when they were discharged. Patients of the virtual hospital also appreciated the comforts of home and the relative ease with which loved ones could visit them. (Experts point out that there is also less exposure to contagion at home.) All in all, the researchers concluded that there is a place for brick-and-mortar hospitals and a place for virtual care.

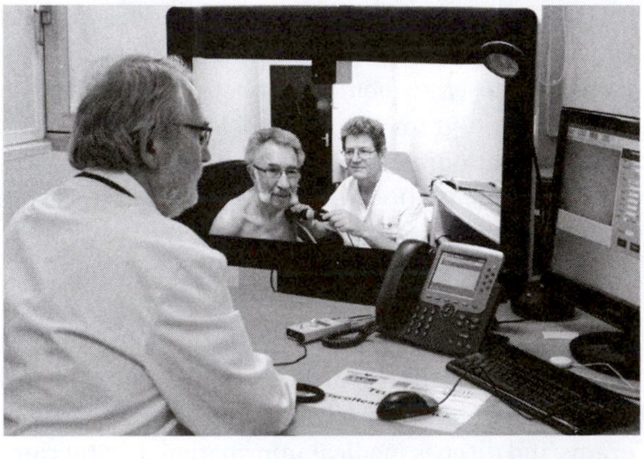

Health professionals in two locations collaborate to care for a patient using telemedicine technology.

So far, telemedicine is most popular among young and affluent patients, who are most likely to be comfortable with technology. They most often use telemedicine (usually via telephone) for occasional and seasonal concerns, such as getting prescriptions refilled or treatment for urinary tract infections (Uscher-Pines & Mehrotra, 2014). Telemedicine may also gain footing with people who have chronic conditions such as Parkinson's disease. For them, long-distance consultations, coupled with regular in-person visits, may provide more contact with medical professionals than they would normally have, as long as the technology is readily available and people on both sides are well trained to use it (Qiang & Marras, 2015).

PATIENT PORTALS

If you have not already been granted access to a **patient portal**, you probably will be soon. These are password-protected websites, usually sponsored by people's physicians, at which patients can view lab results, schedule appointments, see their medical records and immunization history, view information and educational videos, email health professionals, make payments, and more.

Patient portals are designed to put patients in the driver's seat concerning their own care and to reduce busy work for health professionals. In a study of prostate cancer survivors who were given access to online patient portals, nearly 9 in 10 said they would continue to use them (Pai, Lau, Barnett, & Jones, 2013). The men used the portals mainly to view their medical records, make appointments, and monitor their PSA levels. (*PSA* stands for prostate-specific antigen, a protein that can suggest the presence of cancer).

TELEMONITORING

We have already discussed the leaps being made in mHealth monitoring, but in 2008, Glenn Forbes of Mayo Clinic envisioned an even more futuristic image of telehealth, in which people have small microchips inserted under their skin or carry digitized medical information cards that allow them—and, if they wish, medical personnel anywhere in the world—to monitor their health. Forbes imagined how the process would work if he were traveling in another country:

> *I feel fine, but I check in every once in a while. If I have a chip embedded, I might even be unknowingly "checking in." Every seven days Mayo checks my blood sugar and could send me a message about needing to cut back on the cookies because my sugar level went up from 116 to 124. This information and advice is part of my partnership—part of what I have decided to purchase for my personal benefit. (quoted by Berry & Seltman, 2008, p. 239)*

Or, Forbes said, he might have a plastic card that he inserts into a "Health Maintenance ATM" anywhere in the world if he has a health concern, such as frequent headaches. The card transmits his health information and location to his home clinic, where the staff might respond, "Your genetics suggest that you are prone to headaches if you've been eating too much pasta" (p. 239). The clinic staff could also recommend a nearby clinic that is part of the network and has access to his online medical records.

Health-monitoring chips have not yet become commonplace, but many analysts predict they will be available soon. Less invasive devices are on the horizon as well. Mayo Clinic has teamed up with a technology firm to develop disposable, stick-on biosensor patches that will help transmit information about diabetes, obesity, and other factors to people's smartphones, and with their permission, to their doctors and/or researchers (Pennic, 2015). Wearable technology, such as Apple Watches, Jawbone, Pebble Time, and Fitbit allow people to monitor their own health behaviors and may facilitate sharing that information with health professionals.

Forbes says this futuristic model will not alleviate the need for face-to-face health communication, good listening skills, and sensitivity. Indeed, because patients' information will be so readily available, he says, patients and caregivers might have *more* time to talk about their concerns (quoted by Berry & Seltman, 2008).

TELEHEALTH AT POINT OF SALE

Imagine buying St. John's wort at your local drugstore because friends tell you it's a natural treatment for depression. Along with the receipt, you receive a brief printout that tells you St. John's wort may be harmful if you take birth control pills or a variety of other medications.

Point-of-sale programs such as this one are now available to retailers. They are based on databases that send health information directly to a cashier's printer when triggered by the barcodes on health-related items. In a pilot study, most shoppers said the printouts would be useful, particularly if they were clear and simple and included the logo of a trusted source, such as a medical school (Perlman, Lebow, Raphael, Ali, & Simmons, 2013).

POTENTIAL ADVANTAGES OF TELEHEALTH FOR CONSUMERS

The World Health Organization (WHO) lists the main advantages of telemedicine as "access, equity, quality, and cost-effectiveness" (WHO, 2010a, p. 8). At this point, the pros and cons are largely speculative, but many people are optimistic that telehealth will conserve money and resources without sacrificing quality. Here are a few of the reasons why.

Patient-Centered Communication

Technology may enable people increased access to care providers and more options to talk about a wide range of topics. For example, MyCareTeam.com allows people with diabetes to learn information, log their blood sugar levels, and talk to health care providers. When James D. Robinson and colleagues studied nearly 1,000 emails exchanged by participants in the program, they found that most included helpful information and requests for information, offers of assistance ("I can give you a ride"), social integration ("Stop by next time you are in"), emotional support ("It is really hard to lose weight"), esteem support ("You are one of our best patients"), self-disclosure ("I am getting married"), and technical support ("Is the new monitor working?") (Robinson, Turner, & Levine, 2011, p. 129). Social integration messages were most common, followed by information and requests for information. Robinson and colleagues concluded that the interactions were "in some ways more patient-centered than a traditional office visit" (Robinson et al., p. 132).

Other researchers have also identified a patient-centered advantage. A study of patient–caregiver emails revealed that—in contrast to in-person visits, during which doctors do most of the talking—patients studied did most of the "talking" in emails, outnumbering physicians' comments 2 to 1 (Roter, Larson, Sands, Ford, & Houston, 2008). Patients also seemed more comfortable disclosing emotions and praising and thanking their doctors in emails than in person, perhaps because email communication is less intimidating and less constrained by time limits. Physician responses, although briefer than patients,' were usually informative, confirming, and reassuring. Doctors displayed empathy and reassurance in 53% of the emails Roter and colleagues studied. For example, one doctor told a patient via email, "Please don't ever think of doing so [emailing me] as bothering me—I welcome your participation in these decisions!" (Roter et al., 2008, p. 83). Overall, coders rated physicians' emails to be equally as friendly, respectful, and responsive as patients' emails.

CAN YOU GUESS? PART 3

?

- What percentage of U.S. residents say they would like to have online access to their doctors, their medical records, and their test results?
- What percentage would be willing to pay more for that type of access?

Answers appear at the end of the chapter.

Access to Services

Technology may allow people in underserved communities access to care providers and services usually reserved for big-city dwellers. Doctors, particularly specialists, are disproportionately located in densely populated areas and are relatively scarce in rural ones. With telemedicine, a person can conceivably contact a health professional anywhere in the world by phone, email, voice mail, or computer.

Cost Savings

Telehealth may save organizations and individuals money. For one thing, it reduces the need for each small town to have its own set of medical specialists. At an individual level, patients in smaller markets can stay close to home rather than transferring to major medical centers. Additionally, easier access may mean identifying and treating illnesses before they become severe and more costly to treat.

Patient Education

People may become better educated about health matters through long-distance consultations and access to computer databases. For many people with health concerns, such information is a way to feel more in control. The majority of participants in Alex Broom's (2008) study of men with prostate cancer say they appreciate the information they find online and feel that it helps them manage the uncertainties of treatment decisions. Said one man in the study, "Knowledge is power. I like to be in control of my situation and the way I want to do that is by knowing what is going to happen. . . . I really need that information to feel ok" (p. 98).

POTENTIAL ADVANTAGES OF TELEHEALTH FOR HEALTH PROFESSIONALS

Caregivers may benefit from telemedicine as well.

Efficiency

Being able to communicate with patients and colleagues in remote locations reduces travel time and the demands on office space and staff. There are even benefits closer to home. "Email is a timesaver," declares Shelly Reese (2008, para. 5). A heath professional can email a patient when he or she has time, rather than playing phone tag. Email also allows caregivers to think through patient questions and to research them before replying.

One physician Reese (2008) interviewed said his staff is able to respond to about 80% of the emails he receives. Because emails are more detailed than the typical phone message, he can quickly scan the contents to see who should best respond to them. Furthermore, emails can reduce the number of unnecessary office visits and after-hours phone calls. Patients who are able to access their physicians via secure email require 7% to 10% fewer office visits and make 14% fewer after-hours calls to their doctors ("The EMail," 2007; Reese, 2008). Texts and emails are also time savers for office staff members, who can use software to send out appointment reminders (Reese, 2008).

If health professionals are worried about numerous and rambling emails, the evidence suggests they can rest easy most of the time. In a review of 24 studies about emails between patients and health professionals, Jiali Ye and colleagues (2010) found that the emails were usually concise and medically relevant. This was true of both patients' and doctors' emails. Patients typically addressed only one concern per email and avoided making urgent or inappropriate requests. In sum, patients who were invited to email seldom abused the privilege, but the knowledge that they *could* email their doctors made them feel significantly more satisfied about their care than patients without email access (Ye, Rust, Fry-Johnson, & Strothers, 2010).

Improved Care

Social media applications may also improve medicine. Between 60% and 80% of physicians either already communicate with patients online or predict that they will in the near future (Modahl, Tompsett, & Moorhead, 2011). Most believe it will make communication easier and more convenient and will provide innovative means to monitor patients' health. As one doctor put it, online applications have the potential for "better education, increased compliance, and better outcomes" (Modahl et al., 2011, p. 7).

Teamwork

Vital information can be transmitted from one location to another instantly or with only a brief delay, amplifying opportunities for immediate response and medical teamwork. A cardiologist, for example, can monitor a patient's heart activity and direct paramedics' efforts even before the patient arrives at the hospital. At least 64% of the caregivers at one telemedicine site say they have learned valuable skills and information while participating in exams with other doctors and specialists (Whitten, Sypher, & Patterson, 2000).

Accessible Information

Diagnostic images and patient records can be electronically stored and quickly retrieved, even by people in different locations. Caregivers may be able to access the medical charts of patients they are seeing for the first time. This could save time in emergencies and allow medical teams to coordinate patient care more effectively. The ability to quickly and consistently share information also helps with routine decision making and teamwork. Says a radiology manager:

> *The biggest advantage is having images available all the time to everyone. So as soon as I take a picture of you, somebody can see it. In fact, everybody can see it. So where, if you were to come in . . . and you've broken an arm and you have to be referred to the orthopaedic surgeons, there is no backwards and forwards of one piece of film following you around or not as the case may be.* (*quoted by E. Murray et al., 2011, p. 6*)

If the systems are well designed, online medical records can help physicians and researchers collect data on the usefulness of various drugs and therapies (Kush, Helton, Rockhold, & Hardison, 2008). Online records can also help health professionals share notes and guarantee that a patient's records will not be destroyed in a fire or natural disaster.

POTENTIAL DISADVANTAGES OF TELEHEALTH

With so many advantages, it may seem puzzling that telemedicine is not more prevalent. Although the technology continues to improve, much of it has been available for years.

Scheduling Challenges

One concern involves scheduling. Nearly half of the participants in one telemedicine center said it is a challenge to schedule two teams of medical caregivers (one on-site and one remote) to take part in telemedicine consultations (Whitten et al., 2000).

Liability

There are also concerns about legal liability, especially concerning advice given online without the benefit of a full medical exam. In a study of more than 4,000 physicians in the United States, 73% said they worry they will be sued for malpractice if they offer advice online (Modahl et al., 2011). Legal experts caution doctors offering guidance or assistance online, especially if they have not treated the patient personally, to include disclaimers such as the following: "This is not an official medical opinion because I haven't performed an examination. If you need specific medical advice, make an appointment with me or with a physician in the appropriate specialty in your area" (Johnson, 2007, p. 30).

Threats to Privacy

Some people worry about electronic eavesdropping and the possibility that hackers could gain access to confidential patient records. Some 71% of physicians surveyed said they are worried about privacy violations (Modahl et al., 2011). To restrict access, medical networks rely on encryption (secret coding) and electronic "firewalls" designed to stop unauthorized users from reaching confidential data. Secure email systems endorsed by the AMA and many private insurers are also available. By most accounts, these systems are good, although not perfect. But the human component is worrisome as well. Online access means more people would have the chance to view patients' private information than ever before.

Unorganized Information

Information in patients' electronic health records can be restrictive and hard to use if the platforms are not well designed and if physicians are not careful about what they include. Some online forms require caregivers to fill in lengthy amounts of patient information. For example, a pediatrician may be required to ask every patient a time-consuming list of safety questions (use of bike helmets, seatbelts, etc.). This leaves less time to focus on the patient's immediate concerns (Hartzband & Groopman, 2008).

Physicians Pamela Hartzband and Jerome Groopman (2008) describe an additional concern—namely, their frustration with doctors who include inappropriate or too much information in patients' online health records. In some cases, doctors plagiarize. "We have seen portions of our own notes inserted verbatim into another doctor's note," say Hartzband and Groopman (p. 1656). In addition to being unethical, this practice results in repetitive, too-long medical records that fail to present each physician's thoughtful analysis of the patient's condition.

Another factor that bogs down medical records is a lengthy hodgepodge of test results. If such information is not well organized, more is not better—it is just overwhelming. Write Hartzband and Groopman:

> *A colleague at a major cancer center that recently switched to electronic medical records said that chart review during rounds has become nearly worthless. He bemoaned the vain search through meaningless repetition in multiple notes for the single line that represented a new development. "It's like 'Where's Waldo?'" he said bitterly. Ironically, he has started to handwrite a list of new developments on index cards so that he can refer to them at the bedside.* (p. 1656)

Compensation Questions

It is still somewhat unclear how caregivers can or should be compensated for services rendered long distance. Should they charge for phone conversations, email correspondence, and the like? If so, how should those rates compare to the cost of face-to-face visits? Reservations about this issue and the fear of being inundated by patient messages and questions have made some caregivers leery of opening up new lines of communication.

The issue is becoming clearer, however, as reimbursement agencies—mindful that a phone call or email can prevent a more expensive outcome—are increasingly willing to reimburse providers for technology-mediated communication. A group of health insurance companies launched a project in Pennsylvania in which they pay doctors to keep close tabs on patients using email and websites. Another part of the agreement is that participating physicians will keep a percentage of office hours open so that sick patients can schedule appointments within 48 hours (Goldstein, 2008). The hope is that technology and quick-response protocols will save money in the long run.

Restricted Communication

Finally, some worry that telemedicine will become a less effective substitute for face-to-face communication. No one expects (or even wants) telemedicine to replace face-to-face medical visits entirely. Still, the limits of technology may restrict what patients and caregivers are able to convey to each other (Baur, 2000).

Researchers in Japan found that patients who took part in both face-to-face interactions and telemedicine visits were equally satisfied with them, but doctors were less satisfied with the telemedicine visits, feeling that the technology limited communication (Lui et al., 2007). Considering the limitations, some people worry that medical decisions will be made on the basis of incomplete or misleading information. Chamberlain (1994) cautions that high-tech methods cannot make up for poor communication: "No amount of technology is going to compensate for an ill-conceived or ill-designed message. The buck stops there . . . with the communicator" (para. 4).

All in all, the World Health Organization urges the creation of international guidelines in regard to privacy, access, and liability (WHO, 2010a). The authors of the Global Observatory for eHealth report write:

> *It is imperative that telemedicine be implemented equitably and to the highest ethical standards, to maintain the dignity of all individuals and ensure that differences in education, language, geographic location, physical and mental ability, age, and sex will not lead to marginalization of care.* (WHO, 2010b, p. 11)

If you are interested in the changes and opportunities involved with health information technology, see career resources in Box 9.3.

BOX 9.3 CAREER OPPORTUNITIES

Health Information Technology

Computer and Information Systems Manager
Health Information Administrator or Technician
Software Developer

Career Resources and Job Listings

- American Health Information Management Association: http://www.ahima.org
- Association for Computing Machinery: http://www.acm.org
- Commission on Accreditation for Health Informatics and Information Management Education: http://www.cahiim.org
- Health Buzz by the U.S. Department of Health and Human Services: http://www.healthit.gov/buzz-blog/university-based-training/helping-students-launch-health-information-technology-careers-oregon-health-science-universitybased-training-program
- U.S. Bureau of Labor Statistics Occupational Outlook Handbook: http://www.bls.gov/ooh

Summary

Communication technology has the capacity to revolutionize medicine. Some people feel it will give everyday people more information and power than ever before, whereas others worry that it will affect patient–caregiver relationships for the worse.

Whereas information in public media was once filtered through gatekeepers, the gates are now open. eHealth resources allow people to look up information quickly and easily and to engage with people they do not know personally, blurring the lines between information creator and information consumer as well as the boundaries between the public, technical, and personal spheres. At the same time, issues related to access, trust, coping ability, and self-efficacy influence the degree to which people seek out and believe online health information.

The proliferation of mobile devices represents a promising avenue. Mobile apps now allow people around the globe to capture and share data and advice about many health conditions and to monitor their activity levels, fitness goals, vital signs, and more.

Rather than passively attending to messages that come our way, most of us tend to be relatively proactive in seeking information we believe will reduce our health risk and help manage our anxiety. However, health-seeking behaviors may be muted by distrust, lack of confidence, and the belief that such messages do not apply to us.

All in all, the Internet has the potential to educate people in the greatest need of health information, but, overwhelmingly, the people who have Internet access and the ability to use it are already information rich. A knowledge gap exists because of access, information preference, perceived relevance, and reading ability. (We discuss the knowledge gap more in Chapter 13.)

We may happen upon electronic health information accidentally if it turns up in an Internet search or a pop-up message, but unlike television, we mostly control the content of what we see online. A quick click can make something appear or disappear from our screen at will. This has given theorists something new to think about as they explore the reasons that we search for health information.

Telemedicine offers many opportunities, but issues of cost, access, privacy, and legal liability continue to hamper full-scale implementation. It is likely that we will overcome many of these barriers as we renegotiate what it means to be health professionals and patients.

Overall, technology expands the options and the challenges for health communication. Patients and caregivers may have access to more information and more means of message transmission than ever before, but eHealth is not likely to replace face-to-face communication. The most optimistic possibility is that it will allow for higher quality and more inclusive communication at all levels.

Key Terms and Theories

eHealth
mHealth
telehealth
telemedicine
three spheres
personal sphere
technical sphere
public sphere
Web 2.0
social network theory
strong ties
weak ties
ePatients
information sufficiency threshold
health information acquisition model
Theory of Motivated Information Management (TMIM)
Integrative Model of Online Health Information Seeking
health information seeking
health information scanning
health information efficacy
uses and gratifications theory
social entrepreneurs
short message services (SMS)
patient portal

Discussion Questions

1. Think of a widespread health concern, such as disaster preparedness, safer sex, or responsible drinking. In what way is the issue represented in the personal sphere? In the technical sphere? In the public sphere? Which of these spheres influences you most? Why?
2. Think of a person with whom you have a weak-tie relationship (perhaps a classmate, professor, or casual acquaintance) and a person with whom you have a strong tie (maybe a family member, best friend, or romantic partner). What might you gain by communicating with the weak-tie acquaintance? By communicating with a loved one? What roles might people in both categories play during a long-term health crisis?
3. How likely are you to sign up for texts and/or email services designed to help you reach particular health goals, such as eating better, working out more, or quitting smoking? Why? What aspects of these programs do you find most appealing (e.g., encouraging messages, online options to track your improvement, personal coaching, helpful hints, and so on)? What aspects, if any, do you find unappealing?
4. Do you think it is mostly a good idea or a bad idea for people to use mobile apps that diagnose their health conditions and suggest a course of action? Why?
5. Describe some of the most common reasons people seek health information online and the factors that might discourage them from doing so. Your answer should integrate the following terms and theories: information sufficiency threshold, the health information acquisition model, the Theory of Motivated Information Management, and the Integrative Model of Online Health Information Seeking.
6. How does uses and gratifications theory help to explain eHealth behavior? Give an example from your own experience.
7. Imagine that you are miserable with a head cold. For what reasons, if any, might you seek information online? If you have the option, would you like to have a phone conversation or an email exchange with a health care provider, or would you rather meet with that person face to face? Why?

Answers to *Can You Guess?*

Part 1

A. Black Americans—Most likely to rely on TV
B. Hispanic Americans—Most likely to rely on family and friends
C. Non-Hispanic White Americans—Most likely to rely on health care providers (Smith, 2011)

Part 2

People in good to excellent health use the Internet more and trust it more than people in fair to poor health, who are more likely to rely on TV (Smith, 2011).

Part 3

Some 60% of U.S. residents surveyed said they would like to have online access to their doctors, their medical records, and their test results, and 25% said they would be willing to pay more for it (Deloitte, 2008a).

PART V

Communication in Health Organizations

People who devote their lives to serving others deserve excellent leaders who support their efforts and remove obstacles that might limit their effectiveness. In this section, which consists of one very important chapter, we look at what it takes to be a great leader in health care. As you will see, leaders have the potential to transform how health care is provided. They do not call all the shots. Instead, they bring out the best in people and enable them to create powerful systems designed to succeed. Leadership involves health care administrators, but also the work of human resources, marketing, and public relationships professionals, whose job it is to build great teams, support outstanding service, and serve the community. Ultimately, the communication abilities of people in these diverse roles help to determine how health care happens, who is involved, how people regard health care organizations, and whether work is a joy or a daily exercise in frustration.

Good leaders make people feel that they're at the very heart of things, not at the periphery. Everyone feels that he or she makes a difference to the success of the organization. When that happens people feel centered and that gives their work meaning.

—WARREN BENNIS

CHAPTER 10

Health Care Administration, Human Resources, Marketing, and PR

The call came in: "The helicopters are having a hard time identifying the hospital with all the power out in the city," they said, "Find the biggest American flag you can find." When you're in marketing and public relations, you do all sorts of things!—**KENDRICK DOIDGE**

As vice president of marketing and public relations at West Florida Hospital, Kendrick Doidge[1] (pronounced *dodge*) is no stranger to the unexpected demands of crisis management. Less than a year before Hurricane Katrina, he was marketing and public relations coordinator at another hospital when Ivan, a Category 3 hurricane, hit closer to home in Pensacola, Florida.

During Ivan, 4,000 members of the community took refuge in the hospital, joining patients and staff members who were there as well. "The storm raged all night," Doidge remembers:

> *At one point, when we had over 2,000 people camped out in the lobby of the hospital, the winds were blowing so hard the windows were starting to bow inward. Staff members physically held the front doors shut while we evacuated everyone to the basement. . . . Then the basement began taking in water during the night.*

Meanwhile, personnel who were caring for patients worried about their own homes and families. (Indeed, more than 30 hospital employees lost their

[1]Unless otherwise indicated, all quotes attributed to Doidge are from a personal interview conducted by the author.

As a marketing and public relations professional at a large hospital, Kendrick Doidge stays in touch with internal and external stakeholders.

homes and nearly everything they owned that night.) Touched by their selflessness, Doidge worked hard to keep everyone well informed. All the while, he helped supervise an emergency contact center in the hospital, monitored communication with the National Guard and other emergency personnel, stayed in touch with the media, and kept tabs on conditions in the hospital. The team's meticulously rehearsed crisis management plan was in full operation.

But that was not all. Doidge's motto is "be willing to do anything, and don't mind doing the little things" (Outzen, 2005, para. 16). So he also helped with the innumerable tasks that emerge without warning in a crisis. For example, Doidge joined colleagues in hauling 50-pound oxygen tanks up several flights of stairs.

"That's one thing I learned about crisis management," he says, laughing, "move the oxygen tanks out of the basement before the electricity goes out and the elevators stop working!" Like most of the region, the hospital was without electricity and running water during the storm and for days afterward. In the thick of things, the staff wheeled patients into hallways so they would not be near windows. They even delivered five babies during the overnight storm, sometimes by flashlight.

For weeks after the storm, Doidge handled media inquiries from around the country, publicized the hospital's makeshift triage unit for people hurt during the hurricane and recovery effort, and organized assistance for staff members who had lost their homes. "You do everything you can to prepare for a crisis, and you keep learning while you're in the middle of one and ever afterward," he says, adding, "We learned a lot during Ivan that helped us 9 months later when Dennis, a Category 2 storm, hit the area."

Now, just a few months after Dennis, Pensacola was safe, but Tulane Medical Center in New Orleans, a sister institution to West Florida Hospital, was in trouble. In the tense days before and after Katrina, choppers evacuated as many patients as possible from New Orleans to the Pensacola facility.

"After the helicopters landed here and unloaded patients, the staff at our hospital would fill them up with supplies to take back to New Orleans," Doidge says. Now his task was to find an American flag quickly enough to make the next return flight. "I started calling around and found that the biggest flag around was flying over Joe Patti's Seafood across town. I called and asked if we could have it. They immediately said yes," he says. "Then I got in the car and realized, 'I didn't tell them my name. They won't know who I am.'" But, as a testament to community spirit, the flag was folded and ready for him when he walked in the door. "They said, 'Are you the one who called about the flag? Here it is,' and I rushed back to the hospital with it," Doidge says.

In New Orleans, crews draped the flag over the edge of the roof and down the exterior wall of the Tulane Medical Center. It became a recognizable symbol of the rescue effort. "That flag had a life of its own," Doidge says. "There were rumors that it was from the World Trade Towers, that it had flown in Iraq—you name it. There's a book about Katrina, and a part in the middle is devoted to that flag."

Doidge, who has a bachelor's degree in political science and a master's degree in health communication leadership, is lauded for his skill in marketing, public relations, and crisis management. As a health care administrator, he is also involved in long-term planning and staffing decisions. He has a reputation for being honest and compassionate, even in tough situations.

We will hear more about Doidge's experiences as well as others' in this chapter, which focuses on the work of health care administrators, human resource specialists, marketing and public relations professionals, and crisis management experts. We will explore some of the key issues and goals within each profession and learn from the experts which communication strategies are most effective. We cannot cover the full range of activities these professionals accomplish, but hopefully your curiosity will be piqued to learn more. (See Box 10.1 for information about career opportunities and Box 10.2 for related journals.) The chapter culminates with strategies for offering outstanding service to patients and their loved ones.

As you read, notice how central communication is in each profession. Also keep in mind the overlap between job responsibilities. Some of us will serve as specialists in these areas, but everyone in health care is involved with them. As we discussed in Chapter 5, systems are interrelated collections of people and ideas. What happens in one part of the system affects what happens everywhere else within it. In health care, in particular, leadership, human resources, public relations, and crisis management are part of everyone's job.

Health Care Administration

Irving S. Shapiro, the legendary CEO of DuPont and long-time trustee of the Howard Hughes Medical Center, was fond of saying that leaders are "first and foremost in the human relations and communication business" (1984, p. 157). He expanded on the idea this way:

> *One important day-to-day task for the CEO is communication, digesting information and shaping ideas, yes, but even more centrally, the business of listening and explaining. . . . One of the first lessons a manager learns while climbing the corporate*

BOX 10.1 CAREER OPPORTUNITIES

Health Care Administration

- President or CEO
- Chief operating officer
- Chief financial officer
- Health information manager
- Director of human resources
- Strategic planning director
- Medical director
- Nursing director
- Departmental director (e.g., departments such as Nursing, Surgery, Medical Records, Human Resources, Marketing, Public Relations, Education, Information Technology, Billing, and Risk Management)
- Medical office manager

Career Resources and Job Listings

- U.S. Bureau of Labor Statistics: http://www.bls.gov/ooh/Management/Medical-and-health-services-managers.htm
- Association of University Programs in Health Administration: www.aupha.org
- American College of Health Care Administrators: www.achca.org
- American College of Health Care Executives: www.healthmanagementcareers.org

Health Care Human Resources

- Human resource manager
- Recruiter
- Training and development specialist
- Compensation and benefits manager
- Customer service representative

Career Resources and Job Listings

- American Society for Healthcare Human Resources Administration: http://www.ashhra.org/
- Society of Human Resource Management: http://www.shrm.org/Pages/default.aspx
- U.S. Bureau of Labor Statistics: http://www.bls.gov/ooh/Business-and-Financial/Human-resources-specialists.htm

Health Care Marketing and Public Relations

- Public relations professional
- Strategic planning manager
- Marketing professional
- Advertising designer
- Physician marketing coordinator
- Community services director
- In-house communication director
- Pharmaceutical sales representative

Career Resources and Job Listings

- Society for Health care Strategy & Market Development: www.shsmd.org/shsmd_app/index.jsp
- International Association of Business Communicators: www.iabc.com
- Public Relations Society of America: www.prsa.org
- Public Relations Society of America Health Academy: www.healthacademy.prsa.org
- American Association of Advertising Agencies: www.aaaa.org
- American Advertising Federation: www.aaf.org
- U.S. Bureau of Labor Statistics: http://www.bls.gov/ooh/Management/Public-relations-managers-and-specialists.htm

ladder is how little he [or she] can accomplish by relying on his [or her] own brains alone. (Shapiro, 1984, pp. 157–158)

Health care administrators range from CEOs and vice presidents to clinical managers and directors of admissions, medical records, education, business affairs, and many other units. Success in the field usually requires a graduate degree in a field such as health care administration, public health, business administration, or health communication. People are seldom hired directly into administrative roles. They tend to work their way up the ladder instead ("Career," 2012). Candidates for administrative positions have usually gained experience in any number of health care agencies, such as nonprofit organizations, clinics, nursing homes, mental health facilities, hospitals, and more. Experience in other fields may also be relevant.

CAN YOU GUESS? PART 1

1. How many health care administrators are there in the United States?
2. What is their average salary?
3. What is the employment outlook for health care administrators?

Answers appear at the end of the chapter.

As a case in point, Doidge's first job after college was at a visitor information and convention center, where he says he "learned to treat people how you would want someone to treat you or a member of your family. . . . We assisted several hundred people a day, and I really learned the importance of customer service," Doidge says of that experience. He then further honed his skills working in membership development for the Chamber of Commerce before he applied for a job in hospital marketing and public relations.

"I didn't know anything about health care when I got that job," he says. "I knew about strategic communication, and I set out to learn everything I could about health care." Part of his education involved enrolling in a graduate program in health communication. "Never assume you know it all," he advises others. "You have to keep learning."

Part of the learning curve involves understanding current issues and collaborating with others. We next explore a variety of factors that are changing the way health care is provided in the United States and the role of communication in guiding that process.

Reimagining Health Care

One driver of change is health care reform. "The Affordable Care Act has created unprecedented opportunities to transform the health care system," say analysts for the Commonwealth Fund, a nonprofit organization that monitors health care performance (McCarthy, Hostetter, & Klein, 2015). Like other analysts, McCarthy and colleagues observe that superficial changes will not suffice in the current climate. The challenge is greater—to fundamentally *reimagine* the way health care is provided. The goals of the redesign are threefold: to enhance the quality of health care experiences, to improve people's health across the board, and to lower costs. We take a closer look at those three goals here.

ENHANCING HEALTH CARE EXPERIENCES

"Being a patient is about the least amount of fun anyone can have as a consumer," point out Leonard Berry and Kent Seltman (2008, p. 167). Even more than in other industries, every customer/patient in health care wants and deserves to be treated as an individual with unique needs and perceptions. And patients have choices—a reality underlined by highly visible advertising and marketing efforts and by an unprecedented amount of health information available in the news media and on the Internet. In this context, patients are well-informed consumers who are asked to choose between different health services vying for their business.

People in health organizations realize like never before the value of consumer satisfaction, and many are taking steps to eliminate unnecessary irritants. For example, some hospital staffs have redesigned the admissions process. Rather than fill out lengthy paperwork the day of admission, they now obtain information over the phone in advance so that people feel less hassled when they arrive for treatment. Others have authorized employees to reimburse patients for

BOX 10.2 RESOURCES

Journals in the Field

Health Care Administration

Advances in Developing Human Resources
The Health Care Manager
Health Care Management Review
Health Care Management Science
Health Sciences Management Research
International Journal for Quality in Health Care
International Journal of Integrated Care
Journal of the American Medical Directors Association
Journal of Health Administration Education
Journal of Health Management
Journal of Health, Organisation and Management
Journal of Healthcare Management
Journal for Healthcare Quality
Journal of Public Health Management & Practice
Managed Health Care Executive

Health Care Human Resources

Human Resources Development Journal
Human Resources for Health
Journal of Health & Human Resources
Journal of Health & Human Services Administration

Health Care Marketing and Public Relations

Cases in Public Health Communication & Marketing
Health Marketing Quarterly
International Journal of Pharmaceutical and Healthcare Marketing
Journal of Health Care Marketing
Journal of Hospital Marketing and Public Relations
Journal of Management and Marketing in Healthcare
Marketing Health Services
Public Relations Journal
Public Relations Review

lost items (dentures, eyeglasses, pillows, clothing, and so on) and to award gift certificates and coupons when they see fit. As one nurse said, "It's amazing how much good will you can inspire with a free lunch!" After employees at the hospital where she worked were given cafeteria coupons to pass along to others, patient satisfaction increased considerably. Says the nurse:

> *Now, when we see a patient's family that has been waiting around for results or a procedure, we can say, "I'm sorry you have had to wait so long. Please have lunch on us. We'll have everything ready by the time you get back." There's no amount of advertising that can outmatch a free meal when you are hungry, tired, and frustrated. And it makes us feel good to help. We're not the bad guys. We're the ones who understand and help, not just the patients, but their families, too.*

As these examples illustrate, improving health care experiences involves listening and responding to patients and their families, collaborating to improve services and procedures, and fostering mutually satisfying relationships. As the next section shows, these are not only good for morale, but important to health and the bottom line as well.

IMPROVING COMMUNITY HEALTH

As you may remember from Chapter 1, the Affordable Care Act offers incentives to health organizations that keep their clients healthy while simultaneously cutting costs. It's a simple goal, but not an easy one to fulfill. Experts suggest that keeping people healthy requires relinquishing some fundamental "old rules" in health care, such as these: (1) Health care happens mostly in health care organizations, (2) one size fits all in terms of health services, and (3) patients are followers (McCarthy et al., 2015).

Health care organizations in the United States have traditionally offered acute care for injuries and illnesses, within the walls of health care organizations, based on practices and procedures established by professionals rather than patients. This works reasonably well in terms of *reactive* care if people have specific, easily resolved illnesses or injuries. However, the system is not well designed to manage chronic health concerns or to proactively keep people well—two goals that are essential to cutting costs and improving community health.

One idea for tearing down the old walls involves establishing a health-bolstering presence in everyday places. For example, health organizations might partner with schools, community centers, employers, and churches to offer on-site classes, conduct health screenings, and provide care for minor injuries and illnesses (McCarthy et al., 2015). The new rulebook has yet to be written, so the possibilities are as endless as people's imagination. Perhaps they will involve low-cost, healthy meals provided in your workplace, or personalized care teams that visit you at home periodically to see how you are doing in terms of your weight loss, stress reduction, and fitness goals. Maybe they will include low-cost day centers where your elder loved ones can enjoy companionship and receive medical care while you are at work. The emerging model will almost certainly involve team efforts by diverse health professionals who work as hard to help people stay healthy as they do to heal and cure them. Although this new model of health care may sound expensive, it may prove to be more effective and affordable than the current system, which is fragmented and reactionary by comparison.

With so much on the line and a future filled with question marks, people are needed who can organize community efforts, listen to constituents, build teams, stimulate creative thinking, and strategize.

CONTROLLING COSTS

Health care has already changed dramatically in the last few decades, primarily because of efforts to control costs. Two of the most notable responses involve sharing resources and boosting efficiency.

Mergers, Alliances, and Buyouts

To consolidate resources, many health organizations have merged with competitors or been bought out by large corporations. **Integrated health systems** offer a spectrum of health services that may include hospitals, outpatient surgery centers, doctors' offices, fitness centers, nursing homes, rehabilitation centers, hospices, and more (Slusarz, 1996). The idea is that, by sharing resources, integrated health systems can reduce operating costs and be more competitive.

Takeovers, mergers, and alliances present communication challenges, however. For one, long-standing competitors may suddenly find themselves working together. Health care executive Eleanor McGee recalls a consolidation this way: "We went from 2,000 employees to 5,000 employees in two years. We didn't know each other. We didn't like each other. We didn't have a common vision. We didn't even have a common mission" (quoted by du Pré, 2005, p. 312). In circumstances such as this, organizational members may struggle to form new relationships and to find ways to integrate their ideas, or they may do as people in many health systems have done and continue to operate as separate entities under one (rather invisible) umbrella. Partitioning is understandable, but it hampers people's ability to share resources and coordinate patient care.

Another challenge of integration is that, as organizations become more complex, it is difficult to manage them by the old rules.

"Make creativity a habit," encourages one health care consultant, who suggests that health organizations invest in communication-friendly meetings spaces, bulletin boards, white boards, and "sticky" areas where patients and health care associates can post ideas and suggestions (Innovations in Health Care, n.d.).

In *Good to Great*, Jim Collins (2001b) summarized the challenge:

> *Entrepreneurial success is fueled by creativity, imagination, bold moves into uncharted waters, and visionary zeal. As a company grows and becomes more complex, it begins to trip over its own success—too many new people, too many new customers, too many new orders, too many new products. What was once great becomes an unwieldy ball of disorganized stuff.* (p. 121)

It is hard to maintain clarity as an organization grows. Rapid change can feel disorienting and overwhelming. And whereas people in small organizations often perceive themselves to be one cohesive team, factions and division are common in larger ones.

Leaders often react to these forces by establishing hierarchies and complex chains of command. This may help team members feel more organized, but it can also suppress creativity and make it seem that upper-level leaders, not frontline employees, are in charge of the organization's design and destiny. In Collins's terms, an "executive class" with most of the power and perks begins to emerge, distinctly separate from others in the organization. As this happens, "the creative magic begins to wane as some of the most innovative people leave, disgusted by the burgeoning bureaucracy and hierarchy" (Collins, 2001b, p. 121). In short, centralized, bureaucratic decision making is an effort to keep everyone marching in the same direction, but it can be sluggish and inhibiting. We will talk more about these challenges and opportunities throughout the chapter.

CAN YOU GUESS? PART 2

?

In what year did *Time* magazine run the following pronouncement?

> *"High prices have hit hospitals with such a staggering blow that many may have to close their doors. . . . In the past year, hospital payrolls jumped 40%, food more than 43%, drugs 38.9%. Meanwhile, the hospitals had an unprecedented horde of patients."*

The answer appears at the end of the chapter.

Efficiency and Six Sigma

> *"In the new market there will be two kinds of organizations—quick and dead."*—ANN L. HENDRICH, NURSE EXECUTIVE

Hendrich's prediction points to another effort to succeed in a competitive market—rethinking processes that waste time and money (Porter-O'Grady, Bradley, Crow, & Hendrich, 1997, para. 10). People in some health organizations are using techniques including Six Sigma to analyze the efficiency of everyday procedures such as sharing information, ordering lab tests, delivering meal trays, dispensing medication, and responding to patient requests.

Six Sigma is a process in which analysts chart each stage in a workplace routine, time how long it takes, and then consider the various outcomes. The goal is to determine which actions add value and which contribute to waste and errors. These considerations are particularly important in health care because of the high costs involved and because even a small error can have drastic consequences. Carolyn Pexton (n.d.) explains:

> *In terms of impact to the patient, a defect in the delivery of health care can range from relatively minor, such as food on a tray that doesn't match the doctor's orders, to significant, such as operating on the wrong limb. In a worst-case scenario, the defect can be fatal, as when a medication error results in the patient's death.* (para. 5)

In the United States, preventable medical errors are now the third leading cause of death, outnumbered only by cancer and heart disease (James, 2013). Even errors that do not harm a patient's health, such as waiting an extra day in the hospital for lab results, are costly.

As you might expect, analysts find that procedures do not always work according to original design, so people adapt **workarounds**—alternative ways of accomplishing tasks. Over time, people may adopt so many workarounds that immense variations and holes in the system develop.

For example, consider discharge procedures in a hospital nursing unit. Using a Six Sigma process at one hospital, DeBusk and Rangel (n.d.) found that it took an average of three hours to discharge a patient—give or take two hours. In other words, some patients left in one hour and some waited five

Effective teamwork and well-designed systems ease the burden on professionals and help them avoid tragic and costly mistakes.

hours. That's a problem, because while one patient is waiting to vacate a bed, very often staff members elsewhere are waiting to transfer another patient (or soon-to-be-patient) into that bed. Bottlenecks in the process mean long wait times, discomfort, compromised care, heightened frustration, and wasted time and money. Imagine waiting five extra hours for your loved one to be discharged. Now double that, considering that somewhere else in the same hospital, a family may be waiting five hours to get *into* that room.

DeBusk and Rangel soon realized why discharge times varied so widely: Every nurse on the unit followed a slightly different procedure. Some placed paperwork awaiting signatures in a bin for others to pick up (usually about 73 minutes later). Other nurses did not use the bin but went directly to people for their signatures (which usually required about 9 minutes). Because staff members at the nurses' desk could not accurately predict how long it would take to get signatures, they typically waited until all signatures were collected to call a social worker to educate a patient about aftercare procedures, resulting in delays as long as 2½ hours. And even when all discharge procedures were final, there was not a standard way to alert transport personnel of that, so patients sometimes waited around until someone happened to notice that their paperwork was complete and initiate the final step.

The Six Sigma analysts were able to work with the nurses to create what they call a lean process map, a streamlined procedure that shaved more than two hours off the average discharge time, with very little variation. The new process reduced patients' average wait to a consistent 48 minutes (shorter than the quickest time previously), made everyone's job easier, and minimized the chances of error and oversight (DeBusk & Rangel, n.d.).

Next we consider some of the skills that help health care administrators inspire the best in people. As you will see, while it is important that leaders require everyone's best efforts, it is inadvisable for leaders to make all the decisions.

COMMUNICATION SKILL BUILDER: SHARED VISION AND DISPERSED LEADERSHIP

> *"Profitability is a necessary condition for existence and a means to more important ends, but it is not the end in itself."* —James Collins and Jerry Porras (1997, p. 57)

It may seem counterintuitive, but decisions made solely in the interest of making money usually do not, at least not in the long run. Evidence we cover more fully later in the chapter suggests that a single-minded focus on profits often leads to questionable judgment and short-term success at best. The more inspiring and more lucrative option is to place the emphasis on people, principles, and sustainability. Following are some tips from the experts on doing that.

Invert the Pyramid

In a classic bureaucratic hierarchy, the people at the top make most of the decisions, get the biggest perks, reap the greatest financial rewards—and seldom see or talk to service-line employees or clients. The inherent tension and lack of communication are problematic. Moreover, whereas everyone in the organization typically tries to please the bosses, patients are not even in the hierarchy.

Some theorists advocate turning the pyramid upside down. In a health care organization, the largest and highest tier is then devoted to patients and customers. Everyone in the organization is oriented to

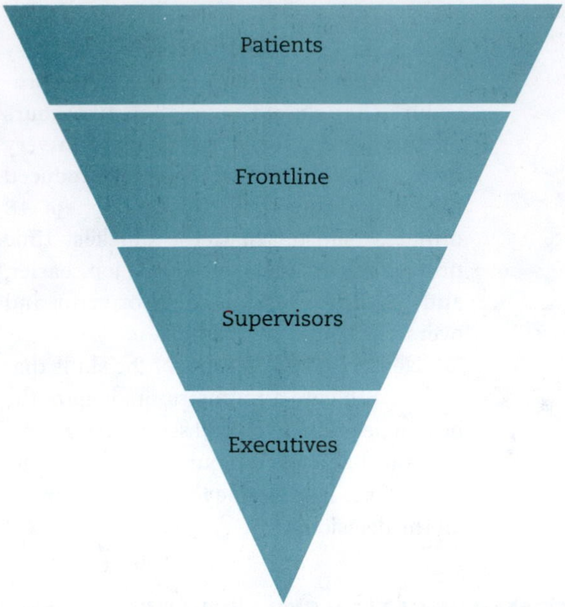

FIGURE 10-1 When the classic hierarchy is inverted, executives act as servant leaders by listening to and supporting the frontline and holding everyone accountable for excellence.

serving *them,* either directly or indirectly. The next-highest tier is made up of frontline service providers—a diverse assortment of everyone who has direct contact with people the organization is designed to serve (patients, families, community members, and so on). In health care, the frontline includes clinicians, volunteers, cafeteria staff, housekeepers, valets, event coordinators, and so on. Subsequent layers are devoted to mid-level supervisors.

In servant-leadership style, CEOs and other executives are on the bottom. From this perspective, their job is to listen, encourage, support, and remove barriers so that people throughout the organization can do what they do best. A classic example of a servant leader was Ken Iverson, former CEO of Nucor Steel. Iverson eliminated executive perks, cut his own salary to be more closely in line with others', reduced the staff at corporate headquarters to 25 people (in a company with 7,000 employees), and put frontline employees' needs first. Nucor—which was nearly bankrupt when Iverson assumed leadership—became a $3.5 billion Fortune 500 company. In his book *Plain Talk,* Iverson (1997) summarizes his philosophy this way:

> *The people at the top of the corporate hierarchy grant themselves privilege after privilege, flaunt those privileges before the men and women who do the real work, then wonder why employees are unmoved by management's invocations to cut costs and boost profitability. . . . When I think of the millions of dollars spent by people at the top of the management hierarchy on efforts to motivate people who are continually put down by that hierarchy, I can only shake my head in wonder.* (pp. 58–59)

Lest this sound too critical of executives, who usually work very hard and bear immense pressure, it's important to note that an inverted pyramid serves them well, too. They are spared the overwhelming burden of being responsible for decisions at all levels. Instead, accountability is dispersed throughout the organization. Leaders in a supportive role are more a part of the overall team and typically enjoy unprecedented appreciation and loyalty from the people they serve.

Empowerment allows teams to create systems and work environments that are tailor made for success. People with adequate training, authority, and resources do not usually need much supervision, particularly if everyone is responsible for meeting clear goals. The typical result is higher morale among both employees and customers. The "We Hate the Rules" feature (Box 10.3) about the Nordstrom department store presents a powerful example of this.

Build Relationships by Listening

Health care leadership expert Quint Studer (2003) maintains that feedback is as crucial as oxygen. As a hospital administrator, he borrowed a technique from physicians and began "rounding" everyday—visiting units throughout the hospital to talk to patients, families, and employees. He typically introduced himself to employees this way: "Hi, I'm Quint Studer. I work for you." After a few questions about the person's experiences and the positive things going on in his or her unit, Studer made it a point to ask, "Do you have the tools and equipment to do your job?" or "What can I do to make your job easier?" And, even more remarkably, he followed through. At one hospital, stories are still told about Studer's influence more than 15 years ago. People continue to marvel that he made hot water reliably available in the ICU, had lights added in the parking lot, provided cleaning supplies in nursing units, and much

BOX 10.3 PERSPECTIVES

"We Hate the Rules"

"We hate rules," says James F. Nordstrom, former cochair of the Nordstrom department store, adding, "The minute you come up with a rule you give an employee a reason to say no to a customer."

There is only one rule in the Nordstrom employee handbook: *Use good judgment in all situations.* Consequently, when a Nordstrom associate learned about a woman who had arrived in the area in the midst of a medical crisis (her husband was about to have emergency brain surgery) and did not have a car or clothing appropriate for the climate, she personally picked the woman up at the hospital, brought her to the store, helped her select clothing, and drove her back to the hospital. The associate knew that in extending this kindness she would be fulfilling Nordstrom's mission of serving customers, and she would not be breaking any rules to do it.

For more about Nordstrom, see Spector and McCarthy (2005). Direct quotes presented here appear on p. 141.

more—usually within 24 hours of learning about a need. Even changes that seem small on the surface resulted in greater efficiency and happier employees and patients (du Pré, 2005).

Doidge adopted a similar strategy when he signed on at West Florida Hospital. He set out to meet everyone he could. "It would sort of surprise people at first when I asked if I could sit with them in the hospital cafeteria," he says. But people soon got used to his friendly manner and willingness to listen. Doidge recalls one nurse who said:

> *Here's what you can do to make my job easier: You can get us different printer paper. The holes in the paper don't match up to the prongs in our patient binders, so we have to fold and bend every page we add to a patient's chart.*

It turned out that the same problem was plaguing nurses throughout the hospital. The paper was frustrating everyone, and it had been for some time. With a quick visit to the supply-chain office, Doidge identified the problem. "Who knows how long ago, someone had apparently bumped the hole-puncher by accident and changed the alignment," says Doidge. With a simple adjustment, a long-standing problem was solved. "You wouldn't believe the response," Doidge recalls, describing the scene:

> *It was the same week we announced a pay raise, but everyone was talking about the hole punches. The nurse who suggested it was a hero. That just shows you, our job is to listen to the people caring for our patients. They'll tell you if you ask. But they don't have time to go looking for the source of problems like that.*

When leaders listen, they send the message that team members matter and are valued. And listening yields valuable information. Frontline employees are typically more familiar than anyone about clients' wishes and the organization's daily routines. Steve Miller, a worldwide manager at Shell Oil Company, emphasizes the need to treat members at every level as intelligent change agents:

> *In the past, the leader was the guy with the answers. Today if you're going to have a successful company, you have to recognize that no leader can possibly have all the answers. The leader may have a vision. But the actual solutions about how best to meet the challenges of the moment have to be made by the people closest to the action.* (*quoted by Pascale, 1999, p. 210*)

With a similar belief, Mayo Clinic staff members attribute a great deal of their success to team spirit and their respect for each other. "I know by name the custodians that work in the emergency department, and I appreciate them as much as I appreciate my physician colleagues," says Anne Sadosty, an emergency care physician with Mayo Clinic (quoted by Berry & Seltman, 2008, p. 58).

Push Decision Making to the Lowest Level Possible

A shared vision is nothing if it has not been integrated into everyday ways of doing things. One strategy is to adopt cohesive guidelines for what to say and do. This is effective in fairly predictable and straightforward situations. There are medical protocols for conducting tests and administering medications, and sometimes communication protocols are effective as well. At one hospital, staff members make it a point to say, "Is there anything else that I may do for you? I have the time." That's a script that seems to work well. Staff members say patients are more forthcoming about their concerns because of it. This ultimately saves time and leads to a better experience. Partly as a consequence, patients' satisfaction scores at that hospital are some of the highest in the country.

WHAT DO YOU THINK?

- If your boss asked you to list the "really stupid rules," what would you include on the list?
- Would you be comfortable making suggestions? Why or why not?

Determining who should be involved in decisions can be tricky. Leadership theorist Wayne Hoy observes that, if you ask human relations theorists if team members should be involved in decision making, they say, "Of course!" Ask people from the scientific management camp and they answer, "Only if they have expertise." Open-systems social scientists usually say, "It depends" (Hoy, 2003, slide 2). The **Hoy-Tarter Model of Shared Decision Making** (Hoy & Tarter, 2008) proposes that leaders consider two main questions when determining whom to include in decision making: *Does the team member have a personal stake in the outcome?* (In other words, is the topic relevant to her or him?) and *Does the team member have expertise on the topic?* If the answer is yes to both, the basic foundations are present for shared decision making. Layered on top of that are other considerations such as: *Is it likely that this person will agree with the decision even without being personally involved in it? Does he or she have the skills to participate effectively in decision making?* and *Do the people involved trust each other?*

One interesting application of the Hoy-Tarter model is that we can apply it to leaders as well as to frontline team members. Compared to the frontline, executive-level leaders often have less personal stake in workplace procedures and less personal knowledge about them, partly because they are not on the frontline as much and partly because people are typically hesitant to be candid with leaders they do not know well. The result, says health care satisfaction expert Irwin Press, can be a lot of top-down rules that do not serve anyone very well.

When assessing employee satisfaction in health care organizations, Press begins by asking employees to list the "really stupid rules" that hamper them from doing a good job. "This is fun and focuses analytical attention on the often arbitrary nature of regulations," says Press (2002, p. 42). Next, he asks people to examine rules that serve a purpose but do not work well. For example, Press asks, is it necessary that nurses deliver meal trays? Could other staff members perform this task and free nurses to respond more quickly to patients' requests?

Press (2002) also advises that, if the rules and paperwork are important, leaders must allow team members the time and space to complete them. For example, it is unrealistic to expect an employee to answer the phone, file reports, and respond to others' needs in the same small space or in brief amounts of time. Frustration and poor service are likely to result. If the regulations are important, Press declares, make fulfilling them part of the job.

Another drawback of centralized decision making is the time it takes. Opportunities for change are often lost or delayed before top-level leaders know about them or can act upon them. This can be fatal in today's fast-moving market. And when service breakdowns occur, frontline team members may have to wait for authorization from "higher-ups" before they can resolve the issues. The result is often a frustrating delay on top of an already disappointing situation.

Health care consultant Fred Lee offers a frustrating example of centralized decision making (Lee, 2004). He arrived at a hospital one morning to conduct a training session, only to find that the classroom was locked. A security officer arrived, but even though he had a key, he was required to get permission from his supervisors across town to open the door, and they were not available. "I'm really sorry," said the security officer while the entire class waited in the hall. Lee reflects,

"How could central dispatch, 20 miles away, have a better understanding of the situation than the officer at the scene? Any information about the problem would be coming from the officer anyway." Lee sympathizes with the employee who was rendered powerless (and no doubt embarrassed) because supervisors did not trust employees to act on their own judgment.

Considerations such as these have led health care experts Thom Mayer and Robert Cates (2004) to advise, "Make no decision at a higher level that can be made at a lower level" (p. 58). They point out that health care is a personal service offered at an individual level; therefore "the people responsible for the service delivery must be entrusted with the power to make service meaningful" (p. 58).

Hold People Accountable

A key component of empowerment is holding people at every level of the organization responsible for goals they help to set and regularly measuring progress to help team members gauge what is working and what is not (Chang, Shih, & Lin, 2010; Donahue, Piazza, Griffin, Dykes, & Fitzpatrick, 2008).

To make the process effective, experts suggest that measurement not be used to punish team members. If so, they will have an incentive to set goals too low and to enhance the results artificially, as in asking patients to give them perfect scores rather than constructive ideas. Feedback mechanisms should be based on what team members *themselves* want to know in the interest of continual self-improvement. In Mayer and Cates's (2004) terms, measurement should be a tool, not a club.

Here is a great example. Lynn Pierce was a nurse manager in a hospital where the staff decided to post the results of weekly patient satisfaction surveys on bulletin boards. That meant that everyone (staff members, patients, visitors, VIPs, and anyone else) could see the scores, as well as charts that compared patient satisfaction scores in various departments. There was no punishment involved, but the numbers were hard to ignore. Pierce says that, although she frequently made excuses for her unit's scores when they were kept private, having them publicly posted changed her point of view. "I started thinking, 'My numbers are going to come up! I won't be left behind,'" she says. Pierce says she began seeing patient requests not as time-consuming chores, but as opportunities. She laughs, "'You want a Coke?' I'd call Dietary and say, '*Send 'em a six-pack!*'" (quoted by du Pré, 2005, p. 317).

Celebrate Successes

One benefit of measuring performance is the opportunity to celebrate when things go well. Experts suggest sending handwritten thank-you letters to employees and their families, posting thank-you letters from patients, holding celebrations when the organization reaches key goals, informally praising people who do good work, and developing formal recognition programs to honor heroic efforts.

In closing this section, it bears emphasizing that leaders are not obsolete once they empower team members. As James Pepicello and Emmett Murphy (1996) point out, empowerment "does not relieve leadership of its responsibility to lead" (para. 17). It does mean that leaders' role is different. No longer is leadership defined by one's position or title. Instead, it is characterized by interpersonal skills, including the ability to inspire, recognize, and reward others (Jobes & Steinbinder, 1996, para. 23).

If it seems overwhelming to contemplate all that health care administrators do, keep in mind that they do not do it alone. Success relies on the integrated efforts of many people. In the next section we will explore how human resources specialists contribute.

Human Resources

Nothing beats being part of a team that is expected to produce great results. . . . If you have the wrong people on the bus, nothing else matters. You may be headed in the right direction, but you still won't achieve greatness. Great vision with mediocre people still produces mediocre results.—**JIM COLLINS (2001A, DISCIPLINED PEOPLE, PARA. 7)**

After studying consistently top-performing companies in the United States, Collins (2001b) debunked the idea that people are a company's most important asset. "People are *not* your most important asset," he clarified, "the *right* people are" (p. 13). Indeed, as we all know, the wrong people, or people who are not well prepared, can be your worst nightmare—damaging trust, running off great team members, causing mistakes, and damaging morale.

In a book with the provocative title *The No Asshole Rule,* Stanford University professor Robert Sutton (2007) presents empirical evidence that people who treat others badly are bad for business, no matter how good they seem to be at some aspects of the job. Sutton calculated what he dubs the TCA (total cost per asshole) of workers in a wide variety of fields and concluded that the disadvantages of people who insult, belittle, and bully others far outweigh the advantages. Even bullies considered to be "top" salespeople, he says, cost companies more than they bring in because of lawsuits, staff turnover, angry clients, and so on. Moreover, their attitudes tend to be contagious, such that the people around them offer poorer service as well. Sutton advises, "Avoid pompous jerks whenever possible. They not only can make you feel bad about yourself, chances are you will eventually start acting like them" ("Work Matters" blog post, n.d.). See the *Check It Out!* box for a chance to test your own bully quotient.

CHECK IT OUT!

Robert Sutton offers a tongue-in-cheek test called "Are You a Certified Asshole?" at http://electricpulp.com/guykawasaki/arse/. Results are scored on a scale from: Not an Asshole ("unless you are fooling yourself"), to Borderline, to Full-Blown Certified, in which case Sutton recommends, "Get help immediately. But, please, don't come to me for help, as I would rather not meet you."

Odds are you have worked with people who evoke fear and anxiety in the people around them. Typically, even their bosses would rather not deal with them, so the bullies often remain where they are, running off clients and colleagues. The challenge of working with hostile team members is unacceptable anywhere, but particularly in health care organizations, where leaders struggle to attract and keep qualified personnel in already stressful environments. Health care staffing shortages (see Box 10.4) make it imperative for leaders to do whatever they can to attract and keep qualified personnel. This includes listening closely to employees' needs, responding to their ideas, and involving them in collaborative efforts to create satisfying environments.

In this section, we look at the contributions of human resource personnel and others who cultivate talent and vision and, ideally, give us the luxury of working with ethical, dedicated people. Human resource specialists are involved in recruiting, hiring, and training staff members; overseeing employee benefits and compensation; mediating employee concerns; providing for mentoring, counseling, and assistance; recognizing outstanding achievements; and monitoring team member satisfaction and retention. Qualifications typically include at least a bachelor's degree in human resources, personnel, communication, psychology, or another field related to human dynamics ("Becoming," 2011).

BOX 10.4

Staffing Shortages in Health Care

Experts estimate that the United States will be short-staffed by nearly 1 million nurses, 124,000 physicians, and 706,000 home health aides by the year 2025 (AHA, 2008; Dill & Salsberg, 2008; U.S. Bureau of Labor Statistics, 2012a, 2012b). There are numerous reasons for the shortfall.

One involves population shifts. A growing elderly population is placing increasing demands on the health care system. The number of people over age 85 will triple between 2008 and 2050, reaching an unprecedented 19 million, and increasing the overall need for health services by at least 40% (U.S. Census Bureau News, 2008).

A second factor is the Affordable Care Act, passed in 2010. By creating provisions for nearly all Americans to be insured and receive regular health care, it will increase the need for qualified caregivers. (The act also includes billions of dollars in grants and training opportunities to prepare new caregivers.)

Third, at the same time health care needs are increasing, the number of trained caregivers, which is already insufficient, is expected to *decrease*. This is partly because many caregivers are at retirement age themselves. Experts predict that about one-half of registered nurses and one-third of physicians currently practicing in the United States will retire by the

continued

year 2025 (Budden, Zhong, Moulton, & Cimiotti, 2013; Dall & West, 2015).

The physician shortage is slightly less extensive than the nursing shortage, partly because some women who might previously have pursued nursing careers are now going to medical school instead. Whereas nursing was once one of the few career paths available to women, the number of first-year college students aspiring to become nurses dropped by 75% between 1974 and 1986, as women began to choose other career options (Green, 1988). As a result of that fairly recent shift, female physicians are younger, on average, than their male counterparts. However, men have not joined nursing at the rate once expected. Today, only about 7% of registered nurses in the United States are male (Budden et al., 2013).

A fourth factor is insufficient funding for colleges and universities. U.S. nursing schools turn away nearly 69,000 qualified applicants a year because they do not have the budgets or faculty necessary to accept more students (American Association of Colleges of Nursing, 2015).

Finally, many health professionals are changing careers. Nearly 1 in 6 registered nurses in the United States is not employed as a nurse. That equates to about 466,564 qualified people who have opted out of the nursing workforce (U.S. DHHS, 2010). The most common reason is burnout from working in understaffed units. Because of the nursing shortage, and to save money, many hospitals and residential care facilities have fewer staff members than before. This includes nurses, nurse aides, technicians, housekeeping staff, and so on. Nurses are often called on to fill the gaps. Stress is also elevated by the demands of caring for sicker patients. Because of reimbursements limits, hospital patients today are "quicker and sicker" than in the past. Rather than a patient load in which some patients are quietly recovering and others are really sick, *everyone* is really sick.

Hospital nurses in Hendrich and colleagues' (2008) study walked an average of 3 miles per 10-hour shift. The researchers conclude, "A picture emerges of the professional nurse who is constantly moving from patient room to room, nurse station to supply closet and back to room, spending a minority of time on patient care activities" (p. 31). The researchers note that it is no surprise that nurses leave the profession. Hendrich and colleagues urge health care leaders to consider ways to make nurses' jobs more efficient and less demanding.

The nursing shortage affects health care professionals. It also hurts patients. An extensive study of 799 hospitals by the U.S. Department of Health and Human Services revealed that patients in understaffed units are significantly more likely than others to have urinary tract infections, pneumonia, shock, and upper gastrointestinal bleeding—conditions that can often be averted or minimized with careful attention ("HHS Study Finds," 2001). Patients in understaffed units are also more likely to have extended hospital stays and less likely to be successfully resuscitated after cardiac arrest. Jack Needleman and associates (2006) found that hospitals can actually save money by hiring more RNs because nurses in well-staffed units have fewer emergencies, patient deaths, and mistakes to manage.

THEORETICAL FOUNDATIONS

Before exploring the research and strategies relevant to human resources, let's consider some of the foundational theories in the field. As you will see, theorists have examined issues such as: *What ethical principles should we consider concerning the treatment of people on our teams? How are people different from other types of resources?* and *What brings out the best in team members so that, together, we have the greatest chance of success?*

Richard de Charms laid the groundwork for many current theories of motivation and workplace dynamics. His (1968) **theory of personal causation** proposes that people naturally resist being treated as **pawns** who are required to relinquish control and blindly follow orders, but people typically respond enthusiastically and with dedication when they are treated as **origins**—active participants in designing and carrying out worthwhile tasks. de Charms's work was as much about ethics as productivity. He felt that people

According to the theory of personal causation, people resist being treated as pawns who are required to relinquish control and blindly follow orders, but they typically respond enthusiastically and with dedication when they are treated as origins—that is, active participants in designing and carrying out worthwhile tasks.

deserve to be treated as something more than cogs in a machine, and he observed that associates make their greatest contributions when they are actively engaged. Consequently, de Charms (1977) advocated a participatory model that he called "plan-choose-act-take responsibility" in which people work together to make decisions, carry them out, and then continually analyze and improve their own performance.

A similar idea is available in Douglas McGregor's (1960) **Theory X and Theory Y** model, which proposes that managers tend to fall into one of two basic camps—those who believe people are naturally lazy and must be prodded and supervised to be productive (Theory X managers) and those who believe people enjoy the inherent rewards of work and are motivated to make a positive difference (Theory Y managers). McGregor observed that managers' attitudes are influential in bringing out either the worst or the best in people. People treated as if they are lazy and untrustworthy are likely to act that way and vice versa. On the other hand, Theory Y managers tend to take a human relations approach, recognizing that people are most effective when they feel appreciated, satisfied, and proud of the work they do. McGregor's theory and relevant research lend further credence to the notion that it is both ethical and expedient to empower team members.

Frederick Herzberg conceived of a more complicated interplay between factors. His **motivation-hygiene theory** suggests that a different set of issues engender satisfaction versus dissatisfaction (Herzberg, 1968; Herzberg, Mausner, & Snyderman, 1959). According to the theory, people are typically satisfied with their work if they believe they are making an important difference, are respected, and are learning and improving. Herzberg called these factors **motivators**. However, dissatisfaction typically arises over a different set of issues, which he called **hygiene factors**. These include feeling underpaid, being forced to work in unhealthy or unproductive conditions, and perceiving that rules and policies are unfair. Herzberg found that, in the absence of such factors, people are typically not dissatisfied. However, it does not follow that they are satisfied, either. To be satisfied, if you recall, we must feel that our work is important and we are respected. The lesson here is that dissatisfaction typically arises from factors (such as pay) that are extrinsic to our work, and motivation arises from the inherent satisfaction of making a difference. Managers who focus on only one or the other are unlikely to create the conditions in which people are both satisfied and highly motivated.

In health care, it is particularly important to recruit outstanding people and to make sure they feel rewarded and valued. Although human resource personnel typically do not work directly with patients, they have immense influence on the quality of those interactions.

COMMUNICATION SKILL BUILDER: BUILDING GREAT TEAMS

When a very ill patient was admitted to a Mayo hospital, her daughter told the care team that she was worried her mother would not live long enough to be present at her upcoming wedding. Sensing that this was important to both mother and daughter, the Mayo team sprang into action. Within hours, they transformed the hospital atrium into a flower- and balloon-filled wedding venue. Personnel from many units volunteered to help out:

> *Staff members provided a cake and a pianist, and nurses arranged the patient's hair and makeup, dressed her, and wheeled her bed to the atrium. The chaplain performed the service. On every floor, hospital staff members, other patients, and visiting family and friends ringed the atrium balconies "like angels from above," to quote the bride. (Berry & Seltman, 2008, p. 57)*

This moving story is evidence of Mayo Clinic's simple vision, known to every employee and used as the basis for all decisions: *The needs of the patient come first* (Berry & Seltman, p. 24). Within that culture, the term *volunteerism* refers to employees' willingness to do more than they have to do because they want to make a difference and they know organizational leaders will back them up.

This level of commitment and compassion does not happen automatically, but results from a concerted effort on many levels. The process begins with selecting the right people, then training them well and weaving the mission into every aspect of daily work. Following are strategies for creating and building outstanding teams from a human resources perspective.

Hire Carefully

The first step toward success, says Collins (2001b), is getting the "right people on the bus." Mayer and Cates (2004) wholeheartedly concur. They ask, "Are there days when you come to work and see the people you are working with and think to yourself, 'Bring it on! Whatever we've got to do today, this team of people can make it happen!'?" (p. 7). If so, they say, you are surrounded by **A-team players**, the type who love a challenge, have a positive attitude, and inspire everyone around them. But if you said no, you understand the concept of **B-team players.** They inspire a different internal dialogue on the way to work, one that sounds more like this: "Shoot me, shoot me, shoot me! I can't work with him—I worked with him yesterday!" (Mayer & Cates, p. 7).

Mayer and Cates describe **B-team players** as negative, lazy, late, confused, and always surprised by the demands of the job. B-team players are "fundamentally toxic" and quite potent, in that it just takes one to poison things for everyone. A major part of a leader's job, maintain Mayer and Cates, is getting B-team members either to reform (which might involve moving them to positions more in line with their talents and passions) or to leave. An even better strategy, they say, is to hire the right people in the first place.

Linda Minton of Parkwest Medical Center in Knoxville, Tennessee, describes how she knew that a new nurse, Paul, would be an A-team member. A woman in her eighties with Alzheimer's was admitted for a blood transfusion under Paul's supervision. When the woman became afraid and pulled out her IVs, her daughter was tearful and distraught. The patient repeatedly requested to be left alone and allowed to go home, but Paul knew that she needed the lifesaving treatment. Minton recalls,

> *Paul again quietly explained that she could not go home, but he also asked if there were anything else she might like to do. Quickly she responded, with a big smile on her face, "I would like to dance." Paul, who is not a dancer, said, "You will have to lead." She agreed, and so—they danced. What a wonderful sight, seeing this lovely lady calmed by the impromptu dance. It was at that moment that we all knew Paul had a place at Parkwest Medical Center.* (*What's Right in Health Care, 2007, p. 666*)

Human resource personnel can be influential in recruiting and selecting A-team players. Experts remind us that it is important to find people with the right attitude and passion as well as the right credentials. Before making hiring decisions, members of highly successful organizations typically conduct multiple interviews with candidates, invite input from people with whom they would work, and consider candidates' intangible qualifications such as patience, appreciation for diversity, and interpersonal skills.

Teach the Culture and Values

This section began with an example of the volunteer spirit of Mayo Clinic. By helping to teach the organization's culture and values, human resource personnel are involved in making such remarkable encounters possible. At Mayo, employees hear the clinic's motto, "The needs of the patient come first," within the first five minutes of new-employee orientation and several times a day ever after. As one employee said, "Mayo becomes part of your DNA" (quoted by Berry & Seltman, 2008, p. 26). Having a strong, clear purpose provides unity, even among diverse people and departments. Team members contribute in different ways, but because they are united by a clear mission, they all know and agree on what they are trying to achieve together.

Continually Recruit Internal Talent

By most estimates, it costs about $75,000 to replace an employee who earns $50,000, and even more for people in higher pay grades (Bliss, 2012). Expenses involve lost productivity and the cost of recruiting, interviewing, and training new employees. That does not even include the frustration of disrupted relationships and being short-staffed in the meantime. It is to everyone's benefit to keep great team members on board. Human resources personnel can help retain talented people in the following ways:

- *Provide ongoing leadership training.* Ideally, leadership training and development do not begin or end when people become designated leaders. The process begins long before that and continues throughout a person's career.

- *Keep no secrets.* If people are to be accountable, they must know where they stand and how the organization is performing. One strategy is to make financial records and satisfaction survey reports available to all employees so they can chart their success and receive immediate market feedback on what works well and what does not (Studer, 2003).
- *Make organizational leaders accessible.* Avoid placing administrative officers in far-off or segregated areas. Encourage leaders to interact freely throughout the organization and to share conversations, praise, and ideas.
- *Reward people for sharing ideas.* Develop a program that invites employees' suggestions and rewards them for submitting workable ideas that improve services, save money, and increase employee morale.
- *Respond to ideas.* Even when the ideas cannot be implemented, people want to know they have been heard. Designate committees to review ideas, respond to them all, and initiate implementation whenever possible. (See Box 10.5 for more on innovative, inclusive leadership.)
- *Prepare people to participate actively.* In the previous section, we explored reasons to invest in dispersed leadership. Empowered team members typically perform at higher levels, are more creative, and more satisfied than others (Fernandez & Moldogaziev, 2013). Human resource personnel can help people build the skills to effectively engage in shared governance.

Based on the theories we have reviewed, encouraging people to use and develop their talents is productive for health care organizations and enriching for the people who comprise them. Recruitment is the first step, but it also pays to continually re-recruit talented team members and hire from within when the talent is available. In a way, point out Berry and Seltman (2008), employment is a job interview "that lasts for years" (p. 29).

Now let's look at the contributions of marketing and public relations professionals, who work both internally and externally to help health care organizations succeed.

BOX 10.5

A Model for Innovative Leadership

When writers for the *Harvard Business Review* interviewed 100 innovative business leaders, they identified some common characteristics among them (Davenport, Prusak, & Wilson, 2003). For one, innovators are *idea scouts*, always looking for new ideas within the organization and outside it. They talk to people and really listen. They are also *tailors* who modify new ideas to suit the organization's needs, while inviting frequent and candid input from others. As the process continues, the best innovators are *promoters* who sell their ideas to people throughout the organization, communicating effectively and enthusiastically with top and middle management as well as frontline employees and clients. Finally, innovators are *experimenters*. They pilot and test new ideas on a small scale to prepare them for wider adoption. Importantly, innovators are *not* do-it-all-myself types. When an innovation has been tested and refined, they "get out of the way and let others execute" (Davenport et al., 2003, p. 58). The implications for communication are clear: Observe, listen, invite feedback, sell your ideas, experiment, and enable others.

What Do You Think?

1. In what ways are you an idea scout? Think of the best idea scout you know. How does he or she do it?
2. What steps might you follow to tailor ideas to a particular organization or group of people?
3. What skills are needed to promote new ideas?
4. Have you ever been part of (or coordinated) a pilot study or experimental program? Did you feel it was worthwhile? What did you learn during the process?
5. Why are skillful innovators not "do-it-myself" types when it comes to implementing widespread changes?

Marketing and Public Relations

We began this chapter with Kendrick Doidge's observation that, "When you're in marketing and public relations, you do all sorts of things!" As you can see from the examples of his work so far, that is certainly true. In this section we talk more about health care marketing and public relations, two career fields that, while not the same, are often interrelated.

Traditionally, health care marketing has been concerned mostly with promoting business and profitability, and public relations has focused on enhancing an organization's image and larger mission. Marketing professionals are likely to be involved with stakeholder groups who are central to business development. This may include marketing directly to physicians who might make patient referrals, conducting market research, helping develop new services to meet market needs, branding and promoting an organization through advertising and other means, communicating internally, and engaging in strategic planning. Results are often measured in terms of financial success and organizational growth.

Public relations professionals in health care are usually involved in such activities as media relations and publicity, publication design, internal communication, strategic planning, special events, health education and promotion, fundraising, volunteer recruitment, and crisis management. The most coveted public relations professionals are those who work in an integrated fashion both within an organization and with external stakeholders. "Long gone are the days when public relations practitioners could claim they were successful after getting their organization positive publicity in the local newspaper," says PR theorist and researcher Kurt Wise (2007), pointing out that "CEOs now expect public relations professionals to demonstrate they can contribute to the bottom-line success of an organization" (p. 162).

Although marketing and public relations are not the same, if they are done well they complement each other. An organization that is not financially sustainable will accomplish very little. At the same time, an organization without a strong reputation and mission is unlikely to be financially successful. It is common in health care for marketing and public relations professionals to work closely together. And sometimes people do both.

FOUNDATIONS FOR THEORY AND PRACTICE

Following are communication best practices from marketing and public relations experts, as well as the theories behind them. As a foundation for the rest, we will spend the most time on cultivating mutually beneficial relationships.

Focus on Relationships

Relationship management and relationship marketing emerged in the late 1980s and have been received with particular enthusiasm in health care. They reflect the idea that transactions do not always (or even, usually) have a distinct beginning, middle, and end (Dwyer, Schurr, & Oh, 1987). For example, if you undergo surgery, your impression of the hospital probably does not begin when you walk in the door. It begins much earlier, perhaps with friends' stories about their experiences there, the hospital's generosity in sponsoring your niece's softball team, the general friendliness of people you know who work there, and so on. And what happens while you are a patient is likely to influence your willingness to seek care there in the future. Considering these factors, marketing and public relations professionals who focus on ongoing relationships are more effective than others in attracting and sustaining not only consumers and partners, but loyal fans of the organization.

Relationships of all types matter. Coworker relationships influence organizational culture and set the tone for consumer interactions. Relationships with external stakeholders play a powerful role as well. Their support (or lack of it) can be the difference between building a new wing and going without. As Berkowitz (2007) points out, "it is extremely difficult to seek donations to build a cancer center, heart center, or women's health program, and ask for a donation from any individual before the organization has a relationship with that donor" (p. 128). In health care, even supposed competitors often team up to fund community clinics for the uninsured, host health fairs, coordinate care in crisis situations, and more. "The demands on and responsibilities of today's health care organizations are too difficult and overwhelming to accomplish without the assistance of strategic partners and other publics," attest Guy, Williams, Aldridge, and Roggenkamp (2007, p. 2).

Many people feel that relationship development is not only good business but is also the key to improving health care and lowering costs. As marketing theorist Lawrence Crosby (2011) puts it:

> *Quality and cost issues are not about healthy individuals collapsing on the street and being rushed to the hospital for a sophisticated diagnosis by TV's Dr. House. They are about chronic problems that have been simmering for years that eventually boil over into far bigger problems. Managing the prevention/treatment/follow-up life cycle requires a relationship approach.* (p. 13)

Crosby posits that today's often-fragmented approach to health care encourages treatment overlaps, inconsistencies, distrust, and neglect that could be overcome with stronger, more trusting relationships.

Robert Morgan and Shelby Hunt's (1994) **commitment-trust theory of relationships** proposes that people make relatively enduring judgments between alternatives based on trust, shared values, loyalty, and commitment—and that, of these, *commitment* and *trust* are the greatest predictors of relationship strength. The theory further posits that, once enduring relationships are formed, we (as consumers, providers, or colleagues) benefit from a sense of stability, uncertainty reduction, and enhanced identity, and we are likely to remain invested in those relationships as long as the benefits outweigh the relational costs, which may include conflict and a sense that other alternatives have emerged that are even more rewarding. This means it is important to foster relationships, to continually nurture them, and to work through relationship threats.

Relationship management has dispelled the notion that marketing and public relations professionals can be effective engaging in only one-way communication with the public (Berkowitz, 2007). Actually, that notion was never very satisfying, particularly in health care. As early as 1939, Alden Brewster Mills prescribed that health care public relations should be, more than anything else, an effort to develop "mutual understanding, good will and respect" (Mills, 1939, p. 3).

With the same conviction, James Grunig and colleagues advocate **two-way symmetrical communication**, meaning ongoing, open dialogue between members of an organization and the larger publics it serves (see, e.g., Grunig, 1992; Grunig, Grunig, & Dozier, 2002). The lesson is that, as in any relationship, listening is as important as talking.

In sum, many people believe that relationship management—with its focus on enduring, mutual benefits for everyone involved—is the most important focus of public relations and marketing. As you might imagine, communication is central to relationship management, being the mechanism by which we convey trust and commitment and manage conflict. And it is not enough for only marketing and public relations professionals to engage in relationship development. Everyone must be involved. We focus next on efforts to integrate marketing and public relations throughout an organization.

Integrate

"Selling is trying to get people to want what you have. Marketing is trying to have what people want," says health care consultant Terrance Rynn (quoted by Lee, 2004. p. 5).

One mistake professionals make is trying to boost business by promoting substandard services. Not only will that not work, says Fred Lee (2004), it will make matters worse. He advises that if a service is subpar, do not promote it. "The worst thing you can do for a poorly delivered service is to get more physicians or patients to try it and find out how bad it is" (p. 6). For this reason, it is important not to consider marketing and public relations as "add-ons" to a health care system, but as integral components in strategic planning and organizational design.

Because marketing and PR professionals are continually involved in scanning the larger environment and listening to what people want and need, they can be valuable players in internal decision making. Besides, the more they know about services, the better and more authentically they can promote them to others.

An interesting example of internal public relations is provided in Trent Seltzer and colleagues' (2012) article "PR in the ER" in which they describe communication in a busy, university-affiliated emergency department. The researchers observed and interviewed staff members, most of whom felt they were "under bombardment" (p. 131), unprepared for the communication challenges they faced every day and discouraged by the hostile attitudes of their coworkers. Worst of all, perhaps, the staff largely perceived that administrators were indifferent to their concerns; thus they were helpless in a bad situation. The researchers observed that the personnel who were confused, frustrated, and anxious were hampered in their ability to do a good job and were poor ambassadors for the organization. Based on these observations, the researchers encouraged leaders to focus on employee concerns, recognizing that public relations is as much an internal function as an external one.

Develop Reputation, Not Only Image

An organization's greatest competitive advantage is not its size, location, or prices. The greatest predictor of success is its character and the constancy of its reputation (Jackson, 2004). In the book *Building Reputational Capital,* Jackson (2004) presents compelling evidence supporting a simple but powerful idea: *Organizations flourish when people are loyal to them.* The principle applies to clients as well as employees. Jackson found that the best employees—the kind with strong integrity, lasting commitment, and goodwill themselves—flock to companies that make them feel proud to work there. In appreciation of being treated well, the people served by those organizations are likely to come back again and again.

In contrast, organizations that defy public trust, no matter how large they are (think Enron, Rupert Murdoch's media empire, and Tyco), are often eventually toppled by scandal. These companies experience what Jackson (2004) calls "relational bankruptcy," which no amount of marketing or public relations can undo. Jackson proposes that "the things that matter most to your business, that enable it to work, to be productive—trust, integrity, fair dealing—exist beyond conventional measurements of the firm's value" (p. 2).

Promoting an image that does not reflect an organization's true character is likely to cause disappointment and foster a poor reputation.

This is particularly true in health care. It is difficult to judge a clinic, hospital, or nonprofit organization except on the basis of its reputation. No matter how high-tech or beautiful a medical center is, it is unlikely that people will trust their lives or their donations to people they do not trust.

Jackson (2004) distinguishes between **corporate identity** (what makes an organization recognizable in comparison to others), **image** (an overall but sometimes fleeting feeling about a company based on its "personality"), and **reputation** (a long-term assessment by a range of constituencies about the "character, conscience, and credibility" of an organization; p. 43). He presents a model of three different types of companies, described here.

People in what we might call **Point-A-to-Point-B companies** are motivated primarily by profits and are willing to engage in questionable means to reach profitable ends. Although the bottom line might look healthy for a while, people in these companies usually experience short-term success at best. They engender little loyalty from customers or employees, and in the end, they may expend a great deal of time and money dealing with legal troubles and scandals, if the company survives at all.

People in the second type of company, which we will call **superficially image based**, realize the value of a positive image, but they seek it through advertising campaigns and slogans that sound good but do not necessarily reflect the true nature of the company. In this company, principles are espoused, but they are not always enacted. This approach is not likely to engender long-term success.

The third company is **reputation based**, meaning that it has a positive image, but more importantly, people throughout the organization consistently embody high principles in all that they do. This is possible because people know the principles and because leaders and policies support those principles, even when it takes a little more time and money to live up to them. Jackson (2004) demonstrates that only in this type of organization can people afford to engage in transparent decision making, which is important because transparency is the key to lasting trust. His research suggests that reputation-based companies are the only ones that experience long-term success.

In summary, Jackson (2004) makes the point that image can be superficial, but an organization's reputation—good or bad—is based on how its members treat people every day in every situation.

So far we have been talking mostly about guiding principles. We will close this section with a skill-builder about one of the many communication tools marketing and public relations professionals use.

HEALTH AND COMMUNICATION TECHNOLOGY

Research about social media and health communication published between 2002 to 2012 showed six main benefits: (1) increased opportunities for interaction, (2) ability to tailor and share information, (3) enhanced access to health information, (4) ability to offer and receive social support, (5) better monitoring of public health issues, and (6) greater voice in health policy matters. However, researchers caution that, if information is inaccurate and unreliable, it can cause more harm than good (Moorhead et al., 2013).

COMMUNICATION SKILL BUILDER: TWO-WAY COMMUNICATION AND SOCIAL MEDIA

Throughout much of the past 100 years, marketing and public relations professionals have worked in concert with journalists to educate and inform the public. That is still an important part of what they do, but as you know, technologies such as the Internet, Facebook, and Twitter now make it possible to disseminate messages without going through formal media channels—and relatively inexpensively. That does not mean social media campaigns are always easy or effective. Here are some experts' suggestions for making the most of them.

- *Be interactive.* Health journalist Carrie Vaughan (2012) describes a hospital that had only 80 "friends" (most of them employees) on Facebook until the PR and marketing staff hosted an online cute-baby contest in conjunction with an upcoming event. The number of friends quickly soared to 1,153.
- *Link messages to key services.* To make the most of high readership numbers, link social media messages to services you would like to promote. Vaughan (2012) gives the example of a "What Do You Heart?" online contest linked to publicity about cardiac services.
- *Be educational.* Social media can allow people to watch medical procedures and receive other health-related information not previously available. The staff at Henry Ford Hospital in Detroit uses Twitter to record and broadcast some surgeries, along with the surgeons' comments. "Doing this removes a real communication barrier," says health care technology expert Charles Parks. "It helps make something scary much more comprehendable" (quoted by Cohen, 2009, para. 12). (If you are comfortable viewing surgery, enter search terms "Henry Ford Hospital" and "Twitter surgery" at YouTube.com to see samples for yourself.)
- *Integrate a range of channels.* The most effective campaigns involve a range of media—such as Facebook, Twitter, and blogs—and link one to the others (Vaughan, 2012).
- *Update people during a crisis.* Social media offer a quick and inexpensive way to keep people abreast of developments in a crisis. For example, when a broken water main left two million people near Boston without water, experts at Tufts University and the Boston Public Health Commission used brief text messages, emails, and Twitter feeds to notify people about water outages and to warn them to boil water that might have been contaminated by the breach. City officials also used computerized phone messages and megaphones to alert residents without access to social media (Gualtieri, 2011). Based on experiences such as these, experts recommend that organizations planning to use social media in crises enlist volunteers and train them in advance, keep messages succinct, monitor incoming messages, avoid sending inconsistent messages, and have a backup plan in case technology or connections fail (Currie, 2009).
- *Do not forget the "worried well."* Nathan Huebner of the CDC urges crisis managers to consider people who are not directly affected by a crisis but are distressed by it or anxious about loved ones. The "worried well" typically outnumber the people who are directly affected, Huebner points out, and keeping them well informed prevents undue anxiety and may keep them out of harm's

way themselves (Currie, 2009). For more on this topic, see Chapter 13 on public health and crisis communication.

- *Maintain relationships.* As we have discussed, strong relationships may enhance patient outcomes, build loyalty, and help with fundraising. Social media can help. A surgical weight loss center in Las Vegas regularly sends Facebook messages with encouraging words and links to healthy information to friends of the site (Patterson, 2012).
- *Develop a social media policy.* The downside of social media is that it is quick, accessible, and inexpensive for *everybody.* Comments posted on an employee's personal Facebook page can violate patient confidentiality or endanger partnerships with other organizations. Consequently, many organizations are educating employees about social media practices and establishing policies such as the following: Be respectful (avoid offensive, profane, embarrassing, or slanderous statements), uphold copyright laws, obtain approval before linking to the company website, maintain confidentiality concerning patients and proprietary information about the company, and do not speak as a member of the organization without getting approval to do so.

Crisis Management

Time magazine proclaimed it the "Summer of the Shark" in July 2001. One of the lead stories was about Jessie Arbogast, an 8-year-old who was bitten by a 7-foot shark while he waded knee-deep in the Gulf of Mexico.

Shark attacks are rare enough to be newsworthy no matter what, but this one was especially spellbinding. While the shark still had the boy's arm in its jaws, Jessie's uncle and another man grabbed the enormous animal by the tail and prevented it from dragging Jessie into deeper water. They were able to save the boy, but not his arm, which was severed by the shark's teeth.

Remarkably, the men managed to wrestle the 200-pound shark onto the beach while others carried Jessie to shore. Then, after medics loaded the boy onto an airmed helicopter, a park ranger and a lifeguard/firefighter recovered the boy's arm from the shark's mouth and sent it to the hospital via an ambulance. Jessie Arbogast suffered massive injuries and brain damage, but he lived, and surgeons were able to reattach his arm during a 12-hour surgery (Roche, 2001).

The remarkable story was covered by media outlets around the world, including CNN, ABC, NBC, CBS, and Fox News. Kendrick Doidge remembers because they were camped out in his parking lot. Soon after the shark attack occurred, Arbogast was a patient at Sacred Heart Hospital in Pensacola, where Doidge was marketing and public relations coordinator. "I received over 300 calls in 24 hours," he remembers. "As soon as Jessie Arbogast was transferred to our hospital, the parking lot filled with media live-remote trucks."

One of the crucial components of crisis management, says Doidge, is communicating well with everyone involved. After quickly securing permission to have the media trucks move to a shopping mall across the street so patients and their families would not be inconvenienced, Doidge and a diverse team of hospital personnel convened to put their crisis management plan into action.

"You have the most thorough crisis management plan you can, but every crisis is different," he says. "We got everyone together to organize how we would handle this one." During that meeting someone made a comment that set the tenor for the entire experience. Doidge explains:

> *The thing about a crisis is that it gets a lot of attention, but you still have other responsibilities you can't neglect. At that first meeting, someone said, "We're going to give Jessie Arbogast the best care possible. But we have 30 other children in that same unit. We can't lose sight of that either."*

From that point on, says Doidge, everyone thought in those terms. When the Mars candy company offered to send Snickers bars to Jessie because they heard he loved them, Doidge and his team were ready with an answer: "We said, 'Only if you send enough for all the kids on that unit,'" Doidge says. As a result, the company sent enough for all the young patients.

"When the governor of Florida and the governor of Alabama asked to visit Jessie in the hospital, we said, 'Okay, if you visit with *all* the patients and all their families,'" Doidge recalls. And they did. "When we had press conferences, we stressed to people, 'This is a team effort. This is what we do. We're doing everything possible for Jesse Arbogast, the same as we do for every child in our care,'" Doidge explains.

It's important to decide in advance who will be a spokesperson for the organization in the event of a crisis.

A cool head has earned Doidge accolades in crisis management. "I've learned you take your time, you listen to people, and you do the right thing," he says. "I'm a parent, and I know if my child were in the hospital, I wouldn't want to think that anything distracted the staff from providing the best care possible. That's what it comes down to, even in a crisis."

By their very nature, health organizations are likely to be part of crises. As Kathleen Fearn-Banks (1996) defines it, from an organizational perspective, a **crisis** is "a major occurrence with a potentially negative outcome affecting an organization, company, or industry, as well as its publics, products, services, or good name" (p. 1). In health care, the crisis usually has an external origin: a natural disaster, an accident, or an outbreak of contagious disease. In such cases, members of health care organizations (especially hospitals and health departments) may be called on to explain the crisis and to keep the public informed about it. In some cases, the crisis originates within the organization—a fire, a baby kidnapped from the nursery, charges of extortion. In any case, it is important to have a well-developed plan for handling crises, collecting information, and making information available to members of the organization, the media, and the public.

In Chapter 12, we talk extensively about handling public health crises, and many of the same principles apply, so we will keep this overview brief. But it is worth mentioning that crises have implications not just for the public. There is an organizational component as well. Crisis management is a job for communication specialists, especially those in public relations. Here are some helpful tips for preparing a crisis plan and managing publicity during a crisis, based on Fearn-Banks's book *Crisis Communication* (1996):

- Let people within the organization know what constitutes a crisis and whom to contact at the first sign of crisis.
- Designate a primary spokesperson for the organization (usually the CEO or public relations director), and help that person decide what information to release and how.
- Develop good relationships with media professionals before a crisis occurs, and do not play favorites during a crisis.
- Educate people in the organization about how to handle a crisis and how to get information.
- Keep up-to-date contact information for designated spokespersons, media professionals, stakeholders, and emergency management professionals.
- Maintain supplies that will be necessary if electricity or Web access is unavailable.
- Plan ahead how you will accommodate members of the media on site.

As you can see, none of the strategies outlined in this chapter occurs in isolation. Public relations specialists usually head crisis management teams, but they are the first to admit that outstanding team members make it possible to offer excellent service on an everyday basis and in extraordinary times. Leaders, human resource personnel, and others make that possible. Let's conclude the chapter with advice from service excellence experts.

Service Excellence Is Everyone's Job

Many of the ideas in this chapter are oriented to service excellence. Based on decades of experience conducting patient satisfaction surveys, Irwin Press (2002) presents five reasons to focus on patient satisfaction:

1. Patients are satisfied when they receive great care, even when that involves frightening and uncomfortable procedures.

2. Satisfied patients experience less stress than others.
3. Highly satisfied patients actually *feel* better than others and recover more quickly.
4. Patients who have positive experiences become "apostles" for the organization, promoting it to others.
5. There is a high correlation between satisfied employees and satisfied patients.

All of these add up to competitive strength and bottom-line gains. As much as 30% of profits are based on patient satisfaction (Press, 2002). And there is another reason not to be overlooked. In their book *Leadership for Great Customer Service,* Mayer and Cates (2004) suggest:

6. The number-one reason "to get customer service right in health care is . . . it makes the job easier" (p. 5).

Mayer and Cates observe that team members *like* coming to work when they feel they are making a difference rather than swimming upstream, when they enjoy the work they do and are able to have creative input, and when they feel valued and supported by coworkers and supervisors. Here are some tips from the experts on building cultures that sustain these ideals. You will see that much of the emphasis is on employee satisfaction. As many have observed, it is unlikely that dissatisfied employees will lead to happy customers, but happy employees will go far beyond the job description to do a good job.

BLOW THEIR MINDS

Doing the job right is not enough. People expect that. Inspiring customer loyalty requires giving people *more* than they expect. Mayer and Cates (2004) put it this way:

> *How much credit do we give airlines for getting us from point A to point B and not killing us? How about none—we expect that. Your patients expect excellent clinical care (the destination). But they also expect excellence service (the journey). (p. 26)*

The team at the Nordstrom department store calls it "fabled service"—the kind that people tell their friends about for years to come. By most estimates, customers who indicate they are "satisfied" (4 on a 5-point scale) may or may not come back to the organization. People *expect* to be satisfied. Only those who rate themselves "very satisfied" (5 on a 5-point scale) are likely to be loyal customers. Some organizations miss this distinction when they combine scores and conclude that, say, "95% of our customers are satisfied or very satisfied." Cognizant of the immense difference between "satisfied" and "very satisfied," for example, Disney considers anything less than a 5 to be a failing score (Lee, 2004).

RECOGNIZE AND CREATE MOMENTS OF TRUTH

Jan Carlzon, the highly successful CEO of Scandinavian Airlines, titled his 1987 memoir *Moments of Truth.* In the book Carlzon advanced the idea that satisfaction and loyalty are made or broken during 50,000 moments of truth every day. These occur any time people develop an impression of the organization based on how they are treated. The Mayo Clinic staff encountered a moment of truth when a woman seeking care in the emergency department declined to be admitted although she was quite ill. In encouraging her to share her concerns, the staff learned that she was from out of town and had left her dog in her truck, parked in the hospital lot. The staff might have discharged her as she requested. Instead, a nurse volunteered to take care of the woman's truck and her dog. The nurse was not even dissuaded when he realized the truck was an 18-wheeler. He got permission to park the truck at a local shopping mall for a few days and recruited a fellow nurse with a commercial license and truck-driving experience to move it there. Then the nurse looked after the woman's dog until she was well enough to leave the hospital.

USE SERVICE FAILURES AS A SPRINGBOARD

When employees of a large hospital were asked to think of times they had experienced outstanding customer service, their answers were inspiring, especially because many of their experiences began on a disappointing note.

One woman ordered a dress from a department store to attend her niece's wedding out of town. First, the store's tailor made a mistake with the alterations. Then the dress was not ready when it was promised. Eventually, it was the day before she was to fly out for the wedding and the woman still did not have her dress. She was frustrated and ready to buy something off the rack at another store and never do business with the original store again. But then a gracious sales associate called her to apologize and to say that she would personally drive to the tailor's, retrieve the dress, and deliver it to the woman's home that evening. The associate arrived on her doorstep with the dress as promised, and the woman was so touched by her apologies and extra effort that she has been a loyal customer ever since.

Another employee said she bought a new car, but two days later it died on her way to work. Frustrated and fearing that she had just invested in a lemon, the woman called the dealership. An associate answered immediately, apologized, and said he would be there (on the roadside where she was stranded) in 10 minutes. To her astonishment, he arrived even sooner, handed her the keys to a new loaner car, and encouraged her to be on her way. He waited for the tow truck, had the woman's car fixed (a minor adjustment to the computer), and delivered it to her driveway a few days later. She proclaims herself a lifelong customer.

These are not only stories of service; they are *service-recovery* stories. Things did not go perfectly. Indeed, in nearly every instance, the customer was ready to walk away forever—frustrated and inclined to tell everyone he or she knew about the poor treatment. But in each case, an associate (who was often not to blame for the service failure) turned the situation around by apologizing and giving far-better-than-expected service. The moral is that service recovery is often an opportunity to turn a customer into a loyal fan.

Mayer and Cates (2004) offer the following tips for service recovery:

- Address the issue immediately. Denying or ignoring a complaint is the worst thing you can do.
- Listen without interrupting, acknowledge the problem or mistake, and apologize for it.
- Ask for another chance to get it right.
- Ask how you can fix the problem, and tell the customer what to expect next.
- Fix it—and then some!
- Follow up, and let the person know what you have done to ensure that such mistakes do not happen in the future.

TELL STORIES AND HONOR HEROES

Stories such as the ones in this chapter become guiding principles for others. They portray what is best and most noble in the things we do. One of the most effective ways to support a culture is to encourage its stories. Good leaders appreciate their value and share them often.

Here is one more story, from Lafayette General Hospital in Lafayette, Louisiana. An ambulance arrived late in the evening on Christmas Eve with a woman and her two young children, who had been involved in an automobile accident. The children were okay, but the woman died soon after arriving at the hospital. Her husband was working on an offshore oil rig, and police were unable to reach him.

The emergency department staff was devastated for these two children who had just lost their mother and were stranded in a hospital with no family on Christmas Eve. The nurses, doctors, and unit receptionist tried to comfort and entertain the children as best they could until their shift change. The stores were closed, so they took turns driving to their homes to get supplies and gifts to create a makeshift holiday for the children. Sacrificing time they might have spent relaxing with their own families, the nurses worked into the night so that, when the children awoke on Christmas morning, the room was decorated with a tree surrounded by presents. Many staff members had brought their families to the hospital to share Christmas morning with the children.

"The employees' kids were amazing," remembers one nurse. "Here they were, in a hospital on Christmas morning, watching children they didn't know open gifts that had been under *their* trees with *their* names on them the day before. And they were just so happy to share. There wasn't a dry eye in the place, I can tell you!"

Summary

There is currently an opportunity and incentive to reimagine health care. The best ways to accomplish that are still emerging, but experts agree that it is crucial to transcend the traditional boundaries of health care to reach people where they live, work, and play. By empowering and supporting people in terms of their everyday behaviors, professionals may be able to improve overall health and reduce costs.

Health care administrators play a key role in uniting diverse people toward a common mission and enabling team members to do their best. Well-designed systems can also reduce stress and minimize errors.

Processes such as Six Sigma are designed to analyze workplace procedures carefully so that people can avoid wasting time and money. True empowerment means that administrators are servant leaders who are open to the ideas and concerns of team members who are encouraged to be decisive and accountable. In many health care organizations, employees are increasingly encouraged to think of ways to please customers, solve problems, work together in teams, and come up with innovative methods to improve care and conserve resources.

It is important to create appealing work environments and to retain and develop talented people in health care. Human resource personnel play an important role by helping to recruit, train, support, and retain outstanding team members. Informed by evidence that people perform best when they are actively engaged, human resource personnel can help people develop the skills and confidence to participate in decision making and leadership. To navigate the challenges ahead and offset staffing shortages, we must help health care professionals do their jobs without burning out. This means giving them the freedom to create pleasant work environments that foster teamwork and relieve stress, resisting the temptation to overwork staff members, and providing frequent breaks and replenishment.

With health care dollars limited and competition steep, people in health organizations are challenged to anticipate as accurately as possible what health services people are likely to want and need. Marketing and public relations professionals can help with this. They work to build trusting relationships with internal and external stakeholders to promote business, encourage healthy habits, and attract loyal patients and benefactors. Social media is emerging as a tool in the effort to maintain relationships, promote key services, educate people, and manage crisis communication.

Public relations professionals are often in charge of creating crisis communication plans on which they rely during natural disasters, image-threatening or high-profile events, health scares, and other situations that put health care organizations in the limelight. Handling crises well requires communication skills, preparation, a commitment to key values, and a willingness to handle unexpected demands.

Finally, excellence is everyone's job. People throughout health care organizations are called upon to offer legendary service, recognize moments of truth, overcome service obstacles, and honor the noble spirit of helping other people.

Key Terms and Theories

integrated health systems
Six Sigma
workarounds
Hoy-Tarter Model of Shared Decision Making
theory of personal causation
pawns
origins
Theory X and Theory Y managers
motivation-hygiene theory
motivators
hygiene factors
A-team and B-team players
commitment-trust theory of relationships
two-way symmetrical communication
corporate identity, image, and reputation
Point-A-to-Point-B companies
superficially image-based companies
reputation-based companies
crisis

Discussion Questions

1. If you had the opportunity to redesign health care, what might you do? Your ideas might focus on a doctor's visit or hospital stay in terms of how people would communicate; what would happen first, second, and third; what the environment would like or include; and so on. Or you might imagine services that are not currently offered, such as programs at work, home, community centers, supermarkets, or shopping malls.
2. Conduct an informal Six Sigma analysis of a process familiar to you, such as registering for classes or paying bills. Chart the steps involved, then identify aspects of the process that are more difficult or time consuming than they need to be. Brainstorm how you would improve the process to make it easier and more efficient.
3. Describe the best boss or teacher you have ever had. How did he or she communicate with others? How did he or she make you and other people feel? Which of the behaviors described in this chapter did that person embody?
4. Describe the best team you have ever been part of. What made the team successful? Describe how members communicated with one another.

What advice would you offer to human resources personnel to help them cultivate the same level of outstanding teamwork on the job?

5. Describe the factors that have contributed to staffing shortages in health care. Brainstorm ways we might minimize the barriers and encourage more people to pursue and maintain careers in health care.
6. Describe the significance of pawns and origins in de Charms's theory of personal causation. Give an example from your own experience in which you felt like a pawn and an example in which you were treated as an origin.
7. Imagine that you have been promoted to supervisor. If you adopt a Theory X approach, how will you treat team members? How will you treat them if you adopt a Theory Y approach? Which do you think will be more effective? Why?
8. Imagine that you do not make a lot of money, but you feel good every day thinking about the lives you change as a result of the work you do. Describe these factors based on motivation-hygiene theory.
9. Explain the concept of relationship marketing and relationship management. What are some of the main ideas that support a relationship approach to marketing and public relations? Include a description of the commitment-trust theory of relationships and two-way symmetrical communication in your answer.
10. What are the differences between corporate identity, image, and reputation? How do these concepts characterize Point-A-to-Point-B companies, superficially image-based companies, and reputation-based companies?
11. Identify several current examples of health-related social media messages. How effective do you think each message is? Why? How many of the tips presented in this chapter do the messages reflect?
12. How did Kendrick Doidge and the rest of the crisis management team respond when the hospital was besieged with media attention after a shark-attack patient was admitted? Do you agree with the way they handled the situation? Why or why not?
13. What are some suggestions for improving service excellence? Which are your favorites among the ones listed in this chapter?

Answers to *Can You Guess?*

Part 1

1. There are about 315,500 health care administrators in the United States.
2. They make an average of $88,580 per year ($42.59 per hour).
3. Employment prospects are expected to increase 23% between 2012 and 2022.

Source: U.S. Department of Labor, 2012

Part 2

The notice about hospital closures appeared in 1947, soon after the end of World War II ("Hospitals in the Red"). It does not make current challenges any less real, but sometimes it is nice to know we are not the first to face such a crisis, isn't it?

PART VI

Media, Public Policy, and Health Promotion

In this section we look at people and events that change the world. We explore the role of mass media in shaping cultural and global ideas about what it means to be healthy and successful. We also look at the efforts of public health experts and consider how we might apply the lessons from Ebola, AIDS, and terrorism to our own efforts. In the final two chapters, we use theory and expert advice to create a hypothetical public health campaign.

As you end this unit, I hope you will feel that your understanding of health communication has deepened and broadened. Keep an eye on the news. Health care is ever changing, and perhaps with the insights and examples we have discussed, you can take an active role yourself in shaping the future of health and health communication.

How wonderful it is that nobody need wait a single moment before starting to improve the world.

—ANNE FRANK

CHAPTER 11

Health Images in the Media

Most photos in popular magazines have been "airbrushed to perfection," in the words of researchers Lindsey Conlin and Kim Bissell (2014, p. 2.). To illustrate the point, the nonprofit advocacy group Global Democracy released a YouTube video showing how such a transformation occurs ("Body Evolution," 2012). In 71 seconds, viewers can watch a time-lapse process in which professionals add makeup and hair extensions to the model and then employ computer graphics to visually move her eyebrows higher on her forehead, change her skin tone, slim her torso and limbs, and lengthen her neck, arms, and legs.

The same illusionary tactics lie behind many media images, with the result that what *appears* to be real is not. Even the models themselves do not look like the stylized images others see of them. These unrealistic depictions have an influence on health when they affect people's self-esteem, their eating patterns, and more. About 24 million Americans (75% of them female) suffer from eating disorders, which represent the leading cause of death among women ages 15 to 24 years old (Alliance for Eating Disorders, 2015).

Women are not the only ones affected by media content, of course. In this chapter, we also explore the impact of mass-communicated messages on men, children, and adolescents. **Mass communication** is defined as the dissemination of messages from one person or group to large numbers of people via media including television, radio, computers, newspapers, magazines, billboards, video games, and other means. As you will see, there is evidence that media messages encourage people to overeat, doubt their attractiveness, drink alcohol, smoke, and neglect physical activity. However, the outlook is not entirely grim. Although media content can have harmful effects on health, it is also a means of sharing information that may enable people to better understand their health and health-related options.

As we explore the ways that mass media messages shape our ideas about health, we begin with health images in advertising, news, and entertainment. As you will see, research often shows a link between media use and behaviors such as overeating and drinking. Remember that this does not prove that the media, or the media alone, *cause* these behaviors. Mass-mediated messages are only one of many influences on health. Their effects are likely to be lessened or exaggerated by a range of other factors, including personal preferences, culture, social networks, and health status. The chapter concludes with information about media literacy—a systematic process of becoming more skeptical and better informed mass-media consumers so we do not unwittingly buy into harmful and unrealistic ideas.

HEALTH AND COMMUNICATION TECHNOLOGY

Nearly 8 in 10 teens in the United States have their own mobile phones, and 9 in 10 have computer access at home (Madden, Lenhart, Duggan, Cortesi, & Gasser, 2013). Teens in the lowest income brackets are most likely to rely on phones for internet access rather than logging on via desktop computers or electronic tablets. For this reason, health messages communicated via mobile technology may have the greatest chance of reaching youth in need.

Most of us feel that we are not personally susceptible to persuasive messages in the media, but we think other people are. W. Phillips Davison (1983) coined the term **third-person effect** to describe this perception. For example, teens often believe their peers will be more likely to smoke if they see pro-smoking messages in the media, but they tend to feel immune from that effect themselves (Gunther, Bolt, Borzekowski, Liebhart, & Dillard, 2006). Here is a look at some theories behind media effects, followed by some examples of the health-related messages we encounter every day.

WHAT DO YOU THINK?

- How much time, per day, do you spend watching television? Playing video games? Texting? Talking on the phone?
- Are you influenced by media messages? If so, how?
- Do you assume that other people are influenced by media messages? Why or why not?

Theoretical Foundations

In a video about sexist images in advertising, Jean Kilbourne (2000) observes that people frequently tell her they are not affected by the media. "Of course, they are usually standing there in their Gap t-shirt while they say this," she laughs.

In reality, we are all affected by media messages to varying extents, and the impact is greatest if we spend a lot of time with media and have limited personal experience with the phenomena we see depicted. The two theories described here—cultivation theory and social comparison theory—consider how media messages influence our attitudes and expectations about the world. Before we look at them, let's review the figures on media use among children and teens today.

What used to be considered heavy media use is now the norm. According to an extensive study by the Henry J. Kaiser Family Foundation (2010), U.S. children ages 8 to 18 spend slightly more than 7½ hours a day (about 2,786 hours a year) engaged with entertainment media devices such as smartphones, MP3 players, computer tablets, and television—sometimes several of them at once. The average is lower (about 4½ hours per day) among children whose parents have set time limits on media use, but only about 30% of youth fall into that category. And the average is much higher (about 13 hours a day) among heavy users, who tend to make poor grades, experience more sadness, and get into more trouble than their peers. Black and Hispanic children tend to fall disproportionately in the range of heavy media use, especially TV watching.

Cultivation theory helps to explain why children may be especially vulnerable to advertising messages. According to the theory, people develop beliefs about the world based on a complex array of influences, including the media. Media's influence is not uniform or automatic, but it is likely to be most profound if (a) media images are highly consistent, (b) people are exposed to large amounts of media, and (c) these people have a limited basis for evaluating what they see and hear (Gerbner, Gross, Morgan, & Signorielli, 1994). To clarify, consider that children have fewer experiences and less knowledge than adults. Because of this, they are less able to perceive that media images may be wrong or unrealistic. The same principle would hold true if you watched a documentary about a faraway land about which you knew very little. People familiar with that land might see inaccuracies in the documentary that you would be unable to identify.

The effect is compounded among high media users because not only is their exposure high, but the more time they spend tuned into mass media, the less opportunity they have to experience activities that might provide a basis for comparison. Children in the

United States who watch a lot of television aimed at young audiences are inundated with depictions of heterosexual romance in which boys mostly value females for their physical appearance and girls spend their time trying to look attractive for boys and complimenting boys on their personalities and accomplishments (Kirsch & Murnen, 2015). Considering that children typically regard media characters as peer role models, these consistent characterizations are likely to influence how they view themselves and those around them.

Social comparison theory helps to explain why people yearn to emulate the models they see in the media. Proposed by Leon Festinger (1957), **social comparison theory** suggests that people judge themselves largely in comparison to others. Want to know if you are attractive, popular, healthy, or smart? The only answer may lie in how you stack up to the people around you. Social comparisons can be useful when they enhance self-esteem or serve as the basis for reasonable self-improvement. However, they become dysfunctional when the comparison establishes an unrealistic standard (like being supermodel thin or weightlifter strong).

WHAT DO YOU THINK?

- Researchers have found that some people suffer low self-esteem because they regularly compare themselves to unrealistic standards such as supermodels or bodybuilders. Do you find yourself doing that? Why or why not?
- If you are around children, what reactions do you observe as they are exposed to messages in the media?
- How do you think we can minimize the effects of media images that establish unrealistic standards of attractiveness?

Next, let's look at deliberate attempts to influence people's behavior through advertisements for health-related products.

Advertising

Can you fill in the blanks to complete the following slogans?

Melts in your mouth, not in your ____________.
*Tastes great, less*______.
Just ________ *it.*
*I'm*_________ *it.*

If you guessed *hands* (M&Ms), *filling* (Miller Lite), *do* (Nike), and *lovin'* (McDonalds), you are right. But perhaps you do not usually stop to think about the connection between brand-name exposure and health. In this section we explore the impact of mass media advertising in terms of prescription drugs, nutrition, tobacco and alcohol use, and body image.

PHARMACEUTICAL ADVERTISEMENTS

> *This product may cause headaches, drowsiness, stomach upset, liver problems, heartbeat irregularities . . .*

Side effects such as these probably sound familiar. But that was not always the case. Brand-name pharmaceutical ads were not allowed in the United States until 1997. Before that, pharmaceutical companies marketed their products to physicians. Now, **direct-to-consumer (DTC)** advertisements—those that encourage everyday people to consider and ask about particular drugs—comprise a $3-billion-a-year industry in the United States (Swanson, 2015).

Brand names such as Claritin, Lipitor, and Viagra have become as familiar as Coca-Cola and Tide. (See Box 11.1 for more about Viagra advertising.) And along with the ads have come a now-familiar list of disclaimers—so familiar that one guest on an online medical site asked the doctor, "Do *all* prescription drugs cause diarrhea and dry mouth?" These *are* common side effects, but you hear about them so much because of a rather nebulous FDA guideline known as "fair balance," which states that, if advertisers present the potential benefits of a drug, they must also report potentially harmful side effects. In the name of fairness (sort of), for every promise of relief you are likely to hear a list of disagreeable outcomes you might also experience. The "sort of" means that the guideline is only loosely and rather lopsidedly upheld. For quick evidence of this, compare the lengthy information in a magazine pharmaceutical ad to the brief disclaimer you hear on a TV or radio commercial for the same drug.

IN YOUR EXPERIENCE

- Have you ever become interested in a drug because you saw it advertised? If so, why?
- Have you done research or asked your doctor or pharmacist about a particular drug? Why or why not?

BOX 11.1 PERSPECTIVES

Viagra Ads Promise Male Transformation

Commercials for erectile dysfunction have varied over time. The *Viva Viagra!* series showed an awkward man taking dance lessons with a Latina instructor, then the same man Viagra-transformed to "impress his partner." Then there were the "get things done" commercials. In one, a handsome man driving a muscle-car along a country road deftly gets his wheels rolling again after the car overheats, with the implication that he is also able to "get things done" in the bedroom with help from Viagra.

In 2014, Pfizer pharmaceuticals shed innuendo with a series of beautiful women who speak directly to men. In one, a woman lounges on a daybed in a tropical setting. "Plenty of guys have this issue—not just getting an erection, but keeping it," she says directly into the camera. "Well, Viagra helps. . . . Good to know, right?"

Jay Baglia, author of *The Viagra Ad Venture* (2005), challenges viewers to think carefully about these ads. For one thing, he says, notice the age of the actors. Although erectile dysfunction (ED) is most common among men age 65 and older, Pfizer tends to target younger men, insinuating that their sexual performance could use a pharmaceutical boost as well. As a case in point, the provocative blonde in the "good to know" commercials is 44-year-old Linette Beaumont. She is presumably closer in age to the *sons* of most men for whom Viagra is medically indicated than to the men themselves.

Nevertheless, the ads seem to work. About 1 in 5 healthy men ages 18 to 30 have taken some form of erectile dysfunction drug, usually, they say, to boost their "sexual confidence" or "sexual performance" (Bechara, Casabé, De Bonis, Hellen, & Bertolino, 2010). The notion of Viagra as a recreational drug is serious, considering that the active ingredient, sildenafil, has been linked to 1,824 deaths as well as 14,818 instances of other serious adverse effects (Lowe & Costabile, 2012).

Baglia (2005) also challenges the insinuation that men's penises reflect their worth as people. The message in Viagra ads is clear, he says: "Nothing tells a man he is masculine—not muscles, earning potential, an attractive partner, or even height—so much as his erection does" (p. 9). And if that is not reductive and intimidating enough, Pfizer has raised the bar on acceptable "male sexual performance" so high that men are nearly certain to feel inadequate. A man who scores 21 points or fewer on Pfizer's 25-point Sexual Health Inventory for Men is instructed to ask his doctor for help. In the tricky game of measuring up to social expectations, it seems Pfizer has defined *normal* and *masculine* to suit its own ends (Baglia).

Judging by the 25 million males who have secured Viagra prescriptions so far (*Viva Viagra*, 2008), men are buying it—literally and figuratively. "You get the 24-year-old who thinks he has erectile dysfunction if they stay up all night and can't get up and do it five times the next morning," says Thomas Jarrett, MD, head of urology at George Washington University (quoted by James, 2011, para. 19).

Baglia (2005) also points out that, in the pervasive images that Pfizer presents, masculinity is portrayed in mostly White, relentlessly heterosexual ways. In this context, "other ways of being a socio/sexual human being don't exist" he says (2005, p. 98).

Finally, the suggestion that Viagra yields virility, confidence, and sexual fulfillment is so palpable that it overshadows what Viagra does *not* do. "What happens when a man first takes a Viagra pill? Absolutely nothing," writes Tara Parker-Pope (2002, para. 10). She explains that the drug is not an aphrodisiac, adding that "the nothingness is so intense that the most common reaction is a slight panic that the drug isn't going to work" (para. 11).

Just as Viagra does not produce sexual feelings in men, neither does it create intimacy between people. True intimacy, Baglia (2005) reminds us, does not come in a pill but through communication, closeness, trust, and mutual respect. And sex comes in many forms that do not require a rigid member, served up pronto. Baglia quotes a *Newsweek* reporter who made the point that "a poor lover plus Viagra does not make a good lover, but merely a poor lover with an erection" (p. 37).

The "fair balance" guideline also explains why some prescription drug ads make no claims at all. The announcer might just say, "Ask your doctor about Zyrtec." Based on FDA guidelines, an ad that does not make a *positive* claim does not have to provide cautionary information either. In the case of no-claim ads, sponsors apparently believe that you will recognize the drug and its purpose by name, that the disclaimers, if mentioned, would scare you away, or that you will be curious enough to ask about or research the drug.

Advantages of DTC Advertising

From one angle, advertisements for needed products are beneficial. Without them, consumers might not know that treatment options are available for indigestion, asthma, allergies, depression, restless legs, and the like. That is not to say that a large percentage of people actually ask health care providers about advertised drugs. Only about 1 in 4 patients actually raises the topic of a specific drug (Wood & Cronley, 2014). When they do raise the subject, it is usually with their doctors (43% of the time) and their pharmacists (25% of the time) (A. Lee, 2010). Although people consult pharmacists less frequently than doctors, they tend to put great stock in pharmacists' opinions, even to the extent of switching doctors if they are unreceptive to pharmacists' advice (A. Lee, 2010).

Another advantage of DTC advertising is that active competition can inspire product development. We presumably benefit when drug companies strive to offer the most appealing and useful products. Marketplace stimulation has not lived up to its full potential, however. A substantial number of "new" drugs are actually what Marcia Angell (2004) calls "me too" drugs—close copycats of already existing products.

Disadvantages of DTC Advertising

Although health information is beneficial within limits, expensive advertising has drawbacks. First, big drug companies now spend more on advertising than they do on research and development (Swanson, 2015). At the same time, prescription drug prices have risen by more than 26% since 2005 for the drugs used the most by older Americans (Thomas, 2012). That is double the average price increase on consumer goods during that time.

Second, health professionals worry that, based on the dazzling scenarios in prescription-drug commercials, people may believe that high-priced designer drugs are better than others and that drugs will not only cure anything that ails them, but will yield increased happiness and excitement as well. Consider a few examples from Rebecca Cline and Henry Young's (2004) content analysis of pharmaceutical ads:

- 93% of the models in arthritis drug ads were shown engaging in physical activity,
- 100% of the models in ads for HIV treatments appeared healthy, and
- 85.7% of models in cancer-related ads appeared healthy.

"The message is obvious," the researchers conclude. "With treatment by prescription drugs, the consumer with the associated condition can be attractively healthy looking and lively" (Cline & Young, 2004, p. 151). As a result of such unrealistic expectations, consumers may squander money on unnecessary medications, seek prescriptions for the wrong reasons, feel disappointed when their doctors do not prescribe the drugs they see in the media, and feel discouraged when the results are less dramatic than advertisers have led them to believe. Critics also worry that ads promising "quick and easy" cures will dissuade people from taking care of themselves in the first place.

Third, in the interest of attracting consumers, drug companies sometimes downplay their products' risks. When Wendy Macias and colleagues studied 106 pharmaceutical TV commercials, they found that 2 violated the FDA's "fair balance" requirement and another 10 were borderline. The rest gave customary, but minimal, amounts of information about potential side effects (Macias, Pashupati, & Lewis, 2007). Even more frightening is evidence that the side effects drug companies report often come from research they have funded and overseen themselves. Researcher Sergio Sismondo (2008) concluded that pharmaceutical companies "not only fund clinical trials but also routinely design and shape them" (para. 5). He reports that these companies often have their staff statisticians perform data analyses and then hire people to write the research reports and corral them through the publication process. For example, after years of denying that its top-selling pain medication (Vioxx) posed significant health risks, Merck Pharmaceutical officials finally withdrew the drug in 2004. By that time, between 27,000 and 60,000 people had died from the drug's side effects (Lyon, 2007). In studying Merck documents and communiqués, researcher Alexander Lyon found that a pervasive "market mentality" led Merck decision makers to suppress and minimize information about Vioxx's harmful side effects.

Fourth, some experts worry that Americans are developing an unhealthy preoccupation with their own health, based largely on the amount of health care products and information now surrounding them. Some analysts have coined the term *cyberchondriacs* to describe people who are habitually fearful about their health because of how many health conditions and risk actors are brought to their attention every day (Vardigan, 2015).

Finally, while some people are overrepresented in DTC images, others are left out of the picture, reinforcing health disparities. For example, although heart disease is the leading cause of death among both men and women, nearly two in three ads show only men (Cline & Young, 2004). And African American and Hispanic models almost always play minor roles in general-audience DTC advertising, if they are pictured at all (Ball, Liang, & Wei-Na, 2009; Cline & Young, 2004; Mastin, Andsager, Choi, & Lee, 2007).

There are exceptions to the mostly White rule, but you have to look in Black-oriented publications to find most of them. According to research by Teresa Mastin and colleagues (2007), about 75% of the pharmaceutical ads in Black-oriented magazines feature only Black models. But even these ads present a distorted picture of what African Americans need. There are four times as many heart-care ads in magazines targeted to women in general than in magazines targeted specifically to African American women, although African Americans are at higher risk for heart disease than other groups. And 80% of the ads directed to Black females are for birth control pills, a bias that is not present in general-readership women's magazines. Mastin and colleagues conclude that direct-to-consumer ads are not educating *all* consumers about health risks and treatment options (Mastin et al., 2007).

Communication Skill Builder: Evaluating Medical Claims

As you have seen, consumers who rely on advertisements for health information do not always (or even often) get a clear picture. Here are some tips for evaluating the claims in medication ads.

- *Do not put too much stock in the wording.* Joel Davis (2007) found that people were most optimistic about drugs when the side effects were presented in language that downplayed their severity, such as "Side effects were mild and might include . . . ," "Side effects tend to be mild and often go away," and "Few people were bothered enough to stop taking the drug." Keep in mind that reassuring word choices do not necessarily mean these drugs are safer than others.
- *Look to print sources for detailed information.* Broadcast commercials mention potential side effects only briefly. Magazine ads include a great deal more information (Boden & Diamond, 2008).
- *"Newer" does not necessarily mean better.* Pharmaceutical companies vie for the public's attention by advertising the "newest" and "latest" therapies. But the rush to the marketplace does not actually mean the medication is "improved," or even that it is safe (Lyon, 2007).

Even advertisements that seem unrelated to health care often affect our health by influencing social expectations about how we should behave, what we should eat and drink, and how we should look. The remainder of this section discusses advertising's impact on nutrition, alcohol, and body image.

NUTRITION

It has been called the "coach potato physique," characterized by soft bulges where muscle ought to be. Heavy TV viewing is consistently linked to obesity, partly because television offers a triple punch to good nutrition. People usually burn few calories while watching, they have a tendency to snack while viewing, and the commercials usually encourage consumption of non-nutritious foods. In addition, commercials sometimes distort people's knowledge of nutrition and influence their food preferences for the worse. For example, teens who are heavy TV viewers tend to overestimate the nutritional value of fast food, perhaps because they see numerous commercials for it in the context of viewing mostly slim and fit people (Russell & Buhrau, 2015).

Obesity

The prevalence of TV commercials for fatty and sugary foods may have serious implications for health, considering that overweight people are at elevated risk for heart disease, cancer, diabetes, and sudden death.

African American women are at especially high risk for obesity and related concerns. This may be partly because of advertisements. When Linda Godbold Kean and Laura Prividera (2007) compared ads in *Essence* (aimed mostly at female African Americans) and *Cosmopolitan* (targeted to women in general), they found that 13% of the ads in *Essence* were for fast food, compared to 1% of the ads in *Cosmopolitan.*

In contrast to the average woman, who wears a size 12 to 14, fashion models typically wear sizes 0 or 2 (Betts, 2002).

Furthermore, *Cosmopolitan* readers were exposed to more weight-loss products and claims (mentioned in 41% of the ads) than were *Essence* readers (12% of ads). (While these messages may be helpful to *Cosmopolitan* readers trying to maintain a healthy weight, it should also be noted that many of the weight-loss claims—such as those for low-carbohydrate whiskey—were not exactly health conscious.)

The editorial content in women's magazines is not making up the difference. When Conlin and Bissell (2014) studied women's magazines, they found that both fashion and fitness magazines focused mostly on women's appearance rather than their health. In the fashion magazines, references to appearance outnumbered references to health nearly 19 to 1. But even in the fitness magazines, diet and physical activity were typically framed in terms of enhancing one's appearance rather than one's health. And appearance was measured mostly in terms of a "thin ideal" in all the magazines. Although many of the models appeared to be dangerously thin, they were promoted as being physically fit and appealing. The researchers concluded that women's magazines tend to frame health in terms of "thinness and glamor" (p. 12).

As the next section shows, weight and nutrition issues often begin in childhood.

Effects on Children

There is a consistent correlation between children's body mass index and their brand-name recognition of unhealthy products such as chips and cookies (Cornwell, McAlister, & Polmear-Swendris, 2014). This is a serious concern, considering that about 1 in 3 children and teens in the United States is overweight or obese (Ogden, Carroll, Kit, Flegal, 2014).

It seems to be no coincidence that weight has increased along with the availability of television, computers, and mobile devices. In the last 30 years, the number of obese children in the United States has doubled, and the number of obese adolescents has quadrupled (Ogden et al., 2014; National Center for Health Statistics, 2012).

Children are exposed to an average of 5,500 televised food commercials per year (Desrochers & Holt, 2007), and the commercials often misrepresent good nutrition. For example, no matter how much TV they watched at home, first through third graders in Kristin Harrison's (2005) study were roughly equivalent in their nutritional knowledge of products, such as fruit and dairy, that are not heavily advertised. But when Harrison asked the children to choose the more nutritional option between cottage cheese and fat-free ice cream and between orange juice and Diet Coke those who watched a lot of television were more likely to consider (incorrectly) that the highly advertised diet products were better for them. The chances are high, Harrison concluded, that children exposed to a lot of commercials will assume that diet products are, by nature, more nutritious than other foods.

When researchers showed preschoolers in the Netherlands fresh banana slices and banana candy, the children preferred the candy. But when they packaged the fresh fruit in packages decorated with popular cartoon characters, the children considered the fruit to be just as appealing as the candy (de Droog, Valkenburg, & Buijzen, 2011). The researchers propose that pairing fruit with images that children already view favorably may increase its appeal.

The distortion continues in the supermarket. A Canadian study of 367 products marketed to children revealed that 89% of them were unhealthy (Elliott, 2007). Nevertheless, 62% of the products with high levels of sugar, fat, and sodium came in packages that touted their "nutritional value."

CAN YOU GUESS? PART 1

1. Worldwide, how does the number of people who are obese today compare with the number in 1980?
2. What percentage of children in the United States are obese today?

Answers appears at the end of this chapter.

Activity Levels

It should be noted that advertising is not entirely to blame for the obesity linked to TV viewing. Some researchers suggest that the sedentary nature of heavy viewing is as unhealthy as the content. Children and teens with televisions in their bedrooms are heavier, on average, than their peers (Rey-Lopez et al., 2012). And heavy television viewing may lead to other unhealthy behaviors. For example, youngsters with high media exposure are more likely than their peers to smoke (Yang, Salmon, Pang, & Cheng, 2015). Researchers speculate that extensive viewing substitutes for physical activities and social development that might otherwise help teens avoid peer pressure.

High media use is also linked to sleep deprivation. Children today sleep an average of two hours less per night than children in the early 1980s (Zimmerman, 2008). Authorities blame TV, video, the Internet, and computer games. They say these activities sometimes cut into sleep time and leave children too excited to sleep when the lights go out. Children may also feel less sleepy because they are not getting much exercise and because the glow from TV and computer screens inhibits melatonin secretion, an important chemical in sleep functioning (Zimmerman, 2008).

If media messages influence the way we eat, they are also likely to influence the way we drink and whether we use tobacco. Particularly worrisome are appeals to youthful audiences, as we will discuss next.

TOBACCO

In 1994, some 46 states entered an agreement with the tobacco industry that included restrictions on the number and placement of tobacco advertisements. The Master Settlement Agreement (MSA), as it is called, bans tobacco advertising in public transit systems, on television, and in the movies, and it severely limits the placement of tobacco billboards near sports stadiums, shopping malls, arcades, and other places that youth frequent. The MSA is meant to restrict tobacco marketing overall, but in particular, to shield youthful audiences from it. Beyond requiring a warning label, the rules do not restrict the content of tobacco ads or packaging, however.

To see how promotional efforts have changed over time, Tae Hyun Baek and Mark Mayer (2010) compared tobacco ads in *Cosmopolitan, Sports Illustrated,* and *Rolling Stone* in 1994 with those that ran nearly 10 years later. They found that the ads have become more sexually suggestive since 1994—frequently featuring young, scantily clad women—and more, rather than fewer, youthful models. "This use of models, especially women, as sexual objects or decoration in advertisement is not a new phenomenon," the researchers reflect, but it is disappointing, they say, that companies continue to depict smokers as young and sexy.

There is further evidence that tobacco companies have stepped up their implicit marketing efforts since the MSA. When Hye-Jin Paek and colleagues (2010) studied nearly 50 years of cigarette advertising in U.S. magazines, they identified a trend. Beginning in the 1930s, tobacco companies often touted the "health benefits" of smoking, such as soothing the throat, preventing coughs, and enhancing relaxation. (Yes, they actually claimed that cigarettes *prevent* coughs and throat irritation.) Those false claims ended in the 1950s, under pressure from the Federal Trade Commission (FTC). After that, tobacco ads and packages included implicit, rather than outright, claims in favor of smoking. For example, marketers began relying on visual cues suggesting that smokers are popular, attractive, healthy, and relaxed, and that smoking is natural and soothing (associated with pleasant scenes from nature). Paek and collaborators found that pleasing images, such as attractive models interacting socially while smoking, are even more prevalent since the MSA than they were before it (Paek, Reid, Choi, & Jeong, 2010).

ALCOHOL

Beer commercials often show drinkers surrounded by beautiful women, fun-loving friends, and exotic locales. But the reality is not nearly so glamorous. Alcohol-related accidents kill 5,000 underage drinkers per year in the United States, and the risk of drinking problems later in life is 5 times greater for people who begin drinking before age 15 than for those who wait until they are 21 ("Underage Drinking," 2012). Heavy drinkers risk liver damage, hypertension, and strokes, and they are more likely than their peers to hurt others, and to be hurt, in accidents and acts of violence (Nestle, 1997). Considering these risks, beer companies are sometimes criticized for portraying drinking episodes as fun and sexy.

Health warnings all but drown in the ocean of pro-alcohol messages. Alcoholic beverage ads outnumber responsible drinking PSAs at least 22 to 1 ("Youth Exposure," 2010). And the ads have appeal. When market researchers asked teens to name their five favorite Super Bowl commercials, three of them were for beer ("Beer Commercials," 2009). Young people may remember and like these commercials so much because the spots are designed for them. Consider the following:

- Youth ages 21 and younger were exposed to 71% more alcohol advertising in 2009 than were youth of the same age in 2001 ("Youth Exposure," 2010).
- More alcoholic beverage commercials air before 9 p.m.—when you might expect young viewers to be watching—than later in the evening. Additionally, there is a spike in the number of commercials on weekdays from 3 p.m. to 5 p.m. Researchers speculate that these commercials are intentionally aimed at schoolchildren since "it would be a reasonable assumption that most people in employment will not have returned home until after 5 p.m." (Alcohol Concern, 2007, p. 13).
- Nearly one-third of radio ads for alcoholic beverages are aired when the listening audience is mostly teens rather than adults ("Youth Exposure," 2011).
- Promotional efforts for alcopops (alcoholic beverages mixed with fruit juice or other flavoring) and wine are most often broadcast on the radio when teenage girls, rather than women, are likely to be listening ("Youth Exposure," 2011).
- African American youth see about 42% more ads for distilled spirits than youth in general ("African-American," 2012).

CAN YOU GUESS? PART 2

?

- What percent of eighth graders in the United States has drunk alcohol in the last 30 days?
- Kids are more likely to see alcohol ads than adults are. How many more ads are they likely to see than their parents in a typical year?

Answers appear at the end of the chapter.

Alcoholic beverage companies buy heavily in magazines aimed at young, minority audiences and employ youthful spokespersons designed to catch the attention of young people. Says the director of an alcohol and drug recovery center in San Francisco, "The models they use in the ads have to be 21, but they're the youngest 21-year-olds you'll ever see" (quoted by F. Green, 2003, p. 1C).

This early exposure seems to make a significant difference. Peter Anderson and colleagues (2009) reviewed 13 longitudinal studies about alcohol use. They found that 12 of the 13 studies provided evidence that teens who are regularly exposed to positive messages about drinking, either in movies or advertisements, are more likely than their peers to drink heavily and to start drinking at an early age (Anderson, de Bruijn, Angus, Gordon, & Hastings, 2009).

The good news is that, despite the odds, responsible drinking messages may have some influence. When analysts reviewed 14 years of research about the effects of campaigns to discourage underage drinking, they found that there were small but significant reductions in the number of teen drinkers over time (Kyrrestad Strøm, Adolfsen, Fossum, Kaiser, & Martinussen, 2014).

BODY IMAGE

Jacob saunters in, leanly muscled and confident, armed with darts, knives, guns, and other devices ready at hand. He is a "charismatic brawler," a fearless fighter who impudently wears his top hat into battle (*Corriea, 2015, para. 18.*)

Jacob is one of the main characters in the video game *Assassin's Creed Syndicate*. Some analysts propose that Jacob and similar video heroes provide a healthy outlet for children and their imaginations. Others worry that video game characters present an unattainable version of what it means to be masculine. Male avatars tend to be both dramatically more slender and more muscular than flesh-and-blood men. One result is that male players often report feeling especially confident and powerful while they embody these personae online, but especially *inadequate* in real life, feeling that their weight and muscularity do not measure up (Cacioli & Mussap, 2014).

Video games are not alone in this regard. Media consumers are consistently urged to believe that their skin, weight, hair, breath, clothing, and teeth are "problem areas" requiring vigorous and immediate attention—at a price. Theorists call this **pathologizing the human body**, making natural functions seem weird and unnatural (Wood, 1999). In short, advertisers are accused of making people feel bad about themselves so they will be willing to pay for "needed" changes.

Teenagers are particularly susceptible to these messages. With the physical and social changes of adolescence comes a heightened self-consciousness that makes it easy to escalate (and capitalize on) teens' insecurity. Media messages often encourage an obsessive concern with physical appearance, sometimes to the detriment of people's health and self-esteem. As a case in point, nearly 68,000 people, mostly tweens (ages 10–13) and teens, have posted "Am I Pretty or Ugly?" videos on YouTube, seeking reassurance in the very mass-media environment that often feeds their insecurities in the first place. One 13-year-old, who whispered into the camera, "I could be the ugliest person that could ever be living. Be honest and tell me if I am ugly or not" inspired tens of thousands of viewings. Some people posted reassuring comments, whereas others were demeaning and even suggested that she kill herself (Quenqua, 2014). As one analyst observes, 13-year-olds through the ages have wondered if they are attractive or not, but these days, they have the power to broadcast those feelings of insecurity and curiosity to the world, and perhaps be subjected to insults and bullying that would crumble the confidence of even the most confident adult (Quenqua, 2014).

In the context of their insecurities, teens are encouraged to buy (or convince their parents to buy) skin care creams, lotions, powders, perfume, makeup, shaving cream, shampoo, bath oil, mouthwash, toothpaste, and more. Aside from making teens feel unattractive without them, these products can pose health risks when they cause rashes, hives, eye irritation, or other reactions.

One problem is that many media images and cultural icons are inherently unrealistic. For example, to attain the proportions of a Barbie doll, a woman would have to be more than 7 feet tall, with a bust 5 inches larger than normal and a waist 6 inches smaller (Duewald, 2003). (See Box 11.2 for more about Barbie.) Likewise, many of today's action figure toys bear little resemblance to actual body types (see Box 11.3). "When did male body hair become a bad thing?" asks a reporter for *The Guardian* (Bilmes, 2014). Apparently college women wonder the same thing. Although most female students surveyed said they like or do not mind body hair on men, most male students said they regularly remove body hair and believe it is sexier to be bare (Basow & O'Neil, 2014).

Abercrombie & Fitch models pose at the grand opening of a store in Munich, Germany, representing a trend toward what some analysts call the sanitized male, distinguished by ripped abs, a hairless body, smooth skin, and grooming so meticulous that he nearly looks plastic.

Health Effects

"Self-acceptance has become a movement," says fashion writer Shaun Dreisbach (2014, para. 2). Celebrities now post bare-faced selfies, defend their cellulite, and say they love their bodies. All the while, everyday women

Box 11.2 PERSPECTIVES

Barbie: Feminist Icon or Woman as Sex Object?

By Annina Dahlstrom

When Barbie debuted in 1959, the second wave of feminism was gaining momentum. The doll's long limbs, overtly curvaceous figure, and lavish wardrobe distinguished her in what had mostly been a *baby* doll market until that time. She also represented a shift from the traditional view of women as mothers and housewives. From some perspectives, Barbie represented the new self-confident and independent woman of the future (Forman-Brunell, n.d.)—albeit with outlandishly impossible proportions and a sex-centric appearance (Alter, 2014).

Although it is unclear how much of the resemblance is due to plastic surgery and how much to makeup, one thing is for certain: Real-life Barbie look-alike Valeria Lukyanova has become a celebrity lightning rod for controversy about the notion of Barbie as a role model (Conley, 2012).

In the decades since, Barbie has inspired her share of dismay and revulsion. Diane Levin and Jean Kilbourne feature her in *So Sexy So Soon* (2008), a book about the harmful effects of overexposing young children to sexuality. As Levin puts it, "when Barbie came around, play suddenly became about dressing up and looking right and it eventually played a role in how women wanted to look in real life" (quoted by Conley, 2012, para. 8). Some Barbie admirers have taken that to extremes, having their faces and bodies medically altered to look more like the vinyl and plastic icon. Others fuel the demand for hundreds of YouTube tutorials on how to emulate Barbie's makeup and wardrobe.

Spokespersons for Mattel, which markets Barbie, counter that detractors are being size-ist. They defend their tiny trendsetter (who in real life would be nearing retirement age) by saying that there is room—in the doll world and the people world—for bodies of all sizes. Mattel has launched a Barbie Twitter campaign to declare (in glittery, pink text) *Be You. Be Bold. Be #Unapologetic* (Barbie, 2014) and an "Anything is Possible" campaign that draws attention to the 150+ careers Barbie has pursued, including Entrepreneur Barbie of 2014, who has her own LinkedIn account. Lisa McKnight, senior VP of marketing for Mattel North America, stands firm that Barbie is a hard-working feminist icon and says "we will continue to promote Barbie in this way for many years to come" (Bulik, 2014, para. 16).

Meanwhile, Barbie's market share has been eroded by a new wave of sexed-up dolls, such as the Monster High collection, that are marketed to an even younger demographic. One cultural observer refers to the newcomers as "younger, sluttier dolls with bigger heads" who "dress like prostitutes and have the dimensions of lollipops" (Alter, 2014, paras. 2 and 3).

On the other side of the issue, Lammily dolls have realistic body proportions and come complete with optional cellulite, stretch marks, acne, tattoos, and freckles, among other features, known as "Lammily Marks." When they were introduced on a crowd-funding website, 13,621 supporters preordered 19,000 Lammily dolls. (See more at http://lammily.com/about/.)

continued

What Do You Think?

1. Do you agree more with the idea that Barbie inspires objectification of women and unrealistic standards of beauty or that she is a symbol of feminine diversity and empowerment? Why?
2. Would you prefer that your young daughter or niece play with Barbie or a Lammily doll? Why?

Box 11.3 PERSPECTIVES

Boys' Toys on Steroids

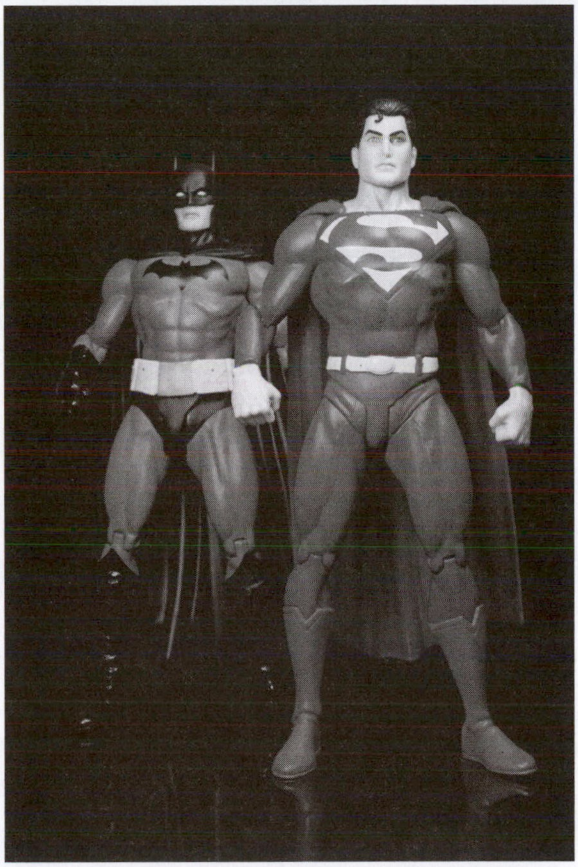

Even with starvation dieting and steroids, it would be impossible for most boys to grow up looking like popular action figures.

At the same time females are encouraged to be thin, boys' toys encourage them to be marathoner sleek and bodybuilder strong. One role model guiding the male psyche toward this conclusion is stiff, smooth, small, and plastic. Many of the male action figures popular today are implausibly slim waisted, hypermuscular, and lean. "Only 1 or 2 percent of [males] actually have that body type," protests psychologist Raymond Lemberg. "We're presenting men in a way that is unnatural" (quoted by Santa Cruz, 2014, para. 8).

Take G.I. Joe as an example. In the 1960s, he had the athletic proportions of a 5-foot-10-inch man with a 32-inch waist and 12-inch biceps. However, if today's G.I. Joe Extreme figurine were inflated to life size, he would have a 29-inch waist (more than 10 inches smaller than the average American man's) and his 32-inch biceps would literally set a new bodybuilding world record (Moss, 2011).

"So here we are," says health sciences professor Tim Olds, "surrounded by images of ideal bodies: actors, sports stars, steroid-pumped bodybuilders, shop mannequins, dolls, dolled-up personal trainers, air-brushed models and digitally-enhanced video game avatars. And not one of them reflects reality" (Olds, 2014, para. 5). His advice? "I'm not G.I. Joe and you're not Barbie, but . . . there are a lot more people in this world like you and me than there are like these dolls. Aim for good health and get comfortable with your normality" (last para.).

are serving as CEOs, adventurers, professional athletes, and more. "So our body confidence should be better, right?" asks Dreisbach (para. 2). As it turns out, progress is marginal at best for women. And for men, it has gotten worse.

Today, about 13% of women and 9% of men in the United States are dissatisfied with their overall appearance, and double or triple that are unhappy with particular areas of their bodies (Fallon, Harris, & Johnson, 2014).

Although obesity is a serious health threat, extreme efforts to change one's weight can also be dangerous or even deadly. About 30 million Americans (two-thirds of them female) will suffer from an eating disorder sometime in their lives, which may damage their hearts and livers, make their bones brittle, and even kill them (National Eating Disorders Association, 2015). Although eating disorders often start in adolescence, they do not end there. In fact, children are likely to feel that their bodies are inferior partly because their parents are preoccupied about their own weight and appearance.

Abusing anabolic steroids to become more muscular is another problem. More than 1 million Americans (most of them male) have abused steroids (National Institute on Drug Abuse [NIDA], 2007). The risks include cardiovascular disease, liver damage, hair loss, sterility, aggressiveness, and depression. Researchers observe that, for most steroid users, the goal is to measure up to Western ideals of masculine attractiveness rather than to excel at sports. Steroid use is unusually high among men ages 22 to 35 who are fans of bodybuilding magazines and TV programs and those who are exposed to explicit pornography (Melki, Hitti, Oghia, & Mufarrij, 2015). They are more likely than other men to think that women like men with large muscles and to feel that muscular men in the media are a realistic benchmark of masculine appearance.

> **CAN YOU GUESS? PART 3**
>
> 1. How many minutes per hour does the typical TV station devote to public service announcements (PSAs)?
> 2. By the time a person is 65, how much time has he or she probably spent watching television?
>
> *Answers appear at the end of the chapter.*

Beauty Sells . . . Sometimes

Why do we buy what the media sells? There is evidence that people sometimes feel a vicarious sense of well-being and optimism when they see idealized models in the media. That's one reason advertisers tend to use beautiful people to sell products that have nothing to do with improving one's appearance. "Seeing a pretty person activates thoughts of 'goodness,' which extends to our evaluations of other things," says one psychology scholar ("Beautiful People," 2011, para. 8). When the advertisement *is* for a beauty enhancement, such as cosmetics or shampoo, people may react one of two ways, she says. Those who think their own appearance will not change substantially are typically skeptical and even angered by the unrealistic depiction. On the other hand, people who are optimistic that the product will make them attractive, too, are usually drawn to it. (Of course, this optimism can backfire if it turns out to be a false hope.)

Let's turn, now, to a different type of programming that often includes health-related messages.

News Coverage

"New Study Suggests that Vaccines Don't Cause Autism"

How do you think people would respond if they saw this banner on the day's news? Christopher Clarke and colleagues (2015) used the headline in a study that compared readers' responses to three slightly different stories about the vaccine controversy.

The issue is an important one. Since 1998, when a medical study (later exposed to be fraudulent) proposed a link between autism and the measles-mumps-rubella (MMR) vaccine, a small but influential percentage of parents have declined to have their children immunized. Since then, outbreaks of the virus have reached record numbers in the United States and Europe among children who have not been immunized and those with medical conditions that make them vulnerable to the virus even if they have been vaccinated (CDC, 2015d; Fox & Connor, 2015). (See Chapter 12 for more about measles as a public health communication issue.)

Clarke and colleagues (2015) explored the conundrum that journalists are expected to present both sides of a controversial issue. At the same time, however, they may be considered irresponsible for presenting information that is not well supported by evidence. Clarke and collaborators created three versions of a *USA Today* story about vaccines. One version included a section describing the preponderance of scientific evidence that vaccines are safe and effective. Another included, instead, a section about advocacy groups and scientists who believe there is a vaccine–autism link. The third version included both of the sections just described. Participants who read the science-only and science-and-opposition versions were more likely to believe there is scientific consensus about the safety of vaccines than those who read only about opposition to vaccines. In other words, the presence of controversy did not significantly diminish most readers' confidence in scientific evidence. Clarke and his team concluded that journalists need not choose between presenting both sides of an issue and letting readers know that the weight of scientific evidence supports one side or the other (Clarke, Dixon, Holton, & McKeever, 2015).

Health news is instrumental in educating people. However, it is not an easy topic to cover. In the rush to provide the latest information, media professionals sometimes oversell scientific findings and overlook ongoing, everyday concerns. This section examines health news in terms of accuracy and sensationalism and discusses the advantages of media coverage.

ACCURACY AND FAIRNESS

Although many media professionals do an admirable job of informing the public about health issues, a sizable amount of health information available in the media is misleading and exaggerated. When researchers compared 462 press releases about health studies to the actual studies they described, they found that at least one-third of the press releases included exaggerated claims or unsupported generalizations. Media outlets often further exaggerated the claims before publishing them, resulting in health science news that was substantially inflated compared to the actual results (Sumner et al., 2014).

Overgeneralizations are common. For instance, a study of older women might be reported simply as a study about women or older adults, although the health concerns of these populations may be significantly different. Such inaccuracies are particularly troubling since it is often difficult for readers to verify scientific information for themselves.

One worry is that overly optimistic news about medical research will give people false hope. As early as 1997, headlines in major publications suggested an imminent cure for AIDS—such as "When AIDS Ends" in the *New York Times Magazine* and "The End of AIDS?" in *Newsweek*. Jon Cohen (1997) cautioned, "If treatments don't live up to unrealistic expectations, researchers fear a public backlash against medical science" (para. 2). Premature reports about cures for cancer raise the same fear. (See the *Check It Out!* box for more on the accuracy of health news sources.)

CHECK IT OUT!

Go to healthnewsreview.org to see how experts rate the accuracy of health news in specific TV programs, networks, magazines, and newspapers. You can also access a list of five-star health stories selected by experts on the basis of their accuracy and usefulness.

Sometimes the concept of "accuracy" is problematic in itself. For example, Brazilian and U.S. newspapers cover the issue of stem cell research differently. Brazilian papers tend to focus on it as a scientific matter, whereas American journalists more often focus on the ethical implications (Reis, 2008). Where health is concerned, there are more than two sides to any coin.

SENSATIONALISM

Media professionals are also criticized for favoring sensational health news rather than useful information about everyday concerns. Heart disease, which is the world's leading cause of death, typically receives less coverage than emergent issues such as Ebola. Coverage of other health issues is also skewed. Newspapers in the United States tend to overreport information on breast cancer, leukemia, pancreatic cancer, and bone/muscle cancer, especially when someone famous had been diagnosed with them. However, they underreport information about male reproductive cancer, lymphatic/Hodgkin's disease, and thyroid cancer (Jensen, Moriarty, Hurley, & Stryker, 2010). Likewise, although HIV and AIDS get a great deal of attention, less than 1% of the stories address their incidence in older adults, which may be one reason that people over age 50 know less about the subject than younger people do and tend to feel particularly shocked and ashamed if they become infected (LaVail, 2010). At the same time, reports about dire health threats, such as a potential bird flu pandemic, rely largely on emotional appeals and do not provide enough information for the public to feel prepared and confident if the crisis arises (Dudo, Dahlstrom, & Broussard, 2007).

In some instances, snappy headlines have little to do with conclusive evidence. In the United States, news coverage (especially TV news coverage) of cancer often highlights potential causes of cancer that have not yet been substantiated, such as dry cleaning chemicals, excessive exercise, and deodorant (Niederdeppe, Fowler, Goldstein, & Pribble, 2010). Partly for that reason, people who rely on TV news coverage a great deal are likely to think that cancer is unavoidable (Niederdeppe et al., 2010).

ADVANTAGES OF HEALTH NEWS

Despite the criticisms, health news does offer several advantages. Media organizations are credited with increasing people's awareness about health. And even when medical news is not what scientists would wish, its presence keeps health on the public agenda and (hopefully) garners support for medical science (Deary, Whiteman, & Fowkes, 1998). For example, coverage of breast cancer has substantially increased since the 1970s and has focused mostly on new treatment methods and scientific breakthroughs (S. Cho, 2006). That is good, except that some other forms of cancer receive minimal coverage by comparison.

It should also be said that news writers are not entirely to blame for misleading health coverage. The fault lies partly with the nature of news and the nature of science. News, especially TV news, is brief by nature. About 74.5% of TV news stories last less than 60 seconds (Wang & Gantz, 2010). Furthermore, it is the nature of news to be unusual and recent. The public is hungry for current and interesting information, and media professionals strive to provide it. However, it is the nature of science to be meticulous and cautious, weighing diverse evidence over long periods of time (Taubes, 1998). Consequently, news writers are at a disadvantage in trying to cover scientific news accurately. The latest groundbreaking study may reach different conclusions from the study before it or after it. Science is full of reliable accounts that, for one reason or another, arrive at different conclusions, so that even experts do not agree.

Furthermore, reporters may be ill prepared to meet the extraordinary challenges that health coverage presents. Medical terminology and statistical analyses make medical science difficult to understand and interpret, and comparatively few reporters are trained to do so (Tanner, Friedman, & Zheng, 2015). On the bright side, with many sources of health news available, the chances are greater that people can evaluate and compare information, judging for themselves what is credible and useful.

COMMUNICATION SKILL BUILDER: PRESENTING HEALTH NEWS

Here are some suggestions offered by Melissa Ludtke and Cathy Trost (1998) and the Association of Health Care Journalists (2015) to help media news writers present fair and accurate coverage.

- *Favor the factual over the sensational and trendy.*
- *Do not allow ongoing issues to fade from coverage.* "Put a fresh face on coverage of long-standing health issues like asthma, lead poisoning and infant mortality" (Ludtke & Trost, 1998, para. 20).
- *Do not forget rural America.* Health issues outside the big city are important in their own right.
- *Never rely on just one source.* Consult a number of experts; read a variety of reliable literature.
- *Seek training.* Seek out lectures, workshops, and conferences at which you can learn the lingo and become proficient at interpreting health science.
- *Set the record straight.* If a health news item is revealed to be untrue or misleading, update the public.

Also see Box 11.4 for career opportunities in health journalism.

Entertainment

In this section we examine how health issues and medical care are portrayed in entertainment programming. We first explore depictions of mental illness and disabilities. We then switch gears to focus on sex and violence in the media and, finally, on fictional portrayals of health care settings. These topics reflect the preponderance of research about entertainment programming and health.

Box 11.4 CAREER OPPORTUNITIES

Health Journalism

Print or broadcast health news reporter
Health news editor
Media relations specialist
Nonprofit organization publicity manager
Health publication editor
Journal or magazine editor

Career Resources and Job Listings

- Association of Health Care Journalists: healthjournalism.org/prof-dev-jobs.php
- Association for Education in Journalism and Mass Communication (includes job listings): aejmc.org
- Broadcast Education Association (includes job listings): beaweb.org
- National Association of Broadcasters (includes job listings): nab.org
- National Press Foundation: nationalpress.org

PORTRAYALS OF HEALTH-RELATED CONDITIONS

For better or worse, even programs designed primarily to entertain can have important implications for health and identity.

Mental Illness

Mentally ill individuals are often portrayed in the media as wild-eyed, disheveled, violent, and dangerous. That characterization has never reflected the reality of most people with psychological disorders. In reality, only about 11% of them are violent, which is roughly equal to the proportion of violent people in the overall population (Hetsroni, 2009). In fact, attests Kristin Fawcett (2015), "Not only are individuals with mental illness less likely [than other people] to commit crimes, they're actually more likely to be victimized" (para. 8).

One harmful effect of stigmatizing images in the media is that people who might benefit from mental health services often consider it personally and socially unacceptable to do so, especially if they perceive the "professionals" and "health care" situations they witness on screen to be negative or hostile (Maier, Gentile, Vogel, & Kaplan, 2014).

Although entertainment programming may dramatize mental illness as diabolical and suspenseful, as one media analyst reminds us, "getting sick is something that happens to everyone, and since our bodies and minds are linked and not separate, mental illness is no more sensational than physical sickness" (Uwujaren, 2012).

Uzo Abuda plays Suzanne "Crazy Eyes" Warren in the TV show *Orange Is the New Black*. Her appearance is altered for the role to make her appear emotionally volatile and eccentric. At the same time, the character is funny and endearing, leading many observers to wonder whether she is mostly reinforcing or dispelling stereotypes about people with mental illnesses.

Disabilities

As the audience watches, a police officer apprehends and arrests a man who has just robbed a cab driver. It might be a scene from any number of television shows or movies. But this one has a twist. The officer, who is partially paralyzed, uses a wheelchair. When researchers showed this clip (from a German television series) to people without physical disabilities, they found that they were significantly more likely than before to believe that people with disabilities can successfully serve as police officers (Reinhardt, Pennycott, & Fellinghauer, 2014). The experiment points to the media's influence in shaping popular opinion, at least some of the time.

People with disabilities are typically underrepresented and misrepresented in mainstream media (Renwick, Schormans, & Shore, 2014). When they are shown, they are typically portrayed in one of three ways—as disadvantaged, as unhealthy victims, or as so-called super crips who do everything able-bodied people can do and even better (L. Zhang & Haller, 2013). As you might imagine, the first two characterizations are associated with stigma and discrimination. By contrast, the super crip image tends to inspire confidence, even among people with disabilities. At the same time, many people worry that over-the-top portrayals will foster unrealistic expectations (L. Zhang & Haller, 2013). In the study involving a fictional cop who is partially paralyzed, viewers with physical disabilities were less likely than other viewers to say that people with paraplegia can successfully serve as police officers, perhaps because they considered the TV behaviors to be unrealistic or because they felt society would not accept them in that role (Reinhardt et al., 2014).

Regular and realistic exposure to people with disabilities is the most successful means of diminishing negative attitudes. Sensitive use of humor may also help. In one study, college students either watched a serious documentary called *Without Pity: A Film About Disabilities* or a video featuring a stand-up comedian sharing funny stories about his experiences since having a leg amputated. On the whole, students who watched the serious film did not experience a change in attitude, but those who watched the stand-up routine were significantly more willing than before to interact with people who have disabilities (Smedema, Ebener, & Grist-Gordon, 2012). Clearly, there are many circumstances in which joking about a physical challenge would be hurtful, but in this case, the researchers speculate that viewers felt they could relate to the comedian, and the humor relieved some of their tension about the topic.

As with mental illness, the reality is that people with disabilities are much like everyone else, regardless of how they are portrayed in the media. "Disability is just one part of a person and one aspect of human diversity," reflect researchers Lingling Zhang and Beth Haller (2013), adding that "the best way to portray people with disabilities is to not use a sticker or label, not to focus on their disability, but to report from their perspectives" (p. 330).

We now turn our attention to another aspect of entertainment programming—the way it depicts health-related behaviors.

PORTRAYALS OF HEALTH-RELATED BEHAVIORS

Two of the most controversial elements of entertainment programming are sex and violence. Here we explore common media depictions and their implications for people's well-being and identity.

Sex

When Rachel Hills began writing a book about sex, she realized, as she puts it, that "the story I had been telling myself all those years had been wrong" (2015a, para. 16). As a college student, she had spent countless hours ironing her hair straight, applying makeup, choosing just the right clothes, walking to class in 3-inch heels, and regularly vomiting in hopes of staying slender. Even so, she never felt as sexy as the women she saw in magazines and movies. After some soul-searching, Hills realized she had "failed" as a sex object, but she had succeeded at something much more important. We will return to her story in a moment. But first, let's consider the ramifications of the way sex is portrayed in the media.

OBJECTIFICATION Few people dispute that, under the right conditions, sex is an intimate and loving act. One concern is that media images often present it in a different way. Take music and music videos, for example. In the last 40 years or so, about 80% of Top 40 songs have focused on love and/or sexual attraction. In that time, an increasing number of them have described casual sex without the love (Madanikia & Bartholomew, 2014). To emphasize the point, music videos, particularly those of rap and hip-hop performers, typically feature women (disproportionately women of color) who are naked or provocatively dressed (Turner, 2011). One analyst observes that many videos have devolved into "twerking competitions" in which the bodies of Black women, particularly their backsides, are dehumanized as mere accessories, and African American men are depicted as sexually voracious (Larasi, 2013).

Sexual objectification occurs when an individual is treated primarily as the object of another person's desire, not as a whole and unique person with needs and desires of his or her own. Objectification is evident when the focus is on particular body parts rather than the whole person, when people are depicted as animals or things (as when a model is dressed to resemble a cheetah or a beer bottle), when people are treated as interchangeable (one person looks and acts so much like another that it is difficult to tell them apart), and when people are treated as commodities to be chosen and used by others (Heldman, 2014).

One result of feeling objectified is a sense of inadequacy. If one's worth is measured in terms of other people's desire—and the terms of that desire are narrow, unrealistic, and impersonal at that—it is difficult to feel appreciated and worthy. "I was a mess of insecurities," remembers Rachel Hills, whose narrative begins this section. "I could never trust that men were interested in me, and on occasions when they seemed to be, I would internally rebut myself with reasons that they never would be" (2015a, para. 8). The worth of an object is how much it is used. Being "used" as a sex object can be demeaning, humiliating, and even dangerous.

A particularly alarming trend involves posting videos of rape episodes on social media. Such glorifications of sexual violence contribute to what some analysts call a **rape culture**, the attitude among some people that it is acceptable, sexy, or even funny to force sex on women, men, or children. Many people feel that *Fifty Shades of Grey* and similar books and movies trivialize rape and abuse and make them seem acceptable.

Rachel Hills, who went on to author the book *The Sex Myth* (2015b), proposes that she truly became attractive in her own mind when she stopped basing her self-worth on other people's opinion of her sex appeal and began celebrating her individuality. "An object may be beautiful, cherished, and adored," she reflects, "but by definition it cannot act; it can only be acted upon by others" (Hills, 2015a, para. 19). These days, she says, she prides herself on being a *subject*, a dynamic creator of her own life story, rather than a mere *object* in someone else's.

Another issue involves the media's treatment of safer sex practices.

SAFER SEX A good deal of evidence suggests that people who regularly watch pornography are more likely than others to be sexually promiscuous and to engage in unsafe sexual practices (Harkness, Mullan, & Blaszczynski, 2015). This may be partly because sexually explicit programming provides a script of sorts for initiating sexual encounters but almost never includes discussion of contraception or disease barriers. Teens who are heavy porn users are more likely than their peers to send and receive sexually explicitly texts (Van Ouytsel, Ponnet, & Walrave, 2014), and college students who frequently view pornography are more likely to initiate casual sex and to engage in risky sex (Braithwaite, Coulson, Keddington, & Fincham, 2015).

Safer-sex practices, such as condom use, are included in only about 1 in 200 sexual references in music, magazines, and movies aimed at teen audiences (Hust, Brown, & L'Engle, 2008). Stacey Hust and colleagues found that these teen-oriented media typically depict talk about condom use as "humiliating and humorous" (p. 14). Boys are most often portrayed as sexually ravenous, and sexual protection is treated as girls' responsibility. The researchers report that "in the rare instances when condoms were discussed or depicted, boys had condoms as a kind of toy, whereas girls were more knowledgeable and more likely to have a condom when it was needed" (p. 17). Even when condoms were present, they were usually treated comically rather than as topics of serious discussion with health consequences.

On the positive side, teens regularly exposed to safer-sex PSAs were subsequently more likely than their peers to use condoms if they were sexually active in the next 18 months, suggesting that the media may be a role model for healthy sexual behaviors, not only risky ones (Hennessy et al., 2013).

SEXUAL ORIENTATION A double standard regarding sexual orientation is also evident in the media. Although relationships between same-sex partners have become more visible on mainstream television, they are depicted as remarkably chaste compared to heterosexual couples' (Bond, 2015). Same-sex couples are seldom shown sharing even mild expressions of affection. As one observer put it, it is now okay in the world of network television to be gay, as long as you don't act "too gay" by behaving like a "real couple" ("But Not," n.d.). Instead, sexuality is still portrayed mostly through a heteronormative lens. For example, gay men are often portrayed as sexually attractive both to women and to men, as if to suggest that their gayness is okay as long as they still appeal to people who aren't (Poole, 2014).

Next we explore an element of entertainment programming that may or may not overlap with depictions of sex.

Violence

"Blood on" versus "blood off" is common parlance in video games. It refers to the level of gore and graphic realism a player may select in games that involve killing other characters. In one study, youth who played a video game with "blood on" were slightly but significantly more likely than "blood off" players to indicate feelings of anger and to say they would react violently if someone ran into them on the sidewalk (Farrar, Krcmar, & Nowak, 2006).

Most researchers agree that there is an association between violence in the media and violence in real life. In one of the broadest studies to date, Brad Bushman and colleagues (2014) surveyed pediatricians, parents, and researchers about the impacts of violent comics, video games, music, TV programs, and more. Although respondents disagreed about the degree to which violent content affects people, all groups agreed that regular exposure to violent content increases the likelihood that young people will act aggressively toward others (Bushman, Gollwitzer, & Cruz, 2014). The only exception was violent literature, which respondents did not feel was predictive of violent behavior.

Of course, not everyone reacts to media violence in the same way, and it is difficult to isolate media effects among the many factors that influence people. Women tend to use the media to moderate their mood when they feel angry (Knobloch-Westerwick & Alter, 2006), whereas males (particularly young men) are more likely to enjoy an adrenaline-pumping sense of fear (Lynch & Martins, 2015). For some people, violence in the media is a substitute for acting out. For others, media images tend to escalate their sense of aggression. One prevalent effect of media violence is called "mean world syndrome"—a tendency among high media users to feel afraid and to overestimate the threat of violence in their environment (Gerbner, Gross, Morgan, & Signorielli, 1980; Jamieson & Romer, 2014).

One criticism of media violence is that the effects are unrealistic. People run through machine gun fire unscathed. They are shot or stabbed but continue to perform like athletes. Evil characters die, but heroes seldom do. George Gerbner (1996) dubbed this *happy violence*: "'Happy violence' is cool, swift, painless, and always leads to a happy ending, so as to deliver the audience to the next commercial in a receptive mood" (para. 10). In a study of PG-13 movies, Theresa Webb and colleagues (2007) report that, although violence was prevalent, enduring harm to victims was "either nonexistent or largely unrealistic" (p. e1226). In the fast-paced world of entertainment, it seems that violence is popular, but lengthy recoveries are boring. The result is an on-screen world in which violence lacks serious consequences.

Media consumers may not be as hooked on violence as content producers think they are. On YouTube, where most content is uploaded by everyday people, there is less violence than on television, and the violence that does appear on YouTube is usually more realistic (Weaver, Zelenkauskaite, & Samson, 2012). The difference is substantial. About 13% of YouTube clips studied involved violence, compared to prior studies that document violence in 61% of TV programs.

PORTRAYALS OF HEALTH CARE SITUATIONS

Medical dramas seem to offer a backstage pass to medicine. What most people "know" about the interior of a surgery unit or a doctor's lounge they learned from television. Areas usually off limits to the public are open for inspection, or at least it seems that way. One upside is that modern medical dramas depict health professionals as less "saintly" than their predecessors, such as *Marcus Welby, M.D.* "Medical shows don't put doctors on as high a pedestal as they used to," says family physician Jason Marker. "They show physicians making poor decisions—that's a major sea change. In some ways it is a much more accurate depiction . . . We are human beings" (Marker, quoted by Krupa, 2012, para. 7–8). In other ways, however, medical dramas are likely to give people mistaken impressions about the way medical work is done.

Diversity is underrepresented on TV medical dramas. For example, although Asian physicians comprise about 25% of U.S. doctors, they make up only 6% of TV doctors (Jain & Slater, 2013). Female physicians now appear on television in a proportion roughly equivalent to real life. However, they are more likely than men to be cast in supporting and minor roles that focus on their sex appeal rather than their professional competence (Jain & Slater, 2013).

The real nature of medicine and healing are also skewed. Based on television portrayals, it may seem that the extremes are the norm. A greater percentage of TV patients die than in real life. However, those who live often experience improbable recoveries. For example, in 136 instances of cardiac arrest on television, care providers performed CPR (cardiopulmonary resuscitation) correctly only once, but were depicted as successfully reviving patients far more often than actually happens (Hinkelbein et al., 2014).

At the same time, medical dramas rely on death as a dramatic element. The mortality rate among TV patients is nearly nine times greater than the norm, prompting the researcher who discovered the disparity to quip, "If you must be hospitalized, television is not the place" (Hetsroni, 2009, p. 311). Most television deaths are quick and dramatic, but do not let them fool you. In actual hospitals, the majority of patients survive, but recovery takes a while.

We might also be misled by the way people look on TV. In real life, about 4 in 10 hospital patients are male. On TV, however, 7 in 10 are male (Hetsroni, 2009). And, whereas men are overrepresented in medical dramas, Hispanic Americans and older adults are underrepresented (Hetsroni, 2009).

Entertainment programming also presents dramatic but untrue information about organ donation. In their study of network television programs, Susan Morgan and colleagues (2007) found numerous story lines about organs sold illegally, people murdered for their organs, doctors giving preferential treatment to their favorite organ recipients, and people allowed to die prematurely so that others could have their organs. The researchers also found fictional accounts of organ recipients who behave criminally or irresponsibly, squandering the life-sustaining gift they have received (Morgan, Harrison, Chewning, Davis, & DiCorcia, 2007, p. 148). All of these depictions—though the stuff of exciting drama—are grossly unrealistic. "We often wonder where members of the public get 'crazy ideas' about organ donation like the existence of the black market, the corruption of the organ allocation system, and the untrustworthiness of doctors," the authors reflect. "The answer may have been quite literally in front of us for years" (Morgan et al., 2007, p. 149).

ENTERTAINMENT AND COMMERCIALISM

It is usually easy to tell the difference between a commercial and a television program or movie. But what if a commercial looks like entertainment or commercial messages are subtly embedded in entertainment programming?

Entertainomercials

Journalists have coined the term **entertainomercials** to characterize sales pitches that resemble entertainment programming ("Entertainomercials," 1996). A classic example involved Joe Camel, the former cartoon-like mascot of Camel cigarettes. R. J. Reynolds Tobacco Company introduced the colorful, sunglasses-wearing camel in 1988 advertising. Although company officials insisted that the animated character was not meant to capture children's interest, it had that effect. Sales of Camel cigarettes to children rose from $6 million per year to $476 million per year (DiFranza et al., 1991). Within a few years, children were as familiar with Joe Camel as with Mickey Mouse (Fischer, Schwartz, Richards, & Goldstein, 1991). Under public and legal pressure, Reynolds ceased using images of Joe Camel after a nine-year run (Vest, 1997).

Product Placement

The tobacco industry is also involved in another type of commercial/entertainment blend called product placement. **Product placement** means that a sponsor pays (with cash, props, services, or so on) to have a product or brand name included in a movie, a television program, a video game, or some other form of entertainment. Subtle product placements (sometimes called *stealth ads*) can be considered a form of subliminal advertising, in that the viewer may not be consciously aware of seeing items displayed but may develop an impression about them based on their association with other elements of the drama (Erdelyi & Zizak, 2004). Many advertisers are turning to product placements as a way to sneak their products into the public eye, realizing perhaps that four out of five TV viewers now ignore commercials or fast-forward through them (Boris, 2014).

WHAT DO YOU THINK?

- Do you think viewers are affected by product placements in the movies and on television? If so, how?
- Do you agree or disagree with the argument that people should be able to enjoy entertainment programming without being wary of embedded sales pitches? Why?

Product placements become health communication when they concern the way people think or behave concerning health issues. A particular concern arises when product placements are used to dodge restrictions on conventional advertising. Although most states forbid tobacco advertisements on radio and TV, tobacco companies have reportedly rewarded movie stars and producers for embedding them in movie scenes. Analysts expect that electronic cigarettes (which deliver nicotine without tobacco) and legalized marijuana—neither of which were addressed in the tobacco advertisement ban—may surface in product placements (D. E. Williams, 2015).

As the next section shows, some people fight fire with fire, using the product placement strategy to promote recommended health behaviors. See Box 11.5 for ethical issues related to health images in entertainment programs.

TIPS FOR TV SHOW AND MOVIEMAKERS

Following are a few of the suggestions (quoted verbatim) from the EIC to people in the entertainment industry:

- Keep in mind that manic depression does not result from isolated personal traumas, such as the death of a loved one or the breakup of a relationship.
- Have one of your characters remind another to apply sunscreen before going outside.
- Consider reflecting the reality that homeowners often freeze up or tremble so badly when trying to use a gun in self-defense that they are unable to deploy it.

For more about these issues and many others, visit the EIC website at http://www.eiconline.org.

ENTERTAINMENT-EDUCATION PROGRAMMING

Producers may embed subtle messages in programs, not to sell products but to educate or persuade people regarding health matters. Efforts to benefit the public using an entertainment format are known as **entertainment-education** or prosocial programming. The idea, say Piotrow and colleagues, is that "no one enjoys being lectured to but everyone enjoys and often learns from entertainment, whether broadcast through radio or television, or performed in person" (Piotrow, Rimon, Merritt, & Saffitz, 2003, p. 5).

Entertainment producers today are likely to be lobbied by health advocates who urge them to incorporate health messages in their scripts, props, and storylines. Organizations such as Hollywood, Health & Society and the Entertainment Industries Council (EIC) encourage entertainment writers to portray health issues in accurate and informative ways. They provide tips, story ideas, and scripts about topics ranging from AIDS to bat bites, car seats, and suicide. For example, the EIC urges writers not to use the term *hard drugs* because it implies incorrectly that drugs that are not "hard" are relatively harmless. It also recommends that characters be shown using seatbelts and other safety devices.

In some countries, entire programs have been created to promote healthy behaviors. After *Nunl Dhuhyo!* (Open Your Eyes!) segments began airing on Korean television, the number of people who signed cornea-donation cards increased from just over 1,000 to nearly 14,000 (Bae & Kang, 2008). In the show, celebrity hosts conduct moving interviews with people who are hoping for cornea transplants to restore their sight.

A radio drama in Ethiopia, *Journal of Life,* depicted a main character who contracted HIV during an isolated sexual indiscretion and then unknowingly infected his wife. A random survey of the radio audience revealed that most listeners became emotionally involved in the storyline and that their resolve to engage in safer sex practices increased the more episodes they heard (Smith, Downs, & Witte, 2007).

IMPACT OF PERSUASIVE ENTERTAINMENT

Before you become too optimistic (or perturbed) about the prospects for incorporating messages within entertainment, it's important to ask: Beyond the effects already mentioned, do messages in entertainment programs make much difference?

Product placements seem to increase brand-name recognition. Although people are seldom motivated to go out and buy a product if they did not already want or need it, brands prominently displayed in entertaining programming have a slight edge over others when people are in the market for similar products (Moonhee & Roskos-Ewoldsen, 2007).

Box 11.5 ETHICAL CONSIDERATIONS

Is the Entertainment Industry Responsible for Health Images?

Does the entertainment industry have a responsibility to promote healthy behaviors? Some claim that entertainment writers and producers behave irresponsibly when they consistently portray unhealthy and unrealistic images of life and health.

One way that the media distort reality is by showing unhealthy and violent behaviors without the natural consequences. People are shot with guns but continue to run and fight. Others overeat but appear to be slender and healthy nevertheless. Another way that media messages often misrepresent health is by depicting ill (especially mentally ill) individuals as dangerous, corrupt, and antisocial.

There is a gray zone where health and entertainment overlap. Even programs presented as healthy sometimes aren't. For example, *The Biggest Loser* and similar reality shows chronicle people involved in multiweek, boot-campish efforts to shed 50, 60, or even 100 pounds. Their experiences can be inspirational, but are they realistic or even healthy? Fitness guru/physician Pamela Peeke (2011) reflects on the show *Heavy*:

> *The people who were chosen are severely obese, with average weights in the range of 400–600 pounds. . . . There are frequent moments of what seems to be embarrassing over exposure of the participants, with numerous half-naked shots revealing enormous rolls of fat. If the producers wanted shock value, they achieved their goal. (para. 5)*

Even worse, she reflects, is the producers' insistence that all the participants need is discipline and sweat, prescribed in a merciless fashion by trainers (always thin) who show the participants little understanding or compassion. The people featured "repeatedly noted that they felt addicted to food, and that food had become the default for life's stresses as well as pleasures. Yet, despite their pleading for help, all they seemed to experience was a grueling workout schedule," Peeke says (para. 6). It's no wonder, she asserts, that most people regain the weight when they leave the show. The routines aren't sustainable, and "biceps curls, although integral to physical health, don't help to change eating behavior" (para. 6).

Some people argue that the entertainment industry need not offer shocking or distorted views of reality. They challenge Hollywood to create engrossing yet realistic programming. Going one step further, some people advocate prosocial programming to educate people while they are entertained.

On the other side of the issue, people argue that entertainment programming should not be harnessed to a social agenda. They feel that artistic creativity is compromised when writers and producers must adhere to social guidelines. Moreover, they say, it is difficult to know whose agenda should prevail. When health professionals disagree about specific guidelines for healthy living, is it entertainers' job to decide which viewpoint should be represented? If the industry is held to a standard of realism, they wonder, what will become of fantasy themes and movies made famous by earlier generations, when different social expectations prevailed?

What Do You Think?

1. Do you think entertainment programming influences people's behavior? For instance, are people more likely to use condoms if they see their favorite characters talking about them in television programs and in the movies?
2. Should entertainers consider how their programs might influence audience members?
3. Do you think it is irresponsible of the entertainment industry to misrepresent the natural consequences of violent or otherwise unhealthy behavior?
4. Do you think it would diminish the entertainment value of your favorite movies and TV shows if they showed healthy behaviors or realistic consequences?
5. Do you believe programs designed specifically to promote healthy behaviors would be popular in the United States? Do you think such programs should be created? Why or why not?

Entertainment-education yields mixed results. When researchers led by Jessie Quintero Johnson (2013) exposed some university students to fact sheets about a health issue and others to a storyline in which the characters experienced that health issue, the students varied in terms of information recall. In some cases, those who read the entertainment-education narrative remembered more about the health issue than those who read the fact sheets. In other cases, however, students were apparently distracted by other details of the storyline so that, even when they were highly engaged in the story, they did not remember key information about the health issue.

One cause for concern is the underlying power dynamic of some education-entertainment programs. From a critical-cultural perspective, Dutta (2006) argues that education-entertainment programs are often designed to serve the goals, values, and priorities of the funding entity, rather than those of the target community. The result can be a form of cultural hegemony in which the values of the dominant culture are imposed on members of the marginalized community, without respect for (or even awareness of) the community's own values, culture, and circumstances. Another danger is that sponsors will focus on individual aspects of a problem—such as having fewer children per family—rather than tackling larger and more systemic issues, such as the need to allocate resources fairly to all people (Dutta, 2006). (We talk more about the critical-cultural perspective in Chapter 14.)

In line with the critical-cultural perspective, **communication infrastructure theory** proposes that people build an integrated sense of community through the interface of resources and storytelling at three levels: a micro level (via interpersonal communication), a meso level (as through businesses, nonprofit organizations, and neighborhood associations), and a macro level (including mass media) (Kim & Ball-Rokeach, 2006; Kim, Jung, & Ball-Rokeach, 2006). The theory acknowledges that communities are constrained by the resources and opportunities available to them, and at the same time, that community members are (and should be) interdependent and active agents in shaping how their resources are interpreted, used, and perhaps expanded. From this perspective, entertainment-education should not be imposed on audience members by outsiders, but instead, arise from the "lived experiences of individual residents in their local community" (Literat & Chen, 2014, p. 96). An example of this might be an effort in which community members help health promoters develop an interactive video game for area schoolchildren about smoking. The video game might allow the children to experiment with various options in a virtual world that mimics the conditions of their own neighborhoods and the realities of smoking as they experience them.

Media Literacy

This chapter concludes where it began, with a reminder that the media's influence is by no means uniform. People are affected differently and to varying extents. Perhaps the best defense against excessive or negative media influence is the ability to analyze messages logically (Austin & Meili, 1994). That is a central tenet of media literacy.

Media literacy is defined as awareness and skills that allow a person to evaluate media content in terms of what is realistic and useful (adapted from Potter, 1998). According to Dorothy Singer and Jerome Singer's (1998) seminal overview, media-literate individuals are aware that advertisers are apt to highlight (and even exaggerate) the attractive aspects of their products and to downplay the disadvantages. They evaluate the creators' intent and try to figure out what is not being said and why. Media-literate individuals are also skillful at identifying portrayals that are unrealistic or have been enhanced by special effects. Overall,

In one study, boys who played video games with highly muscular avatars were more likely to be dissatisfied with their own bodies afterward than boys whose avatars were normally proportioned (Sylvia, King, & Morse, 2014). Media literacy programs can help tykes realize how unrealistic media images can be.

media-literate individuals tend to evaluate messages in terms of fairness and appropriateness, weighing ideas for themselves.

TEACHING MEDIA LITERACY

Media literacy instruction usually involves an informative, an analytic, and an experiential stage. Arli Quesada and Sue Summers (1998) described these stages well, and the discussion here is based on their work.

In the **informative stage,** participants in media literacy programs learn to identify different types of messages (persuasive, informative, and entertaining) and different types of media (television, radio, newspapers, and so on). They learn about the strengths and limitations of various media. For example, Internet resources are vast and accessible, but some sources are not trustworthy. Participants also learn about production techniques and special effects.

In the **analytic stage,** participants discuss their perceptions of media in general and of specific media messages. In this stage they typically deconstruct messages with guidance from a trained leader. **Deconstructing** a message means breaking it down into specific components, such as key points, purpose, implied messages, production techniques, and goals. For example, beer commercials often present a social reality in which drinking is fun and sexy. In deconstructing a beer commercial (or any other media message), participants try to identify the message's purpose, what information is missing from it, and how it compares to their own social reality. They might conclude that beer companies make drinking look fun to sell their products, but the reality is different from what the commercials show.

Finally, in the **experiential stage**, media literacy programs challenge participants to write their own news stories, design ads, perform skits, and participate in other creative efforts to help them understand the process and demystify the way media messages are created. Adolescents who have taken part in tobacco-related media literacy programs are more likely than others to think carefully about tobacco commercials and to decide not to smoke (Pinkleton, Austin, Cohen, Miller, & Fitzgerald, 2007). A particularly useful technique is to have participants create their own anti-smoking messages (Banerjee & Greene, 2006).

Media literacy programs often yield promising results. Adolescent boys who took part in one program were subsequently less likely than their peers to consider advertisements for alcohol to be realistic (Chen, 2013). In another program, teenagers who studied the techniques that advertisers use to change models' appearance in photos were generally more satisfied with their bodies and less likely than their peers to have disordered eating, even more than two years later (Espinoza, Penelo, & Raich, 2013).

Media literacy can be taught at home when parents help children understand aspects of the media messages they encounter. This is known as **parental mediation**. Adults are often able to make children aware of inaccuracies and discrepancies in media messages. For example, "Why does this program show thin people eating fattening foods?" (Austin, 1995) or "Is the violence shown in this program realistic?" (Nathanson & Yang, 2003). Research suggests that children get maximum benefits from media (while minimizing unfavorable influences) when their parents (1) limit media exposure; (2) choose programs with care; (3) watch, listen, or read alongside them; and (4) discuss program content with them (Austin, 1993; Austin, Roberts, & Nass, 1990; Lee, 2013; Singer & Singer, 1998).

Summary

Whether you regard the media as friend or foe, mass-mediated messages are an important component of health communication. The distinction in this chapter between advertising, news, and entertainment is useful for explanatory purposes, but do not forget that actual media exposure involves a great deal of blending and juxtaposing. For instance, a news story about eating disorders may be followed by an advertisement featuring unnaturally thin models. Such clashes are common, and contradictions of this nature may mitigate the effects of health-conscious messages.

Although it is difficult to say to what degree people's actions are affected by advertising, significant influence is suggested by the number of people who eat the unhealthy food advertisers promote, drink the beverages they sell, and strive to emulate supermodels. As Timothy Gibson (2007) puts it, "Our physical health depends, at least in part, upon the health of our media environment" (p. 125). Based on cultivation theory, children and adolescents may be especially susceptible to advertising messages because their frame of reference is limited. Social comparison theory suggests that people strive to measure up to "idealized" characters in the media, even when the ideals are far from attainable. Sometimes advertisers make natural conditions seem bad or unnatural (pathological) so that people will pay money to change them. Although advertising offers many advantages, it can be harmful if it encourages poor nutrition, drug and alcohol abuse, or an unhealthy reliance on cosmetics and fad diets. For example, the severity of mandated warning messages on tobacco packages is offset by other cues, such as soothing, relaxing colors and the word "light" in the product name.

Direct-to-consumer advertisements for pharmaceutical drugs increase consumers' awareness, but present a number of challenges and ethical dilemmas related to social justice, research objectivity, full disclosure, and market agendas versus altruism.

News coverage of health issues is important for sharing valuable knowledge. However, news audiences should remember that scientific findings are usually tentative, news stories tend to focus on unusual concerns, and coverage may be influenced by the desire to please advertisers or attract new audiences. The vaccine–autism controversy is a powerful reminder of how influential the news is in shaping what people believe and how they behave regarding health issues.

Entertainment portrayals may influence what people believe about medical care, risky behavior, and people with disabilities. Sex and violence are shown mostly for entertainment value, not as serious subjects with health consequences. In reality, medical miracles are less common than as shown on television, and people are more diverse.

Do not be surprised if the food, drinks, cigarettes, vehicles, and props in your favorite programs and movies were put in purposefully to please advertisers. Although product placements may not look like commercials, advertisers go to great expense, hoping that they will function like commercials. Health advocates sometimes use the same logic in inserting pro-health messages into entertainment programs, a practice known as education-entertainment programming. Communication infrastructure theory is one critical-cultural perspective that reminds us that even well-intentioned entertainment-education programming can be harmful if it does not honor the values and viewpoints of the people exposed to it.

Finally, media literacy allows people some control over how media messages affect them. Wise consumers learn to distinguish between reliable and unreliable information by critiquing media messages to determine their purposes, strengths, and limitations.

Key Terms and Theories

mass communication
third-person effect
cultivation theory
social comparison theory
direct-to-consumer (DTC) advertising
pathologizing the human body
sexual objectification
rape culture
entertainomercials
product placement
entertainment-education programming
communication infrastructure theory
media literacy
informative stage
analytic stage
deconstructing
experiential stage
parental mediation

Discussion Questions

1. Consider the mediated images and messages that an elementary school student is likely to encounter in a typical day via television, billboards, the news, the Internet, video games, and so on. Based on cultivation theory and social comparison theory, what is the child likely to believe about him- or herself and the larger world based on these messages?
2. Identify several DTC ads for pharmaceutical drugs. In your opinion, are the depictions in the ads realistic? Fair? Culturally inclusive? What are the advantages and disadvantages of these ads, as you see them? In your opinion, do the advantages outweigh the disadvantages or not? Why?
3. In what ways, if any, do media messages affect your food choices? Your body image? Your decision to drink or smoke, or not? Your preference for particular brands? Why do you feel you have been influenced, or why do you think media images have not influenced you?
4. You read about evidence that alcoholic beverage makers target underage youth and particular racial groups? Have you seen evidence of this yourself? If so, how? Do you think it has an effect?
5. In what ways do some advertisers pathologize the human body? In what ways do some music videos

dehumanize women? What are the health implications of these?

6. Identify several health items in the news. Does the information reflect ongoing health concerns (e.g., heart disease, cancer, asthma) or rarer conditions? Is the information helpful in terms of treating or preventing health concerns? What do you like best about the stories you have identified? What would you improve about them?
7. Do you ever struggle with the type of insecurities Rachel Hills describes, in terms of being attractive to others? In what situations, if any, do you feel sexually objectified? What evidence of objectification can you identity in the photos that appear in this chapter and in what you witness in the media?
8. What did Gerbner mean by the term *happy violence*? Can you give some examples from your own media experiences?
9. Based on communication infrastructure theory, brainstorm how you might initiate a respectful and effective community campaign to address the issue of childhood obesity.
10. Analyze several media messages (an advertisement, a news story, a video game, or so on) following the steps in a media literacy program. What conclusions do you reach about the creators' agenda? The explicit and implied messages? The realistic nature of the images and messages?

Answers to *Can You Guess?*

Part 1

1. The number of obese people in the world has nearly doubled since 1980 ("10 Facts," 2012).
2. About 33% of U.S. children (1 in 3) are obese.

Part 2

1. Approximately 14% of eighth graders in the United States have drunk alcohol in the last 30 days.
2. Youth are likely to see about 67,656 more alcohol ads than adults do in a typical year.

Source: *Center on Alcohol Marketing and Youth (2012)*

Part 3

1. On average, broadcast and cable TV stations devote an average of 17 seconds per hour to PSAs. That's less than one-half of 1% of airtime. And 46% of PSAs run between midnight and 6 a.m. (Henry J. Kaiser Family Foundation, 2008).
2. In 65 years, the average person will spend a total of 11.3 years in front of a TV set ("Nielsen Reports," 2008).

CHAPTER 12

Public Health and Crisis Communication

By longstanding tradition, when someone dies in Sierra Leone, loved ones have washed and dressed the body and involved community members in elaborate ceremonies to honor that person's life, assure him or her a peaceful transition to the afterlife, and protect the community from ill omens (Maxmen, 2015). No one dreamed how drastically that would change in 2014, when health officials—encased in plastic suits, masks, gloves, and boots—began whisking the dead away and burying them, as many as 50 bodies a day, in unidentified graves. It was the height of the Ebola epidemic.

This chapter explores the role of communication in promoting public health and managing health risks and crises. In contrast to chronic health conditions (covered in Chapters 13 and 14) that are often difficult to keep in the limelight, here we focus on the challenge of emergent threats that present health communication specialists with a different challenge—to make sense of rapidly emerging details and keep the public vigilant but not terrified. We explore real-life case studies about health crises to identify the best ways to prepare for and manage developing threats to public health. As you will see, an assortment of "lessons learned" appear in italics throughout this chapter and are summarized in Box 12.6 at the end of the chapter. We begin by returning to the Ebola case to see what lessons it holds for us as communicators.

Ebola

Ebola was first detected in humans in 1976, when two people in different regions of Africa were diagnosed with it. One of them lived near the Ebola River of Central Africa, which gave rise to the name. The Ebola virus resurfaced at various times over the next 38 years, killing about 1,000 people, mostly in remote regions of Africa (CDC, 2015e). However, nothing compared to the 2014 epidemic, in which more than 11,000 people died from the disease (WHO, 2015b). The crisis, which was daunting by medical standards, was further exacerbated by mistrust and poor communication.

Part of the fear surrounding Ebola stems from the dreadful nature of the disease. In early stages, the symptoms are much like the flu, making it difficult to diagnose accurately. Left untreated, however, Ebola sufferers are likely to suffer internal and external bleeding and catastrophic organ failure (WHO, 2015c). At least half the people who contract the virus die. Health officials believe that people originally caught Ebola during contact with wild animals and then the virus mutated to spread between people. At the time of the 2014 outbreak, no vaccine was available to protect people from the contagion. (As this book went to press, a preventive treatment was being tested in clinical trials.)

COMMUNICATION WITH THE WORRIED WELL

With sketchy information, except for alarming evidence that Ebola is deadly and contagious, health authorities around the world scrambled to make people aware of the risks without unduly frightening them. When a handful of Ebola cases surfaced in the United States, a variety of authorities, from the CDC to the president, sought to reassure an uneasy public. But their efforts often seemed disjointed and the information unclear and speculative, leading analysts/researchers Scott Ratzan and Kenneth Moritsugu (2014) to identify some of the first communication lessons from the crisis:

- Provide the public with answers to three key questions: "What do I need to know? What do I need to do or not do today to protect my health and that of my family? Where do I find information that I can trust and understand?" (p. 1214).
- Designate a single spokesperson to provide trustworthy, current information that is based on science and evidence.
- Coordinate with local health officials so that advice and information is consistent at every level.

At the height of the crisis, President Barack Obama urged, "We can't give in to hysteria or fear—because that only makes it harder to get people the accurate information they need" (Frizell, 2014). At the same time, however, people hungry for information turned to media outlets presenting images of dead bodies in the streets of western Africa and predictions that Ebola would soon spread and claim more than a million lives (Ratzan & Moritsugu, 2014).

Observing disparate efforts such as these, Gaya Damhewage (2014), coordinator of the World Health Organization Department of Communication in Geneva, urged people to conceive of public health communication as a "four-legged stool." In her model, the stool's legs represent (1) specialists in public health, social science, and communication who engage in ongoing, two-way communication with the public; (2) professionals with expertise in media, media relations, social media, and other means of reaching mass audiences; (3) people engaged in health policy, leadership, and resource management; and (4) scientists and others who can provide data-based information and technical guidance. From a communication perspective, this balance involves specialists in interpersonal, small-group, organizational, and mass communication, as well as leaders and coordinators to help diverse constituents communicate effectively with each other. The overall lesson is: *Engage in coordinated communication at every level—with individuals, community groups, policy-makers, health professionals, and scientists—utilizing media best suited for each type of interaction.*

As it turned out, nowhere did Damhewage's (2014) words ring truer than at the epicenter of the crisis, in western Africa.

COMMUNICATION IN THE MIDST OF TRAUMA

Since Ebola is transmitted via body fluids such as blood, patients in advanced stages of the disease are highly contagious, as are those who have recently died. Authorities believe that many people in Sierra Leone, Guinea, and Liberia contracted the disease while caring for infected loved ones and handling their bodies after death.

"Anyone who touches a droplet of sweat, blood, or saliva from someone about to die or just deceased is at high risk of contracting the disease," explains Amy Maxmen (2015, para. 12). Considering that, it is understandable from a scientific perspective why health authorities were eager to remove ill individuals and corpses from their homes. However, they initially failed to consider other factors that were equally as important to the people involved.

"The problem," says anthropologist Julienne Anoko, "was that the people handling the intervention only looked at this as a health issue; they did not try to understand the cultural aspects of the epidemic" (quoted by Maxmen, 2015, para. 10). In communication terms, they acted on the facts as they saw them, but they frequently overlooked issues of culture and history that made their claims unbelievable to the people they sought to influence.

During the crisis, people in western Africa often refused to believe that Ebola was real. Instead, they suspected that officials were kidnapping and killing their loved ones. As a consequence, citizens often hid their ill and dead family members and unwittingly infected themselves and others (Maxmen, 2015). The citizens' response may seem irrational on the surface. However, it becomes clearer considering their past experiences.

In the areas of Africa hardest hit by Ebola, a history of poverty, corruption, killings, and civil war has made citizens skeptical that local authorities have their best interests at heart. They also tend to be distrustful of foreigners, whom they may associate with violent "blood diamond" warlords of the past who killed and enslaved millions in wars over the region's diamond mines (Thompson, 2014).

As you might imagine, citizens' fears escalated when health officials—many of them from other countries and all of them dressed in what looked like protective spacesuits—began forcibly removing ill people and deceased loved ones from their homes. With inadequate resources, health professionals often sent ill patients from hospital to hospital, hoping to find one that could take them. And to stem the contagion, they quickly buried the dead, often without clearly recording their identities, if they even knew them in the first place. Consequently, once their loved ones had been removed, families were often unable to locate them or even determine if they were alive. They knew only that they had "disappeared" at the hands of people they did not know or trust.

"These disappearances stoked conspiracy theories that Ebola was a hoax," explains Maxmen (2015, para. 21). "In one, doctors were said to be killing patients to steal their organs. The less people believed that Ebola was real, the less likely they were to bring deathly ill relatives to clinics and to stop honoring their dead relatives in the traditional way."

WHAT DO YOU THINK?

- Do you trust information you see in the news about a health crisis? Why or why not?
- Are you likely to tune in to hear a public official update the public about a crisis? Why or why not?

One turning point involved listening and empathic communication. At some point, officials appealed to community chiefs, religious leaders, and healers for insight and help. These leaders, who were trusted within their communities, educated health professionals about local customs and began to reassure their fellow citizens that it was okay to forego the traditional (and highly dangerous) burial rituals (Maxmen, 2015). Officials in charge of confiscating bodies for burial recruited trusted community members to help them communicate with families throughout the process. Together, these teams began explaining their process to family members, assuring them that their loved ones' burials would be "safe and dignified." They also began to pause once they had wrapped an infected body in protective plastic, to allow loved ones to gather around it at a safe distance for prayer and goodbyes. Whenever possible, the officials agreed to dress the deceased loved ones in garments chosen by the family and bury them with family keepsakes.

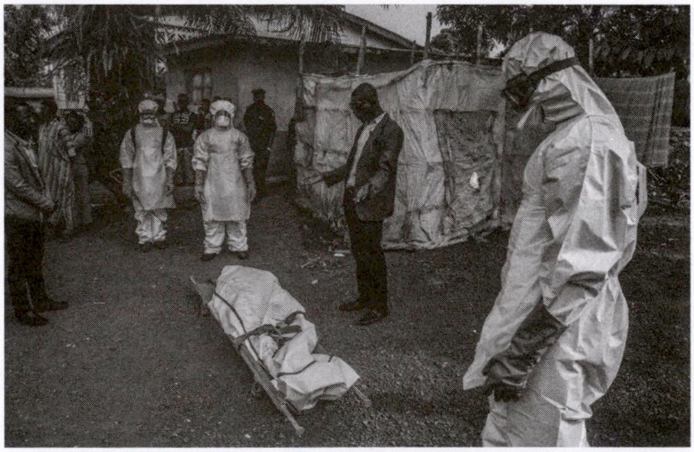

Empathic communication led relief workers in Sierra Leone to rethink the way they intervened when community members died from Ebola. Here, health workers in protective "space suits" pause before removing a body to allow loved ones to pray over it from a safe distance.

Once these changes were made, families began to cooperate more willingly with authorities, which was a vital step in controlling the epidemic. By early 2015, cases had dwindled. Midway through 2015, new cases were as few as nine a week (WHO, 2015b). The lesson was clear: *However well intentioned, communication that is not built on trust and mutual understanding is unlikely to be effective.*

What Is Public Health?

As the Ebola crisis illustrates, public health involves the well-being of entire communities. Mary-Jane Schneider (2006) describes it this way:

> *Just as a doctor monitors the health of a patient by taking vital signs—blood pressure, heart rate, and so forth—public health workers monitor the health of a community by collecting and analyzing health data.* (p. 121)

And public health does not stop there. In the same way that physicians and other caregivers are devoted to keeping people well, public health professionals are concerned with maintaining the good health of the entire population (Schneider, 2006). They seek to accomplish this through education, community partnerships, health campaigns, immunizations, and other medical care by maintaining healthy standards in restaurants, day care centers, schools, and much more. There are more than 2,800 local health departments in the United States (National Association of City & County, 2015). (See Box 12.1 for more on career opportunities in public health.)

In the classic definition presented by Charles-Edward A. Winslow (1923), **public health** is

> *the science and art of preventing disease, prolonging life, and promoting physical health and efficiency through organized community efforts for the sanitation of the environment, the control of community infections, the education of the individual in principles of personal hygiene, the organization of medical and nursing service for the early diagnosis and preventive treatment of disease, and the development of the social machinery which will ensure to every individual in the community a standard*

BOX 12.1 CAREER OPPORTUNITIES

Public Health

Epidemiologist
Health educator
Health researcher
Communication specialist
Media relations professional
Health campaign designer
Environmentalist
Health inspector
Nutritionist
Nurse
Physician
Risk/crisis communication specialist
Nonprofit organization director
Fundraiser
Professor/educator
Public policy advisor
Health department administrator
Business or billing manager
Patient advocate or navigator
Social worker
Emergency management director

Career Resources and Job Listings

- American Public Health Association: apha.org/about-apha
- Partners in Information Access for the Public Health Workforce: phpartners.org/jobs.html
- Public Health Jobs Worldwide: jobspublichealth.com
- U.S. Department of Health & Human Services Careers: hhs.gov/careers/
- Association of Schools in Public Health: asph.org
- World Health Organization: who.int/employment/vacancies/en

Also check the websites of your local hospitals and health departments.

> *of living adequate for the maintenance of health. (Originally published in Winslow's* The Evolution and Significance of the Modern Public Health Campaign, *1923, reprinted in the "History of Public Health," 2002, n.p.)*

This definition prescribes that public health professionals be both proactive—seeking to avoid unhealthy conditions, illnesses, and injuries—and diligent about monitoring and responding to health needs that arise.

Modern thinking about public health recognizes that one-way communication has not worked very well. As Piotrow and colleagues (2003) put it, health communication is "no longer simply repeating untested slogans like 'A small family is a happy family'" (p. 2) or distributing how-to guides on contraceptive methods. Instead, professionals are oriented more toward **social mobilization**, large-scale efforts in which community members and professionals work interactively to define goals, raise awareness, and create hospitable environments for healthy behaviors.

Social mobilization relies on teamwork, diversity, shared leadership, and active involvement (Patel, 2005). For example, in an effort to stop the spread of leprosy in Bihar, India, World Health Organization (WHO) officials met with experts and citizens in the region. They realized that it was uncommon for local residents to check themselves for early signs of leprosy because they had very few full-length mirrors, they typically showered outdoors while partly clothed, and even married couples did not often see each other naked (Renganathan et al., 2005). More than a catchy slogan would be needed for people to establish the habit of checking their skin for subtle changes. Community members would willingly have to alter their lifestyles and customs. Changes of this sort are usually most successful when they are promoted by community opinion leaders rather than by outsiders.

IN YOUR EXPERIENCE

Think of an effort to mobilize the public. It might be a don't-text-while-driving campaign, a stop-smoking PSA, a political campaign, or the like.

- Did it influence you?
- Did you take part?
- Why or why not?

Public health involves an array of health concerns. Traditionally, ongoing concerns such as diabetes, cancer, and heart disease fall within the rubric of *health promotion* (Chapters 13 and 14). *Risk communication* usually refers to health concerns that occur in a particular time and place, such as exposure to harmful substances, workplace dangers, and so on (Glik, 2007).

Risk and Crisis Communication

Risk communication is an ongoing process that involves disseminating information and engaging in interactive discussions about how people perceive the risks and how they feel about the risk messages (The National Research Council, 1989, p. 21). Part of the challenge involves when and how to alert the public.

When people began to fall ill after eating cattle raised in Great Britain in the 1980s and 1990s, officials largely chose to downplay the risk and reassure people that beef was safe to eat. The public gradually became skeptical, and even angry, about this claim. A full six years before officials went public about what came to be known as mad cow disease, the British journal *Nature* chided authorities for keeping people in the dark:

> *Never say that there is not danger (risk). Instead, say that there is always a danger (risk), and that the problem is to calculate what it is. And never say that the risk is negligible unless you are sure that your listeners share your own philosophy of life. ("Mad Cows and the Minister," 1990, p. 278)*

The author of the article stressed that the minister of agriculture "should be obliged to tell it like it is" (p. 278) and admonished that the cost of false reassurance was fear, distrust, and economic instability.

Downplaying risks may ultimately create a sense of distrust that discourages people from believing anything health officials say. Although risk communication professionals are sometimes in the business of soothing fears, in the mad cow disease scenario, they violated an important tenet of risk and crisis communication: *Be open about what you know, even if you do not have all the answers.* False reassurance—what Peter Sandman (2006a) calls "optimism masquerading as information" (para. 9)—can actually heighten fears and mistrust. This is supported by another lesson that belies conventional wisdom: *Citizens rarely panic when they are well informed.* Reporting on 50 years of research about people's behavior during disasters, Lee Clarke (2002) observes that, despite the "panic myth," people rarely act irrationally or selfishly in crisis situations. Instead, emergencies usually bring out the best in people. "When danger arises, the rule—as in normal situations—is for people to help those next to them before they help themselves" (Clarke, 2002, p. 24).

Keeping the public well informed is important for another reason as well. People with good intentions often rush to the scene of disasters, which can be helpful, but it may also expose them to dangerous conditions and make it difficult for first responders to function effectively. After a devastating earthquake in Nepal, so many untrained volunteers rushed to the country that they created a "second disaster"—escalating food shortages, clogging transportation routes, and adding to the chaos (Bennett, 2015).

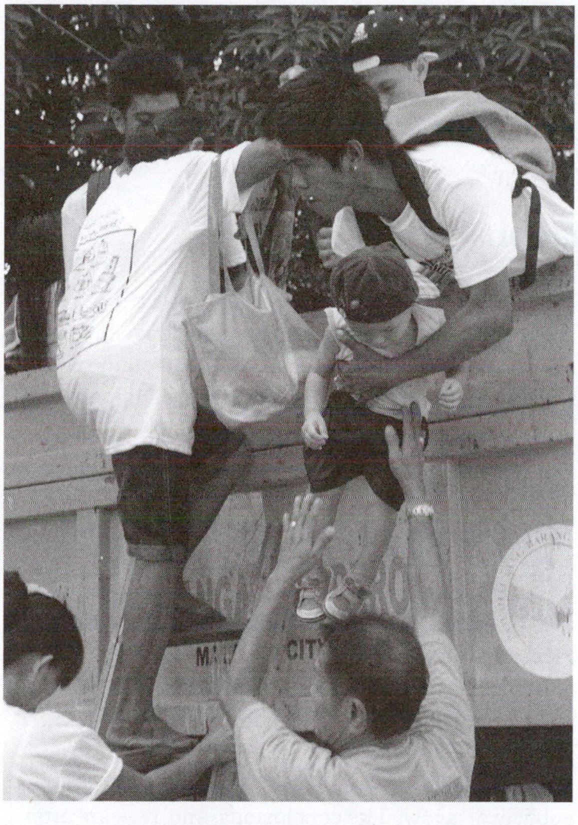

The "panic myth" says people act irrationally or selfishly in crisis situations. Research suggests the opposite, that emergencies usually bring out the best in people. However, timing is crucial. Rushing to the scene of a disaster can make things worse, particularly if you are not trained to offer assistance.

Sandman (2006b) describes three "risk communication traditions": (1) helping people who are *insufficiently concerned* appreciate that a serious risk exists; (2) reassuring and calming people who are *excessively concerned*; and (3) working with people who are *appropriately concerned* (those who are "genuinely endangered and rightly upset") to help them cope and function effectively (p. 257).

In its broadest sense, crisis communication can involve any number of events—a natural disaster, a scandal that rocks a political campaign, an epidemic, a chemical spill, and so on. In this chapter, we focus on communication about crises that involve public health. The Centers for Disease Control and Prevention (CDC, 2008) define health-related **crisis communication** as:

> *An approach used by scientists and public health professionals to provide information that allows an individual, stakeholders, or an entire community to make the best possible decisions about their well-being, under nearly impossible time constraints, while accepting the imperfect nature of their choices.* (para. 2)

The definition is telling in that it acknowledges "the nearly impossible" demands and the inherently "imperfect" nature of crisis management. Public health expert Deborah Glik (2007) observes that a crisis involves "unexpectedness, high levels of threat, an aroused and stressed population, and media looking for breaking news stories" (p. 35). Practitioners work hard to lay solid groundwork and learn everything they can, but overwhelming demands and emotions can challenge even the most experienced professionals.

MANAGING PERCEPTIONS

In her review of risk communication research, Katherine McComas (2006) observes that people tend to perceive some risks, such as being attacked by a shark while swimming at the beach, to be greater than they actually are, whereas people tend to have "optimistic biases" or "illusions of invulnerability" about other, statistically more threatening risks, such as smoking and sun exposure (p. 78). This is particularly true when the risky behavior has pleasant or socially rewarding implications. For example, despite warning messages that we have heard, we may tell

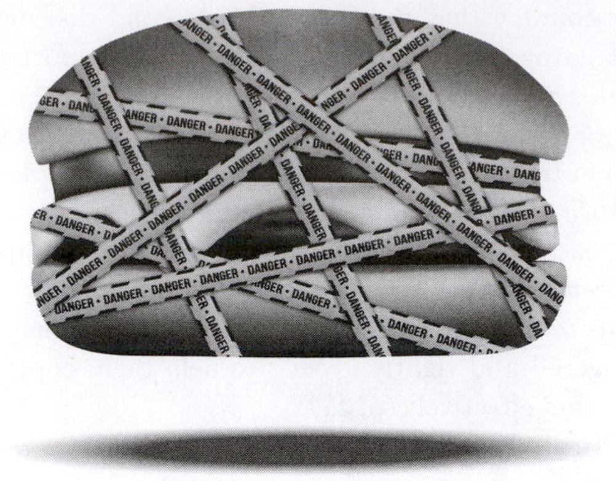

Exposed to too many "fear appeals," people become overwhelmed or indifferent; too few and they do not take risks seriously.

ourselves that we are too young to get skin cancer, that we will put on sunscreen later, or that having a suntan is worth the risk.

Ratzan and Meltzer (2005) point out that consumers are not wrong when they see things differently from experts; they just have a different vantage point. "These two audiences receive different information, process it in unique ways, and respond to conclusions based on their own set of circumstances and concerns" (Ratzan & Meltzer, 2005, p. 324). It is complicated, of course, because members of the public are not uniform in their perceptions. For example, you may have felt your anxiety rise while reading about Ebola, perhaps because you have been to western Africa, you have seen horrifying footage from the region, or your brother is a nurse who may encounter undiagnosed cases of Ebola. Meanwhile, some readers may feel insulated from the issue and wonder what all the fuss is about. There is no right way to feel. Instead, we must remember as health communication practitioners that belittling or ignoring diverse perspectives is typically ineffective and even unethical. (For more about diverse perceptions, see Box 12.2 about the controversy surrounding vaccines.)

BOX 12.2

Parents Grapple with Vaccine Information

By Patricia Barlow

More than 100 children brought home something more than memories when they visited southern California theme parks in 2015. They left with measles. "Disease detectives for months raced to contain the highly contagious disease, which surfaced at Disney theme parks and spread to a half-dozen U.S. states, Mexico and Canada," reported NBC News ("Measles Outbreak," 2015). In the end, 147 people were sickened in the outbreak, most of them children who had not been immunized as recommended or who were too young to be immunized.

Measles is caused by a virus that primarily affects the skin, nose, and throat. About 1 in 4 children with measles will require hospitalization, and 1 in 1,000 will experience swelling of the brain, which may cause brain damage and even death. When pregnant women get the virus, their babies may be born prematurely or of low birth weight (CDC, 2015b).

By 1998, measles had become so rare that experts at the CDC announced that it was "no longer an indigenous disease in the United States" ("Epidemiology of Measles," 1999, para. 1). It had become all but obsolete based on what scientists call herd immunity—people had been immunized with such consistency that the virus could no longer find a stronghold. However, that was about to change.

A 1998 article in the British medical journal *The Lancet* proposed a link between autism and a preservative (thimerosal) in the measles-mumps-rubella (MMR) vaccine (Wakefield et al., 1998). The study was later found to be faulty. It was based on only 12 children, and by the researchers' own admission, they misinterpreted the data (Willingham & Helft, 2014). Six years after the article was published, 10 of the 13 authors publicly disavowed its conclusions, and 12 years after publication, *The Lancet* retracted the story.

Extensive studies by other researchers have failed to indicate a link between autism and thimerosal. However, as a precaution, U.S. authorities ordered

continued

that it be removed from childhood vaccines beginning in 2001. Even so, the original article's impact on public sentiment has been profound.

Some parents (sometimes called anti-vaxxers) remain firm in their belief that vaccines cause autism. Consequently, about 1 in 12 children in the United States has not received the recommended MMR vaccination (Elam-Evans, Yankey, Singleton, & Kolasa, 2014). By 2014, some 16 years after the disease was deemed nearly nonexistent, the United States experienced a record-breaking number of measles cases (668 in all). In Europe, where measles had nearly died out as well, about 3,840 new cases a year are emerging (Fox & Connor, 2015).

Dialogue on the risks and benefits of vaccines has played out in the media with strong feelings on both sides. Actor/comedian Jenny McCarthy has been an outspoken opponent of vaccines. Other stars, such as Kristen Bell, have proclaimed, "No vaccines? You can't hold my children" (Cruz, 2015, headline). Health care providers are divided about whether to see patients who are not vaccinated, some of them fearful that contagious diseases will be spread to other children in their care (Bellafante, 2014). Government entities argue over strengthening mandates, eliminating exceptions, and imposing consequences on anti-vaxxers (Bernstein, 2015). For their part, anti-vaxxers worry that pharmaceutical companies are covering up evidence about vaccines so that people will continue to use their products.

Much of the conversation swirling within the vaccination controversy involves identifying the most effective strategies for communicating with parents who are concerned about the safety of vaccinations (Hendrix, 2015). Communication from public health professionals has emphasized empirical research about the benefits and safety of vaccines. However, this approach has not been highly successful with vaccination-averse parents (Nyhan, Reifler, Richey, & Freed, 2014), perhaps because they distrust government agencies and pharmaceutical companies. Some evidence suggests that the most effective messages emphasize the benefits of vaccinations (Friedersdorf, 2015; Hendrix, 2015), while other research indicates that it is more effective to describe the risks of diseases, especially if the news comes directly from trusted doctors (Nyhan et al., 2014).

What Do You Think?

1. What type of information do you consider most important on the topic of vaccines: news stories, scientific studies, physicians, parents, celebrities, or another source? Why?
2. If information is inconsistent, which sources are you most likely to trust? Why?
3. Are you more concerned about the safety of vaccines, or the ill effects of disease they are meant to prevent? Why?

HOW SCARED IS SCARED ENOUGH?

While interacting with the public about health risks and crises, it is sometimes difficult to judge how much fear is productive and how much is disabling. It sometimes seems that public health advocates want people to be afraid of something nearly all of the time. As Dawn Hillier (2006) puts it, well-meaning health promoters sometimes feed the public "a steady diet of fearful programmes about impending calamities" (p. 30). After a while, people may be either too fearful to make effective choices or so weary of "fear appeals" that they discount them altogether. However, a *rational* fear of horrible outcomes is healthy and motivational. It is a fine line to walk. Sandman (2006b) captured the dilemma well when he wrote:

> *The Holy Grail of crisis communicators is to get people to take precautions without frightening them. This is like trying to write a novel without using the letter "e"; it may be possible, but it's certainly a handicap.* (p. 258)

By way of example, Sandman quotes a *New York Times* headline that read "Fear Is Spreading Faster Than SARS." He retorts, "As if it weren't supposed to. . . . If the purpose of fear is to motivate precautions, after all, then the fear must come before the precautions are needed" (p. 259). We talk more about fear appeals in Chapter 14.

IN YOUR EXPERIENCE

- Have you ever been frightened by a health scare in the news?
- If so, how did you respond?

IN THE HEAT OF THE MOMENT

Crisis communication looks easier on paper than it feels in reality. Vicki Freimuth (2006), former director of communication at the CDC, reflects on crises this way:

> *Health communicators have a particularly difficult time with speed, as they are accustomed to conducting formative research, carefully segmenting audiences, planning messages, and pretesting before releasing them. [In a crisis] all of these activities have to occur in hours, not days, weeks, or months. Theory and research are still critical, but must be internalized by the communicators so they are available to use on the spot.* (p. 144)

And a cool-headed commitment to safety can be even more difficult at the actual site of an emergency. Dave Johnson (2006) recalls the chaos at the World Trade Center in New York when it was attacked in 2001:

> *A violent explosion rips through your office complex. Multiple fires are burning. An ominous plume of heat, fire, dust, debris and an unknowable mixture of perhaps asbestos, silica, lead and other metals floats into the atmosphere. . . . Firefighters and police and EMTs, over which you have no authority, arrive on the scene. The fire chief says "Get out of our way." His guys, and the police, don't wear proper protection. . . . Your own workforce is shocked. Some rush past the fires and debris, into the plume, searching for comrades. . . . It's chaotic. You're operating in a fog of disaster. . . . What do you say to your own workforce? To those outside your control, such as the firefighters? To the crowd of reporters? To threatened residents and business owners? And to your CEO, who won't wear a hard hat or respirator or safety glasses because, "We don't want to scare people"?* (p. 58)

Johnson, who is editor of *Industrial Safety & Hygiene News*, presents some of the lessons learned about risk communication at Ground Zero.

- *"Beware of overly optimistic risk assessments,"* as when an EPA administrator prematurely announced one week after the disaster that the air in New York City was "safe to breathe" (p. 58). False reassurance can undermine experts' credibility and put people in danger.
- *Understand the different information needs of various stakeholders.* The Ground Zero team found that, after workers heard officials reassure the public that the site was safe, supervisors had a hard time convincing workers to use proper safety gear and caution.
- *"Understand the emotions and fears you are dealing with"* (p. 60). People who are worried, anxious, angry, or grief-stricken are likely to brush aside safety concerns and then be sorry later.
- *"Expect resistance to your message" and do not give up* (p. 60). Use a range of methods if necessary. When even New York City mayor Rudy Giuliani balked about wearing a hardhat, the Ground Zero team presented him with one that said "VIP—Mayor" on the front. "It worked," said Stewart Burkhammer, an environmental safety and health consultant working at Ground Zero. At other times, Burkhammer said, bluntness worked better than subtlety. He once told the crew at a morning safety meeting, "I'm not going to be the one to tell the mayor we just killed somebody, so clean up your act" (quoted by Johnson, 2006, p. 62).
- *Foster relationships and open communication with partners (media, emergency personnel, and so on) before, during, and after a crisis.*
- *Be proactive rather than reactive.* "Communicate and instruct as much as possible in advance of an emergency," recommends Burkhammer. "We spent a lot of time being great reactors. . . . A lot of things were done by feel and guess. I think we were very poor proactors" (p. 62).

Box 12.3 presents a framework to help guide your efforts as you prepare for and manage health crises. With these lessons in mind, let's examine a few case studies involving risk and crisis communication around the globe.

BOX 12.3 THEORETICAL PERSPECTIVES

Risk Management/Communication Framework

Imagine that, after eating lunch in their school cafeteria, 125 local children have become ill, some of them requiring hospitalization. As the health education supervisor at the health department, you are expected to help manage the crisis. Your staff has received 25 calls from worried parents and 15 calls from media professionals, and the issue has not even hit the news yet. What do you do first?

You might start by refreshing your knowledge of Scott Ratzan and Wendy Meltzer's (2005) **risk management/communication framework** (RMCF). Drawing on extensive experience in crisis and risk communication, Ratzan and Meltzer developed their model to be an elegant and useful synthesis of guidelines presented in the WHO Maxims for Effective Health and Risk Communication, the U.S. Food and Drug Administration (FDA) Model for Risk Management, Covello's (2003) Best Practices in Public Health Risks and Crisis Communication, and other trusted models.

Establishing the Foundations

If you are wise, the first step in managing the crisis actually began long before it occurred. Experts recommend developing interactive and trusting relationships with stakeholders when things are calm. They also recommend creating teams and crisis management plans and practicing what to do when a crisis occurs. Another precaution is to collect information that will be helpful, quick at hand, and tailored to different audiences. Ratzan and Meltzer (2005) point out that there is not always time in a crisis to construct and pretest new messages carefully. In your case, having ready access to good information about food-borne illnesses will make your job a great deal easier.

Partnering with Stakeholders

Stakeholders are important before, during, and after a crisis. Ratzan and Meltzer (2005) embrace a broad definition of *stakeholders* as "anyone and everyone touched by the event" (p. 325). In your case, this might mean parents, children, school employees, reporters, public officials, health professionals, food distribution and preparation personnel, state agencies, and more. Ratzan and Meltzer observe that there are several benefits of engaging stakeholders: (1) They can give you valuable, diverse input; (2) they can be (and should be) active partners in achieving shared goals; and (3) if you trust each other, you can engage in two-way communication that is honest and open.

In the current crisis, you might not know all of the stakeholders personally, but if you have made it a point to interact with at least a few key people in each group, you will be more effective in this crisis. In addition, you can activate your network to extend outreach to stakeholder groups. For example, if the health department supplies local schools with nurses, you might enlist the nurses' help in communicating with stakeholders. In the same way, you might call on health inspectors, media relations staff, PTA presidents, and others. If you have laid good groundwork and are open and trustworthy with stakeholders, a crisis can renew and strengthen relationships rather than damage them (Ratzan & Meltzer, 2005; Ulmer, Seeger, & Sellnow, 2007).

Communicating with the Public

A portion of the information you want conveyed will be passed along through mass media. Understanding media professionals' goals will help you work as partners rather than as adversaries. Be mindful that reporters have a stake in presenting immediate, accurate, and interesting information to the public. They look as foolish as you do if they pass along inaccurate information. But this does not mean you should keep them waiting until you know everything. "Today's media have a need for constant information updates to fill 24-hour broadcasts," Ratzan and Meltzer (2005) advise, adding, "Crisis communicators need to be aware that if they do not supply information, the media will report what they have" (p. 328).

In communicating with the public (either in person or through media channels), Ratzan and Meltzer (2005) recommend, be "clear, honest and compassionate" (p. 330). Being clear requires that you consider the different needs and literacy levels of stakeholders. Information that might make sense

continued

continued

to researchers and clinicians can bewilder and frighten members of the public. All the while, show that you care and are feeling emotions. "This is the exact reason Mayor Giuliani was so successful at managing a citywide crisis" after the 9/11 terrorist attacks, say Ratzan and Meltzer (p. 331). Citizens believed that he genuinely cared. However, be sure that you do not allow your emotions to exaggerate or minimize the severity of the crisis. Your words and demeanor convey to the public how they should think and feel about the crisis. Always "think before you speak," urge Ratzan and Meltzer (p. 331).

Internal Communication Strategies

In the general rush to meet public and media demands, it is easy to neglect teamwork in a crisis. But this oversight can lead to devastating mistakes. Ratzan and Meltzer (2005) underscore the importance of communicating regularly with members of your team. Depending on the duration of the crisis, you might call daily or twice-a-day briefings at which everyone can compare notes and impressions.

With these principles in mind, RMCF presents five stages of risk management (quoted verbatim from Ratzan & Meltzer, 2005, p. 335):

1. *Risk assessment:* Estimation and evaluation of risk
2. *Risk confrontation:* Determining acceptable level of risk in a larger context
3. *Risk intervention:* Risk control action
4. *Risk communication:* Interactive process of exchanging risk information
5. *Risk management evaluation:* Measure and ensure effectiveness of risk management efforts

As indicated, each of these stages involves partnering with stakeholders (members of the public, experts, media professionals, and others), making decisions, creating messages and communication strategies, and continually monitoring and refining your strategies.

What Do You Think?

With regard to the "sick schoolchildren" crisis described at the opening of this box:

1. Where would you begin? What would you do first?
2. What stakeholders might you involve, and why? What questions would you ask each stakeholder group?
3. How would you enlist the stakeholders as active partners in the process?
4. How will you get (and convey) answers to reporters' questions such as the following: How sick are the children? Could this be deadly? Can you arrange interviews with some of the children or parents? How likely is it that other children will come down sick? Have you definitively linked the illness to food served at school? If so, what food was it? Who is responsible for food at school? Is there a chance that the tainted food was distributed to other schools as well? To restaurants? To grocery stores?
5. What will you do when your staff cannot keep up with all the phone calls, much less research the issue and contact stakeholders?
6. When the crisis has passed, how will you evaluate the success or failure of your efforts?
7. What might you do to prepare for future risks and crises?

Case Studies: A Global Perspective

In the past, it was largely feasible to contain contagious illnesses such as smallpox and yellow fever to geographic sectors. Now, because more than 2 billion people a day fly to locations it would have taken days, weeks, or months to reach in the past, "an outbreak or epidemic in any one part of the world is only a few hours away from becoming an imminent threat somewhere else" ("World Health Report," 2007, p. x). (See Box 12.4 for a profile of famous disease carriers and some tough considerations about personal liberties and public welfare.)

Another problem is that diseases—and their resistance to known drugs—are multiplying. Margaret Chan, director-general of WHO, cautions that, since 1970, about one new disease has surfaced every year, contributing to the incidence of thousands of epidemics around the world ("World Health Report," 2007).

BOX 12.4

Typhoid Mary and TB Andy

Andrew Speaker, an Atlanta resident with drug-resistant tuberculosis (TB), traveled by plane to Europe and back in 2007, even though doctors say they told him not to fly because of the risk to others. Tuberculosis is dangerous and highly contagious, particularly in the recirculated air of an airplane cabin. Nearly 2 million people a year die from TB, mostly in developing countries (WHO, 2008b). The disease has made a deadly comeback in recent years because new strains have emerged that do not respond to drug therapy, and people with immune deficiencies such as HIV and AIDS are particularly susceptible to TB whether they have been immunized or not.

In Speaker's case, authorities in Italy were alerted to his health status and they refused to allow him to board a flight back to the United States. So Speaker and his wife (they were on their honeymoon) flew to Canada instead, where his status went unnoticed, and they were able to fly back to Atlanta. Many fellow airline passengers, angry that Speaker knowingly exposed them to a dangerous disease, later filed charges against him ("Plane Passengers Sue," 2007).

Some journalists nicknamed Speaker "TB Andy," referencing another famous figure in history, Typhoid Mary. In the years preceding 1906, Mary Mallon was a cook for wealthy families in New York. Authorities began to notice that, in the homes where she worked, an extraordinary number of people contracted typhoid fever. At the time, about 10% of people who got typhoid died from it. Mallon resisted being tested or being taken into custody. Indeed, she "brandished a meat fork and threats" so vociferously that it took five police officers to bring her in ("TV Program," 2004, para. 6).

Tests showed that Mallon was a typhoid carrier, although she manifested no symptoms herself. She was forcibly quarantined in a hospital on an island in New York City's East River. Her distraught letters from the time relate that she felt like a kidnap victim and a "peep show" ("In Her Own Words," 2004, last paragraph). Mallon was released after about six years. But when she disobeyed orders and returned to cooking professionally, she was taken into custody for the rest of her life. Historians have mixed feelings about whether Mallon was treated fairly or not.

What Do You Think?

1. Should the state take people into custody if they refuse to take actions (such as wearing gloves or face masks, agreeing not to fly, and so on) that would help protect others from catching their illnesses? Does it matter what illness it is? Do colds and flu count? What about illnesses that are somewhat, but not highly, contagious?
2. Should airlines beef up their "no fly" lists so that people with highly contagious diseases are not permitted aboard? Why or why not?
3. If a person knowingly exposes others to a contagious disease, should the people who are exposed have the right to sue? Would you? Why or why not?
4. Historians have noted that Mary Mallon had little means of earning a living besides being a cook. If protecting others means changing careers, should the government help pay for new vocational training or education?
5. Babies and people whose immune systems are compromised by illness, chemotherapy, or other conditions are particularly susceptible to diseases that would not endanger others. Should we exercise greater-than-usual precautions knowing that such people are in our communities? Why or why not? What precautions would you consider reasonable?
6. In some countries, people who have colds wear disposable face masks (like surgical masks) in public to protect others. Do you think people in other countries should adopt this practice as well? Why or why not? Would you wear a mask when you had a cold? Why or why not?
7. Many illnesses could be prevented if people washed their hands before eating. In Japan, even fast-food restaurants provide moist towelettes with every meal. Do you think other countries should adopt this practice? Why or why not?
8. A common means of transmitting illness is shaking hands with others and then touching food. Some people suggest that we would be healthier (and perhaps avert epidemics) if we bowed or waved in greeting instead of shaking hands. What do you think?

For an excellent video about Mary Mallon as well as discussion guides and ethical analyses, see www.pbs.org/wgbh/nova/typhoid.

Contact with other people, especially a *lot* of other people, can be hazardous to your health. But health risks involve more than communicable diseases. They also encompass environmental issues, safety practices, exposure to hazardous substances, contaminated food and water, natural disasters, and more. The good news is that globalization has also improved worldwide awareness of public health. After a devastating earthquake struck Nepal in 2015, people around the world contributed more than $69 million in the first three days alone (Petroff & Rooney, 2015).

We could fill volumes with descriptions of public health issues around the world. Instead, let's look at a few case studies that illustrate some key principles, challenges, and lessons. The following discussion focuses on AIDS, SARS, bioterrorism, and avian flu.

Children in sub-Saharan Africa can only hope for a brighter future than current conditions predict. That region now has the highest concentration of HIV infection in the world.

AIDS

AIDS has been called the greatest public health challenge of the last half-century. About 35 million people are now living with HIV or AIDS. The crisis is particularly bad in Africa, where about 75% of AIDS-related deaths occur ("Global HIV/AIDS," 2014).

One challenge of AIDS is that related behaviors are sometimes considered taboo, immoral, or too personal to be discussed. Cultural rules about these behaviors vary widely from culture to culture. For example, although members of Western cultures mean well, their Judeo-Christian worldview can be baffling to others. Americans missed the mark when they designed public health messages urging people in Namibia, Africa, to prevent HIV by abstaining from premarital sex and by being faithful to their spouses. These concepts are not meaningful to most Namibian citizens, who are accustomed to polygamy and who tend to define marriage very loosely (Hillier, 2006). Hillier concludes, "Prevention campaigns have been silent about polygamous sexual cultures. . . . [They have] elevated the Christian monogamous marriage to the most desirable norm but it is not the only or most common form of sexual union" (p. 18). As a result, many foreign efforts are culturally unacceptable and are therefore ineffective at changing people's behavior.

Another difficulty is that HIV and AIDS cannot yet be prevented with a pill or a shot. The only way to prevent transmission is by changing people's behavior (Schneider, 2006). That is a tremendous challenge. Some health communication specialists have concluded that it is naive to assume that most people *will not* have sex. The trick, they feel, is to make safer sex sexier. The Pleasure Project, based in Oxford, England, is a cooperative effort to emphasize the erotic appeal of safer sex. The project's website explains:

> *While most safer sex and HIV prevention programmes are negative and disease-focused, The Pleasure Project is different: we take a positive, liberating and sexy approach to safer sex. Think of it is as sex education . . . with the emphasis on "sex." ("About Us," 2013)*

CHECK IT OUT!

You can access the Pleasure Project website at www.thepleasureproject.org. (A word of warning: The website is sexually explicit.)

Project coordinators present condoms and alternatives to sexual intercourse as exciting and erotically stimulating. The website includes a racy directory of related organizations and programs, erotic tips for safer sex, and links to organizations that sell condoms and sex toys and donate the proceeds to the safer sex campaign.

The "safer sex is better sex" effort has been applauded by a range of public health experts. After reviewing relevant research, the authors of a Viewpoint article in *The Lancet* concur:

> *Since pursuit of pleasure is one of the main reasons that people have sex, this factor must be addressed when motivating people to use condoms and participate in safer sexual behaviour.* (*Philpott, Knerr, & Maher, 2006, p. 3*)

These are just a few of the many approaches to preventing HIV and AIDS. The good news is that, although the crisis is still very real, the rate of HIV infection has dropped 33% since 2001, largely because of public health efforts ("UNAIDS Reports," 2013). Some lessons learned include the following.

- *Listen and learn.* Knowing what the public believes and is willing to do is just as important, sometimes more important, than knowing what experts think people *should* do (Covello, 2003).
- *Vary your approach.* Fear appeals can be highly motivational, but particularly for frightening and long-term crises such as AIDS, people may tune out fear messages because they are overwhelming or overly familiar. Innovative, culturally sensitive appeals may regain people's attention.

A high school student in South Korea wears a mask as protection from Middle East respiratory syndrome (MERS). The challenge for public health communicators is to gauge when it is helpful to recommend such precautions and when they might frighten the public unnecessarily.

SARS

One of the great success stories in managing a public health crisis arose from worldwide efforts to contain severe acute respiratory syndrome (SARS). The issue first drew attention in February 2003, when a man in Vietnam was admitted to a hospital with a respiratory disorder. His condition deteriorated, and, although he was transferred to a Hong Kong medical center, he died within four days. Soon, seven caregivers who had been involved with the patient became sick as well. The disorder spread so quickly that, in slightly more than a month, there were 150 cases of SARS in eight countries (WHO, 2003c).

By May 2003, SARS had become a pandemic. New cases were emerging at the rate of 200 a day. The disease had spread to almost every continent. A total of 8,000 people in 28 countries were infected (WHO, 2003b). SARS was especially hard to contain because it was easily spread from person to person, it was infectious for more than a week before symptoms appeared, and it was hard to diagnose because the initial symptoms were similar to those of many other illnesses. Worst of all, SARS was deadly. About 10% of people who were infected (many of them hospital personnel) died.

The authors of the World Health Report (2007) recall:

> *SARS incited a degree of public anxiety that virtually halted travel to affected areas and drained billions of dollars from economies across entire regions. . . . It showed that the danger arising from emerging diseases is universal. No country, rich or poor, is adequately protected from either the arrival of a new disease on its territory or the subsequent disruption this can cause.* (*p. xix*)

However, it might have been worse. Remarkably, just 100 days into the crisis (in June, 2003), spokespersons for WHO announced that the pandemic was under control and that new cases had dwindled to a handful a day. The crisis was over by July. How was that possible? The turnaround resulted partly from effective quarantines. Much of the success also involved communication. Lessons from the experience illustrate the role communication played.

- *Develop strong teams.* WHO credits "monumental efforts" by governments, health professionals, and public health agencies. Because officials around the world reported cases promptly, WHO and other agencies were able to monitor and contain new outbreaks as much as possible. WHO dubbed it "solidarity" and "interdependence" on a global scale never seen before (WHO, 2003b, para. 8).
- *Make the most of communication technology.* Communication technology allowed researchers and health experts to share data and new developments quickly and accurately. Because of this, they figured out how SARS was transmitted "in record time" (WHO, 2003b, para. 11).
- *Keep everyone informed.* Although experts did a good job communicating with each other, members of some affected populations were out of the loop. In China, because of tight government controls on media content, many people were frustrated by the lack of SARS news coverage. Some of them there used the Internet to seek and share information about SARS that they could not get otherwise (Tai & Sun, 2007).
- *Educate the people involved.* Once officials knew that SARS was transmitted via droplets spread through coughing and sneezing, they were able to tell health care workers how to minimize the risk of infection.

In just a few months, SARS took a heavy toll. By the time it was contained, 8,098 people had been infected and 774 of those had died (CDC, 2005). However, containing the disease so quickly saved millions of lives. The SARS case is regarded as a model response to a nearly unthinkable public health threat.

Some people compare SARS to the more recent outbreak of Middle East respiratory syndrome (MERS), which may also be passed from person to person when an infected person sneezes or coughs. As of this writing, more than 1,000 cases of MERS have been reported (WHO, 2015e). Most of them are in Saudi Arabia, but people have been diagnosed with MERS in 25 other countries as well. Nearly 4 in 10 people diagnosed with the virus have died from it, which is a far higher percentage than with SARS (WHO, 2015d). However, MERS has not spread as rapidly. It remains to be seen if MERS will escalate or if health officials will be able to use the lessons from SARS to minimize its impact.

ANTHRAX

Some public health crises are the result of intentional acts. The CDC (2007) defines **bioterrorism** as "the deliberate release of viruses, bacteria, or other germs (agents) used to cause illness or death in people, animals, or plants" (para. 1). Bioterrorism is not new. Schneider (2006) points out that when European settlers purposely gave Native Americans blankets used by people with smallpox, they were engaging in (tragically effective) germ warfare. Today, dense population centers are especially vulnerable to attacks.

One act of bioterrorism on American soil occurred in 2001, when 22 people were sickened and 5 died after contact with letters containing anthrax spores. Anthrax is a potentially deadly disease that people can get by inhaling, touching, or digesting a rare bacterium. In September and October 2001, someone sent four envelopes containing anthrax spores to media professionals and government officials. In doing so, the terrorist put many people, including postal workers and mailroom employees, at grave risk.

Because the anthrax attacks occurred soon after the terrorist attacks of September 11, public anxiety was particularly high. And because the attacks occurred through the mail, it was difficult to know who had been or might be exposed to anthrax. Potentially, anyone in the country might be next. As Haider and Aravindakshan (2005) put it, "The threat turned junk mail into potential parcels of danger" (p. 393). In contrast to a typical illness, which begins in one place and then may spread, this one was immediately a nationwide concern (Gursky, Inglesby, & O'Toole, 2003). At one point, health officials put 32,000 people on antibiotics, a preemptive move that experts speculate saved many lives.

In the article "Order Out of Chaos," Freimuth (2006) describes how the CDC Office of Communication (of which she was director) functioned in the high-pressure weeks following the anthrax attacks. The CDC is the arm of the U.S. Department of Health and Human Services in charge of public health efforts, education, information, and more. Staff members in the media relations office, which is one component of the communication division, usually field about 55 calls a week. But they received an average of 1,283 calls a week in the six weeks following the anthrax attacks (Freimuth, 2006). In addition, the staff coordinated a total of 373 press briefings, press statements, and broadcast interviews in that time. "It was common in a single day to have interview requests from every network morning show, every network evening news hour, and the

Larry King Hour," recalls Freimuth (2006, p. 144). Since there was no way the 10-person media relations staff could meet the demands on their own, Freimuth oversaw a temporary reorganization in which the staff was tripled to 30 people who each worked four days a week, overlapping one day in the middle.

As with many public health crises, one of the greatest hurdles was managing uncertainty. Scientific evidence about inhalable anthrax was scant, and information that emerged was sometimes incomplete and inaccurate. As new information was released, media professionals sometimes treated the old information as "mistakes" (Freimuth, 2006, p. 142). And, in their eagerness to get information, some reporters turned to untrustworthy sources who were willing to offer speculative and self-serving information.

The CDC staff, which prides itself on a "slow, thoughtful scientific" process, was forced to work quickly and with less deliberation than usual (Freimuth, 2006, p. 142). Friction sometimes resulted when scientists were concerned that their research might be oversimplified, but it was necessary to summarize scientific findings quickly and make them easy to understand. All the while, the FBI (which was officially in charge of the case) wanted some details kept secret to avoid compromising the investigation.

To keep up with demands and to ensure that stakeholder groups were not overlooked, members of the CDC communication staff organized themselves into teams. One team communicated with clinicians, another with concerned citizens, still others with media professionals, policy-makers, and the like. As in most crises, success was defined largely by communication. "Not all of these staff had to be communication specialists, but they needed to be managed by communication staff so that messages could be consistent across the agency and delivered in a timely manner," writes Freimuth (2006, p. 146).

WHAT DO YOU THINK?

- Given the opportunity, would you like to be part of a crisis management team such as the CDC communication team? Why or why not?
- What aspects of the job appeal to you most?
- What do you think would be most difficult?

See Career Opportunities (Box 12.1) for relevant resources.

Another challenge was to identify and prepare spokespeople. Freimuth (2006) reflects that the public naturally looks to political leaders for information and updates. But those leaders are often not well informed about scientific details, and they tend to comfort audiences rather than level with them. Scientists, although more knowledgeable, often err in the other direction, coming off as "logical and unemotional" (Freimuth, 2006, p. 142). The process of choosing and preparing spokespeople was difficult, but it was worth the extra effort. Kristen Swain's (2007) study of news coverage during the anthrax crisis shows that audiences responded most favorably when information was specific and was clearly linked to trustworthy sources.

The anthrax case involved people from many agencies and organizations. At the height of the crisis, when a suspicious substance was reported in the western United States, Freimuth was awakened at 3 a.m. to take part in a conference call involving nearly 15 people from a wide range of agencies. "It was impossible to sort out who was with what organization and what position they held," she says, "yet in that phone call, decisions had to be reached" (Freimuth, 2006, p. 143).

Although the anthrax case revealed serious deficits in the government's preparedness for a bioterrorist attack, the CDC Office of Communication was lauded as doing an admirable job during extremely trying circumstances.

WHAT DO YOU THINK?

- If an incident of bioterrorism occurs in your state or community, what spokespeople will you trust most? Why?
- What type of information will you want?
- Through what channels are you most likely to seek information?

The following lessons about public health and risk/crisis communication emerge from the anthrax case:

- *Crisis is a matter of perception.* In the same year that anthrax killed 5 people, 30,000 other people in the United States died from the flu (Lovett, 2003). It is a phenomenon that risk and crisis communicators know well: Fear and uncertainty elevate some health concerns to crisis status, while far more prevalent killers, such as the flu and diabetes, often fail to make headlines.

- *Even if you do not specialize in crisis management, learn as much as you can about it and be prepared to take part.* The media relations restructuring was possible because the CDC staff pulled communication experts from a range of other duties and partnered them with content experts. Freimuth (2006) advises, "Health communicators working in any public health context need to add risk communication and crisis management skills to their repertoire" (p. 148).
- *Even in the midst of a crisis, do not be afraid to restructure the system if it helps you respond to stakeholders more effectively.*
- *Show genuine compassion.* Empathize with people's fears, sadness, and frustration. Crisis communication expert Vincent Covello (2003) advises, "Avoid using distant, unfeeling language when discussing harm, deaths, injuries, and illness" (p. 7).
- *Speaking with many voices is sometimes okay.* This lesson runs counter to crisis management advice for companies, individuals, and political campaigns. In those instances, it is important to deliver a clear, consistent message to the public. But a public health campaign is usually far more complex, and evidence suggests that allowing a range of viewpoints is sometimes effective and even preferable. After studying the anthrax case, L. Clarke and colleagues (2006) concluded that the situation was "naturally given to the expression of many voices" and that "a single voice with a single message would have been so discordant with actual circumstances that it could only misrepresent the risks that people might face" (p. 167). Experience shows that, even in a crisis, people expect and can cope with a range of expert viewpoints on complex issues. One caveat is that audiences who are already distrustful of public health messages may assume that sources are being dishonest if they provide inconsistent information (Meredith et al., 2007). For this reason, it is important not to hide inconsistencies, but to acknowledge and explain why they exist (Seeger, 2006).
- *Do not go it alone.* Covello (2003) advises organizations to "coordinate, collaborate, and partner with other credible sources" (p. 6). Such teamwork can help offset overwhelming demands on any one organization and can demonstrate to the public that multiple sources agree on key issues.
- *Do not overlook "forgotten publics."* In the anthrax case, postal workers were particularly sensitive to any implication that their safety was less important than that of the people to whom the dangerous letters were addressed. Similar tensions arose on a greater scale during the Hurricane Katrina crisis, when government agencies were accused of devaluing New Orleans residents on the basis of race and socioeconomic status (L. Fisher, 2007; Littlefield & Quenette, 2007; Waymer & Heath, 2007).

Next we turn to an issue that, as of this writing, is still in the pre-crisis or perhaps the early-crisis phase.

CHECK IT OUT!

Following are links to some risk and crisis communication centers:

- Center for Risk Communication: www.centerforriskcommunication.org
- The Communication Initiative Network: www.comminit.com
- Peter Sandman's interactive blog about crisis and risk communication: www.psandman.com/gst2006.htm

Also check university websites. Many schools have centers for risk and crisis communication as well as degree programs in the field.

AVIAN FLU

One of the threats keeping public health professionals on high alert is avian flu, also called bird flu and H5N1. As the name suggests, the virus originated in poultry. So far, more than half of the 840 people diagnosed with avian flu had died from it (WHO, 2015a). In serious cases, there is nothing doctors can do. Within days, lung tissue dies, and so does the patient. As in the case studies we have reviewed, communication is likely to play a pivotal role in managing this threat.

The first documented case of H5N1 occurred in Hong Kong in 1997. After that, the government oversaw the killing of every chicken in Hong Kong (about

When tens of millions of poultry in the United States were found to have bird flu, part of public health officials' job was to educate farmers about precautions they could take to minimize the chance of human infection.

1.5 million birds; Appenzeller, 2005). The disease seemed to go away. But it resurfaced in 2003, killing 230 people and millions of birds (WHO, 2007b). In late 2014, officials confirmed that birds in several areas of the United States carried the virus or one similar to it. By May 2015, it hit the media that bird flu was "raging through poultry farms across the United States" ("Secretary of Agriculture," 2015, para. 1). By then, turkeys and chickens in 220 poultry farms in 20 states were affected. No humans had contracted the virus, but farmers slaughtered tens of millions of birds to try to stop the spread.

The virus often kills birds in a matter of hours by destroying their lungs, brains, muscles, and intestines (Appenzeller, 2005). So far, people with H5N1 seem to have caught it from direct contact with affected animals. Although scientists are not certain how the disease jumps to humans, they caution people to cook poultry fully, to use gloves and masks when handling live or dead birds, and not to use bird-dropping fertilizer.

But the danger that worries public health officials the most is that this virus or a similar one will mutate so that it can spread from human to human. Flu viruses in the past have been remarkably adept at doing that. "It's bound to happen," predicts Jeremy Farrar, an Oxford University physician who specializes in avian flu, "and when it does, the world is going to face a truly horrible pandemic" (quoted by Appenzeller, 2005, para. 11).

If H5N1 becomes a pandemic, millions of people could die. It has happened before. During World War I, some 50 million people died from Spanish flu—more than three times the number of soldiers who died in the war (Appenzeller, 2005). Like avian flu, Spanish flu probably jumped from animals to people. That type of mutation is extremely dangerous because humans have few antibodies to protect them from the novel virus.

And if you are thinking that you rarely get the flu or that you get over it quickly when you do, beware. This version of the flu is especially dangerous for people who have well-functioning immune systems. In serious cases, avian flu so overstimulates the body's immune system that the lungs become grossly inflamed with white blood cells, and life-sustaining tissues die (Appenzeller, 2005).

It is difficult to imagine overplanning for a crisis such as avian flu. As Barbara Reynolds (2006) points out, in any health crisis, "the devil is most certainly in the details" (p. 249). WHO (2007a) has released rapid-response guidelines for containing a deadly flu pandemic. Public health personnel in your community are probably already working on the local plan. WHO guidelines include the following: (1) Create a geographic "containment zone" when the first cases surface in order to separate people who have the disease, as well as those who have been exposed to it, from other people; (2) create a "buffer zone" around the containment zone to reduce further the risk of contagion; and (3) communicate effectively with the public to maintain barriers, keep people informed, ensure that people within the containment zone have adequate care and supplies, and minimize stigmatization of people with the disease.

How will this work exactly? It sounds a bit frightening, but it's not as scary as the alternative. Imagine your community partitioned with roadblocks, warning signs, and guarded screening stations. No one except essential personnel will go in or out of containment zones for at least 20 days. It sounds like something from a movie, but it is no exaggeration. Health officials realize that the only way to save lives is to limit the spread of the virus. Inside the containment zone—which could be your neighborhood or a portion of your hometown—health officials will monitor people's health, care for and quarantine (in a hospital or at home) people who are infected, watch for new outbreaks, and help distribute antiviral medication to those who are still healthy. (See Box 12.5 for more about ethical dilemmas concerning who should receive the limited number of vaccines available.)

This means that, if a person in your household becomes ill, you may all be confined to your home until officials can be sure you are not contagious. And even if everyone in your household is healthy, if an outbreak occurs in your area, it would be advisable to remain in your home. Public health experts recommend that everyone maintain a two-week supply of food, water, and needed medications just in case. They also recommend that people wash their hands frequently and cover their mouths when sneezing or coughing.

WHAT DO YOU THINK?

- Would you be frightened if a containment zone were declared in your area? Why or why not?
- Do you feel adequately informed about, and prepared for, such a crisis?

Because we are currently in a pre-crisis, planning phase concerning the next pandemic flu, it is difficult to know what lessons will emerge. But it is interesting to note that health officials are consciously building on what worked well in the SARS case. A visit to the WHO, CDC, or PandemicFlu.gov website reveals an extensive collection of materials, including health-tracking software, government agency contact lists, brochures, and checklists for a wide range of stakeholder groups.

As with many other components of public health and risk/crisis management, success depends largely on effective communication (Seeger, 2006). It is no longer defensible to think of avian flu as an Asian crisis or a future scenario. Sandman (2006b) advises crisis communicators to imagine "that the crisis has just begun and to make a list of things they wish the public had already learned or already done" (p. 259). As members of the public, we might ask ourselves: *Are we aware and prepared for a deadly flu pandemic? If containment zones were created in our community next week or next month, would we understand what was happening? Are we (and our neighbors) prepared to stay in our homes for two weeks or longer?* Ideally, the public should answer yes to these questions well in advance of the crisis.

As we wrap up coverage of international health crises, it helps to remember that challenges are happening all the time, but so are victories. In his article "Still a Privilege to Be a Doctor," pediatrician Lawrence Rifkin (2008) pauses to reflect on the small miracles that health advocates accomplish every day:

BOX 12.5 ETHICAL CONSIDERATIONS

Who Should Be Protected?

The good news is that researchers have created a vaccine for avian flu. It is not perfect because they do not know exactly how the virus will mutate. And researchers must still make sure there are no harmful side effects. But even if the vaccine is approved, there will not be enough for everyone. So public health experts face a dilemma. After reading about bird flu in this chapter, consider what you would do in their shoes.

1. If you had to choose, which of the following populations would you vaccinate and why? (a) people who are most likely to die from the disease if they get it; (b) service providers such as health care professionals, firefighters, and police officers; or (c) another population of your choosing.
2. Would you first vaccinate people in communities in which avian flu cases have already been diagnosed? Why or why not? If those citizens or their governments are unable to afford the vaccine, do you believe people in other countries should help pay for it? Why or why not?
3. Viruses such as the flu often spread quickly among children. Would you vaccinate them early on? Why or why not?
4. Are you in favor of *requiring* people at high risk for avian flu (such as those who regularly handle birds) to get vaccinated? Why or why not?
5. Depending on how the virus mutates, the vaccine might not be especially effective. Do you think governments should invest in it anyway? Why or why not?
6. Given the opportunity, would you choose to be vaccinated? Why or why not?

BOX 12.6

Lessons for Public Health and Crisis Communication

Following is a summary of the tips provided in this chapter.

Have a Plan

- Create a well-developed crisis management plan.
- Designate who will speak on behalf of the issue or organization.
- Practice what to do when a crisis occurs.

Cultivate Ongoing Relationships

- Nurture interactive and trusting relationships with stakeholders (community members, leaders, media, emergency personnel, and so on).
- Listen well. Focus on stakeholders' beliefs, expectations, and information needs.

Build an Information Library

- Collect information in advance that will be helpful, quick at hand, and tailored to different audiences.

Emphasize Teamwork

- Develop strong teams within and between organizations.
- Even if you do not specialize in crisis management, learn as much as you can about it and be prepared to take part.
- Even in the midst of a crisis, do not be afraid to restructure the system if it helps you respond to stakeholders more effectively.

Be Honest and Consistent

- Present trustworthy, current information that is based on science and evidence.
- Provide the public with answers to three key questions: "What do I need to know? What do I need to do or not do today to protect my health and that of my family? Where do I find information that I can trust and understand?" (Ratzan & Moritsugu, 2014, p. 1214).
- Coordinate with local health officials so that advice and information is consistent at every level whenever possible.
- When information is unavoidably inconsistent, acknowledge that and explain why.
- Be proactive rather than simply reacting to developments as they occur.
- Do not downplay legitimate risks and dangers.
- Vary your approach.
- Make the most of communication technology.

Recognize Diversity

- Remember that crisis is a matter of perception. People may assume that issues are more or less threatening than they seem to you.
- Don't overlook "forgotten publics," such as civil servants and the worried well.

Keep Communicating

- Expect resistance to your message and do not give up.
- Keep everyone involved (internally and externally) well informed and educated about risks and precautions.
- Communicate regularly with the public, members of the team, and with external agencies.

Ashley's in Room 3, with a positive rapid strep. It doesn't get more commonplace than that. Then, with a sense of wonder, I remember: A century ago, rheumatic fever complications from strep were the No. 1 cause of death in school-age children. Now, we hardly see rheumatic fever in this country; a few generations ago, Ashley may have been one of the victims. As I write out yet another prescription for amoxicillin, I think maybe I just saved a life. (p. 28)

Summary

A collection of case studies illustrates the complexities and interrelatedness of public health, risk communication, crisis communication, and health care reform.

The Ebola experience reminds us that it is critical for health officials to understand the fears, customs, and expectations of people involved and to communicate with them in respectful and consistent ways.

Largely in response to the widespread coverage of the Disneyland measles outbreaks, anti-vaxxers have been portrayed in the media as selfish, irrational, misinformed, and dangerous to public health (Friedersdorf, 2015). Others urge people to remember that, like most parents, anti-vaxxers care about their children and are trying to make sense of complex information.

From the mad cow disease saga we learn that, even when scientists cannot provide definitive answers, it is dangerous and unethical to keep the public in the dark about a potential health threat. Although public officials naturally worry about creating panic, the majority of evidence suggests just the opposite: People typically want to assist others in emergency situations. This can actually make it difficult to convince citizens and rescue workers to use safety precautions, as we saw following the 9/11 terrorist attacks.

Although people seldom panic, public health experts are advised to use fear appeals with sensitivity. Overloading the public with frightening messages can cause undue worry. Conversely, offering false reassurance can mislead people and damage their trust in public officials.

A different challenge is keeping an ongoing health crisis such as AIDS on the public agenda. Prevention efforts are complicated by the sensitive nature of transmission-related behaviors and the wide diversity of cultures affected. The AIDS case underscores how important it is to listen to, respect, and understand the people we are trying to help.

The global nature of commerce and travel makes it imperative that health advocates around the world work together to monitor emerging concerns, track their incidence, and stop the spread of contagious illnesses as quickly as possible. The SARS case represents a successful effort to do just that. Efforts are already under way to respond to an avian flu pandemic if it occurs.

Although these lessons look easy on paper, the stress and demands of an actual crisis make them difficult to follow. The risk management/communication framework reminds us that the best crisis communicators lay solid groundwork before a crisis emerges so they have information at hand, trusting and open relationships with stakeholders, and well-developed and well-rehearsed plans in place. The anthrax case reminds us that a wide range of professionals is likely to be enlisted for help, making crisis management skills an important part of anyone's professional portfolio. At the same time, ethical dimensions of risk and crisis communication are everyone's businesses.

Key Terms and Theories

public health
social mobilization
risk communication
crisis communication
risk management/communication framework (RMCF)
bioterrorism

Discussion Questions

1. How would you feel if health officials in hazardous-material suits showed up at your home and the homes of your neighbors, demanding that you turn ill family members over to them? What if you heard that many families who turned their loved ones over to authorities never knew what happened to them afterwards?
2. What advice do you have for health crisis communicators who are worried about creating panic? For those who are worried that too many warnings will make people indifferent when true emergencies arise?
3. Of the three risk communication traditions presented by Peter Sandman, which is most descriptive of risk communication? Of crisis communication?
4. Describe the risk management/communication framework (RMCF) that Scott Ratzan and Wendy Meltzer present.
5. Discuss the ethical implications raised by the Andrew Speaker and Mary Mallon (Typhoid Mary) cases. Why might such public health risks be even more salient today than in Mallon's time? What do you think we should do to protect individual liberties while preserving the public's health interest?
6. Describe how the CDC communication staff handled the anthrax crisis and what we can learn from the experience.
7. Trace the development of the H5N1 avian flu case so far. Would you be frightened if a containment zone were declared in your area? Why or why not? Do you feel adequately informed about and prepared for such a crisis? Why or why not?

CHAPTER 13

Planning Health Promotion Campaigns

The truth is all around you, the truth® campaign, that is. You might remember images of public spaces filled with life-sized mannequins, each one representing a person who died as a result of smoking. Or you might have seen "Catmageddon" videos that showcase amusing feline feats while warning viewers that cats are twice as likely as their owners to die from smoking-related cancer. "The Internet is fueled by cat videos, and because cigarettes can kill cats, too, we're freaking out, and you should, too" says a truth® campaign message.

The spots are often irreverent and entertaining, but they mean business. truth® is the nation's longest running and most successful youth smoking-prevention campaign. It is designed for a highly specific target market—youth ages 12 to 17. As truth®'s creators explain:

> **truth** *speaks to youth and young adults on their terms, through the channels they understand and trust. truth delivers the facts about the health effects and social consequences of tobacco and the marketing tactics of the tobacco industry so that youth and young adults can make informed decisions and influence others to do the same.*

The campaign gets results. When it launched in 2000, teens' awareness of antitobacco messages almost immediately doubled (Farrelly, Healton, Davis, Messeri, & Haviland, 2002). Since then, the percentage of teen smokers in the United States has dropped to its lowest level in more than 20 years (Johnston, O'Malley, Miech, Bachman, & Schulenberg, 2014). The truth® campaign is not the only factor involved in reducing teen smoking, but analysts give it kudos for having a huge impact. *Advertising Age* named truth® one of the Top 15 Ad Campaigns of the 21st Century ("truth® Named," 2015).

truth® is sponsored by Truth Initiative, a national public health organization dedicated to achieving a culture in which all youth and young adults reject tobacco. It is funded by a settlement reached between the tobacco industry and 46 states and five U.S. territories in 1998.

In the early years, truth® messages were mostly about the health threats of tobacco use (Lavoie & Quick, 2013). Campaign advocates published the ingredients of cigarettes (including chemicals also found in "cat pee" and "dog poop") and presented the "hard facts" about tobacco companies' deceptions and unfair practices.

CHECK IT OUT!

Visit the truth® website at www.thetruth.com.

More recently, the mischievously named FINISH**IT** campaign encouraged youth to be the generation that ends teen smoking. Based on evidence that the portion of teens who smoke is down to 7%, the website explains, "This isn't about throwing stones at smokers. It's about finding and turbo-charging new fun ways to do what no generation has ever done before—end smoking" (thetruth.com, 2015, "About Us"). Campaign messages encourage teens to post their own photos and videos, recruit their friends to join the FINISH**IT** movement, and engage in a variety of teen-oriented events and online activities.

In this chapter we walk through the first steps in creating an effective health-promotion campaign. In Chapter 12, we discussed the overlap between public health and crisis communication. Here we turn our attention to another side of the same coin—efforts to help people protect themselves from more chronic health threats such as cancer, obesity, diabetes, and accidents. Keeping health issues on the public agenda and working with people to change their everyday behaviors can be as challenging as managing a crisis.

Health-promoting behaviors are those that "enhance health and well-being, reduce health risks, and prevent disease" (Brennan & Fink, 1997, p. 157). These behaviors include lifestyle choices, medical care, prevention efforts, and activities that foster an overall sense of well-being.

Health promotion campaigns are systematic efforts to influence people to engage in health-enhancing behaviors (Backer & Rogers, 1993). These efforts may involve the use of many communication channels, from face-to-face communication to mass media. The term *health promoter* includes anyone involved in the process of creating and distributing health promotion messages. This includes volunteers in the community, employees of nonprofit health agencies, public relations and community relations professionals, production artists, media decision makers, and more. As this list suggests, health promotion offers diverse career opportunities for communication specialists. (See Box 13.1.)

In this chapter we consider the challenges of promoting health behaviors among diverse members of the population. We begin with a brief overview of health campaigns, describing some particularly

BOX 13.1 CAREER OPPORTUNITIES

Health Promotion and Education

Hospital-based health educator
School-based health educator
Community health educator
Director of nonprofit organization
Patient advocate or patient navigator
Professor/educator
Health information publication designer
Corporate wellness director
Fitness instructor

Career Resources and Job Listings

- Society for Public Health Education: sophe.org
- Area Health Education Centers: nationalahec.org
- National Commission for Health Education Credentialing (NCHEC): nchec.org
- U.S. Bureau of Labor Statistics Occupational Outlook: bls.gov/oco/ocos063.htm
- *Chronicle of Higher Education* Job Search: chronicle.com/jobs
- Centers for Disease Control and Prevention Division of Health Communication: cdc.gov/healthcommunication
- National Institutes of Health: nih.gov
- World Health Organization: who.int/employment/vacancies/en

notable ones. Then we follow the first four stages of designing a health promotion campaign:

Step 1: Defining the situation and potential benefits
Step 2: Analyzing and segmenting the audience
Step 3: Establishing campaign goals and objectives
Step 4: Selecting channels of communication

Steps 5 through 7, on designing and implementing a campaign, are covered in the next chapter. Keep in mind that it's important to know all the steps before you actually begin. Although evaluating and refining the campaign is the final step, you must consider from the beginning how you will accomplish those goals later on.

Background On Health Campaigns

"Live long and prosper," the Vulcan salutation on *Star Trek,* seems to say it all. A long and healthy existence—isn't that what life is all about? You might think so. But it turns out that Vulcan logic is not always able to explain human behavior, as Mr. Spock discovered.

Early health campaigns were designed with the confidence that, as humans, we want nothing so much as our own health and longevity. From that viewpoint it follows that, if we know a behavior is unhealthy, we will not act that way. In fact, we should go to great lengths to pursue health-enhancing outcomes. Seen this way, persuasion is not an issue. People only need reliable information. The motivation to comply with it is presumably already there, as innate as the animal instinct for survival.

MOTIVATING FACTORS

It turns out that influencing human behavior is not that simple. We are motivated by a number of factors that make us more or less receptive to health information and more or less motivated to change our behavior. Sometimes we do things we know to be unhealthy because the behavior is inexpensive, convenient, socially rewarding, or fun. For instance, research indicates that people may drink alcoholic beverages even though they believe them to be unhealthy because they are reluctant to give up the social ritual of drinking with friends. Conversely, we sometimes change our behavior without knowing much about the change or the reasons for it. We may try a behavior (like taking vitamins) simply because someone tells us to or because the change seems interesting, easy, fashionable, or so on. In these instances, knowledge may *follow* behavior change.

Research has not always been encouraging about health campaigns' actual effects. Campaigns have been criticized for naively seeking to change people's behavior without changing their circumstances and for assuming that knowledge reaches and affects all people equally.

In reality, campaigns may raise awareness, but, unless the recommended behaviors are compatible with people's beliefs and are supported within their social networks, campaigns are unlikely to change behavior very much. Health promoters have discovered that we cannot simply educate people about health and presume they will adjust their lifestyles accordingly. We must take a range of factors into account. It is crucial to know the audience and to consider not just how they might benefit from certain behaviors, but whether they would find those behavior changes difficult or unacceptable.

> **CAN YOU GUESS? PART 1**
>
> Which kills more people in the United States—tobacco or illegal drugs?
>
> *The answer appears at the end of the chapter.*

EXEMPLARY CAMPAIGNS

This section describes a few exemplary health promotion campaigns. Each provides an inspiring lesson for promoters. Together, these examples illustrate that, as health promoters, we must often do more than simply disseminate information if we are to succeed. Sensitivity to audience needs, problem-solving skills, assessment, community involvement, and careful planning and follow-through are required as well.

Get to Know the Audience

One quality of effective health promoters is that *they know their audiences well and design campaigns to suit those audiences.* Analysts say truth® has been successful largely because its creators take time to understand and engage with the target audience. Whereas health promoters have long been frustrated by teens' tendency to do the opposite of what they are told, the truth® campaign honors their rebellious nature (Farrelly et al., 2002). The campaign "never preaches and never talks down to teenagers," explain truth® sponsors. ("truth® Overview," n.d.). Instead, it honors adolescents' sense of independence and personal choice. As the truth® website puts it:

> *WE DON'T HATE.* ***WE INSTIGATE.***
> *We're not here to criticize your choices, or tell you not to smoke. We're here to arm everyone—smokers and non-smokers—with the tools to make change.*
>
> *EXPOSING* ***BIG TOBACCO***
> *We've always been about exposing Big Tobacco's lies and manipulation. And while they keep adapting their tactics, we keep it real.* (*thetruth, 2015, "About Us"*)

The people behind truth® wager that when teens are exposed to the deceit and manipulation behind tobacco companies' efforts, they will rebel against corporate greed by *not* smoking.

Invest in Communication Infrastructures

A community health initiative involving Matthew Matsaganis, Annis Golden, and Muriel Scott (2014) illustrates another best practice in health promotion: *Create enduring infrastructures that support relationship development and collaborative problem solving.* The members of the research team helped to increase reproductive health care received by low-income African American women in one community by helping underserved community members and service providers get to know each other better. The program was based on four main premises. One was that storytelling can be a powerful means of bridging social gaps. Another was that outreach efforts should be initiated within the places and circumstances of people's everyday lives. A third was that underserved individuals are capable and deserving of collaborating with care providers to structure how services are provided. A fourth premise was that long-term success relies on the creation of an enduring communication infrastructure. For more about this remarkable project, see Box 13.2.

BOX 13.2

Storytelling Connects Underserved Women and Care Providers

It was a common dilemma. A publicly funded health care center was available to the residents of a small, rural community. However, many of the people most in need of its services were not receiving them. Here is what happened when a team of three health communication scholars took on the challenge.

Aware that low-income African American women were underutilizing a reproductive health care center in their community, scholars Matthew Matsaganis, Annis Golden, and Muriel Scott (2014) focused on the reasons why. They soon realized that there was a general disconnect between the women and local services organizations. Although organizational members wished women would make greater use of their services, most of them felt unsure how to bridge the gap that separated them. For their part, the would-be clients were often unsure what was available to them, unable to find reliable transportation, and skeptical that they could trust care providers.

Over the course of four years, principal investigators Matsaganis and Golden served not only as researchers, but as interstitial actors in the effort to help. That is, they were intermediaries who helped to bridge the gaps between people, organizations, and larger public entities. They reached out to underserved women in gathering places (communication hotspots) the women frequented in everyday life. In this way, they sidestepped some of the barriers—such as transportation difficulties and distrust—that might have prevented the women's participation (Matsaganis, Golden, & Scott, 2014).

The objective was to listen to and partner with African American women, not to engage in one-way communication or to privilege organizational agendas. As the women interacted with each other and with organizational representatives, storytelling emerged as a natural means of getting to know each other. As one woman put it, "They was talking to me,

continued

they was real good to me . . . And they was listening and that was making me feel good 'cause they was listening and answering my questions the way that I wanted them answered" (Matsaganis et al., 2014, p. 1503).

Significantly, Matsaganis and colleagues (2014) helped to create enduring communication infrastructures. They founded a community advisory board, recruited and trained peer health advocates, and spearheaded the creation of a field office at a local public housing complex, which they staffed with an African American community outreach associate who was familiar in the community and knowledgeable about health resources.

The field office was critical to the project's success, reflects Matsaganis. It became a "comfort zone" within the community, "a great place to connect with residents and foster the development of trust between the research team and residents" (Matsaganis, personal correspondence). Based on the relationships that emerged in the field office, women in the community were more comfortable taking part in other activities sponsored by the team, such as health fairs and entertainment events, and ultimately, in seeking reproductive health care and other services (Matsaganis et al., 2014).

With a clearer understanding of underserved women's needs, staff members at the field office and other locations initiated new support services. For example, they began to assist women in making health appointments, and they provided taxi vouchers so they could reach the health center.

As with any program of this magnitude, participants faced hurdles in terms of limited resources and resilient distrust. However, with the benefit of a communication infrastructure that invited their involvement, local residents and members of the health community gradually developed more trusting partnerships. Utilization of reproductive health services increased 25% (Matsaganis et al., 2014).

Make Healthy Options Accessible

Another lesson is that health promotion comes in many forms, and *sometimes actions are more empowering than words alone.* For example, realizing that healthy eating is not an affordable option for everyone, programs such as Feeding America offer nutritious take-home food for schoolchildren in need.

Another example involves **nudging**, the practice of making healthy options readily apparent, appealing, and available. Some nudging efforts are nonverbal, as in displaying healthy food in a prominent location of the grocery store. Others are more explicit, as when health promoters provide discount coupons for child safety seats. Astrid Junghans and colleagues (2015) surveyed consumers in the United Kingdom to see whether they mostly considered nudges in the supermarket to be manipulative or empowering. Most of them felt that nudges were helpful if they were not overpowering and if they were motivated by a desire to help people rather than to make a profit (Junghans, Cheung, & De Ridder, 2015). However, some people felt that nudges have a paternalistic downside in that they seek to influence people's behavior at a subconscious level rather than presenting a persuasive message outright. (See the *What Do You Think?* box to consider the implications for yourself.)

WHAT DO YOU THINK?

- Do you feel it is ethical to locate the supermarket bakery near the front of the stores so that shoppers will immediately smell the scent of bread and sweets? Why or why not?
- Do you feel it is ethical for supermarket personnel to display fresh produce in highly visible places throughout the store? Why or why not?
- What might supermarket personnel do to make healthy choices accessible without being unfairly manipulative or paternalistic?

Take a Multimedia Approach

A *multimedia approach may be more beneficial than using only one channel.* To test this idea, Grace Ahn (2015) invited a group of university students to don headsets and experience a virtual world in which they observed time-lapse images of a person drinking sugary soft drinks over a two-year span and gaining 20 pounds. The experiment was immersive in that the students could "look around the virtual world as they would in the physical world" and hear the sound of "fat splattering onto a digital scale" as the person gained weight (Ahn, p. 548). Ahn asked other students to review only a printed pamphlet that described the same process. Still a third group both reviewed the pamphlet and took part in the virtual experience. One week later, participants in the third group were the most likely of all to say that they would not like to have sugary drinks, which suggests that the combined impact of multiple experiences may be a particularly powerful means of conveying health information.

Set Clear Goals and Measure Your Success

Another best practice is to *establish clear goals and measure your success.* A case in point is the designated driver campaign, originally launched in 1988 by members of the Harvard School of Public Health's Center for Health Communication, who were inspired by a similar concept in Scandinavia. It is estimated that the program and related spin-offs have saved the lives of at least 50,000 people ("Designated Driving Statistics," 2015). Public health expert Jay Winsten (2010) proposes that the campaign was successful largely because the goal (to reduce drunk-driving accidents) was clear and measurable, it involved a modest change in behavior (agreeing to be a sober driver for one's friends one occasion at a time), and because the entertainment industry embraced the idea and wove it into prime-time storylines—as many as 160 of them.

Virtual reality headsets such as this one are one means of making health-related images vivid, immersive, and tailored to individuals. In one study, participants were more likely to swear off sugary soft drinks after they read a pamphlet about their ill effects and watched a virtual-reality time-lapse presentation of a soft drink consumer gaining weight (Ahn, 2015).

Next let's consider how we would create our own health campaign.

Step 1: Defining The Situation and Potential Benefits

To illustrate the steps in planning a health campaign, imagine that staff members of a university sports recreation department have asked us to help recruit new participants. Specifically, they would like to increase the number of people who go to the campus fitness center in their free time. The recreation department will not benefit financially from the added enrollment, but the staff wishes to increase participation because physical activity improves people's health. The rest of the chapter guides us through the initial steps of creating a campaign. The hypothetical sports recreation campaign is admittedly a small-scale effort, but many influential campaigns are aimed at limited audiences, and improving health habits among even a small group is a momentous goal. Furthermore, the steps given apply well to large and small campaigns.

If you are like many people, your first instinct is to post fliers and to send a story about the recreation program to the campus newspaper. Those may be effective steps, but before we begin, let's take the advice of professional campaign planners and do some preliminary research.

BENEFITS

At this stage, we should be interested in learning what benefits (if any) our efforts might achieve. Following are some questions we might research.

- Would exercising at the fitness center actually improve people's health?
- Would everybody benefit?

- Are there some people who would not benefit?
- Are there alternative ways to get the same benefits?

Answers to these questions can be obtained by reading published literature and talking with experts in the field. Such preliminary research will prepare us to share useful knowledge with others and may help us decide if the project is worthwhile.

CURRENT SITUATION

Assuming that we find reasonable evidence to believe that people might benefit from exercising at the gym, the next step is to assess the current situation. Following are some questions to guide our preliminary research. The same questions will be useful later in guiding audience analysis. Remember that experts, program leaders, current participants, and nonparticipants are all valuable sources of information. In addition to these general questions, we may want to add some specific questions relevant to the campaign.

- How many people currently participate in the recommended behavior?
- What types of people participate and for what reasons? (Of interest is demographic information, such as age, sex, and income, as well as cultural, personal, social, or personality variables that might be relevant.)
- What are the strengths and weaknesses of the program (from the perspective of participants and nonparticipants)?
- What types of people do not participate?
- What are their reasons for not participating?
- What factors are most important to participants and nonparticipants (e.g., cost, convenience, social interaction)?
- Do people consider the potential benefits of this behavior important? Why or why not?
- Are there any conditions under which nonparticipants might participate?
- How do the people in the audience usually receive information (i.e., fliers, newspaper, radio, email, etc.)?
- Through what channels do they prefer to get information?
- What information sources do they trust?

Preliminary answers to our questions may be surprising. We may find, for instance, that current sports recreation participants are not primarily concerned about health benefits. They go to the fitness center because their friends are there and they enjoy the social interaction. Or we might find that some people will not participate no matter how healthy physical activity is because they are afraid of looking foolish on the basketball court or out of shape in group fitness classes. Perhaps recreational programs are scheduled when many people cannot attend them. If these factors are important, simply educating people about the health benefits of exercise may not do much good.

DIVERSE MOTIVATIONS

Keep in mind that health concerns are not people's only motivation. We are all most receptive to options that satisfy us on many levels (intellectual, emotional, personal, social, and so on). In assessing the situation, it is important not to assume that everyone is motivated in the same way we are. Consider (and ask about) the diversity among people who might participate in the sports recreation program. Our audience is probably not just traditional college students (a diverse group in itself), but international students, people with disabilities, middle-aged and older adults, experienced students and newcomers, university faculty and staff members, and maybe even community members and children.

People have diverse motivations for taking part in health-related behaviors. Some may enjoy the social aspect of going to the gym, whereas others are motivated primarily by the desire to have quiet time, lose weight, or reach other goals.

In Step 2, we will attempt to learn about our audience and choose a portion of it to target. Being sensitive to diverse beliefs and motivations can help us understand why people behave as they do and what is important to them. This understanding is crucial to our success as we partner with them.

Step 2: Analyzing and Segmenting The Audience

After assessing the health benefits and the current situation at the sports recreation department, we are ready to analyze the audience. This will involve asking a larger number of people many of the questions we asked in preliminary research.

Audience research may seem an unnecessary step, but experienced campaign planners know better. Audience analysis allows us to collect important data about people's behaviors and preferences. It pays to know, in advance, what information sources our target audience members use and trust, how they view their overall health, what their main concerns are, and more (Ledlow, Johnson, & Hakoyama, 2008). Edward Maibach and Roxanne Parrott (1995) applaud promoters for considering the audience's needs before they determine campaign goals. As they put it, audience-centered analysis "means that health messages are designed primarily to respond to the needs and situation of the target audience, rather than to the needs and situation of the message designers or sponsoring organizations" (p. 167).

DATA COLLECTION

There are several ways to learn about potential audience members. Preexisting databases are a good place to start. For example, we might request demographics about the student body and usage statistics from the campus recreation department. We should also seek more specific information about the target audience's beliefs, values, and habits.

This section describes how to get started, including how and when to get ethics-board approval for our study and the comparative advantages of using interviews, questionnaires, and focus groups to learn about the people we hope to help.

Ethical Commitments

Before we discuss the research phase, keep in mind that, to uphold the highest standards of ethics, we must get an official go-ahead to implement the research procedure we design. Usually, this means submitting the research plan to an **institutional review board (IRB)**, an ethics panel that reviews and monitors research efforts to ensure that participants are treated fairly. Universities have IRBs, as do many organizations, especially in health care. If our research involves people from more than one organization, it may be necessary to get IRB approval from each of them.

The IRB will be interested to know how we will secure informed consent from participants (see Chapter 4), maintain their anonymity or keep their identities confidential, and avoid causing them unnecessary distress. They will also want to know why the results we are likely to get are worth any risk or commitment we require from participants. We will need to make special efforts to protect the needs and rights of vulnerable populations if they are involved in our study, including children, people with cognitive disabilities, people recovering from abuse, seriously ill people, and so on. It is advisable to check IRB guidelines and timelines early on so that ethics will be first on our minds and we can avoid unexpected delays. (See the *Check It Out!* box for more resources.)

> **CHECK IT OUT!**
>
> - The National Institutes of Health offers a free, online instructional session about research ethics at http://phrp.nihtraining.com/users/login.php.
> - Check out the IRB approval procedures at your university. They are usually available through a department of sponsored research.

Data-Gathering Options

There are a number of ways we might learn more about the audiences involved in our campaign effort. Approach this with avid curiosity and a respect for multiple viewpoints. Here is a quick overview of some information-gathering methods we might consider.

INTERVIEWS. You might be surprised what you can learn from asking and listening. Here are different interview strategies and the advantages and limitations of each (based on Frey, Botan, Friedman, & Kreps, 1999).

- **Highly scheduled interviews**. Interviewers are given specific questions to ask and are not allowed to make comments or ask additional questions. This helps minimize the interviewers' influence on respondents' answers, but it does not allow for follow-up questions or clarifications. Answers are typically brief but easy to tally and compare.
- **Moderately scheduled interviews**. Interviewers are given a set of questions but are allowed to ask for clarification and additional information as they see fit. These interviews are more relaxed and conversational, but less precise, than highly scheduled interviews.
- **Unscheduled interviews**. Interviewers are given a list of topics but are encouraged to phrase questions as they wish and to probe for more information when it seems useful and appropriate. These interviews are useful for collecting information about respondents' feelings, but they do not yield answers that can easily be compared or tallied.

QUESTIONNAIRES. Because they can be administered to large numbers of people in less time than it would take to interview them, questionnaires are a popular way to collect audience information. A **questionnaire** asks respondents to indicate their answers to a list of questions. In general, written responses are more limited than interview responses, but people may be more willing to answer sensitive questions in writing or online, especially if surveys are conducted anonymously.

Here are some guidelines for designing an effective questionnaire:

- *Keep it brief.* People are unlikely to complete surveys that take more than 10 minutes.
- *Seek immediate response.* If people take time to complete the survey right away, the response rate will be higher.
- *Collect demographic information.* This may include factors such as age, sex, income, college major, occupation, and the like, if they are relevant to the campaign. **Fixed-alternative questions** ask respondents to select the appropriate responses from a list of all possibilities. These make it easy to count and compare answers, but it's important to include an "other" option when the list is not comprehensive.
- *Ask about knowledge and behaviors.* A mixture of open and closed questions will yield the most useful information. **Open-ended questions** allow respondents to express ideas in their own words (e.g., *How do you feel about basketball and aerobics?*). **Close-ended questions** require very brief answers (*e.g., Do you prefer to work out with free weights or weight machines?*).
- *Pilot (pretest) the questionnaire.* We will test the questionnaire on a few representative people before administering it to everyone in our sample, and we will ask the respondents to indicate if any questions are confusing or leading, if fixed-alternative questions include all possible answers, and if they can think of other questions we should add.
- *Allow for anonymity.* Whether the questionnaire is on paper or online, it is ideal if people can respond anonymously.

HEALTH AND COMMUNICATION TECHNOLOGY

Here are some tips from the experts on creating online surveys ("Internet Surveys," 2008):

- *Keep it quick, and keep it simple.*
- *Go easy on formatting.* Complex graphics can make surveys difficult to open and to read.
- *Avoid overkill.* We all probably receive more online survey requests than we can fulfill. Respect people's time by sending surveys only to the target audience.
- *Be clear and honest* about whether responses will be anonymous (we do not know the respondent's identity) or confidential (we know, but we will not divulge, his or her identity).

FOCUS GROUPS. A third option for collecting information is the use of focus groups. A **focus group** involves a small number of people who respond to questions posed by a moderator. The moderator encourages the group members to speak openly on topics relevant to the campaign. Members' comments are usually recorded so that they can be studied later. Focus groups are useful for learning the target audience's feelings about an issue. For example, a research team led by Rose Clark-Hitt conducted focus groups with military members to see how they reacted to campaign materials that encouraged them to "help a buddy take a knee"; that is, to support their comrades in seeking mental health counseling without shame (Clark-Hitt, Smith, & Broderick, 2012).

Whether we use surveys, questionnaires, or focus groups, it is important to think carefully about whom to include. Choosing people to include is called **sampling** the population. Interviews and surveys allow us to collect information from people who reflect the diversity in the population we are considering. In contrast, focus group participants are members of a target group such as nontraditional students or freshmen. Too much diversity within one group of respondents can make it hard to develop a focused discussion. For example, when Mary Frances Casper and colleagues (2006) conducted focus groups about college students' drinking patterns, they had student participants fill out questionnaires in advance. Then they assigned students to one of three focus groups. The students did not know it, but the groups reflected their typical drinking levels—nondrinkers, moderate, and more-than-average drinkers (Casper, Child, Gilmour, McIntyre, & Pearson, 2006). The researchers knew that participants were more likely to engage in open discussion if it emerged that other people in the room had similar feelings.

Although we should keep membership in any one focus group fairly homogenous, it is important to hold focus groups that, together, represent a wide array of perspectives. Depending on the campaign, consider how you might include diversity in terms of culture, race and ethnicity, gender identity, age, ability, and other factors.

In our case, we might conduct separate focus groups with people who use the workout facilities and those who do not. Throughout the process, we must be careful not to assume that one group speaks for the others or for the population overall.

Following are some tips for conducting effective focus groups:

- *Determine what type of information you most want to collect.* For example, concerning our fitness campaign, consider whether you are more interested in the opinions of people who already use the fitness center or people who are not yet involved.
- *Design a list of open questions to get the information you most want.*
- *Appoint (or hire) a facilitator to lead the focus group discussion.* A good facilitator helps people feel comfortable expressing their opinions, allows everyone to contribute to the discussion, and does not influence members' responses. Many experts recommend using a facilitator not associated with the promotion effort because focus group members may feel more comfortable voicing criticisms and because the facilitator may be more objective.
- *Choose 7 to 10 people from the target audience to make up each focus group.*
- *Arrange to conduct the focus group in a conference room or other comfortable area.* (It is customary to provide refreshments for focus group participants.)
- *Arrange to audio- and video-record the session unobtrusively (with participants' permission).*
- *Review the information collected.*
- *Consider conducting multiple focus groups with different members of the target audience.*

CULTURE AND HEALTH

Hispanic adults in the United States with literacy challenges seem to benefit from high exposure to health-related media messages even more than their more language-proficient peers do (De Jesus, 2013). This is important considering that patients are increasingly expected to be proactive and well-informed consumers.

CHOOSING A TARGET AUDIENCE

It is not only effective to identify the group that we most want to reach and to make every effort to understand that audience; it is part of our ethical responsibility as health promoters. In this section we talk about the vulnerabilities and needs of various groups we might target. We start by examining the irony that the people who are easiest to reach and who are most receptive are probably already aware of what we would like to tell them. Often, a more worthwhile challenge is to connect with people who are not already information rich.

Theoretical Foundations

The **knowledge gap hypothesis** proposes that people with plentiful information resources (such as televisions, computers, and well-informed friends and advisors) are likely to know more and to continue learning more than people with fewer information resources (Tichenor, Donohue, & Olien, 1970). Income and education are highly linked to resource availability and media habits. Consequently, people of high socioeconomic status tend to be knowledge rich, and people of low status tend to be knowledge poor. New information often increases the knowledge gap rather than diminishing it. In other words, the people who already know a lot learn more, and the others fall farther behind.

Unfortunately, people who are information poor are often most in need of health information. Here are just a few examples.

- Three years after a state medical assistance program for the uninsured was implemented in their community, 50% of low-income families were still unaware of it (Rucinski, 2004).
- Mexican American women in rural areas more frequently die from breast cancer than other women, but they often know little about breast self-exams and the severity of the disease (Hubbell, 2006).
- Girls who have sex before age 16 are at highest risk for sexually transmitted infections, but they are the least likely to know about or to be offered preventive care such as the human papillomavirus (HPV) vaccine (Sacks, Copas, Wilkinson, & Robinson, 2014).

There are several reasons that underprivileged persons are hard to reach with health messages. One barrier involves trust. Underprivileged audiences tend disproportionately to be people from minority cultures. They may be skeptical about mainstream messages, either because they seem irrelevant (aimed at Whites rather than Blacks, for example) or because they mistrust the sources (Holland, 2014).

Second, underprivileged individuals are more likely than others to rely on television than on more detailed sources such as online medical information. A so-called **digital divide** separates the information rich, who have easy access to the Internet (predominantly young, well-educated city dwellers), and the information poor, who are often rural residents with limited or no online access (Rains, 2008b). As you might expect, people with quick, convenient access to online sources are more likely to use them to access health information (Rains, 2008b). Thus, underprivileged persons' media habits often put them at a disadvantage.

Third, although they may watch television, members of ethnic cocultures are more likely to believe interpersonal sources (such as friends and health professionals) than the mainstream media (Cheong, 2007). That is fine if they have ready access to health experts, but many do not. Female African American and Latina adolescents in one study were familiar with breast and lung cancer because they knew of people with those diseases. However, most of the girls had never heard of cervical cancer, even though it was receiving abundant media attention in connection with a new HPV vaccine (Mosavel & El-Shaarawi, 2007). Their lack of knowledge is especially unfortunate because the vaccine is designed primarily for girls their age (Mosavel & El-Shaarawi, 2007).

Fourth, people may filter out new information because it does not mesh with what they know or believe. For example, Mexican American women over age 65 often feel that they are expected to spend their time cooking, cleaning, caring for children, and going to church rather than engaging in physical activity for the purpose of staying fit (Balbale, Schwingel, Wojtek, & Huhman, 2014). This proposes a dilemma, as Dutta-Bergman (2005) explains: "Campaign materials that propose to alter the belief structure of the receiver of the message are not likely to be adhered to. Instead, those individuals who are already interested in the issue end up learning more from the message" (p. 112).

Finally, underprivileged audiences may have different priorities. People who are worried about violence and hunger may feel that long-term health issues are the least of their concerns.

Reaching Underinformed Audiences

In their article "Lessons From the Field," three noted health promotion specialists urge campaign designers not to overlook marginalized members of society. They write:

> *Conducting communication research within diverse ethnic/racial/underserved communities will be especially important in the future. Attention to these audiences is a necessity, not a nicety. . . . Working with an audience for the first time inevitably brings frustrations as one discovers that principles applied successfully in the past with other populations*

do not necessarily fit in other contexts. Our experience has been that the potential payoff is worth the initial frustration. (*Edgar, Freimuth, & Hammond, 2003, p. 627*)

It is not enough to encourage people to engage more with media. We must think, as well, about the subtext, values, and trust issues involved. For example, we know that, as a general rule, frequent mass-media consumption correlates with being well informed and resource rich. But media exposure benefits some groups more than others. The term **social capital** encompasses the benefits possible when members of a community build positive social connections and a mutual sense of trust. In terms of social capital, Christopher Beaudoin and Esther Thorson (2006) found that watching television news benefits European Americans significantly more than African Americans. This mostly because African Americans are so often portrayed negatively in news and entertainment that media images may strengthen prejudice and powerlessness rather than provide information they feel they can trust and use. This may be true even when the messages are well intentioned. For example, highlighting the high incidence of HIV among African Americans and among gay men may get their attention, but it may also strengthen prejudice against them.

The challenge for health promoters is to earn trust, respond to community needs, and inform and enable people, at the same time being careful to avoid stigmatizing communities at risk (Smith, 2007). Here are a few suggestions:

- *Focus on social capital.* Recognize that health is not merely a matter of individual control. Prejudice, trust, community resources, social networks, and confidence have profound effects as well. (We cover this idea more thoroughly in Chapter 14.)
- *Tailor materials to audiences' literacy levels.* For example, clinics might educate people with low reading skills by showing instructional health videos in medical waiting rooms.
- *Help build online skills and confidence.* For some people, access to health information is limited because they lack a computer or online capability. Even for those with access, a sense of self-efficacy is often missing (Rains, 2008a). Evidence suggests that members of underinformed audiences benefit when they are coached to use the Web knowledgeably and confidently. The National Cancer Institute has helped fund a number of projects to narrow the digital divide by designing websites tailored to the needs of underserved populations and offering community workshops to teach people how to use them (Kreps, 2005).

With these issues in mind, let's turn to the important task of determining exactly whom to target with our campaign.

SEGMENTING THE AUDIENCE

As we consider who should receive information about the sports recreation program, it may be tempting to target everyone possible. However, research suggests that appealing to an entire population at one time usually does not pay off. Because people tend to evaluate information based on its relevance to them, a broad message may seem too general for anyone to take personally. On the other hand, people tend to take messages more seriously when they identify with the people in them (Moran & Sussman, 2014). The odds are that, even on small campuses, the population is varied enough to make audience segmentation preferable.

Segmenting an audience means identifying specific groups who are alike in important ways and whose involvement is important to the purpose of the campaign. As we attempt to segment the audience, we must avoid grouping people based on superficial attributes. Characteristics such as race and income are not reliable indicators of how people think and behave. People within those categories may have very divergent viewpoints. Identifying groups on the basis of similar goals and experiences is harder to do but is usually more productive. Following are some questions to consider:

- Who is currently involved (and not involved) in the recommended activity?
- What are people's reasons for participating (or not)?
- Who stands to benefit from the recommended behaviors?
- Who is in most need of these benefits?
- Who might reasonably be expected to adopt these behaviors?
- Is there anyone who should *not* be encouraged to participate?

Remember that some campaigns do more harm than good by recommending behaviors inappropriate for the audience. For example, vigorous exercise is not right for everybody.

Keep in mind that indirect approaches sometimes work well for hard-to-reach audiences. People who plan campus lectures often ask professors to publicize them in class and to consider offering students extra credit for attendance. They recognize that students might be more influenced by their professors' encouragement than by flyers or word of mouth. A similar effect seems to be true concerning physical activities. Young people's inclination to work out is influenced by their parents, friends, and teachers (Olivares, Cossio-Bolaños, Gomez-Campos, Almonacid-Fierro, & Garcia-Rubio, 2015).

Also be open to unexpected combinations. For instance, freshmen and university staff members may be alike in feeling out of place at the campus gym. Where our campaign is concerned, this similarity may be more important than the differences between these groups. Based on these similarities, we might decide that both freshman and staff members would respond more enthusiastically to personal invitations than to bulletin board notices.

It is sometimes difficult to decide where to draw the line in segmenting an audience. The choice may be to target a small audience of high-need individuals or a large audience whose needs are less severe. Sometimes campaign designers overlook great opportunities to help small audiences. For example, tobacco harvesters are a relatively isolated and overlooked community within the overall population, but they have serious health concerns. For one, they often suffer from nausea, dizziness, and heart rate disruptions caused by exposure to green tobacco leaves (Parrott & Polonec, 2008). They can minimize their risk simply by wearing thicker clothing and changing into dry clothes when moisture from the plants soaks them, but little effort has been devoted to educating farmers about this (Parrott & Polonec, 2008). This health concern might not be as widespread as some others, but it is a serious issue for the people involved, and results are reasonably attainable. All in all, there is no definitive rule for choosing between highly focused and more generalized approaches, but health promoters who are sensitive to audience needs and health benefits are most likely to make reasonable judgments.

WHAT DO YOU THINK?

Evidence suggests that young people are more receptive to messages that focus on social implications, such as offending others with secondhand smoke, than on personal consequences, such as getting lung cancer (Keller & Lehmann, 2008). Why do you think this is the case?

Based on our audience analysis, we might decide to target our sports recreation campaign toward people new on campus (students, staff, or both), to community members, or to nontraditional students. We might find that current participants do not reflect the racial and ethnic diversity on campus, or that the current membership is mostly men or women, or that people with disabilities are not as involved as they could be. Consequently, we might direct the campaign toward groups that are currently underutilizing the sports recreation program or those people who most need the benefits it offers. And do not forget the current participants. Maybe their involvement can be improved. The possibilities are numerous, making it especially important to know the audience well before choosing a segment of it to target.

AUDIENCE AS A PERSON

Once a target focus community has been identified, imagine the audience as a single person, complete "with name, gender, occupation, and lifestyle" (R. Lefebvre et al., 1995, p. 221). With this "person" in mind, Lefebvre and colleagues (1995) pose the following questions for consideration:

- What is important to this person?
- What are the person's feelings, attitudes, and beliefs about the behavior change (including perceived benefits and barriers)?
- What are his or her media habits?

Imagining the audience as a person is useful in focusing the campaign and in creating messages that seem personal and immediate.

Every audience and every audience member is unique, but some overall characteristics may help guide our efforts. Here is some information that may be useful to us as we attempt to understand our focus community.

YOUNG AUDIENCES

Age may have some effect on how members perceive health messages. Although it is difficult to make generalizations about adult audiences, the developmental stages of youth often have relatively predictable effects.

Children are an important audience. As Erica Weintraub Austin (1995) points out, it is easier to prevent bad habits than to break them. Sending consistent messages to children early on may prevent them from developing unhealthy behaviors later. Evidence supports that children are strongly influenced by adults. On the bright side, young people tend to follow their parents' advice (Moran & Sussman, 2014). However, children often seek to emulate adult behaviors—even the unhealthy ones. Portraying behaviors such as smoking as "adult-only" may actually make them seem more appealing to youngsters.

Adolescents often believe they are unlike other people and that others do not understand them (this is called **personal fable**). Consequently, they are likely to assume that health warnings do not apply to them (Effertz, Franke, & Teichert, 2014). Teenagers also tend to be extremely self-conscious and to feel that people are scrutinizing their appearance and behavior (this is called **imaginary audience**). This makes them sensitive to peer pressure and social approval, which can work for or against health promotion efforts (Helms et al., 2014). A third factor, called **psychological reactance**, characterizes adolescents' desire to assert their independence and sense of personal control (Brehm, 1966). They often resent it when they feel that other people are telling them what to do, and they may rebel just to avoid feeling controlled.

Despite the challenges, there is some promising research about reaching adolescents.

- *Focus on immediate concerns.* Austin (1995) reminds health promoters that teens' immediate social concerns may outweigh their long-term health considerations. In Austin's words, adolescents may "care more that smoking will make their breath smell bad than that they could develop cancer" (p. 115).
- *Emphasize personal choice.* Adolescents tend to react negatively to messages that restrict their freedom of choice (Rains & Turner, 2007; M. J. Lee, 2010). Their inclination to resist the message might be reduced with a passage such as this: "You might feel that your freedom to choose how you will consume alcohol is being threatened. However, the facts about binge drinking . . . are pretty powerful when you think about them" (Richards & Banas, 2015, p. 455). It may also be useful to conclude messages with "restoration of freedom" passages such as, "We all make our own decisions and act as we choose to act. Obviously, you make your own decisions too. The choice is yours. You're free to decide for yourself" (Miller, Lane, Deatrick, Young, & Potts, 2007, p. 240).
- *Remember that there are many stages of youth.* A few years can make a big difference in how young audiences respond. Hye-Jin Paek's (2008) data indicate that younger children respond well to school-based programs, whereas older teens benefit more from high-sensation appeals and fact-based information, such as the truth® campaign's presentation of tobacco-related statistics and tobacco-industry memos.

The danger with high sensation-seekers is that risky behaviors appeal to them. Not only are they less likely than others to take recommended precautions, they are more likely to be in dangerous situations in the first place.

SENSATION-SEEKERS

The **activation model for information exposure** supports two premises: first, that persuasive messages are most effective when they stimulate an optimal amount of arousal in the reader/viewer, and second, that what is "optimal" for one person may be boring or too intense for another (Donohew, Palmgreen, & Duncan, 1980). For example, reactions were mixed when a police department in Wales released don't-text-while-driving PSAs that showed bloody images from automobile accidents. American broadcasters declined to air the PSAs, but the campaign's creators argued that people should know how horrific the outcomes of distracted driving can be (Inbar, 2009). Graphic images on cigarette packages (photo 13.5) are another example. Some countries now require that tobacco companies dispense with attractive colors and brand names and instead package their products with realistic images of tobacco and nicotine's effects on the body. The argument is the same—that, while some people may be offended, the shock value is necessary to impact audiences who tend to ignore health threats otherwise.

The activation model can apply to audiences of any age or description. So far, researchers and campaign designers have used it most extensively for adolescent and young-adult audiences, who are more likely than others to be high **sensation-seekers**, meaning that they enjoy new and intense experiences (Everett & Palmgreen, 1995; Zuckerman, 1994). The danger with high sensation-seekers is that risky behaviors appeal to them. Not only are they less likely than others to take precautions, they are more apt to be in dangerous situations in the first place. For instance, compared to their peers, high sensation-seekers are more likely to think smoking is appealing (Paek, 2008). They are typically more impulsive about having sex, yet less willing than others to use condoms (Noar, Zimmerman, Palmgreen, Lustria, & Horosewski, 2006). And they tend to associate with other high sensation-seekers, which can make their behaviors seem normal rather than dangerous or extreme (Wang et al., 2014). These factors may be challenging for health promoters. But also keep in mind that, because high sensation-seekers are receptive to novel situations, they typically welcome diversity and intercultural communication (Arasaratnam & Banerjee, 2011). Thus, they may be less ethnocentric and more open-minded than normal, which may make them receptive to a range of health-related messages and spokespeople.

Here are a few promising lines of research about appealing to high sensation-seekers:

- *Make messages varied and intense.* Messages that have quick and vivid visual edits and loud and fast music typically have the most impact on high sensation-seekers, teens, and tweens (9- to 12-year-olds) (Lang, Schwartz, Lee, & Angelini, 2007; Niederdeppe, Davis, Farrelly, & Yarsevich, 2007).
- *Make the most of low-distraction environments.* Both intense- and mild-content antismoking PSAs had an impact on high sensation-seekers when they were exposed to the messages in a classroom environment (Helme, Donohew, Baier, & Zittleman, 2007).
- *Run PSAs during popular programs.* High sensation-seekers who watch a lot of television do not necessarily remember a lot about the PSAs they see. But they do typically remember the PSAs that appear during their favorite programs (typically sports, comedy, and cartoons for 16- to 25-year-olds) (D'Silva & Palmgreen, 2007).

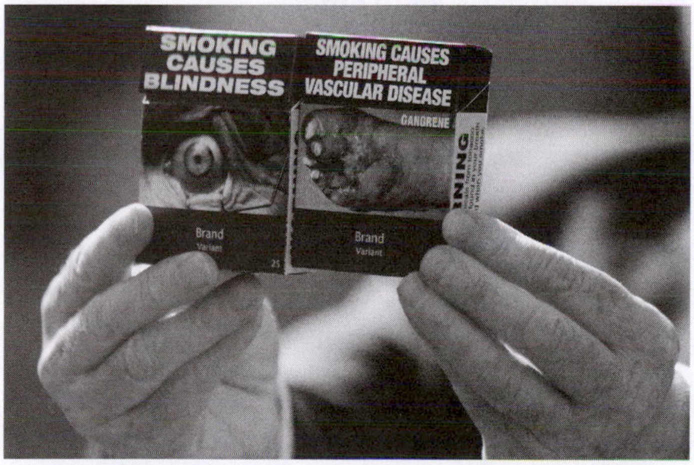

In 2015, regulators in Ireland followed Australia's example by ruling that cigarette packages depict graphic warning images such as these rather than splashy brand-name packaging. There is some evidence that graphic images discourage teens from smoking, particularly if they are not already heavy smokers (Andrews, Netemeyer, Kees, & Burton, 2014).

Part of the dilemma, of course, is that the intense messages that sensation-seekers enjoy may be too much for most audiences, making it difficult to target high-risk individuals without offending others. (For other ethical considerations about health promotion, see Box 13.3.)

As we complete Step 2 in creating a health campaign, it may seem that, although we have already done a lot of work, we still do not know what the campaign

BOX 13.3 ETHICAL CONSIDERATIONS

The Politics of Prevention—Who Should Pay?

Health promotion may seem like a win–win situation. If people can be encouraged to prevent disease and injuries, they will enjoy better health and the nation's health costs will be minimized. How far should we carry this line of reasoning? Should people who work hard to be healthy get discount prices on health care and insurance? Should they be given advantages when competing for jobs? If people knowingly engage in unhealthy behaviors, should society help pay for their medical bills?

Some 86% of America's health care dollar pays for care of people with chronic health conditions, many of which could have been avoided with healthier diets, more exercise, and abstention from alcohol and tobacco (CDC, 2015a). The added expense eats up tax money and leads to hikes in health insurance rates. As Daniel Wikler (1987) puts it, "The person who takes risks with his [or her] own health gambles with resources which belong to others" (p. 14). Some theorists argue that people who continue risky behavior (like smoking, overeating, or driving without seatbelts) when they know it is bad for them should pay from their own pockets when their behavior leads to medical expenses.

In a related issue, some feel that companies that profit from selling unhealthy products should pay part of the health bill. State governments have successfully sued tobacco companies for damages, charging that it is unfair for them to make huge profits while others foot the enormous bill of treating tobacco-related illnesses. Experts estimate that smoking costs Americans $193 billion a year in medical expenses and lost productivity (CDC, 2011). Around the world, more than 5 million people a year die from tobacco-related illnesses, including 600,000 who are killed by the effects of secondhand smoke (WHO, 2012b).

Some companies now refuse to hire smokers or people who are extremely overweight because they are at greater health risk, and thus are likely to cost the company more money than others in terms of health benefits and sick leave. Similarly, some insurance companies offer a discount to people who do not smoke and those who remain accident free or who complete informational programs such as defensive-driving courses.

On the other side of the issue, some worry that governments and employers are becoming too involved in people's lifestyle decisions. Some charge that groups like Mothers Against Drunk Driving (MADD) are taking a good thing too far by seeking to punish people for drinking even small amounts of alcohol. Some people say that increasing the "sin taxes" on alcohol and tobacco will hurt consumers, not companies, and they are afraid the taxes will be extended to cover snack foods and other not-so-healthy items. A third argument is that health concerns such as obesity are not always matters of individual control. Obesity has many causes, including social norms and heredity. People may gain weight because of medications or other health conditions. However, media coverage tends to sway the public toward considering obesity as either an individualistic or a societal issue (Kim & Willis, 2007). All in all, opponents of tighter health requirements say you cannot assume people are fully in control of their health, and you cannot control the risks people take without controlling their freedom of choice.

What Do You Think?

1. Should people who knowingly take health risks pay more than others for health insurance? Should they be denied insurance? Should they be denied health services?
2. Should people be required by law to engage in healthy practices such as being immunized and exercising regularly?
3. Should it be against the law to sell or advertise products known to have a high health risk? Does it matter if such products are addictive?
4. Do you agree with the rationale behind many states' seatbelt and motorcycle helmet laws—that people who neglect safety precautions not only endanger their own lives but increase the trauma and expense for everybody?
5. How do you weigh the argument that some people are not well informed about health issues (perhaps because they cannot read or cannot

continued

afford a computer) and that it is unfair to expect them to follow health guidelines about which they know little?

6. In your opinion, which of the following behaviors (if any) should be grounds for denying or limiting health benefits? On what criteria do you make your judgments?

   Smoking
   Engaging in unprotected sex
   Exceeding the speed limit
   Snow skiing
   Neglecting to exercise regularly
   Overeating
   Playing football
   Rescuing accident victims

7. If a person has a family history of a disease, should he or she be required by society to take extra health precautions?

will involve. Our efforts will not go to waste. Research shows that campaigns launched without a clear understanding of the audience, current situation, and potential benefits are often frustrating to create and ineffective at reaching their goals. With a focus community in mind, we are ready for Step 3.

Step 3: Establishing Campaign Goals and Objectives

By this point we should have a fairly clear impression of the sports recreation department, its potential benefits, and the people we most want to reach with our campaign. Collecting and analyzing data have prepared us to establish specific objectives for our campaign. **Objectives** state in clear, measurable terms exactly what we hope to achieve with the campaign. We might consider the following questions:

- What exactly do we want people to start/stop/continue doing?
- If we hope to encourage a particular behavior, when (and for how long) should it occur to be of benefit?
- How will we know if our campaign has been successful?

Relevant to the sports recreation campaign, we may decide that signing up 40 freshmen in three months would constitute success. Or perhaps we have decided to focus on students with disabilities or on newcomers. Our objective may be to get at least 20 current participants to bring an individual from one of those groups to an event.

We must make sure our objectives are oriented to the overall purpose of the campaign. For instance, if people participate in only one climbing-wall session, will there be health benefits? If not, it may be important to aim for continued participation—perhaps attendance once a week for at least two months.

CAN YOU GUESS? PART 2

One challenge of health promotion is monitoring which threats are most prevalent and most deadly. Worldwide, which of the following causes of death have become less prevalent since 2000? Which of the following have become more prevalent?

HIV/AIDS, heart disease, road injuries, premature birth, stroke, tuberculosis, diabetes, hypertension, cancer of the trachea or lungs, diarrhea

Answers appear at the end of the chapter.

Let's think ahead about exactly how we will measure the effects of the campaign. This may involve follow-up surveys or sign-up sheets to keep track of participation. Setting measurable goals will allow us (and others) to determine if the campaign has been a success.

Health promoters are increasingly being held accountable for their efforts. **Accountability** means demonstrating how the results of a project compare to the money and time invested in it. A useful means of tracking health risks and changes is the use of **disease maps**, which look like regular maps but are color coded to show health deficits (such as disease) and health assets (such as areas in which people live longer than usual). These maps present a great deal of information in a way that is clear and visually appealing (Parrott, Hopfer, Ghetian, & Lengerich, 2007). (See the *Check It Out!* Box for links to online disease maps.) For example, you might look up a cancer map of the United States and feel either alarmed or encouraged by how your state, community, or neighborhood compares to others. If they are accurate and up to date, disease maps have an advantage over complex reports. Imagine scanning tables of disease statistics about every area of your community and state. It might take you hours and many volumes of paperwork to show what a simple map can convey in a few minutes. And even if you carefully reviewed the data in table format, it would be easy to overlook health patterns that show up vividly on a disease map—like cancer rates that are particularly high around an industrial plant or river. This information is useful in accomplishing what some researchers call *environmental justice* or *environmental equity*, meaning that attention is given to demographically situated populations that lag behind others or require more resources than they currently have to ensure citizens' health (Waller, Carlin, Xia, & Gelfand, 1997).

Keeping in mind the factors involved in understanding a target audience, let's consider how we might appeal to the people we chose to target with our campaign.

CHECK IT OUT!

Disease maps are available at:

- CDC Map Gallery: cdc.gov/gis/gallery.htm
- U.S. Department of the Interior: diseasemaps .usgs.gov/index.html

Step 4: Selecting Channels of Communication

A **channel** is a means of communicating information, either directly (in person) or indirectly (through media such as TV or radio or computers). To select the best channels for our campaign, let's consider which ones our target audience uses and trusts most.

Sometimes channel selection is limited by time or money. Our sports recreation enrollment effort will probably not involve full-color magazine ads or sophisticated television commercials. Nevertheless, as health promoters, we should be familiar with all types of channels. Moreover, let's not assume too quickly that a channel is out of our reach. For example, we may not produce television commercials, but we might book appearances on campus or community television talk shows.

CHANNEL CHARACTERISTICS

Let's consider the advantages and limitations of different channels. Experts suggest that channels for a health campaign be evaluated in terms of reach, specificity, and impact (Schooler, Chaffee, Flora, & Roser, 1998). **Reach** refers to the number of people who will be exposed to a message via a particular channel. **Specificity** refers to how accurately the message can be targeted to a specific group of people. **Impact** is how influential a message is likely to be.

Television and the Internet usually have larger and more diverse audiences than other media. As such, they have immense reach. However, when audiences are large and diverse, it can be hard to tailor messages to particular people. Television, especially, has low specificity, although that has changed somewhat with the creation of special-interest cable and satellite programs. The Internet can be more specific, if we put the effort into selecting people within the target audience and/or posting information with specific identifiers that will lead interested people to it.

Although it may be tempting to aim for the broadest reach possible, it is advisable to focus on our target audience. Exposure that is broader than necessary can waste resources and contribute to information overload, making it difficult for people to identify which messages are most important and relevant to them (Lang, 2006).

MESSAGE IMPACT

The channels we select influence the nature and impact of our messages. In the interest of selecting the most effective channels, we next consider two factors relevant to message impact: arousal and involvement.

Arousal

Arousal refers to how emotionally stimulating and exciting a message is (Schooler et al., 1998).

When we view words and images about risky products—such as condoms, liquor, and cigarettes—we typically experience greater emotional and physical arousal than with more innocuous images such as water bottles and vegetables (Lang, Chung, Lee, & Zhao, 2005). We tend to identify the risky products more quickly and remember them longer (Lang et al., 2005). This can make it difficult for healthy campaign messages (especially if they are sedate) to compete with advertisements for unhealthy products.

Audiences in positive moods, as when they are watching comedies, tend to be more receptive than others to detection messages (e.g., breast self-exam, cancer screening, and so on). Audiences in negative moods—when, say, they are watching dramas or news shows—are typically more receptive to prevention messages, such as using sunscreen (Anghelcev & Sar, 2011).

Interactive computer programs are a good example of high-arousal messages that can be used to promote healthy behaviors. Interactive, on-screen messages are often very engrossing, with colorful graphics, moving images, and sound. Roberto and colleagues (2007) report success using an interactive computer program to involve high school students in safer sex and pregnancy-prevention efforts. Compared to other students, those who took part in the online program were more knowledgeable about STDs, more aware of their personal risk, more reluctant to have sex, and more confident about their ability to use safer sex practices if they did have sex.

Involvement

Involvement is the amount of mental effort required to understand a message. Interpersonal communication is high involvement. It requires a great deal of thought and action. Thus, health professionals, family members, and friends tend to have high impact. Newspapers are also high-involvement channels, because people must read and use their imaginations. Television is low involvement, because viewers passively observe the sounds and sights displayed for them.

The **elaboration likelihood model** proposes that when we are highly involved with a message, we pay close attention to details and evaluate the message thoroughly. As a consequence, we tend to remember high-involvement messages longer than others and are more likely to act on them (Briñol & Petty, 2006; Petty & Cacioppo, 1981). In short, people usually pay closer attention when using high-involvement channels, such as reading and talking, and this affects how much they are influenced by the information. Surveys show that people who use high-involvement channels are usually better informed about health than people who rely on low-involvement channels such as television.

Evidence suggests that **tailored messages**—those that are designed to be personally relevant to the recipients—generally have greater impact on recipients' behaviors than messages that are more generic in nature (Lustria et al., 2013). The impact and degree of tailoring differs widely. At one level, images might be tailored to match the age group and general appearance of a media consumer (Ahn, 2015). At another level, messages may be tailored in multiple ways using complex computer algorithms. For example, rather than sift through dozens of web pages for information that is useful to you, you might log onto an interactive site and answer a number of questions about your background, lifestyle, goals, frustrations, and so on. Based on your responses, the system will sift through information for you and present a collection of resources (information, videos, photos, community resources, live links, and so on) chosen specifically to suit your needs. Some programs paraphrase and reflect your input much like a real-life counselor would.

For example, you might get an on-screen message that reads something like this:

> *On the one hand you think it is not that important to become more physically active because you have a very busy life. On the other hand you do think it is important to become more active because physical activity helps you to relax.... This is a very common and very understandable situation. Many people find it convenient to deal with this situation by assessing what their current activity schedule is like on a typical day in their lives. As the next step, they decide whether they spend enough time doing things they really think are important. Maybe this could be an interesting idea for you, too?* (Friederichs et al., 2014, p. 11)

Based on the tenets of the elaboration likelihood model, we are likely to pay close attention to messages such as these that feel relevant to us as individuals.

Valerie Pilling and Laura Brannon (2007) took a tailored approach in creating a responsible-drinking website for college students. Some students in the study viewed a website tailored to suit their personalities (either responsible, communicative, logical, or adventuresome), while others viewed more general messages about the dangers of binge drinking. Students who viewed the tailored messages were significantly more likely than the others to consider the website interesting, to predict that it would be effective, and to say that the materials affected their attitudes about drinking.

Even if we cannot create tailored versions of our campus fitness campaign for individual users, it is clear that directing our messages to a clear target audience is likely to enhance their impact.

MULTICHANNEL CAMPAIGNS

As you have seen, broadcasting and narrowcasting have advantages. Many times, the best chance of making a difference is to reach people through several channels. Multichannel efforts are important because people have different communication patterns and preferences. What appeals to some people may not appeal to others. For example, when researchers studied the impact of campaign messages in Hawaii encouraging people to eat healthy foods and walk regularly, they found that television PSAs were seen about equally by all members of the population (Buchthal et al., 2011). However, residents with low incomes and with literacy challenges benefited less than others from printed messages. On the bright side, they benefited more than others from radio PSAs and campaign posters in supermarkets. The researchers suggest that reaching members of the target audience where they are (as in the fruit and vegetable aisle), with messages they can easily understand, is critical to minimizing knowledge gaps.

Mass-mediated and interpersonal channels are also complementary, in that the media messages typically influence what people think about and talk about. However, people do not simply buy into everything the media says. They are also likely to be influenced by discussions with neighbors and family members. **Diffusion of innovations** theory refers to a multistep process in which new information is filtered and passed along throughout a community (Brosius & Weimann, 1996; Lazarsfeld, Burleson, & Gaudet, 1948; Rogers, 1983). Research shows that some community members are opinion leaders who have credibility by virtue of their expertise or social standing. They often pass along new ideas and information from the media to other people. In this way, mass media messages may influence people indirectly, whether they use the media or not. When Uriyoan Colon-Ramos and colleagues studied survey responses from nearly 13,000 adults in the United States, they found that about 2 in 100 had extensive social networks of 75 people or more, to whom they regularly offered guidance about a range of matters, including health. It seems like a small proportion of people, but the effects may be significant. Most of the highly networked opinion leaders were eager to learn health information, were tuned into a variety of health information sources, and were likely to engage in healthy behaviors themselves (Colon-Ramos et al., 2009).

Summary

Successful health promotion recognizes that people do not necessarily change their behaviors because they have been presented with new health information. As campaign designers, we must take into account the concerns, habits, and preferences of the people we wish to influence. Campaigns with the best chance of succeeding talk to people where they are, whether it is the beauty salon, the athletic field, or the doctor's office. Good health campaigns are thorough and are backed by long-term commitment. The best campaigns involve members of the focus population as active participants and recruit social support for healthy behaviors. Furthermore, they speak with many voices, including the concerned tones of loved ones, the calm assurance of experts, and the printed and recorded messages of mass media. They also make it practical for people to adopt healthy behaviors, even if it means changing public policy, offering free or easy-to-access options, and building communication infrastructures.

Because people are inclined to pay more attention to messages that seem relevant to them, campaigns directed at "everyone" may not pique the interest of anyone. Health campaign success stories show that it is important to know the audience well, take positive action, establish clear goals, measure success, and make behaviors socially rewarding.

Whereas illness and disease prevention seem to benefit everyone, ethical dilemmas are involved, such as: Should people be rewarded or penalized based on their health-related behavior? How should we balance people's right to choose for themselves with society's interest in keeping costs down? Where do we draw the line between healthy and unhealthy behaviors?

The first step in creating a health campaign is to research potential benefits of the campaign. Find out who stands to gain, who is already behaving according to campaign recommendations, and what alternatives exist.

The second step is to choose a target audience. Interviews, questionnaires, and focus groups are useful ways to learn about potential audience members—what they like, what they know, how they typically behave, what they consider important, and more. We may wish to target people in great need or those who are most likely to respond to the campaign. At the same time, keep in mind audience characteristics such as self-consciousness, sensation hunger, confidence, need for independence, and psychological reactance. It is often challenging to reach audiences who are culturally different from the mainstream. However, considering the knowledge gap hypothesis, these audiences are often the most in need of health information and assistance.

With a target audience in mind, the third step in creating a health campaign is to establish clear and measurable objectives so we can accurately assess a campaign's effects. Fourth, we select channels through which to communicate campaign messages. Channels typically differ in terms of reach, specificity, and impact. Sometimes tailored messages are more effective than broadcast ones, in that tailored messages focus on information that is well suited to an individual's interests, abilities, and resources. Often, the best campaigns make use of several channels. All in all, the media play an important role in promoting health issues, but media impact is limited without interpersonal reinforcement.

Key Terms and Theories

health-promoting behaviors
health promotion campaigns
nudging
institutional review board (IRB)
highly scheduled interviews
moderately scheduled interviews
unscheduled interviews
questionnaire
fixed-alternative questions
open-ended questions
close-ended questions
focus group
sampling
knowledge gap hypothesis
digital divide
social capital
segmenting an audience
personal fable
imaginary audience
psychological reactance
activation model for information exposure
sensation-seekers
objectives
accountability
disease maps
channel
reach
specificity
impact
arousal
involvement
elaboration likelihood model
tailored messages
diffusion of innovations

Discussion Questions

1. Describe the strategy and principles of the truth® campaign. How do they relate to the principles suggested throughout the chapter?
2. What are five qualities of good campaigns, as illustrated by the exemplary campaigns in this chapter? Find or think of other campaigns that embody one or more of these best practices.
3. Using your classmates as a target audience, conduct a quick focus group to identify an important health interest they have in common. Then develop a simple survey to find out more about their current practices, goals, barriers, and preferences regarding this health issue.
4. Using the knowledge gap hypothesis, explain why people of low socioeconomic status are often underinformed about health issues. How does the digital divide figure in? What are some tips for reaching underinformed audiences?
5. Explain the activation model for information exposure. Link it to the concept of sensation seeking.
6. Choose campaign messages delivered via a variety of channels. Compare them in terms of reach, specificity, impact, arousal, and involvement.

Answers to *Can You Guess?*

Part 1

Tobacco kills more people. Indeed, more people die from tobacco-related illnesses than from motor vehicle accidents, HIV, murder, illegal drug use, and suicide *combined* (CDC, 2011, "Tobacco-Related Mortality," 2011).

Part 2

Declining Death Rates

HIV/AIDS
Premature birth
Tuberculosis
Diarrhea

Escalating Death Rates

Heart disease
Stroke
Cancer of the trachea or lungs
Diabetes
Road injuries
Hypertension

Source: *World Health Organization (2014b)*

CHAPTER 14

Designing and Implementing Health Campaigns

One of the most widely emulated health communication campaigns on college campuses is RU SURE, developed in the 1990s at Rutgers University to curb the incidence of dangerous alcohol consumption. The campaign challenges students to reconsider the notion that most young adults drink to excess. RU Sure materials make the point (as in the graphic at right) that two-thirds of Rutgers students actually stop after three or fewer drinks ("RU Sure," 2015). By providing students with accurate statistics, campaign sponsors hope to clarify that the norm is less extreme than students think; thus students need not drink excessively to fit in with their peers (Lederman & Stewart, 2005; Lederman et al., 2001; Menegatos, Lederman, & Hess, 2010).

The RU SURE campaign is famous for its high level of student involvement and its novel ways of integrating campaign messages into everyday campus life. The campaign is designed by students for students. "Communication majors are involved in all aspects of this campaign, from designing ways to deliver campaign messages to gathering evaluation data," says Lea Stewart, professor and director of the Rutgers Center for Communication and Health Issues. "Since no one works on the campaign without first learning about the scope and consequences of dangerous drinking among college students, we reach two audiences: our target audience of first-year students and a secondary audience of upper-level students."

Through the years, students in the campaign have designed and distributed free T-shirts featuring a "Top Ten Misperceptions" list about life at Rutgers, including three misperceptions about drinking as well as humorous myths such as, "You don't need shower shoes for the dorms." They have also engaged students in RU SURE Bingo games, developed curricula supplements for campus courses, and developed partnerships with community leaders and others. The campaign seems to be effective. Students' estimates of peer drinking at Rutgers dropped considerably once RU SURE began (Stewart et al., 2002; Lederman, Stewart, & Russ, 2007).

IN YOUR EXPERIENCE

Have you noticed social-norm campaigns similar to RU Sure on your campus?

- If so, what do you think of them?
- How much alcohol do most college students drink on a typical night out? How often?
- If you learned that your estimates were inaccurate, would it influence the way you behave?

Like many health-promotion efforts, the RU Sure campaign is based partly on social marketing. **Social marketing** is an approach wherein campaign designers apply principles of commercial advertising to prosocial campaigns such as health-promotion efforts (Lefebvre & Flora, 1988). The rationale is that many of the techniques used to sell goods and services also work well when promoting healthy lifestyles.

WHAT DO YOU THINK?

- What is the first health-related PSA or campaign that comes to your mind? Why do you think it is so memorable?
- What is your favorite PSA or campaign? Why?
- Do you think health campaigns influence the choices you make? Why or why not?

Because the concern in social marketing is primarily with what the "consumer" needs, health promoters make a great effort to understand the audience, assess its needs, and target specific people. Social marketing also involves using multiple channels and conducting follow-up research to measure the success of campaign efforts.

Social marketers may be guided by the classic 4Ps of marketing: price, product, promotion, and place (Borden, 1964). From a social marketing perspective,[1] health-related behaviors have a price tag of sorts. They cost something in terms of money, time, energy, or some other investment. The product may be tangible (such as healthy food, condoms, or cleaner drinking water) or intangible (better health, more opportunities, or greater control over one's circumstances). Promotion describes the process, design, and means of sharing information. Place refers to where messages are received (such as online, at a friend's house, or on television) and where the effects may be most felt (within the family, at school or in the workplace, or so on.)

While the 4Ps may serve as a checklist of sorts, many theorists question their utility as a stand-alone model for social marketing. Some advocate adding additional Ps to the model, to recognize the importance of people, public policy, physical evidence (used to weigh various options and to evaluate outcomes), purse strings (resources), and processes (conventional ways of doing things and potential alternatives) (Booms & Bitner, 1981; Goyal Wasan & Tripathi, 2014; Kotler & Zaltman, 1971). The most fundamental challenges to the 4P model are that it focuses on "sellers" and their needs more than on "buyers" and that it is more oriented to one-time transactions than to ongoing efforts and relationship-building (Grönroos, 1994; Gordon, 2012). In contrast to commercial marketing efforts, social marketers sometimes function more as lobbyists, advocates, and facilitators than as salespeople. For example, they may "go upstream" to address the source of a health issue, as when they advocate for new legislation or stand up to factories that pollute the environment (Gordon, 2012).

Components of social marketing appear throughout the chapter, as we talk about campaign strategies. But first let's recap. Chapter 13 provided a guide to the first four stages of creating a health campaign:

Step 1: Defining the situation and potential benefits
Step 2: Analyzing and segmenting the audience

[1]Be careful not to confuse social marketing with social norms theory, which we talk about later in the chapter. Social marketing is a general approach, whereas social norms theory proposes that people base their behavior partly on what they consider to be normal among their peers.

Step 3: Establishing campaign goals and objectives
Step 4: Selecting channels of communication

The process continues in this chapter with a description of key theories and techniques to create health-promotion campaigns. The hypothetical sports recreation campaign we began in Chapter 13 helps illustrate how a health-promotion effort comes together. We will continue it in this chapter. Keep in mind that the same steps apply to campaigns of various sizes on any number of health topics.

This chapter begins by introducing four influential models of behavior change: the health belief model, social cognitive theory, the theory of reasoned action, and the transtheoretical model. We then explore the critical-cultural approach and describe the three final stages in campaign development:

Step 5: Designing campaign messages
Step 6: Piloting and implementing the campaign
Step 7: Evaluating and maintaining the campaign

Along the way, we will touch on a number of message-design perspectives, including the role of affect, social norms theory, the theory of normative social behavior, and the extended parallel process model.

Theories of Behavior Change

The theories described here emphasize that people make lifestyle decisions based on a complex array of factors, including personal perceptions, skills, social pressure, convenience, and more. Each of these theories has earned considerable respect among health communication scholars and health promoters. Space is not available to discuss each model in great detail, but this introduction should help orient you to the rich scholarship behind health campaign efforts and provide opportunities for further investigation. Applying these theories to health campaigns can have a positive effect—at least sometimes. Keep in mind that theories are only guiding principles, not magic formulas. No one theory works all of the time or with every audience.

HEALTH BELIEF MODEL

The **health belief model** proposes that we base our behavior choices on five primary considerations (Rosenstock, 1960; Stretcher & Rosenstock, 1997). Namely, we are most motivated to change our behaviors if we believe that

- we will be adversely affected if we do not change;
- the adverse effects will be considerable;
- behavior change will be effective in preventing the undesired outcome;
- the effort and cost of preventive behavior is worthwhile; and
- we are moved to action by a novel or eye-opening occurrence, such as a brush with danger, a compelling warning message, or an alluring incentive.

In short, motivation is based on an individual's perception of personal susceptibility, serious consequences, worthwhile benefits, justifiable costs, and cues to actions.

The health belief model is used widely for assessing audiences and organizing campaigns. For example, Kami Silk and colleagues (2006) used components of the model to guide focus groups with female adolescents and adults prior to developing breast cancer prevention materials. They found that participants of all ages understood the severity of breast cancer, but they defined the consequences somewhat differently. The adolescents tended to emphasize the appearance-altering effects of the disease, such as hair loss during chemotherapy. The adults were more likely to know someone with breast cancer, to know a lot about the disease, and to feel personally susceptible.

The health belief model also reminds us to keep renewing our familiarity with target audiences. Jon Krosnick and coauthors report that, although the adverse affects of smoking are well known to many, about 34% of the public is still unaware that smoking causes or worsens oral cancer, and 35% is not aware that smoking increases one's risk for stroke (Krosnick, Chang, Sherman, Chassin, & Presson, 2006). Campaign designers who overlook these knowledge gaps may miss important opportunities.

Considering all of these factors, it seems naive to assume that people will change simply because someone tells them to do so. A campaign message may be a cue to action, but unless someone has reason to believe that the recommended behavior is useful and worthwhile and that it will prevent an outcome that is otherwise likely to occur, the recommendation will probably not be motivation enough.

If we are trying to increase participation in our university's sports recreation program, we might consider how strongly members of our target audience believe the benefits we propose would actually help them. Let's say that audience analysis reveals a common sentiment such as this: "I know exercise is good for people. But I'm young and healthy. I don't have to worry about that yet." According to the health belief model, people who feel this way will not be motivated to seek the benefits proposed because they do not believe they need them. Therefore we might focus on other goals—such as looking good, meeting people, and winning awards—that are relevant to gym membership and more important to members of the target audience. Conversely, if people do not know about the benefits of exercise, the health belief model advocates educating them. Knowledge does not ensure behavior change, but it is an important foundation for it.

IN YOUR EXPERIENCE

- Can you think of a time when an event or message spurred you to action?
- If so, why do you think it had that effect?

SOCIAL COGNITIVE THEORY

Returning to the sports recreation campaign, imagine that everything seems to be in our favor. People are aware of the recreation program. They know about the benefits. They even feel they would benefit personally. Yet they do not plan to participate. This may seem very puzzling.

A promoter familiar with social cognitive theory would consider the environment. **Social cognitive theory** holds that we make decisions by considering the interplay of internal and environmental factors (Bandura, 1986, 1994). **Internal factors** include knowledge, skills, emotions, habits, and so on. **Environmental factors** include social approval, physical environment, institutional rules, and the like. According to the theory, we are most comfortable when internal and environmental factors are in sync. This may explain why changing people's minds does not necessarily change their behavior. Elements of the environment have a persuasive appeal of their own, which may run counter to experts' advice. For example, people may knowingly expose themselves to the risks of indoor tanning because they believe it will make them more attractive (Noar et al., 2015). Or they may believe that poor oral health is to be expected because many people around them have tooth decay and because they do not feel they have the skills, time, or money to avoid that fate themselves (Savage, Scott, Aalboe, Stein, & Mullins, 2014).

IN YOUR EXPERIENCE

- What behaviors are embedded in your lifestyle? Which of them are healthy? Unhealthy?
- What would it take to change those behaviors?

Let's apply social cognitive theory to our sports recreation campaign. The theory suggests that, as health promoters, we must do more than make people aware of health risks. We must make healthy behaviors practical and socially acceptable. We may find that people believe it's healthy to work out, but they are discouraged from doing so because they fear others will laugh at them, the hours are not convenient, or they do not know anyone at the gym. If so, we may dedicate our efforts to improving the social atmosphere at the fitness center, suggesting different hours, or making other changes that build people's confidence and reduce the perceived risks of participating.

CAN YOU GUESS?

1. People who smoke tend to die at a younger age than others. How many years of their lives do smokers usually lose?
2. How much does the tobacco industry spend every day to advertise its products?
3. The World Health Organization has named tobacco one of the most severe health threats of modern times. In what percentage of the world is tobacco advertising banned?

Answers appear at the end of the chapter.

THEORY OF REASONED ACTION

The **theory of reasoned action (TRA)** is based on the assumption that we are rational decision makers. We do not just *happen* to behave one way or another. Instead, we make decisions and deliberate choices based on two primary considerations: (1) how strongly we believe a behavior will lead to positive outcomes, and (2) the perceived social implications of performing that behavior (Ajzen & Fishbein, 1980).

TRA is similar to social cognitive theory in that both consider personal and social influences. However, TRA is more global in focus. Its predictive power lies in assessing the attitudes and behaviors of large numbers of people (Ajzen & Fishbein, 1980). Because TRA is designed to make generalizations, its founders do not consider it necessary (or even helpful) to focus on specifics such as personality, rules, and emotions. The effects of these variables tend to even out over large populations. By the same token, TRA does not assume that small changes will make much difference overall. As Ajzen and Fishbein put it, "Changing one or more beliefs may not be sufficient to bring about change in the overall attitude" (p. 81).

According to the theory of planned behavior, the difference between wanting to do something healthy and actually doing it lies partly in the strength of our intentions and partly in how confident we are that we can actually follow through with them.

Icek Ajzen, one of the cofounders of TRA, extended the theory several years after its inception with the theory of planned behavior (Ajzen, 1985, 1991), which addresses circumstances in which the conditions set forth in TRA are met—that is, we believe strongly in a behavior and perceive it to be socially supported—but we encounter circumstances in which it is difficult to follow through. For example, maybe we have said for months that we are going to start a new diet, but something always seems to prevent us from doing it. According to the **theory of planned behavior**, the difference between wanting to do something and actually doing it may lie partly in the strength of our intentions, which are shaped by three main factors: our attitudes about the issue and behaviors (*maybe we're not sure which diet to choose*), how socially rewarding and acceptable we consider it to be (*it might be easier if our friends were not always eating hamburgers and French fries*), and the extent to which we feel—all things considered—that we can carry out the behavior (*we mean to make healthy dishes but it seems there is never time to buy and prepare them*). The theory is empowering in that it sensitizes us to some of the factors that underlie our choices. Without thinking about it too carefully, maybe we have been putting off a diet because no one around us is on one. Perhaps we can change that or make a choice to overcome it.

The theory also reminds us that our intentions often affect the people around us. When Kyle Andrews and collaborators studied the link between parental behavior and childhood obesity, they found that parents are least likely to proactively guide their children's eating and TV-watching habits if (1) they do not feel strongly that those behaviors are important; (2) they do not see other parents they admire doing so; and/or (3) they are not sure those behaviors make much difference anyway—perhaps, the authors point out, because the parents have been frustrated by their attempts to manage their own weight (Andrews, Silk, & Eneli, 2010). The researchers suggest that health promoters keep in mind that knowledge is part of the equation, but attitudes, role models, and confidence are also significant factors in achieving long-lasting change.

It may seem that the macro focus of TRA is not very helpful in planning our sports recreation campaign. Indeed, our target audience may be too small to make broad generalizations very useful. But TRA is of interest theoretically because it suggests that people make behavior changes based on their *overall* beliefs and perceptions. Small changes may not have much effect if they are outweighed by larger concerns. For example, imagine that a new study suggests that the best sunscreen is a thick coat of zinc oxide ointment. Do you suppose you could get students at your school to color their noses and other body parts white everyday? Probably not. Their belief in the health benefits is probably outweighed by their desire to be socially acceptable. Luckily for us, physical exercise *is* widely accepted. What we propose is already in line with most people's overall intentions.

TRANSTHEORETICAL MODEL

In analyzing the audience for our sports recreation campaign, imagine that we find some people *want* to exercise but that many of them are not doing so. We may even find that people *plan* to go to the gym but do not make it there. This is an important finding because it helps us understand our audience's state of mind. According to the **transtheoretical model**, we may not proceed directly from thinking about a problem to changing our behavior (Holtgrave, Tinsley, & Kay, 1995; Prochaska & DiClemente, 1983; Prochaska, DiClemente, & Norcross, 1992). Instead, we tend to change in stages. According to the model, change typically involves the following five stages:

Precontemplation: Not aware of a problem
Contemplation: Thinking about a problem
Preparation: Deciding to take action
Action: Making a change
Maintenance: Sticking to the change for six months or more

The Pink Ribbon campaign has raised awareness about breast cancer, but some critics charge that the rhetoric has not translated into effective support for cancer research (Jenkins, 2012), highlighting the lesson that publicity is not the only measure of a health campaign's success.

IN YOUR EXPERIENCE

- Can you think of behaviors you engage in even though you know they are unhealthy?
- What are the rewards of these behaviors?
- What would it take (if anything) to get you to quit?
- What advice do you have for health campaign designers trying to target this behavior?

The implication is that we react differently to health-promotion efforts depending on our current stage. Attention-getting information is called for when we are unaware of a problem. But skills training and encouragement may be more useful if we are already prepared to make a change. Furthermore, if we have already adopted the recommended behavior, we should be encouraged to continue it.

Hyunyi Cho and Charles Salmon (2007) found support for this concept when they exposed students to a variety of messages about skin cancer. Participants in precontemplation stages who viewed highly threatening messages were highly motivated to protect themselves, but they also reported higher-than-average feelings of hopelessness and fatalism. The authors concluded that fear appeals can call attention to previously unattended issues, but they may be counterproductive unless accompanied by clear and useful guidance.

Considering change as a stage-based process reveals some key challenges and opportunities for health campaign managers. One challenge is that we do not simply overhaul our behavior as soon as we hear new information. Change agents must be sensitive to barriers and motivations as well. Second, the transtheoretical model reveals why prevention efforts are particularly challenging. Inundating audience members with messages inappropriate to their stage of change may actually discourage them from proceeding. Rather than accelerate the change process, people may avoid the issue entirely.

The transtheoretical model presents opportunities for important contributions as well. Without motivational health campaigns, members of at-risk populations are likely to "remain stuck in the early stages" (Prochaska, Johnson, & Lee, 1998, p. 64). The model also suggests that changes, once initiated, must be supported. A team led by Elisia Cohen (2015) showed a video about the importance of HPV vaccines to women who had just had the first dose of the vaccine. Those women were subsequently 2.5 times more likely than others to return for the second and third dose of the vaccine than women who did not view the video. Cohen's team also found that, with slight modifications, the video was helpful for women in other stages of decision making as well. The project is a good reminder that effective campaigns are not simply one-shot affairs, but ongoing programs that support change and commitment.

WRAPPING IT UP

In closing our discussion of behavior change theories, it is important to point out that, as health promoters, we need not limit ourselves to any one model. The beauty of these theories is that they often overlap and call attention to different shades of meaning within the same process. Theories are like camera lenses, in that they help us achieve focus and clarity. This can be immensely helpful. But if we are not careful, a focus can be a limitation. In the next section we explore a different perspective. (Box 14.1 provides a brief overview of these theories and others in the chapter.)

BOX 14.1 THEORETICAL FOUNDATIONS

Synopsis of Campaign-Related Theories

CULTURAL-CRITICAL PERSPECTIVE: Health is not simply a matter of personal agency, but is inextricably linked to larger issues of culture, power, control, identity, and social consciousness.

HEALTH BELIEF MODEL: People are more or less motivated to change their behavior based on their perception of personal susceptibility, serious consequences, worthwhile benefits, justifiable costs, and cues to actions.

EXTENDED PARALLEL PROCESS MODEL: People evaluate threatening messages; first, to determine if they are personally at risk, and second, to judge whether they can prevent a harmful outcome. If they perceive a risk but do not feel they can avoid a bad outcome, they are likely to avoid the issue.

NORMATIVE SOCIAL BEHAVIOR THEORY: People are influenced by social norms to a greater or lesser degree, depending on how much they value the social approval to be gained by conforming, what outcomes they expect from the behavior, and how much they identify with the group.

SOCIAL COGNITIVE THEORY: People make decisions by considering the interplay of internal factors, such as skills and knowledge, and environmental factors, such as environment and social approval.

THEORY OF PLANNED BEHAVIOR: The difference between wanting to do something and actually doing it lies partly in the strength of a person's intentions, which are shaped by attitudes about the issue and behaviors, how socially rewarding and acceptable the person considers the behavior to be, and the extent to which she or he feels able to carry out the behavior.

THEORY OF REASONED ACTION: People make rational and deliberate choices based on how strongly they believe a behavior will lead to positive outcomes and the perceived social implications of performing that behavior.

TRANSTHEORETICAL MODEL: People tend to change in stages, ranging from precontemplation to contemplation, preparation, action, and maintenance.

Critical-Cultural Perspective

Return for a moment to the idea of a camera. When you look through the viewfinder you can zoom in on elements of the environment. But while you are focusing on one thing—even a very big thing like a sunset—there are other things you do not see. That's natural. The problem occurs when it begins to feel that what we see in the viewfinder is all there is. No matter what our perspective, there is usually more there than meets the eye. In this spirit, critical theorists remind us that—for all the many contributions of the cognitive theories we have just discussed—they share a common focus: They treat health as primarily the product of choices we make as individuals (Dutta-Bergman, 2005). Granted, cognitive theories acknowledge that our choices are influenced by a range of factors. But the nexus is still individual thought and decision making. What if we assume that this is only part of the story and look at health issues through a wider angle lens?

Communication theorist Mohan J. Dutta has emerged as a leading advocate of the **critical-cultural approach**, which proposes that health is not merely the result of individual choices, but is intertwined with issues of culture, power, control, identity, and social consciousness. From this perspective, health-related behaviors are profoundly influenced by dynamics that are larger and more pervasive than any individual (Dutta-Bergman, 2005).

There is plentiful evidence to support the idea that health is, to a great extent, a socially enacted phenomenon. As you may remember from Chapter 6, health disparities typically observe social boundaries. The overall health of some groups is worse or better than the health of others for a range of reasons such as resources, prejudice and discrimination, trust, cultural mores, information, stress, living and working conditions, and more. Assuming that people who are poor in information and resources have the same choices as other people requires that we overlook a host of factors that are very real to the people who experience them.

Moreover, it is not simply a question of having or not having. Cultural values and identities influence what is "good," "healthy," and "acceptable." The way a health expert views a particular behavior (such as smoking, drug use, driving fast, wearing a helmet, monogamy, and so on) may be very different from the way members of diverse cultures view it. Slater (2006) observes that health-related behaviors are often tied to issues of personal identity:

> *Risk-taking teens may believe that alcohol or marijuana experimentation is part of what defines them as adventurous, fun party people. Farmers may believe that accepting risk of injury [as in deciding not to have roll-bars mounted on their tractors] in the interest of keeping costs low is part of what makes them farmers.* (p. 155)

Conversely, scientific evidence suggests that these behaviors are dangerous. And health-related behaviors may also be attributed moral qualities such that they are considered bad, irresponsible, or evil. (This is especially true of issues such as drug use and sex.)

IN YOUR EXPERIENCE

- What factors influence your own health-related behaviors (e.g., how often you visit a doctor, whether you exercise every day, eat right, and so on)?
- How are these behaviors affected by larger issues such as resources, culture, and social support?

Considering these diverse viewpoints, a number of questions present themselves: Whose view is right? Who should decide how people ought to behave? And how is one's quality of life improved or diminished by the behaviors in question? These are difficult questions. The answers, say critical theorists, are not simple or universal. Rather than privileging one perspective over another, they advocate open and respectful dialogue about the issues—dialogue that involves the active participation of theorists, practitioners, and, most notably, members of the social group themselves (Dutta-Bergman, 2005).

Critical-cultural theorists observe that health promotion efforts that do not recognize the social contexts in which people live often fail to do much good. In fact, they often do harm—by reifying power differences, dominating the cultural landscape, and reinforcing the idea that people whose health is "poor" are not trying very hard or are like children who should be instructed by others. (See Box 14.2 for more on these ethical dilemmas.)

BOX 14.2 ETHICAL CONSIDERATIONS

Three Issues for Health Promoters to Keep in Mind

Health promoters are faced with a number of ethical considerations. Among them is deciding how to warn audiences without needlessly frightening them. They must also be careful not to blame people for ill health, while also encouraging people to prevent any illnesses and injuries they can. All the while, they must walk a fine line between making people concerned about illness and making them worried sick.

Timing

When early evidence of a health risk surfaces, is it better to warn the public right away or to wait for more conclusive evidence? This question poses a dilemma for health promoters. On the one hand, researchers suggest that people are wary of premature announcements that are later shown to be inaccurate. For example, people were long urged to increase their exposure to sunlight to ensure sufficient amounts of vitamin D. Now people are encouraged to avoid sunlight to lower their risk of skin cancer. Conflicting messages such as these may confuse people and cause them to ignore health advisories.

On the other hand, it may take months or years to compile conclusive evidence. During that time, people may be exposed to health risks they might have avoided. People are likely to be angry if health officials are aware of potential risks yet do not warn the public.

Scapegoating

It is difficult to know where the responsibility for personal health lies. For example, if children with the flu go to school and spread it to others, is it (1) the parents' fault for not keeping them home, (2) employers' fault for making it difficult for parents to stay home with sick children, or (3) health officials' fault for not educating parents about the need to keep children home? Although all of these factors probably contribute to the problem, part of a health promoter's job is to identify the conditions that most need improvement. In doing so, however, it is easy to **scapegoat**—to blame one person or group for the whole problem.

Scapegoating presents an ethical dilemma. It makes sense to focus attention on the condition or people with the greatest chance of making a difference. The typical health-promotion message cannot describe all the factors that contribute to a problem. However, focusing on one aspect or group of people may seem to place blame. For example, a campaign that admonishes parents to keep their sick children home may alienate parents who cannot afford to miss a day of work. These parents may feel frustrated and criticized, and they may resent promoters' efforts. Second, people not held to blame may feel that the problem is no longer their responsibility. Ruth Faden (1987) asserts that government officials sometimes promote the idea that people are personally responsible for their health partly because this lets government off the hook. There is little imperative to make sweeping social changes or health care reform if it seems that health is solely the product of voluntary lifestyle changes.

Evidence fuels both sides of the debate, suggesting that personal choices and empowerment are important to health but that, at the same time, personal efforts are often constrained by environmental factors beyond individuals' control (such as money to afford medical care or sanitary living conditions). Health promoters may find themselves trying to identify key objectives without ignoring that every objective is intertwined with others.

Stigmatizing

Prevention is the process of avoiding undesirable outcomes. People wear helmets to avoid head injuries, they are immunized to avoid diseases, and so on. Typically, the worse the potential outcome, the more people try to prevent it. Therefore health promoters try to motivate people by showing them how bad undesirable outcomes can be.

continued

continued

The dilemma is that, in portraying some *conditions* as undesirable, promoters may stigmatize some *people* as undesirable. People may become so frightened of diseases that they avoid the people who have them. For instance, an image of a child with a disability may be frightening enough to make children observe safety rules, but how are they likely to feel about children with disabilities? The same dilemma applies to AIDS publicity. People may become so frightened that they overprotect themselves by avoiding people who have AIDS.

What Do You Think?

1. Should health promoters release information about potential health risks immediately or wait for more conclusive evidence?
   a. How long is it reasonable to wait?
   b. What constitutes conclusive evidence?
2. Can you think of a way to promote public health without seeming to place the blame on certain people or groups?
3. Do you think it is possible to warn people about health hazards without stigmatizing people who have already been affected? Why or why not?

This is not to say that health promoters mindfully oppress the people they are trying to serve. It is more that their good intentions are often based on tacitly held assumptions about whose ideas are most valuable and who should be telling whom how to behave. You may say, "But they are only trying to teach people how to have better health." That's undoubtedly true. But let's unpack the baggage within that assertion. The idea of teaching implies that one person has knowledge or insight that he or she helps others comprehend. That is relatively unproblematic if we assume that the information is straightforward and value-free. One thing we know about health: It is never impersonal or value-free. So who defines what "better health" means? And who decides the best ways to accomplish that? When health promoters assume they have the answers to these questions, the result is often a paternalistic "I know what's best for you" mind-set. Actually, critical theorists argue, what is "best" is largely a matter of interpretation and value.

WHAT DO YOU THINK?

- What do you think of the idea that health-promotion experts, although they mean well, often reinforce a group's marginal status by adopting a paternalistic "this is what you should do" mind-set?
- Have you ever felt misunderstood or belittled by people who were trying to help you? If so, describe the experience.

In the end, privileging one perspective, even if it seems to be "for people's own good," is an exercise in power and often serves to marginalize and alienate people who see the world differently. Mohan Dutta and Rebecca de Souza (2008) trace the history of health-promotion efforts, showing that the tradition has largely been for those "in the center" to assist those "in the margins." They write:

> *This position was based on the assumption of the expertise of those at the center, who could examine an underdeveloped community, evaluate its needs based on scientific instruments, and propose solutions that would supposedly propel the community toward development; the category of the "underdeveloped" was fixed in its position as the object of interventions, its people portrayed as the "primitive" receivers of campaign messages who were incapable of development without the helping hand of the interventionists.* (p. 327)

Such efforts have often been experienced as insulting and naive, and, despite (and perhaps partly because of) widespread health-promotion campaigns, the gap between the health rich and the health poor around the world continues to widen at a staggering pace (Dutta & de Souza, 2008).

One approach recommended by the critical-cultural perspective involves embracing the notion of "many realities," none more correct or dominant than another (Dutta-Bergman, 2005, p. 117). This means shedding the notion that health promoters should set the agenda. Instead, it requires that they immerse themselves in the communities they serve, acting as facilitators who support community members' efforts to decide for themselves what they consider important and how they can best attain their goals (Dutta-Bergman, 2005). Health experts can share what they know of science and theory, but it's important that they not presume (or behave as if) that information is more right or important than participants' own perspectives. In other words, knowledge is one of many resources to be shared, not a tool to be used in the process of controlling others (Dutta, 2008). The goal is an interactive, ongoing process in which "problems are configured and reconfigured; solutions are generated and worked on based on the needs of the community as defined by community members" (Dutta-Bergman, 2005, p. 116). One objective is to build social consciousness about health and to engender a sense of **collective efficacy**, a communal sense that positive change can be accomplished. Dutta-Bergman (2005) also emphasizes the necessity of **community capacity**, the resources needed for good health, such as healthy food and water, safe shelter, and medical care. These basics are lacking in many parts of the country and the world.

Considering our campus campaign, we might choose to work with people who are frequently "in the margins" of fitness efforts. For example, we might focus on students and employees with physical disabilities. To accomplish this, we will want to immerse ourselves, as best we can, in the concerns and viewpoints of the people in the focus community. (Even if you have a disability yourself, it is risky to make assumptions from your own perspective.) Perhaps there is an organization or support group at which people with disabilities openly discuss their goals and concerns. With permission, we might attend meetings, or, if such a format does not already exist, we might organize a series of meetings. The process of encouraging people with disabilities to talk about fitness goals may be powerful in itself. There is likely to be great diversity among the people who participate, but we might learn that they share some common goals and face some common barriers they would like to overcome. Perhaps they are already involved in fitness efforts we do not know much about. We may find that, like many other people, they dread feeling conspicuous at the gym. Or perhaps they require specialized equipment or space that is not currently available. It may be that health professionals focus mostly on their other concerns and do not encourage them to pursue fitness goals much, so they do not feel confident about exercising. Already, you can probably imagine how issues of collective efficacy and community capacity might emerge and how you might help. Also keep in mind that—while it might seem patently audacious to tell people with disabilities how to behave if we do not understand their worldview—it can be equally as presumptuous to tell people from other cultures and communities how to think and act. Critical-cultural theory requires us to be respectful of "diverse realities" at every level.

WHAT DO YOU THINK?

You might be a member of the target audience for the sports recreation campaign. Take a moment to reflect on your own characteristics as an audience member.

- Do you exercise frequently? Why or why not?
- How do your considerations match up with the theories in this chapter?

The critical-cultural approach reminds us that nothing happens in isolation. What seem to be individual choices are often patterns of behavior shaped and reinforced by the systems in which they occur (Bohm, 1996; Senge, 2006). Ignoring the larger patterns can result in unproductive attempts at localized change. For example, health campaign designers frequently appeal to people to avoid or quit smoking, but they rarely tackle the larger issues of public policy and tobacco-industry standards (Dutta, 2008; Smith & Wakefield, 2006). Health promoters can help equalize disparities by advocating for community resources, public policies, and issues of social justice to help communities overcome their marginalized status.

The medical director of a free, walk-in clinic experienced a related dilemma when the clinic received a grant to publicize its services but did not receive funds to cover additional operating expenses. "The staff is already overwhelmed," he said. "It's kind of crazy to think publicity will solve the problem. Before we can serve more people, we need more staff." Another dilemma is that patients often cannot make scheduled appointments. "Maybe their boss won't let them off, or they don't have reliable transportation, or they work assorted day jobs and they can't afford to pass up an opportunity," explains the medical director, adding, "If we make appointments, the staff ends up

BOX 14.3 RESOURCES

Designing Campaign Materials

The details and techniques of campaign design are beyond the scope of this book, but here are some resources to guide your efforts.

Alstiel, T. B., & Grow, J. M. (2016). *Advertising creative: Strategy, copy, and design* (4th ed.). Thousand Oaks, CA: Sage.

Choi, H. (Ed.). (2013). *Health communication message design: Theory and practice*. Thousand Oaks, CA: Sage.

Drewlany, B. L., & Jewler, A. J. (2015). *Creative strategy in advertising* (10th ed.). Boston, MA: Wadsworth.

Parente, D. E., & Strausbaugh-Hutchinson, K. L. (2004). *Advertising campaign strategy: A guide to marketing communication plans* (3rd ed.). Boston, MA: Cengage.

Rice, R. E., & Atkin, C. K. (Eds.). (2013). *Public communication campaigns* (4th ed.). Thousand Oaks, CA: Sage.

Shea, A. (2012). *Designing for social change: Strategies for community-based graphic design*. New York: Princeton Architectural Press.

sitting around when we could have been caring for other people." So the clinic maintains a come-anytime policy. But he says that is problematic as well: "You might get in right away, or you might have to wait for hours to see a doctor. People on hourly wages can't afford to do that. We're in a fix. We're here to serve, but limitations pop up every day." The issues the clinic faces are large ones. Health experts who are not aware of the systems, structures, and assumptions that relegate some people to "the margins" and others to "the center" risk being ineffective in accomplishing true change. And even worse, they may contribute to the very disparities they are trying to overcome.

Let's take this knowledge of theories and power differences back to our own campaign, as we discuss the three final stages: designing campaign messages, piloting and implementing the campaign, and evaluating and maintaining the effort. (See Box 14.3 for additional resources about designing campaigns and Box 14.4 for more career options related to health campaigns.)

Step 5: Designing Campaign Messages

As we discussed in Chapter 13, the first step in designing an effective campaign is to listen and ask questions. Experts recommend that campaign designers work closely with members of the focus community to determine what aspect of the problem is most important to them and then make that concern a focal point. Critical-cultural theory also behooves us to look at cultural values and the macro-level, systemic factors that affect the people we want to help.

It may turn out that our campaign does not involve the traditional step of creating messages that will be widely distributed to audience members. Instead, we might advocate for new hours at the fitness center, specialized fitness classes, more space or resources, skills training, or some other effort. Most campaigns, however, involve some degree of message creation and dissemination. Even if our principal effort is changing the structure, we will want to get the word out somehow. In this section we focus on the central principles of message design.

CHOOSING A VOICE

Campaign messages have a voice. The voice may seem masculine, feminine, young, old, friendly, casual, stern, or so on. Whatever its character, this voice embodies the mood and personality of the campaign. Here are some questions to consider in finding that voice.

- What is the campaign's personality and mood?
- Is it an authority figure or a friend?
- Is it a logical person or an emotional person?
- Is it the sort of person to whom the audience is likely to respond?

Even when words appear in print, the tone of the message gives the reader a sense of who is "talking" and what type of relationship the writer wishes to establish with the reader.

BOX 14.4 CAREER OPPORTUNITIES

Health Campaign Design and Management

Campaign director
Publication designer
Communication director
Media relations specialist
Public relations specialist
Director of nonprofit organization
Professor/educator

Career Resources and Job Listings

- Chronicle of Philanthropy: philanthropy.com/jobs
- Wellness Council of America: welcoa.org
- American Journal of Health Promotion: healthpromotionjournal.com
- National Institutes of Health: nih.gov
- World Health Organization: who.int/employment/vacancies/en

Of course, the source is even more apparent when the audience can see or hear a spokesperson deliver the message. Messages typically have more impact when the target audience trusts the spokesperson and thinks that he or she is capable and attractive. Celebrities can sometimes fill the bill. The *NO MORE Excuses* campaign to overcome domestic violence and sexual assault features more than 40 well-known spokespeople from the arts, entertainment, sports, and more. An evolving collection of spokespersons attracts regular media attention.

There are sometimes drawbacks to using well-known spokespersons, however. When cyclist Lance Armstrong admitted to using performance-enhancing drugs in 2013, his Livestrong charity to benefit cancer research took a hit as well. Megasponsors Nike and RadioShack pulled out, and individual contributions plummeted (Lapowsky, 2014).

There is considerable evidence that audiences are most likely to believe people who are similar to them, an effect called **source homophily** (Rogers, 1973). Not only do people pay more attention when the spokesperson is similar to them, they feel more personally vulnerable to the health risk (Rimal & Morrison, 2006). For example, African Americans typically prefer and are more likely to trust PSAs that feature African Americans rather than people of other races (Wang & Arpan, 2008). In a national survey, 50% of African Americans interviewed said they trust Black-oriented media, but only 34% trusted mainstream media sources (Brodie, Kjellson, Hoff, & Parker, 2008). This may be partly because 78% of the African American respondents felt that they are often left out of health-related news stories, and 76% felt they are overrepresented in stories about crime (Brodie et al., 2008).

DESIGNING THE MESSAGE

In designing an effective health campaign message, it's important to consider community expectations and the role of logic, emotion, and novelty. We begin by exploring the different ways that messages about the same health behavior can be framed. Then we will talk about the art of matching messages to audience needs and emotions.

Theoretical Foundations: Message Framing

You are walking through the mall with a friend when you come upon a booth proclaiming "Free Health Screening." The health professionals staffing the booth say they can give you a relatively accurate cholesterol score. They just need a drop or two of blood from your finger. And they can tell your body-fat percentage by gently pinching and measuring the skin on your upper arm. One of you says, "Sure! What do I have to lose?" and steps up to participate. The other says, "No thanks," and backs away quickly. Why do you and your friend respond so differently?

Message-frame theorists are interested in the way people interpret health-related behaviors and in health promoters' efforts to affect those interpretations

(Slater, 2006). A famous example involves smoking. For years, health promoters tried to get people to quit because it was bad for their health. But the real turning point occurred when researchers discovered the dangers of secondhand smoke. The issue was reframed from endangering self to endangering others. Whereas the personal risk seemed acceptable—even cool and rebellious to some—many people found it unacceptable to put others at risk. It was the same behavior, but framed differently.

As with most things health-related, effects are not simple or predictable. Men in the United States are still at particularly high risk for smoking. One reason may be that advertisers have done a good job framing smoking in culturally masculine terms. In a study of smoking references in men's magazines, Mohan Dutta and Josh Boyd (2007) found that smoking was consistently framed as a sensual pleasure, as independent and mysterious, and as occurring in places of power, in exotic lands, or in appealing outdoor locations. The researchers suggest that antismoking campaigns might turn around the masculine appeal of these themes by framing antismoking messages in similar ways.

Messages may be framed in respect to potential gains, losses, and risks (Rothman & Salovey, 1997). A **gain-frame appeal** illustrates the advantages of performing the recommended behavior. For example, people might be persuaded that eating a low-carbohydrate diet will keep their weight down and help prevent diabetes and heart disease. They gain something by following the diet. Conversely, a **loss-frame appeal** emphasizes the negative repercussions of not taking action. For example, cigarette labels might show the harmful effects of smoking either in words or in graphic photos (Nan, Zhao, Yang, & Iles, 2015), as we discussed in Chapter 13.

There is some evidence that gain-frame appeals are more effective than loss-frame appeals at getting people to engage in preventive behaviors, especially when people know someone who has been adversely affected by the issue. For example, women whose loved ones have experienced breast cancer tend to find loss-frame messages about breast cancer distressing. They tend to respond more favorably to gain-frame appeals (H. J. Kim, 2014).

Health messages may not always change our minds, but they can boost us from *believing* in a behavior to actually carrying it out. For example, adults over age 24 who watched a video about the positive benefits of dental flossing were more likely to make flossing a habit if they already felt confident that they could avoid tooth decay and gum disease (Updegraff, Brick, Emanuel, Mintzer, & Sherman, 2015).

The issue gets a little more complicated when the goal shifts from disease prevention to disease detection. For example, you may willingly stock your beach bag with sunscreen, but imagine that you notice a suspicious mole on your shoulder. If you are like most people, you will feel a range of complicated emotions. Seeking a diagnosis is emotionally risky. You might learn that you have cancer and need treatment. It is emotionally self-protective to avoid what might be an anxiety-producing outcome. In fact, such avoidance can, and often does, last months or years.

But perhaps something else happens. You hear about someone who died of skin cancer or you see an alarming PSA. These are loss-frame messages, in that they highlight bad things that might happen if you do not take action. It's possible that you will become so frightened about what might be happening with your body that your anxiety will outweigh your desire to ignore the issue. Perhaps you will make a doctor's appointment after all.

One rule of thumb is to promote disease *prevention* with gain-frame messages and disease *detection* behaviors (such as doctor visits and health screenings) with loss-frame messages. But actual evidence on the value of loss-frame messages is inconclusive. That is probably because of the complex interplay of factors and emotions that surround health decisions. In our hypothetical example of the health booth at the mall, one of you is willing to be tested but the other is not. Research is filled with such inconsistencies. In the suspicious mole scenario, maybe you would not delay seeing a doctor if you noticed a suspicious mole. Perhaps you do not like uncertainty, you want to be sure it does not get any worse, you are pretty sure it is no big deal, or you have a checkup scheduled anyway so you will mention the mole to avoid a second visit. In contrast, another person might see the same frightening PSA yet still put the issue off, perhaps reasoning that "If it hasn't killed me yet, it must not be too bad" or "I'll die when it's my time to die and there's not much I can do about it anyway." People are complicated, to say the least. Although we seem to share the basic desire to maximize gains and minimize losses, there are numerous reasons we might weigh these factors differently.

WHAT DO YOU THINK?

- What factors might influence your decision to take part in a free health screening at the mall? What might you gain if you are tested? On the other hand, what unpleasant outcomes might result if you participate?
- What if the stakes were higher? If you suspected that you had been exposed to HIV, what factors would influence whether you got tested or not? Why?

Community Expectations

Health message are only useful if people consider them to be relevant and meaningful. When researchers noted that many older African American women consider faith to be central to their lives, they interviewed women to see if spirituality might be a helpful component of messages about breast cancer screening (Best, Spencer, Hall, Friedman, & Billings, 2015). The women they interviewed suggested that such messages reflect three themes—that one's body is a temple, that faith will help women cope if they find out they have breast cancer, and that consulting a physician is not inconsistent with having faith in God. As one woman put it, "You have to do your part so that God can do His part" (Best et al., 2015, p. 296). The women also suggested that messages be spiritual without being "pushy" or specific to any one religion. Best and colleagues concluded that listening to members of the target audience was helpful, respectful, and practical.

Sometimes community beliefs misrepresent the actual occurrence of health-related behaviors. For example, a good deal of research has focused on college students' alcohol consumption. There is consistent evidence that students who drink typically believe that alcohol frees their inhibitions and makes them less shy and more socially engaging (Sopory, 2005). That is a tough perception to overcome. And it is one reason students and health advocates often disagree about how much drinking is too much. Although researchers tend to define five or more drinks as "binge drinking," students typically perceive that five drinks are within the normal range for their peers (Lederman, Stewart, Goodhart, & Laitman, 2008). They define a binge in more extreme terms. Consequently, researchers who survey students about "binge drinking" may be measuring something different from what they think. And students may feel that warnings about "binge drinking" do not apply to them because their behavior is within "normal" bounds (Lederman et al., 2008). (For more on social norms as the basis for safe-drinking campaigns, see Box 14.5.)

Narrative Messages

Lupita, the oldest of three girls in a Mexican American family, has HPV, a sexually transmitted infection that can cause cancer. As viewers watch, Lupita shares details about the virus with her boyfriend, her younger sister, her mother, and a friend of the family, proposing that her 15-year-old sister Rosita be vaccinated for HPV so she can avoid getting it once she becomes sexually active.

Lupita and the others are characters in *Tamale Lessons*, a brief film designed to convey the facts about HPV, its consequences, and prevention options. The film is an example of a health message presented in a narrative storytelling format. Researchers led by Lauren Frank (2015) surveyed 450 women who watched *Tamale Lessons* to see how the film impacted their ideas about HPV. They found that viewers who identified strongly with the characters were most likely to take the HPV threat to heart and to maintain that concern six months later (Frank, Murphy, Chatterjee, Moran, & Baezconde-Garbanati, 2015).

Narratives often inspire a greater sense of realism, identification, and emotional and cognitive engagement than more didactic approaches do (Miller-Day & Hecht, 2013). They can transport people to scenarios they have not experienced personally and convey complex information in a way that is not overwhelming (Niederdeppe, Shapiro, Kim, Bartolo, & Porticella, 2014; Sanders-Jackson, 2014; Stavrositu & Kim, 2015).

In the *keepin' it REAL* (*kiR*) program, children are encouraged to write and create audio and video PSAs in which they share their personal stories about issues such as resisting peer pressure to drink and do drugs. These narrative messages, created for kids by kids, may have an advantage in terms of empowering young people to set agendas and address concerns in their own ways (Krieger et al., 2013).

BOX 14.5 THEORETICAL FOUNDATIONS

What Does Science Say About Peer Pressure?

I think that alcohol is a huge part of adult life. It's like a rite of passage when you finally turn 21.

Every college student I know drinks.

College students love to party. It's tradition.

Thinking of your own undergraduate experience, you might find yourself nodding in agreement as you read these comments made by college students in Casper and colleagues' (2006) study (p. 295). Or you might shake your head in doubt. Experiences vary. And conventional wisdom suggests that your experience has a lot to do with the company you keep. It feels normal for partiers to party and nondrinkers not to drink. But in some instances, some people don't follow the crowd. What *does* science say about fitting in with the crowd?

On the one hand, there is ample evidence that people are more likely to engage in risky behaviors if their friends do. Having peers who smoke and approve of smoking is the single greatest predictor of a teen's decision to smoke cigarettes (Krosnick et al., 2006; Miller, Burgoon, Grandpre, & Alvaro, 2006). The same goes for kicking the habit. The overall decline in smoking has not occurred so much here and there as in distinct social clusters. In studying the issue, Nicholas Christakis and James Fowler (2008) found that smoking had persisted in some circles but that in others "whole groups of people were quitting in concert" (p. 2249).

One foundation for the RU SURE campaign that begins this chapter is **social norms theory**, which suggests that people base their behavior partly on what they consider appropriate and socially acceptable (Haines & Spear, 1996). The idea is that such campaigns may be especially influential in settings such as college campuses, where students are part of novel situations in which they are not immediately aware of cultural expectations. As you know, that campaign has had demonstrable success curbing student alcohol abuse.

But some social norm campaigns have been less successful. In a study of students at 37 colleges, Wechsler and colleagues (2003) found that drinking was the same on campuses with social norm campaigns as on those without them. In another study, 72.6% of college students surveyed disbelieved the assertion that "most students drink 0 to 4 drinks when they party" (Polonec, Major, & Atwood, 2006, p. 23). And Shelly Campo and Kenzie Cameron (2006) found that, after viewing social-norming messages, light drinkers were even more determined to keep their drinking within healthy bounds, but heavier drinkers often went the other way. Their drinking intentions were *more* intense after viewing the normative messages. Another challenge to the power of social norms is that, in some cases, people find nonconformity appealing. People of varying ages who rank high on individualism or rebellious tendencies are likely to go *against* the norm (Lapinski, Rimal, DeVries, & Lee, 2007; M. Lee & Bichard, 2006).

Rajiv Rimal and Kevin Real (2005) have sought to make sense of the complexity with their **theory of normative social behavior (TNSB)**. The theory proposes that we *are* influenced by perceived social norms but that a variety of factors either strengthen or weaken how much those perceptions affect us. These include (1) how much we value the social approval to be gained from conforming, (2) the outcomes we expect from engaging in the behavior, (3) the degree to which we identify with the group, and (4) how confident we feel in our ability to say no to the behavior in question (Jang, Rimal, & Cho, 2013; Rimal & Real, 2005). In other words, if we like and value the group, we may want to "fit in" by acting in accordance with its norms, especially if the behavior offers rewards we like. However, our desire to fit in may be outweighed by other factors—as when the behavior seems inconsequential, we do not value or identify with the group very much, we enjoy being different, or we like the behavior so much we are willing to buck convention to do it. There is evidence that college students drink if/when they perceive that the rewards (such as loss of social inhibitions) outweigh the potential for negative repercussions, such as getting in trouble or getting hurt. And this is particularly true if they also perceive that drinking is accepted and approved by their friends (Rimal & Real, 2005).

continued

So back to the initial question: *Does believing that "most people drink" or "drink a lot" mean we are likely to do the same?* So far, the best answer is that it depends. For one, it depends on how we define "most people." The "norm" that researchers often use (as in "two of three college students stop at three or fewer drinks") is an aggregate statistic. It might change your mind about typical college student behavior. Or you might think, "They clearly haven't met *my* friends." Evidence suggests that, if the overall statistic seems different from what you perceive strongly within your own social network, you are likely to disbelieve or disregard it (Polonec et al., 2006; Yanovitzky, Stewart, & Lederman, 2006). A second consideration concerns the perceived value of the behavior (Rimal, 2008). Whereas a **descriptive norm** describes "what most people do," an **injunctive norm** characterizes the perception that people *should* do it based on particular values (Boer & Westhoff, 2006; Rimal, 2008). For example, even if you believe that most of your friends occasionally drink and drive, you may refuse to do so yourself because you consider it wrong or irresponsible. Finally, TNSB suggests that norms affect us to the degree that it is socially and personally rewarding to live up to them. If any of a complex array of factors change (rewards, penalties, group membership, or so on), the power of the norm may change considerably.

Here are a few implications for health campaigns.

- *Correct misperceptions about descriptive norms.* Although descriptive norms do not tell the whole story, nearly everyone agrees that people who overestimate the prevalence of risky behaviors are more likely than others to feel that the behaviors are acceptable and even socially preferred.
- *Emphasize descriptive and injunctive norms.* For example, a sun safety program was particularly effective when the health promoters presented both an injunctive norm (photos that showed undesirable skin damage) and a descriptive norm (information that most people now use sunscreen) (Mahler, Kulik, Butler, Gerrard, & Gibbons, 2008).
- *Do not rely solely on norming messages.* Norms sometimes take a backseat to other factors, such as personal enjoyment. College students in Cameron and Campo's (2006) study were most likely to smoke, exercise, and drink if they enjoyed those behaviors, even when there was no strong peer support for them. It may help to emphasize the negative repercussions of unhealthy behaviors as well as social norms.
- *Target social networks.* A common suggestion among social norm researchers is that campaigns address alcohol abuse as a social network issue. This often involves developing partnerships with sororities and fraternities, sports teams, student governments, and other groups.

The debate continues to be lively and productive. The success of the RU SURE campaign at Rutgers may be based partly on its social norm foundation and partly on the integrated and multifaceted nature of the campaign itself. TNSB offers a rich, contextual understanding of the facets that figure into social norming, a concept that continues to evolve and to influence theorists as well as practitioners.

CULTURE AND HEALTH

Cultural traditions may make smoking seem appealing, even in the face of evidence about its health effects. Chinese Canadian participants in one study said that it is customary for them to offer and accept cigarettes from each other as a show of hospitality and friendship (Poureslami, Shum, Cheng, & FitzGerald, 2014).

Logical Appeals

A **logical appeal** attempts to demonstrate an evidentiary (demonstrable) link between a behavior and a result. For example, it may seem logical to eat less if it will result in greater health and a longer life. Logical appeals are often based on the results of scientific studies. Quoting science is not as clear cut as it sounds, however.

Daniel O'Keefe (2015) proposes that, to present evidence fairly and responsibly, health promoters should rely on data that are consistent across studies that involve a representative range of people and message types. He also urges health promoters to avoid unsupported generalizations by taking into account the effect sizes (how strongly two or more variables are related) and confidence intervals (the likelihood that the results are accurate and consistent rather than the result of chance variations). Other theorists echo the call that it is important to present clear and convincing evidence rather than "scientific flourishes" such as fancy words and irrelevant numbers (Hample & Hample, 2014).

As we have discussed, scientific evidence is not always the only, or even the most compelling, factor that people consider when making health choices. Community standards, emotions, and preferences play a role as well.

Emotional Appeals

An **emotional appeal** (also called an *affect appeal*) suggests that people feel a certain way regarding their health and their behaviors. For example, they may be afraid to engage in unprotected sex, proud if they have quit smoking, or guilty if they are endangering others. Ellen Peters and colleagues (2006) propose that persuasive appeals that involve affect typically make one of four general claims: (1) they campaign for particular interpretations, as when we think, "The people in that commercial look really happy; it must be a good product"; (2) they grab or hold our attention; (3) they motivate us to think carefully or take action; and (4) they link behaviors with community values, as when a message encourages us to recycle because it is good for the earth or to stop smoking because it puts our children in danger (Peters et al., 2006). Although emotions occur along a complex continuum, Peters and colleagues observe that there are two basic "flavors"—positive and negative. For the most part, campaigns encourage people to strive for positive outcomes and to avoid negative ones. Research discussed in this section describes the usefulness and the limitations of various emotional appeals.

POSITIVE-AFFECT APPEALS. Campaigns may promote positive emotional rewards in the form of popularity, a sense of accomplishment, honor, fun, happiness, or so on. As we discussed in Chapter 11, pharmaceutical ads are famous for implying that people who take those drugs are remarkably healthy, active, and attractive.

Campaigns may also inspire positive affect because the messages themselves are pleasant or entertaining. For example, people sometimes remember more about humorous messages than others because they pay more attention to them (Blanc & Brigaud, 2014). In a similar way, a fun computer game about food choices boosted university students' knowledge of nutrition as well as their confidence and intention to eat healthy foods (Peng, 2009).

Positive affect can be the honey that draws people to health messages they might otherwise ignore. But that is no guarantee that they will be influential. Sometimes people pay attention to the humor, graphics, or music but not to the main information, especially if the issue is not one that concerns them very much.

NEGATIVE-AFFECT APPEALS. Some campaign designers attempt to motivate people by making them feel anxious, fearful, or guilty. There is evidence that fearful appeals are effective at convincing people to be tested for AIDS and to take other health precautions (Green & Witte, 2006; Hullett, 2006).

Communication theorist Kim Witte proposes that, if people are not at all anxious about a health topic, then they probably are not motivated to learn about it or to take action. However, if they are overly anxious, they may avoid the subject. Witte's **extended parallel process model** (EPPM) proposes that people evaluate a threatening message, first, to determine if they are personally at risk and, second, to judge whether they can prevent a harmful outcome. If they perceive a risk but do not feel they can avoid a bad outcome, they are likely to soothe their anxiety by avoiding the issue (Witte, 1997, 2008). Some evidence suggests that a 1-to-1 ratio of threatening messages and confidence-building (efficacy) messages seems most effective (Carcioppolo et al., 2013).

Simon-Arndt and associates (2006) used EPPM principles to test an interactive program for Marines. Marines in the study answered online questions about their alcohol consumption. Then they received online feedback about their risk levels and potential ways to prevent unhealthy outcomes. About 85% of the Marines who took part preferred this program to other alcohol-use campaigns, perhaps because it seemed highly targeted to their own behaviors (Simon-Arndt, Hurtado, & Patriarca-Troyk, 2006).

Guilt, a feeling of remorse about having done something wrong, is a particularly strong emotion. Consequently, it is a popular tool for advertisers and health campaigners. People typically feel sorry or ashamed when they have behaved badly, especially when others are hurt by their actions. Advertisers who bring these feelings to the surface and offer a way to make retribution may find that people are willing to cooperate to soothe their consciences. For example, people are more likely to sign up as organ donors if they think they will feel guilty for saying no (Wang, 2011).

Overall, negative affect is a popular component of persuasive messages, but it must be used carefully. Health promoters have overshot the mark in some cases. Women in the United States now consistently overestimate their risk of breast cancer (Jones, Denham, & Springston, 2007). And it is not easy to reassure them. Amanda Dillard and colleagues found that it was just as difficult to reduce women's sense of breast cancer danger as it was to *stimulate* their concern about other health risks (Dillard, McCaul, Kelso, & Klein, 2006).

Heidi Klum obliges Tim Gunn with an Ice Bucket Challenge to raise awareness about amyotrophic lateral sclerosis (ALS). The challenge was to dump ice water over one's head or make a donation to the ALS Association. More than 3 million celebrities and everyday people took an ice bath for the cause, often capturing the experience on video and posting it online. The novel approach and publicity inspired donations as well, about $115 million worth within a few months (Tirrell, 2015).

CHECK IT OUT!

For guidance on creating your own health campaign, visit the following websites.

- The Community Tool Box: ctb.ku.edu
- The American Public Health Association: apha.org
- Making Health Communication Programs Work: A Planner's Guide available at cancer.gov/pinkbook
- Communication Planning with CDCynergy available at cdc.gov/healthmarketing

Novel and Shocking Messages

Novel messages tend to catch people's attention and stick in their memory (Parrott, 1995). Some messages are novel (new or different) without being **shocking** (intense or improper). For instance, London residents were surprised to find that the names of famous shops and landmarks had changed overnight as part of a National Health Services campaign (see Box 14.6). The novel approach was attention getting but not edgy enough to offend. At other times, novel messages may be shocking because they deal with topics not usually discussed in public or because they are purposefully controversial to attract attention. One difficulty about using novel images to attract attention is that the novelty wears off. Keeping novelty alive may mean becoming ever more risqué. It's sometimes difficult to balance decorum with the need for public awareness.

One difficulty surrounding AIDS awareness is that health promoters must deal with delicate issues like premarital sex and anal intercourse. Even when promoters do not mean to be shocking, they often are. Particularly when AIDS first became a health concern, condoms and gay sex were not socially acceptable topics for mass-media campaigns. In the 1990s, controversy arose concerning a poster campaign in New York City. The posters (which were hung in subway terminals) read "Young, Hot, Safe!" and showed images of homosexual couples kissing while holding condoms ("Controversy Heats Up," 1994). Some people felt the posters were indecent, while others argued that they communicated an important message to a high-risk group. (The poster campaign was discontinued soon thereafter.)

LESSONS ABOUT EMOTIONAL APPEALS. Here are a few guidelines, suggested by theorists and researchers, about using emotional appeals.

- *Match the emotion to the goal.* Emotional appeals are most persuasive when they are appropriate to the desired response. For example, fear appeals can alert people to danger, disgust appeals can make unhealthy behaviors unappealing, hope appeals can convince people it is worth taking action, and so on (Dillard & Nabi, 2006).

- *Build empathy.* "It won't happen to me" is a common response to health messages, even when they are highly arousing. For example, we may feel concerned about intravenous drug users because they are at risk for AIDS but perceive our own risk to be negligible because we are not part of that group. We usually feel a sense of personal relevance only if we understand the message cognitively, the speaker effectively conveys his or her feelings of vulnerability, and we perceive that those feelings are relevant to our own situations (Campbell & Babrow, 2004).
- *Don't overdo it.* Too much affect can be counterproductive and cause people to avoid the issue or to worry unnecessarily (Peters et al., 2006, p. S155).

IN YOUR EXPERIENCE

- Have you ever seen a PSA you did not like?
- If so, what made it unappealing?

Step 6: Piloting and Implementing The Campaign

It is important to pilot (pretest) a campaign before launching it full scale. **Piloting** usually involves selecting members from the target audience to review the campaign materials and comment on them. Salmon and Atkin (2003) state that early feedback is crucial:

> *The feedback from the audience can reveal whether the tone is too righteous (admonishing unhealthy people about their incorrect behavior), the recommendations too extremist (rigidly advocating unpalatable ideas of healthy behavior), the execution too politically correct (staying within tightly prescribed boundaries of propriety to avoid offending overly sensitive authorities and interest groups), and the execution too self-indulgent (letting creativity and style overwhelm substance and substantive content). (p. 453)*

Some questions to consider include the following:

- Are written messages easy to read and understand?
- Are recorded messages easy to understand?
- Do messages seem relevant and important?
- Are the messages appealing? Why or why not?

BOX 14.6

S-mething Is Missing

By Elizabeth McPherson

In June 2015, names of famous landmarks in the United Kingdom suddenly lost three important letters: A, O, and B. Overnight, world-renowned Downing Street became "D-wning Street" and the *Daily Mirror* became the "*D-ily M-rror.*" In an online article, British Broadcasting Corporation (BBC) Newsbeat asked: "S- who is d-ing it, -nd why -re they d-ing it?" (BBC Newsbeat, 2015).

The missing letters, A, O and B, all refer to blood groups in short supply. As part of a carefully crafted health campaign to raise awareness during the UK's National Blood Week, companies, individuals, and the media deleted the three letters on signs, messages, and headlines, then used the hashtag #missingtype to promote their activities on social media. Within days the campaign attracted international attention.

The high-profile campaign, started by the National Health Service (NHS), was designed to attract 204,000 new blood donors across England and North Wales (NHS, 2015). The NHS is funded through taxes. In return, all services—from preventive care to extensive medical procedures like transplants—are free to residents at the point of use (NHS, 2015).

- Is the spokesperson effective?
- Does the information seem controversial or offensive?

It may be useful to survey people before and after they are exposed to campaign materials to see if there is any change in their knowledge, attitudes, and intentions. When possible, it is also advisable to survey people a week or a month after they were initially exposed to campaign materials to see how much they remember and whether message effects are still present. Remember to allow time to refine campaign messages based on the results of pretesting. Planning ahead will improve the campaign's likelihood of success.

Once campaign messages have been created, piloted, and refined, it's time to distribute them through chosen channels. In many cases (as with one-on-one communication, community presentations, online messages, and social media), health promoters have direct contact with community members and thus have control over what is conveyed. For some channels, however, health promoters must rely on others to share, and sometimes to edit, their messages. For instance, editors and news directors choose what PSAs to publicize and when, and what topics to cover in the news. On a social level, community opinion leaders focus on some issues more than others, affecting what the people around them think and believe. People in the media and the community who decide what information will be publicized and how are known as **gatekeepers**.

Good campaign designers employ a variety of communication channels to help ensure that messages make it to focus community members through one gate or another. Wise health promoters realize the importance of gatekeepers, include them in campaign planning, and consider their points of view. Media gatekeepers are bound by multiple pressures (e.g., operating budgets, community demands, and time constraints). The promoter who gets to know gatekeepers personally and makes it easy for them to pass along information has a better chance of getting messages to community members.

Step 7: Evaluating and Maintaining The Campaign

A campaign is not over when it has been released to the public. Effective health promotion requires that campaign managers evaluate the success of the project, help community members maintain any positive changes they may have made, and refine and develop future campaign messages.

EVALUATION

The effects of a campaign may be evaluated in several ways. A **pretest–posttest design** means that campaigners survey people before the campaign is released and then survey them again afterward to see if their knowledge, intentions, or behaviors have changed. You might go about this in two different ways—by exposing people to campaign materials in a controlled environment such as classroom or community center and evaluating their immediate responses (an **efficacy study**), or by studying campaign effects in the context of people's everyday lives (an **effectiveness study**) (Evans, Uhrig, Davis, & McCormack, 2009, p. 315). W. Douglas Evans and colleagues (2009) found that efficacy studies offer several advantages: (1) You can make sure the participants are exposed to your campaign messages before they respond to your questions, (2) you minimize the likelihood that responses have been affected by extraneous factors, and (3) you can expose members of the target audience to multiple messages and see how their responses to them differ. Of course, efficacy studies may not tell you how many people in the larger population are affected or how, so you may want to use both.

You collect data to determine if people's attitudes, knowledge, or actions have changed since the campaign. Just keep in mind that if changes have occurred, they may or may not be the result of campaign exposure.

To evaluate the impact of the truth® campaign described in Chapter 13, researchers conducted telephone surveys with 6,897 youth ages 12 to 17 before the campaign began (Farrelly, Healton, Davis, Messeri, & Haviland, 2002). The survey participants were chosen to represent teens in different ethnic and racial groups, urban and nonurban areas, and areas with and without other antitobacco campaigns. Researchers asked the youth to indicate their level of agreement or disagreement with statements about the tobacco industry, the social acceptability of smoking, and their intention to smoke within the next year. In follow-up interviews after the campaign's release, researchers asked 10,692 youth if they remembered seeing any antitobacco campaigns and, if so, what they remembered about them. They also asked about perceptions of the tobacco industry, the social acceptability of smoking, and the youths' intention to smoke in the next year. To factor out as many intervening variables as possible, researchers statistically controlled for such factors as the number of parents in the household, amount of television viewing, the presence of smokers in the household, and parental messages about smoking. With the data collected, researchers were able (1) to gauge the extent to which community members saw and remembered the campaign, and (2) to compare youth attitudes before and after the campaign.

Another way to evaluate a campaign's success is to study actual behavior changes, such as the number of people who sign up for basketball or the number of hospital admissions or calls to a hotline. These evaluation techniques are useful, but it is always difficult to know precisely what effects a campaign has had. For one thing, the campaign is not the only factor influencing people's attitudes and behavior. They may be affected by personal experiences, natural disasters, news stories, or other occurrences. Second, campaigns often have indirect effects. For instance, the campaign may have reached influential members of the community, who in turn spread the word to others. Thus, people who were not exposed to campaign messages personally may still be affected by them. Third, sometimes the success of a health campaign is reflected in what does *not* occur over the long run. For example, the coordinators of a drug-free program in elementary schools may not know if they have been successful until the children involved are adolescents or adults, by which time they will have been influenced by many other factors as well. When undesired behaviors do not occur, it is difficult to know how many people might have adopted those behaviors if not for the campaign.

For better or worse, sometimes the best that campaigners can do is evaluate the **reach** (number of people exposed to campaign messages) and **specificity** (the type of people exposed to the messages) of a campaign. For this purpose, promoters can survey community members and keep track of when and where campaign messages are publicized.

MAINTENANCE

Maintaining behaviors that have been positively influenced by a campaign involves continued encouragement and skills training. Keep in mind that people are most likely to continue new behaviors if they fully understand the benefits of doing so. Because some people try new behaviors without first fully understanding them, do not assume that people who begin a behavior are fully educated about it. Encouragement, incentives, and continued skills training can help people overcome setbacks they are likely to encounter.

Summary

Social marketers conduct extensive audience analyses and strive to create messages with the same appeal as commercial messages. The results of social marketing are measured, not in sales figures or profit margins, but in public awareness and improved health. These outcomes are often realized in subtle ways over long periods of time, but social marketers work hard to gauge the success of their efforts and apply what they learn to future campaigns.

Theories of behavior change explain the conditions under which people are likely to make lifestyle changes. The overall message is that behavior is influenced by a complex array of factors, both internal and external. Failing to consider these can lead to health campaigns that look good but have very little social value. In addition, campaign designers who fail to consider and accommodate audience members' beliefs and opportunities can alienate the people they hope to influence and can actually make things worse by promoting behaviors that people find offensive, puzzling, or even impossible to carry out. One alternative is for health advocates to serve as facilitators and enablers who help communities set their own agendas and build collective efficacy and social capacity.

In designing campaign messages, health promoters should consider ethical implications concerning timing, scapegoating, and stigmatizing, as well as audience needs, campaign goals, and benefits of the recommended behaviors.

Campaign messages have different voices, ranging from stern to casual and friendly. Often, the spokesperson influences how the message is perceived. Research suggests that people typically respond most favorably to spokespersons who are similar to them, likable, and attractive. A celebrity may be an effective spokesperson or a public liability.

The same behavior may be framed in a number of ways to emphasize potential gains, losses, or social implications. Narrative storytelling is a promising way to engage people who relate to the storytellers and to provide culturally appealing information. Some campaign messages also appeal to our logic and emotions. Messages may motivate people through positive affect, such as the promise of pleasure and happiness or the desire to fit in with social norms. Negative-affect appeals may induce people to change by stirring up feelings of anxiety, fear, and guilt. According to the extended parallel process model, anxiety is a powerful motivator, except when the threat is so overwhelming that people would rather avoid the issue. Novel and shocking messages typically create interest, but they may be controversial and offensive to some people.

Experts recommend that health promoters pilot new campaigns before implementing them. Testing campaign messages on sample community members can reveal unanticipated reactions and ambiguities so messages can be improved before they are publicly released. Finally, health promoters should evaluate campaigns once they are released, apply what they have learned to future efforts, and compare the results with their goals.

Key Terms and Theories

social marketing
health belief model
social cognitive theory
internal factors
environmental factors
theory of reasoned action (TRA)
theory of planned behavior
transtheoretical model
critical-cultural approach
scapegoat
collective efficacy
community capacity
source homophily
gain-frame appeal
loss-frame appeal
social norms theory
theory of normative social behavior (TNSB)
descriptive norm
injunctive norm
logical appeal
emotional appeal
extended parallel process model (EPPM)
guilt
novel messages
shocking messages
piloting
gatekeepers
pretest–posttest design
efficacy study
effectiveness study
reach
specificity

Discussion Questions

1. Identify several campaign messages.
   a. From the perspective of social marketing, what are the "costs" and rewards of the recommended behavior in each message?
   b. Analyze how the messages reflect components of the following theories: health belief model, social cognitive theory, theory of planned behavior, and transtheoretical model.
   c. Analyze the same messages from the critical-cultural perspective. Do they seem culturally inclusive and sensitive? What role do issues such as power, control, identity, and social consciousness play? Do the messages seem to build collective efficacy and/or community capacity? If so, how? How might you reframe these messages to reflect the goals and realities of a community with which you identify?
2. Think of a health-related behavior (e.g., drinking water, avoiding sweets, getting enough sleep). Brainstorm ways you can frame the behavior in terms of potential losses, gains, and risks. What do you think would be most effective? Why?
3. In what circumstances are positive-affect messages usually effective? Negative-affect appeals? Think of as many examples as you can. Which type of appeal do you typically prefer, and why?
4. Explain the extended parallel process model as it relates to negative-affect appeals. Give an example from your own experience.

Answers to *Can You Guess?*

1. Smoking cuts an average of 15 years off a person's life (WHO, 2008a).
2. Tobacco companies spend $26 million a day on advertising—in the United States alone. Their *daily* budget is more than the *annual* budget of the truth® campaign, which is the largest anti-tobacco campaign in history (CDC, 2015f; "New Research," 2008).
3. Only 5% of the world's population is shielded from tobacco advertising.

References

Abelson, R. (2012, March 15). Recession's toll on health coverage [Blog post]. Economix. *The New York Times*. Retrieved from http://economix.blogs.nytimes.com/2012/03/15/recessions-toll-on-health-coverage/

About us. (2012). Washington, DC: American Legacy Foundation. truth® website. Retrieved from https://www.thetruth.com/about-truth

About us. (2013). Oxford, England: The Pleasure Project website. Retrieved from http://thepleasureproject.org/about-us/

Abroms, L. C., Ahuja, M., Kodl, Y., Thaweethai, L., Sims, J., Winickoff, J. P., & Windsor, R. A. (2012). Text2Quit: Results from a pilot test of a personalized, interactive mobile health smoking cessation program. *Journal of Health Communication, 17*, 44–53.

Accreditation Council to Graduate Medical Education (ACGME). (2006, April). Introduction to competency-based education. Facilitator's guide. Chicago: Author. Retrieved from http://www.acgme.org/outcome/e-learn/21M1_FacManual.pdf

Accreditation Council to Graduate Medical Education (ACGME). (2015). Common program requirements. Chicago: Author. Retrieved from http://www.acgme.org/acgmeweb/Portals/0/PFAssets/ProgramRequirements/CPRs_07012015_TCC.pdf

Adams, J., Braun, V., & McCreanor, T. (2014). "Aren't labels for pickle jars, not people?" Negotiating identity and community in talk about "being gay." *American Journal of Men's Health, 8*(6), 457. doi:10.1177/1557988313518800

Adams, J. R., Elwyn, G., Légaré, F., & Frosch, D. L. (2012). Communicating with physicians about medical decisions: A reluctance to disagree. *Archives of Internal Medicine, 172*(15), 1184–1186.

Adams, N., & Field, L. (2001). Pain management 1: Psychological and social aspects of pain. *British Journal of Nursing, 10*(14), 903–911.

Adams, R. J., & Parrott, R. (1994, February). Pediatric nurses' communication of role expectations to parents of hospitalized children. *Journal of Applied Communication Research, 22*, 36–47.

Adams, R., Price, K., Tucker, G., Nguyen, A.-M., & Wilson, D. (2012). The doctor and the patient—How is a clinical encounter perceived? *Patient Education and Counseling, 86*(1), 127–133.

Adelman, S. A. (2008, January 4). Be careful what you promise. *Medical Economics, 85*(1), 14.

A doctor's advice, a patient's race influence flu shot rates. (2015, February 24). *Health*. Retrieved from http://news.health.com/2015/02/24/a-doctors-advice-a-patients-race-influence-flu-shot-rates/

Afifi, W. A., & Weiner, J. L. (2004). Toward a theory of motivated information management. *Communication Theory, 14*, 167–190.

African-American youth and alcohol advertising. (2012). Center on Alcohol Marketing and Youth. Retrieved from http://www.camy.org/resources/fact-sheets/african-american-youth-and-alcohol-advertising/index.html

Ahmad, N. N. (2004, April 15). Arab-American culture and health care. Retrieved from http://www.cwru.edu/med/epidbio/mphp439/Arab-Americans.htm

Ahn, S. J. (2015). Incorporating immersive virtual environments in health promotion campaigns: A construal level theory approach. *Health Communication, 30*(6), 545–556.

Ajzen, I. (1985). From intentions to actions: A theory of planned behavior. In J. Kuhl & J. Beckman (Eds.), *Action control: From cognition to behavior* (pp. 11–39). Heidelberg: Springer.

Ajzen, I. (1991). The theory of planned behavior. *Organizational Behavior and Human Decision Processes, 50*, 179–211.

Ajzen, I., & Fishbein, M. (1980). *Understanding attitudes and predicting behavior.* Englewood Cliffs, NJ: Prentice Hall.

Alam, R., Barrera, M., D'Agostino, N., Nicholas, D. B., & Schneiderman, G. (2012). Bereavement experiences of mothers and fathers over time after the death of a child due to cancer. *Death Studies, 36*, 1–22. doi:10.1080/07481187.2011.553312

Albrecht, T. L., & Adelman, M. B. (1987). Communicating social support: A theoretical perspective. In T. L. Albrecht & M. B. Adelman (Eds.), *Communicating social support* (pp. 18–39). Newbury Park, CA: Sage.

Alcohol Concern. (2007, July). *Not in front of the children—child protection and advertising.* London: Author. Retrieved from http://www.alcoholpolicy.net/files/Not_in_front_of_the_children.pdf

Alden, D. L., Merz, M. Y., & Thi, L. M. (2010). Patient decision-making preference and physician decision-making style for contraceptive method choice in an Asian culture: Does concordance matter? *Health Communication, 25*, 718–725.

Al-Janabi, H., Coast, J., & Flynn, T. N. (2008). What do people value when they provide unpaid care for an older person? A meta-ethnography with interview follow-up. *Social Science & Medicine, 67*, 111–121.

Allen, K. A., Blascovich, J., & Mendes, W. B. (2002). Cardiovascular reactivity and the presence of pets, friends, and spouses: The truth about cats and dogs. *Psychosomatic Medicine, 64*, 727–739.

Alliance for Eating Disorders Awareness. (2015). Truth in numbers. West Palm Beach, FL: Author. Retrieved from http://www.allianceforeatingdisorders.com/portal/did-you-know#.VYROphNViko

Al-Samarrie, N. (2014). When doctors don't listen: Tell your story. *Diabetes Health, 23*(1), 22–25.

Alston, S. (2007). Nothing to laugh at: Humour as a means of coping with pain and stress. *Australian Journal of Communication, 34*(1), 77–89.

Alter, C. (2014, February 6). In defense of Barbie: Why she might be the most feminist doll around. *Time.* Retrieved from http://time.com/4597/in-defense-of-barbie-why-she-might-be-a-feminist-doll-after-all/

American Association of Colleges of Nursing (AACN). (2012, March 22). 2012–2013 enrollment and graduations in baccalaureate and graduate programs in nursing. Washington, DC: Author. Retrieved from http://www.aacn.nche.edu/news/articles/2012/enrollment-data

American Association of Colleges of Nursing. (2015). 2014–2015 enrollment and graduations in baccalaureate and graduate programs in nursing. Washington, DC: Author. Retrieved from http://www.aacn.nche.edu/research-data/standard-data-reports

American Association of Colleges of Osteopathic Medicine. (2012). What is osteopathic medicine? Chevy Chase, MD: Author. Retrieved from http://www.aacom.org/about/osteomed/Pages/default.aspx

American Hospital Association (AHA). (2008, March). Hospital facts to know. Washington, DC: Author. Retrieved from http://www.aha.org/aha/content/2008/pdf/08-issue-facts-to-know-.pdf

American Medical Association (AMA). (2003). Low literacy has a high impact on patients' ability to follow doctors' orders. Retrieved from www.ama-assn.org/ama/pub/print/article/4197-7395.html

American Medical Association. (2005, April). Quality health care for minorities: Understanding physicians' experience. Retrieved from http://www.ama-assn.org/ama/pub/physician-resources/public-health/eliminating-health-disparities/commission-end-health-care-disparities/quality-health-care-minorities-understanding-physicians.page

Ammentorp, J., Kofoed, P., & Laulund, L. (2011). Impact of communication skills training on parents' perceptions of care: Intervention study. *Journal of Advanced Nursing, 67*(2), 394–400.

Anderson, J. O., & Geist-Martin, P. (2003). Narratives and healing: Exploring one family's stories of cancer survivorship. *Health Communication, 15*(2), 133–143.

Anderson, P., de Bruijn, A., Angus, K., Gordon, R., & Hastings, G. (2009). Impact of alcohol advertising and media exposure on adolescent alcohol use: A systematic review of longitudinal studies. *Alcohol and Alcoholism, 44*, 229–243.

Andrews, J. C., Netemeyer, R. G., Kees, J., & Burton, S. (2014). How graphic visual health warnings affect young smokers' thoughts of quitting. *Journal of Marketing Research, 51*(2), 165–183.

Andrews, K. R., Silk, K. S., & Eneli, I. U. (2010). Parents as health promoters: A theory of planned behavior perspective on the prevention of childhood obesity. *Journal of Health Communication, 15*, 95–107. doi:10.1080/10810730903460567

Angell, M. (2004, July 15). The truth about drug companies. *The New York Review of Books, 51*(12), n.p. Retrieved from http://www.nybooks.com/articles/17244

Anghelcev, G., & Sar, S. (2011). The influence of pre-existing audience and message relevance on the effective of health PSAs: Differential effects by message type. *Journal and Mass Communication Quarterly, 88*, 481–501.

Apker, J. (2001). Role development in the managed care era: A case in hospital-based nursing. *Journal of Applied Communication Research, 29*(2), 117–136.

Appenzeller, T. (2005, October). Tracing the next killer flu. *National Geographic, 208*(4), 2–31.

Arasaratnam, L. A., & Banerjee, S. C. (2011). Sensation seeking and intercultural communication competence: A model test. *International Journal of Intercultural Relations, 35*, 226–233. doi: 10.1016/j.ijintrel.2010.07.003.

Armstrong, K., Putt, M., Halbert, C., Grande, D., Schwartz, J., Liao, K., . . . Shea, J. (2013). Prior experiences of racial discrimination and racial differences in health care system distrust. *Medical Care, 51*(2), 144–150.

Arnquist, S. (2009, August 25). Health care abroad: Japan [Blog post]. Prescriptions. *The New York Times.* Retrieved from http://prescriptions.blogs.nytimes.com/2009/08/25/health-care-abroad-japan/

Arrington, M. I. (2003). "I don't want to be an artificial man": Narrative reconstruction of sexuality among prostate cancer survivors. *Sexuality & Culture, 7*(2), 30–58.

Ashley, B. M., & O'Rourke, K. D. (1997). *Health care ethics: A theological analysis* (4th ed.). Washington, DC: Georgetown University Press.

Ashraf, A. A., Colakoglu, S., Nguyen, J. T., Anastasopulos, A. J., Ibrahim, A. M., Yueh, J. H., . . . Lee, B. T. (2013). Association for Academic Surgery: Patient involvement in the decision-making process improves satisfaction and quality of life in postmastectomy breast reconstruction. *Journal of Surgical Research, 184*, 665–670.

Ask me 3. (n.d.). American Medical Association and National Patient Safety Foundation. Retrieved from http://www.npsf.org/?page=askme3

Association of American Medical Colleges. (2014). MCAT and GPA grid for applicants and acceptees to U.S. medical schools, 2012–2014 (aggregated). (2014). Washington, DC: Author. Retrieved from https://www.aamc.org/data/facts/applicantmatriculant/157998/factstablea24.html

Association of Health Care Journalists. (2015). Main web page. Retrieved from http://healthjournalism.org/

Atherly, A., Kane, R. L., & Smith, M. A. (2004). Older adults' satisfaction with integrated capitated health and long-term care. *The Gerontologist, 44*(3), 348–357.

Augusta Health. (n.d.). Pushing the limits: Two-time breast cancer survivor planning her next race. Retrieved from http://www.augustahealth.com/foundation/grateful-patient-stories/pushing-the-limits

Aulagnier, M., Verger, P., Ravaud, J. F., Souville, M., Lussault, P. Y., Garnier, J. P., & Paraponaris, A. (2005). General practitioners' attitudes towards patients with disabilities: The need for training and support. *Disability and Rehabilitation, 27*(22), 1343–1352.

Austin, E. W. (1993). Exploring the effects of active parental mediation of television content. *Journal of Broadcasting & Electronic Media, 37*, 147–158.

Austin, E. W. (1995). Reaching young audiences: Developmental considerations in designing health messages. In E. Maibach & R. L. Parrott (Eds.), *Designing health messages* (pp. 114–144). Thousand Oaks, CA: Sage.

Austin, E. W., & Meili, H. K. (1994). Effects of interpretations of televised alcohol portrayals on children's alcohol beliefs. *Journal of Broadcasting & Electronic Media, 38*, 417–435.

Austin, E. W., Roberts, D. F., & Nass, C. I. (1990). Influences of family communication on children's television-interpretation process. *Communication Research, 17*, 545–564.

Azevedo, D. (1996). Taking back health care: Doctors must work together. *Medical Economics, 73*, 156–162.

Babrow, A. S. (1992). Communication and problematic integration: Understanding diverging probability and value, ambiguity, ambivalence, and impossibility. *Communication Theory, 2*, 95–130.

Babrow, A. S. (2001). Uncertainty, value, communication, and problematic integration. *Journal of Communication, 51*(3), 553–573.

Backer, T. E., & Rogers, E. M. (1993). Introduction. In T. E. Backer & E. M. Rogers (Eds.), *Organizational aspects of health communication campaigns: What works?* (pp. 1–9). Newbury Park, CA: Sage.

Bae, H.-S., & Kang, S. (2008). The influence of viewing an entertainment-education program on cornea donation intention: A test of the theory of planned behavior. *Health Communication, 23*(1), 87–95.

Baek, T., & Mayer, M. (2010). Sexual imagery in cigarette advertising before and after the Master Settlement Agreement. *Health Communication, 25*, 747–757. doi:10.1080/10410236.2010.521917

Baglia, J. (2005). *The Viagra ad venture*. New York: Peter Lang.

Balbale, S. N., Schwingel, A., Wojtek, C., & Huhman, M. (2014). Visual and participatory research methods for the development of health messages for underserved populations. *Health Communication, 29*(7), 728–740.

Balint, J., & Shelton, W. (1996). Regaining the initiative: Forging a new model of the patient–physician relationship. *Journal of the American Medical Association, 275*, 887–892.

Ball, J., Liang, A., & Wei-Na, L. (2009). Representation of African Americans in direct-to-consumer pharmaceutical commercials: A content analysis with implications for health disparities. *Health Marketing Quarterly, 26*, 372–390. doi:10.1080/07359680903304328

Baltes, M. M., & Wahl, H.-W. (1996). Patterns of communication in old age: The dependence-support and independence-ignore script. *Health Communication, 8*, 217–231.

Bandura, A. (1986). *Social foundations of thought and action: A social cognitive approach*. Englewood Cliffs, NJ: Prentice Hall.

Bandura, A. (1994). Social cognitive theory of mass communication. In J. Bryant & D. Zillman (Eds.), *Media effects: Advances in theory and research* (pp. 61–90). Hillsdale, NJ: Lawrence Erlbaum.

Banerjee, S. C., & Greene, K. (2006). Analysis versus production: Adolescent cognitive and attitudinal responses to antismoking interventions. *Journal of Communication, 56*, 773–794.

Banja, J. D. (2005). *Medical errors and medical narcissism*. Boston: Jones and Bartlett.

Banja, J. D., & Amori, G. (2005). The empathic disclosure of medical error. In *Medical errors and medical narcissism* (pp. 173–192). Boston: Jones and Bartlett.

Bao, Y., Fox, S. A., & Escarce, J. J. (2007). Socioeconomic and racial/ethnic differences in the discussion of cancer screening: "Between-" versus "within-" physician differences. *Health Services Research, 42*(3), 950–970.

Barbie. [Barbie]. (2014, February 1). Be YOU. Be bold. Be #Unapologetic [Tweet]. Retrieved from https://twitter.com/barbie/status/429673457127657472

Barker, S. A., & Dawson, K. S. (1998). The effects of animal-assisted therapy on anxiety ratings of hospitalized psychiatric patients. *Psychiatric Services, 49*, 797–801.

Barnard, A. (2003, January 22). Doctors brace for changes on patient privacy. *Boston Globe*, National/Foreign, p. A1.

Barnes, D. (2015, May 1). TeleMIND brings specialty health care to rural clinic. The University of Mississippi Medical Center. Retrieved from https://www.umc.edu/News_and_Publications/Press_Release/2015-05-01-00_TeleMIND_brings_specialty_health_care_to_rural_clinic.aspx

Barnes, L. (n.d.). I am not a victim of breast cancer. Great Inspirational Quotes. Retrieved from http://www.great-inspirational-quotes.com/i-am-not-a-victim-of-breast-cancer.html

Barnes, M. K., & Duck, S. (1994). Everyday communicative contexts for social support. In B. R. Burleson, T. L. Albrecht, & I. G. Sarason (Eds.), *Communication of social support: Messages, interactions, relationships, and community* (pp. 175–194). Thousand Oaks, CA: Sage.

Barnett, G. V., Hollister, L., & Hall, S. (2011). Use of the standardized patient to clarify interdisciplinary team roles. *Clinical Simulation In Nursing, 7*, e169–e173.

Barnlund, D. (1970). A transactional model of communication. In K. K. Sereno & C. D. Mortensen (Eds.), *Foundations of communication theory* (pp. 83–102). New York: Harper.

Basow, S. A., & O'Neil, K. (2014). Men's body depilation: An exploratory study of United States college students' preferences, attitudes, and practices. *Body Image, 11*, 409–417.

Basu, A., & Dutta, M. J. (2008). The relationship between health information seeking and community participation: The roles of health information orientation and efficacy. *Health Communication, 23*(1), 70–79.

Bauer, G. R. (2014). Incorporating intersectionality theory into population health research methodology: Challenges and the potential to advance health equity. *Social Science & Medicine, 110*, 10–17. doi:10.1016/j.socscimed.2014.03.022

Baur, C. (2000). Limiting factors on the transformative powers of e-mail in patient–physician relationships: A critical analysis. *Health Communication 12*(3), 239–259.

Baxter, L. A. (1988). A dialectic perspective of communication strategies in relationship development. In S. Duck (Ed.), *Handbook of personal relationships* (pp. 257–273). New York: Wiley.

BBC Newsbeat. (2015, June 8). The letters A, O & B are vanishing around the UK. Why? *BBC Newsbeat*. Retrieved from http://www.bbc.co.uk/newsbeat/article/33046805/the-letters-a-o—b-are-vanishing-around-the-uk-why?ocid=socialflow_facebook

Beach, M. C., Roter, D., Korthuis, P. T., Epstein, R. M., Sharp, V., Ratanawongsa, N., . . . Saha, S. (2013). A multicenter study of physician mindfulness and health care quality. *Annals of Family Medicine, 11*(5), 421–428.

Beach, W. A. (2002). Between dad and son: Initiating, delivering, and assimilating bad cancer news. *Health Communication, 14*(3), 271–298.

Beach, W. A., Buller, M. K., Dozier, D. M., Buller, D. B., & Gutzmer, K. (2014). The Conversations about Cancer (CAC) Project: Assessing feasibility and audience impacts from viewing the cancer play. *Health Communication, 29*(5), 462–472.

Bealieu-Volk, D. (2014). Motivating patients with diabetes. *Medical Economics, 91*(10), 36–39.

Beaudoin, C. E., & Thorson, E. (2006). The social capital of Blacks and Whites: Differing effects of the mass media in the United States. *Human Communication Research, 32*, 157–177.

Beautiful people, beautiful products. (2011, July 2). Psysociety. Retrieved from https://psysociety.wordpress.com/2011/07/02/beautiful-people-beautiful-products/

Bebinger, M. (2014, June 10). Mass. inches toward health insurance for all. Kaiser Health News. Retrieved from http://khn.org/news/massachusetts-nears-zero-percent-uninsured/

Bechara, A., Casabé, A., De Bonis, W., Hellen, A., & Bertolino, M. V. (2010). Recreational use of phosphodiesterase type 5 inhibitors by healthy young men. *The Journal of Sexual Medicine, 7*, 3736–3742.

Beck, C. S., Ragan, S. L., & du Pré, A. (1997). *Partnership for health: Building relationships between women and health caregivers*. Mahwah, NJ: Lawrence Erlbaum.

Becker, G., & Newsom, E. (2003). Socioeconomic status and dissatisfaction with health care among chronically ill African Americans. *American Journal of Public Health, 93*(5), 742–748.

Beckman, H. B., & Frankel, R. M. (1984). The effect of physician behavior on the collection of data. *Annals of Internal Medicine, 101*, 692–696.

Becoming a hospital human resource manager. (2011). HealthcareAdministration.com. Retrieved from http://www.healthcareadministration.com/what-is-the-function-of-hospital-human-resource-management/

Beer commercials among favorite Super Bowl ads for teens. (2009, February 5). Drug-Free Action Alliance: Alexandria, VA. Retrieved from http://50-201-129-166-static.hfc.comcastbusiness.net/resources/detail/beer-commercials-among-favorite-super-bowl-ads-teens

Bell, D. J., Bringman, J., Bush, A., & Phillips, O. P. (2006). Job satisfaction among obstetrician-gynecologists: A comparison between private practice physicians and academic physicians. *American Journal of Obstetrics and Gynecology, 195*(5), 1474–1478.

Bellafante, G. (2014, October 10). Fear of vaccines goes viral. *The New York Times*. Retrieved from http://www.nytimes.com/2014/10/12/nyregion/fear-of-vaccines-goes-viral.html

Benjamin, J. M., Cox, E. D., Trapskin, P. J., Rajamanickam, V. P., Jorgenson, R. C., Weber, H. L., . . . Lubcke, N. L. (2015). Family-initiated dialogue about medications during family-centered rounds. *Pediatrics, 1*, 94.

Bennett, C. (2015, April 27). Don't rush to Nepal to help. Read this first. *The Guardian*. Retrieved from http://www.theguardian.com/commentisfree/2015/apr/27/earthquake-nepal-dont-rush-help-volunteers-aid

Berger, P., & Luckmann, T. (1966). *The social construction of reality*. New York: Doubleday.

Bergstrom, M. J., & Holmes, M. E. (2000). Lay theories of successful aging after the death of a spouse: A network text analysis of bereavement advice. *Health Communication, 12*(4), 377–406.

Bergstrom, M. J., & Nussbaum, J. F. (1996). Cohort differences in interpersonal conflict: Implications for the older patient–younger care provider interaction. *Health Communication, 8*, 233–248.

Berkman, N. D., Sheridan, S. L., Donahue, K. E., Halpern, D. J., Viera, A., . . . Viswanathan, M. (2011, March). Health literacy interventions and outcomes: A systematic review. AHRQ Evidence Report/Technology Assessment No. 199. AHRQ Publication No. 11-E006. Retrieved from http://www.ncbi.nlm.nih.gov/books/NBK82434/?report=reader

Berkowitz, E. N. (2007). The evolution of public relations and the use of the Internet: The implications for health care organizations. *Health Marketing Quarterly, 24*(3–4), 117–130.

Bernheim, S. M., Ross, J. S., Krumholz, H. M., & Bradley, E. H. (2008). Influence of patients' socioeconomic status on clinical management decisions: A qualitative study. *Annals of Family Medicine, 6*(1), 53–59.

Bernstein, S. (2015, May 14). California Senate votes to end beliefs waiver for school vaccinations. *Reuters*. Retrieved from http://www.reuters.com/article/us-usa-measles-vaccinations-idUSKBN0O003320150515

Berry, L. L., & Seltman, K. D. (2008). *Management lessons from Mayo Clinic: Inside one of the world's most admired service organizations*. New York: McGraw-Hill.

Best, A. L., Spencer, M., Hall, I. J., Friedman, D. B., & Billings, D. (2015). Developing spiritually framed breast cancer screening messages in consultation with African American women. *Health Communication, 30*(3), 290–300.

Bethea, L. S., Travis, S. S., & Pecchioni, L. (2000). Family caregivers' use of humor in conveying information about caring for dependent older adults. *Health Communication, 12*(4), 361–376.

Betts, K. (2002, March 31). The tyranny of skinny, fashion's insider secret. *New York Times*. Retrieved from http://www.nytimes.com/2002/03/31/style/the-tyranny-of-skinny-fashion-s-insider-secret.html?pagewanted=all

Bevan, J. L., Rogers, K. E., Andrews, N. F., & Sparks, L. (2012). Topic avoidance and negative health perceptions in the distant family caregiving context. *Journal of Family Communication, 12*(4), 300–314.

Bhopal, P. (1998, June 27). Spectre of racism in health and health care: Lessons from history and the United States. *British Medical Journal, 7149*, 1970–1973.

Bias, S. (2014, November 7). Self acceptance vs. self esteem [Blog post]. Retrieved from http://stacybias.net/2014/11/self-acceptance-vs-self-esteem/

Bias, S. (2015, January 20). I stood up to a fat-shaming bully on a train because I'm tired of fighting for the right to exist. *xoJane*. Retrieved from http://www.xojane.com/issues/fat-shaming-train-bully

Bibace, R., & Walsh, M. E. (1981). Children's conceptualizations of illness. In R. Bibace & M. E. Walsh (Eds.), *Children's conceptualizations of health, illness, and bodily functions* (pp. 31–48). San Francisco: Jossey-Bass.

Bickmore, T. W., Pfeifer, L. M., Byron, D., Forsythe, S., Henault, L. E., Jack, B. W., & Paasche-Orlow, M. K. (2010). Usability of conversational agents by patients with inadequate health literacy: Evidence from two clinical trials. *Journal of Health Communication, 15*, 197–210. doi:10.1080/10810730.2010.499991

Bilmes, A. (2014, October 8). When did male body hair become a bad thing? *The Guardian*. Retrieved from http://www.theguardian.com/fashion/shortcuts/2014/oct/08/when-did-male-body-hair-become-such-a-bad-thing

Bindler, R. C., Richardson, B., Daratha, K., & Wordell, D. (2012). Clinical method: Interdisciplinary health science research collaboration. Strengths, challenges, and case example. *Applied Nursing Research, 25*, 95–100.

Birkeland, S., Murphy-Graham, E., & Weiss, C. (2005). Good reasons for ignoring good evaluation: The case of the drug abuse resistance education (D.A.R.E.) program. *Evaluation and Program Planning, 28*, 247–256.

Blanc, N., & Brigaud, E. (2014). Humor in print health advertisements: Enhanced attention, privileged recognition, and persuasiveness of preventive messages. *Health Communication, 29*, 669–677.

Blavin, F., Buettgens, M., & Roth, J. (2012, January). State progress toward health reform implementation: Slower moving states have much to gain. Urban Institute. Retrieved from http://www.urban.org/research/publication/state-progress-toward-health-reform-implementation-slower-moving-states-have/view/full_report

Bleustein, C., Valaitis, E., & Jones, R. (2010). Effect of wait room time on ambulatory patient satisfaction. *Otolaryngology—Head and Neck Surgery, 143*, P38–P39.

Bliss, W. G. (2012, January 24). Cost of employee turnover. *Small Business Advisor*. Retrieved from http://www.hermangroup.com/store/bliss_article.html

Block, S. D. (2001). Psychological considerations, growth, and transcendence at the end of life. *Journal of the American Medical Association, 285*(22), 2898–2905.

Bochner, S. (1983). Doctors, patients and their cultures. In D. Pendleton & J. Hasler (Eds.), *Doctor-patient communication* (pp. 127–138). London: Academic Press.

Bock, B. C., Becker, B. M., Niaura, R. S., Partridge, R., Fava, J. L., & Trask, P. (2008). Smoking cessation among patients in an emergency chest pain observation unit: Outcomes of the Chest Pain Smoking Study (CPSS). *Nicotine & Tobacco Research, 10*(10), 1523–1531.

Boden, W. E., & Diamond, G. A. (2008, May 22). DTCA for PTCA—Crossing the line in consumer health education? *The New England Journal of Medicine, 358*(21), 2197.

Body evolution: Model before and after. (2012). GlobalDemocracy.com. Retrieved from https://www.youtube.com/watch?v=17j5QzF3kqE

Boer, H., & Westhoff, Y. (2006, February). The role of positive and negative signaling communication by strong and weak ties in the shaping of safe sex subjective norms of adolescents in South Africa. *Communication Theory, 16*(1), 75–90.

Bohm, D. (1980). *Wholeness and the implicate order*. London: Routledge & Kegan Paul.

Bohm, D. (1996). *On dialogue*. L. Nichol (Ed.). London: Routledge & Kegan Paul.

Bond, B. (2015). Portrayals of sex and sexuality in gay- and lesbian-oriented media: A quantitative content analysis. *Sexuality & Culture, 19*(1), 37–56.

Bonsteel, A. (1997, March–April). Behind the white coat. *The Humanist, 57*, 15–19.

Boodman, S. (1997, February 25). Silent doctors more likely to be sued; malpractice study suggests that physicians' manner affects patients' readiness to go to court. *Washington Post*, p. WH9.

Boodman, S. G. (2011, February 28). Many Americans have poor health literacy. *The Washington Post*. Retrieved from http://www.washingtonpost.com/wp-dyn/content/article/2011/02/28/AR2011022805957.html

Booms, B. H., & Bitner, M. J. (1981). Marketing strategies and organization structures for service firms. In J. H. Donnelly & W. R. George (Eds.), *Marketing of services* (pp. 47–51). Chicago: American Marketing Association.

Booth-Butterfield, M., Anderson, R., & Booth-Butterfield, S. (2000). Adolescents' use of tobacco, health locus of control, and self-monitoring. *Health Communication, 12*, 137–148.

Borden, N. H. (1964). The concept of the marketing mix. *Journal of Advertising Research, 4*(2), 2–7.

Boris, C. (2014, October 20). TV viewers would rather skim social media than watch TV commercials. *Marketing Pilgrim*. Retrieved from http://www.marketingpilgrim.com/2014/10/

tv-viewers-would-rather-skim-social-media-than-watch-tv-commercials.html

Borkhoff, C. M., Hawker, G. A., Kreder, H. J., Glazier, R. H., Mahomed, N. N., & Wright, J. G. (2013). Influence of patients' gender on informed decision making regarding total knee arthroplasty. *Arthritis Care & Research, 65*(8), 1281. doi:10.1002/acr.21970

Borreani, C., Brunelli, C., Miccinesi, G., Morino, P., Piazza, M., Piva, L., & Tamburini, M. (2008). Eliciting individual preferences about death: Development of the End-of-Life Preferences Interview. *Journal of Pain and Symptom Management, 36(4)*, 335–350.

Botta, R. A., & Dumlao, R. (2002). How do conflict and communication patterns between fathers and daughters contribute to or offset eating disorders? *Health Communication, 14*, 199–219.

Boukus, E. R., Cassil, A., & O'Malley, A. S. (2009, September). A snapshot of U.S. physicians: Key findings from the 2008 health tracking physician survey. Center for Studying Health System Change. Retrieved from http://www.hschange.com/CONTENT/1078/

Bowleg, L. (2008). When black + lesbian + woman ≠ black lesbian woman: The methodological challenges of qualitative and quantitative intersectionality research. *Sex Roles, 59*(5/6), 312–325.

Bowleg, L. (2012). The problem with the phrase women and minorities: Intersectionality—an important theoretical framework for public health. *American Journal of Public Health, 102*(7), 1267–1273.

Boyd, J. E., Adler, E. P., Otilingam, P. G., & Peters, T. (2014). Internalized stigma of mental illness (ISMI) scale: A multinational review. *Comprehensive Psychiatry, 55*, 221–231. doi:10.1016/j.comppsych.2013.06.005

Boylstein, C., Rittman, M., & Hinojosa, R. (2007). Metaphor shifts in stroke recovery. *Health Communication, 21*, 279–287.

Brady, M. J., & Cella, D. F. (1995, May 30). Helping patients live with their cancer. *Patient Care*, pp. 41–49.

Braithwaite, D. O. (1996). "Persons first": Expanding communicative choices by persons with disabilities. In E. B. Ray (Ed.), *Communication and disenfranchisement: Social health issues and implications* (pp. 449–464). Mahwah, NJ: Lawrence Erlbaum.

Braithwaite, D. O., & Harter, L. M. (2000). Communication and the management of dialectic tensions in the personal relationships of people with disabilities. In D. O. Braithwaite & T. L. Thompson (Eds.), *Handbook of communication and people with disabilities: Research and applications* (pp. 17–36). Mahwah, NJ: Lawrence Erlbaum.

Braithwaite, D. O., & Japp, P. (2005). "They make us miserable in the name of helping us": Communication of persons with visible and invisible disabilities. In E. B. Ray (Ed.), *Health communication in practice: A case study approach* (pp. 171–179). Mahwah, NJ: Lawrence Erlbaum.

Braithwaite, D. O., & Thompson, T. L. (Eds.). (2000). *Handbook of communication and people with disabilities: Research and applications.* Mahwah, NJ: Lawrence Erlbaum.

Braithwaite, S. R., Coulson, G., Keddington, K., & Fincham, F. D. (2015). The influence of pornography on sexual scripts and hooking up among emerging adults in college. *Archives of Sexual Behavior, 44*(1), 111–123.

Branch, W. T., Jr., Levinson, W., & Platt, F. W. (1996). Diagnostic interviewing: Make the most of your time. *Patient Care, 30*(12), 68–76.

Branch, W. T., Jr., & Malik, T. K. (1993). Using "windows of opportunities" in brief interviews to understand patients' concerns. *Journal of the American Medical Association, 269*, 1667–1668.

Brann, M. (2007). Health care providers' confidentiality practices and perceptions: Expanding a typology of confidentiality breaches in health care communication. *Qualitative Research Reports in Communication, 8*(1), 45–52.

Brann, M., Himes, K. L., Dillow, M. R., & Weber, K. (2010). Dialectic tensions in stroke survivor relationships. *Health Communication, 25*, 323–332.

Brann, M., & Mattson, M. (2004). Toward a typology of confidentiality breaches in health care communication: An ethic of care analysis of provider practices and patient perceptions. *Health Communication, 16*, 229–251.

Brashers, D. E., & Babrow, A. S. (1996). Theorizing health communication. *Communication Studies, 47*, 237–251.

Brehm, J. W. (1966). *A theory of psychological reactance.* New York: Academic Press.

Brennan, P. F., & Fink, S. V. (1997). Health promotion, social support, and computer networks. In R. L. Street, Jr., W. R. Gold, & T. Manning (Eds.), *Health promotion and interactive technology: Theoretical implications and future directions* (pp. 157–169). Mahwah, NJ: Lawrence Erlbaum.

Brett, A. L., Branstetter, J. E., & Wagner, P. D. (2014). Nurse educators' perceptions of caring attributes in current and ideal work environments. *Nursing Education Perspectives, 35*(6), 360–366.

Brett, R. (2003, February 21). Life's great, say area survivors. *The Plain Dealer*, p. B1.

Briñol, P., & Petty, R. E. (2006). Fundamental processes leading to attitude change: Implications for career prevention communications. *Journal of Communication, 56*, S81–S104.

Britton, P. C., Williams, G. C., & Conner, K. R. (2008). *Journal of Clinical Psychology, 64*(1), 52–66.

Brodie, M., Kjellson, N., Hoff, T., & Parker, M. (2008). Perceptions of Latinos, African Americans, and Whites on media as a health information source. In L. C. Lederman (Ed.), *Beyond these walls: Readings in health communication* (pp. 378–394). New York: Oxford University Press.

Broom, A. (2008). Virtually healthy: The impact of Internet use on disease experience and the doctor–patient relationship. In L. C. Lederman (Ed.), *Beyond these walls: Readings in health communication* (pp. 92–109). New York: Oxford University Press.

Brosius, H., & Weimann, G. (1996). Who sets the agenda? Agenda-setting as a two-step flow. *Communication Research, 23*, 561–580.

Brown, J., & Addington-Hall, J. (2007). How people with motor neuron disease talk about living with illness: A narrative study. *Journal of Advanced Nursing, 62*(2), 200–208.

Brown, T. (2012, March 14). Hospitals aren't hotels. *The New York Times.* Retrieved from http://www.nytimes.com/2012/03/15/opinion/hospitals-must-first-hurt-to-heal.html

Brown, T. N., Ueno, K., Smith, C. L., Austin, N. S., & Bickman, L. (2007). Communication patterns in medical encounters for the treatment of child psychosocial problems: Does pediatrician–parent concordance matter? *Health Communication, 21,* 247–256.

Brown, V. A., Parker, P. A., Furber, L., & Thomas, A. L. (2011). Patient preferences for the delivery of bad news—The experience of a UK Cancer Centre. *European Journal of Cancer Care, 20*(1), 56–61.

Buchholz, B. (1992, January–February). Psyching yourself: How to prepare for medical procedures. *Arthritis Today, 6*(1), 20–24.

Buchthal, O., Doff, A. L., Hsu, L. A., Silbanuz, A., Heinrich, K. M., & Maddock, J. E. (2011). Avoiding a knowledge gap in a multiethnic statewide social marketing campaign: Is cultural tailoring sufficient? *Journal of Health Communication, 16,* 314–327. doi:10.1080/10810730.2010.535111

Buckley, L. M. (2008). *Talking with patients about the personal impact of illness: The doctor's role.* New York: Radcliffe.

Budden, J. S., Zhong, E. H., Moulton, P., & Cimiotti, J. P. (2013, July). Highlights of the National Workforce Survey of Registered Nurses. *Journal of Nursing Regulation, 4*(2), 5–14.

Bulik, B. S. (2014, September 2). Mattel pushes as model of empowerment for young girls. *Advertising Age.* Retrieved from http://adage.com/article/news/mattel-pushes-barbie-model-empowerment-young-girls/294755/

Burda, D. (2008, April 28). The perfection injection; Not paying for "never events" is a slippery slope. *Modern Healthcare, 38*(17), 20.

Burgoon, M. H., & Burgoon, J. K. (1990). Compliance-gaining and health care. In J. P. Dillard (Ed.), *Seeking compliance: The production of interpersonal influence messages* (pp. 161–188). Scottsdale, AZ: Gorsuch Scarisbrick.

Burleson, B. R. (1990). Comforting as social support: Relational consequences of supportive behaviors. In S. Duck & R. C. Silver (Eds.), *Personal relationships and social support* (pp. 66–82). London: Sage.

Burleson, B. R. (1994). Comforting messages: Significance, approaches, and effects. In B. R. Burleson, T. L. Albrecht, & I. G. Sarason (Eds.), *Communication of social support: Messages, interactions, relationships, and community* (pp. 175–194). Thousand Oaks, CA: Sage.

Bushman, B. J., Gollwitzer, M., & Cruz, C. (2014). There is broad consensus: Media researchers agree that violent media increase aggression in children, and pediatricians and parents concur. *Psychology of Popular Media Culture, 4*(3), 200–214.

But not too gay. (n.d.). TV Tropes. Retrieved from http://tvtropes.org/pmwiki/pmwiki.php/Main/ButNotTooGay

Bute, J. J., Donovan-Kicken, E., & Martins, N. (2007). Effects of communication-debilitating illnesses and injuries on close relationships: A relational maintenance perspective. *Health communication, 21*(3), 235–246.

Butler, J. (1999). *Gender trouble: Feminism and the subversity of identity* (2nd ed.). New York: Routledge.

Byck, R. (1986). *The encyclopedia of psychoactive drugs: Treating mental illness.* New York: Chelsea House.

Bylund, C. L., D'Agostino, T. A., Ho, E. Y., & Chewning, B. A. (2010). Improving clinical communication and promoting health through concordance-based patient education. *Communication Education, 59,* 294–311.

Budzi, D., Lurie, S., Singh, K., & Hooker, R. (2010). Veterans' perceptions of care by nurse practitioners, physician assistants, and physicians: A comparison from satisfaction surveys. *Journal of the American Academy of Nurse Practitioners, 22*(3), 170–176.

Bundgaard, K., Sørensen, E. E., & Nielsen, K. B. (2011). The art of holding hands: A fieldwork study outlining the significance of physical touch in facilities for short-term stay. *International Journal for Human Caring, 15*(3), 34–41.

Caba, J. (2016, February 24). Gigantism and acromegaly explained: Why taller people die earlier than most. *Medical Daily.* Retrieved from http://www.medicaldaily.com/gigantism-acromegaly-why-tall-people-die-374890

Cacioli, J., & Mussap, A. J. (2014). Avatar body dimensions and men's body image. *Body Image, 11*(2), 146–155.

Caldroney, R. D. (2008, March 21). Why we've never been sued: This doctor and his partners have stayed out of the courtroom for nearly 30 years. Learn how to follow their lead. *Medical Economics, 85*(6), 30–32.

Cameron, K. A., & Campo, S. (2006). Stepping back from social norms campaigns: Comparing normative influences to other predictors of health behaviors. *Health Communication, 20,* 277–288.

Campbell, R. G., & Babrow, A. S. (2004). The role of empathy in responses to persuasive risk communication: Overcoming resistance to HIV prevention messages. *Health Communication, 16,* 159–182.

Campo, S., & Cameron, K. A. (2006). Differential effects of exposure to social norm campaigns: A cause for concern. *Health Communication, 19,* 209–219.

Candib, L. M. (1994). Reconsidering power in the clinical relationship. In E. S. More & M. A. Milligan (Eds.), *The empathic practitioner: Empathy, gender, and medicine* (pp. 135–155). New Brunswick, NJ: Rutgers University Press.

Cantor, J. C., Schoen, C., Belloff, D., How, S. K. H., & McCarthy, D. (2007, June). Aiming higher: Results from a State Scorecard on Health System Performance. New York: The Commonwealth Fund Commission on a High Performance Health System. Retrieved from www.commonwealthfund.org/publications/publications_show.htm?doc_id=494551

Caplan, S. E., Haslett, B. J., & Burleson, B. R. (2005). Telling it like it is: The adaptive function of narratives in coping with loss in later life. *Health Communication, 17,* 233–251.

Capriotti, T. (1999, February 1). Exploring the "herbal jungle." *MedSurg Nursing, 8,* 53.

Carcioppolo, N., Jensen, J. D., Wilson, S. R., Collins, W. B., Carrion, M., & Linnemeier, G. (2013). Examining HPV threat-to-efficacy ratios in the Extended Parallel Process Model. *Health Communication, 28,* 20–28.

Career: Health care administrator. (2012). *The Princeton Review* online bulletin. Retrieved from http://www.princetonreview.com/careers.aspx?cid=76

Caregiving in the U.S. (2009). National Alliance of Caregiving and the American Association of Retired Persons. Retrieved from http://www.caregiving.org/data/Caregiving_in_the_US_2009_full_report.pdf

Carlzon, J. (1987). *Moments of truth: New strategies for today's customer-driven economy.* New York: Harper & Row.

Carpiac-Claver, M. L., & Levy-Storms, L. (2007). In a manner of speaking: Communication between nurse aides and older adults in long-term care settings. *Health Communication, 22,* 59–67.

Casper, M. F., Child, J. T., Gilmour, D., McIntyre, K. A., & Pearson, J. C. (2006). Healthy research perspectives: Incorporating college student experiences with alcohol. *Health Communication, 20,* 289–298.

Cassedy, J. H. (1991). *Medicine in America: A short history.* Baltimore: Johns Hopkins University Press.

Cassell, E. J. (1991). *The nature of suffering.* New York: Oxford University Press.

Catlin, A., Armigo, C., Volat, D., Vale, E., Hadley, M. A., Gong, W., Bassir, R., & Anderson, K. (2008). Conscientious objection: A potential neonatal nursing response to care orders that cause suffering at the end of life? Study of a concept. *Neonatal Network, 27*(2), 101–108.

Cegala, D. J., & Broz, S. L. (2003). Provider and patient communication skills training. In T. L. Thompson, A. M. Dorsey, K. I. Miller, & R. Parrott (Eds.), *Handbook of health communication* (pp. 95–119). Mahwah, NJ: Lawrence Erlbaum.

Cegala, D. J., Street, R. L., Jr., & Clinch, C. R. (2007). The impact of patient participation on physicians' information provision during a primary care medical interview. *Health Communication, 21,* 177–185.

Center on Alcohol Marketing and Youth website. (2012). Available at http://www.camy.org/

Center on Budget and Policy Priorities. (2015, March 11). Policy basics: Where do our federal tax dollars go? Washington DC: Author. Retrieved from http://www.cbpp.org/cms/?fa=view&id=1258

Centers for Disease Control and Prevention (CDC). (2005, May 3). Frequently asked questions about SARS. Atlanta: Author. Retrieved from http://www.cdc.gov/sars/about/faq.html

Centers for Disease Control and Prevention (CDC). (2007, February 12). What is bioterrorism? Atlanta: Author. Retrieved from http://emergency.cdc.gov/bioterrorism/overview.asp

Centers for Disease Control and Prevention (CDC). (2008, July 1). Overview of crisis & emergency risk communication. Atlanta: Author. Retrieved from http://emergency.cdc.gov/cerc

Centers for Disease Control and Prevention (CDC). (2011, March 21). Tobacco-related mortality. Atlanta: Author. Retrieved from http://www.cdc.gov/tobacco/data_statistics/fact_sheets/health_effects/tobacco_related_mortality/

Centers for Disease Control and Prevention (CDC). (2012). Suicide: Facts at a glance. Atlanta, GA: Author. Retrieved from http://www.cdc.gov/violenceprevention/pdf/Suicide-DataSheet-a.pdf

Centers for Disease Control and Prevention (CDC). (2013). Deaths. Final data for 2013. Table 12, number of deaths from 113 selected causes. Atlanta, GA: Author. Retrieved from http://www.cdc.gov/nchs/fastats/homicide.htm

Centers for Disease Control and Prevention (CDC). (2014a). Deaths: Final data for 2013, Table 13. Atlanta, GA: Author. Retrieved from http://www.cdc.gov/nchs/fastats/life-expectancy.htm

Centers for Disease Control and Prevention (CDC). (2014b). Health literacy for public health professionals. Atlanta, GA: Author. Retrieved from http://www.cdc.gov/healthliteracy/findtraining/onlinecourse.html

Centers for Disease Control and Prevention (CDC). (2014c). The national intimate partner and sexual violence survey. Atlanta, GA: Author. Retrieved from http://www.cdc.gov/violenceprevention/NISVS/index.html

Centers for Disease Control and Prevention (CDC). (2015a). Chronic disease prevention and health promotion. Atlanta, GA: Author. Retrieved from http://www.cdc.gov/chronicdisease/

Centers for Disease Control and Prevention (CDC). (2015b, February 17). Complications of measles. Atlanta, GA: Author. Retrieved from http://www.cdc.gov/measles/about/complications.html

Centers for Disease Control and Prevention (CDC). (2015c). Leading causes of death among females United States, 2011. Atlanta, GA: Author. Retrieved from http://www.cdc.gov/Women/lcod/2011/index.htm

Centers for Disease Control and Prevention (CDC). (2015d, June 2). Measles cases and outbreaks. Atlanta, GA: Author. Retrieved from http://www.cdc.gov/measles/cases-outbreaks.html

Centers for Disease Control and Prevention (CDC). (2015e, March 24). Outbreaks chronology: Ebola virus disease. Atlanta, GA: Author. Retrieved from http://www.cdc.gov/vhf/ebola/outbreaks/history/chronology.html

Centers for Disease Control and Prevention (CDC). (2015f). Tobacco industry marketing. Atlanta, GA: Author. Retrieved from http://www.cdc.gov/tobacco/data_statistics/fact_sheets/tobacco_industry/marketing/

Chaiken, S. (1980). Heuristic versus systematic information processing and the use of source versus message cues in persuasion. *Journal of Personality and Social Psychology, 39,* 752–766.

Chaiken, S., Giner-Sorolla, R., & Chen, S. (1996). Beyond accuracy: Defense and impression motives in heuristic and systematic information processing. In P. M. Gollwitzer & J. A. Bargh (Eds.), *The psychology of action: Linking cognition and motivation to behavior* (pp. 553–578). New York: Guilford.

Chamberlain, M. A. (1994). New technologies in health communication: Progress or panacea? *American Behavioral Scientist, 38*, 271–285.

Chan, E. A., Jones, A., & Wong, K. (2013). The relationships between communication, care and time are intertwined: A narrative inquiry exploring the impact of time on registered nurses' work. *Journal of Advanced Nursing, 69*(9), 2020–2029.

Chang, L.-C., Shih, C.-H., & Lin, S.-M. (2010). The mediating role of psychological empowerment and organizational commitment for school health nurses: A cross-sectional questionnaire survey. *International Journal on Nursing Studies, 47*, 427–433.

Charchuk, M., & Simpson, C. (2005). Hope, disclosure, and control in the neonatal intensive care unit. *Health Communication, 17*, 191–203.

Charlton, C. R., Dearing, K. S., Berry, J. A., & Johnson, M. J. (2008). Nurse practitioners' communication styles and their impact on patient outcomes: An integrated literature review. *Journal of the American Academy of Nurse Practitioners. 20*(7), 382–388.

Charmaz, K. (1987). Struggling for a self: Identity levels of the chronically ill. In J. Roth & P. Conrad (Eds.), *Research in the sociology of health care* (pp. 283–321). Greenwich, CT: JAI Press.

Charon, R. (2006). *Narrative medicine: Honoring the stories of illness*. New York: Oxford University Press.

Charon, R. (2009a). Narrative medicine as witness for the self-telling body. *Journal of Applied Communication Research, 37*, 118–131.

Charon, R. (2009b). The polis of a discursive narrative medicine. *Journal of Applied Communication Research, 37*, 196–201.

Chen, H., Tu, H., & Ho, C. (2013). Understanding biophilia leisure as facilitating well-being and the environment: An examination of participants' attitudes toward horticultural activity. *Leisure Sciences, 35*(4), 301–319.

Chen, Y.-C. (2013). The effectiveness of different approaches to media literacy in modifying adolescents' responses to alcohol. *Journal of Health Communication, 18*, 723–739.

Cheong, P. H. (2007). Health communication resources for uninsured and insured Hispanics. *Health Communication, 21*, 153–163.

Chesler, M. A., & Barbarin, O. A. (1984). Difficulties of providing help in a crisis: Relationships between parents of children with cancer and their friends. *Journal of Social Issues, 40*, 113–134.

Chia, H. L. (2009). Exploring facets of a social network to explicate the status of social support and its effects on stress. *Social Behavior & Personality: An International Journal, 37*(5), 701–710.

Cho, H., & Salmon, C. T. (2007). Unintended effects of health communication campaigns. *Journal of Communication, 57*, 293–317.

Cho, S. (2006). Network news coverage of breast cancer. *Journalism and Mass Communication, 83*(1), 116–130.

Cho, S.-H., Lee, J.-S., Thabane, L., & Lee, J. (2009). Acupuncture for obesity: A systematic review and meta-analysis. *International Journal of Obesity, 33*, 183–196.

Chou, W.-Y., Wang, L. C., Finney Rutten, L. J., Moser, R. P., & Hesse, B. W. (2010). Factors associated with Americans' ratings of health care quality: What do they tell us about the raters and health care systems? *Journal of Health Communication, 15*, 147–156.

Christakis, N. A., & Fowler, J. H. (2008, May 22). The collective dynamics of smoking in a large social network. *New England Journal of Medicine, 358*, 2249.

Christian Science Board of Directors. (n.d.). A closer look at health: The next breakthrough is here. Retrieved from http://christianscience.com/what-is-christian-science/a-closer-look-at-health

Christmas, C., Park, E., Schmaltz, H., Gozu, A., & Durso, S. C. (2008). A model intensive course in geriatric teaching for non-geriatric educators. *Journal of General Internal Medicine, 23*(7), 1048–1052.

Chung, S. (2008, April 18). When a balance makes patients avoid you. Letter to the editor. *Medical Economics, 85*(8), 17.

Ciechanowski, P., & Katon, W. J. (2006). The interpersonal experience of health care through the eyes of patients with diabetes. *Social Science & Medicine, 63*, 3067–3079.

Clarke, C. E., Dixon, G. N., Holton, A., & McKeever, B. W. (2015). Including "evidentiary balance" in news media coverage of vaccine risk. *Health Communication, 30*, 461–472.

Clarke, J. N., & Binns, J. (2006). The portrayal of heart disease in mass print magazines, 1991–2001. *Health Communication, 19*, 39–48.

Clarke, L. (2002, Fall). Panic: Myth or reality? *Contexts, 1*(3), 21–26.

Clarke, L. Chess, C., Holmes, R., & O'Neill, K. M. (2006, September). Speaking with one voice: Risk communication lessons from the U.S. anthrax attacks. *Journal of Contingencies and Crisis Management, 14*(3), 160–169.

Clarke, L. H., & Griffin, M. (2008). Visible and invisible ageing: Beauty work as a response to ageism. *Aging & Society, 28*(5), 653–674.

Clark-Hitt, R., Smith, S. W., & Broderick, J. S. (2012). Help a buddy take a knee: Creating persuasive messages for military service members to encourage others to seek mental health help. *Health Communication, 27*, 429–438. doi:10.1080/10410236.2011.606525

Clements, B. (1996). Talk is cheaper than three extra office visits. *American Medical News, 39*, 17–20.

Cline, R. J. W., & Young, H. N. (2004). Marketing drugs, marketing health care relationships: A content analysis of visual cues in direct-to-consumer prescription drug advertising. *Health Communication, 16*, 131–157.

Cohen, C. (2009, February 17). Surgeons send "tweets" from operating room. CNN.com/technology. Retrieved from http://www.cnn.com/2009/TECH/02/17/twitter.surgery/index.html

Cohen, E. L., Head, K. J., McGladrey, M. J., Hoover, A. G., Vanderpool, R. C., Bridger, C., . . . Winterbauer, N. (2015). Designing for dissemination: Lessons in message design from "1-2-3 Pap." *Health Communication, 30*, 196–207.

Cohen, J. (1997). The media's love affair with AIDS research: Hope vs. hype. *Science, 275*, 289–299.

Cohen, S., & Wills, T. A. (1985). Stress, social support, and buffering hypothesis. *Psychological Bulletin, 98*, 310–357.

Coleman, K. (2009). Personal and communal reactions to cancer: An interpretative phenomenological analysis of the beliefs held by charedi Jewish breast cancer patients. *At The Interface/Probing The Boundaries, 55*, 75–97.

Collins, J. C. (2001a). Good to great (article). *Fast Company*. Retrieved from http://www.jimcollins.com/article_topics/articles/good-to-great.html

Collins, J. C. (2001b). *Good to great: Why some companies make the leap . . . and others don't.* New York: HarperCollins.

Collins, J. C., & Porras, J. I. (1997). *Built to last: Successful habits of visionary companies.* Harper Business.

Collins, S. R., Garber, T., & Davis, K. (2011, September 13). Number of uninsured in United States grows to 49.9 million; young adults benefitting from the Affordable Care Act. The Commonwealth Fund. Retrieved from http://www.commonwealthfund.org/Blog/2011/Sep/Number-of-Uninsured-in-United-States-Grows.aspx

Collins, S. R., Rasmussen, P. W., Doty, M. M., & Beutel, S. (2015a). Americans' experiences with marketplace and Medicaid coverage. Findings from the Commonwealth Fund Affordable Care Act Tracking Survey, March–May 2015. Retrieved from http://www.commonwealthfund.org/publications/issue-briefs/2015/jun/experiences-marketplace-and-medicaid

Collins, S. R., Rasmussen, P. W., Doty, M. M., & Beutel, S. (2015b). The rise in health care coverage and affordability since health care reform took effect—Findings from the Commonwealth Fund Biennial Health Insurance Survey, 2014. Retrieved from http://www.commonwealthfund.org/publications/issue-briefs/2015/jan/biennial-health-insurance-survey

Colon-Ramos, U., Atienza, A. A., Weber, D., Taylor, M., Uy, C., & Yaroch, A. (2009). Practicing what they preach: Health behaviors of those who provide health advice to extensive social networks. *Journal of Health Communication, 14*, 119–130. doi:10.1080/10810730802659111

The Commonwealth Fund. (2008a). Doctor–patient communication by race/ethnicity, family income, insurance, and residence, 2004. Results of the National Scorecard on U.S. Health System Performance, 2008. Retrieved from http://www.commonwealthfund.org/chartcartcharts/chartcartcharts_show.htm?doc_id=694048

The Commonwealth Fund. (2008b, January 15). National survey on public's health care reform views: Americans favor keeping employer role in paying for health insurance; believe covering all should be shared responsibility of employers, individuals, and government. New York: Author. Retrieved from http://www.commonwealthfund.org/newsroom/newsroom_show.htm?doc_id=646974

The Commonwealth Fund. (2011). Why not the best? Results from the National Scorecard on U.S. Health System Performance, 2011. New York: Author. Retrieved from http://www.commonwealthfund.org/~/media/files/publications/fund-report/2011/oct/1500_wntb_natl_scorecard_2011_web_v2.pdf

The Commonwealth Fund. (2013, September 18). Health care in the two Americas: Findings for the scorecard on state health system performance for low-come populations, 2013. New York: Author. Retrieved from http://www.commonwealthfund.org/publications/fund-reports/2013/sep/low-income-scorecard

The Commonwealth Fund. (2014). Mirror, mirror on the wall, 2014 update: How the U.S. health care system compares internationally. New York: Author. Retrieved from http://www.commonwealthfund.org/publications/fund-reports/2014/jun/mirror-mirror

The Commonwealth Fund. (2015, March 16). Washington health policy week in review. New York: Author. Retrieved from http://www.commonwealthfund.org/publications/newsletters/washington-health-policy-in-review/2015/mar/mar-16-2015/many-households-lack-liquid-savings-to-pay-deductibles

Conan, N. (2002, August 12). Medical privacy. National Public Radio's *Talk of the Nation*. Retrieved http://www.npr.org/templates/story/story.php?storyId=1148101.

Congressional Budget Office (CBO). (2012, March 13). CBO releases updated estimates for the insurance coverage predictions of the Affordable Care Act. Washington, DC: Author. Retrieved from http://www.cbo.gov/publication/43080

Congressional Budget Office (CBO). (2014, June 5). Payments of penalties for being uninsured under the Affordable Care Act: 2014 update. Washington, DC: Author. Retrieved from http://www.cbo.gov/publication/45397

Conley, M. (2012, April 23). The real-life Ukrainian Barbie doll. Retrieved from http://abcnews.go.com/blogs/health/2012/04/23/the-real-life-ukrainian-barbie-doll/

Conlin, L., & Bissell, K. (2014). Beauty ideals in the checkout aisle: Health-related messages in women's fashion and fitness magazines. *Journal of Magazine & New Media Research, 15*(2), 1–19.

Conrad, P. (1988). Learning to doctor: Reflections on recent accounts of the medical school years. *Journal of Health and Social Behavior, 29*, 323–332.

Controversy heats up over subway's safer sex ads. (1994, February 7). *AIDS Weekly, 9*, 9–10.

COPD [Chronic Obstructive Pulmonary Disease] Foundation. (n.d.) What is COPD? Washington, DC: Author. Retrieved from http://www.copdfoundation.org/

Corbin, J., & Strauss, A. L. (1988). Experiencing body failure and a disrupted self image. In J. Corbin & A. L. Strauss (Eds.), *Unending work and care: Managing chronic illness at home* (pp. 49–67). San Francisco: Jossey-Bass.

Cornwell, T. B., McAlister, A. R., & Polmear-Swendris, N. (2014). Research report: Children's knowledge of packaged and fast food brands and their BMI. Why the relationship matters for policy makers. *Appetite, 81,* 277–283.

Corriea, A. R. (2015, May 12). *Assassin's Creed Syndicate* story, characters, and setting breakdown. Two heads are better than one. *E3.* Retrieved from http://www.gamespot.com/articles/assassin-s-creed-syndicate-story-characters-and-se/1100-6427217/

Cortés, D. E., Drainoni, M.-L., Henault, L. E., & Paasche-Orlow, M. K. (2010). How to achieve informed consent for research from Spanish-speaking individuals with low literacy: A qualitative report. *Journal of Health Communication, 15,* 172–182.

Cottingham, H. (1992). Cartesian dualism: Theology, metaphysics, and science. In J. Cottingham (Ed.), *The Cambridge companion to Descartes* (pp. 236–257). Cambridge: Cambridge University Press.

Coupland, N., Coupland, J., & Giles, H. (1991). *Language, society & the elderly.* Oxford: Blackwell.

Cousin, G., Mast, M. S., Roter, D. L., & Hall, J. A. (2012). Concordance between physician communication style and patient attitudes predicts patient satisfaction. *Patient Education and Counseling, 87,* 193–197.

Covello, V. T. (2003). Best practices in public health risk and crisis communication. *Journal of Health Communication, 8,* 5–8.

Coward, D. D. (Fall 1990). The lived experience of self-transcendence in women with advanced breast cancer. *Nursing Science Quarterly, 3*(3), 162–169.

Cowart, D., & Burt, R. (1998). Confronting death: Who chooses, who controls? *The Hastings Center Report, 28,* 14–24.

Cox, R. (2010). *Environmental communication and the public sphere* (2nd ed.). Thousand Oaks, CA: Sage.

Cozma, R. (2009, Fall). Online health communication: Source or eliminator of health myths? *Southwestern Mass Communication Journal, 24*(2), 69–80.

Crenshaw, K. (1991). Mapping the margins: Intersectionality, identity politics, and violence against women of color. *Stanford Law Review, 6,* 1241–1299.

Crenshaw, K. W. (1989). Demarginalizing the intersection of race and sex: A black feminist critique of antidiscrimination doctrine, feminist theory and antiracist politics. *University of Chicago Legal Forum, 1989,* 139–167.

Crosby, L. A. (2011, Spring). Healthy relationships: Think relationship management when it comes to solving the health care crisis. *Marketing Management, 20*(1), 12–13.

Crowder, M. K., & Kemmelmeier, M. (2014). Untreated depression predicts higher suicide rates in U.S. honor cultures. *Journal of Cross-Cultural Psychology, 45*(7), 1145–1161. doi:10.1177/0022022114534915

Cruz, D. (2015). Kristen Bell: No vaccines? You can't hold my children. *Parenting.* Retrieved from http://www.parenting.com/news-break/kristen-bell-no-vaccines-you-cant-hold-my-children

Cruz, G. G. (2014). Oral health disparities: Opportunities and challenges for policy communication. *Journal of Communication in Healthcare, 7*(2), 74–76. doi:10.1179/1753807614Y.0000000049

Currie, D. (2009). Special report: Crisis communication and social media. Expert roundtable on social media and risk communication during times of crisis: Strategic challenges and opportunities. Sponsored by American Public Health Association, the George Washington University School of Public Health and Health Services, International Association of Emergency Managers, and National Association of Government Communicators. Retrieved from http://www.boozallen.com/insights/insight-detail/42420696

Curtin, R. B., Walters, B. A., Schatell, D., Pennell, P., Wise, M., & Klicko, K. (2008). Self-efficacy and self-management behaviors in patients with chronic kidney disease. *Advances in Chronic Kidney Disease, 15*(2), 191–205.

Cutrona, C. E., & Suhr, J. A. (1994). Social support communication in the context of marriage: An analysis of couples' supportive interactions. In B. R. Burleson, T. L. Albrecht, & I. G. Sarason (Eds.), *Communication of social support: Messages, interactions, relationships, and community* (pp. 113–135). Thousand Oaks, CA: Sage.

Dahm, M. R. (2012). Tales of time, terms, and patient information-seeking behavior—An exploratory qualitative study. *Health Communication,* 27, 682–689.

Dalgliesh, J., & Nutt, K. (2013). Treating men with eating disorders in the NHS. *Nursing Standard, 27*(35), 42–46.

Dall, T., & West, T. (2015). The complexities of physician supply and demand: Projections from 2013 to 2025. Association of American Medical Colleges. Retrieved from https://www.aamc.org/download/426242/data/ihsreportdownload.pdf?cm_mmc=AAMC-_-ScientificAffairs-_-PDF-_-ihsreport

Damhewage, G. M. (2014). Complex, confused, and challenging: Communicating risk in the modern world. *Journal of Communication in Healthcare, 7*(4), 252–254. doi:10.1179/1753806814Z.00000000094

Davenport, T. H., Prusak, L., & Wilson, H. J. (2003). Who's bringing you hot ideas and how are you responding? *Harvard Business Review, 81*(2), 58–64, 124.

Davis, J. (2007). The effect of qualifying language on perceptions of drug appeal, drug experience, and estimates of side-effect incidence in DTC advertising. *Journal of Health Communication, 12,* 617–622.

Davison, W. P. (1983). The third-person effect in communication. *Public Opinion Quarterly, 47,* 1–13.

Dean, M., & Street, J. L. (2014). Review: A 3-stage model of patient-centered communication for addressing cancer patients' emotional distress. *Patient Education and Counseling, 94,* 143–148.

Deary, I. J., Whiteman, M. C., & Fowkes, F. G. R. (1998). Medical research and the popular media. *The Lancet, 351,* 1726–1727.

de Charms, R. (1968). *Personal causation: The internal effective determinants of behavior.* New York: Academic Press.

de Charms, R. (1977). Students need not be pawns. *Theory into Practice, 16*(4), 296–301.

de Droog, S. M., Valkenburg, P. M., & Buijzen, M. (2011). Using brand characters to promote young children's liking of and purchase requests for fruit. *Journal of Health Communication, 16*, 79–89. doi:10.1080/10810730.2010.529487

Defenbaugh, N., & Chikotas, N. E. (2015). The outcome of interprofessional education: Integrating communication studies into a standardized patient experience for advanced practice nursing students. *Nurse Education In Practice* (electronic publication).

Defenbaugh, N. L. (2013). Revealing and concealing ill identity: A performance narrative of IBD disclosure. *Health Communication, 28*, 159–169.

Definitive Healthcare. (2015, April 14). Controversy over telemedicine in Texas. Retrieved from http://www.definitivehc.com/news/2015/04/14/controversy-over-telemedicine-texas-medical-board-votes-to-restrict-and-limit-telemedicine-practices/

Dehning, S., Reiß, E., Krause, D., Gasperi, S., Meyer, S., Dargel, S., . . . Siebeck, M. (2014). Provider attitudes: Empathy in high-tech and high-touch medicine. *Patient Education and Counseling, 95*, 259–264.

De Jesus, M. (2013). The impact of mass media health communication on health decision-making and medical advice-seeking behavior of U.S. Hispanic population. *Health Communication, 28*, 525–529.

Deloitte. (2008a). Online usage: 2008 survey of health care consumers. Retrieved from http://www.deloitte.com/dtt/article/0,1002,cid%253D192702,00.html

Deloitte. (2008b). Reality check: 2008 survey of health care consumers. Retrieved from http://www.deloitte.com/dtt/article/0,1002,cid=192468,00.html

DeLucia, M. (2011, December 14). Dogs offer patient care that cannot be matched. Fox5 News, Las Vegas, Nevada. Retrieved from http://www.fox5vegas.com/story/16157761/pets-overcome-adversity-to-help-sunrise-patients-dogs-vegas-sunrise-hospital

Dennis, M. R. (2006). Compliance and intimacy: Young adults' attempts to motivate health-promoting behaviors for romantic partners. *Health Communication, 19*, 259–267.

Derschowitz, J. (2015, February 3). Bruce Jenner to discuss transition in Diane Sawyer interview. CBS News. Retrieved from http://www.cbsnews.com/news/bruce-jenner-to-discuss-transition-in-diane-sawyer-interview/

Dervin, B. (1999, May). Sense-making's theory of dialogue: A brief introduction. Paper presented at a nondivisional workshop held at the meeting of the International Communication Association, San Francisco.

Dervin, B., & Frenette, M. (2001). Sense-making methodology: Communicating communicatively with campaign audiences. In R. Rice & C. Atkin (Eds.), *Public communication campaigns* (3rd ed., pp. 69–87). Thousand Oaks, CA: Sage.

Designated driving statistics. (2015). Designated Driving.net. Retrieved http://www.designateddriving.net/designateddrivingstatistics.html

de Souza, R. (2009, November). Women living with HIV/AIDS: Stories of power and powerlessness. Presented at the conference of the National Communication Association. Chicago, IL.

Desrochers, D. M., & Holt, D. J. (2007). Children's exposure to television advertising: Implications for childhood obesity. *Journal of Public Policy & Marketing, 26*(2), 182–201.

deBusk, C., & Rangle, A., Jr. (nd). Creating a lean Six Sigma hospital discharge process. An iSixSigma case study. iSix Sigma Healthcare. Retrieved from http://healthcare.isixsigma.com/library/content/c040915a.asp

Dharmananda, S. (2010) FENG: The meaning of wind in Chinese medicine. Institute of Traditional Medicine. Portland, OR: Author. Retrieved from http://www.itmonline.org/articles/feng/feng.htm

DiFranza, J. R., Richard, J. W., Paulman, P. M., Wolf-Gillespie, N., Fletcher, C., Jaffe, R. D., & Murray, D. (1991). RJR Nabisco's cartoon camel promotes Camel cigarettes to children. *Journal of the American Medical Association, 266*, 3149–3153.

Dilger, D. (2013, November 16). The emotional health literacy block. KevinMD.com. Retrieved from http://www.kevinmd.com/blog/2013/11/emotional-health-literacy-block.html

Dill, M. J., & Salsberg, E. S. (2008, November). The complexities of physician supply and demand projections through 2025. Center for Workforce Studies, American Association of Medical Colleges. Retrieved from http://www.innovationlabs.com/pa_future/1/background_docs/AAMC%20Complexities%20of%20physician%20demand,%202008.pdf

Dillard, A. J., McCaul, K. D., Kelso, P. D., & Klein, W. M. P. (2006). Resisting good news: Reactions to breast cancer risk communication. *Health Communication, 19*, 115–123.

Dillard, J. P., Carson, C. L., Bernard, C. J., Laxova, A., & Farrell, P. M. (2004). An analysis of communication following newborn screening for cystic fibrosis. *Health Communication, 16*, 195–206.

Dillard, J. P., & Nabi, R. L. (2006). The persuasive influence of emotion in cancer prevention and detection messages. *Journal of Communication, 56*, S123–S139.

Dillard, J. P., Shen, L., Laxova, A., & Farrell, P. (2008). Potential threats to the effective communication of genetic risk information: The case of cystic fibrosis. *Health Communication, 23*, 234–244.

Dillon, P. J. (2012). Assessing the influence of patient participation in primary care medical interviews on recall of treatment recommendations. *Health Communication, 27*, 58–65.

Dinwiddie, G. Y., Zambrana, R. E., & Garza, M. A. (2014). Exploring risk factors in Latino cardiovascular disease: The role of education, nativity, and gender. *American Journal of Public Health, 104*(9), 1742–1750.

Do, T.-P., & Geist, P. (2000). Embodiment and disembodiment: Identity transformation and persons with physical disabilities. In D. O. Braithwaite & T. L. Thompson (Eds.), *Handbook of communication and people with disabilities: Research and applications* (pp. 49–65). Mahwah, NJ: Lawrence Erlbaum.

Donahue, M. O., Piazza, I. M., Griffin, M. Q., Dykes, P. C., & Fitzpatrick, J. J. (2008). The relationship between nurses' perceptions of empowerment and patient satisfaction. *Applied Nursing Research, 21*, 2–7.

Donohew, L., Palmgreen, P., & Duncan, J. (1980). An activation model of information exposure. *Communication Monographs, 47*, 295–303.

Donovan-Kicken, E., Tollison, A. C., & Goins, E. S. (2011). A grounded theory of control over communication among individuals with cancer. *Journal of Applied Communication Research, 39*, 310–330.

Dorsey, J. L., & Berwick, D. M. (2008, February 27). Dirty words in healthcare. *Boston Globe*, Op-Ed, p. A9.

Douki, S., Zineb, S. B., Nacef, F., & Halbreich, U. (2007). Women's mental health in the Muslim world: Cultural, religious, and social issues. *Journal of Affective Disorders, 102*(1–3), 177–189.

Dranove, D. (2008). *Code red: An economist explains how to revive the healthcare system without destroying it.* Princeton: NJ: Princeton University Press.

Dreisbach, S. (2015). How do you feel about your body? *Glamour.* Retrieved from http://www.glamour.com/health-fitness/2014/10/body-image-how-do-you-feel-about-your-body

Drucker, P. F. (1993). *Post-capitalistic society.* New York: HarperCollins.

D'Silva, M. U., & Palmgreen, P. (2007). Individual differences and context: Mediating recall of anti-drug public service announcements. *Health Communication, 21*, 65–71.

Dube, S. P., Ghadlinge, M. S., Mungal, S. U., Saleem, B. T., & Kulkarni, M. B. (2014, May). Students perception towards problem based learning. *IOSR Journal of Dental and Medical Sciences, 13*(5), 49–53.

DuBois, J. M., Anderson, E. E., Carroll, K., Gibb, T., Kraus, E., Rubbelke, T., & Vasher, M. (2012). Environmental factors contributing to wrongdoing in medicine: A criterion-based review of studies and cases. *Ethics & Behavior, 22*(3), 163–188.

Dudo, A. D., Dahlstrom, M. F., & Broussard, D. (2007). Reporting a potential pandemic: A risk-related assessment of avian influenza coverage in U.S. newspapers. *Science Communication, 28*(4), 429–454.

Duewald, M. (2003, June 22). Body and image; one size definitely does not fit all. *The New York Times.* Retrieved from http://query.nytimes.com/gst/fullpage.html?sec=health&res=9F0DE7DD1638F931A15755C0A9659C8B63

Duggan, A. (2006). Understanding interpersonal communication processes across health contexts: Advances in the last decade and challenges for the next decade. *Journal of Health Communication, 11*, 93–108.

Duggan, A., Bradshaw, Y. S., Carroll, S. E., Rattigan, S. H., & Altman, W. (2009). What can I learn from this interaction? A qualitative analysis of medical student self-reflection and learning in a standardized patient exercise about disability. *Journal of Health Communication, 14*, 797–811. doi:10.1080/10810730903295526

Duggleby, W. (2003). Helping Hispanic/Latino home health patients manage their pain. *Home Healthcare Nurse, 21*(3), 174–179.

Duke, A. (2014, August 12). Robin Williams dead; family, friends, and fans are "totally devastated." CNN Online. Retrieved from http://www.cnn.com/2014/08/11/showbiz/robin-williams-dead/

Duplaga, M. (2015). A cross-sectional study assessing determinants of the attitude to the introduction of eHealth services among patients suffering from chronic conditions. *BMC Medical Informatics & Decision Making, 15*(1), 1–15.

du Pré, A. (1998). *Humor and the healing arts: Multimethod analysis of humor use in health care.* Mahwah, NJ: Lawrence Erlbaum.

du Pré, A. (2002). Accomplishing the impossible: Talking about body and soul and mind during a medical visit. *Health Communication, 14*, 1–22.

du Pré, A. (2005). Making empowerment work: Medical center soars in satisfaction ratings. In E. B. Ray (Ed.), *Health communication in practice: A case study approach* (pp. 311–322). Mahwah, NJ: Lawrence Erlbaum.

du Pré, A., & Ray, E. B. (2008). Comforting episodes: Transcendent experiences of cancer survivors. In L. Sparks, H. D. O'Hair, & G. L. Kreps (Eds.), *Cancer, communication and aging* (pp. 99–114). Cresskill, NJ: Hampton Press.

Durà-Vilà, G., & Hodes, M. (2012). Cross-cultural study of idioms of distress among Spanish nationals and Hispanic American migrants: *Susto, nervios* and *ataque de nervios. Social Psychiatry & Psychiatric Epidemiology, 47*(10), 1627–1637. doi:10.1007/s00127-011-0468-3

Dutta, M. J. (2006). Theoretical approaches to entertainment education campaigns: A subaltern critique. *Health Communication, 20*, 221–231.

Dutta, M. J. (2008). *Communicating health: A culture-centered approach.* Cambridge, MA: Polity Press.

Dutta, M. J., Bodie, G. D., & Basu, A. (2008). Health disparity and the racial divide among the nation's youth: Internet as a site for change? In A. Everett (Ed.), *Learning race and ethnicity: Youth and the digital media* (pp. 175–198). Cambridge, MA: MIT Press.

Dutta, M. J., & Boyd, J. (2007). Turning "smoking man" images around: Portrayals of smoking in men's magazines as a blueprint for smoking cessation campaigns. *Health Communication, 22*, 253–263.

Dutta, M. J., & de Souza, R. (2008). The past, present, and future of health development campaigns: Reflexivity and the critical-cultural approach. *Health Communication, 23*, 326–339.

Dutta-Bergman, M. J. (2005). Theory and practice in health communication campaigns: A critical interrogation. *Health Communication, 18*, 103–122.

Dwyer, F. R., Schurr, P. H., & Oh, S. (1987). Developing buyer-seller relationships. *Journal of Marketing, 51*(2), 11–27.

Dyche, L., & Swiderski, D. (2005). The effect of physician solicitation approaches on ability to identify patient concerns. *Journal of General Internal Medicine, 20*(3), 267–270.

Dyer, J. (1996). *In a tangled wood: An Alzheimer's journey.* Dallas: Southern Methodist University Press.

Dym, H. (2008). Risk management techniques for the general dentist and specialist. *Dental Clinics of North America, 52*(3), 563–577.

Dyrbye, L. N., Varkey, P., Boone, S. L., Satele, D. V., Sloan, J. A., & Shanafelt, T. D. (2013). Physician satisfaction and burnout at different career stages. *Mayo Clinic Proceedings, 88*(12), 1358–1367.

Dyrbye, L. N., West, C. P., Satele, D., Boone, S., Tan, L., Sloan, J., & Shanafelt, T. D. (2014). Burnout among U.S. medical students, residents, and early career physicians relative to the general U.S. population. *Academic Medicine: Journal of the Association of American Medical Colleges, 89*(3), 443–451.

Dziengel, L. (2014). Renaming, reclaiming, renewing the self: Intersections of gender, identity, and health care. *Affilia: Journal of Women & Social Work, 29*(1), 105. doi:10.1177/0886109913510660

Eastman, J. K., Eastman, K. L., & Tolson, M. A. (1997). The ethics of managed care: An initial look at physicians' perspectives. *Marketing Health Services, 17,* 26–40.

Economic Research Initiative on the Uninsured. (2005, December). Rising health care costs frustrate efforts to reduce uninsured rate. *ERIU Research Highlight* No. 10. Retrieved from eriu.sph.umich.edu/pdf/highlight-chernew.pdf

Economic Research Institute. (2012). Top managed care executive salary survey data. Irvine, CA: Author. Retrieved from http://www.erieri.com/index.cfm?fuseaction=research.Top-Managed-Care-Executive-salary-data-details&PositionId=7545&CityId=300

Edgar, T., Freimuth, V., & Hammond, S. L. (2003). Lessons learned from the field on prevention and health campaigns. In T. L. Thompson, A. M. Dorsey, K. I. Miller, & R. Parrott (Eds.), *Handbook of health communication* (pp. 625–636). Mahwah, NJ: Lawrence Erlbaum.

Edgar, T. M., Satterfield, D. W., & Whaley, B. B. (2005). Explanations of illness: A bridge to understanding. In E. B. Ray (Ed.), *Health communication in practice: A case study approach* (pp. 95–109). Mahwah, NJ: Lawrence Erlbaum.

Edwards, H., & Noller, P. (1998). Factors influencing caregiver–care receiver communication and the impact on the well-being of older care receivers. *Health Communication, 10,* 317–342.

Effertz, T., Franke, M., & Teichert, T. (2014). Adolescents' assessments of advertisements for unhealthy food: An example of warning labels for soft drinks. *Journal of Consumer Policy, 2,* 279–299.

Egan, T. (1988, May 1). Rebuffed by Oregon, patients take their life-or-death cases public. *The New York Times.* Retrieved from http://www.nytimes.com/1988/05/01/us/rebuffed-by-oregon-patients-take-their-life-or-death-cases-public.html

Egbert, N., Koch, L., Coeling, H., & Ayers, D. (2006). The role of social support in the family and community integration of right-hemisphere stroke survivors. *Health Communication, 20,* 45–55.

Egbert, N., Sparks, L., Kreps, G. L., & du Pré, A. (2008). Finding meaning in the journey: Methods of spiritual coping for aging patients with cancer. In L. Sparks, H. D. O'Hair, & G. L. Kreps (Eds.), *Cancer, communication and aging* (pp. 277–291). Cresskill, NJ: Hampton Press.

Egerton, J. (2007, September 21). 11 ways to keep your patients satisfied: Your front-desk staff can make the patient experience positive or turn them off. Here's how to make sure that all goes well. *Medical Economics, 84*(18), 50–52.

Eggly, S. (2002). Physician–patient co-construction of illness narratives in the medical interview. *Health Communication, 14,* 339–360.

Eisenberg, E. M., Baglia, J., & Pynes, J. E. (2006). Transforming emergency medicine through narrative: Qualitative action research at a community hospital. *Health Communication, 19,* 197–208.

Elam-Evans, L. D., Yankey, D., Singleton, J. A., Kolasa, M. (2014, August 29). National, state, and selected local area vaccination coverage among children aged 19–35 months—United States, 2013. *Morbidity and Mortality Weekly Report 63*(34), 741–748. Retrieved from http://www.cdc.gov/mmwr/preview/mmwrhtml/mm6334a1.htm

Ellingson, L. L. (2007). The performance of dialysis care: Routinization and adaptation on the floor. *Health Communication, 22,* 103–114.

Ellingson, L. L. (2011). The poetics of professionalism among dialysis technicians. *Health Communication, 26,* 1–12.

Elliott, C. (2007). Assessing "fun foods": Nutritional content and analysis of supermarket foods targeted at children. *Obesity Reviews, 9*(4), 368–377.

The e-mail advantage. (2007, September 7). *Medical Economics, 84*(17), 28.

Emanuel, E. J., & Emanuel, L. L. (1995). Four models of the physician–patient relationship. In J. D. Arras & B. Steinbock (Eds.), *Ethical issues in modern medicine* (4th ed., pp. 67–76). Mountain View, CA: Mayfield.

Emanuel, E. J., & Emanuel, L. L. (1998, May 16). The promise of a good death. *The Lancet, 351,* S21–S29.

Emme, C., Rydahl-Hansen, S., Østergaard, B., Schou, L., Svarre Jakobsen, A., & Phanareth, K. (2014). How virtual admission affects coping—telemedicine for patients with chronic obstructive pulmonary disease. *Journal of Clinical Nursing, 23*(9/10), 1445–1458.

English, J., Wilson, K., & Keller-Olaman, S. (2008). Health, healing and recovery: Therapeutic landscapes and the everyday lives of breast cancer survivors. *Social Science & Medicine, 67,* 68–78.

Entertainomercials. (1996, November 4). *Forbes, 158,* 322–323.

Epidemiology of measles—United States, 1998. (1999, September 3). *Morbidity and Mortality Weekly Reports, 48*(34), 749–753. Retrieved from http://www.cdc.gov/mmwr/preview/mmwrhtml/mm4834a1.htm

Epstein, R. M. (1999). Mindful practice. *Journal of the American Medical Association, 282*(9), 833–839.

Epstein, R. M., Fiscella, K., Lesser, C. S., & Stange, K. C. (2010). Why the nation needs a policy push on patient-centered health care. The Commonwealth Fund. Retrieved from http://www.commonwealthfund.org/Publications/In-the-Literature/2010/Aug/Why-the-Nation-Needs-a-Policy-Push.aspx

Erdelyi, M, H., & Zizak, D. M. (2004). Beyond gizmo subliminality. In L. J. Shrum (Ed.), *The psychology of entertainment media: Blurring the lines between entertainment and persuasion* (pp. 13–44). Mahwah, NJ: Lawrence Erlbaum.

Erdman, L. (1993). Laughter therapy for patients with cancer. *Journal of psychosocial oncology, 11*, 55–67.

Erickson, S. (2008, May 16). The day I received my final verdict: A lawsuit left the author with worries about his reputation, until a surprising visit took place. *Medical Economics, 85(10)*, 32–33.

Espinoza, P., Penelo, E., & Raich, R. M. (2013). Prevention programme for eating disturbances in adolescents. Is their effect on body image maintained at 30 months later? *Body Image, 10*, 175–181.

Evans, B. C., & Ume, E. (2012). Psychosocial, cultural, and spiritual health disparities in end-of-life and palliative care: Where we are and where we need to go. *Nursing Outlook, 60* (Special Issue: State of the Science: Palliative Care and End of Life), 370–375. doi:10.1016/j.outlook.2012.08.008

Evans, W. D., Uhrig, J., Davis, K., & McCormack, L. (2009). Efficacy methods to evaluate health communication and marketing campaigns. *Journal of Health Communication, 14*, 315–330. doi:10.1080/10810730902872234

Evercare study of the economic downturn and its impact on family caregiving. (2009, April). Evercare by United Healthcare (Minnetonka, MN) and the National Alliance for Caregiving (Bethesda, MD). Retrieved from http://www.caregiving.org/data/EVC_Caregivers_Economy_Report%20FINAL_4-28-09.pdf

Everett, M. W., & Palmgreen, P. (1995). Influences of sensation seeking, message sensation value, and program context on effectiveness of anticocaine public service announcement. *Health Communication, 7*, 225–248.

Faces of the fallen. (2015, February 21). *The Washington Post*. Retrieved from http://apps.washingtonpost.com/national/fallen/

Faden, R. R. (1987). Ethical issues in government sponsored public health campaigns. *Health Education Quarterly, 14*, 27–37.

Fadiman, A. (1997). *The spirit catches you and you fall down: A Hmong child, her American doctors, and the collision of two cultures*. New York: Farrar, Straus and Giroux.

Fahey, K. F., Rao, S. M., Douglas, M. K., Thomas, M. L., Elliott, J. E., & Miaskowski, C. (2008). Nurse coaching to explore and modify patient attitudinal barriers interfering with effective cancer pain management. *Oncology Nursing Forum, 35*(2), 234–240.

Fallon, E. A., Harris, B. S., & Johnson, P. (2014). Prevalence of body dissatisfaction among a United States adult sample. *Eating Behaviors, 15*(1), 151–158.

Farber, N. J., Novack, D. H., & O'Brien, M. K. (1997). Love, boundaries, and the patient–physician relationship. *Archives of Internal Medicine, 157*, 229–294.

Farrar, K. M., Krcmar, M., & Nowak, K. L. (2006). Contextual features of violent video games, mental models, and aggression. *Journal of Communication, 56*, 387–405.

Farrelly, M. C., Healton, C. G., Davis, K. C., Messeri, P., & Haviland, M. L. (2002, June). Getting to the truth: Evaluating national tobacco countermarketing campaigns. *American Journal of Public Health, 92*(6), 901–907.

Fawcett, K. (2015, April 16). How mental illness is represented in the media. *US News & World Report*. Retrieved from http://health.usnews.com/health-news/health-wellness/articles/2015/04/16/how-mental-illness-is-misrepresented-in-the-media

Fearn-Banks, K. (1996). *Crisis communication: A casebook approach*. Mahwah, NJ: Lawrence Erlbaum.

Feldman, S. (2008, January 25). Dr.Score releases its first Annual Report Card on Patient Satisfaction in the U.S., to coincide with the observance of National Medical Practice Group Week. Retrieved from www.drscore.com/press/report/012508.pdf

Fenton, J. J., Jerant A. F., Bertakis, K. D., & Franks, P. (2012). The cost of satisfaction: A national study of patient satisfaction, health care utilization, expenditures, and mortality. *Archives of Internal Medicine, 172*, 405–411. doi:10.1001/archinternmed.2011.1662

Ferguson, B., Lowman, S. G., & DeWalt, D. A. (2011). Assessing literacy in clinical and community settings: The patient perspective. *Journal of Health Communication, 16*, 124–134. doi:10.1080/10810730.2010.535113

Ferguson, T. (1997, November–December). Health care in cyberspace: Patients lead a revolution. *The Futurist, 31*(6), 29–34.

Fernandez, S., & Moldogaziev, T. (2013). Employee empowerment, employee attitudes, and performance: Testing a causal model. *Public Administration Review, 73*(3), 490–506.

Fertility acupuncture: Fear and discovery. (2012, May 23). Path to Fertility [Blog post]. Retrieved from http://fertility-news.rmact.com/Path-To-Fertility-Blog/bid/105392/Fertility-Acupuncture-My-Personal-Experience-with-RMACT-Experts

Festinger, L. (1957). *A theory of cognitive dissonance*. Stanford, CA: Stanford University Press.

Fiabane, E., Giorgi, I., Sguazzin, C., & Argentero, P. (2013). Work engagement and occupational stress in nurses and other healthcare workers: The role of organisational and personal factors. *Journal of Clinical Nursing, 22*(17/18), 2614–2624.

File, T., & Ryan, C. (2014, November). Computer and Internet use in the United States: 2013. American Community Survey Reports, U.S. Census Bureau. Retrieved from http://www.census.gov/content/dam/Census/library/publications/2014/acs/acs-28.pdf

Finney Rutten, L. J., Agunwamba, A. A., Greene, S. M., Mazor, K. M., Ebbert, J. O., St. Sauver, J. L., & Dearing, J. W. (2014). Enabling patient-centered communication and care through health information technology. *Journal of Communication in Healthcare, 7*(4), 255–261.

Fischer, P. M., Schwartz, M. P., Richard, J. W., & Goldstein, A. O. (1991). Brand logo recognition by children aged 3 to 6 years: Mickey Mouse and Old Joe the Camel. *Journal of the American Medical Association, 266*, 3154–3158.

Fisher, J. A. (1994). *The plague makers*. New York: Simon & Schuster.

Fisher, L. B. (2007, March). President Bush's major post-Katrina speeches: Enhancing image repair. Discourse theory applied to the public sector. *Public Relations Review, 33*(1), 40–48.

Florida hospital surgeons mistakenly amputate wrong leg of patient. (1995, March 20). *Jet*. Retrieved from http://findarticles.com/p/articles/mi_m1355/is_n19_v87/ai_16717100

Floyd, K., Hesse, C., & Haynes, M. T. (2007, January). Human affection exchange: SV. Metabolic and cardiovascular correlates of trait expressed affection. *Communication Quarterly, 55*(1), 79–94.

Flynn, J. J., Hollenstein, T., & Mackey, A. (2010). The effect of suppressing and not accepting emotions on depressive symptoms: Is suppression different for men and women? *Personality and Individual Differences, 49*, 49582–49586. doi:10.1016/j.paid.2010.05.022

Fonarow, G. C., Abraham, W. T., Albert, N. M., Stough, W. G., Gheorghiade, M., Greenberg, B., . . . Young, J. B. (2008). Factors identified as precipitating hospital admissions for heart failure and clinical outcomes: Findings from OPTIMIZE-HF. *Archives of Internal Medicine, 168*(8), 847–854.

Ford, L. A., Babrow, A. S., & Stohl, C. (1996). Social support messages and the management of uncertainty in the experience of breast cancer: An application of problematic integration theory. *Communication Monographs, 63*, 189–208.

Ford, L. A., & Christmon, B. C. (2005). "Every cancer is different": Illness narratives and the management of identity in breast cancer. In E. B. Ray (Ed.), *Health communication in practice: A case study approach* (pp. 157–170). Mahwah, NJ: Lawrence Erlbaum.

Forman-Brunell, M. (n.d.). What Barbie dolls have to say about postwar American culture. Smithsonian Center for Education and Museum Studies. Retrieved from http://www.smithsonianeducation.org/idealabs/ap/essays/barbie.htm

Former UCLA employee indicted for HIPAA violations over celebs. (2008, May 5). *Modern Healthcare, 38*(18), 4.

Forrest, C. B., Shadmi, E., Nutting, P. A., & Starfield, B. (2007). Specialty referral completion among primary care patients: Results from the ASPN referral study. *Annals of Family Medicine, 5*(4), 361–367.

Forsythe, L. P., Alfano, C. M., Kent, E. E., Weaver, K. E., Bellizzi, K., Arora, N., . . . Rowland, J. H. (2014). Social support, self-efficacy for decision-making, and follow-up care use in long-term cancer survivors. *Psycho-Oncology, 23*(7), 788–796.

Foster, E. (2007). *Communicating at the end of life: Finding magic in the mundane*. Mahwah, NJ: Lawrence Erlbaum.

Fowler, B. A. (2006). Claiming health: Mammography screening decision making of African American women. *Oncology Nursing Forum, 33*(5), 969–975.

Fowler, C., & Nussbaum, J. (2008). Communicating with the aging patient. In K. B. Wright & S. D. Moore (Eds.), *Applied health communication* (pp. 159–178). Cresskill, NJ: Hampton Press.

Fox, M. (2014, May 21). The future of health care in America? Think Hispanic. NBC News. Retrieved from http://www.nbcnews.com/storyline/obamacare-deadline/future-health-care-america-think-hispanic-n111461

Fox, M., & Connor, T. (2015, February 7). Think the U.S. has a measles problem? Just look at Europe. NBC News. Retrieved from http://www.nbcnews.com/storyline/measles-outbreak/think-u-s-has-measles-problem-just-look-europe-n301726

Frank, E., Carrera, J. S., Stratton, T., Bickel, J., & Nora, L. M. (2006). Experiences of belittlement and harassment and their correlates among medical students in the United States: Longitudinal survey. *British Medical Journal, 333*, 682–684.

Frank, E., Modi, S., Elon L., & Coughlin, S. S. (2008). U.S. medical students' attitudes about patients' access to care. *Preventive Medicine, 47*(1), 140–145.

Frank, L. B., Murphy, S. T., Chatterjee, J. S., Moran, M. B., & Baezconde-Garbanati, L. (2015). Telling stories, saving lives: Creating narrative health messages. *Health Communication, 30*, 154–163.

Frankel, R. M., & Beckman, H. B. (1989). Conversation and compliance with treatment recommendations: An application of micro-interactional analysis in medicine. In L. Grossberg, B. J. O'Keefe, & E. Wartella (Eds.), *Rethinking communication: Vol. 2. Paradigm exemplars* (pp. 60–74). Newbury Park, CA: Sage.

Frankl, V. E. (1959). *Man's search for meeting*. Boston: Beacon Press.

Frates, J., Bohrer, G. G., & Thomas, D. (2006). Promoting organ donation to Hispanics: The role of the media and medicine. *Journal of Health Communication, 11*(7), 683–698.

Freimuth, V. S. (2006). Order out of chaos: The self-organization of communication following the anthrax attacks. *Health Communication, 20*, 141–148.

Freimuth, V. S., Stein, J. A., & Kean, T. J. (1989). *Searching for health information: The cancer information service model*. Philadelphia: University of Pennsylvania Press.

Frey, L. R., Botan, C. H., Friedman, P. G., & Kreps, G. (1999). *Investigating communication: An introduction to research methods* (2nd ed.). New York: Pearson.

Friederichs, S. H., Oenema, A., Bolman, C., Guyaux, J., van Keulen, H. M., & Lechner, L. (2014). I Move: systematic development of a web-based computer tailored physical activity intervention, based on motivational interviewing and self-determination theory. *BMC Public Health, 14*(1), 1–29.

Friedersdorf, C. (2015, February 3). Should anti-vaxers be shamed or persuaded? The backlash to a measles outbreak—and a case against politicizing it. *The Atlantic*. Retrieved from http://www.theatlantic.com/politics/archive/2015/02/should-anti-vaxxers-be-shamed-or-persuaded/385109/

Friedman, D. B., Hooker, S. P., Wilcox, S., Burroughs, E. L., & Rheaume, C. E. (2012). African American men's perspectives on promoting physical activity: "We're not that difficult to figure out!" *Journal of Health Communication, 17,* 1151–1170.

Friedman, H. S., & DiMatteo, M. R. (1979). Health care as an interpersonal process. *Journal of Social Issues, 35,* 1–11.

Friedmann, E., & Thomas, S. A. (1995). Pet ownership, social support, and one-year survival after acute myocardial infarction in the cardiac arrhythmia suppression trial. *American Journal of Cardiology, 76,* 1213–1217.

Frizell, S. (2014, October 18). Obama on Ebola: "We can't give in to hysteria." *Time.* Retrieved from http://time.com/3520341/obama-ebola-fear/

Frosch, D. L., May, S. G., Rendle, K. A. S., Tietbohl, C., & Elwyn, G. (2012). Authoritarian physicians and patients' fear of being labeled "difficult" among key obstacles to shared decision making. *Health Affairs, 31*(5), 1030–1038.

Fry, R. B., & Prentice-Dunn, S. (2005). Effects of coping information and value affirmation on responses to a perceived health threat. *Health Communication, 17,* 133–147.

Fuchs-Lacelle, S., Hadjistavropoulos, T., & Lix, L. (2008). Pain assessment as intervention: A study of older adults with severe dementia. *Clinical Journal of Pain, 24*(8), 697–707.

Fuller, J. (2003). Intercultural health care as reflective negotiated practice. *Western Journal of Nursing Research, 7,* 781.

Gade, C. J. (2007). Understanding and defining roles in the pharmacist-patient relationship. *Journal of Communication in Healthcare, 1,* 88–98.

Galanti, G.-A. (2014). *Caring for patients from different cultures* (5th ed.). Philadelphia, PA: University of Pennsylvania Press.

Gallagher, S., Phillips, A. C., Ferraro, A. J., Drayson, M. T., & Carroll, D. (2008). Social communication is positively associated with the immunoglobulin M response to vaccination with pneumococcal polysaccharides. *Biological Psychology, 78*(2), 211–215.

Gamble, M. (2012, April 30). 30 statistics on global patient satisfaction. Becker's Hospital Review. Retrieved from http://www.beckershospitalreview.com/hospital-management-administration/30-statistics-on-global-patient-satisfaction.html

Gamlin, R. (1999). Sexuality: A challenge for nursing practice. *Nursing Times, 95*(7), 48–50.

Geertz, C. (1973). *The interpretation of cultures.* New York: Basic Books.

Geist, P., & Dreyer, J. (1993). The demise of dialogue: A critique of medical encounter dialogue. *Western Journal of Communication, 57,* 233–246.

Geist, P., & Gates, L. (1996). The poetics and politics of recovering identities in health communication. *Communication Studies, 47,* 218–228.

Geist, P., & Hardesty, P. (1992). Negotiating the crisis: DRGs and the transformation of hospitals. In J. Bryant (Ed.), *Organizational communication* (pp. 19–42). Mahwah, NJ: Lawrence Erlbaum.

Geist-Martin, P., & Bell, K. K. (2009). "Open your heart first of all": Perspectives of holistic providers in Costa Rica about communication in the provision of health care. *Health Communication, 24,* 631–646. doi:10.1080/10410230903242234

Geller, G., Bernhardt, B. A., Carrese, J., Rushton, C. H., & Kolodner, K. (2008). What do clinicians derive from partnering with their patients? Reliable and valid measure of "personal meaning in patient care." *Patient Education and Counseling, 72,* 293–300.

Gelsema, T. I., van der Doef, M., Maes, S., Janssen, M., Akerboom, S., & Verhoeven, C. (2006). A longitudinal study of job stress in the nursing profession: Causes and consequences. *Journal of Nursing Management, 14*(4), 289–299.

Gerbner, G. (1996, Fall). TV violence and what to do about it. *Nieman Reports, 50,* 10–12.

Gerbner, G., Gross, L., Morgan, M., & Signorielli, N. (1980). The "mainstreaming" of America: Violence profile no. 11. *Journal of Communication, 30*(3), 10–29.

Gerbner, G., Gross, L., Morgan, M., & Signorelli, N. (1994). *Living with television: The dynamics of the cultivation process.* In J. Bryant & D. Zillmann (Eds.), *Perspectives on media effects* (pp. 17–40). Hillsdale, NJ: Lawrence Erlbaum.

Getting doctors out in the neighborhoods. (2002, June 17). Davis, CA: University of California Newsroom. Retrieved from http://www.universityofcalifornia.edu/news/article/4472

Gibson, T. A. (2007, May). WARNING—the existing media system may be toxic to your health: Health communication and the politics of media reform. *Journal of Applied Communication Research, 35*(2), 125–132.

Giles, H., Ballard, D., & McCann, R. M. (2002). Perceptions of intergenerational communication across cultures: An Italian case. *Perceptual and Motor Skills, 95,* 583–591.

Giles, L. C., Glonek, G. F., Luszcz, M. A., & Andrews, G. R. (2005, July). Effect of social networks on 10-year survival in very old Australians: The Australian longitudinal study of aging. *Journal of Epidemiology & Community Health, 59*(7), 574–579.

Gill, E. A., & Babrow, A. S. (2007). To hope or to know: Coping with uncertainty and ambivalence in women's magazine breast cancer articles. *Journal of Applied Communication Research, 35*(2), 133–155.

Gillespie, S. R. (2001). The politics of breathing: Asthmatic Medicaid patients under managed care. *Journal of Applied Communication Research, 29*(2), 97–116.

Gillisen, A. (2007). Patient's adherence in asthma. *Journal of Physiology and Pharmacology,* 58[Suppl. 5,] 205–222.

Gilstrap, C. M., & White, Z. M. (2015). Interactional communication challenges in end-of-life care: dialectical tensions and management strategies experienced by home hospice nurses. *Health Communication, 30,* 525–535.

Ginossar, T. (2014). Disparities and antecedents to cancer prevention information seeking among cancer patients and caregivers attending a minority-serving cancer center. (2014). *Journal of Communication in Healthcare, 7*(2), 93–105.

Glass, R. M. (1996). The patient–physician relationship: JAMA focuses on the center of medicine. *Journal of the American Medical Association, 275*, 147–148.

Glik, D. C. (2007, April). Risk communication for public health emergencies. *Annual Review of Public Health, 28*, 33–54.

Global HIV/AIDS overview. (2014). AIDS.gov. Retrieved from https://www.aids.gov/federal-resources/around-the-world/global-aids-overview/

Goffman, E. (1963). *Stigma: Notes on the management of spoiled identity*. Englewood Cliffs, NJ: Prentice Hall.

Goffman, E. (1967). *Interaction rituals*. New York: Pantheon.

Goffman, E. (1974). *Frame analysis: An essay on the organization of experience*. New York: Harper Colophon.

Goins, E. S., & Pye, D. (2013). Check the box that best describes you: Reflexively managing theory and praxis in LGBTQ health communication research. *Health Communication, 28*, 397–407. doi:10.1080/10410236.2012.690505

Gold, J. (2013, November 21). In Iowa, accountable care begins to make a difference. Kaiser Health News and National Public Radio. Retrieved from http://khn.org/news/iowa-accountable-care-organization-aco/

Goldstein, J. (2008, May 13). Insurers pay caregivers to track patients. *Philadelphia Inquirer*, Health Daily, p. A01.

Goode, E. E. (1993, February 15). The cultures of illness. *U.S. News & World Report, 114*, 74–76.

Goodnight, T. G. (1982). The personal, technical, and public spheres of argument: A speculative inquiry into the art of public deliberation. *Journal of the American Forensic Association, 18*, 214–227.

Gorawara-Bhat, R., Gallagher, T. H., & Levinson, W. (2003). Patient–provider discussions about conflicts of interest in managed care: Physicians' perceptions. *American Journal of Managed Care, 9*(8), 564–571.

Gordon, E. J., Leon, J. B., & Sehgal, A. R. (2003). Why are hemodialysis treatments shortened and skipped? Development of a taxonomy and relationship to patient subgroups. *Nephrology Nursing Journal, 30*(2), 209–217.

Gordon, R. (2012). Re-thinking and re-tooling the social marketing mix. *Australasian Marketing Journal, 20*, 122–126.

Govindarajan, A., & Schull, M. (2003). Effect of socioeconomic status on out-of-hospital transport delays of patients with chest pain. *Annals of Emergency Medicine, 41*(4), 481–490.

Goyal Wasan, P., & Tripathi, G. (2014). Revisiting social marketing mix: A socio-cultural perspective. *Journal of Services Research, 14*(2), 127–144.

Grady, M., & Edgar, T. (2003). Racial disparities in healthcare: Highlights from focus group findings. In B. D. Smedley, A. Y. Stith, & A. R. Nelson (Eds.), *Unequal treatment: Confronting racial and ethnic disparities in health care* (pp. 392–405). Washington, DC: Board on Health Sciences Policy, Institute of Medicine. Retrieved from http://books.nap.edu/openbook.php?isbn=030908265X

Granovetter, M. S. (1973). The strength of weak ties. *American Journal of Sociology, 78*, 1360–1380.

Granovetter, M. S. (1983). The strength of weak ties: A network theory revisited. *Sociological Theory, 1*, 201–233.

Grant, A., Kinnersley, P., & Field, M. (2012). Learning contexts at two UK medical schools: A comparative study using mixed methods. *BMC Research Notes, 5*(1), 153–160.

Grant, C. J., III, Cissna, K. N., & Rosenfeld, L. B. (2000). Patients' perceptions of physicians' communication and outcomes of the accrual to trial process. *Health Communication, 12*, 23–39.

Green, E. C., & Witte, K. (2006). Can fear arousal in public health campaigns contribute to the decline of HIV prevalence? *Journal of Health Communication, 11*(3), 245–259.

Green, F. (2003, June 20). Booze ads target Black teens, report finds. *San-Diego Union-Tribune*, p. C1.

Green, K. C. (1988, January). Who wants to be a nurse? *American Demographics, 10*, 46–49.

Green, R. (1999). *The Nicholas Effect: A boy's gift to the world*. Cambridge, MA: O'Reilly.

Green, R. (2003). A child's legacy of love. The Nicholas Green Foundation. Retrieved from http://www.nicholasgreen.org/articles.html

Greene, J. (2008, February 25). Turning the tables: Insurers win low marks in doc-satisfaction survey. *Modern Healthcare*, 38(8), 58.

Greene, K. (2009). An integrated model of health disclosure decision-making. In T. D. Afifi & W. A. Afifi (Eds.), *Uncertainty and information regulation in interpersonal contexts: Theories and applications* (pp. 226–253). New York: Routledge.

Greene, K., Magsamen-Conrad, K., Venetis, M. K., Checton, M. G., Bagdasarov, Z., & Banerjee, S. C. (2012). Assessing health diagnosis disclosure decisions in relationships: Testing the disclosure decision-making model. *Health Communication, 27*, 356–368.

Greene, M. G., Adelman, R. D., & Majerovitz, S. D. (1996). Physician and older patient support in the medical encounter. *Health Communication, 8*, 263–279.

Griffin, R. J., Dunwoody, S., & Neuwirth, K. (1999). Information insufficiency and risk communication. *Media Psychology, 6*, 23–61.

Grönroos, C. (1994). From marketing mix to relationship marketing: Towards a paradigm shift in marketing. *Management Decision, 32*(2), 4–20.

Groopman, J. (2007). *How doctors think*. Boston: Houghton Mifflin.

Gruber, T. (2014, June). Growth and variability in health plan premiums in the individual insurance market before the Affordable Care Act. The Commonwealth Fund. Retrieved from http://www.commonwealthfund.org/~/media/files/publications/issue-brief/2014/jun/1750_gruber_growth_variability_hlt_plan_premiums_ib_v2.pdf

Grunig, J. E. (Ed.). (1992). *Excellence in public relations and communication management.* Hillsdale, NJ: Lawrence Erlbaum.

Grunig, L. A., Grunig, J. E., & Dozier, D. M. (2002) *Excellent public relations and effective organizations: A study of communication management in three countries.* Mahwah, NJ: Lawrence Erlbaum.

Gunther, A. C., Bolt, D., Borzekowski, D. L. G., Liebhart, J. L., & Dillard, J. P. (2006). Presumed influence on peer norms: How mass media indirectly affect adolescent smoking. *Journal of Communication, 56,* 52–68.

Gupta, V. (2010). Impact of culture on healthcare seeking behavior of Asian Indians. *Journal of Cultural Diversity, 17*(1), 13–19.

Gur-Arie, M. (2014, March 4). How mHealth will change the doctor-patient culture. KevinMD.com. Retrieved from http://www.kevinmd.com/blog/2014/03/mhealth-change-doctorpatient-culture.html

Gursky, E., Inglesby, T. V., & O'Toole, T. (2003). Anthrax 2001: Observations on the medical and public health response. *Biosecurity and Bioterrorism, 1*(2), online version, n.p. Retrieved from http://online.liebertpub.com/doi/pdfplus/10.1089/153871303766275763

Gustavo, S. A., Parsons-Perez, C., Goltz, S., Bhadelia, A., Durstine, A., Knaul, F., . . . Lu, R. (2013). Recommendations towards an integrated life-course approach to women's health in the post-2015 agenda. *Bulletin of the World Health Organization, 91,* 704–706.

Guy, B., Williams, D. R., Aldridge, A., & Roggenkamp, S. D. (2007). Approaches to organizing public relations functions in healthcare. *Health Marketing Quarterly, 24(3-4),* 1–18. doi: 10.1080/07359680802118969.

Hagemeier, N. E., Hess Jr., R., Hagen, K. S., & Sorah, E. L. (2014). Impact of an interprofessional communication course on nursing, medical, and pharmacy students' communication skill self-efficacy beliefs. *American Journal of Pharmaceutical Education, 78*(10), 1–10.

Haider, M., & Aravindakshan, N. P. (2005). Content analysis of anthrax in the media. In M. Haider (Ed.), *Global public health communication: Challenges, perspectives, and strategies* (pp. 391–406). Boston: Jones and Bartlett.

Hain, D. J., & Sandy, D. (2013). Partners in care: Patient empowerment through shared decision-making. *Nephrology Nursing Journal, 40*(2), 153–157.

Haines, M. P., & Spear, S. F. (1996). Changing the perceptions of the norm: A strategy to decrease binge drinking among college students. *Journal of American College Health, 45,* 134–140.

Halbesleben, J. R. (2006). Patient reciprocity and physician burnout: What do patients bring to the patient–physician relationship? *Health Services Management Research, 19*(4), 215–222.

Halbesleben, J. R., & Rathert, C. (2008). Linking physician burnout and patient outcomes: Exploring the dyadic relationship between physicians and patients. *Health Care Management Review, 33*(1), 29–39.

Halkowski, T. (2006). Realizing the illness: Patients' narratives of symptom discovery. In J. Heritage & D. W. Maynard (Eds.), *Communication in medical care: Interactions between primary care physicians and patients* (pp. 86–114). Cambridge: Cambridge University Press.

Hall, A. (2014, November 13). Eco advocates for a 20 percent increase in green space by 2020. USA News.com.

Hall, A. K., Bernhardt, J. M., Dodd, V., & Vollrath, M. W. (2015). The digital health divide: Evaluating online health information access and use among older adults. *Health Education & Behavior, 42*(2), 202.

Hample, D., & Hample, J. M. (2014). Persuasion about health risks: Evidence, credibility, scientific flourishes, and risk perceptions. *Argumentation & Advocacy, 51*(1), 17–29.

Han, J. Y., Hou, J., Kim, E., & Gustafson, D. H. (2014). Lurking as an active participation process: A longitudinal investigation of engagement with an online cancer support group. *Health Communication, 29,* 911–923.

Han, J. Y., Shah, D. V., Kim, E., Namkoong, K., Lee, S.-Y., Moon, J., . . . Gustafson, D. H. (2011). Empathic exchanges in online cancer support groups: Distinguishing message expression and reception effects. *Health Communication, 26,* 185–197.

Hankivsky, O. (2012). Women's health, men's health, and gender and health: Implications of intersectionality. *Social Science & Medicine, 74,* 1712–1720. doi:10.1016/j.socscimed.2011.11.029

Hankivksy, O., Grace, D., Hunting, G., Giesbrecht, M., Fridkin, A., Rudrum, S., . . . Clark, N. (2014). An intersectionality-based policy analysis framework: Critical reflections on a methodology for advancing equity. *International Journal for Equity in Health, 13*(1), 50–78. doi:10.1186/s12939-014-0119-x

Happell, B., Dwyer, T., Reid-Searl, K., Burke, K. J., Caperchione, C. M., & Gaskin, C. J. (2013). Nurses and stress: Recognizing causes and seeking solutions. *Journal of Nursing Management, 21*(4), 638–647.

Hardey, M. (2008). e-Health: The Internet and the transformation of patients into consumers and producers of health knowledge. In L. C. Lederman (Ed.), *Beyond these walls: Readings in health communication* (pp. 154–164). New York: Oxford University Press.

Harkness, E. L., Mullan, B. M., & Blaszczynski, A. (2015). Association between pornography use and sexual risk behaviors in adult consumers: a systematic review. *Cyberpsychology, Behavior and Social Networking, 18*(2), 59–71.

Harres, A. (2008). "But basically you're feeling well, are you?" Tag questions in medical consultations. In L. C. Lederman (Ed.), *Beyond these walls: Readings in health communication* (pp. 49–57). New York: Oxford University Press.

Harrington, N. G., Norling, G. R., Witte, F. M., Taylor, J., & Andrews, J. E. (2007). The effects of communication skills training on pediatricians' and parents' communication during "sick child" visits. *Health Communication, 21,* 105–114.

Harrison, K. (2005). Is "fat free" good for me? A panel study of television viewing and children's nutritional knowledge and reasoning. *Health Communication, 17,* 117–132.

Hart, C. N., Kelleher, K. J., Drotar, D., & Scholle, S. H. (2007). Parent–provider communication and parental satisfaction with care of children with psychosocial problems. *Parent Education and Counseling, 68*, 179–185.

Hart, J. L., & Walker, K. L. (2008). Communicating health beliefs and practices. In K. B. Wright & S. D. Moore (Eds.), *Applied health communication* (pp. 125–142). Cresskill, NJ: Hampton Press.

Harter, L. M. (2009). Narratives as dialogic, contested, and aesthetic performances. *Journal of Applied Communication Research, 37*, 140–150.

Hartzband, P., & Groopman, J. (2008). Off the record: Avoiding the pitfalls of going electronic. *New England Journal of Medicine, 358*(16), 1656.

Harwood, J., & Sparks, L. (2003). Social identity and health: An intergroup communication approach to cancer. *Health Communication, 15*, 145–159.

Haskard, K. B., Williams, S. L., DiMatteo, R., Rosenthal, R., White, M. K., & Goldstein, M. G. (2008). Physician and patient communication training in primary care: Effects on participation and satisfaction. *Health Psychology, 27*(5), 513–522.

Haskell, H., Mannix, M. E., James, J. T., & Mayer, D. (2012). Parents and families as partners in the care of pediatric cardiology patients. *Progress in Pediatric Cardiology, 33*, 67–72.

Hatch, J., & Clinton, A. (2000). Job growth in the 1990s: A retrospect. *Monthly Labor Review* online. Retrieved from http://www.bls.gov/opub/mlr/2000/12/art1full.pdf

Hawkley, L. C., Masi, C. M., Berry, J. D., & Cacioppo, J. T. (2006). Loneliness is a unique predictor of age-related differences in systolic blood pressure. *Psychology and Aging, 21*(1), 152–164.

Health care delivery, quality and transformation. (2015). American Telemedicine Association. Retrieved from http://www.americantelemed.org/ata-2015/ata-2015-awards#.VWI9JVnBzGd

Health economics: Soaring healthcare premiums seen as threat to managed care. (2003, July 14). *Health & Medicine Week*, p. 56.

Health expenditures per capita. (2009). Henry J. Kaiser Family Foundation. Retrieved from http://www.globalhealthfacts.org/data/topic/map.aspx?ind=66

Health insurance coverage of the total population. (2013). Henry J. Kaiser Family Foundation. Retrieved from http://www.statehealthfacts.org/comparetable.jsp?ind=125&cat=3

Health Privacy Project. (2003). Myths and facts about the HIPAA privacy rule. U.S. Department of Health and Human Services. Retrieved from www.healthprivacy.org

Heath, C. (2006). Body work: The collaborative production of the clinical object. In J. Heritage & D. W. Maynard (Eds.), *Communication in medical care: Interactions between primary care physicians and patients* (pp. 184–213). Cambridge: Cambridge University Press.

Hegedus, K., Zana, Á., & Szabó, B. (2008). Effect of end-of-life education on medical students' and health care workers' death attitude. *Palliative Medicine, 22*, 264–269.

Heldman, C. (2014, Feburary 9). The sexy lie. TEDxYouth. Retrieved from http://everydayfeminism.com/2014/02/the-sexy-lie/

Helme, D. W., Donohew, R. L., Baier, M., & Zittleman, L. (2007). A classroom-administered simulation of a television campaign on adolescent smoking: Testing an activation model of information exposure. *Journal of Health Communication, 12*, 399–415.

Helms, S. W., Choukas-Bradley, S., Widman, L., Giletta, M., Cohen, G. L., & Prinstein, M. J. (2014). Adolescents misperceive and are influenced by high-status peers' health risk, deviant, and adaptive behavior. *Developmental Psychology, 50*, 2697–2714.

Hendrich, A., Chow, M., Skierczynski, B. A., & Lu, Z. (2008). A 36-hospital time and motion study: How do medical-surgical nurses spend their time? *The Permanente Journal, 12*(3), 25–34.

Hendrix, K. S. (2015, March 9). What doctors should tell parents who are afraid of vaccines. *The Washington Post*. Retrieved from https://www.washingtonpost.com/posteverything/wp/2015/03/09/what-doctors-should-tell-parents-who-are-afraid-of-vaccines/

Hennessy, M., Romer, D., Valois, R. F., Vanable, P., Carey, M. P., Stanton, B., . . . Salazar, L. F. (2013). Safer sex media messages and adolescent sexual behavior: 3-year follow-up results from project iMPPACS. *American Journal of Public Health, 103*(1), 134–140.

Henrietta Lacks Foundation. (2015). Chicago, IL: Author. Retrieved from http://henriettalacksfoundation.org/

Henry J. Kaiser Family Foundation. (2008, January). Study finds television stations donate an average of 17 seconds an hour to public service advertising. Retrieved from http://www.kff.org/entmedia/entmedia012408pkg.cfm

Henry J. Kaiser Family Foundation. (2010, January 20). Generation M2: Media in the lives of 8- to 18-year-olds. Author: Menlo Park, CA. Retrieved from http://kff.org/other/event/generation-m2-media-in-the-lives-of/

Henry J. Kaiser Family Foundation. (2014). 2014 employer health benefits survey. Menlo Park, CA: Author. Retrieved from http://kff.org/health-costs/report/2014-employer-health-benefits-survey/

Henson, N. (2007). Mosquito-style communication. *Dental Assistant, 76*(3), 32–35.

Heritage, J., & Robinson, J. D. (2006). The structure of patients' presenting concerns: Physicians' opening questions. *Health Communication, 19*, 89–102.

Herman, A., & Jackson, P. (2010). Empowering low-income parents with skills to reduce excess pediatric emergency room and clinic visits through a tailored low literacy training intervention. *Journal of Health Communication, 15*, 895–910. doi:10.1080/10810730.2010.522228

Hermann, J. (2010, August 24). Giz explains: How blind people see the Internet. Gizmodo. Retrieved from http://gizmodo.com/5620079/giz-explains-how-blind-people-see-the-internet

Herzberg, F. (1968, January/February). One more time: How do you motivate employees again? *Harvard Business Review, 46*, 53–62.

Herzberg, F., Mausner, B., & Snyderman, B. B. (1959). *The motivation to work*. New York: Wiley.

Hesson, A. M., Sarinopoulos, I., Frankel, R. M., & Smith, R. C. (2012). A linguistic study of patient-centered interviewing: Emergent interactional effects. *Patient Education and Counseling, 88*, 373–380.

Hetsroni, A. (2009). If you must be hospitalized, television is not the place: Diagnoses, survival rates and demographic characteristics of patients in TV hospital dramas. *Communication Research Reports, 26*, 311–322.

HHS [Health and Human Services] study finds strong link between patient outcomes and nursing staffing in hospitals. (2001, April 20). Washington, DC: U.S. Department of Health and Human Services. Retrieved from newsroom.hrsa.gov

Hillier, D. (2006). *Communicating health risks to the public: A global perspective*. Burlington, VT: Gower.

Hills, R. (2015a, August 4). I failed at being a "sex object"—and became something so much hotter. The Blog. Retrieved from http://www.huffingtonpost.com/rachel-hills/failed-at-being-a-sex-object-and-became-something-hotter_b_7933376.html

Hills, R. (2015b). *The sex myth: The gap between our fantasies and reality*. New York: Simon & Schuster.

Himmelstein, D. U., Warren, E., Thorne, D., & Woolhandler, S. (2005, February 2). Market watch: Illness and injury as contributors to bankruptcy. *Health Affairs* Web Exclusive, w5–w73. Retrieved from http://content.healthaffairs.org/content/early/2005/02/02/hlthaff.w5.63.short

Hines, S. C. (2001). Coping with uncertainties in advance care planning. *Journal of Communication, 51*(3), 498–513.

Hinkelbein, J., Spelten, O., Marks, J., Hellmich, M., Böttiger, B. W., & Wetsch, W. A. (2014). Simulation and education: An assessment of resuscitation quality in the television drama Emergency Room: Guideline non-compliance and low-quality cardiopulmonary resuscitation lead to a favorable outcome? *Resuscitation, 85*, 1106–1110.

Hinton, L., Kurinczuk, J. J., & Ziebland, S. (2010). Infertility; isolation and the Internet: A qualitative interview study. *Patient Education and Counseling, 81*, 436–441.

Hirschmann, K. (2008). Blood, vomit, and communication: The days and nights of an intern on call. In L. C. Lederman (Ed.), *Beyond these walls: Readings in health communication* (pp. 58–73). New York: Oxford University Press.

History of public health. (2002). *Encyclopedia of public health*. Farmington Hills, MI: Gale Cengage.

Ho, D. (2002, January 18). Eli Lilly settles charges of violating the privacy of Prozac patients. Associated Press, Business News. Retrieved from LexisNexis.

Ho, E. Y. (2006). Behold the power of *Qi*: The importance of *Qi* in the discourse of acupuncture. *Research on Language and Social Interaction, 39*(4), 411–440.

Ho, E. Y., & Bylund, C. L. (2008). Models of health and models of interaction in the practitioner–client relationship in acupuncture. *Health Communication, 23*, 506–515.

Hofstede, G. (2001). *Culture's consequences: Comparing values, behaviors, institutions, and organizations across nations* (2nd ed.). Thousand Oaks, CA: Sage.

Holland, J. C., & Zittoun, R. (1990). Psychosocial issues in oncology: A historical perspective. In J. C. Holland & R. Zittoun (Eds.), *Psychosocial aspects of oncology* (pp. 1–10). New York: Springer-Verlag.

Holland, J. J. (2014, September 16). Blacks, Hispanics have doubts about media accuracy. *AP*. Retrieved from http://bigstory.ap.org/article/blacks-hispanics-have-doubts-about-media-accuracy

Holmes, O. W. (1891). *Medical essays: 1842–1882*. Boston: Houghton Mifflin.

Holohan, J., & Chen, V. (2011, December). Changes in health insurance coverage in the great recession, 2007–2010. Menlo Park, CA: Kaiser Commission on Medicaid and the Uninsured. Retrieved from http://www.kff.org/uninsured/upload/8264.pdf

Holtgrave, D. R., Tinsley, B. J., & Kay, L. S. (1995). Encouraging risk reduction: A decision-making approach to message design. In E. Maibach & R. L. Parrott (Eds.), *Designing health messages: Approaches from communication theory and public health practice* (pp. 24–40). Thousand Oaks, CA: Sage.

Holton, A., & Love, B. (2013). Lonely no more: Remembering text messaging in mHealth conversations. *Health Communication, 28*, 530–532. doi:10.1080/10410236.2012.713776

Hong, S. G., Kim, D. W., Trimi, S., & Hyun, J. H. (2015). A Delphi study of factors hindering web accessibility for persons with disabilities. *Journal of Computer Information Systems, 55*(4), 28–34.

Horowitz, A. M., Wang, M. Q., & Kleinman, D. V. (2012). Opinions of Maryland adults regarding communication practices of dentists and staff. *Journal of Health Communication, 17*(10), 1204–1214.

Horstmann, S. (2013, September 13). When nurses bond with their patients [Blog post]. *Well*. Retrieved from http://well.blogs.nytimes.com/2013/09/13/when-nurses-bond-with-their-patients/?_r=0

Horvath, K. J., Harwood, E. M., Courtenay-Quirk, C., McFarlane, M., Fisher, H., Dickenson, T., . . . Simon Rosser, B. R. (2010). Online resources for persons recently diagnosed with HIV/AIDS: An analysis of HIV-related webpages. *Journal of Health Communication, 15*, 516–531.

Hospice care in America. (2012). National Hospice and Palliative Care Organization. Alexandria, VA: Author. Retrieved from http://www.nhpco.org/sites/default/files/public/Statistics_Research/2011_Facts_Figures.pdf

Hospitals in the red. (1947, November 24,). *Time, L*(21), nonpaginated online version. Retrieved from http://www.time.com/time/magazine/article/0,9171,887776,00.html

Hou, J., & Shim, M. (2010). The role of provider-patient communication and trust in online sources in Internet use of health-related activities. *Journal of Health Communication, 15*, 186–199.

Hovick, S. R., Liang, M., & Kahlor, L. (2014). Predicting cancer risk knowledge and information seeking: The role of social and cognitive factors. *Health Communication, 29*, 656. doi:10.1080/10410236.2012.763204

How, S. K. H., Fryer, A.-K., McCarthy, D., Schoen, C., & Schor, E. L. (2011, February). Securing a healthy future: The Commonwealth Fund State Scorecard on Health System Performance. Retrieved from http://www.commonwealthfund.org/~/media/Files/Publications/Fund%20Report/2011/Feb/Child%20Health%20Scorecard/1468_How_securing_a_healthy_future_state_scorecard_child_hlt_sys_performance_2011_web_final_v8.pdf

Hoy, W. (2003). Shared decision making: The Hoy-Tarter Simplified Model. PowerPoint available at http://www.waynekhoy.com/shared_dm_model.html

Hoy, W. K., & Tarter, C. J. (2008). *Administrators solving the problems of practice: Decision-making cases, concepts, and consequence* (3rd ed.). Boston: Allyn & Bacon.

Hrisanfow, E., & Hägglund, D. (2013). Impact of cough and urinary incontinence on quality of life in women and men with chronic obstructive pulmonary disease. *Journal of Clinical Nursing, 22*(1/2), 97–105. doi:10.1111/j.1365-2702.2012.04143.x

Hsiao, W. C., Knight, A. G., Kappel, S., & Done, N. (2011). What other states can learn from Vermont's bold experiment: Embracing a single-payer health care financing system. *Health Affairs, 30*, 1232–1241.

Hubbell, A. P. (2006). Mexican American women in a rural area and barriers to their ability to enact protective behaviors against breast cancer. *Health Communication, 20*, 35–44.

Hufford, D. J. (1997). Gender, culture and experience: A painful case. *Southern Folklore, 54*, 114–123.

Hullett, C. R. (2006). Using functional theory to promote HIV testing: The impact of value-expressive messages, uncertainty, and fear. *Health Communication, 20*, 57–67.

Human genome project information. (2008). Website sponsored by the U.S. Department of Energy Office of Science, Office of Biological and Environmental Research, & Human Genome Program. Retrieved from http://www.ornl.gov/sci/techresources/Human_Genome/home.shtml

Hummert, M. L., & Mazloff, D. C. (2001). Older adults' responses to patronizing advice. *Journal of Language & Social Psychology, 20*(1/2), 167–196.

Hummert, M. L., & Shaner, J. L. (1994). Patronizing speech to the elderly as a function of stereotyping. *Communication Studies, 45*, 145–158.

Hust, S. J. T., Brown, J. D., & L'Engle, K. L. (2008). Boys will be boys and girls better be prepared: An analysis of the rare sexual health messages in young adolescents' media. *Mass Communication and Society, 11*(1), 3–23.

Hutch, R. (2013). Health and healing: Spiritual, pharmaceutical, and mechanical medicine. *Journal of Religion & Health, 52*(3), 955–965. doi:10.1007/s10943-011-9545-x

Huvane, K. (2008, October). Quick check-in: Kiosks are emerging as a potentially "easy win" that can increase patient satisfaction and improve staff efficiency. *Healthcare Informatics, 25*(10), 22–29.

Imes, R. S., Bylund, C. L., Sabee, C. M., Routsong, T. R., & Sanford, A. A. (2008). Patients' reasons for refraining from discussing Internet health information with their healthcare providers. *Health Communication, 23*, 538–547.

Improving Americans' health literacy. (2011, January). T. H. Chan School of Public Health at Harvard University. Retrieved from http://www.hsph.harvard.edu/news/multimedia-article/healthliteracy/

Inbar, M. (2009). Is PSA about driving while texting too graphic? NBCNews. Retrieved from http://www.today.com/id/32551351/ns/today-money/t/psa-about-texting-while-driving-too-graphic/#.VZL0gxNViko

Indian Health Service. (n.d.). Cross culture medicine. Rockville, MD: Author: Retrieved from http://www.ihs.gov/navajo/index.cfm?module=nao_cross_culture_medicine

Information and communication technology facts and figures. (2011, December). International Telecommunication Union /Information and Communication Technology database. Author: Geneva, Switzerland. Retrieved from http://www.itu.int/ITU-D/ict/statistics/

In her own words. (2004). Commentary about *The most dangerous woman in America* [video documentary], Nancy Porter (Writer/Director). NOVA in association with WGBH/Boston. Retrieved from http://www.pbs.org/wgbh/nova/typhoid

Innovations in health care. (n.d.) Miron Healthcare Services. Retrieved from http://miron-construction.com/wp-content/files/2012/11/50InspiringHCIdeas.pdf

Internet surveys. (2008). In P. J. Lavrakas (Ed.), *Encyclopedia of survey research methods* (p. 356–359). Thousand Oaks, CA: Sage

Iverson, K. (1997). *Plain talk: Lessons from a business maverick*. Somerset, NJ: John Wiley & Sons.

Jackson, K. T. (2004). *Building reputational capital: Strategies for integrity and fair play that improve the bottom line*. Oxford: Oxford University Press.

Jadad, A. R., & Rizo, C. A. (2003). I am a good patient believe it or not. *British Medical Journal, 326*(7402), 1293–1294.

Jahns, R.-G. (2013, March 7). The market for mHealth app services will reach $26 billion by 2017. Research2Guidance. Retrieved from http://research2guidance.com/the-market-for-mhealth-app-services-will-reach-26-billion-by-2017/

Jain, P., & Slater, M. D. (2013). Provider portrayals and patient–provider communication in drama and reality medical entertainment television shows. *Journal of Health Communication,18*(6), 703–722.

James, A. S., Hall, S., Greiner, K. A., Buckles, D., Born, W. K., & Ahluwalia, J. S. (2008). The impact of socioeconomic status on perceived barriers to colorectal cancer testing. *American Journal of Health Promotion, 23*(2), 97–100.

James, J. T. (2013). A new, evidence-based estimate of patient harms associated with hospital care. *Journal of Patient Safety, 9*(3), 122–128.

James, S. D. (2011, June 9). Honeymoon with Viagra could be over. ABC News. Retrieved from http://abcnews.go.com/Health/viagra-prescription-sales-sexual-expectations/story?id=13794726#.T_by6BzHSCA

Jamieson, P. E., & Romer, D. (2014). Violence in popular U.S. prime time TV dramas and the cultivation of fear: A time series analysis. *Media and Communication, 2*, 31–41.

Jang, S. A., Rimal, R. N., & Cho, N. (2013). Normative influences and alcohol consumption: The role of drinking refusal self-efficacy. *Health Communication, 28*, 443–451.

Jangland, E., Gunningberg, L., & Carlsson, M. (2009). Patients' and relatives' complaints about encounters and communication in health care: Evidence for quality improvement. *Patient Education and Counseling, 75*, 199–204.

Janis, I. (1972). *Victims of groupthink* (2nd ed.). Boston: Houghton Mifflin.

Jauhar, S. (2008a, June 17). Eyes bloodshot, doctors vent their frustration. *New York Times*, Late Edition, Section F, Science Desk Essay, p. 5.

Jauhar, S. (2008b). *Intern: A doctor's initiation*. New York: Farrar, Straus and Giroux.

Jenkins, H. S. (2008, February 15). Patients love my broken Spanish: This determined ER physician taught himself a second language so he could communicate with all his patients. *Medical Economics*, 85(4), 42–43.

Jenkins, M. (2012, May 31). "Pink ribbons," tied up with more than hope. National Public Radio. Retrieved from http://www.npr.org/2012/05/31/153912165/pink-ribbons-tied-up-with-more-than-hope

Jensen, J. D., King, A. J., Guntzviller, L. M., & Davis, L. A. (2010). Patient–provider communication and low-income adults: Age, race, literacy, and optimism predict communication satisfaction. *Patient Education and Counseling, 79*, 30–35.

Jensen, J. D., Moriarty, C. M., Hurley, R. J., & Stryker, J. (2010). Making sense of cancer news coverage trends: A comparison of three comprehensive content analyses. *Journal of Health Communication, 15*, 136–151. doi:10.1080/10810730903528025

Jeong, S.-H. (2007). Effects of news about genetics and obesity on controllability attribution and helping behavior. *Health Communication, 22*, 221–228.

Jessica's story. (n.d.). Memorial Sloan Kettering Cancer Center. Retrieved from https://www.mskcc.org/experience/hear-from-patients/jessica-tar

Jobes, M., & Steinbinder, A. (1996). Transitions in nursing leadership roles. *Nursing Administration Quarterly, 20*, 80–84.

Johnson, D. (2006, November.) Risk communication in the fog of disaster. Lessons from ground zero. *Industrial Safety & Hygiene News, 40*(11), 58, 60, 62.

Johnson, L. J. (2007, August 3). Patient e-mail perils. *Medical Economics, 84*(15), 30.

Johnston, L. D., O'Malley, P. M., Miech, R. A., Bachman, J. G., & Schulenberg, J. E. (2014). Monitoring the future national results on drug use: 1975–2013: Overview, key findings on adolescent drug use. Institute for Social Research at the University of Michigan. Retrieved from http://www.monitoringthefuture.org/pubs/monographs/mtf-overview2013.pdf

Jones, D., Gill, P., Harrison, R., Meakin, R., & Wallace, P. (2003). An exploratory study of language interpretation services provided by videoconferencing. *Journal of Telemedicine and Telecare, 9*(1), 51–56.

Jones, K. O., Denham, B. E., & Springston, J. K. (2007). Differing effects of mass and interpersonal communication on breast cancer risk estimates: An exploratory study of college students and their mothers. *Health Communication, 21*, 165–175.

Jones, R. K., & Biddlecom, A. E. (2011). Is the Internet filling the sexual health information gap for teens? An exploratory study. *Journal of Health Communication, 16*, 112–123.

Joy, S. V. (2008). Clinical pearls and strategies to optimize patient outcomes. *The Diabetes Educator, 34*, 54S–59S.

Julliard, K., Vivar, J., Delgado, C., Cruz, E., Kabak, J., & Sabers, H. (2008). What Latina patients don't tell their doctors: A qualitative study. *Annals of Family Medicine, 6*(6), 543–549.

Junghans, A. F., Cheung, T. L., & De Ridder, D. T. (2015). Under consumers' scrutiny—An investigation into consumers' attitudes and concerns about nudging in the realm of health behavior. *BMC Public Health, 15*(1), 1–13.

Kaiser Family Foundation and Pew Research Center's Project for Excellence in Journalism. (2008, December). *Health news coverage in the U.S. media. January 2007–June 2008*. Retrieved from http://www.journalism.org/files/HealthNewsReportFinal.pdf

Kakai, H. (2002). A double standard in bioethical reasoning for disclosure of advanced cancer diagnosis in Japan. *Health Communication, 14*, 361–376.

Kaplan, R. M. (1997). Health outcomes and communication research. *Health Communication, 9*, 75–82.

Katz, E., Blumler, J., & Gurevitch, M. (1974). Uses of mass communication by the individual. In J. G. Blumler & E. Katz (Eds.), *The uses of mass communication* (pp. 19–32). Newbury Park, CA: Sage.

Katz, J. (1984). *The silent world of doctor and patient*. New York: Free Press.

Katz, J. (1995). Informed consent: Ethical and legal issues. In J. D. Arras & B. Steinbock (Eds.), *Ethical issues in modern medicine* (4th ed., pp. 87–97). Mountain View, CA: Mayfield.

Kealey, E., & Berkman, C. S. (2010). The relationship between health information sources and mental models of cancer: Findings of the 2005 Health Information National Trends Survey. *Journal of Health Communication, 15*, 236–251.

Kean, L. G., & Prividera, L. C. (2007). Communicating about race and health: A content analysis of print advertisements in African American and general readership magazines. *Health Communication, 21*, 289–297.

Kean, S. (2012). *The violinist's thumb: And other lost tales of love, war, and genius, as written by our genetic code*. New York: Back Bay Books.

Kearney, M. (1978). Spiritualistic healing in Mexico. In P. Morley & R. Wallis (Eds.), *Culture and curing* (pp. 19–39). Pittsburgh: University of Pittsburgh Press.

Keeley, M. P. (2004). Final conversations: Survivors' memorable messages concerning religious faith and spirituality. *Health Communication, 16,* 87–104.

Keller, P. A., & Lehmann, D. R. (2008). Designing effective health communications: A meta-analysis. *American Marketing Association, 27,* 117–130.

Kennedy, J., Chi-Chuan, W., & Wu, C.-H. (2007, May 17). Patient disclosure about herb and supplement use and adults in the US. *eCam*, pp. 1–6.

Kenney, C. (2010). *Transforming health care: Virginia Mason Medical Center's pursuit of the perfect patient experience.* New York: Taylor & Francis.

Keyhani, S., & Federman, A. (2009). Doctors on coverage—physicians' views on a new public insurance option and Medicare expansion. *The New England Journal of Medicine, 361*(14), e24. doi:10.1056/NEJMp0908239

Kilbourne, J. (2000). *Killing us softly 3: Advertising's image of women.* North Hampton, MA: Media Education Foundation.

Kim, H. (2011). Pharmaceutical companies as a source of health information: A pilot study of the effects of source, web site interactivity, and involvement. *Health Marketing Quarterly, 28,* 57–85.

Kim, H. J. (2014). The impacts of vicarious illness experience on response to gain- versus loss-framed breast cancer screening (BCS) messages. *Health Communication, 29,* 854–865.

Kim, J. (2014). Mobile health platforms take sides in the operating system fight. TechTarget. Retrieved from http://searchhealthit.techtarget.com/tip/Mobile-health-platforms-take-sides-in-the-operating-system-fight

Kim, K., & Kwon, N. (2010). Profile of e-patients: Analysis of their cancer information-seeking from a national survey. *Journal of Health Communication, 15,* 712–733.

Kim, S.-H., & Willis, L. A. (2007, June). Talking about obesity: News framing of who is responsible for causing and fixing the problem. *Journal of Health Communication, 12,* 359–376.

Kim, Y.-C. & Ball-Rokeach, S. J. (2006). Civic engagement from a communication infrastructure perspective. *Communication Theory, 16,* 173–197.

Kim, Y.-C., Jung, J.-Y., & Ball-Rokeach, S. J. (2006). "Geo-ethnicity" and neighborhood engagement: A communication infrastructure perspective. *Political Communication, 23*(4), 421–441.

King, S. (2010). Pink diplomacy: On the uses and abuses of breast cancer awareness. *Health Communication, 25,* 286–289.

Kirkham, S. R. (2003). The politics of belonging and intercultural health care. *Western Journal of Nursing Research, 7,* 762.

Kirsch, A. C., & Murnen, S. K. (2015). "Hot" girls and "cool dudes": Examining the prevalence of the heterosexual script in American children's television media. *Psychology of Popular Media Culture, 4*(1), 18–30.

Kisa, K., Kawabata, H., Itou, T., Nishimoto, N., & Maezawa, M. (2011). Survey of patient and physician satisfaction regarding patient-centered outpatient consultations in Japan. *Internal Medicine, 50*(13), 1403–1410.

Klass, P. (1987). *A not entirely benign procedure: Four years as a medical student.* New York: Penguin.

Kleinman, A., Eisenberg, L., & Good, B. (1978). Culture, illness, and care: Clinical lessons from anthropological and cross-cultural research. *Annals of Internal Medicine, 88,* 251–258.

Knight-Agarwal, C. R., Kaur, M., Williams, L. T., Davey, R., & Davis, D. (2014). The views and attitudes of health professionals providing antenatal care to women with a high BMI: A qualitative research study. *Women and Birth, 27,* 138–144.

Knobloch-Westerwick, S., & Alter, S. (2006). Mood adjustment to social situations through mass media use: How men ruminate and women dissipate angry moods. *Human Communication Research, 32*(1), 58–73.

Koch-Weser, S., Bradshaw, Y, S., Gualtieri, L., & Gallagher, S. S. (2010). The Internet as a health information source: Findings from the 2007 Health Information National Trends Survey and Implications for health communication. *Journal of Health Communication, 15,* 279–293.

Koermer, C. D., & Kilbane, M. (2008). Physician sociality communication and its effect on patient satisfaction. *Communication Quarterly, 56,* 69–86.

Koh, G. C., Khoo, H. E., Wong, M. L., & Koh, D. (2008). The effects of problem-based learning during medical school on physician competency: A systematic review. *Canadian Medical Association Journal, 178*(1), 34–41.

Komaroff, A. L., & Fagioli, J. (1996). *Medical assessment of fatigue and chronic fatigue syndrome: An integrative approach to evaluation and treatment* (pp. 154–181). New York: Guilford Press.

Kopfman, J. E., & Ray, E. B. (2005). Talking to children about illness. In E. B. Ray (Ed.), *Health communication in practice: A case study approach* (pp. 111–119). Mahwah, NJ: Lawrence Erlbaum.

Korsch, D. M., & Negrete, V. F. (1972). Doctor–patient communication. *Scientific American, 227,* 66–74.

Koszalinski, R. S., & Williams, C. (2012). Embodying identity in chemotherapy-induced alopecia. *Perspectives in Psychiatric Care, 48,* 116–121.

Kotler, P., & Zaltman, G. (1971). Social marketing: An approach to planned social change. *Journal of Marketing, 35*(3), 3–12.

Koven, S. (2012, June 29). Marriage equality, in sickness and in health. BostonGlobe.com. Retrieved from http://www.boston.com/lifestyle/health/2012/06/24/marriage-equality-sickness-and-health/MwK6A6R0iQxTlT4iMdJ3sI/story.html

Kowalski, K. M. (1997, October). On guard against health rip-off. *Current Health, 24,* 6–11.

Krajewski, L. A., & Beach Slatten, T. (2013). The changing roles of Japanese women in the Japanese business world. *Business Studies Journal, 5*(1), 29–41.

Kramer, H., & Kramer, K. Conversations at midnight. (1993, March–April). *Psychology Today, 26,* 26–27.

Kramer, J., Boon, B., Schotanus-Dijkstra, M., van Ballegooijen, W., Kerkhof, A., & van der Poel, A. (2015).

The mental health of visitors of web-based support forums for bereaved by suicide. *Crisis: The Journal of Crisis Intervention and Suicide Prevention, 36*(1), 38–45.

Kreps, G. L. (1988). Relational communication in health care. *Southern Speech Communication Journal, 53*, 344–359.

Kreps, G. L. (1990). Applied health communication research. In D. O'Hair & G. L. Kreps (Eds.), *Applied communication theory and research* (pp. 313–330). Hillsdale, NJ: Lawrence Erlbaum.

Kreps, G. L. (2005). Narrowing the digital divide to overcome disparities in care. In E. B. Ray (Ed.), *Health communication in practice: A case study approach* (pp. 357–364). Mahwah, NJ: Lawrence Erlbaum.

Kreps, G. L., Query, J. L., Jr., & Bonaguro, E. W. (2008). In L. C. Lederman (Ed.), *Beyond these walls: Readings in health communication* (pp. 3–14). New York: Oxford University Press.

Kreps, G. L., & Thornton, B. C. (1992). *Health communication: Theory & practice* (2nd ed.). Prospect Heights, IL: Waveland Press.

Krieger, J. L., Coveleski, S., Hecht, M. L., Miller-Day, M., Graham, J. W., Pettigrew, J., & Kootsikas, A. (2013). From kids, through kids, to kids: Examining the social influence strategies used by adolescents to promote prevention among peers. *Health Communication, 28*, 683–695.

Kroll, T., Beatty, P. W., & Bingham, S. (2003). Primary care satisfaction among adults with physical disabilities: The role of patient–provider communication. *Managed Care Quarterly, 11*(1), 11–19.

Krosnick, J. A., Chang, L., Sherman, S. J., Chassin, L., & Presson, C. (2006). The effects of beliefs about the health consequences of cigarette smoking on smoking onset. *Journal of Communication, 56*, S18–S37.

Krug, P. (1998). Where does physician-assisted suicide stand today? *Association of Operating Room Nurses Journal, 68*, 869.

Krupa, C. (2012, November 19). TV doctors' portrayal evolves from saintly to human. AMEDnews.com. Retrieved from http://www.amednews.com/article/20121119/profession/311199949/4/

Kübler-Ross, E. (1969). *On death and dying.* New York: Macmillan.

Kulich, K. R., Berggren, U., & Hallberg, I, R.-M. (2003). A qualitative analysis of patient-centered dentistry in consultations with dental phobic patients. *Journal of Health Communication, 8*, 171–187.

Kumar, R., Warnke, J. H., & Karabenick, S. A. (2014). Arab-American male identity negotiations: Caught in the crossroads of ethnicity, religion, nationality and current contexts. *Social Identities, 20*(1), 22–41.

Kundrat, A. L., & Nussbaum, J. F. (2003). The impact of invisible illness on identity and contextual age. *Health Communication, 15*, 331–347.

Kush, R. D., Helton, E., Rockhold, F. W., & Hardison, C. D. (2008). Electronic health records, medical research, and the Tower of Babel. *New England Journal of Medicine, 358*, 1738.

Kyrrestad Strøm, H., Adolfsen, F., Fossum, S., Kaiser, S., & Martinussen, M. (2014). Effectiveness of school-based preventive interventions on adolescent alcohol use: A meta-analysis of randomized controlled trials. *Substance Abuse Treatment, Prevention & Policy, 9*(1), no pagination specified.

The Lacks family [blog]. (2012). Retrieved from http://www.lacksfamily.net/.

Laframboise, D. (1998). When home is the hospital. *Chatelaine, 71*, 26–31.

Laine, C., & Davidoff, F. (1996). Patient-centered medicine: A professional evolution. *Journal of the American Medical Association, 275*, 152–155.

Lambert, B. L., Street, R. L., Cegala, D. J., Smith, D. H., Kurtz, S., & Schofield, T. (1997). Provider–patient communication, patient-centered care, and the mangle of practice. *Health Communication, 9*, 27–43.

Lang, A. (2006). Using the limited-capacity model of motivated mediated message processing to design effective cancer communication messages. *Journal of Communication, 56*, S57–S80.

Lang, A., Chung, Y., Lee, S., & Zhao, X. (2005). It's the product: Do risky products compel attention and elicit arousal in media users? *Health Communication, 17*, 283–300.

Lang, A., Schwartz, N., Lee, S., & Angelini, J. R. (2007, September). Processing radio PSAs: Production pacing, arousing content, and age. *Journal of Health Communication, 12*, 581–599.

Lansdale, D. (2002). Touching lives: Opening doors for elders in retirement communities through e-mail and the Internet. In R. W. Morrell (Ed.), *Older adults, health information, and the World Wide Web* (pp. 133–151). Mahwah, NJ: Lawrence Erlbaum.

Lapinski, M. K., Rimal, R. N., DeVries, R., & Lee, E. L. (2007). The role of group orientation and descriptive norms on water conservation and behaviors. *Health Communication, 22*, 133–142.

Lapowsky, I. (2014, April 1). Livestrong without Lance. *Moneybox.* http://www.slate.com/blogs/moneybox/2014/04/01/lance_armstrong_livestrong_how_the_charity_came_back_from_the_scandal.html

Larasi, I. (2013, September 2). Why do music videos portray black women as exotic sex objects? *The Guardian.* Retrieved from http://www.theguardian.com/lifeandstyle/the-womens-blog-with-jane-martinson/2013/sep/02/music-video-black-women-sex-objects

Larkin, M. (2014, October 27). Dr. Eric Topol: Digital healthcare will put the patient in charge. ElsevierConnect. Retrieved from http://www.elsevier.com/connect/Dr-Eric-Topol-Digital-healthcare-will-put-the-patient-in-charge

Lauer, C. S. (2008b, March 10). The unwritten curriculum. Writer: Medical students learn from elders' cynicism. *Modern Healthcare, 38*(10), 50.

LaVail, K. H. (2010). Coverage of older adults and HIV/AIDS: Risk information for an invisible population. *Communication Quarterly, 58*, 170–187.

Lavoie, N. R., & Quick, B. L. (2013). What is the truth? An application of the extended parallel process model to televised truth® ads. *Health Communication, 28*, 53–62.

Lazarsfeld, P., Burleson, B., & Gaudet, H. (1948). *The people's choice*. New York: Columbia University Press.

Lederman, L. C., & Stewart, L. P. (2005). *Changing the culture of college drinking: A socially situated health communication campaign*. Cresskill, NJ: Hampton Press.

Lederman, L. C., Stewart, L. P., Barr, S. L., Powell, R. L., Laitman, L., & Goodhart, F. W. (2001). Using communication theory to reduce dangerous drinking on a college campus. In R. E. Rice & C. K. Atkin (Eds.), *Public communication campaigns* (3rd ed., pp. 295–299). Thousand Oaks, CA: Sage.

Lederman, L. C., Stewart, L. P., Goodhart, F. W., & Laitman, L. (2008). A case against "binge" as the term of choice. In L. C. Lederman (Ed.), *Beyond these walls: Readings in health communication* (pp. 292–303). New York: Oxford University Press.

Lederman, L. C., Stewart, L. P., & Russ, T. L. (2007). Addressing college drinking through curriculum infusion: A study of the use of experience-based learning in the communication classroom. *Communication Education, 56*(4), 476–494.

Ledlow, G. R., Johnson, J. A., & Hakoyama, M. (2008). Social marketing and organizational efficacy. In K. B. Wright & S. D. Moore (Eds.), *Applied health communication* (pp. 85–103). Cresskill, NJ: Hampton Press.

Lee, A. (2010). Who are the opinion leaders? The physicians, pharmacists, patients, and direct-to-consumer prescription drug advertising. *Journal of Health Communication, 15*, 629–655. doi:10.1080/10810730.2010.499594

Lee, C., Ramírez, A. S., Lewis, N., Gray, S. W., & Hornik, R. C. (2012). Looking beyond the Internet: Examining socioeconomic inequalities in cancer information seeking among cancer patients. *Health Communication, 27*, 806–817. doi:10.1080/10410236.2011.647621

Lee, F. (2004). *If Disney ran your hospital: 9½ things you would do differently*. Bozeman, MT: Second River Healthcare Press.

Lee, J. Y., & Sundar, S. S. (2013). To tweet or to retweet? That is the question for health professionals on Twitter. *Health Communication, 28*, 509–524.

Lee, M. J. (2010). The effects of self-efficacy statements in humorous anti-alcohol abuse messages targeting college students: Who is in charge? *Health Communication, 25*, 638–646. doi:10.1080/10410236.2010.521908

Lee, M. J., & Bichard, S. L. (2006). Effective message design targeting college students for the prevention of binge-drinking: Basing design on rebellious risk-taking tendency. *Health Communication, 20*, 299–308.

Lee, S.-J. (2013). Parental restrictive mediation of children's Internet use: Effective for what and for whom? *New Media & Society, 15*(4), 466.

Lee, S. Y., & Hawkins, R. (2010). Why do patients seek an alternative channel? The effects of unmet needs on patients' health-related Internet use. *Journal of Health Communication, 15*, 152–166.

Lee, Y. J., Park, J., & Widdows, R. (2009). Exploring antecedents of consumer satisfaction and repeated search behavior on e-health information. *Journal of Health Communication, 14*, 160–173.

Lefebvre, C. (2009, October). Integrating cell phones and mobile technologies into public health practice: A social marketing perspective. *Health Promotion Practice, 10*, 490–494.

Lefebvre, R. C., Doner, L., Johnston, D., Loughrey, K., Balch, G. I., & Sutton, S. M. (1995). Use of database marketing and consumer-based health communication in message design: An example for the Office of Cancer Communications' "5 a Day for Better Health" program. In E. Maibach & R. L. Parrott (Eds.), *Designing health messages: Approaches from communication theory and public health practice* (pp. 217–246). Thousand Oaks, CA: Sage.

Lefebvre, R. C., & Flora, J. A. (1988). Social marketing and public health intervention. *Health Education Quarterly, 15*, 299–315.

Légaré, F., & Witteman, H. O. (2013). Shared decision making: examining key elements and barriers to adoption into routine clinical practice. *Health Affairs, 32*(2), 276–284.

Lehman, D. R., Ellard, J. H., & Wortman, C. B. (1986). Social support for the bereaved: Recipients' and providers' perspectives on what is helpful. *Journal of Consulting and Clinical Psychology, 54*, 438–446.

Leventhal, R. (2014, July-August). How a N.J. medical center saved millions with mHealth technology: A smartphone app has improved efficiency through better communications across the medical staff. *Healthcare Informatics*. Retrieved from http://www.healthcare-informatics.com/article/how-nj-medical-center-has-saved-millions-mhealth-technology

Levin, D. E., & Kilbourne, K. (2008). *So sexy so soon: The new sexualized childhood and what parents can do to protect their kids*. New York: Ballantine Books.

Levine, D. A. (2013). Office-based care for lesbian, gay, bisexual, transgender, and questioning youth. *Pediatrics, 132*(1), 198–203. doi:10.1542/peds.2013-1282

Levinsky, N. (1995). The doctor's master. In J. D. Arras & B. Steinbock (Eds.), *Ethical issues in modern medicine* (4th ed., pp. 116–119). Mountain View, CA: Mayfield.

Levy, B. R., Chung, P. H., Bedford, T., & Navrazhina, K. (2014). Facebook as a site for negative age stereotypes. *Gerontologist, 54*(2), 172–176.

Li, H. Z., Krysko, M., Desroches, N. G., & Deagle, G. (2004). Reconceptualizing interruptions in physician–patient interviews: Cooperative and intrusive. *Communication & Medicine, 1*(2), 145–157.

Lief, H. L., & Fox, R. C. (1963). Training for "detached concern" in medical students. In J. I. Lief, V. F. Lief, & N. R. Lief (Eds.), *The psychological basis of medical practice*. New York: Harper & Row.

"Life interrupted" by cancer diagnosis at 22. (2012, May 15). National Public Radio. *Talk of the Nation* broadcast. Transcript retrieved at http://www.npr.org/2012/05/16/152840031/life-interrupted-by-cancer-diagnosis-at-22

Lindberg, D. A. B. (2002). Older Americans, health information, and the Internet. In R. W. Morrell (Ed.), *Older adults, health information, and the World Wide Web* (pp. 13–19). Mahwah, NJ: Lawrence Erlbaum.

Lindley, L. L., Friedman, D. B., & Struble, C. (2012). Becoming visible: Assessing the availability of online sexual health information for lesbians. *Health Promotion Practice, 13*(4), 472. doi:10.1177/1524839910390314

Literat, I., & Chen, N. N. (2014). Communication infrastructure theory and entertainment-education: An integrative model for health communication. *Communication Theory. 24*(1), 83–103.

Littlefield, R. S., & Quenette, A. M. (2007, February). Crisis leadership and Hurricane Katrina: The portrayal of authority by the media in natural disasters. *Journal of Applied Communication Research, 35*(1), 26–47.

Living with cancer. (1997, September). *Harvard Health Letter, 22*, 4–5.

Lo, M.-C. M. (2010). Cultural brokerage: Creating linkages between voices of lifeworld and medicine in cross-cultural clinical settings. *Health: An Interdisciplinary Journal for the Social Study of Health, Illness & Medicine, 14*(5), 484–504.

Loane, S. S., & D'Alessandro, S. (2013). Communication that changes lives: Social support within an online health community for ALS. *Communication Quarterly, 61*(2), 236–251.

Lockwood, N. L., & Yoshimura, S. M. (2014). The heart of the matter: The effects of humor on well-being during recovery from cardiovascular disease. *Health Communication, 29*, 410–420.

Longino, C. F. (1997, December). Beyond the body: An emerging medical paradigm. *American Demographics, 19*, 14–18.

Lovell, B., Moss, M., & Wetherell, M. A. (2011). Perceived stress, common health complaints and diurnal patterns of cortisol secretion in young, otherwise healthy individuals. *Hormones and Behavior, 60*, 301–305.

Lovett, R. A. (2003, May–June). Fact versus fear: We worry too much about man-made catastrophe. *Psychology Today, 36*(3), 14.

Lowe, G., & Costabile, R. A. (2012). 10-year analysis of adverse event reports to the Food and Drug Administration for phosphodiesterase type-5 inhibitors. *Journal of Sexual Medicine, 9*, 265–270. doi: 10.1111/j.1743-6109.2011.02537

Lowes, R. (2008, May 2). Open access, extended hours: Seeing patients when they want to be seen helps you respond to their needs and stay competitive. *Medical Economics, 85*(9), 62–72.

Lowrey, W., & Anderson, W. B. (2006). The impact of Internet use on the public perception of physicians: A perspective from the sociology of professions literature. *Health Communication, 19*, 125–131.

Ludtke, M., & Trost, C. (1998). Covering children's health. *American Journalism Review, 20*, 81–88.

Lui, X., Sawada, Y., Takizawa, T., Sato, H., Sato, M., Sakamoto, H., . . . Sakamaki, T. (2007). Doctor-patient communication: A comparison between telemedicine consultation and face-to-face consultation. *Internal Medicine, 46*, 227–232.

Lumma-Sellenthin, A. (2009). Talking with patients and peers: Medical students' difficulties with learning communication skills. *Medical Teacher, 31*, 528–534.

Lund, C. C. (1995). The doctor, the patient, and the truth. In J. D. Arras & B. Steinbock (Eds.), *Ethical issues in modern medicine* (pp. 55–57). Mountain View, CA: Mayfield.

Lundine, K., Buckley, R., Hutchinson, C., & Lockyer, J. (2008). Communication skills training in orthopedics. *Journal of Bone and Joint Surgery, 90*(6), 1393–1400.

Lustria, M. A., Noar, S. M., Cortese, J., Van Stee, S. K., Glueckauf, R. L., & Lee, J. (2013). A meta-analysis of web-delivered tailored health behavior change interventions. *Journal of Health Communication, 18*, 1039–1069.

Lynch, T., & Martins, N. (2015). Nothing to fear? An analysis of college students' fear experiences with video games. *Journal of Broadcasting & Electronic Media, 59*(2), 298–317.

Lyon, A. (2007, November). "Putting patients first": Systematically distorted communication and Merck's marketing of Vioxx. *Journal of Applied Communication Research, 35*(4), 376–398.

MacDonald, M. (1981). *Mystical bedlam: Madness, anxiety, and healing in seventeenth-century England*. Cambridge: Cambridge University Press.

Macias, W., & McMillan, S. (2008). The return of the house call: The role of Internet-based interactivity in bringing health information home to older adults. *Health Communication, 23*, 34–44.

Macias, W., Pashupati, K., & Lewis, L. S. (2007). A wonderful life or diarrhea and dry mouth? Policy issues of direct-to-consumer drug advertising on television. *Health Communication, 22*, 241–252.

Mackert, M., Donovan, E. E., Mabry, A., Guadagno, M., & Stout, P. A. (2014). Stigma and health literacy: An agenda for advancing research and practice. *American Journal of Health Behavior, 38*(5), 690–698. doi:10.5993/AJHB.38.5.6

MacLellan, D. L., & Lordly, D. (2008). The socialization of dietetic students: Influence of the preceptor role. *Journal of Allied Health, 37*(2), E81–E92.

Madanikia, Y., & Bartholomew, K. (2014). Themes of lust and love in popular music lyrics from 1971 to 2011. *Sage Open*. Retrieved from //sgo.sagepub.com/content/spsgo/4/3/2158244014547179.full.pdf

Mad cows and the minister. (1990, May 24). *Nature, 345*, 277–278.

Madden, M., Lenhart, A., Duggan, M., Cortesi, S., & Gasser, U. (2013, March 13). Teens and technology 2013. Pew Research Center's Internet & American Life Project. Retrieved from http://www.pewinternet.org/files/old-media/Files/Reports/2013/PIP_TeensandTechnology2013.pdf

Magee, M., & D'Antonio, M. (2003). *The best medicine: Stories of doctors and patients who care for each other* (2nd ed.). New York: Spencer Books.

Mahler, H. I. M., Kulik, J. A., Butler, H. A., Gerrard, M., & Gibbons, F. X. (2008). Social norms information enhances the efficacy of an appearance-based sun protection intervention. *Social Science & Medicine, 67*, 321–329.

Mahomed, R., St. John, W., & Patterson, E. (2012). Understanding the process of patient satisfaction with nurse-led chronic disease management in general practice. *Journal of Advanced Nursing, 68*(11), 2538–2549.

Mahon, M., & Weymouth, J. (2012, May 3). U.S. spends far more for health care than 12 industrialized nations, but quality varies. The Commonwealth Fund. Retrieved from http://www.commonwealthfund.org/News/News-Releases/2012/May/US-Spends-Far-More-for-Health-Care-Than-12-Industrialized-Nations-but-Quality-Varies.aspx

Maier, J. A., Gentile, D. A., Vogel, D. L., & Kaplan, S. A. (2014). Media influences on self-stigma of seeking psychological services: The importance of media portrayals and person perception. *Psychology of Popular Media Culture, 3*(4), 239–256.

Makarem, S. C., Smith, M. F., Mudambi, S. M., & Hunt, J. M. (2014). Why people do not always follow the doctor's orders: The role of hope and perceived control. *Journal of Consumer Affairs, 48*(3), 457–485.

Maibach, E. W., & Parrott, R. L. (Eds.). (1995). *Designing health messages*. Thousand Oaks, CA: Sage.

Malinski, V. M. (Ed.). (1986). *Explorations on Martha Rogers' science of unitary human beings*. Norwalk, CT: Appleton-Century-Crofts.

Malis, R. S., & Roloff, M. E. (2007). The effect of legitimacy and intimacy on peer interventions into alcohol abuse. *Western Journal of Communication*, 71(1), 49–68.

Manfredi, C., Kaiser, K., Matthews, A. K., & Johnson, T. P. (2010). Are racial differences in patient-physician cancer communication and information explained by background, predisposing, and enabling factors? *Journal of Health Communication, 15*, 272–292. doi: 10.1080/10810731003686598

Mann, D. (2009). Electronic medical records: The promise. *Web*MD. Retrieved from http://www.webmd.com/health-insurance/technology-plays-key-role-in-health-care-reform

Marantz, P. R. (1990). Blaming the victim: The negative consequences of preventive medicine. *American Journal of Public Health*, *80*, 1186–1187.

Margonelli, L. (2010, February 5). Eternal life. Sunday book review. *The New York Times*. Retrieved from http://www.nytimes.com/2010/02/07/books/review/Margonelli-t.html?pagewanted=all&_r=0

Marion, G. S., Hildebrandt, C. A., Davis, S. W., Marin, A. J., & Crandall, S. J. (2008). Working effectively with interpreters: A model curriculum for physician assistant students. *Medical Teacher, 30*(6), 612–617.

Mars, R. (Producer). (2011, June 30). The blue yarn. *99% invisible* [podcast]. Distributed by Public Radio Exchange.

Martin, L. R., Williams, S. L., Haskard, K. B., & Dimatteo, M. R. (2005). The challenge of patient adherence. *Therapeutics and Clinical Risk Management, 1*(3), 189–199.

Marwick, C. (1997). Proponents gather to discuss evidence-based medicine. *Journal of the American Medical Association, 278*, 531–532.

Maslach, C. (1982). *Burnout: The cost of caring*. Englewood Cliffs, NJ: Prentice Hall.

Mast, M. S. (2007). On the importance of nonverbal communication in the physician–patient interaction. *Patient Education and Counseling, 67*(3), 315–318.

Mastin, T., Andsager, J. L., Choi, J., & Lee, K. (2007). Health disparities and direct-to-consumer prescription drug advertising: A content analysis of targeted magazine genres, 1992–2002. *Health Communication, 22*, 49–58.

Mathew: Surving lymphoma. (n.d.). Children's Cancer Research Fund. Retrieved from http://learn.childrenscancer.org/personal-stories.html

Matsaganis, M. D., Golden, A. G., & Scott, M. E. (2014). Communication infrastructure theory and reproductive health disparities: Enhancing storytelling network integration by developing interstitial actors. *International Journal of Communication*, 1495–1515.

Maxmen, A. (2015, January 30). How the fight against Ebola tested a culture's traditions. *National Geographic*. Retrieved from http://news.nationalgeographic.com/2015/01/150130-ebola-virus-outbreak-epidemic-sierra-leone-funerals/

Mayer, G., & Kuklierus, A. (1999). *What to do when your child gets sick*. La Habra, CA: Institute for Healthcare Advancement.

Mayer, T. A., & Cates, R. J. (2004). *Leadership for great customer service: Satisfied patients, satisfied employees*. Chicago: Health Administration Press.

Maynard, D. W., & Frankel, R. M. (2006). On diagnostic rationality: Bad news, good news, and the symptoms residue. In J. Heritage & D. W. Maynard (Eds.), *Communication in medical care: Interactions between primary care physicians and patients* (pp. 248–278). Cambridge: Cambridge University Press.

Mayo Clinic. (2015). Post-traumatic stress disorder (PTSD). Rochester, MN: Author. Retrieved from http://www.mayoclinic.org/diseases-conditions/post-traumatic-stress-disorder/basics/symptoms/con-20022540

McCague, J. J. (2001, May 21). On today's older patients. *Medical Economics, 78*(10), 104.

McCarley, P. (2009). Patient empowerment and motivational interviewing: Engaging patients to self-manage their own care. *Nephrology Nursing Journal, 36*(4), 409–413.

McCarthy, D., Hostetter, M., & Klein, S. (2015, June 3). "New rules" to guide health care redesign. The Commonwealth Fund. Retrieved from http://www.commonwealthfund.org/publications/blog/2015/jun/new-rules-guide-health-care-redesign

McComas, K. A. (2006). Defining moments in risk communication research: 1996–2005. *Journal of Health Communication, 11*, 75–91.

McConatha, D. (2002). Aging online: Toward a theory of e-equality. In R. W. Morrell (Ed.), *Older adults, health information, and the World Wide Web* (pp. 21–41). Mahwah, NJ: Lawrence Erlbaum.

McCormick, T. R., & Conley, B. J. (1995). Patients' perspectives on dying and the care of dying patients. *Western Journal of Medicine, 163*, 236–243.

McCreaddie, M., & Payne, S. (2012). Humour in health-care interactions: A risk worth taking. *Health Expectations, 17*(3), 332–344.

McCue, J. D. (1995). The naturalness of dying. *Journal of the American Medical Association, 273*, 1039–1044.

McCune, S. K., Beck, A. M., & Johnson, R. A. (2011). *The health benefits of dog walking for people and pets: Evidence and case studies*. West Lafayette, IN: Purdue University Press.

McGregor, D. (1960). *The human side of organization*. New York: McGraw-Hill.

McKinley, C. J., & Perino, C. (2013). Examining communication competence as a contributing factor in health care workers' job satisfaction and tendency to report errors. *Journal of Communication in Healthcare, 6*(3), 158–165.

McKnight, J. (2004). Sentinel disparity in health care: a uniquely unacceptable phenomenon. *Harvard Journal of African American Public Policy, 10*, 85–98.

McMullen, M., & Netland, P. A. (2013). Wait time as a driver of overall patient satisfaction in an ophthalmology clinic. *Clinical Ophthalmology, 7*, 1655.

McWhinney, I. (1989). The need for a transformed clinical method. In M. Stewart & D. Roter (Eds.), *Communicating with medical patients: Vol. 9. Interpersonal communication* (pp. 25–40). Newbury Park, CA: Sage.

Mead, E. L., Doorenbos, A. Z., Javid, S. H., Haozous, E. A., Arviso Alvord, L., Flum, D. R., & Morris, A. M. (2013). Shared decision-making for cancer care among racial and ethnic minorities: A systematic review. *American Journal of Public Health, 103*(12), e15–e29.

Mead, G. H. (1934). *Minds, self, and society*. Chicago: University of Chicago Press.

Measles outbreak traced to Disneyland is declared over. (2015, April 17). NBC News. Retrieved from http://www.nbcnews.com/storyline/measles-outbreak/measles-outbreak-traced-disneyland-declared-over-n343686

Medical cost trend: Behind the numbers 2015. (2015). Pricewaterhouse Coopers. Retrieved from http://www.pwc.com/us/en/health-industries/behind-the-numbers/infographics.jhtml

Medical records: The growing threat to patient privacy. (2001, November 28). *San Diego Union-Tribune*, p. B8.

Melki, J. P., Hitti, E. A., Oghia, M. J., & Mufarrij, A. A. (2015). Media exposure, mediated social comparison to idealized images of muscularity, and anabolic steroid use. *Health Communication, 30*(5), 473–484.

Mendenhall, E., Fernandez, A., Adler, N., & Jacobs, E. (2012). *Susto, coraje*, and abuse: Depression and beliefs about diabetes. *Culture, Medicine & Psychiatry, 36*(3), 480–492. doi:10.1007/s11013-012-9267-x

Menegatos, L., Lederman, L. C., & Hess, A. (2010). Friends don't let Jane hook up drunk: A qualitative analysis of participation in a simulation of college drinking-related decisions. *Communication Education, 3*, 374–388.

Meredith, L. S., Eisenman, D. P., Rhodes, H., Ryan, G., & Long, A. (2007, April–May). Trust influences response to public health messages during a bioterrorist event. *Journal of Health Communication, 12*, 217–232.

Metts, S., & Manns, H. (1996). Coping with HIV and AIDS: The social and personal challenges. In E. B. Ray (Ed.), *Communication and disenfranchisement: Social issues and implications* (pp. 347–364). Mahwah, NJ: Lawrence Erlbaum.

Micalizzi, D. A. (2008, March 3). The aftermath of a "never event": A child's unexplained death and a system seemingly designed to thwart justice. *Modern Healthcare, 38*(9), 24.

Milika, R. M., & Trorey, G. M. (2008). Patients' expectations of the maintenance of their dignity. *Journal of Clinical Nursing, 17*, 2709–2717.

Miller, C. H., Burgoon, M., Grandpre, J. R., & Alvaro, E. M. (2006). Identifying principal risk factors for the initiation of adolescent smoking behaviors: The significance of psychological reactance. *Health Communication, 19*, 241–252.

Miller, C. H., Lane, L. T., Deatrick, L. M., Young, A. M., & Potts, K. A. (2007). Psychological reactance and promotional health messages: The effects of controlling language, lexical concreteness, and the restoration of freedom. *Human Communication Research, 33*, 219–240.

Miller, K. I., Birkholt, M., Scott, C., & Stage, C. (1995). Empathy and burnout in human service work: An extension of the communication model. *Communication Research, 22*, 123–147.

Miller, K. I., Stiff, J. B., & Ellis, B. H. (1988). Communication and empathy as precursors to burnout among human service workers. *Communication Monographs, 55*, 250–265.

Miller, L. E. (2014). Uncertainty management and information seeking in cancer survivorship. *Health Communication, 29*, 233–243.

Miller, W. R., & Rollnick, S. (2002). *Motivational interviewing: Preparing people for change*. New York: Guilford Press.

Miller-Day, M., & Hecht, M. L. (2013). Narrative means to preventative ends: A narrative engagement framework for designing prevention interventions. *Health Communication, 28*, 657–670.

Miller-Day, M., & Marks, J. (2006). Perceptions of parental communication orientation, perfectionism, and disordered eating behaviors of sons and daughters. *Health Communication, 19*, 153–163.

Mills, A. W. (1939). *Hospital public relations*. Chicago: Physicians Record Company.

Mills, C. B. (2005). Catching up with Down syndrome: Parents' experiences in dealing with the medical and therapeutic communities. In E. B. Ray (Ed.), *Health communication in practice: A case study approach* (pp. 195–210). Mahwah, NJ: Lawrence Erlbaum.

Mishler, E. G. (1981). The social construction of illness. In E. B. Mishler, L. R. Amarasingham, S. D. Osherson, S. T. Hauser, & R. Leim (Eds.), *Social contexts of health*, *illness, and patient care* (pp. 141–168). Cambridge: Cambridge University Press.

Mishler, E. G. (1984). *The discourse of medicine: Dialectics of medical interviews.* Norwood, NJ: Ablex.

Modahl, M., Tompsett, L., & Moorhead, T. (2011, September). Doctors, patients and social media. Study conducted by the Care Continuum Alliance. Retrieved from http://www.quantiamd.com/q-qcp/doctorspatientsocialmedia.pdf

Modave, F., Shokar, N. K., Peñaranda, E., & Nguyen, N. (2014). Analysis of the accuracy of weight loss information search engine results on the Internet. *American Journal of Public Health, 104*(10), 1971–1978.

Moldovan-Johnson, M., Tan, A. S. L., & Hornik, R. C. (2014). Navigating the cancer information environment: The reciprocal relationship between patient-clinician information engagement and information seeking from nonmedical sources. *Health Communication, 29,* 974–983.

Molina, M. A., Cheung, M. C., Perez, E. A., Byrne, M. M., Franceschi, D., Moffat, F. L., . . . Koniaris, L. G. (2008). African American and poor patients have a dramatically worse prognosis for head and neck cancer: An examination of 20,915 patients. *Cancer, 113*(10), 2797–2806.

Moonhee, Y., & Roskos-Ewoldsen, D. R. (2007). The effectiveness of brand placements in the movies: Levels of placements, explicit and implicit memory, and brand-choice behavior. *Journal of Communication, 57,* 469–489.

Moore, L. G., Van Arsdale, P. W., Glittenberg, J. E., & Aldrich, R. A. (1987). *The biocultural basis of health: Expanding views of medical anthropology.* Prospect Heights, IL: Waveland Press.

Moore, L. W., & Miller, M. (2003). Older men's experiences of living with severe visual impairment. *Journal of Advanced Nursing, 43*(1), 10–18.

Moorhead, S. A., Hazlett, D. E., Harrison, L., Carroll, J. K., Irwin, A., & Hoving, C. (2013). A new dimension of health care: Systematic review of the uses, benefits, and limitations of social media for health communication. *Journal of Medical Internet Research, 15*(4). doi:10.2196/jmir.1933

Moran, M. B., & Sussman, S. (2014). Translating the link between social identity and health behavior into effective health communication strategies: An experimental application using antismoking advertisements. *Health Communication, 29,* 1057–1066.

Morgan, L. A., & Brazda, M. A. (2013). Transferring control to others: Process and meaning for older adults in assisted living. *Journal of Applied Gerontology, 32*(6), 651.

Morgan, R. M., & Hunt, S. D. (1994). The commitment-trust theory of relationship marketing. *Journal of Marketing, 58*(3), 20–38.

Morgan, S. E., Harrison, T. R., Afifi, W. A., Long, S. D., & Stephenson, M. T. (2008). In their own words: The reasons why people will (not) sign an organ donor card. *Health Communication, 23,* 23–33.

Morgan, S. E., Harrison, T. R., Chewning, L., Davis, L., & DiCorcia, M. (2007). Entertainment (mis)education: The framing of organ donation in entertainment television. *Health Communication, 22,* 143–151.

Morris, D., & Matthews, J. (2014). Communication, respect, and leadership: Interprofessional collaboration in hospitals of rural Ontario. *Canadian Journal of Dietetic Practice & Research, 75*(4), 173–179. doi:10.3148/cjdpr-2014-020

Morris, J. L., Lippman, S. A., Philip, S., Bernstein, K., Neilands, T. B., & Lightfoot, M. (2014). Sexually transmitted infection related stigma and shame among African American male youth: Implications for testing practices, partner notification, and treatment. *AIDS Patient Care & STDs, 28*(9), 499–506. doi:10.1089/apc.2013.0316

Morse, D. S., Edwardsen, E. A., & Gordon, H. S. (2008). Missed opportunities for interval empathy in lung cancer communication. *Archives of Internal Medicine, 168,* 1853–1858.

Mosavel, M., & El-Shaarawi, N. (2007, December). "I have never heard of that one": Young girls' knowledge and perception of cervical cancer. *Journal of Health Communication, 12,* 707–719.

Moss, M. (2011). *The media and the models of masculinity.* Lanham, MD: Lexington Books.

Mulac, A., & Giles, H. (1996). "You're only as old as you sound": Perceived vocal age and social meanings. *Health Communication, 8,* 199–215.

Muller, J. H., Jain, S., Loeser, H., & Irby, D. M. (2008). Lessons learned about integrating a medical school curriculum: Perceptions of students, faculty and curriculum leaders. *Medical Education, 42*(8), 778–785.

Murdock, D. (2012, March 16). The unaffordable care act. *National Review Online.* Retrieved http://www.nationalreview.com/article/293612/unaffordable-care-act-deroy-murdock

Murgatroyd, C. (2015). Disease and sport. *Power of the gene* (blog). Retrieved from http://powerofthegene.com/joomla/index.php/conversational-genetics/genetics-in-sport

Murray, D. (2007, November 2). Hospitals vow a better response. *Medical Economics, 85*(21), 18.

Murray, E., Burns, J., May, C., Finch, T., O'Donnell, C., Wallace, P., & Mair, F. (2011). Why is it difficult to implement e-health initiatives? A qualitative study. *Implementation Science, 6*(6), nonpaginated. Retrieved from http://www.implementationscience.com/content/6/1/6

Muskin, P. R. (1998). The request to die: Role for a psychodynamic perspective on physician-assisted suicide. *Journal of the American Medical Association, 279,* 323–328.

Naeem, A. G. (2003). The role of culture and religion in the management of diabetes: A study of Kashmiri men in Leeds. *Journal of the Royal Society of Health, 123*(2), 110–116.

Nan, X., Zhao, X., Yang, B., & Iles, I. (2015). Effectiveness of cigarette warning labels: Examining the impact of graphics, message framing, and temporal framing. *Health Communication, 30,* 81–89.

Napier, A. D., Ancarno, C., Butler, B., Calabrese, J., Chater, A., Chatterjee, H., . . . Tyler, N. (2014). Culture and health. *Lancet, 384*(9954), 1607–1639.

Nathanson, A. I., & Yang, M.-S. (2003, January). The effects of mediation content and form on children's responses to violent television. *Human Communication Research, 29*, 111–134.

National Assessment of Adult Literacy. (2014). Fast facts. National Center for Education Statistics. Retrieved from http://nces.ed.gov/fastfacts/display.asp?id=69

National Association of City & County Health Officials. (2015). About NACCHO. Washington, DC: Author. Retrieved from http://www.naccho.org/about/

National Center for Complementary and Alternative Medicine at the National Institutes of Health. (2012). The use of complementary and alternative medicine in the United States. Washington, DC: Author. Retrieved from http://nccam.nih.gov/news/camstats/2007/cam-survey_fs1.htm#use

National Center for Health Statistics. (2012). Health, United States, 2011: with special features on socioeconomic status and health. Hyattsville, MD: U.S. Department of Health and Human Services. Retrieved from http://www.cdc.gov/nchs/data/hus/hus11.pdf

National Eating Disorders Association. (2015). Statistics on eating disorders. New York: Author. Retrieved from http://www.nationaleatingdisorders.org/general-statistics

National health care expenditure data. (2014). NHE summary share of GDP. Table 1. Center for Medicare and Medicaid Services, Office of the Actuary. Retrieved from http://www.cms.gov/Research-Statistics-Data-and-Systems/Statistics-Trends-and-Reports/NationalHealthExpendData/NationalHealthAccountsHistorical.html

National Health Service (NHS). (2015). National Blood Week #Missing Type. Retrieved from http://www.blood.co.uk/news-media/campaigns/national-blood-week/

National Institute of Medicine. U.S. Committee on the Use of Complementary and Alternative Medicine by the American Public. (2005). *Complementary and alternative medicine in the United States. Prevalence, cost, and patterns of CAM use.* Washington, DC: Author. National Academies Press. Retrieved from http://www.ncbi.nlm.nih.gov/books/NBK83794/

National Institute on Drug Abuse (NIDA). (2007, December). *InfoFacts: High school and youth trends.* Bethesda, MD: Author. Retrieved from http://www.drugabuse.gov/infofacts/hsyouthtrends.html

National Research Council. (1989). *Improving risk communication.* Washington, DC: National Academy Press. Retrieved from http://www.nap.edu/openbook.php?isbn=0309039436

Native American religions: Balance and harmony. (2010, October 4). Native American Netroots. Retrieved from http://nativeamericannetroots.net/diary/705

Needleman, J., Buerhaus, P. I., Stewart, M., Zelevinsky, K., & Marrke, S. (2006, February). Market watch. Nursing staffing in hospitals: Is there a business case for quality? *Health Affairs, 25*(1), 204–211.

Neihardt, J. G. (1932). *Black Elk speaks: Being the life story of a holy man of the Oglala Sioux.* New York: Morrow.

Nelkin, D., & Gilman, S. L. (1991). Placing blame for devastating disease. In A. Mack (Ed.), *In time of plague: The history and social consequences of lethal epidemic disease* (pp. 39–56). New York: New York University Press.

Nemeth, S. A. (2000). Society, sexuality, and disabled/able bodied romantic relationships. In D. O. Braithwaite & T. L. Thompson (Eds.), *Handbook of communication and people with disabilities: Research and applications* (pp. 37–48). Mahwah, NJ: Lawrence Erlbaum.

Nestle, M. (1997, March–April). Alcohol guidelines for chronic disease prevention: From prohibition to moderation. *Nutrition Today, 32*, 86–92.

Neuberger, J. (1999, June 22). Let's do away with "patients." *British Medical Journal, 318*, 1756–1757.

Newman, M. A. (1986). *Health as expanding consciousness.* St. Louis, MO: C. V. Mosby.

Newman, M. A. (1995). *A developing discipline: Selected works of Margaret Newman.* New York: National League for Nursing Press.

Newman, M. A. (2000). *Health as expanding consciousness* (2nd ed.). Boston: Jones & Bartlett.

New report: More than $5 billion in total consumer benefits from Affordable Care Act's medical loss ratio provision. (2015, March 26). The Commonwealth Fund. Retrieved from http://www.commonwealthfund.org/publications/press-releases/2015/mar/medical-loss-ratio-year-3

New research shows the national truth: Youth smoking prevention campaign offset negative effects of decreased state tobacco control funding. (2008, April 3). Washington, DC: American Legacy Foundation.

Nicholas, A. (2014, April 6). Ayubowan: A medical student's encounter with healthcare in Kandy, Sri Lanka. Global health. Rutgers Robert Wood Johnson Medical School [blog]. Retrieved from http://rwjms.rutgers.edu/global_health/ihig/experiences.html

Nicolai, J., Demmel, R., & Farsch, K. (2010). Effects of mode of presentation on ratings of empathic communication in medical interviews. *Patient Education and Counseling, 80*, 76–79.

Niederdeppe, J., Davis, K. C., Farrelly, M. C., & Yarsevich, J. (2007). Stylistic features, need for sensation, and confirmed recall of national smoking prevention advertisements. *Journal of Communication, 57*, 272–292.

Niederdeppe, J., Fowler, E. F., Goldstein, K., & Pribble, J. (2010). Does local television news coverage cultivate fatalistic beliefs about cancer prevention? *Journal of Communication, 60*, 230–253.

Niederdeppe, J., Hornick, R. C., Kelly, B. J., Frosch, D. L., Romantan, A., Stevens, R. S., . . . Schwartz, J. S. (2007). Examining the dimensions of cancer-related information seeking and scanning behavior. *Health Communication, 22*, 153–167.

Niederdeppe, J., Shapiro, M. A., Kim, H. Y., Bartolo, D., & Porticella, N. (2014). Narrative persuasion, causality, complex integration, and support for obesity policy. *Health Communication, 29*, 431–444.

Nielsen reports TV, Internet and mobile usage among Americans. (2008, July 8). New York: Nielsen Company. Retrieved from http://www.nielsen.com/media/2008/pr_080708.html

Noar, S. M., Myrick, J. G., Zeitany, A., Kelley, D., Morales-Pico, B., & Thomas, N. E. (2015). Testing a social cognitive theory-based model of indoor tanning: Implications for skin cancer prevention messages. *Health Communication, 30*, 164–174.

Noar, S. M., Zimmerman, R. S., Palmgreen, P., Lustria, M., & Horosewski, M. L. (2006). Integrating personality and psychosocial theoretical approaches to understanding safer sexual behavior: Implications for message design. *Health Communication, 19*(2), 165–174.

Noland, C., & Walter, J. C. (2006). "It's not our ass": Medical resident sense-making regarding lawsuits. *Health Communication, 20*, 81–89.

Nordby, H., & Nøhr, Ø. N. (2011). Care and empathy in ambulance services: Paramedics' experiences of communicative challenges in transports of patients with prolonged cancer. *Journal of Communication in Healthcare, 4*, 215–226.

Norling, G. R. (2005). Developing a theoretical model of rapport building: Implications for medical education and the physician–patient relationship. In M. Haider (Ed.), *Global public health communication* (pp. 407–414). Boston: Jones and Bartlett.

Novack, D. H., Suchman, A. L., Clark, W., Epstein, R. M., Najberg, G. E., & Kaplan, C. (1997). Calibrating the physician: Personal awareness and effective patient care. *Journal of the American Medical Association, 278*, 502–510.

Nussbaum, J. F. (2007). Life span communication and quality of life. Presidential address. *Journal of Communication, 57*, 1–7.

Nussbaum, J. F., Baringer, D., Fisher, C. L., & Kundrat, A. L. (2008). Connecting health, communication, and aging. In L. Sparks, H. D. O'Hair, & G. L. Kreps (Eds.), *Cancer, communication and aging* (pp. 67–76). Cresskill, NJ: Hampton Press.

Nussbaum, J. F., Pecchioni, L., Grant, J. A., & Folwell, A. (2000). Explaining illness to older adults: The complexities of the provider–patient interaction as we age. In B. B. Whaley (Ed.), *Explaining illness* (pp. 171–194). Mahwah, NJ: Lawrence Erlbaum.

Nussbaum, J. F., Ragan, S., & Whaley, B. (2003). Children, older adults, and women: Impact on provider–patient interaction. In T. L. Thompson, A. M. Dorsey, K. I. Miller, & R. Parrott (Eds.), *Handbook of health communication* (pp. 183–204). Mahwah, NJ: Lawrence Erlbaum.

Nyhan, B., Reifler, J., Richey, S., & Freed, G. L. (2014). Effective messages in vaccine promotion: A randomized trial. *Pediatrics, 133*(4). doi: 10.1542/peds.2013-2365

O'Connell, B., Bailey, S., & Pearce, J. (2003). Straddling the pathway from pediatrician to mainstream health care: Transition issues experienced in disability care. *Australian Journal of Rural Health, 11*(2), 57–63.

Ogden, C. L., Carroll, M. D., Kit, B. K., Flegal, K. M. (2014). Prevalence of childhood and adult obesity in the United States, 2011–2012. *Journal of the American Medical Association, 311*, 806–814.

Oetzel, J., Simpson, M., Berryman, K., Iti, T., & Reddy, R. (2015). Managing communication tensions and challenges during the end-of-life journey: Perspectives of Māori kaumātua and their whānau. *Health Communication, 30*, 350–360.

O'Keefe, D. J. (2015). Message generalizations that support evidence-based persuasive message design: Specifying the evidentiary requirements. *Health Communication, 20*, 106–113.

Older adults' health and age-related changes: Reality versus myth. (n.d.). American Psychological Association. Retrieved from http://www.apa.org/pi/aging/resources/guides/older-adults.pdf

Olds, T. (2014, June 1). You're not Barbie and I'm not GI Joe, so what is a normal body? *The Conversation*. Retrieved from http://theconversation.com/youre-not-barbie-and-im-not-gi-joe-so-what-is-a-normal-body-14567

O'Leary, S. C. B., Federico, S., & Hampers, L. C. (2003). The truth about language barriers: One residency program's experience. *Pediatrics, 111*(5), 1100.

Olivares, P. R., Cossio-Bolaños, M. A., Gomez-Campos, R., Almonacid-Fierro, A., & Garcia-Rubio, J. (2015). Influence of parents and physical education teachers in adolescent physical activity. *International Journal of Clinical Health & Psychology, 15*(2), 113–120.

O'Reilly, K. B. (2012, March 19). The ABCs of health literacy. *American Medical News*. Retrieved from http://www.amednews.com/article/20120319/profession/303199949/4/

Organ donation: Don't let these myths confuse you. (2008). Rochester, MN: Mayo Clinic. Retrieved from http://www.mayoclinic.com/health/organ-donation/FL00077

OrganDonor.Gov. (2008). Access to U.S. government information on organ & tissue donation and transplantation. Washington, DC: U.S. Department of Health and Human Services. Retrieved from http://www.organdonor.gov

Ortman, J. M., Velkoff, V. A., & Hogan, H. (2014, May). An aging nation: The older population in the United States. U.S. Census Bureau. Retrieved from http://www.census.gov/prod/2014pubs/p25-1140.pdf

Outzen, R. (2005, November 3). Rising stars. *Independent News, 5*(42), np. Retrieved from http://inweekly.net/article.asp?artID=2040

Overton, B. C., du Pré, A., & Pecchioni, L. L. (2015). Media portrayals of aging: Women's sexuality concealed and revealed. In N. Jones & B. Batchelor (Eds.), *Aging heroes: Growing old in popular culture* (pp. 181–197). New York: Rowman & Littlefield.

Padela, A., Killawi, A., Forman, J., DeMonner, S., & Heisler, M. (2012). American Muslim perceptions of healing: Key agents in healing, and their roles. *Qualitative Health Research, 22*(6), 846–858.

Paek, H.-J. (2008). Mechanisms through which adolescents attend and respond to antismoking media campaigns. *Journal of Communication, 58*, 84–105.

Paek, H.-J., Reid, L. N., Choi, H., & Jeong, H. J. (2010). Promoting health (implicitly)? A longitudinal content analysis of implicit health information in cigarette advertising, 1954–2003. *Journal of Health Communication, 15*, 769–787. doi: 10.1080/10810730.2010.514033

Page-Reeves, J., Niforatos, J., Mishra, S., Regino, L., Gingrich, A., & Bulten, J. (2013). Health disparity and structural violence: How fear undermines health among immigrants at risk for diabetes. *Journal of Health Disparities Research & Practice, 6*(2), 30–47.

Pahal, J. S. (2006). The dynamics of resident-patient communication: Data from Canada. *Communication & Medicine, 3*(2), 161–170.

Pai, H. H., Lau, F., Barnett, J., & Jones, S. (2013). Meeting the health information needs of prostate cancer patients using personal health records. *Current Oncology, 20*(6), e561–e569.

Palmer-Wackerly, A. L., & Krieger, J. L. (2015). Dancing around infertility: The use of metaphors in a complex medical situation. *Health Communication, 30*, 612–623.

Paris, M., & Hoge, M. A. (2010). Burnout in the mental health workforce: A review. *Journal of Behavioral Health Services and Research, 37*, 519–528.

Parker-Pope, T. (2002, November 11). Viagra is misunderstood despite name recognition. *Wall Street Journal*, online. Retrieved December 23, 2008, from http://www.usrf.org/breakingnews/bn_111202_viagra/bn_111202_viagra.html

Parkes, C. M. (1998). The dying adult. *British Medical Journal, 316*, 1313–1315.

Parrott, R. (1995). Motivation to attend to health messages: Presentation of content and linguistic considerations. In E. Maibach & R. L. Parrott (Eds.), *Designing health messages: Approaches from communication theory and public health practice* (pp. 7–23). Thousand Oaks, CA: Sage.

Parrott, R., Hopfer, S., Ghetian, C., & Lengerich, E. (2007). Mapping as a visual health communication tool: Promises and dilemmas. *Health Communication, 22*, 13–24.

Parrott, R., & Polonec, L. (2008). Preventing green tobacco sickness in farming youth: A behavioral adaptation to health communication in health campaigns. In K. B. Wright & S. D. Moore (Eds.), *Applied health communication* (pp. 341–359). Cresskill, NJ: Hampton Press.

Parry, R. (2008). Are interventions to enhance communication performance in allied health professionals effective, and how should they be delivered? Direct and indirect evidence. *Patient Education and Counseling, 73*, 186–195.

Pascale, R. T. (1999). Leading from a different place: Applying complexity theory to tap potential. In J. A. Conger, G. M. Spreitzer, & E. E. Lawler, III (Eds.), *The leader's change handbook: An essential guide to setting direction and taking action* (pp. 195–220). San Francisco: Jossey-Bass.

Pateet, J. R., Fremonta, L. M., & Miovic, M. K. (2011). Possibly impossible patients: Management of difficult behavior in oncology patients. *Journal of Oncology Practice, 7*, 242–246.

Patel, D. S. (2005). Social mobilization as a tool for outreach programs in the HIV/AIDS crisis. In M. Haider (Ed.), *Global public health communication: Challenges, perspectives, and strategies* (pp. 91–102). Boston: Jones and Bartlett.

Patel, S., Schnall, R., Little, V., Lewis-Fernández, R., & Pincus, H. (2014). Primary care professionals' perspectives on treatment decision making for depression with African Americans and Latinos in primary care practice. *Journal of Immigrant & Minority Health, 16*(6), 1262. doi:10.1007/s10903-013-9903-8

Paterniti, D. A., Pan, R. J., Smith, L. F., Horan, N. M., & West, D. C. (2006). From physician-centered to community-centered perspectives on health care: Assessing the efficacy of community-based training. *Academic Medicine, 81*(4), 347–353.

Patient satisfaction planner: Unsatisfactory stay sparks Planetree care model. (2007, September 1). *Hospital Peer Review*, n.p.

Patterson, J. (2012, March 4). Social media linking Las Vegas doctors, patients. *Las Vegas Review-Journal*. Retrieved from http://www.lvrj.com/health/social-media-linking-las-vegas-doctors-patients-141389473.html

Pearce, C., Arnold, M., Phillips, C. B., Trumble, S., & Dwan, K. (2012). The many faces of the computer: An analysis of clinical software in the primary care consultation. *International Journal of Medical Informatics, 81*, 475–484.

Peate, I. (2012). Breaking the silence: Helping men with erectile dysfunction. *British Journal of Community Nursing, 17*(7), 310–317.

Peeke, P. (2011, March 29). Reality shows abut the obese: Empowering or exploitative? *Everyday Fitness* (blog). Retrieved from http://blogs.webmd.com/pamela-peeke-md/2011/03/reality-shows-about-the-obese-empowering-or-exploitative.html

Pelto-Piri, V., Engström, K., & Engström, I. (2013). Paternalism, autonomy and reciprocity: ethical perspectives in encounters with patients in psychiatric in-patient care. *BMC* [Biomed Central] *Medical Ethics, 14*, 49.

Pendleton, D., Schofield, T., Tate, P., & Havelock, P. (1984). *The consultant: An approach to learning and teaching.* Oxford: Oxford University Press.

Peng, W. (2009). Design and evaluation of a computer game to promote a healthy diet for young adults. *Health Communication, 24*, 115–127. doi:10.1080/10410230802676490

Penn, C., Watermeyer, J., & Evans, M. (2011). Why don't patients take their drugs? The role of communication, context and culture in patient adherence and the work of the pharmacist in HIV/AIDS. *Patient Education and Counseling, 83*, 310–318.

Pennic, J. (2015, March 4). Mayo Clinic, Gentag partner to develop wearable biosensors for obesity and diabetes. *Health Information Technology*. Retrieved from http://hitconsultant.net/2015/03/04/mayo-clinic-gentag-partner-to-develop-wireless-sensors/

Pepicello, J. A., & Murphy, E. C. (1996). Integrating medical and operational management. *Physician Executive, 22*, 4–9.

Peretti-Watel, P., Seror, V., Verger, P., Guignard, R., Legleye, S., & Beck, F. (2014). Smokers' risk perception, socioeconomic status and source of information on cancer. *Addictive Behaviors, 39*(9), 1304–1310. doi:10.1016/j.addbeh.2014.04.016

Perlman, A. I., Lebow, D. G., Raphael, K., Ali, A., & Simmons, L. A. (2013). A point-of-sale communications campaign to provide consumers safety information on drug-dietary supplement interactions: A pilot study. *Health Communication, 28*, 729–739.

Perry, B. (2002, November). Growth and satisfaction: "I became a nurse because I wanted to help others." *Canadian Business and Current Affairs, 98*(10), nonpaginated.

Peters, E., Lipkus, I., & Diefenbach, M. A. (2006). The functions of affect in health communications and in the construction of health preferences. *Journal of Communication, 56*, S140–S162.

Peterson, E. D., Shah, B. R., Parsons, L., Pollack, C .V., Jr., French, W. J., Canto, J. G., . . . Rogers, W. J. (2008). Trends in quality of care for patients with acute myocardial infarction in the National Registry of Myocardial Infarction from 1990 to 2006. *American Heart Journal, 156*(6), 1045–1055.

Peterson, T. M. (2012, April 2). The Batista "health" rights [Blog post]. *TiffanyAndLupus.com*. Retrieved from http://www.tiffanyandlupus.com/2012/04/my-miranda-health-rights.html

Pet Partners video: The health benefits of pets. (n.d.). Bellevue, WA: Author. Retrieved from http://www.deltasociety.org/page.aspx?pid=642

Petroff, A., & Rooney, B. (2015, April 28). Nepal earthquake donations: Who's sending what. *CNN Money*. Retrieved from http://money.cnn.com/2015/04/27/news/nepal-earthquake-donations/

Petty, R. E., & Cacioppo, J. T. (1981). *Attitudes and persuasion: Classic and contemporary approaches*. Dubuque, IA: Wm. C. Brown.

Pexton, C. (n.d.). Framing the need to improve health care using Six Sigma methodologies. iSixSigma. Retrieved from http://www.isixsigma.com/industries/healthcare/framing-need-improve-health-care-using-six-sigma/

Pham, J. C., Story, J. L., Hicks, R. W., Shore, A. D., Morlock, L. L., Cheung, D. S., . . . Pronovost, P. J. (2011). National study on the frequency, types, causes, and consequences of voluntarily reported emergency department medication errors. *Journal of Emergency Medicine, 40*, 485–492.

Philpott, A., Knerr, W., & Maher, D. (2006). Promoting protection and pleasure: Amplifying the effectiveness of barriers against sexually transmitted infections and pregnancy. Viewpoint. *The Lancet, 368*, pp. 1–4. Retrieved from http://www.thelancet.com/journals/lancet/article/PIIS0140673606698103/abstract

Physician assistant program. (2015). *Peterson's*. Retrieved from http://www.petersons.com/graduate-schools/duke-university-school-of-medicine-physician-assistant-program-000_10047331.aspx

Physicians and surgeons. (2008). *Occupational outlook handbook, 2008–09 edition*. Washington, DC: U.S. Department of Labor.

Physicians report growing dissatisfaction with "business" of medicine. (2008). Locum Tenens. Retrieved from www.locumtenens.com/physician-careers/Business-of-Medicine.aspx

Pickering, A. (1995). *The mangle of practice: Time, agency, and science*. Chicago: University of Chicago Press.

Pighin, S., & Bonnefon, J.-F. (2011). Facework and uncertain reasoning in health communication. *Patient Education and Counseling, 85*, 169–172.

Pilling, V. K., & Brannon, L. A. (2007). Assessing college students' attitudes toward responsible drinking messages to identify promising binge drinking intervention strategies. *Health Communication, 22*, 265–276.

Pincus, C. R. (1995). Why medicine is driving doctors crazy. *Medical Economics, 72*, 40–44.

Pinkleton, B. E., Austin, E. W., Cohen, M., Miller, A., & Fitzgerald, E. (2007). A statewide evaluation of the effectiveness of media literacy training to prevent tobacco use among adolescents. *Health Communication, 21*, 23–34.

Piotrow, P. T., Rimon, J. G., II, Payne Merritt, A., & Saffitz, G. (2003). *Advancing health communication: The PCS experience in the field*. Center Publication 103. Baltimore: Johns Hopkins Bloomberg School of Public Health/Center for Communication Programs. Retrieved from http://pdf.usaid.gov/pdf_docs/Pnact765.pdf

Plane passengers sue TB patient. (2007, July 13). CNN.com/health. Retrieved from http://www.cnn.com/2007/HEALTH/conditions/07/12/tb.suit/index.html

Platt, F. W. (1995). *Conversation repair: Case studies in doctor–patient communication*. Boston: Little, Brown.

Platt, F. W., & Gordon, G. H. (2004). *Field guide to the difficult patient interview* (2nd ed.). Philadelphia: Lippincott Williams & Wilkins.

Plews-Ogan, M., Owens, J. E., & May, N. B. (2013). Medical errors: Wisdom through adversity: Learning and growing in the wake of an error. *Patient Education and Counseling, 91*, 236–242.

Polonec, L. D., Major, A. M., & Atwood, L. E. (2006). Evaluating the believability and effectiveness of the social norms message "Most students drink 0 to 4 drinks when they party." *Health Communication, 20*, 23–34.

Poole, J. (2014). Queer representations of gay males and masculinities in the media. *Sexuality & Culture, 18*(2), 279–290.

Porter-O'Grady, T., Bradley, C., Crow, G., & Hendrich, A. L. (1997, Winter). After a merger: The dilemma of the best leadership approach for nursing. *Nursing Administration Quarterly, 21*, 8–19.

Potter, E. (n.d.). We used to love to travel and eat out . . . now, nothing. Caregiver stories. Family Caregiver Alliance. Retrieved from https://caregiver.org/we-used-love-travel-and-eat-out-now-nothing

Potter, J. E. (2002). Do ask, do tell. *Annals of Internal Medicine, 137*(5), 341–343.

Potter, W. J. (1998). *Media literacy.* Thousand Oaks, CA: Sage.

Poureslami, I. M., Shum, J., Cheng, N., & FitzGerald, J. M. (2014). Does culture or illness change a smoker's perspective on cessation? *American Journal of Health Behavior, 38*(5), 657–667.

Press, I. (2002). *Patient satisfaction: Defining, measuring, and improving the experience of care.* Chicago: Health Administration Press.

Prochaska, J. O., & DiClemente, C. C. (1983). Stages and processes of self-change of smoking: Toward an integrative model of change. *Journal of Consulting and Clinical Psychology, 51,* 390–395.

Prochaska, J. O., DiClemente, C. C., & Norcross, J. C. (1992). In search of how people change applications to the addictive behaviors. *American Psychologist, 47,* 1102–1114.

Prochaska, J. O., Johnson, S., & Lee, P. (1998). The transtheoretical model of behavior change. In S. A. Shumaker, E. B. Schron, J. K. Ockene, & W. L. McBee (Eds.), *The handbook of behavior change* (2nd ed., pp. 59–84). New York: Springer-Verlag.

Puhl, R., & Heuer, C. (2010). Obesity stigma: Important considerations for public health. *American Journal of Public Health, 100*(6), 1019–1028.

Purnell, L. D. (2008, February). Traditional Vietnamese health and healing. *Urologic Nursing, 28*(1), 63–67.

Qiang, J. K., & Marras, C. (2015). Short communication: Telemedicine in Parkinson's disease: A patient perspective at a tertiary care centre. *Parkinsonism and Related Disorders, 21,* 525–528.

Quenqua, D. (2014, August 1). Tell me what you see, even if it hurts me. *The New York Times.* Retrieved from http://www.nytimes.com/2014/08/03/fashion/am-i-pretty-videos-posed-to-the-internet-raise-questions.html

Query, J. L., Jr., & Kreps, G. L. (1996). Testing a relational model for health communication competence among caregivers for individuals with Alzheimer's disease. *Journal of Health Psychology, 1,* 335–351.

Quesada, A., & Summers, S. L. (1998, January). Literacy in the cyberage: Teaching kids to be media savvy. *Technology & Learning, 18,* 30–36.

Quintero Johnson, J. M., Harrison, K., & Quick, B. L. (2013). Understanding the effectiveness of the entertainment-education strategy: An investigation of how audience involvement, message processing, and message design influence health information recall. *Journal of Health Communication, 18,* 160–178.

Radley, D. C., McCarthy, D. . Lippa, J. A., Hayes, S. L., & Schoen, C. (2014, May). Aiming higher: Results from a scorecard on state health system performance. The Commonwealth Fund. Retrieved from http://www.commonwealthfund.org/publications/fund-reports/2014/apr/2014-state-scorecard

Raffel, M. W., & Raffel, N. K. (1989). *The U.S. health system: Origins and functions* (3rd ed.). New York: John Wiley & Sons.

Ragan, S. L., & Goldsmith, J. (2008). End-of-life communication: The drama of pretense in the talk of dying patients and their M.D. In K. B. Wright & S. D. Moore (Eds.), *Applied health communication* (pp. 207–227). Cresskill, NJ: Hampton Press.

Ragan, S. L., Wittenberg, E., & Hall, H. T. (2003). The communication of palliative care for the elderly cancer patient. *Health Communication, 15*(2), 219–226.

Ragan, S. L., Wittenberg-Lyles, E. W., Goldsmith, J., & Sanchez-Reilly, S. (2008). *Communication as comfort: Multiple voices in palliative care.* New York: Routledge.

Rains, S. A. (2008a, June). Health at high speed: Broadband Internet access, health communication, and the digital divide. *Communication Research, 35*(3), 283–297.

Rains, S. A. (2008b, January/March). Seeking health information in the information age: The role of Internet self-efficacy. *Western Journal of Communication, 72*(1), 1–18.

Rains, S. A., & Keating, D. M. (2011, December). The social dimension of blogging about health: Health blogging, social support, and well-being. *Communication Monographs, 78,* 511–534.

Rains, S. A., & Turner, M. M. (2007). Psychological reactance and persuasive health communication: A test and extension of the intertwined model. *Human Communication Research, 33*(2), 241–269.

Ramanadhan, S., & Viswanath, K. (2006). Health and the information nonseeker: A profile. *Health Communication, 20,* 131–139.

Ramchand, R., Karney, B. R., Osilla, K. C,. Burns, R. M., & Caldarone, L. B. (2008). Prevalence of PTSD, depression, and TBI among returning service members. In Tanielian, T., & Jaycox, L. J. (Eds.), *Invisible wounds of war: Psychological and cognitive injuries, their consequences, and services to assist recovery* (pp. 35–85). Santa Monica, CA: RAND Center for Military Health Policy Research. Retrieved from http://www.rand.org/content/dam/rand/pubs/monographs/2008/RAND_MG720.pdf

Rampell, C. (2014, November 6). Many more men say they want to be stay-at-home dads than actually are. *The Washington Post.* Retrieved from http://www.washingtonpost.com/news/rampage/wp/2014/11/06/many-more-men-say-they-want-to-be-stay-at-home-dads-than-actually-are/

Rao, J. K., Anderson, L. A., Lin, F., & Laux, J. P. (2014). Completion of advance directives among U.S. consumers. *American Journal of Preventive Medicine, 46,* 65–70. doi:10.1016/j.amepre.2013.09.008

Ratzan, S., & Meltzer, W. (2005). State of the art in crisis communication: Past lessons and principles of practice. In M. Haider (Ed.), *Global public health communication: Challenges, perspectives, and strategies* (pp. 321–347). Boston: Jones and Bartlett.

Ratzan, S. C., & Moritsugu, K. P. (2014). Ebola crisis-communication chaos we can avoid. *Journal of Health Communication, 19*(11), 1213–1215.

Rawlins, W. K. (1989). A dialectical analysis of the tensions, functions, and strategic challenges of communication in young adult friendships. *Communication Yearbook, 12*, 157–189.

Rawlins, W. K. (1992). *Friendship matters: Communication, dialectics, and the life course*. New York: Aldine De Gruyter.

Rawlins, W. K. (2009). Narrative medicine and the stories of friends. *Journal of Applied Communication Research, 37*, 167–173.

Redfern, J. S., & Sinclair, B. (2014). Improving health care encounters and communication with transgender patients. *Journal of Communication in Healthcare, 7*(1), 25–40. doi:10.1179/1753807614Y.0000000045

Reducing health disparities in Asian American and Pacific Islander populations. (2005). Management Sciences of Health. Office of Minority Health and Bureau of Primary Health Care. Retrieved from http://erc.msh.org/aapi/ca6.html

Reese, S. (2008, April 18). Pick up the mouse, put down the phone: Trading e-mails with patients is easier than playing phone tag, and you may even get paid for it. *Medical Economics, 85*(8), 24–28.

Reilly, P. (1987). *To do no harm: A journey through medical school*. Dover, MA: Auburn House.

Reinhardt, J. D., Pennycott, A., & Fellinghauer, B. G. (2014). Impact of a film portrayal of a police officer with spinal cord injury on attitudes towards disability: A media effects experiment. *Disability & Rehabilitation, 36*(4), 289–294.

Reinhardt, J. P., Boerner, K., & Horowitz, A. (2006). Good to have but not to use: Differential impact of perceived and received support on well-being. *Journal of Social and Personal Relationships, 23*(1), 117–129.

Reinhardt, U. W. (2014, July 1). The illogic of employer-sponsored health insurance [Blog post]. *The Upshot*. Retrieved from http://www.nytimes.com/2014/07/03/upshot/the-illogic-of-employer-sponsored-health-insurance.html?abt=0002&abg=0

Reis, R. (2008). How Brazilian and North American newspapers frame the stem cell research debate. *Science Communication, 29*(3), 316–334.

Renganathan, E., Hosein, E., Parks, W., Lloyd, L., Suhaili, M. R., & Odugleh, A. (2005). Communication-for-behavioral-impact (COMB): A review of WHO's experiences with strategic social mobilization and communication in the prevention and control of communicable diseases. In M. Haider (Ed.), *Global public health communication: Challenges, perspectives, and strategies* (pp. 305–320). Boston: Jones and Bartlett.

Renwick, R., Schormans, A. F., & Shore, D. (2014). Hollywood takes on intellectual/ developmental disability: cinematic representations of occupational participation. *Occupation, Participation and Health, 34*(1), 20–31.

Rey-Lopez, J. P., Ruiz, J. R., Vicente-Rodriguez. G., Gracia-Marco, L., Manios, Y., Sjostrom, M., De Bourdeaudhuij, I., & Moreno, L. A. (2012). Physical activity does not attenuate the obesity risk of TV viewing in youth. *Pediatric Obesity, 7*, 240–250.

Reynolds, B. (2006, August). Response to best practices. *Journal of Applied Communication Research, 34*(4), 249–252.

Rhodes, S. D., Yee, L. J., & Hergenrather, K. C. (2003). Hepatitis A vaccination among young African American men who have sex with men in the Deep South: Psychosocial predictors. *Journal of the American Medical Association, 95*(4), 31S–36S.

Richards, A. S., & Banas, J. A. (2015). Inoculating against reactance to persuasive health messages. *Health Communication, 30*, 451–460.

Rifkin, L. (2008, March 21). Still a privilege to be a doctor: Though not immune to the hassles and hardships of practice, this physician tells why he experiences the joy of medicine. *Medical Economics, 85*(6), 28–29.

Riiser, K., Løndal, K., Ommundsen, Y., Småstuen, M. C., Misvær, N., & Helseth, S. (2014). The outcomes of a 12-week Internet intervention aimed at improving fitness and health-related quality of life in overweight adolescents. *Plos ONE, 9*(12), 1–21.

Rimal, R. (2000). Closing the knowledge–behavior gap in health promotion: The mediating role of self-efficacy. *Health Communication, 12*, 219–238.

Rimal, R. N. (2008, March/April). Modeling the relationship between descriptive norms and behaviors: A test and extension of the theory of normative social behavior (TNSB). *Health Communication, 23*, 103–116.

Rimal, R. N., & Morrison, D. (2006). A uniqueness to personal threat (UPT) hypothesis: How similarity affects perceptions of susceptibility and severity in risk assessment. *Health Communication, 20*, 209–219.

Rimal, R. N., Ratzan, S. C., Arnston, P., & Freimuth, V. S. (1997). Reconceptualizing the "patient": Health care promotion as increasing citizens' decision-making competencies. *Health Communication, 9*, 61–74.

Rimal, R. N., & Real, K. (2005, June). How behaviors are influenced by perceived norms: A test of the theory of normative social behavior. *Communication Research, 32*, 389–414.

Robert Wood Johnson Foundation. (2008, April 29). Cost of insurance far outpaces income. Princeton, NJ: Author. Retrieved August 14, 2008, from http://www.rwjf.org/en/library/articles-and-news/2008/04/cost-of-insurance-far-outpaces-income.html

Robert Wood Johnson Foundation. (2010). Report projects up to 66 million Americans could be uninsured by 2019 unless health reform is enacted. Princeton, NJ: Author. Retrieved from http://www.rwjf.org/en/library/articles-and-news/2009/05/report-projects-up-to-66-million-americans-could-be-uninsured-by.html

Roberto, A. J., Zimmerman, R. S., Carlyle, K. E., Abner, E. L., Cupp, P. K., & Hansen, G. L. (2007). The effects of computer-based pregnancy, STD, and HIV prevention intervention: A nine-school trial. *Health Communication, 21*, 115–124.

Roberts, J. A., Luc Honore Petnji, Y., & Manolis, C. (2014). The invisible addiction: Cell-phone activities and addiction among male and female college students. *Journal of Behavioral Addictions, 3*(4), 254–265.

Roberts, L., & Bucksey, S. J. (2007). Communicating with patients: What happens in practice? *Physical Therapy, 87*(5), 587–594.

Robertson, T. (1999, March 26). Michigan jury gets Kevorkian case: Defendant cites civil rights leaders. *Boston Globe*, p. A3.

Robinson, J. D. (2003). An interactional structure of medical activities during acute visits and its implications for patients' participation. *Health Communication, 15*, 27–58.

Robinson, J. D., & Tian, Y. (2009). Cancer patients and the provision of informational social support. *Health Communication, 24*, 381–390. doi:10.1080/10410230903023261

Robinson, J. D., Turner, J. W., & Levine, Y. (2011). Expanding the walls of the health care encounter: Support and outcomes for patients online. *Health Communication, 26*, 125–134.

Robinson, T., Callister, M., Magoffin, D., & Moore, J. (2006). The portrayal of older characters in Disney animated films. *Journal of Aging Studies, 21*, 203–213.

Rocha, T. (2010, Fall). Transforming patient care through the Planetree approach. NorthwestQuarterly.com. Retrieved from http://northwestchicagoland.northwestquarterly.com/2011/01/transforming-patient-care-through-the-planetree-approach/

Roche, T. (2001, July 30). Saving Jessie Arbogast. *Time, 158*(4), 40–41. Retrieved from http://www.time.com/time/magazine/article/0,9171,1000445-1,00.html

Rodriguez, H. P., Anastario, M. P., Frankel, R. M., Odigie, E. G., Rogers, W. H., von Glahn, T., & Safran, D. G. (2008). Can teaching agenda-setting skills to physicians improve clinical interaction quality? A controlled intervention. *BMC Medical Education, 8*, 3–7.

Rogers, E. M. (1973). *Communication strategies for family planning*. New York: Free Press.

Rogers, E. M. (1983). *Diffusion of innovations* (3rd ed.). New York: The Free Press.

Rogers, L. E., & Escudero, V. (2004). Theoretical foundations. In L. E. Rogers & V. Escudero (Eds.) *Relational communication: An interactional perspective to the study of process and form* (pp. 3–21). Mahwah, NJ: Lawrence Erlbaum.

Rollnick, S., & Miller, W. (1995). What is motivational interviewing? *Behavioural and Cognitive Psychotherapy, 23*, 325–334. Reprinted online. Retrieved from http://www.motivationalinterview.net/clinical/whatismi.html

Roscoe, L. A., Tullis, J. A., Reich, R. R., & McCaffrey, J. C. (2013). Beyond good intentions and patient perceptions: Competing definitions of effective communication in head and neck cancer care at the end of life. *Health Communication, 28*, 183–192.

Rose, I. D., & Friedman, D. B. (2013). We need health information too: A systematic review of studies examining the health information seeking and communication practices of sexual minority youth. *Health Education Journal, 72*(4), 417–430.

Rosen, I. M., Gimotty, P. A., Shea, J. A., & Bellini, L. M. (2006). Evolution of sleep quantity, sleep deprivation, mood disturbances, empathy, and burnout among interns. *Academic Medicine, 81*(1), 82–85.

Rosenstein, A. H., & O'Daniel, M. (2008). Managing disruptive physician behavior: Impact on staff relationships and patient care. *Neurology, 70*(17), 1564–1570.

Rosenstock, I. M. (1960). What research in motivation suggests for public health. *American Journal of Public Health, 50*, 295–301.

Roser, M. (2015). Life expectancy. OurWorldinData.Org. Retrieved from http://ourworldindata.org/data/population-growth-vital-statistics/life-expectancy.

Ross, S., Ryan, C., Duncan, E. M., Francis, J. J., Johnston, M., Ker, J. S., . . . Bond, C. (2013). Perceived causes of prescribing errors by junior doctors in hospital inpatients: A study from the PROTECT programme. *British Medical Journal Quality & Safety, 2*, 97.

Rossiter, C. M., Jr. (1975). Defining "therapeutic communication." *Journal of Communication, 25*(3), 127–130.

Roter, D. L., Larson, S., Sands, D. Z., Ford, D. E., & Houston, T. (2008). Can e-mail messages between patients and physicians be patient-centered? *Health Communication, 23*, 80–86.

Rothman, A. J., & Salovey, P. (1997). Shaping perceptions to motivate healthy behavior: The role of message framing. *Psychological Bulletin, 121*, 3–19.

Rubenstein, A., & Macías-González, V. M. (2012). *Masculinity and sexuality in Modern Mexico*. Albuquerque, NM: University of New Mexico Press.

Rucinski, D. (2004, August). Community boundedness, personal relevance, and the knowledge gap. *Communication Research, 31*(4), 472–495.

Rudolph, J. (2008, March 7). Bonding with patients when time is scarce: Even the busiest physician can find time to convey caring and concern. *Medical Economics, 85*(5), 50–51.

Ruppert, R. A. (1996, March). Caring for the lay caregiver. *American Journal of Nursing, 96*, 40–46.

Russell, C. A., & Buhrau, D. (2015). Research report: The role of television viewing and direct experience in predicting adolescents' beliefs about the health risks of fast-food consumption. *Appetite, 92*, 200–206.

Russell, L. D., & Babrow, A. S. (2011). Risk in the making: Narrative, problematic integration, and the social construction of risk. *Communication Theory, 21*(3), 239–260. doi:10.1111/j.1468-2885.2011.01386.x

RU Sure. (2015). Rutgers University Center for Communication and Health Studies. Retrieved from http://commandhealthissues.rutgers.edu/ru-sure.html

Ryan, C. (2013, August). Language use in the United States: 2011. Table 2. Languages spoken at home for the population 5 years and over: 1980, 1990, 2000, and 2010. U.S. Census Bureau. Retrieved from https://www.census.gov/prod/2013pubs/acs-22.pdf

Ryan, E. B., Anas, A. P., & Vuckovich, M. (2007). The effects of age, hearing loss, and communication difficulty on first impressions. *Communication Research Reports, 24*(1), 13–19.

Ryan, E. B., & Butler, R. N. (1996). Communication, aging, and health: Toward understanding health provider relationships with older clients. *Health Communication, 8*, 191–197.

Ryan, L., Logsdon, M. C., McGill, S., Stikes, R., Senior, B., Helinger, B., . . . Davis, D. W. (2014). Evaluation of printed health education materials for use by low-education families. *Journal of Nursing Scholarship, 46*(4), 218–228. doi:10.1111/jnu.12076

Ryan-Wenger, N., & Gardner, W. (2012). Hospitalized children's perspectives on the quality and equity of their nursing care. *Journal of Nursing Care Quality, 27*(1), 35–42.

Sachdeva, N., Tuikka, A., Kimppa, K. K., & Suomi, R. (2015). Digital disability divide in information society. *Journal of Information, Communication & Ethics In Society, 13*(3/4), 283.

Sacks, R. J., Copas, A. J., Wilkinson, D. M., & Robinson, A. J. (2014). Uptake of the HPV vaccination programme in England: A cross-sectional survey of young women attending sexual health services. *Sexually Transmitted Infections, 90*(4), 315–321.

Saha, S., Guiton, G., Wimmers, P. F., & Wilkerson, L. (2008). Student body racial and ethnic composition and diversity-related outcomes in U.S. medical schools. *Journal of the American Medical Association, 300*(10), 1135–1145.

Salamon, J. (2008, May 26). My year inside Maimonides: A hospital with a polyglot patient body learns the importance of communication. *Modern Healthcare, 38*(21), 24.

Salander, P. (2002). Bad news from the patient's perspective: An analysis of the written narratives of newly diagnosed cancer patients. *Social Science & Medicine, 55*, 721–732.

Salas, E., Wilson, K. A., Murphy, C. E., King, H., & Salisbury, M. (2008, June). Communicating, coordinating, and cooperating when lives depend on it: Tips for teamwork. *Joint Commission Journal on Quality and Patient Safety, 34*, 333–341.

Salmon, C. T., & Atkin, C. (2003). Using media campaigns for health promotion. In T. L. Thompson, A. M. Dorsey, K. I. Miller, & R. Parrott (Eds.), *Handbook of health communication* (pp. 449–472). Mahwah, NJ: Lawrence Erlbaum.

Salonen, H., Lahtinen, M., Lappalainen, S., Nevala, N., Knibbs, L. D., Morawska, L., & Reijula, K. (2013). Physical characteristics of the indoor environment that affect health and well-being in healthcare facilities: A review. *Intelligent Buildings International, 5*(1), 325.

Samovar, L. A., & Porter, R. E. (2007). *Communication between cultures* (6th ed.). Belmont, CA: Wadsworth.

Sanders, L. (2003). The ethics imperative. *Modern Healthcare, 33*(11), 46.

Sanders-Jackson, A. (2014). Rated measures of narrative structure for written smoking-cessation texts. *Health Communication, 29*, 1009–1019.

Sandman, P. M. (2006a, August). Crisis communication best practices: Some quibbles and additions. *Journal of Applied Communication Research, 34*(3), 257–262.

Sandman, P. M. (2006b). Telling 9/11 emergency responders to wear their masks. In Comments and questions (and some answers). The Peter Sandman Risk Communication Website. Retrieved from http://www.psandman.com/gst2006.htm

Santa Cruz, J. (2014, March 10). Body-image pressure increasingly affects boys. *The Atlantic*. Retrieved from http://www.theatlantic.com/health/archive/2014/03/body-image-pressure-increasingly-affects-boys/283897/

Sastre, M. T. M., Sorum, P. C., & Mullet, E. (2011). Breaking bad news: The patient's viewpoint. *Health Communication, 26*, 649–655.

Savage, M. W., Scott, A. M., Aalboe, J. A., Stein, P. S., & Mullins, R. (2014). Perceptions of oral health in Appalachian Kentucky: Implications for message design. *Health Communication, 30*, 186–195.

Schein, E. H. (1986). *Organizational culture and leadership*. San Francisco: Jossey-Bass.

Schmid Mast, M., Hall, J. A., & Roter, D. (2008). Caring and dominance affect participants' perceptions and behaviors during a virtual medical visit. *Journal of General Internal Medicine, 23*(5), 523–527.

Schneider, M.-J. (2006). *Introduction to public health* (2nd ed.). Boston: Jones and Bartlett.

Scholl, J. C. (2007). The use of humor to promote patient-centered care. *Journal of Applied Communication Research, 35*(2), 156–176.

Schooler, C., Chaffee, S. H., Flora, J. A., & Roser, C. (1998). Health campaign channels: Tradeoffs among reach, specificity, and impact. *Health Communication Research, 24*, 410–432.

Schreiber, L. (2005). The importance of precision in language: Communication research and (so-called) alternative medicine. *Health Communication, 17*, 173–190.

Schulman, K. A., Berlin, J. A., Harless, W., Kerner, J. F., Sistrunk, S., Gersh, B. J., . . . Escarce, J. J. (1999). The effect of face and sex on physicians' recommendations for cardiac catheterization. *New England Journal of Medicine, 340*, 618–626.

Schur, L. (director and producer), & Thompson, L. (producer). (2008). *Greedy for life*. Arlington, VA: Schur Schot Productions.

Schur, L. (director and producer), & Thompson, L. (producer). (2012). *The beauty of aging*. Arlington, VA: Schur Schot Productions.

Schwade, S. (1994, December). Hospitals with the human touch. *Prevention, 46*, 96–99.

Scommegna, P. (2013, July). Exploring the paradox of U.S. Hispanics' longer life expectancy. Population Reference Bureau. Retrieved from http://www.prb.org/Publications/Articles/2013/us-hispanics-life-expectancy.aspx

Secretary of Agriculture: Bird flu poses "no health issue" to humans. (2015, May 31). *NPR*. Retrieved from http://www.npr.org/2015/05/31/410924073/secretary-of-agriculture-bird-flu-poses-no-health-issue-to-humans

Seeger, M. W. (2006, August). Best practices in crisis communication: An expert panel process. *Journal of Applied Communication Research, 34*(3), 232–244.

Segrin, C., & Domschke, T. (2011). Social support, loneliness, recuperative processes, and their direct and indirect effects on health. *Health Communication, 26*, 221–232. doi:10.1080/10410236.2010.546771

Segrin, C., & Passalacqua, S. A. (2010). Functions of loneliness, social support, health behaviors, and stress in association with poor health. *Health Communication, 25*, 312–322.

Seltzer, T., Gardner, E., Bichard, S., & Callison, C. (2012). PR in the ER: Managing internal organization-public relationships in a hospital emergency department. *Public Relations Review, 38*, 128–136.

Senge, P. M. (2006). *The fifth discipline: The art and practice of the learning organization.* New York: Doubleday/Currency.

Sentell, T., & Braun, K. L. (2012). Low health literacy, limited english proficiency, and health status in Asians, Latinos, and other racial/ethnic groups in California. *Journal of Health Communication, 17*, 82–99. doi:10.1080/10810730.2012.712621

Seo, M., & Matsaganis, M. D. (2013). How interpersonal communication mediates the relationship of multichannel communication connections to health-enhancing and health-threatening behaviors. *Journal of Health Communication, 18*(8), 1002–1020. doi:10.1080/10810730.2013.768726

Seymour, B., Getman, R., Saraf, A., Zhang, L. H., & Kalenderian, E. (2015). When advocacy obscures accuracy online: Digital pandemics of public health misinformation through an antifluoride case Study. *American Journal of Public Health, 105*(3), 517–523.

Shapiro, I. S. (1984, Fall). Executive forum. Managerial communication: The view from the inside. *California Management Review, 27*, 157–172.

Sharf, B. (2010). The day Patrick Swayze died. *Health Communication, 25*, 628–631.

Sharf, B. F., Haidet, P., & Kroll, T. L. (2005). "I want you to put me in the grave with all my limbs": The meaning of active health participation. In E. B. Ray (Ed.), *Health communication in practice: A case study approach* (pp. 39–51). Mahwah, NJ: Lawrence Erlbaum.

Shepard, D. S., & Rabinowitz, F. E. (2013). The power of shame in men who are depressed: Implications for counselors. *Journal of Counseling & Development, 91*(4), 451–457. doi:10.1002/j.1556-6676.2013.00117.x

Should the government provide free universal health care to all Americans? (n.d.). BalancedPolitics.org. Retrieved from http://www.balancedpolitics.org/universal_health_care.htm

Shue, C. K., O'Hara, L. L. S., Marini, D., McKenzie, J., & Schreiner, M. (2010). Diabetes and low-health literacy: A preliminary outcome report of a mediated intervention to enhance patient-physician communication. *Communication Education, 59*, 360–373.

Shuler, S. (2011). Social support without strings attached. *Health Communication, 26*, 198–201.

Siegel, J. T., Alvaro, E. M., Crano, W. D., Lienemann, B. A., Hohman, Z. P., & O'Brien, E. (2012). Increasing social support for depressed individuals: A cross-cultural assessment of an affect-expectancy approach. *Journal of Health Communication, 17*(6), 713–732.

Silk, K. J., Bigbsy, E., Volkman, J., Kingsley, C., Atkin, C., Ferrara, M., & Goins, L.-A. (2006). Formative research on adolescent and adult perceptions of risk factors for breast cancer. *Social Science & Medicine, 63*, 3124–3136.

Silver, M. (2013, August 17). A new chapter in the immortal life of Henrietta Lacks. *National Geographic.* Retrieved from http://news.nationalgeographic.com/news/2013/08/130816-henrietta-lacks-immortal-life-hela-cells-genome-rebecca-skloot-nih/

Silvester, J., Patterson, F., Koczwara, A., & Ferguson, E. (2007). "Trust me . . . ": Psychological and behavioral predictors or perceived physician empathy. *Journal of Applied Psychology, 92*(2), 519–527.

Simon-Arndt, C. M., Hurtado, S. L., & Patriarca-Troyk, L. A. (2006). Acceptance of Web-based personalized feedback: User ratings of an alcohol misuse prevention program targeting U.S. Marines. *Health Communication, 21*, 13–22.

Singer, D. G., & Singer, J. L. (1998). Developing critical viewing skills and media literacy in children. *Annals of the American Academy of Political and Social Science, 557*, 164–179.

Siskin, A. (2011, March 22). Treatment of noncitizens under the Patient Protection and Affordable Care Act. Washington, DC: Congressional Research Service. Retrieved from https://www.ciab.com/WorkArea/DownloadAsset.aspx?id=2189&libID=2211

Sismondo, S. (2008). How pharmaceutical industry funding affects trial outcomes: Causal structures and responses. *Social Science & Medicine, 66*(9), 1909–1914.

Skluth, M. (2007, September 7). Get patients involved. *Medical Economics, 84*(17), 16.

Slack, P. (1991). Responses to plague in early modern Europe: The implications of public health. In A. Mack (Ed.), *In time of plague: The history and social consequences of lethal epidemic disease* (pp. 111–132). New York: New York University Press.

Slater, M. D. (2006). Specification and misspecification of theoretical foundations and logic models for health communication campaigns. *Health Communication, 20*, 149–158.

Slusarz, M. (1996). From fried rice to sushi: To market an integrated delivery system throw out the old menu. *Journal of Health Care Marketing, 16*, 12–15.

Smedema, S. M., Ebener, D., & Grist-Gordon, V. (2012). The impact of humorous media on attitudes toward persons with disabilities. *Disability & Rehabilitation, 34*(17), 1431–1437.

Smedley, B. D., Stith, A. Y., & Nelson, A. R. (2003). *Unequal treatment: Confronting racial and ethnic disparities in health care.* Washington, DC: National Academies Press. Retrieved December 3, 2008, from http://books.nap.edu/openbook.php?isbn=030908265X

Smith, D. (2011). Health care consumer's use of trust and health information sources. *Journal of Communication in Healthcare, 4*, 200–209.

Smith, K. C., & Wakefield, M. (2006). Newspaper coverage of youth and tobacco: Implications for public health. *Health Communication, 19*, 19–28.

Smith, R. (2007, April/May). Media depictions of health topics: Challenge and stigma formats. *Journal of Health Communication, 12*, 233–249.

Smith, R. A., Downs, E., & Witte, K. (2007, June). Drama theory and entertainment education: Exploring the effects of a radio drama on behavioral intentions to limit HIV transmission in Ethiopia. *Communication Monographs, 74*(2), 133–153.

Smith, R. C., & Hoppe, R. B. (1991). The patient's story: Integrating the patient- and physician-centered approaches to interviewing. *Annals of Internal Medicine, 115*, 460–477.

Smith, S. G., Wolf, M. S., & Wagner, C. V. (2010). Socioeconomic status, statistical confidence, and patient-provider communication: An analysis of the Health Information National Trends Survey (HINTS 2007). *Journal of Health Communication, 15*, 169–185. doi:10.1080/10810730.2010.522690

Smith-du Pré, A., & Beck, C. S. (1996). Enabling patients and physicians to pursue multiple goals in health care encounters: A case study. *Health Communication, 8*, 73–90.

Smith-McLallen, A., Fishbein, M., & Hornik, R. C. (2011). Psychosocial determinants of cancer-related information seeking among cancer patients. *Journal of Health Communication, 16*, 212–225.

Sobo, E. J., & Loustaunau, M. O. (2010). *The cultural context of health, illness, and medicine*. Santa Barbara, CA: Praeger.

Solomon, J., Knapp, P., Raynor, D., & Atkin, K. (2013). Worlds apart? An exploration of prescribing and medicine-taking decisions by patients, GPs and local policy makers. *Health Policy, 112*, 264–272. doi:10.1016/j.healthpol.2013.08.004

Sontag, S. (1978). *Illness as metaphor*. New York: Farrar, Straus and Giroux.

Sopory, P. (2005). Metaphor in formative evaluation and message design: An application to relationship and alcohol use. *Health Communication, 17*, 149–172.

Soule, K. P, & Roloff, M. E. (2000). Help between persons with and without disabilities from a resource theory perspective. In D. O. Braithwaite & T. L. Thompson (Eds.), *Handbook of communication and people with disabilities: Research and applications* (pp. 67–83). Mahwah, NJ: Lawrence Erlbaum.

Sparks, L., Villagran, M. M., Parker-Raley, J., & Cunningham, C. B. (2007). A patient-centered approach to breaking bad news: Communication guidelines for health care providers. *Journal of Applied Communication, 35*(2), 177–196.

Spector, R., & McCarthy, P. (2005). *The Nordstrom way to customer service excellence: A handbook for implementing great service in your organization*. Hoboken, NJ: John Wiley & Sons.

Stavrositu, C. D., & Kim, J. (2015). All blogs are not created equal: The role of narrative formats and user-generated comments in health prevention. *Health Communication, 30*, 485–495.

Stephens, N. M., Markus, H. R., & Fryberg, S. A. (2012). Social class disparities in health and education: Reducing inequality by applying a sociocultural self model of behavior. *Psychological Review, 119*, 723–744.

Stewart, L. P., Lederman, L. C., Golubow, M., Cattafesta, J. L., Godhart, F. W., Powell, R. L., & Laitman, L. (2002, Winter). Applying communication theories to prevent dangerous drinking among college students: The RU SURE campaign. *Communication Studies, 53*(4), 381–399.

Street, J. L., & De Haes, H. C. (2013). Medical education: Designing a curriculum for communication skills training from a theory and evidence-based perspective. *Patient Education and Counseling, 93*, 27–33.

Street, R. L., Jr., Gordon, H. S., Ward, M. M., Krupat, E., & Kravitz, R. L. (2005). Patient participation in medical consultations: Why some patients are more involved than others. *Medical Care, 43*(10), 960–969.

Stretcher, V. J., & Rosenstock, I. M. (1997). The health belief model. In K. Glanz, F. M. Lewis, & B. K. Rimer (Eds.), *Health behavior and health education* (pp. 41–59). San Francisco: Jossey-Bass.

Studer, Q. (2003). *Hardwiring excellence: Purpose, worthwhile work, making a difference*. Gulf Breeze, FL: Fire Starter.

Studts, C. T., Tarasenko, Y. Y., & Schoenberg, N. (2013). Barriers to cervical cancer screening among middle-aged and older rural Appalachian women. *Journal of Community Health, 38*(3), 500–512.

Stynes, T. (2014, July 29). HCA holdings profit rises 14%. *The Wall Street Journal*. Retrieved from http://www.wsj.com/articles/hca-holdings-profit-rises-14-1406640706

Suchman, A. L., Markakis, K., Beckman, H. B., & Frankel, R. (1997). A model of empathic communication in the medical interview. *Journal of the American Medical Association, 277*, 678–683.

Sudore, R. L., Schillinger, D., Knight, S. J., & Fried, T. R. (2010). Uncertainty about advance care planning treatment preferences among diverse older adults. *Journal of Health Communication, 15*, 159–171.

Sugai, W. J. (2008, June 20). Taking a hard line with compliant patients. Talk back. Letter to the editor. *Medical Economics, 85*(12), 14.

Sumner, P., Vivian-Griffiths, S., Boivin, J., Williams, A., Venetis, C. A., Davies, A., . . . Chambers, C. D. (2014). The association between exaggeration in health related science news and academic press releases: Retrospective observational study. BMJ *(Clinical Research Ed.), 349*, g7015.

Sutton, R. L. (2007). *The no asshole rule: Building a civilized workplace and surviving one that isn't*. New York: Warner Business.

Sutton, S. (2014, April 25). Stephen's story—when life gives you cancer [YouTube video]. Retrieved from https://www.youtube.com/watch?v=MvG3ifEd0t0

Swain, K. A. (2007, Summer). Outrage factors and explanations in news coverage of the anthrax attacks. *Journalism and Mass Communication Quarterly, 84*(2), 335–352.

Swanson, A. (2015, February 11). Big pharmaceutical companies are spending far more on marketing than research. *Washington Post*. Retrieved from http://www.washingtonpost.com/blogs/wonkblog/wp/2015/02/11/big-pharmaceutical-companies-are-spending-far-more-on-marketing-than-research/

Swazey, J. P., & Reeds, K. (1978). *Today's medicine, tomorrow's science: Essays on paths of discovery in the biomedical sciences.* U.S. Department of Health, Education, and Welfare. Washington, DC: Author. Retrieved from http://www.baruch.cuny.edu/library/alumni/online_exhibits/digital/2001/swazey_reeds_1978/default.htm

Swedish, J. (April 28, 2008). Our carpe diem moment; execs, clinicians must help policymakers find the way to universal coverage (Opinions Commentary). *Modern Healthcare,* 38(17), 22.

Swiderski, R. M. (1976). The idiom of diagnosis. *Communication Quarterly, 24,* 3–11.

Sylvia, Z., King, T. K., & Morse, B. J. (2014). Virtual ideals: The effect of video game play on male body image. *Computers in Human Behavior, 37,* 183–188.

Szanton, S., Rifkind, J., Mohanty, J., Miller, E., Thorpe, R., Nagababu, E., . . . Evans, M. (2012). Racial discrimination is associated with a measure of red blood cell oxidative stress: A potential pathway for racial health disparities. *International Journal of Behavioral Medicine, 19*(4), 489–495.

Taha, H., Al-Qutob, R., Nyström, L., Wahlström, R., & Berggren, V. (2013). "Would a man smell a rose then throw it away?" Jordanian men's perspectives on women's breast cancer and breast health. *BMC Women's Health, 13*(1), 1–21. doi:10.1186/1472-6874-13-41

Tai, Z., & Sun, T. (2007, December). Media dependencies in a changing media environment: The case of the 2003 SARS epidemic in China. *New Media & Society, 9*(6), 987–1009.

Talen, M. R., Muller-Held, C. F., Eshleman, K. G., & Stephens, L. (2011). Patients' communication with doctors: A randomized control study of a brief patient communication intervention. *Families, Systems, & Health, 29*(3), 171–183. doi:10.1037/a0024399

Tan, G., Jensen, M. P., Thornby, J. I., & Anderson, K. O. (2006). Are patient ratings of chronic pain services related to treatment outcome? *Journal of Rehabilitation Research and Development, 43*(4), 451–460.

Tanner, A. H., Friedman, D. B., & Zheng, Y. (2015). Influences on the construction of health news: The reporting practices of local television news health journalists. *Journal of Broadcasting & Electronic Media, 59*(2), 359–376.

Tardy, C. H. (1994). Counteracting task-induced stress: Studies of instrumental and emotional support in problem-solving contexts. In B. R. Burleson, T. L. Albrecht, & I. G. Sarason (Eds.), *Communication of social support: Messages, interactions, relationships, and community* (pp. 71–87). Thousand Oaks, CA: Sage.

Tarrant, C., Windridge, K., Boulton, J., Baker, R., & Freeman, G. (2003, June 14). How important is personal care in general practice? *British Medical Journal (Clinical Research Edition), 326,* 1310.

Tauber, M. (2014, August 13). How Robin Williams fought, and lost, his battles with addiction and depression. *People.* Retrieved from http://www.people.com/article/robin-williams-dies-depression-addiciton-struggles

Taubes, G. (1998). Telling time by the second hand. *Technology Review, 101,* 76–78.

Tellis-Nayak, V. (2005). Who will care for the caregivers? *Health Progress, 86*(6), 37–43.

10 facts on obesity. (2012, May). Geneva, Switzerland: World Health Organization. Retrieved from http://www.who.int/features/factfiles/obesity/en/

Terrell, G. E. (2007, September/October). "Can't get no (physician) satisfaction?" *Physician Executive,* pp. 12–15.

thetruth.com. (2015). Legacy Foundation. Retrieved from http://www.thetruth.com/?video=LvgUUeSu9tA&gclid=CJfStovwtcYCFY89gQodNnYMFg

Thomas, K. (2012, March 6). AARP study says price of popular drugs rose 26%. *The New York Times* reprints online, n.p. Retrieved from http://www.nytimes.com/2012/03/07/business/aarp-study-says-price-of-popular-drugs-rose-26.html

Thompson, D. (2014, July 2). Ebola's deadly spread in Africa driven by public health failures, cultural beliefs. *National Geographic.* Retrieved from http://news.nationalgeographic.com/news/2014/07/140702-ebola-epidemic-fever-world-health-guinea-sierra-leone-liberia/

Thompson, T. L. (1984). The invisible helping hand: The role of communication in the health and social service professions. *Communication Quarterly, 32,* 148–161.

Thompson, T. L. (2011). Hope and the act of informed dialogue: A delicate balance at the end of life. *Journal of Language and Social Psychology, 30,* 177–192.

Thompson, T. L., & Gillotti, C. (2005). Staying out of the line of fire: A medical student learns about bad news delivery. In E. B. Ray (Ed.), *Health communication in practice: A case study approach* (pp. 11–25). Mahwah, NJ: Lawrence Erlbaum.

Thompson, T. L., Parrott, R., & Nussbaum, J. F. (2011). *The Routledge handbook of health communication.* New York: Taylor & Francis.

Thomsen, T., Rydahl-Hansen, S., & Wagner, L. (2010). A review of potential factors relevant to coping in patients with advanced cancer. *Journal of Clinical Nursing, 19,* 3410–3426. doi:10.1111/j.1365-2702.2009.03154.x

Thomtén, J., Soares, J., & Sundin, Ö. (2011). The role of psychosocial factors in the course of pain: A 1-year follow-up study among women living in Sweden. *Archives of Women's Mental Health, 14,* 493–503. doi:10.1007/s00737-011-0244-0

Tichenor, P. J., Donohue, G. A., & Olien, C. N. (1970). Mass media flow and differential growth in knowledge. *Public Opinion Quarterly, 34,* 159–170.

Tiedtke, C., de Rijk, A., Donceel, P., Christiaens, M., & Dierckx de Casterl, B. (2012). Survived but feeling vulnerable and insecure: A qualitative study of the mental preparation for RTW after breast cancer treatment. *BMC Public Health, 12*(1), 538–550.

Tirrell, M. (2015, February 9). Ice Bucket Challenge: 6 months later. *CNBC.* Retrieved from http://www.cnbc.com/id/102405889

Topol, E. (2015). *The patient will see you now: The future of medicine is in your hands.* New York: Basic Books.

Tough, E. A., & White, A. R. (2011). Effectiveness of acupuncture/dry needling for myofascial trigger point pain. *Physical Therapy Reviews, 16*, 147–154.

Tourangeau, A. E., & Cranley, L. A. (2005). Nurse intention to remain employed: Understanding and strengthening determinants. *Journal of Advanced Nursing, 55*(4), 497–509.

Tovey, P., & Broom, A. (2007). Oncologists' and specialist cancer nurses' approaches to complementary and alternative medicine and their impact on patient action. *Social Science & Medicine, 64*, 2550–2564.

Transue, E. R. (2004). *On call: A doctor's days and nights in residency*. New York: St. Martin's Griffin.

Troth, A., & Peterson, C. C. (2000). Factors predicting safe-sex talk and condom use in early sexual relationships. *Health Communication, 12*, 195–218.

Troy, D. T., & Wilson, D. M. (2014). The cost of the Affordable Care Act to large employers. American Health Policy Institute. Retrieved from http://www.americanhealthpolicy.org/content/documents/resources/2014_ACA_Cost_Study.pdf

Trujillo, J. M., & Hardy, Y. (2009). A nutrition journal and diabetes shopping experience to improve pharmacy students' empathy and cultural competence. *American Journal of Pharmaceutical Education, 73*(2), 1–10.

truth® named one of the top 15 ad campaigns of 21st century. (2015, January 12). *PR Newswire*.

truth® overview. (n.d.). Legacy Foundation. Retrieved from http://www.legacyforhealth.org/content/download/621/7337/file/truth_fact_sheet_January_2012.PDF

Tu, H. T. (2005, June). Medicare seniors much less willing to limit physician-hospital choice for lower costs. Center for Studying Health System Change, Issue Brief No. 96, nonpaginated. Retrieved from www.hschange.org/CONTENT/744

Tuffrey-Wijne, I., Hollins, S., & Curfs, L. (2005). Supporting patients who have intellectual disabilities: A survey investigating staff training needs. *International Journal of Palliative Nursing, 11*(4), 182–188.

Turner, J. T. (2011). Sex and the spectacle of music videos: An examination of the portrayal of race and sexuality in music videos. *Sex Roles, 64*(3/4), 173–191.

Turpin, T. P. (2013). Unintended consequences of a segmentation strategy: Exploring constraint recognition among black women targeted in HIV/AIDS campaigns. *Public Relations Journal, 7*(2), 96–127.

Tustin, N. (2010). The role of patient satisfaction in online health information seeking. *Journal of Health Communication, 15*, 3–17.

TV program description. (2004). *The most dangerous woman in America* [video documentary], Nancy Porter (Writer/Director). NOVA in association with WGBH/Boston. Retrieved from http://www.pbs.org/wgbh/nova/typhoid/about.html

Twaddle, A. C., & Hessler, R. M. (1987). *A sociology of health* (2nd ed.). New York: Macmillan.

Uba, L. (1992). Cultural barriers to health care for Southeast Asian refugees. *Public Health Reports, 107*, 544–548.

Ugarte, W. J., Högberg, U., Valladares, E. C., & Essén, B. (2013). Measuring HIV- and AIDS-related stigma and discrimination in Nicaragua: Results from a community-based study. *AIDS Education & Prevention, 25*(2), 164–178. doi:10.1521/aeap.2013.25.2.164

Ulmer, R. R., Seeger, M. W., & Sellnow, T. L. (2007, June). Post-crisis communication and renewal: Expanding the parameters of post-crisis discourse. *Public Relations Review, 33*(2), 130–134.

UNAIDS reports a 52% reduction in new HIV infections. (2013). Joint United Nations Programme on HIV/AIDS. Retrieved from http://www.unaids.org/en/resources/presscentre/pressreleaseandstatementarchive/2013/september/20130923prunga

Ünal, S. (2012). Evaluating the effect of self-awareness and communication techniques on nurses' assertiveness and self-esteem. *Contemporary Nurse: A Journal for the Australian Nursing Profession, 43*(1), 90–98.

Underage drinking. (2012). National Institute on Alcohol Abuse and Alcoholism. Retrieved from http://pubs.niaaa.nih.gov/publications/UnderageDrinking/Underage_Fact.pdf

Uninsured in America. Key facts. (2000, March). Menlo Park, CA: Kaiser Commission on Medicaid and the Uninsured. Retrieved from http://www.pbs.org/newshour/health/uninsured/kaiserstudy/kaiser_key_facts.pdf

United Health Foundation. (2015). Preventable hospitalizations. United States. Minnetonka, MN: Author. Retrieved from http://www.americashealthrankings.org/ALL/preventable

Unsworth, C. (1996). Team decision-making in rehabilitation. *American Journal of Physical Medicine & Rehabilitation, 75*, 483–486.

Updegraff, J. A., Brick, C., Emanuel, A. S., Mintzer, R. E., & Sherman, D. K. (2015). Message framing for health: Moderation by perceived susceptibility and motivational orientation in a diverse sample of Americans. *Health Psychology, 34*(1), 20–29.

U.S. Bureau of Labor Statistics. (2009, November). Spotlight on statistics. Health care. Washington, DC: Author. Retrieved from http://www.bls.gov/spotlight/2009/health_care/

U.S. Bureau of Labor Statistics. (2012a, February 1). Employment projections 2010–2020. Washington, DC: Author. Retrieved from http://bls.gov/news.release/ecopro.nr0.htm

U.S. Bureau of Labor Statistics. (2012b). Occupational outlook handbook. Washington, DC: Author. Retrieved from http://www.bls.gov/ooh/Healthcare/Registered-nurses.htm

U.S. Bureau of Labor Statistics. (2013, December 19). Employment projections 2012–2022. Washington, DC: Author. Retrieved from http://www.bls.gov/news.release/pdf/ecopro.pdf

U.S. Bureau of Labor Statistics. (2014a). Employed persons by detailed occupation, sex, race, and Hispanic or Latino ethnicity. Washington, DC: Author. Retrieved from http://www.bls.gov/cps/cpsaat11.pdf

U.S. Bureau of Labor Statistics. (2014b). Healthcare occupations. Occupational outlook handbook. Washington, DC: Author. Retrieved from http://www.bls.gov/ooh/healthcare/home.htm

U.S. Bureau of Labor Statistics. (2015). Employed persons. Washington, DC: Author. Retrieved from http://www.bls.gov/cps/cpsaat11.htm

U.S. Census Bureau. (2009, June 23). Census Bureau reports world's older population projected to triple by 2050. Washington, DC: Author. Retrieved from https://www.census.gov/newsroom/releases/archives/international_population/cb09-97.html

U.S. Census Bureau. (2011, November). The older population: 2010. Washington, DC: Author. Retrieved from http://www.census.gov/prod/cen2010/briefs/c2010br-09.pdf

U.S. Census Bureau. (2012). Table 104. Expectations of life at birth, 1970 to 2008, and projections, 2010 to 2020. Washington, DC: Author. Retrieved from http://www.census.gov/compendia/statab/2012/tables/12s0104.pdf

U.S. Census Bureau. (2014). Population estimates. Washington, DC: Author. Retrieved from http://www.census.gov/popest/data/national/asrh/2014/index.html

U.S. Census Bureau News. (2008, August 14). An older and more diverse nation by midcentury. Washington, DC: Author. Retrieved from http://www.census.gov/Press-Release/www/releases/archives/population/012496.html

Uscher-Pines, L., & Mehrotra, A. (2014). Analysis of Teladoc use seems to indicate expanded access to care for patients without prior connection to a provider. *Health Affairs*, 33(2), 258–264.

U.S. Department of Education. (2015). Digest of education: Statistics 2014, Table 507. Literacy skills of adults, by type of literacy, proficiency levels, and selected characteristics: 1992-2003. Retrieved from https://nces.ed.gov/fastfacts/display.asp?id=69

U.S. Department of Health and Human Services (DHHS), Health Resources and Services Administration. (2010). The registered nurse population: Findings from the 2008 national sample survey of registered nurses. Washington, DC: Author. Retrieved from http://bhpr.hrsa.gov/healthworkforce/rnsurveys/rnsurveyfinal.pdf

U.S. Department of Labor. (2012, March 29). Occupational outlook handbook, 2012–13 edition. Medical and health services managers. Washington, DC: Author. Retrieved from http://www.bls.gov/ooh/management/medical-and-health-services-managers.htm

U.S. Food and Drug Administration (FDA). (2008). Beware of online cancer fraud. Washington, DC: Author. Retrieved from http://www.fda.gov/ForConsumers/ConsumerUpdates/ucm048383.htm

Usta, J., Antoun, J., Ambuel, B., & Khawaja, M. (2012). Involving the health care system in domestic violence: What women want. *Annals of Family Medicine, 10*(3), 213–220.

Uwujaren, J. (2012, December 9). Mental illness: How the media contributes to its stigma. *Everyday Feminism*. Retrieved from http://everydayfeminism.com/2012/12/mental-illness-stigma/

Vangeest, J. B., Welch, V. L., & Weiner, S. J. (2010). Patients' perceptions of screening for health literacy: Reactions to the newest vital sign. *Journal of Health Communication, 15*, 402–412.

van der Riet, P., Rossiter, R., Kirby, D., Dluzewska, T., & Harmon, C. (2015). Piloting a stress management and mindfulness program for undergraduate nursing students: Student feedback and lessons learned. *Nurse Education Today, 35*(1), 44–49.

Van Ouytsel, J., Ponnet, K., & Walrave, M. (2014). The associations between adolescents' consumption of pornography and music videos and their sexting behavior. *Cyberpsychology, Behavior and Social Networking, 17*(12), 772–778.

van Zanten, M., Boulet, J. R., & McKinley, D. (2007). Using standardized patients to assess the interpersonal skills of physicians: Six years' experience with a high-stakes certification examination. *Health Communication, 22*(3), 195–205.

Vardigan, B. (2015, March 11). Fear of illness is the illness itself, and health information on the Internet is fueling the phobia. *Health Day*. Retrieved from http://consumer.healthday.com/encyclopedia/diseases-and-conditions-15/misc-diseases-and-conditions-news-203/hypochondria-647704.html

Vaughan, C. (2012, March 8). 4 social media strategies to build patient loyalty. *HealthLeaders Media*. Retrieved from http://www.healthleadersmedia.com/page-1/MAR-277456/4-Social-Media-Strategies-to-Build-Patient-Loyalty

Veatch, R. M. (1983). The physician as stranger: The ethics of the anonymous patient–physician relationship. In E. E. Shelp (Ed.), *The clinical encounter: The moral fabric of the patient–physician relationship* (pp. 187–207). Dordrecht, The Netherlands: D. Reidel.

Veatch, R. M. (1991). *The patient–physician relation: The patient as partner, Part 2*. Bloomington: Indiana University Press.

Venetis, M. K., Robinson, J. D., & Kearney, T. (2015). Breast-cancer patients' participation behavior and coping during presurgical consultations: A pilot study. *Health Communication, 30*(1), 19–25.

Verlinde, E., De Laender, N., De Maesschalck, S., Deveugele, M., & Willems, S. (2012). The social gradient in doctor-patient communication. *International Journal for Equity in Health, 11*(1), 12–25. doi:10.1186/1475-9276-11-12

Vernon, J. A., Trujillo, A., Rosenbaum, S., & DeBuono, B. (2007). Low health literacy: Implications for national health policy. Retrieved from http://publichealth.gwu.edu/departments/healthpolicy/CHPR/downloads/LowHealthLiteracyReport10_4_07.pdf

Vest, J. (1997, July 21). Joe Camel walks his last mile. *U.S. News & World Report, 123*, 56.

Vickers C., & Goble, R. (2011). Well, now, okey dokey: English discourse markers in Spanish-language medical consultations. *The Canadian Modern Language Review, 67*, 536–567.

Vilhauer, R. P. (2011). "Them" and "us": The experiences of women with metastatic disease in mixed-stage versus stage-specific breast cancer support groups. *Psychology & Health, 26*(6), 781–797.

Viva Viagra. (2008). TV spots. Pfizer. Retrieved from https://www.youtube.com/watch?v=NyMXahpRVV4

Vogt, D. (2013). Research on women, trauma and PTSD. Washington, DC: National Center for PTSD. Retrieved from http://www.ptsd.va.gov/professional/treatment/women/women-trauma-ptsd.asp

Waitzkin, H. (1991). *The politics of medical encounters: How patients and doctors deal with social problems.* New Haven, CT: Yale University Press.

Wakefield, A. J., Murch, S. H., Anthony, A., Linnell, J., Casson, D. M., Malik, M., . . . Walker-Smith, J. A. (1998). Ileal-lymphoid-nodular hyperplasia, non-specific colitis, and pervasive developmental disorder in children. *The Lancet, 351*, 637–641. [Retracted]

Walker, K. L., Arnold, C. L., Miller-Day, M., & Webb, L. M. (2002). Investigating the physician–patient relationship: Examining emerging themes. *Health Communication, 14*, 45–68.

Waller, M, L. A., Carlin, B. P., Xia, H., & Gelfand, A. E. (1997, June). Hierarchical spatio-temporal mapping of disease rates. *Journal of the American Statistical Association, 92*(438), 607–617.

Walsh, K., Jordan, Z., & Apolloni, L. (2009). The problematic art of conversation: Communication and health practice evolution. *Practice Development in Health Care, 8*, 166–179.

Walters, E. (2015, February 12). Virtual doctors making medical board really nervous. *Weeks*MD. Retrieved from http://weeksmd.com/2015/02/virtual-medicine-vs-standard-care/

Wang, B., Deveaux, L., Li, X., Marshall, S., Chen, X., & Stanton, B. (2014). The impact of youth, family, peer and neighborhood risk factors on developmental trajectories of risk involvement from early through middle adolescence. *Social Science & Medicine, 106*, 43–52.

Wang, X. (2011). The role of anticipated guilt in intentions to register as organ donors and to discuss organ donation with family. *Health Communication, 26*, 683–690. doi:10.1080/10410236.2011.563350

Wang, X., & Arpan, L. M. (2008, January/March). Effects of race and ethnic identity on audience evaluation of HIV public service announcements. *Howard Journal of Communications, 19*(1), 44–63.

Wang, Z., & Gantz, W. (2010). Health content in local television news: A current appraisal. *Health Communication, 25*, 230–237. doi:10.1080/10410231003698903

Wanzer, M. B., Booth-Butterfield, M., & Gruber, K. (2004). Perceptions of health care providers' communication: Relationships between patient-centered communication and satisfaction. *Health Communication, 16*, 363–384.

Wanzer, M. B., Sparks, L., & Frymier, A. B. (2009). Humorous communication within the lives of older adults: The relationships among humor, coping efficacy, age, and life satisfaction, *Health Communication, 24*, 128–136.

Wanzer, M. B., Wojtaszczyk, A. M., Schimert, J., Missert, L., Baker, S., Baker, R., & Dunkle, B. (2010). Enhancing the "informed" in informed consent: A pilot test of a multimedia presentation. *Health Communication, 25*, 365–374.

Warren-Jeanpiere, L., Miller, K. S., & Warren, A. M. (2010). African American women's retrospective perceptions of the intergenerational transfer of gynecological health care information received from mothers: Implications for families and providers. *Journal of Family Communication, 10*(2), 81–98. doi:10.1080/15267431003595454

Waseem, M., & Ryan, M. (2005). "Doctor" or "doctora": Do patients really care? *Pediatric Emergency Care, 21*(8), 515–517.

Watson, T. J. (2014). What we have here is a failure to communicate! Communication mistakes account for 25 percent of malpractice claims at WILMIC and are among the most frequent grievances filed with the OLR; avoid communication breakdown with clients by following effective communication practices. *The Wisconsin Lawyer, 11*, 51.

Watzlawick, P., Beavin, J. H., & Jackson, D. D. (1967). *Pragmatics of human communication.* New York: W. W. Norton.

Waymer, D., & Heath, R. L. (2007, February). Emergent agents: The forgotten publics in crisis communication and issues management research. *Journal of Applied Communication Research, 35*(1), 88–108.

Weaver, A. J., Zelenkauskaite, A., & Samson, L. (2012). The (non)violent world of YouTube: Content trends in Web video. *Journal of Communication, 62*(6), 1065–1083.

Webb, T., Jenkins, L., Browne, N., Abdelmonen, A. A., & Kraus, J. (2007). Violent entertainment pitched to adolescents: An analysis of PG-13 films. *Pediatrics, 119*(6), e1219–e1229.

Wechsler, H., Nelson, T. F., Lee, J. E., Seibring, M., Lewis, C., & Keeling, R. P. (2003, July). Perception and reality: A national evaluation of social norms marketing interventions to reduce college students' heavy alcohol use. *Journal of Studies on Alcohol, 64*(4), 484–494.

Weinberg, D. (2011, May 2). U.S. hospital turns to Toyota for management inspiration. Voice of America. Retrieved from http://www.voanews.com/content/us-hospital-turns-to-toyota-for-management-inspiration—121165799/163553.html

Weinrich, S., Vijayakumar, S., Powell, I. J., Priest, J., Hamner, C. A., McCloud, L., & Pettaway, C. (2007). Knowledge of hereditary prostate cancer among high-risk African American men. *Oncology Nursing Forum, 34*(4), 854–860.

Weir, K. (2013, November). Feel like a fraud? American Psychological Association. Retrieved from http://www.apa.org/gradpsych/2013/11/fraud.aspx

Weiss, C. (2013, July 20). Patient comes to Mayo for foot surgery, receives lifesaving surprise. Mayo Clinic. Retrieved from http://sharing.mayoclinic.org/discussion/patient-comes-to-mayo-for-foot-surgery-receives-lifesaving-surprise/

Weiss, G. G. (2008, June 20). The new doctor–patient paradigm: How the shift from the "physician as wise parent" model to one of more shared responsibility is playing out in the exam room. *Medical Economics, 85*(12), 48–52.

Welch, G., Rose, G., & Ernst, D. (2006). Motivational interviewing and diabetes: What is used, and does it work? *Diabetes Spectrum, 19*(1), 5–11.

Wells, D. L. (2009). The effects of animals on human health and well-being. *Journal of Social Issues, 65*, 1540–4560.

West, C. P., Dyrbye, L. N., Rabatin, J. T., Call, T. G., Davidson, J. H., Multari, A., . . . Shanafelt, T. D. (2014). Intervention to promote physician well-being, job satisfaction, and professionalism: A randomized clinical trial. *Journal of the American Medical Association Internal Medicine, 174*(4), 527–533. doi:10.1001/jamainternmed.2013.14387.

Weston, W. W., & Lipkin, M., Jr. (1989). Doctors learning communication skills: Developmental issues. In M. Stewart & D. Roter (Eds.), *Communicating with medical patients. Vol. 9. Interpersonal communication* (pp. 43–57). Newbury Park, CA: Sage.

Whaley, B. B. (1999). Explaining illness to children: Advancing theory and research by determining message content. *Health Communication, 11*, 185–193.

Whaley, B. B. (2000). Explaining illness to children: Theory, strategies, and future inquiry. In B. B. Whaley (Ed.), *Explaining illness* (pp. 195–207). Mahwah, NJ: Lawrence Erlbaum.

Whaley, B. B., & Edgar, T. (2008). Explaining illness to children. In K. B. Wright & S. D. Moore (Eds.), *Applied health communication* (pp. 145–158). Cresskill, NJ: Hampton Press.

What's right in health care: 365 stories of purpose, worthwhile work, and making a difference. (2007). Compiled by Studer Group. Gulf Breeze, FL: Fire Starter.

White, A., Philogene, G., Fine, L., & Sinha, S. (2009). Social support and self-reported health status of older adults in the United States. *American Journal of Public Health, 99*(10), 1872–1878.

White, A. D. (1925). *A history of the warfare of science with theology in Christendom* (vol. 2). New York: D. Appleton (originally published in 1896).

Whitten, P., Sypher, B. D., & Patterson, J. D., III. (2000). Transcending the technology of telemedicine: An analysis of telemedicine in North Carolina. *Health Communication, 12*, 109–135.

Wicks, R. J. (2008). *The resilient clinician.* Oxford: Oxford University Press.

Wikler, D. (1987). Who should be blamed for being sick? *Health Education Quarterly, 14*, 11–25.

Wilkinson, S., Perry, R., Blanchard, K., & Linsell, L. (2008). Effectiveness of a three-day communication skills course in changing nurses' communication skills with cancer/palliative care patients: A randomized controlled trial. *Palliative Medicine, 22*(4), 365–375.

Willems, S. J., Swinnen, W., & De Maeseneer, J. M. (2005). The GP's perception of poverty: A qualitative study. *Family Practice, 22*(2), 177–183.

Williams, B., Brown, T., Boyle, M., McKenna, L., Palermo, C., & Etherington, J. (2014). Levels of empathy in undergraduate emergency health, nursing, and midwifery students: A longitudinal study. *Advances in Medical Education & Practice, 5*, 299–306.

Williams, D. E. (2015). Take a deep breath: Marijuana product placement is on the way. *Health Business Blog.* Retrieved from http://healthbusinessblog.com/2014/09/17/take-a-deep-breath-marijuana-product-placement-is-on-the-way/

Williams, T. (2012, June 8). Suicides outpacing war deaths for troops. *New York Times.* Retrieved from http://www.nytimes.com/2012/06/09/us/suicides-eclipse-war-deaths-for-us-troops.html?_r=0

Willing, R. (1999, April 14). Kevorkian sentenced to 10–25 years. *USA Today*, p. 1A.

Willingham, E., & Helft, L. (2014, September 5). The autism-vaccine myth. NOVA. Retrieved from http://www.pbs.org/wgbh/nova/body/autism-vaccine-myth.html

Wilson, K. (2003). Therapeutic landscapes and the First Nations people: An exploration of culture, health and place. *Health & Place, 9*(2), 83–93.

Winkelman, M. (2009). *Culture and health: Applying medical anthropology.* San Francisco: Jossey-Bass.

Winslow, C.-E. A. (1923). *The evolution and significance of the modern public health campaign.* New Haven, CT: Yale University Press.

Winsten, J. (2010, March 18). The Designated Driver Campaign: Why it worked. Media. *Huffington Post.* Retrieved from http://www.huffingtonpost.com/jay-winston/designated-driver-campaig_b_405249.html

Wise, K. (2007). The organization and implementation of relationship management. *Health Marketing Quarterly, 24*(3–4), 151–166.

Witte, K. (1997). Preventing teen pregnancy through persuasive communications: Realities, myths, and hard-fact truths. *Journal of Community Health, 22*, 137–154.

Witte, K. (2008). Putting the fear back into fear appeals: The extended parallel process model. In L. C. Lederman (Ed.), *Beyond these walls: Readings in health communication* (pp. 273–291). New York: Oxford University Press.

Wittenberg-Lyles, E., Washington, K., Demiris, G., Oliver, D. P., & Shaunfield, S. (2014). Understanding social support burden among family caregivers. *Health Communication, 29*, 901.

Wolf, M. S., Williams, M. V., Parker, R. M., Parikh, N. S., Nowlan, A. W., & Baker, D. W. (2007). Patients' shame and attitudes toward discussing the results of literacy screening. *Journal of Health Communication, 12*, 721–732.

Wood, J. (1999). *Gendered lives* (3rd ed.). Belmont, CA: Wadsworth.

Wood, K. S., & Cronley, M. L. (2014). Then and now: Examining how consumer communication and attitudes of direct-to-consumer pharmaceutical advertising have changes in the last decade. *Health Communication, 29*, 814–825.

Woodyard, C. (2011). Exploring the therapeutic effects of yoga and its ability to increase quality of life. *International Journal of Yoga, 4*(2), 49–54. doi:10.4103/0973-6131.85485

Work matters. Bob Sutton blog. (n.d.). Retrieved from http://bobsutton.typepad.com/
World Health Organization (WHO). (1948). Preamble to the Constitution of the World Health Organization. Official records of the World Health Organization, no. 2, p. 100. Retrieved from www.who.int/about/definition/en
World Health Organization (WHO). (1998). Health promotion glossary. Geneva, Switzerland: Author. Retrieved from www.who.int/hpr/ncp/support.documents.shtml
World Health Organization (WHO). (2003a). Update 83—one hundred days into the outbreak. Retrieved from http://www.who.int/csr/don/2003_06_18/en/
World Health Organization. (2003b, June 18). Epidemic and pandemic alert and response (EPR). Update 83. One hundred days into the outbreak. Geneva, Switzerland: Author. Retrieved from http://www.who.int/csr/don/2003_06_18/en/index.html
World Health Organization. (2003c, March 16). Epidemic and pandemic alert and response (EPR). Severe acute respiratory syndrome (SARS). Multi-country Outbreak. Update. Geneva, Switzerland: Author. Retrieved from http://www.who.int/csr/don/2003_03_16/en/index.html
World Health Organization. (2007a, October). Interim protocol: Rapid operations to contain the initial emergence of pandemic influenza. Geneva, Switzerland: Author. Retrieved from http://www.who.int/influenza/resources/documents/RapidContProtOct15.pdf
World Health Organization. (2007b, October). Options for the use of human H5N1 influenza vaccines and the WHO H5N1 vaccine stockpile. Geneva, Switzerland: Author. Retrieved from http://www.who.int/csr/resources/publications/WHO_HSE_EPR_GIP_2008_1d.pdf
World Health Organization. (2008a). Traditional medicine. Geneva, Switzerland: Author. Retrieved from http://www.who.int/mediacentre/factsheets/fs134/en/
World Health Organization (WHO). (2008b). World health statistics. Part 2. Global health indicators. Global health indicators. Geneva, Switzerland: Author. Retrieved from www.who.int/whosis/whostat/EN_WHS08_Table4_HSR.pdf
World Health Organization. (2010a). Telemedicine: Opportunities and developments in member states. *Global Observatory for eHealth series. Volume 2*. Geneva, Switzerland: Author. Retrieved from http://www.who.int/goe/publications/ehealth_series_vol3/en/index.html
World Health Organization. (2010b). The world health report. Executive summary. Geneva, Switzerland: Author. Retrieved from http://www.who.int/whr/2010/10_summary_en.pdf
World Health Organization. (2011a). Compendium of new and emerging health technologies. Geneva, Switzerland: Author. Retrieved from http://www.who.int/goe/call2012/en/index.html
World Health Organization. (2011b). New horizons for health through mobile technologies. Based on the findings of the second global survey on eHealth. Global Observatory for eHealth series. Volume 3. Geneva, Switzerland: Author. Retrieved at http://www.who.int/goe/publications/ehealth_series_vol3/en/index.html
World Health Organization. (2012a). Life expectancy. Data by country. Geneva, Switzerland: Author. Retrieved from http://apps.who.int/gho/data/node.main.688
World Health Organization. (2012b, May). Tobacco. Geneva, Switzerland: Author. Retrieved from http://www.who.int/mediacentre/factsheets/fs339/en/index.html
World Health Organization (WHO). (2012c). World health statistics. Geneva, Switzerland: Author. Retrieved from http://apps.who.int/iris/bitstream/10665/44844/1/9789241564441_eng.pdf
World Health Organization. (2013). Interprofessional collaborative practice in primary health care: Nursing and midwifery perspectives. Geneva, Switzerland: Author. Retrieved from http://www.who.int/hrh/resources/IPE_SixCaseStudies.pdf
World Health Organization (WHO). (2014a, November). Violence against women. Geneva, Switzerland: Author. Retrieved from http://www.who.int/mediacentre/factsheets/fs239/en/
World Health Organization (WHO). (2014b, May). The top ten causes of death. Geneva, Switzerland: Author. Retrieved from http://www.who.int/mediacentre/factsheets/fs310/en/
World Health Organization (WHO). (2014b). World health statistics. Health expenditure. Geneva, Switzerland: Author. Retrieved from http://apps.who.int/iris/bitstream/10665/112738/1/9789240692671_eng.pdf
World Health Organization (WHO). (2015a, May). Cumulative number of confirmed human cases of avian influenza A(H5N1) reported to WHO, 2003–2015. Geneva, Switzerland: Author. Retrieved from http://www.who.int/influenza/human_animal_interface/EN_GIP_20150501CumulativeNumberH5N1cases.pdf?ua=1
World Health Organization (WHO). (2015b, June 10). Ebola situation report. Geneva, Switzerland: Author. Retrieved from http://apps.who.int/ebola/en/current-situation/ebola-situation-report-10-june-2015
World Health Organization (WHO). (2015c, April). Ebola virus disease. Geneva, Switzerland: Author. Retrieved from http://www.who.int/mediacentre/factsheets/fs103/en/
World Health Organization (WHO). (2015d, June). Middle East respiratory syndrome coronavirus (MERS-CoV). Geneva, Switzerland: Author. Retrieved from http://www.who.int/emergencies/mers-cov/en/
World Health Organization (WHO). (2015e, June). Public health roundup. Geneva, Switzerland: Author. Retrieved from http://www.who.int/bulletin/volumes/93/4/15-010415/en/
World Health Report, 2000. (2000). Health systems: Improving performance. Geneva, Switzerland: World Health Organization. Retrieved from http://www.who.int/whr/2000/en/
World Health Report, 2007. (2007). A safer future: Global public health security in the 21st century. Geneva, Switzerland: World Health Organization. Retrieved from http://www.who.int/whr/2007/en/index.html

Wright, K. (2002). Social support within an on-line cancer community: An assessment of emotional support, perceptions of advantages and disadvantages, and motives for using the community from a communication perspective. *Journal of Applied Communication Research, 31*(3), 195–209.

Wright, K. B., & Rains, S. A. (2014). Weak tie support preference and preferred coping styles as predictors of perceived credibility within health-related computer-mediated support groups. *Health Communication, 29*, 281–287.

Wright Nunes, J. A., Wallston, K. A., Eden, S. K., Shintani, A. K., Ikizler, T. A., & Cavanaugh, K. L. (2011). Associations among perceived and objective disease knowledge and satisfaction with physician communication in patients with chronic kidney disease. *Kidney International, 80*(12), 1344–1351.

Wynia, M. K., VanGeest, J. B., Cummins, D. S., & Wilson, I. B. (2003). Do physicians not offer useful services because of coverage restrictions? *Health Affairs, 22*(4), 190–197.

Xutian, S., Cao, D., Wozniak, J., Junion, J., & Boisvert, J. (2012). Comprehension of the unique characteristics of Traditional Chinese Medicine. *American Journal of Chinese Medicine, 40*(2), 231–244.

Yang, F., Salmon, C. T., Pang, J. S., & Cheng, W. J. (2015). Media exposure and smoking intention in adolescents: A moderated mediation analysis from a cultivation perspective. *Journal of Health Psychology, 20*(2), 188–197.

Yanovitzky, I., Stewart, L. P., & Lederman, L. C. (2006). Social distance, perceived drinking by peers, and alcohol use by college students. *Health Communication, 19*, 1–10.

Ye, J., Rust, G., Fry-Johnson, Y., & Strothers, H. (2010). E-mail in patient-provider communication: A systematic review. *Patient Education and Counseling, 80*, 266–273.

Yee, A. M., Puntillo, K., Miaskowski, C., & Neighbor, M. L. (2006). What patients with abdominal pain expect about pain relief in the emergency department. *Journal of Emergency Nursing, 32*(4), 281–287.

Yeon-Hwan, P., & HeeKyung, C. (2014). Effect of a health coaching self-management program for older adults with multimorbidity in nursing homes. *Patient Preference & Adherence, 8*, 959–970. doi:10.2147/PPA.S62411

Young, A. (2004). *What patients taught me: A medical student's journey*. Seattle: Sasquatch Books.

Young, A., & Flower, L. (2002). Patients as partners, patients as problem-solvers. *Health Communication, 14*, 69–97.

Youth exposure to alcohol advertising on television. (2010, December 15). A study sponsored by Johns Hopkins University and the Center on Alcohol Marketing and Youth. Retrieved from http://www.camy.org/research/Youth_Exposure_to_Alcohol_Ads_on_TV_Growing_Faster_Than_Adults/_includes/CAMYReport2001_2009.pdf

Youth exposure to alcohol product advertising on local radio in 75 U.S. markets, 2009. (2011, September 13). A study sponsored by Johns Hopkins University and the Center on Alcohol Marketing and Youth. Retrieved from http://www.camy.org/research/Youth_Exposure_to_Alcohol_Advertising_on_Local_Radio_2009/_includes/report.pdf

Zakrzewski, P. A., Ho, A. L., & Braga-Mele, R. (2008). Should ophthalmologists receive communication skills training in breaking bad news? *Canadian Journal of Ophthalmology, 43*(4), 419–424.

Zaner, R. M. (2009). Narrative and decision. *Journal of Applied Communication Research, 37*, 174–187.

Zhang, L., & Haller, B. (2013). Consuming image: How mass media impact the identity of people with disabilities. *Communication Quarterly, 61*(3), 319–334.

Zhang, Z.-J., Chen, H.-Y., Yip, K.-C., Ng, R., & Wong, V. T. (2010). The effectiveness and safety of acupuncture therapy in depressive disorders: Systematic review and meta-analysis. *Journal of Affective Disorders, 124*, 9–21. doi: 10.1016/j.jad.2009.07.005

Zickuhr, K., & Madden, M. (2012, June 6). Older adults and Internet use. Pew Research Center. Retrieved from http://www.sainetz.at/dokumente/Older_adults_and_internet_use_2012.pdf

Zikmund-Fisher, B. J., Couper, M. P., Singer, E., Ziniel, S., Fowler, F., . . . Fagerlin, A. (2010) The DECISIONS study: A nationwide survey of U.S. adults regarding nine common medical decisions. *Medical Decision Making, 30*(5S), S20–S34.

Zimmerman, B., & Zimmerman, D. (2002). *Killer germs: Microbes and diseases that threaten humanity*. New York: McGraw-Hill.

Zimmerman, F. J. (2008, June). Children's media use and sleep problems: Issues and unanswered questions. Prepaid for the Henry J. Kaiser Family Foundation. Retrieved from http://www.kff.org/entmedia/upload/7674.pdf

Zoller, H. M., & Dutta, M. J. (Eds.). (2008). *Emerging perspectives in health communication: Meaning, culture, and power*. New York: Routledge.

Zook, E. (1993). Diagnosis HIV/AIDS: Caregiver communication in the crisis of terminal illness. In E. B. Ray (Ed.), *Case studies in health communication* (pp. 113–128). Hillsdale, NJ: Lawrence Erlbaum.

Zook, R. (1997, April). Handling inappropriate sexual behavior with confidence: Here are nine tips for keeping the boundaries clear. *Nursing, 27*, 65.

Zoucha, R., & Broome, B. (2008, April). The significance of culture in nursing: Examples from the Mexican-American culture and knowing the unknown. *Urologic Nursing, 28*(2), 140–142.

Zuckerman, M. (1994). *Behavioral expressions and biosocial bases of sensation seeking*. Cambridge: Cambridge University Press.

Credits

CHAPTER 1

Page 2, Photo by Jenny Gold/Kaiser Health News; page 8, © Image Source/Alamy Stock Photo; page 12, Spotmatik Ltd/Shutterstock.com

CHAPTER 2

Page 24, Andy Dean Photography/Shutterstock.com; page 26, © Design Pics Inc/Alamy Stock Photo; page 34, © Richard Levine/Alamy Stock Photo

CHAPTER 3

Page 46, ©iStockphoto/Yuri_Arcurs; page 51, Monkey Business Images/Shutterstock.com; page 57, ©iStockphoto/Cathy Yeulet; page 63, Olimpik/Shutterstock.com

CHAPTER 4

Page 71, ©iStockphoto/Pamela Moore; page 73, Steve Mack/Getty Images Entertainment/Getty Images; page 76, Monkey Business Images/Shutterstock.com; page 79, ©iStockphoto/Cathy Yeulet; page 81, Pressmaster/Shutterstock.com; page 84, ©iStockphoto/zhudifeng; page 87, Stephen's Story/Facebook/PA Wire; page 88, ©iStockphoto/nano

CHAPTER 5

Page 96, ©iStockphoto/coffeeyu; page 99, Olesia Bilkei/Shutterstock.com; page 108, michaeljung/Shutterstock.com; page 114, wavebreakmedia/Shutterstock.com; page 118, Rido/Shutterstock.com

CHAPTER 6

Page 128, Courtesy of Public Health—Seattle & King County; page 131, Rex Features via AP Images; page 135, © Terry Smith Images/Alamy Stock Photo; page 139, AP Photo/The Spokesan-Review, Colin Mulvany; page 147, ©iStockphoto/EdStock

CHAPTER 7

Page 158, © Image Source/Alamy Stock Photo; page 163, Courtesy of Stacy Bias; page 166, NBC/NBCUniversal/Getty Images; page 169, Jaguar PS/Shutterstock.com; page 175, © TongRo Images/Alamy Stock Photo

CHAPTER 8

Page 184, Monkey Business Images/Shutterstock.com; page 191, Stock-Asso/Shutterstock.com; page 200, StockLite/Shutterstock.com; page 203, Oleksiy Mark/Shutterstock.com

CHAPTER 9

Page 213, AP Photo/Tony Dejak; page 214, Tharakorn/Shutterstock.com; page 217, Monkey Business Images/Shutterstock.com; page 219, ©iStockphoto/Stepan Popov; page 222, cunaplus/Shutterstock.com; page 225, Vlad Teodor/Shutterstock.com; page 226, ©iStockphoto/Yuri; page 228, © Phanie/Alamy Stock Photo

CHAPTER 10

Page 241, Rawpixel/Shutterstock.com; page 243, Syda Productions/Shutterstock.com; page 250, Amnarj Tanongrattana/Shutterstock.com; page 255, Naypong/Shutterstock.com; page 258, ©iStockphoto/Dean Mitchell

CHAPTER 11

Page 270, AP Photo/Diane Bondareff; page 273, Hannes Magerstaedt/Getty Images Entertainment/Getty Images; page 274, Vincenzo Lombardo/Getty Images Entertainment/Getty Images; page 275, ©iStockphoto/Brendan Hunter; page 279, Photo by Diane Bondareff/Invision/AP; page 286, ©iStockphoto/Imgorthand

CHAPTER 12

Page 292, © Tommy E Trenchard/Alamy Stock Photo; page 295, Jay Directo/AFP/Getty Images; page 296, VitaminCo/Shutterstock.com; page 303, AP Photo/Ahn Young-joon; page 307, ©iStockphoto/Edward Westmacott

CHAPTER 13

Page 316, Barone Firenze/Shutterstock.com; page 317, antoniodiaz/Shutterstock.com; page 324, © age fotostock/Alamy Stock Photo; page 325, Press Assocation via AP Images; page 329, ©iStockphoto/Christopher Futcher

CHAPTER 14

Page 337, ©iStockphoto/EduLeite; page 338, © marc macdonald/Alamy Stock Photo; page 351, Photo by Andy Kropa/Invision/AP

Author Index

Note: *b* refers to box and *f* refers to figure.

Subject Index

Note: *b* refers to box, *f* refers to figure, and *t* refers to table.